Other Kaplan Books for College-Bound Students

College Admissions and Financial Aid

Straight Talk on Paying for College

Parent's Guide to College Admissions

The Unofficial, ~~Un~~biased Guide to the 328 Most Interesting Colleges

The *Yale Daily News* Guide to Succeeding in College

Test Preparation

SAT 1600

Ring of McAllister

Smart Girl's guide to the SAT

SAT Vocabulary Flashcards: Flip-O-Matic

SAT Verbal Velocity

SAT Math Mania

SAT II: Biology

SAT II: Chemistry

SAT II: Literature

SAT II: Mathematics

SAT II: Physics

SAT II: Spanish

SAT II: U.S. History

SAT II: World History

SAT II: Writing

SAT Verbal Workbook

SAT Math Workbook

ACT

SAT*
& PSAT†

2004

BY THE STAFF OF KAPLAN, INC.

Simon & Schuster

NEW YORK · LONDON · SINGAPORE · SYDNEY · TORONTO

Kaplan Publishing
Published by Simon & Schuster
1230 Avenue of the Americas
New York, NY 10020

Contributing Editors: Seppy Basili, Dan McGrew, Justin Serrano, and Barry Tonoff

Project Editor: Charli Engelhorn

Cover Design: Cheung Tai

Production Manager: Michael Shevlin

Managing Editor: Déa Alessandro

Executive Editor: Del Franz

Thanks to: Renée Mitchell, Laurel Douglas, Grace Begany, Michael Bitz, Joanna Cohen, and Darcy Galane

July 2003

10 9 8 7 6 5 4 3 2 1

Manufactured in the United States of America

Published simultaneously in Canada

ISBN 0-7432-4156-8

ISSN 1093-3395

Table of Contents

Section 6: Practice Tests and Explanations

Section 7: SAT Study Aids

Dear Student:

For more than 60 years, Kaplan has been helping students meet their academic and admissions goals. More than three million students have passed through our doors, and as their evaluations of our courses have repeatedly shown, one thing stands out that sets Kaplan apart from the rest: our teachers.

We have long known that our outstanding teaching staff is Kaplan's most important asset. Throughout the years we have committed ourselves to finding expert, enthusiastic, and engaging teachers for every Kaplan course. That's why we interview only those candidates who scored high on the test they are to teach and from this pool select only the most promising candidates: individuals who are enthusiastic about helping students reach their goals. All prospective teachers complete an intensive Kaplan training, and from ongoing observations, evaluations, and reviews of student feedback, they get even better as they teach.

The knowledge and experience that our teachers have acquired from working with students like you—about standardized tests, study habits, test panic, and more—is something we'd like to share outside of the classroom. We're pleased to incorporate the wisdom, tips, and inspiration of Kaplan's teachers in this test-prep guide so that you may benefit from the best we have to offer. I hope you find their expertise useful in your quest for academic success. If you decide you'd also like to work with our first-rate instructors in person, give us a call at (800) KAP-TEST.

Sincerely,

Jonathan Grayer

CEO, Kaplan, Inc.

SAT 2004 Update

SAT COMPETITION

Getting into college has never been more competitive. More students are applying to more colleges with some predictable results: more rejection letters going out, and significantly more wait-list notices. Here's a snapshot of what you're up against when it comes to the SAT:

- In 2002, the mean score on the Verbal section was 504; while this represents a two-point drop from 2001, it is also a four-point increase since 1992. On the Math section, the mean score was 516 in 2002—a 32-year high and a 15-point increase since 1992.

- In 2002, 1,327,831 high school graduates took the SAT (a 4 percent rise over 2001). Twenty-two percent of SAT I test takers attained a combined (Verbal and Math) score of 1200 or higher. Twenty-six percent of test takers had GPAs that placed them in the top 10 percent of their high school class.

SAT TEST DATES

The competitive college admissions landscape has changed testing patterns: more students are taking the SAT earlier. To some degree, this trend is the result of an increased number of students applying to early decision programs. Another factor is that more students are taking the SAT more than once. In general, the shift to taking the SAT earlier reflects the importance of getting your SAT scores under your belt by the end of your junior year so that you know where you stand and can plan accordingly.

Here are the SAT dates for the remaining part of the 2003–2004 test cycle:

2003–2004 Saturday Administrations			
National Test Dates	**Tests Offered**	**Registration Deadlines**	
		U.S. and International	**U.S. Late**
October 11, 2003 November 1, 2003	SAT I & SAT II SAT I, SAT II, and Language Tests with Listening including ELPT (English Language Proficiency Test)	September 9, 2003 September 26, 2003	September 13, 2003 October 8, 2003
December 6, 2003 January 24, 2004 March 27, 2004** May 1, 2004	SAT I & SAT II SAT I, SAT II, and ELPT SAT I only SAT I & SAT II	October 31, 2003 December 22, 2003 February 20, 2004 March 26, 2004	November 12, 2003 December 31, 2003 March 4, 2004 April 7, 2004
June 5, 2004	SAT I & SAT II	April 30, 2004	May 12, 2004

A NEW PSAT IN 2004

Changes are on the way for the PSAT/NMSQT. This test was developed in part to give high school sophomores a preview of the SAT. The changes in the PSAT are intended to make sure that the test continues to reflect the SAT, which is undergoing a major revision. The PSAT, like the SAT, will drop two question types—Analogies and Quantitative Comparisons—but gain more reading passages and harder math questions. For the specifics of what will be changing on the PSAT, go to page 230 in the PSAT section in this book. The first administration of the new PSAT will be in October 2004; the October 2003 test is unchanged.

CHANGES FOR THE SAT IN 2005

The SAT is getting a major overhaul. A new version of the SAT will replace the current test beginning in March 2005. The changes are designed to align the test more closely to high school curricula and college skills, thus making the test a more accurate predictor of college performance. There will be changes not only in the content tested but also in the types of questions used. Here are the most important changes.

The New Writing Section

The biggest change in the SAT will be the addition of a writing test. The SAT Writing Section will include multiple choice questions and a written essay. The multiple choice questions will test the students ability to identify sentence errors and to make improvements in sentences and paragraphs. The essay section will assess the student's writing ability. Plans call for the student to be asked to write a persuasive essay taking a position on a particular issue given them in the test and support their position with reasons and evidence.

Changes to the Verbal Section

First, the Verbal section is getting a new name to reflect its new focus: Critical Reading. The Analogies questions, which required test takers to understand the meanings of specific words and analyze the relationship between them (see chapter 5 for examples) are being dropped. In their place there will be short reading passages added with two to three multiple choice questions following each passage.

Changes to the Math Section

Some questions of greater difficulty will be added to the SAT Mathematical section; these will cover the topics usually taught in algebra II in U.S. high schools. In addition, the Quantitative Comparison questions, which require a comparison of a quantity in column A to a quantity in column B to determine which is larger, are being eliminated entirely (see chapter 12 for examples). They will be replaced by additional regular multiple choice questions and Grid-in questions.

Scoring the New Test

The new writing test will be scored on a scale 200-800, the same scale currently used for the Mathematical and Verbal sections of the SAT. The composite scores on the new test will be between 600-2400, instead of the 400-1600 now used.

SAT Time Breakdown		
	Current SAT	**New SAT**
Math	75 minutes	70 minutes
Verbal/Critical Reading	75 minutes	70 minutes
Writing	None	50 minutes
Experimental Section	30 minutes	25 minutes
TOTAL	3 hours	3 hours, 35 minutes

How to Use This Book:

THE CLASSIC PLAN

Ideally, you should take a couple of months to work through the book and CD-ROM in this package, though it's certainly possible to do so in far less time. Below you'll find some suggestions as to how you can effectively use both the book and CD-ROM in your SAT/PSAT preparation. (Refer to the "User's Guide to the CD-ROM" at the end of this book for technical instructions on how to use the software.)

1. Read through each chapter completely, learning from the example problems and trying the practice problems. In the "SAT Study Aids" section, you'll find a list of 2,200 SAT vocabulary words complete with example sentences, a root list, and a word families list, as well as a review of the 100 most important math concepts to know for the SAT.

2. At the beginning of each chapter in the book, there is a Highlights box containing the most important concepts in the chapter. At the end of most chapters, you'll find a Checklist that allows you to check off the concepts as you master them.

3. On the *Higher Score on the SAT and PSAT* CD-ROM, fill out the student profile and take the diagnostic test. This will allow the software to assign you a personalized study plan that is customized to your individual needs. Follow this study plan as you work through the interactive lessons and practice tests, review the reference sections and flashcards, and play games that will help reinforce the skills you'll need to perform well on the SAT.

4. Read the chapter in the book entitled "Stress Management" to set the stage for your training and testing success.

5. Take a full-length practice test under strictly timed conditions. You can take Practice Test One in the book or one of the full-length tests on the CD-ROM, depending on your preference.

6. Score your Practice Test. Find out where you need help and then review the appropriate chapters in the book and/or lessons on the CD-ROM.

7. Reread all the Highlights boxes in the book once more before trying your luck at the other Practice Tests in the book and on the CD-ROM. Repeat the process of reviewing your areas of weakness.

8. Give yourself a day of rest right before the real exam.

If you have time, do just two or three chapters and/or CD-ROM practice lessons a week, and let the material sink in slowly. Don't hesitate to take some time off from your SAT preparation when you need to. Nobody can take this stuff day in and day out for weeks at a time without a break.

Taking the PSAT?

If you are taking the PSAT, you'll face the same subject matter and types of questions that you would if you were taking the SAT. So you should follow the SAT test preparation study plan described above and work through this book in exactly the same way as any SAT test taker would. The main difference between the SAT and the PSAT is that since 1997, the PSAT has included a Writing Skills section. You'll find a chapter on this section that provides content review, skills, and strategies at the end of the book. (For a closer look at this test, and more practice with PSAT question types, check out Kaplan's *PSAT* book.) Work through Kaplan's strategic approaches for each question type, and learn about the most common grammar concepts on which you'll be tested. Also covered is important information on test format, scoring, and National Merit scholarships.

THE SAT EMERGENCY PLAN

Maybe you have only two or three weeks—or even less time than that. Don't freak! *SAT and PSAT* has been designed to work for students in your situation, too. If you go through a chapter or two every day, you can finish this book in a couple of weeks. If you have limited time to prepare for the SAT (fewer than two weeks), we suggest you do the following:

1. If you feel totally stressed out, take a slow, deep breath. Read chapter 16, "Stress Management," to maximize your study and testing time.

2. Check out the "CD-ROM User's Guide" to find out how to use the *Higher Score on the SAT and PSAT* software.

3. Read the "SAT Mastery" chapter.

4. Read the "SAT Emergency" sidebar at the beginning of each chapter. The suggestions in these sidebars can really streamline your study strategy as well as ensure that you cover the vital concepts before Test Day.

5. Take as many of the Practice Tests as you can—in the book or on the CD-ROM, depending on your preference—*under timed conditions.*

6. Review your results, with special attention to the questions you missed.

7. Give yourself the day before the test off.

Scattered throughout the text you'll find "hints"—special points that we feel deserve emphasis and amplification. Pay special attention to these hints, which spotlight some very important test prep information. Sidebars also highlight key concepts and strategies, fun facts, and real-world stories.

SAT Emergency FAQs

Q. It's two days before the SAT and I'm clueless. What should I do?

A. First of all, don't panic. If you only have a day or two to prepare for the test, then you don't have time to prepare thoroughly. But that doesn't mean you should just give up. There's still a lot you can do to improve your potential score. First and foremost, you should become familiar with the test. Read chapter 1, "SAT Mastery." And if you don't do anything else, take one of the full-length practice tests at the back of this book under reasonably testlike conditions. When you finish the practice test, check your answers and look at the explanations to the questions you didn't get right.

Q. Math is my weak spot. What can I do to get better at math in a big hurry?

A. Review the "SAT Math in a Nutshell" chapter, which highlights the 100 Key Math Concepts for the SAT. Then do as many of the sample problems in chapter 13, "Classic Problem-Solving Techniques," as you have time for. If you don't have time to do the sample problems, just read the sidebars in the math chapters. They contain really helpful facts and tips.

Q. I'm great at Math, but Verbal scares me. How can I improve my Verbal score right away?

A. Go straight to the section called "Decoding Strange Words on the Test" in chapter 4. Much of the SAT Verbal depends on your ability to work with unfamiliar words. It's also a good idea to check out the SAT Word Families, as well as the SAT Root List. Then do as many of the sample problems in the Verbal chapters as you have time for. If you don't have time to do the sample problems, just read the sidebars in those chapters. These strategies can help boost your score.

Q. I get to use a calculator on the SAT! Does that mean I don't have to worry about learning math?

A. Not exactly. You ARE allowed to bring a calculator to the SAT, but that's actually a mixed blessing. If you don't use your calculator wisely, you could actually end up wasting time or, even worse, generating wrong answers. Make sure to read the chapter on "Calculators and the SAT," particularly the pages on Common Calculator Mistakes, before you take the test. Knowing when and how to use your calculator will help you immeasurably. And remember, your calculator won't think for you!

Q. My parents are upset with me for waiting till the last minute to study, and now I can't concentrate. Help!

A. Take a deep breath! Anxiety and stress are the enemies of all test takers—no matter how much time they have to prepare. Turn to chapter 16 and read through Kaplan's suggestions for managing stress. Do the suggested exercises. And don't forget to think positively!

Q: The SAT is tomorrow. Should I stay up all night studying geometry formulas?

A: The best thing to do right now is to try to stay calm. Read the "What Do I Do Now?" chapter to find out the best way to survive, and thrive, on Test Day. And get a good night's sleep.

Q: *I don't feel confident. Should I just guess?*

A: You should always guess if you can do so intelligently. The SAT does have a wrong-answer penalty for most question types, but that doesn't mean you should never guess. If you can rule out even ONE answer choice, you should guess, because you have significantly increased your chances of guessing correctly. Also, on questions that appear early in a section, more obvious answers will tend to be correct, so you can guess more confidently on those questions. Finally, always guess on Grid-ins, since there is no wrong-answer penalty on that question type.

Q: *What's the most important thing I can do to get ready for the SAT quickly?*

A. In addition to basic Math and Verbal skills, the SAT mainly tests your ability to take the SAT. Therefore, the most important thing you can do is to familiarize yourself with the directions, the question types, the answer grid, and the overall structure of the test. Make sure you feel comfortable with the logistics—how to get to your test center, how to fill in Grid-ins, how (and when) to use your calculator. Read every question carefully—many mistakes are the result of simply not reading thoroughly.

Q. *So it's a good idea to panic, right? RIGHT?*

A. No! No matter how prepared you are for the SAT, stress will hurt your performance, and it's really no fun. Stay confident, and don't cram. So . . . breathe. Stay calm, and remember, it's just a test.

How to Team Up for a Better Score on the SAT

Being a loner has a certain mystique, it's true. Loners seem cool and aloof, which has some benefits when it comes to cultivating a rock star image. But when it comes to preparing for the SAT, there is safety in numbers. Even if the term "group work" makes you cringe, you should think about setting up an SAT study team—what we call an **SAT Power Pack**.

Why Join an SAT Power Pack?

- *An SAT Power Pack keeps you committed.* You are far less likely to blow off studying if your friends are depending on you to show up at meetings and be useful.

- *An SAT Power Pack points out the error of your ways.* It is sometimes hard to see your own weaknesses. Your SAT Power Pack will help you recognize and correct your trouble spots.

- *An SAT Power Pack calms you down.* Preparing for the SAT is stressful. With so much riding on your score, it's no wonder some students get a bit frayed around the edges as test day approaches. Your SAT Power Pack is there to give you the support you need. It is always comforting to know that you are not alone.

How to Get Started

Having a successful study group takes a lot more than a box of doughnuts and a dining room table. It takes careful planning and a little negotiation. Use the list below to get off to the right start.

- *Choose your Power Pack wisely.* This doesn't mean you can only team up with straight-A students. But you should steer clear of people who are not as serious as you are about preparing well for the SAT. They will only waste your time. The right number of partners is important, too: we recommend limiting your group to three to six members. That way you have all the benefits of teaming up, but no one gets overshadowed or left behind.

- *Set realistic goals from the outset.* Everyone in your Power Pack needs to take a practice test from section 6 of this book before the first meeting. Once you know what your strengths and weaknesses are, you should have a discussion with your partners about what you hope to gain from the SAT Power Pack. A 100-point score improvement? Better math skills? Reduced anxiety? You can certainly have individual goals, but your pack needs to be heading in the same general direction for you to work together well.

- *Find the right meeting place.* You need a place where you can all sit comfortably for a couple of hours free from distraction. You need room to spread out your materials. Some access to food and drinks is a nice bonus.

- *Make an ironclad schedule.* Get out your calendars and mark down every meeting in advance. Commit to those times. We recommend at least four meetings of at least one hour each; two hours is better. It's hard to get anything accomplished in less time than this. Decide in advance what material you will cover at each meeting.

General Guidelines

OK, you've got the members, you've got the place, you've got the time. But exactly what are you all supposed to do for two hours?

The Best Way to Learn Is to Teach

To make every minute count, you need to agree on a procedure for learning. One effective way to use your meeting time is to pick a "teacher" from the group for each chunk of material you want to cover.

For example, Bianca takes chapter 8, "Critical Reading Skills." Everyone reads chapter 8 in advance, but it is Bianca's job to set up a lesson on Critical Reading for the rest of the group. It is up to her to set the agenda. This takes a lot of preparation and extra planning, but the advantage is that by the time Bianca has taught the session, she will be an expert on critical reading.

Warning: *Do* Attempt This at Home

To make your SAT Power Pack meetings more productive, you will all have to do some preparation on your own. This means reading chapters in advance, taking practice tests, and bringing in whatever extra materials your pack thinks are necessary.

Practice, Practice, Practice

Take at least two of the three practice tests in this book. You should take the first before your initial meeting so you have an idea of your skill level. Take another test after a couple of meetingsm and discuss your results in a Power Pack meeting. This will help you pinpoint trouble areas, gauge your progress, and build your familiarity with the test format. If you like, you can take a final practice test after your last meeting to measure your improvement.

I'm a Tutor, You're a Tutor

The children of millionaires aren't the only ones who can get one-on-one SAT tutoring. Your SAT Power Pack can provide that, too. Just have every member of your group pair up with a partner. Partners should evaluate one another's practice tests to locate weaknesses and give some focused help in those areas.

Get Hooked on Mnemonics

Performing well on the SAT Verbal section does take more than a good vocabulary . . . but a good vocabulary sure will help a lot. It makes sense to spend some time studying the SAT Word List in section 7. There are several tried-and-true memorization techniques you can use on your own, like making flashcards with the vocabulary word on one side and the definition on another.

But in an SAT Power Pack, you can get more creative and have a little more fun. One activity you can try is having each member select ten words from the SAT Word List and come up with a mnemonic device for each one to share with the pack. A mnemonic (pronounced "nuh-MON-ik") device is just a memory aid—something catchy that helps you remember a piece of information.

For example, take the word *florid*, which means "ruddy" or "flushed." You might remember this definition by thinking of the state of Florida, which sounds like *florid*. Florida has lots of sunny beaches where tourists get badly sunburned. Imagine the red-faced tourists of Florida, and you will probably remember *florid*. Mnemonic devices can be as weird or creative as you want. In fact, you may find you can remember weird ones better than straightforward ones.

Run a Math Guess-a-Thon

As you'll learn, there's a so-called "guessing penalty" on most sections of the SAT. That means that on everything but Math Grid-In questions, you lose part of a point for every wrong answer, while leaving a question blank costs you nothing. This spooks a lot of students into skipping questions they find tough. Wrong strategy! If you can cross out even one answer choice using the process of elimination, it is in your best interest to take a good guess. The odds are that over the course of the whole test, you will wind up with a better score. Aggressive guessing takes some guts, so you'd better practice. Try this exercise during your SAT Power Pack meetings:

- Throughout this book, you'll find tons of practice questions. Review the chapter on "Math Guessing," then try any of the practice questions in the Math section without actually working the problems. Eliminate answers you think seem unlikely, then guess. (You can also try this on the Critical Reading practice questions in chapters 7 and 8 by answering the questions without reading the passages and sentences associated with the questions.) See which one of your Power Pack members is the best guesser. Then talk about some of the reasons you used for eliminating answer choices. You may even develop some guessing strategies of your own!

Above All: Don't Panic

To quote the science fiction classic *Dune*, "Fear is the mind killer." If you are super-stressed during the test, you won't think clearly and you won't perform well. Chapters 16 and 17 contain some very effective tips for handling stress. Here are some of the ways you can put these tips into action with your pack:

- *Work out with your SAT Power Pack:* Exercise is an ideal stress reducer. Take an SAT Power Pack partner—or your whole group—and do a quick walk around the block. Get together and go jogging or play basketball. Anything that gets your heart pounding for a little while will take the edge off your anxiety.

- *Get into group meditation:* You might want to close each of your meetings with a short meditation period. We're not talking about chanting and incense here, don't worry. Just have everyone close their books, close their eyes, breathe in and out slowly and deeply, and empty their minds of all worry.

- *Compliment each other:* Sometimes it's hard to focus on the positive when you're stressed out. Make it an SAT Power Pack activity for each group member to point out the strengths of other members (like "Bianca is an ace on Critical Reading passages"). Do this regularly. You will see that new strengths will develop as you continue studying.

- *Celebrate together:* Don't forget to get together one last time after the test to celebrate a job well done!

A Special Note for
International Students

If you are an international student considering attending an American university, you are not alone. Over 582,000 international students pursued academic degrees at the undergraduate, graduate, or professional school level at U.S. universities during the 2001–2002 academic year, according to the Institute of International Education's Open Doors report. Almost 50 percent of these students were studying for a bachelor's or first university degree. This number of international students pursuing higher education in the United States is expected to continue to grow. Business, management, engineering, and the physical and life sciences are particularly popular majors for students coming to the United States from other countries.

If you are not a U.S. citizen and you are interested in attending college or university in the United States, here is what you'll need to get started.

- If English is not your first language, you'll probably need to take the TOEFL* (Test of English as a Foreign Language) or provide some other evidence that you are proficient in English. Colleges and universities in the United States will differ on what they consider to be an acceptable TOEFL score. A minimum TOEFL score of 213 (550 on the paper-based TOEFL) or better is often required by more prestigious and competitive institutions. Because American undergraduate programs require all students to take a certain number of general education courses, all students—even math and computer science students—need to be able to communicate well in spoken and written English.

- You may also need to take the SAT* or the ACT*. Many undergraduate institutions in the United States require both the SAT and TOEFL of international students.

- There are over 3,400 accredited colleges and universities in the United States, so selecting the correct undergraduate school can be a confusing task for anyone. You will need to get help from a good advisor or at least a good college guide that gives you detailed information on the different schools available. Since admission to many undergraduate programs is quite competitive, you may want to select three or four colleges and complete applications for each school.

- You should begin the application process at least a year in advance. An increasing number of schools accept applications year round. In any case, find out the application deadlines and plan accordingly. Although September (the fall semester) is the traditional time to begin university study in the United States, you can begin your studies at many schools in January (the spring semester).

- In addition, you will need to obtain an I-20 Certificate of Eligibility from the school you plan to attend if you intend to apply for an F-1 Student Visa to study in the United States.

Kaplan International Programs

If you need more help with the complex process of university admissions, assistance preparing for the SAT, ACT, or TOEFL, or help building your English language skills in general, you may be interested in Kaplan's programs for international students.

Kaplan International Programs were designed to help students and professionals from outside the United States meet their educational and career goals. At locations throughout the United States, international students take advantage of Kaplan's programs to help them improve their academic and conversational English skills, raise their scores on the TOEFL, SAT, ACT, and other standardized exams, and gain admission to the schools of their choice. Our staff and instructors give international students the individualized attention they need to succeed. Here is a brief description of some of Kaplan's programs for international students:

General Intensive English

Kaplan's General Intensive English classes are designed to help you improve your skills in all areas of English and to increase your fluency in spoken and written English. Classes are available for beginning to advanced students, and the average class size is 12 students.

TOEFL and Academic English

This course provides you with the skills you need to improve your TOEFL score and succeed in an American university or graduate program. It includes advanced reading, writing, listening, grammar, and conversational English. You will also receive training for the TOEFL using Kaplan's exclusive computer-based practice materials.

SAT Test Preparation Course

The SAT is an important admission criterion for American colleges and universities. A high score can help you stand out from other applicants. This course includes the skills you need to succeed on each section of the SAT, as well as access to Kaplan's exclusive practice materials.

Other Kaplan Programs

Since 1938, more than 3 million students have come to Kaplan to advance their studies, prepare for entry to American universities, and further their careers. In addition to the above programs, Kaplan offers courses to prepare for the ACT, GMAT*, GRE*, MCAT*, DAT*, USMLE*, NCLEX*, and other standardized exams at locations throughout the United States.

*All test names used in this section are registered trademarks of their respective owners.

KAPLAN

Applying to Kaplan International Programs

To get more information, or to apply for admission to any of Kaplan's programs for international students and professionals, contact us at:

Kaplan International Programs
700 South Flower, Suite 2900
Los Angeles, CA 90017, USA
Phone (if calling from within the United States): 800-818-9128
Phone (if calling from outside the United States): 213-452-5800
Fax: 213-892-1364
Website: www.kaplaninternational.com
Email: world@kaplan.com

Kaplan is authorized under federal law to enroll nonimmigrant alien students. Kaplan is accredited by ACCET (Accrediting Council for Continuing Education and Training).

The Basics

1

SAT Mastery

HIGHLIGHTS

- Learn how to use the structure of the SAT to your advantage
- Formulate a plan for attacking the questions

To perform well on the SAT, you need to draw on a set of skills that the College Board does not mention in any of their materials. You need to be a good SAT test taker.

Acquiring this ability, and the confidence it produces, is what this book is about.

There are three simple things you need to master the SAT:

- You need to have a basic understanding of SAT content.
- You need to hone the thinking and testing skills that underlie the SAT.
- You need to know the nature of the SAT.

Content and skills are obviously important. You can't do well without them. But understanding the nature of the SAT, its setup, its structure, and the traps it often sets for you will allow you to gain points on the test that you might not otherwise have earned.

USING THE STRUCTURE OF THE SAT TO YOUR ADVANTAGE

The SAT is different from the tests that you're used to taking. On a school test, you probably go through the problems in order. You spend more time on the hard questions than on easy ones, since this is where you get more points. And

> **SAT Emergency**
>
> If you have just a few weeks to prep for the SAT, don't panic. The first thing you should do is become familiar with the test. This chapter is the place to start.

you often show your work since the teacher tells you that how you approach a problem is as important as getting the answer right.

None of this works on the SAT. You can benefit from moving around within a section, the hard questions are worth the same as the easy ones, and it doesn't matter how you answer the question—only what your answer is.

To succeed in this peculiar context, you need to know some fundamentals about the overall structure of the SAT.

The SAT Is Highly Predictable

Because the format and directions of the SAT remain unchanged from test to test, you can learn the setup in advance. On the day of the test, Analogies, QCs, Grid-ins—or the setup of any other question type or section—shouldn't be new to you.

One of the easiest things you can do to help your performance on the SAT is to understand the directions before taking the test. Since the instructions are always exactly the same, there's no reason to waste your time on the day of the test reading them. Learn them beforehand, as you go through this book, and skip them during the test.

Most SAT Questions Are Arranged by Order of Difficulty

You've probably noticed that not all the questions on the SAT are equally difficult. Except for the Critical Reading problems, the questions are designed to get tougher as you work through a set.

Here's how to use this pattern to your advantage. As you work, you should always be aware of where you are in the set. When working on the easy problems, you can generally trust your first impulse—the obvious answer is likely to be right.

As you get to the end of the set, you need to become more suspicious. Now the answers probably won't come easy. If they do, look at the problem again, because the obvious answer is likely to be wrong. Watch out for the answer that just "looks right." It may be a *distractor*—a wrong answer choice meant to entice you.

There's No Mandatory Order to the Questions

You're allowed to skip around within each section of the SAT. High scorers know this. They move through the test efficiently. They don't dwell on any one question, even a hard one, until they've tried every question at least once.

When you run into questions that look tough, circle them in your test booklet and skip them for the time being. Go back and try again after you have answered the easier ones if you have time. On a second look, troublesome questions can turn out to be amazingly simple.

If you've started answering a question and get confused, quit and go on to the next question. Persistence may pay off in school, but it usually hurts your SAT score. Don't spend so much time answering one tough question that you use up three or four questions' worth of time. That costs you points, especially if you don't get the hard question right.

There's a Guessing Penalty That Can Work in Your Favor

The test makers like to talk about the guessing penalty on the SAT. This is a misnomer. It's really a *wrong answer* penalty. If you guess wrong you get penalized. If you guess right, you're in great shape.

The fact is, if you can eliminate one or more answers as definitely wrong, you'll turn the odds in your favor and *actually come out ahead* by guessing.

Here's how the penalty works:

- If you get an answer wrong on a Quantitative Comparison, which has four answer choices, you lose 1/3 point.

- If you get an answer wrong on other multiple-choice questions, which have five answer choices, you lose 1/4 point.

- If you get an answer wrong on a Grid-in math question, for which you write in your own answers, you lose nothing.

> **Kaplan Rules**
>
> DON'T GUESS, unless you can eliminate at least one answer choice.
>
> DON'T SKIP IT, unless you have absolutely no idea.

The fractional points you lose are meant to offset the points you might get "accidentally" by guessing the correct answer. With practice, however, you'll learn that it's often easy to eliminate several answer choices on some of the problems that you see. By learning the techniques for eliminating wrong answer choices, you can actually turn the guessing "penalty" to your advantage.

The Answer Grid Has No Heart

It sounds simple but it's extremely important: Don't make mistakes filling out your answer grid. When time is short, it's easy to get confused going back and forth between your test book and your grid. If you know the answer, but misgrid, you won't get the points. To avoid mistakes on the answer grid:

Always Circle the Questions You Skip

Put a big circle in your test book around any question numbers you skip. When you go back, these questions will be easy to locate. Also, if you accidentally skip a box on the grid, you can check your grid against your book to see where you went wrong.

> **Circle Before You Skip**
>
> A common cause of major SAT disasters is filling in all of the questions with the right answers—in the wrong spots.
>
> Every time you skip a question, circle it in your test book and make doubly sure that you skip it on the answer grid as well.

Always Circle the Answers You Choose

Circling your answers in the test book makes it easier to check your grid against your book.

Grid Five or More Answers at Once

Don't transfer your answers to the grid after every question. Transfer your answers after every five questions, or at the end of each reading passage. That way, you won't keep breaking your concentration to mark the grid. You'll save time and you'll gain accuracy.

Transferring Your Answers

You need to be careful at the end of a section when time may be running out. You don't want to have your answers in the test booklet and not be able to transfer them to your answer grid because you have run out of time.

These fundamentals apply to every section of the test. But each question type also has its own structural peculiarities that make them easy to prep for. Some examples: On Grid-ins, the grid cannot accommodate five-digit answers, negatives, or variables. If you get such an answer, you know you've made a mistake and need to redo the problem.

Analogy answer choices are always ordered with the same parts of speech; this helps you determine if you're building an appropriate bridge.

Critical Reading questions with line references, "Little Picture" questions, can often be done quickly and don't require you to read the entire passage. You can do these first in a later reading passage if you're running out of time.

We'll show you lots of these structural elements, and the strategies you can use to take advantage of them, throughout this book.

APPROACHING SAT QUESTIONS

Apart from knowing the setup of the SAT, you've got to have a system for attacking the questions. You wouldn't travel around a foreign city without a map and you shouldn't approach the SAT without a plan. Now that you know some basics about how the test is set up, you can approach each section a little more strategically. What follows is the best method for approaching SAT questions systematically.

Teacher Tip

"Mark up your test book—it's going to be thrown away anyway! Don't waste time considering answers you've already eliminated in your head but not on paper."

—Ed Cottrell
Kaplan Teacher
Houston, TX

Think about the Question Before You Look at the Answer

The people who make the test love to put distractors among the answer choices. Distractors are answer choices that look like the right answer, but aren't. If you jump right into the answer choices without thinking first about what you're looking for, you're much more likely to fall for one of these traps.

Use Backdoor Strategies If the Answer Doesn't Come to You

There are usually a number of ways to get to the right answer on an SAT question. Most of the questions on the SAT are multiple-choice. That means the answer is right in front of you—you just have to find it. This makes SAT questions open to a lot of ways of finding the answer. If you can't figure out the answer in a straightforward way, try other techniques. We'll talk about specific Kaplan methods such as backsolving, picking numbers, and eliminating weak Analogy bridges in later chapters.

Guess Only When You Can Eliminate One Answer Choice

You already know that the wrong answer "penalty" can work in your favor. Don't simply skip questions that you can't answer. Spend some time with them to see if you can eliminate any of the answer choices. If you can, it pays for you to guess.

Pace Yourself

The SAT gives you a lot of questions in a short period of time. To get through a whole section, you can't spend too much time on any one question. Keep moving through the test at a good speed; if you run into a hard question, circle it in your test booklet, skip it, and come back to it later if you have time.

In the sidebar to the right are recommended average times per question. This doesn't mean that you should spend exactly 40 seconds on every Analogy. It's a guide. Remember, the questions get harder as you move through a problem set. Ideally, you can work through the easy problems at a brisk, steady clip, and use a little more of your time for the harder ones that come at the end of the set.

One caution: Don't completely rush through the easy problems just to save time for the harder ones. These early problems are points in your pocket, and you're better off not getting to the last couple of problems than losing these easy points.

Recommended Timing

Section	On Average
Analogies	40 seconds
Sentence Completions	40 seconds
Critical Reading*	75 seconds
Regular Math	70 seconds
QCs	45 seconds
Grid-ins	90 seconds

* Average time for Critical Reading includes time to read the passage. Spend about 30 secs. per question.

Locate Quick Points If You're Running Out of Time

Some questions can be done quickly; for instance, some reading questions will ask you to identify the meaning of a particular word in the passage. These can be done at the last minute, even if you haven't read the passage. On most Quantitative Comparisons, even the hardest ones, you can quickly eliminate at least one answer, improving your chances of guessing correctly. When you start to run out of time, locate and answer any of the quick points that remain.

When you take the SAT, you have one clear objective in mind—to score as many points as you can. It's that simple. The rest of this book will help you do it.

2

Inside the SAT

- Familiarize yourself with the breakdown of questions

- Learn how the test is timed and scored

Because it's a standardized test, you can feel safe in knowing that the structure, contents, and questions on the SAT will be pretty much what you should expect after working your way through this book. In this chapter, we will walk you through the structure of the SAT. When you sit down to take the test, you should already know what kind of questions you'll find, what the instructions say, how the test will be scored, and how you will be timed.

STRUCTURE OF THE TEST

There are six types of questions on the SAT, three Verbal and three Math. The likely number of questions you'll see of each type is shown below.

SAT Emergency

If you have only a week or two to prep for the SAT, you should spend time getting familiar with the test. Be sure to read this chapter.

Verbal

On the Verbal section of the SAT you'll find:

- 19 *Analogies*—Analogies test your ability to see relationships between words.

- 19 *Sentence Completions*—These test your ability to see how the parts of a sentence relate. About half will have one word missing from a sentence; the rest will have two words missing. Both types test vocabulary knowledge and reasoning ability.

- *40 Critical Reading questions*, in four separate sets—Critical Reading tests your ability to read and understand a passage. The passages are long (400–850 words), and at least one passage contains two related readings. Some reading questions test your understanding of the content of the passage; others will require you to draw conclusions. Some will also explicitly test vocabulary in context.

Kaplan Rules

Getting familiar with the SAT can get you a higher score on the SAT. Once you know the setup of the test and you've learned what to expect, you'll be more confident about your ability to master every section and question type. Familiarity gives you confidence and confidence gets you points.

Math

On the Math section you'll find:

- 15 *Quantitative Comparisons*—QCs, as they're called, give you two quantities and ask you to compare them. You have to determine if one quantity is larger, if they're equal, or if you don't have enough information to decide. They test your knowledge of math, your ability to apply that knowledge, and your reasoning ability. They're also designed to be done quickly, making them a good source of quick points.

- 35 *Regular Math* questions—These are straightforward multiple-choice math questions, with five answer choices.

- 10 *Grid-ins*—These questions are open-ended, with no answer choices. Instead, you enter your response into a small grid. These questions test the same math concepts as the other types of questions.

SECTION BREAKDOWN

The SAT is divided into seven sections, which can appear in any order:

- Two 30-minute Verbal sections with Analogies, Sentence Completions, and Critical Reading

- One 15-minute Verbal section with Critical Reading

- One 30-minute section with QCs and Grid-ins

- One 30-minute section with Regular Math

- One 15-minute section with Regular Math

There is also one 30-minute Experimental section. This section does not affect your score and is used to try out new questions. It can show up anyplace and it will look like any other Verbal or Math section. Don't try to figure out which section is experimental so you can nap during that period. First of all, you'll lose your momentum in the middle of the test. Second, and more important, you might be wrong.

SCORING

You get one point added to your score for each correct answer on the SAT, and lose a fraction of a point for each wrong answer (except for Grid-ins—but we'll go into that later). If you leave a question blank, you neither gain nor lose points. The totals are added up for all the Verbal and Math questions, and that produces two raw scores.

These numbers aren't your SAT scores. The raw scores are converted into scaled scores, each on a scale of 200 to 800, and these are the scores that are reported to you and the colleges you choose. (The reports include subscores as well, but most colleges focus on the two main scores.)

In April of 1995, the College Board adjusted or "recentered" the scoring of the SAT. The average scaled score (on a 200- to 800-point scale) for either Math or Verbal is now 500, for an average combined score of 1,000 points. This is almost 100 points higher than the old combined averages. The test isn't any easier or harder; only the scoring has changed.

Bottom line: If you compared your SAT score with that of someone who took the test before 1995 (someone who got the exact number of questions right as you did), your score would probably be higher. Sounds great, right?

Well, it's not so cut-and-dried. Remember, everyone's score is adjusted, so you'll fall in the same percentile range using this new scale as you would using the old. The percentile is the percentage of SAT takers scoring at or below a given score.

> **Did You Know . . .**
>
> . . . that a little bit of improvement on the SAT can go a long way? Getting just one extra question right every ten minutes on the SAT translates to 15 more questions right over the entire test. This improvement could boost your scaled score by close to 150 points.

SAT TIMING

The SAT:

- Is three hours long
- Includes two ten-minute breaks (after Sections 2 and 4)

There are some rules about how you can and cannot allocate this time:

- You are not allowed to jump back and forth between sections.
- You are not allowed to return to earlier sections to change answers.
- You are not allowed to spend more than the allotted time on any section.
- You can move around within a section.
- You can flip through your section at the beginning to see what type of questions you have.

You'll get more familiar with the format and setup of the SAT as you work your way through this book. For now, just remember the basics we covered in chapter 1: The SAT is predictable, there are elements built right into the test that allow you to prep for it, and you need to develop an approach to answering the questions.

SAT Registration Overview

- Check the College Board website at www.collegeboard.com for complete information about registering for the SAT.

- To register for the SAT by mail, you'll need to get a Registration Bulletin from your high school guidance counselor.

- You can also register online at www.collegeboard.com/sat/html/satform.html. The website contains easy, step-by-step instructions for electronically submitting your registration. Not all students are eligible to register online; read the instructions and requirements carefully.

- You may register by telephone, for a fee of $10, only if you've previously registered for the SAT and you require no special forms (like a fee waiver). If you have a touch-tone phone and a major credit card, you can reregister by calling (800) SAT-SCORE. If you need assistance, you can reach a customer service representative at (609) 771-7600.

- Register early to secure the time you want at the test center of your choice and to avoid late registration fees.

- Students with Disabilities can call (609) 771-7137 (TTY: (609) 882-4118) for more information.

- The basic fee at press time is $26 in the United States. This price includes reports for you, your high school, and up to four colleges and scholarship programs. There are additional fees for late registration, standby testing, international processing, changing test centers or test dates, rush reporting, and for additional services and products.

- The SAT is administered on select Saturdays during the school year. Sunday testing is available for students who cannot take the Saturday test because of religious observances.

- You will receive an admission ticket at least a week before the test. The ticket confirms your registration at a specified date, at a specified test center. Make sure to bring it, and proper identification, with you to the test center. Some acceptable forms of identification include photo IDs such as a driver's license, a school identification card, or a valid passport. Unacceptable forms of identification include a social security card, credit card, or birth certificate.

- Check with the College Board for all the latest information on the test. Every effort is made to keep the information in this book up to date, but changes may occur after the book is published.

- You might be considering whether to take the SAT, ACT, or both. For more information on the ACT, go to the ACT website at www.act.org/aap/.

- SAT scores will be available online approximately three weeks after the test. If you can't wait that long, you can get your scores eight days earlier with Scores by Web or Scores by Phone. Both services are $13. Please visit www.collegeboard.com for more information.

PSAT Registration Overview

- For complete information about the PSAT/NMSQT, visit the College Board's website at www.collegeboard.com/psat/student/html/indx001.html or the National Merit Scholarship Corporation's website, www.nationalmerit.org.

- To register for the PSAT, you must contact your high school guidance counselor. Your counselor can also provide complete information on dates, times, fees, etc. This test is not administered through test centers but rather by the high schools themselves.

- At press time, the basic fee for the PSAT/NMSQT is $10.50. Please note that schools sometimes charge an additional fee to cover administrative costs. Contact your school counselor for information regarding fee waivers.

- The PSAT is administered twice a year in October. Your school will probably administer the test on one of these two dates. You can check out the new College Board home page created specifically for your school to learn what day the PSAT is being given there. Go to www.collegeboard.com/psat/student/html/home_bridge.html.

- Taking the PSAT/NMSQT may qualify you to compete for a variety of college scholarships. For more information, check out www.nationalmerit.org.

Verbal Skills Workout

3

Introducing SAT Verbal

- Understand the breakdown and setup of the Verbal section
- Tap into existing Verbal skills such as paraphrasing and making inferences

Imagine yourself driving through Paris, France. As you approach an intersection, you see a red octagonal sign with the word *arrêtez* on it. Even if you don't speak a word of French, you come to a stop and look down the crossroads before driving on through the city.

If you didn't know the language, you probably took the information given to you—the shape, color, and location of the sign—and related it to what you already know. You may also have noticed, maybe subconsciously, that *arrêtez* sounds something like *arrest*, which means "stop."

The skills you displayed by making this deduction are skills of inference. To do well on the SAT Verbal section, you need to apply these same skills. The SAT does not test spelling or grammar. It does not test your knowledge of English literature or literary terms. It will never ask you to interpret a poem. SAT Verbal questions cover a fairly predictable, fairly limited body of skills and knowledge: vocabulary, verbal reasoning, and reading skills.

There are three scored Verbal sections on the SAT. The breakdown of the questions will go something like this:

SAT Emergency

This chapter will help you get a handle on the SAT Verbal section. You should read this chapter even if you have two weeks or fewer to prep.

- One 30-minute section with nine Sentence Completions, 13 Analogies, and 13 Critical Reading questions

- One 30-minute section with 10 Sentence Completions, six Analogies, and 14 Critical Reading questions

- One 15-minute section with 13 Critical Reading questions

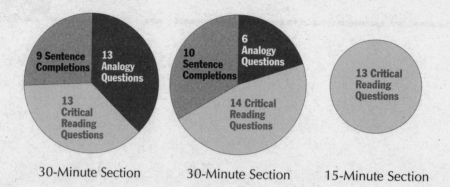

30-Minute Section   30-Minute Section   15-Minute Section

The Sentence Completions and Analogy sets are arranged by order of difficulty. The first few questions in a set are meant to be fairly straightforward and manageable. The middle few questions will be a little harder and the last few are the most difficult. Keep this in mind as you work and move through the early questions a little more quickly to leave yourself more time for the difficult ones. Work through the Sentence Completions and Analogies quickly and efficiently. Make sure you get all the points you can there, and then move on to Reading.

Critical Reading is not arranged by difficulty. Any time you find yourself beginning to spend too much time on a question, you should skip it and return to it later.

What Matters

Your score on the Verbal section is based on your ability to do the following:

- Solve analogies by finding two words that are related in the same way as the two words they give you.

- Fill in the blanks in sentences that are missing one or two words.

- Read a passage and answer a bunch of questions about it.

HOW TO APPROACH SAT VERBAL

To do well on SAT Verbal, you need to be systematic in your approach to each question type and each of the three Verbal sections. Sentence Completions and Analogies are designed to be done relatively quickly. That means you can earn points fast, so you should do these first. Critical Reading takes a lot longer, so you can't just leave yourself five minutes to do a passage. Remember, you earn just as many points for an easy question as you do for a hard one.

Tapping Your Verbal Skills

Although the test materials never explain this, a big key to doing well on the verbal part of the SAT is sharpening your verbal critical thinking skills—skills that you already use every day.

If you get to a movie ten minutes late, do you give up and walk out, deciding you'll never understand what's going on? Probably not. Instead, you use your inference skills—the ability to draw valid conclusions from limited information—to catch up and enjoy the rest of the film.

If you have a sudden urge for a tub of popcorn, do you leave during the climactic scene? More likely, you use your ability to distinguish important concepts from minor details to pick a dull moment to make your move.

When your younger brother asks you what the movie was about, do you take two hours to explain it to him? You probably use your paraphrasing skills—the ability to condense complex ideas into a few words—to give him the highlights in a few minutes before you go back to ignoring him.

Know What to Expect

Doing your best on SAT Verbal comes from knowing what to expect, and knowing that you have the skills to handle it. You use words every day. You make your own ideas clear and you understand and respond to those of others. In all of these cases—talking with friends or talking with teachers, reading a textbook or reading a billboard, listening to lyrics or listening to your SAT proctor's instructions—you take limited information, process it through your own intellect and experience, and make sense of it. If you can learn to make the most of these skills on the test, you'll be well on the road to a great Verbal score.

What Doesn't Matter

You don't need to know pronunciation, antonyms, foreign languages, creative writing, spelling, or anything about literature.

Teacher Tip

"Write all over your test booklet. Crossing out wrong answers eliminates confusion and helps you to see clearly which answer is correct. Underlining key points when reading passages helps you to determine the main idea, and underlining key words in Sentence Completions helps you to predict which word fits correctly in the blank."

—Jennifer Killmer
Kaplan Teacher
Coral Gables, FL

4

Vocabulary

- Practice working with unfamiliar words and familiar words with secondary meanings

- Improve your vocabulary by studying word roots and families

- Find out how to decode strange words

You know how to read. You can explain the relationship between *kitten* and *cat* to a three-year-old. You can finish a friend's sentence when she sneezes in the middle. So what makes the Verbal section such a challenge? Vocabulary. You may have a solid understanding of a Critical Reading passage but then get thrown by one tough vocabulary word. You may know the relationship between the original pair of words in an Analogy, but have a tough time finding the answer because all the choices have words you've never seen before. You may know precisely what kind of word to fill in on a Sentence Completion, and then find that all the answer choices look like they're in a foreign language.

All three Verbal question types—Analogies, Sentence Completions, and Critical Reading—depend upon your ability to work with unfamiliar words. You won't be asked to define words on the SAT. But you'll need to have a sense of their meaning in order to answer the questions.

SAT Emergency

If you have only a week or two to prep for the SAT, go straight to the section called "Decoding Strange Words on the Test" and try to master those skills.

TWO TYPES OF HARD WORDS

There are two types of hard SAT words:

- Unfamiliar words

- Familiar words with secondary meanings

Some words are hard because you haven't seen them before. The words *scintilla* or *circumlocution*, for instance, are probably not part of your everyday vocabulary. But they might pop up on your SAT.

Easy words, such as *recognize* or *appreciation*, may also trip you up on the test because they have secondary meanings that you aren't used to. Analogies and Critical Reading in particular will throw you familiar words with unfamiliar meanings.

To get a sense of your vocabulary strength, we've provided a representative list of words you might find on the SAT. Take a couple of minutes to look through it and see how many you know. Write your answer right in the book. Give yourself one point for each word you know. (Answers follow the quiz.)

<table>
<tr><td>*irritate*</td><td>to annoy</td></tr>
<tr><td>*truthful*</td><td>speaking truth</td></tr>
<tr><td>*conquer*</td><td>to win by taking over</td></tr>
<tr><td>*passionate*</td><td>emotional; strong feelings for something</td></tr>
<tr><td>*inactive*</td><td>not moving; dormant</td></tr>
<tr><td>*eliminate*</td><td>to get rid of</td></tr>
<tr><td>*benevolent*</td><td>kind; generous</td></tr>
<tr><td>*elocution*</td><td>study + practice of public speaking
pronunciation of words</td></tr>
<tr><td>*irk*</td><td>annoy; bother</td></tr>
<tr><td>*pragmatic*</td><td>practical</td></tr>
<tr><td>*breadth*</td><td>width across the surface of something</td></tr>
</table>

Who Cares?

Somewhere in the process of studying for the Verbal section, you may decide that learning the difference between *taciturn* and *tenacious*, *obdurate*, and *obloquy*, and even *plaudit* and *pusillanimous* is among the silliest things you've ever done. After all, no one on TV talks that way.

Your vocabulary says a lot about your ability to express yourself, as well as giving some valuable hints as to how well read you are. Colleges like students with big vocabularies, so humor them. Learn some new words.

The single best way to do well on SAT verbal is to read as much as possible. Read newspapers and magazines to see words in use. Underline the ones you need to look up. If you recognize the words you see on the exam, you'll be on your way to acing the SAT.

rectify — _to correct_ / _to make holy_

duplicity — _deception; dishonesty_ / _doubtful_

impartial — _not biased_

abandon (n.) — _without inhibitions_

vie — _compete_

overt — _unconcealed; obvious_ / _under cover_

august (adj.) — _dignified; venerable_ / _old_

laud — _to praise_ / _call attention to; talk about_

voluble — _lengthy in words; talkative_

flag (v.) — _to call / signal; to lose energy_

perspicacity — _shrewdness_

maladroit — _clumsy; tactless_

sonorous — _of sound_

doleful — _sad_

serpentine — _twisting, winding_ / _long, slender_

rail (v.) — _complain (of injustice); to scold_

quiescence — _inactivity; stillness_ / _accepting_

idiosyncrasy — _eccentricity_ / _accepted forms in society_

kudos — _fame; glory; honor_ / _something good_

Teacher Tip

"Many students worry that they do not know enough vocabulary to perform well on the Verbal section, but even someone with the most basic vocabulary background can conquer the SAT with the correct preparation."

—Suzanne Riskin
Kaplan Teacher
Miami, FL

Strange Word Origins

Learning the derivation of words can often help you remember the meaning of words. Did you know . . .

- *Jovial* (joyful) comes from the Roman deity Jove, who was known for his pleasant disposition.

- *Sardonic* (characterized by bitter mockery) comes from sardinia, a mythical plant from the island of the same name. Ingestion of the plant caused convulsive laughter followed by death.

- *Maudlin* (overly sentimental) comes from Mary Magdalene, a follower of Christ who is shown weeping in many paintings. *Maudlin* is an alternate pronunciation of Magdalene.

Here are the definitions of the words in the list on the previous page:

irritate	to annoy, bother
truthful	honest, straightforward, trustworthy
conquer	to defeat, overthrow
passionate	emotional, ardent, enthusiastic
inactive	not active, not moving
eliminate	to get rid of
benevolent	generous, kind
elocution	the study and practice of public speaking
irk	to irritate, anger, annoy
pragmatic	practical; moved by facts rather than abstract ideal
breadth	broadness, wideness
rectify	to correct
duplicity	deception, dishonesty, double-dealing
impartial	fair, just, unbiased, unprejudiced
abandon (n.)	total lack of inhibition
vie	to compete, contend
overt	apparent, unconcealed
august (adj.)	dignified, awe-inspiring, venerable
laud	to praise, applaud, honor
voluble	speaking much and easily, talkative; glib
flag (v.)	to droop, lose energy; to signal, to mark
perspicacity	shrewdness, astuteness, keenness of wit
maladroit	clumsy, tactless
sonorous	producing a full, rich sound
doleful	sad, mournful
serpentine	serpentlike; twisting, winding
rail (v.)	to scold with bitter or abusive language
quiescence	inactivity, stillness
idiosyncrasy	peculiarity of temperament, eccentricity
kudos	fame, glory, honor

If you got ten definitions or fewer right, you should probably work on building your vocabulary. The techniques and tools in this chapter will help you improve your vocabulary and make the most out of what you do know about words.

If you got between 10 and 20 right, your vocabulary is average. If you're willing to put in the time, using these techniques and tools can help you do better.

If you got 20 definitions or more right, your vocabulary is in great shape. You can polish it further, but you don't have to. If time is short, learn the strategies in the "Decoding Strange Words" section and concentrate on other aspects of the SAT that you find difficult.

A VOCABULARY-BUILDING PLAN

A great vocabulary can't be built overnight, but you can develop a better SAT vocabulary with a minimum of pain. Here's a plan:

Learn Words Strategically

The best words to learn are words that have appeared often on the SAT. The test makers are not very creative in their choice of words for each test; words that have appeared frequently are likely bets to show up again.

The word lists in the "SAT Study Aids" section of this book give you a jump on some common SAT words. Learn a few words a day from these lists, spreading them over the time remaining before the SAT. Keep reviewing those you've already studied.

The Word Families list groups words into common meaning families. For example, *loquacious, verbose,* and *garrulous* all mean "wordy, talkative." *Taciturn, laconic, terse, concise,* and *pithy* all mean "not talkative, not wordy." Instead of learning just one of these words, learn them all together—you get eight words for the price of one definition.

Be strategic. How well you use your time between now and the day of the test is just as important as how much time you spend prepping.

> **Teacher Tip**
>
> "Take five vocabulary flashcards a day and learn them thoroughly—flip through them at least three times. Each day take on five more, adding them to the cards from the previous day. Review your collection as it grows. Vocabulary skills will build dramatically if this is kept up until Test Day!"
>
> —Jennifer Killmer
> Kaplan Teacher
> Coral Gables, FL

Work with Word Roots

Most SAT words are made up of prefixes and roots that can get you at least partway to a definition. Often, that's all you need to get a right answer.

Use the Root List in the "SAT Study Aids" section to pick up the most valuable SAT roots. Target these words in your vocabulary prep. Learn a few new roots a day, familiarizing yourself with the meaning.

Personalize Your Vocabulary Study

Figure out a study method that works best for you, and stick to it.

- Use flashcards: Write down new words or word groups and run through them whenever you have a few spare minutes. Put one new word or word group on one side of a 3 × 5 index card and a short definition on the back.

- Make a vocabulary notebook: List words in one column and their meaning in another. Test yourself. Cover up the meanings, and see which words you can define from memory. Make a sample sentence using each word in context.

- Make a vocabulary tape: Record unknown words and their definitions. Pause for a moment before you read the definition. This will give you time to define the word in your head when you play the tape back. Quiz yourself. Listen to your tape in your portable cassette player. Play it in the car, on the bus, or whenever you have a few spare moments.

- Think of hooks that lodge a new word in your mind: Create visual images of words.

- Use rhymes and other devices that help you remember the words.

It doesn't matter which techniques you use, as long as you learn words steadily and methodically. Doing so over several months is ideal.

DECODING STRANGE WORDS ON THE TEST

Trying to learn every word that could possibly appear on the SAT is like trying to memorize the license plate number of every car on the freeway. It's not much fun, it'll give you a headache, and you probably won't pull it off.

No matter how much time you spend with flashcards, vocabulary tapes, or word lists, you're bound to face some mystery words on your SAT. No big deal. Just as you can use your basic multiplication skills to find the product of even the largest numbers, you can use what you know about words to focus on likely meanings of tough vocabulary words.

Go with Your Hunches

When you look at an unfamiliar word, your first reaction may be to say, "Don't know it. Gotta skip it." Not so fast. Vocabulary knowledge on the SAT is not an all-or-nothing proposition.

- Some words you know so well you can rattle off a dictionary definition of them.

- Some words you "sort of" know. You understand them when you see them in context, but don't feel confident using them yourself.

- Some words are vaguely familiar. You know you've heard them somewhere before.

If you think you recognize a word, go with your hunch!

Try to Recall Where You've Heard the Word Before

If you can recall a phrase in which the word appears, that may be enough to eliminate some answer choices, or even zero in on the right answer.

EXAMPLE

Between the two villages was a ---- through
which passage was difficult and hazardous.

(A) precipice

(B) beachhead

(C) quagmire

(D) market

(E) prairie

To answer this question, it helps to know the word *quagmire*. You may remember *quagmire* from news reports referring to "a foreign policy *quagmire*" or "a *quagmire* of financial indebtedness." If you can remember how *quagmire* was used, you'll have a rough idea of what it means, and you'll see it fits. You may also be reminded of the word *mire*, as in "We got *mired* in the small details and never got to the larger issue." Sounds something like stuck, right? You don't need an exact definition. A *quagmire* is a situation that's difficult to get out of, so (C) is correct. Literally, a *quagmire* is a bog or swamp.

Decide If the Word Has a Positive or Negative "Charge"

Simply knowing that you're dealing with a positive or negative word can earn you points on the SAT. For example, look at the word *cantankerous*. Say it to yourself. Can you guess whether it's positive or negative? Often words that sound harsh have a negative meaning, while smooth-sounding words tend to have positive meanings. If *cantankerous* sounded negative to you, you were right. It means "difficult to handle."

You can also use prefixes and roots to help determine a word's charge. *Mal, de, dis, un, in, im, a,* and *mis* often indicate a negative, while *pro, ben,* and *magn* are often positives.

Not all SAT words sound positive or negative; some sound neutral. But if you can define the charge, you can probably eliminate some answer choices on that basis alone.

EXAMPLE

He seemed at first to be honest and loyal, but
before long it was necessary to ---- him for his
---- behavior.

(A) admonish . . steadfast

(B) extol . . conniving

(C) reprimand . . scrupulous

(D) exalt . . insidious

(E) castigate . . perfidious

All you need to know to answer this question is that negative words are needed in both blanks. Then you can scan the answer choices for a choice that contains two clearly negative words. Choice (E) is right. *Castigate* means "punish or scold harshly," and *perfidious* means "treacherous."

Use Your Foreign Language Skills

Many of the roots you'll encounter in SAT words come from Latin. Spanish, French, and Italian also come from Latin, and have retained much of it in their modern forms. English is also a cousin to German and Greek. That means that if you don't recognize a word, try to remember if you know a similar word in another language.

Look at the word *carnal*. Unfamiliar? What about *carne*, as in *chili con carne*? *Carn* means "meat" or "flesh," which leads you straight to the meaning of *carnal*—pertaining to the flesh. You could decode *carnivorous* ("meat eating") in the same way.

You can almost always figure out something about strange words on the test because SAT words are never all that strange. Chances are that few words on the SAT will be totally new to you, even if your recollection is more subliminal than vivid.

When All Else Fails

Eliminate choices that are clearly wrong and make an educated guess from the remaining choices. A wrong answer won't hurt you much; a right answer will help you a lot.

Don't forget to study the word lists in the "SAT Study Aids" section!

Checklist

Once you've mastered a concept, check it off.

Vocabulary:

❏ A vocabulary-building plan

❏ Decoding strange words

5

Analogies

- Become proficient in building bridges

- Study the Kaplan Three-Step Method for Analogies

- Review the nine classic bridges

- Use process of elimination as a backup strategy

- Complete the Analogies Practice Set

Analogies may seem frightening at first because they don't look like anything you've ever done before. But you'll feel better about them as soon as you realize that you speak and think in analogies all the time. Any time you say "my sister is like a slug," you're drawing an analogy between your sister and slugs—perhaps your sister is as gross as a slug. That may not be the kind of relationship that will appear on your SAT, but the way of thinking is the same.

Once you get familiar with the Analogy format, you'll find there's a simple method for mastering this question type. In fact, prepping often gains you more points on Analogies than on any other Verbal question type. With practice, you can even learn to get the Analogy right when you don't know all of the vocabulary words involved.

SAT Emergency

If you don't have much time to prep for the SAT, here's the best way to spend your time:

- Learn the Kaplan Three-Step Method for Analogies.

- Do the practice set in this chapter.

- If you miss an answer, review the tips in this chapter.

THE FORMAT

There are 19 Analogies in all on the SAT. You'll probably see one set of 13 and one set of six. Each 30-minute Verbal section contains a set of Analogies. A question looks like this:

EXAMPLE

FLAKE : SNOW ::

(A) storm : hail

(B) drop : rain

(C) field : wheat

(D) stack : hay

(E) cloud : fog

The two words in capital letters are called the *stem words*. The instructions will tell you to choose the pair of words from the five answer choices that is related in the same way as this pair. In this example, the answer above is (B). A flake is a small unit of snow, just as a drop is a small unit of rain.

BUILDING BRIDGES

In every Analogy question, there exists a strong, definite connection between the two stem words. Your task is to identify this relationship, and then to look for a similar relationship among the answer pairs.

What's a strong, definite relationship?

- The words *library* and *book* have a strong, definite connection. A library is defined as a place where books are kept. LIBRARY : BOOK could be a question stem.

- The words *library* and *child* do not have a strong, definite connection. A child may or may not have anything to do with a library. LIBRARY : CHILD would never be a question stem.

Teacher Tip

"Analogies are not just about knowing the words, they are also about knowing how to spot a strong bridge. Right answers are chosen based on good elimination strategies."

—Suzanne Riskin
Kaplan Teacher
Miami, FL

The best way to pinpoint the relationship between the stem words is to build a bridge. A bridge is a short sentence that relates the two words. Often, a bridge reads like a definition of one of the two words. For instance: "A *library* is a place where BOOKS are kept."

The ability to find bridges is fundamental to Analogy success. Your bridge needs to capture the strong, definite connection between the words.

KAPLAN

KAPLAN'S THREE-STEP METHOD

The Kaplan Method for solving Analogies has three simple steps:

1. Build a bridge between the stem words.

2. Plug in the answer choices.

3. Adjust your bridge, if you need to.

Here's an Analogy stem. We've left out the answer choices because you need to focus first on the stem.

EXAMPLE

LILY : FLOWER ::

1. Build a Bridge

The best bridge here is, "A LILY is, by definition, a type of FLOWER."

2. Plug in the Answer Choices

Here is the complete question.

EXAMPLE

LILY : FLOWER ::

(A) rose : thorn

(B) cocoon : butterfly

(C) brick : building

(D) maple : tree

(E) sky : airplane

> ### What Makes a Strong Bridge?
>
> You might be lured into thinking the words *trumpet* and *jazz* have a strong bridge. They don't.
>
> You can play lots of things on trumpets other than jazz—fanfares, taps, whatever. You can also play jazz on things other than trumpets.
>
> *Trumpet* and *instrument* do have a strong bridge. A trumpet is, by definition, a type of instrument. This is always true—it's a strong, definite relationship.

Take the bridge you have built and plug in answer choices (A) through (E). If only one pair fits, it's the answer.

HINT: *Be sure to try all five choices.*

Here's how plugging in the answer choices works:

(A)   A *rose* is a type of *thorn*? No.

(B)   A *cocoon* is a type of *butterfly*? No.

(C)   A *brick* is a type of *building*? No.

(D)   A *maple* is a type of *tree*? Yes.

(E)   A *sky* is a type of *airplane*? No.

We've got four nos and only one yes, so the answer is (D).

3. Adjust Your Bridge If You Need To

If no answer choice seems to fit, your bridge is too specific and you should go back and adjust it. If more than one answer choice fits, your bridge is not specific enough. Look at this example:

> EXAMPLE
>
> SNAKE : SLITHER ::
>
> (A) egg : hatch
>
> (B) wolf : howl
>
> (C) rabbit : hop
>
> (D) turtle : snap
>
> (E) tarantula : bite

With a simple bridge, such as "a snake slithers," you'd have a hard time finding the answer. All the answer choices make sense: an *egg hatches*, a *wolf howls*, a *rabbit hops*, a *turtle snaps*, and a *tarantula bites*. Don't worry. Go back to step one and build another bridge, this time making it more specific. Think about what *slither* means.

New bridge: "Slithering is how a snake gets around."

> (A)   *Hatching* is how an *egg* gets around? No.
>
> (B)   *Howling* is how a *wolf* gets around? No.
>
> (C)   *Hopping* is how a *rabbit* gets around? Yes.
>
> (D)   *Snapping* is how a *turtle* gets around? No.
>
> (E)   *Biting* is how a *tarantula* gets around? No.

Four nos and one yes; the answer is (C).

HINT: *If no answer fits, or too many answers fit, build a new bridge and plug in again.*

WHAT PART OF SPEECH IS A STEM WORD?

Occasionally with an Analogy you might have to take a quick peek at the answer choices before you can build a bridge for the stem. The part of speech of a stem word may be ambiguous. When you're not sure whether a stem word is a noun, verb, adjective, or adverb, look at the words directly beneath that stem word. As a rule, the words in a vertical row are all the same part of speech.

For example, you might see this:

> VERB : NOUN ::
>
> (A) verb : noun
>
> (B) verb : noun
>
> (C) verb : noun
>
> (D) verb : noun
>
> (E) verb : noun

or this:

> ADJECTIVE : NOUN ::
>
> (A) adjective : noun
>
> (B) adjective : noun
>
> (C) adjective : noun
>
> (D) adjective : noun
>
> (E) adjective : noun

but you'll *never* see this on an SAT Analogy:

> NOUN : NOUN ::
>
> (A) verb : noun
>
> (B) noun : noun
>
> (C) verb : verb
>
> (D) verb : noun
>
> (E) verb : noun

To establish the part of speech of a stem word, you don't usually have to look at more than choice (A).

How would you think through the following example?

> EXAMPLE
>
> PINE : DESIRE ::
>
> (A) laugh : sorrow
>
> (B) drink : thirst
>
> (C) watch : interest
>
> (D) listen : awe
>
> (E) starve : hunger

The word *pine* can be a noun, but that's not likely here. You can't build a bridge between a tree with needlelike leaves and *desire*. Try another part of speech. A glance at the answer choices below *pine* (*laugh, drink, watch, listen,* and *starve*) tells you *pine* is being used as a verb.

What about *desire*? It could be a noun or a verb, but the answer choices beneath it (*sorrow, thirst, interest, awe,* and *hunger*) tell you it's used as a noun.

You've probably heard of someone pining away from unrequited love. As a verb, *pine* means "to yearn or suffer from longing." A good bridge would be: "By definition, to pine is to suffer from extreme desire." Plugging in the answer choices, you get:

(A)   To *laugh* is to suffer from extreme *sorrow*? No.

(B)   To *drink* is to suffer from extreme *thirst*? No.

(C)   To *watch* is to suffer from extreme *interest*? No.

(D)   To *listen* is to suffer from extreme *awe*? No.

(E)   To *starve* is to suffer from extreme *hunger*? Yes.

Once again, four nos and one yes; the answer is (E).

TEST YOUR ANALOGY SMARTS

Try out what you've learned on these Analogies. (Answers on p. 36.)

1. SWEEP : BROOM ::

(A) cut : scissors
(B) soil : cloth
(C) dry : bucket
(D) thread : needle
(E) wash : dish   Ⓐ Ⓑ Ⓒ Ⓓ Ⓔ

2. MAP : ATLAS ::

(A) lock : key
(B) road : highway
(C) recipe : cookbook
(D) concept : encyclopedia
(E) theory : hypothesis   Ⓐ Ⓑ Ⓒ Ⓓ Ⓔ

3. HUNGRY : FAMINE ::

(A) thirsty : rainfall
(B) sick : plague
(C) sated : dinner
(D) dry : flood
(E) sore : injury   Ⓐ Ⓑ Ⓒ Ⓓ Ⓔ

NINE CLASSIC BRIDGES

It's easier to build bridges when you know the types of bridges that have appeared on the SAT in the past. While no one can give you a list of the words that will appear on SAT Analogies, you can learn what types of relationships to expect. The following classic bridges appear over and over again on the SAT. Don't memorize these bridges, or lists of words that fit these bridges. Instead, learn which types of bridges can lead you to the right answer on SAT Analogies and which cannot.

HINT: *Become familiar with the types of bridges that connect stem words on the SAT. They can lead you to the right answer.*

Classic bridges may take different forms, depending on what parts of speech are used. But the underlying concepts are what matter. Here are examples of nine classic types:

Bridge Type #1: Description

In many Analogies, one stem word is a person, place, or thing, and the other word is a characteristic of that person, place, or thing.

Look at these examples:

> PAUPER : POOR—A PAUPER is always POOR.
>
> GENIUS : INTELLIGENT—A GENIUS is always INTELLIGENT.
>
> TRAGEDY : SAD—A TRAGEDY is always SAD.

This classic bridge can also describe a person, place, or thing by what it is *not*.

> PAUPER : WEALTHY—A PAUPER is never WEALTHY.
>
> GENIUS : STUPID—A GENIUS is never STUPID.
>
> TRAGEDY : HAPPY—A TRAGEDY is never HAPPY.

Here are more types of classic bridges. Fill in each blank with a stem word that will complete the bridge. There is more than one way to fill in each blank. The important thing is to get the right idea. Suggested answers follow.

Bridge Type #2: Characteristic Actions

> An INSOMNIAC can't ----.
>
> A GLUTTON likes to ----.
>
> A PROCRASTINATOR tends to ----.

Bridge Type #3: Lack

> Something MURKY lacks ----.
>
> A PESSIMIST lacks ----.
>
> A PAUPER lacks ----.

Do It Yourself

One way to see the inner workings of Analogies is to put some together yourself. Make sure you include five answer choices. This exercise will give you a good feel for the structure of SAT Analogies and may help you spot and avoid bad answer choices.

Answers to Analogy Questions on p. 34

1. (A) (A broom is used to sweep.)

2. (C) (An atlas is made up of many maps.)

3. (B) (Many are hungry during a famine.)

Bridge Type #4: Categories

MEASLES is a type of ----.

A MOTORCYCLE is a type of ----.

A POLKA is a type of ----.

Bridge Type #5: Size/Degree

To SPEAK very quietly is to ----.

To LIKE strongly is to ----.

To BRUSH is to ---- lightly.

Bridge Type #6: Causing/Stopping

A REMEDY stops or cures an ----.

An OBSTACLE prevents ----.

Something INCENDIARY causes ----.

Bridge Type #7: Places

A JUDGE works in a ----.

A PLAY is performed on a ----.

BREAD is made in a ----.

Bridge Type #8: Function

GILLS are used for ----.

A PAINTBRUSH is used to ----.

A HELICOPTER is used for ----.

Bridge Type #9: Part/Whole

An ARMY is made up of ----.

A CROWD is made up of many ----.

An arrangement of FLOWERS is a ----.

Suggested Answers to Bridge Types

Your answers may vary from our suggested answers. As long as you've got the basic idea, that's okay.

Characteristic Actions:

An INSOMNIAC can't SLEEP.

A GLUTTON likes to EAT.

A PROCRASTINATOR tends to DELAY.

Lack:

Something MURKY lacks CLARITY.

A PESSIMIST lacks OPTIMISM.

A PAUPER lacks MONEY.

Categories:

MEASLES is a type of ILLNESS.

A MOTORCYCLE is a type of VEHICLE.

A POLKA is a type of DANCE.

Size/Degree:

To SPEAK very quietly is to WHISPER.

To LIKE strongly is to LOVE (or ADORE).

To BRUSH is to TOUCH lightly.

Causing/Stopping:

A REMEDY stops or cures an ILLNESS.

An OBSTACLE prevents PROGRESS (or MOVEMENT).

Something INCENDIARY causes FIRE.

Places:

A JUDGE works in a COURTROOM.

A PLAY is performed on a STAGE (or in a THEATER).

BREAD is made in a BAKERY.

Function:

GILLS are used for BREATHING.

A PAINTBRUSH is used to PAINT.

A HELICOPTER is used for FLYING.

Part/Whole:

An ARMY is made up of SOLDIERS.

A CROWD is made up of many PEOPLE.

An arrangement of FLOWERS is a BOUQUET.

HOW TO FILL VOCABULARY GAPS

Sometimes on an SAT Analogy, you simply don't know one of the stem words. When this happens, the basic three-step process won't do much good. You can't even do step one; you can't build a bridge using a word you don't know. You need another plan.

The best backup strategy is not to focus on the stem pair. Instead, try looking at the answer pairs and eliminate those that simply can't be right. If you can knock out even one, guessing from the remaining choices is to your advantage. You may be surprised at how far this strategy can take you.

Teacher Tip

"In an analogy question there are usually at least two or three answer choices with weak bridges that can be eliminated right away, dramatically increasing your chances of getting a correct answer."

—Jennifer Killmer
Kaplan Teacher
Coral Gables, FL

Before you guess, take these three steps to eliminate some answer choices. (And remember, even if you can eliminate only one answer choice, guessing comes out in your favor.)

1. Eliminate answer choices with weak bridges.

2. Eliminate any two answer choices with identical bridges.

3. Eliminate answer choices with bridges that couldn't work with the stem pair no matter what that unknown word means.

Here's how you do it.

Eliminate Answer Choices with Weak Bridges

You learned earlier that a strong, definite relationship always exists between the pair of stem words. The answer pairs, however, don't always have a good bridge—and any choice without a good bridge can't be right. In other words, you can eliminate certain answer choices without looking at the stem at all.

Try this exercise. Here is a list of six answer pairs without any stem pairs—answers without questions. Try to make a bridge for each pair. If no strong bridge is possible, mark the pair with an *X*. (Answers on p. 40.)

1. DOG : HOUSE

2. AQUATIC : WATER

3. NOCTURNAL : ANIMAL

4. INFANTILE : TOY

5. STEAK : POTATOES

6. RAISIN : GRAPE

Kaplan Rules

The following relationships are not SAT-type bridges. If you encounter one, it's wrong.

- synonyms (example: PREDICT : FORETELL)

- antonyms (example: WEALTHY : IMPOVERISHED)

- members of the same category (example: DOG : CAT)

In many cases, this method alone will allow you to eliminate one, two, or even three answer choices.

Eliminate Answer Choices with Identical Bridges

There's another way of eliminating some wrong choices that's so obvious you might not think of it. If two choices have the same bridge, it follows that neither one can be more right than the other. And since they can't both be right, they must both be wrong. For example, look at the following question:

EXAMPLE

LEGERDEMAIN : MAGICIAN ::

(A) baggage : immigrant

(B) justice : pragmatist

(C) sluggishness : racer

(D) diplomacy : diplomat

(E) indifference : fanatic

What if you don't know what *legerdemain* means? (C) seems like a possible answer because this pair of words has a strong bridge: "Sluggishness is the opposite of what you'd expect from a racer." But choice (E) has a very similar bridge: "Indifference is the opposite of what you'd expect from a fanatic."

Since a question can't have two right answers, and both (C) and (E) have the same bridge, both must be wrong. The correct answer is (D).

Eliminate Answer Choices with Bridges That Can't Fit the Stem

What do you do with answer pairs that can't be eliminated by either of the first two methods? The next step is to find bridges for the remaining answers, and then to plug in the stem word pair. It's true that you don't even know what one of the stem words means. But in some cases you'll see that the stem word pair can't fit the answer bridge no matter what that unknown word means. Here's an example:

EXAMPLE

GENUFLECT : KNEE ::

(A) pierce : ear

(B) hold : hand

(C) nod : neck

(D) stub : toe

(E) pick : tooth

You may not know what *genuflect* means. Since you can't work directly with this stem, take a look at the answer choices instead.

Answer pair (A) has a strong bridge: To *pierce* an *ear* is to put a hole in it. Now try plugging *genuflect* and *knee* into this same bridge: To *genuflect* a *knee* is to put a hole in it. Hmmm. Can you really imagine that there exists a verb in the English language that means "to put a hole in a knee"? No way. The concept doesn't even make sense. So GENUFLECT : KNEE and pierce : ear can't possibly have the same bridge. (A) can't be the right answer.

The same technique can be used to eliminate choice (E). *Picking* your *teeth* is a way of cleaning between them. Is there a comparable way of cleaning between your knees? Not likely.

So you've been able to eliminate two of the answer choices—without knowing what *genuflect* means. Sometimes, of course, this technique demands a bit more intuition. Without knowing for sure, you might just have a feeling that there wouldn't be a word for a very large telephone or for a group of hammers. If you're guessing anyway, go with these hunches. The correct answer is (C).

Putting It Together

Now apply all three answer-eliminating techniques to one question. (Pretend that you don't know the word *scimitar* even if you do.)

EXAMPLE

SCIMITAR : SWORD ::

(A) diamond : ring

(B) greyhound : dog

(C) saddle : horse

(D) lance : shield

(E) forest : tree

(A) A *diamond* may adorn a *ring*, but plenty of rings don't have diamonds, and plenty of diamonds don't have rings. Choice (A) has a weak bridge. Eliminate.

(B) A *greyhound* is a kind of *dog*. Could a *scimitar* be a kind of *sword*? It sounds possible.

(C) A *saddle* is used for riding a *horse*. A *scimitar* is used for *riding* a sword? That can't make sense. Eliminate.

(D) A *lance* and a *shield* are both part of the traditional gear of a knight, but that's all we can say to connect them. Again, a weak bridge. Eliminate.

(E) A *forest* is a group of *trees*. Could a *scimitar* be a group of *swords*? Maybe.

Without knowing a stem word, you've gotten down to two answer choices—(B) and (E). Is there more likely to be a word for a kind of sword or for a group of swords? Take your best guess.

(B) is, in fact, the answer.

A DOUBLE VOCABULARY GAP

What if you don't know either of the stem words? You can still eliminate weak bridges and identical bridges. For example:

MANUMISSION : THRALL ::

(A) submission : employee

(B) prediction : artist

(C) promotion : rank

(D) tip : waiter

(E) parole : prisoner

> **Kaplan Rules**
>
> Not all bridges are classic bridges, but there is always a strong and definite relationship between the stem words.

Promotion is the act of raising an employee in rank. A *tip* is a type of gratuity or reward given to a waiter. *Parole* is the act of freeing a prisoner. These are all good bridges, and none of them repeat, so (C), (D), and (E) are all possible answers. But *submission* is not a characteristic of every *employee*, and there's no particular connection between *prediction* and *artist*. So eliminate (A) and (B).

To make your final decision, of course, you still have to guess. But now that you've eliminated answer choices, guessing works in your favor. The answer here happens to be (E), since *manumission* is, by definition, the act of freeing a *thrall*, or slave.

Now test your Analogy skills on the questions in the Analogies Practice Set that starts on the next page.

ANALOGIES PRACTICE SET

1. COPPER : METAL ::

   (A) grain : sand
   (B) helium : gas
   (C) stem : flower
   (D) tree : trunk
   (E) stone : clay

   Ⓐ Ⓑ Ⓒ Ⓓ Ⓔ

2. BROOM : DIRT ::

   (A) brush : bristles
   (B) fork : plate
   (C) rake : leaves
   (D) mirror : face
   (E) scissors : blades

   Ⓐ Ⓑ Ⓒ Ⓓ Ⓔ

3. COWARD : BRAVERY ::

   (A) eccentric : conformity
   (B) hero : fortitude
   (C) prophet : vision
   (D) sage : wisdom
   (E) comedian : humor

   Ⓐ Ⓑ Ⓒ Ⓓ Ⓔ

4. REVERE : ADMIRE ::

   (A) cherish : conceive
   (B) release : reject
   (C) guess : solve
   (D) propose : change
   (E) despise : disdain

   Ⓐ Ⓑ Ⓒ Ⓓ Ⓔ

5. PERPLEXING : CONFUSION ::

   (A) appalling : dismay
   (B) static : change
   (C) unpleasant : chaos
   (D) dignified : pride
   (E) grave : regret

   Ⓐ Ⓑ Ⓒ Ⓓ Ⓔ

6. AMUSING : MIRTH ::

   (A) ailing : health
   (B) painful : sympathy
   (C) optimistic : objectivity
   (D) protective : insecurity
   (E) terrifying : fear

7. FOOD : MENU ::

   (A) accounting : inventory
   (B) index : foreword
   (C) silverware : spoon
   (D) merchandise : catalog
   (E) films : credits

8. IMPERCEPTIBLE : DETECT ::

   (A) fundamental : begin
   (B) inconceivable : imagine
   (C) rugged : seize
   (D) costly : overcharge
   (E) immense : notice

Ⓐ Ⓑ Ⓒ Ⓓ Ⓔ

9. PERSEVERE : DOGGED ::

   (A) comply : obedient
   (B) inspire : pompous
   (C) hesitate : reckless
   (D) speak : laconic
   (E) retard : expeditious

Ⓐ Ⓑ Ⓒ Ⓓ Ⓔ

10. ENTHRALLING : TEDIUM ::

    (A) witty : frivolity
    (B) insipid : appetite
    (C) glaring : illumination
    (D) wearisome : redundancy
    (E) trite : originality

Answers and Explanations for Analogies Practice Set

1. (B) (Copper is a kind of metal.)

2. (C) (A broom is used to clear away dirt.)

3. (A) (A coward does not display bravery.)

4. (E) (By definition, to revere is to admire very much.)

5. (A) (Something that is perplexing causes confusion.)

6. (E) (Something that is amusing causes mirth.)

7. (D) (A menu is, by definition, a list of available food.)

8. (B) (If something is imperceptible, you cannot detect it.)

9. (A) (A dogged person is one who perseveres.)

10. (E) (Something that is enthralling lacks tedium.)

Checklist

Once you've mastered a concept, check it off.

Analogies:

❑ The format

❑ Building bridges

❑ Kaplan's Three-Step Method

❑ Test your analogy smarts

❑ Nine classic bridges

❑ How to fill vocabulary gaps

❑ Analogy practice set

6

Sentence Completions

HIGHLIGHTS

- Master the Kaplan Four-Step Method for Sentence Completions

- Learn to pick up on clues and predict answers

- Practice special techniques for tackling hard or tricky questions

- Complete the Sentence Completions Practice Set

Of all the Verbal question types, Sentence Completions are probably the most student-friendly. Unlike Analogies, they give you some context in which to think about vocabulary words, and unlike Critical Reading, they only require you to pay attention to a single sentence at a time. The 19 Sentence Completions count for about one-fourth of your verbal score.

THE FORMAT

There are 19 Sentence Completions in all on the SAT. You'll probably see one set of nine and one set of ten. They appear in both 30-minute Verbal Sections. The instructions for Sentence Completions look something like this:

Select the lettered word or set of words that best completes the sentence.

SAT Emergency

If you have only a week or two to prep for the SAT, here's the best way to spend your time:

- Learn the Kaplan Four-Step Method for Sentence Completions (pp. 46–47).

- Do the practice set starting on p. 56. If you miss an answer, skim through the chapter and look at the examples.

EXAMPLE

Today's small, portable computers contrast markedly with the earliest electronic computers, which were ----.

(A) effective

(B) invented

(C) useful

(D) destructive

(E) enormous

In the example, the new computers, which are small and portable, are contrasted with old computers. You can infer that the old computers must be the opposite of small and portable, so (E), *enormous*, is right.

KAPLAN'S FOUR-STEP METHOD

Here's the basic method for Sentence Completions:

1. Read the Sentence for Clue Words

Think about the sentence before looking at the answer choices. Figure out what the sentence means, taking special note of clue words.

HINT: *Clue words such as* and, but, such as, *and* although *tell you where a sentence is heading.*

2. Anticipate the Answer

You can see the direction some sentences are headed in from a mile away. Consider these examples:

"I still want to be your friend . . . ."

"Despite your impressive qualifications . . . ."

"If I ever get my hands on you, you little . . . ."

You could probably finish off these sentences on your own with pretty much the same language that the speaker would use. That's because the tone and structure of a sentence often clue you in to the meaning of the sentence.

On SAT Sentence Completions, you need to fill in missing pieces. Predict the word that goes in the blanks before looking at the answer choices. Do this by using the sentence's clue words (e.g., *despite, although*) and structural clues (construction and punctuation) to determine where the sentence is headed.

Kaplan Rules

To solve a Sentence Completion question:

1. Read the sentence for clue words.

2. Anticipate the answer.

3. Compare your prediction with each answer choice, and pick the best match.

4. Read the sentence with your answer choice in the blank or blanks.

You don't have to make an exact prediction. A rough idea of the kind of word you'll need will do. Often enough, it's simple to predict whether the missing word is positive or negative.

3. Compare Your Prediction with Each Answer Choice, and Pick the Best Match

Scan every answer choice before deciding.

4. Read the Sentence with Your Answer Choice in the Blank or Blanks

Keep in mind that only one choice will make sense.

If you've gone through the four steps and more than one choice seems possible, don't get stuck on the sentence. If you can eliminate at least one answer as wrong, guess and move on. If a question really stumps you, skip it and come back when you're done with the section.

Let's take a look at how the Four-Step Method works on some examples.

Kaplan Rules

Timing Tip: Spend no more than 40 seconds per Sentence Completion question. Don't read the sentence five times, plugging in every answer choice. That method takes too much time and makes you vulnerable to traps. Think about the question before you look for the answer.

EXAMPLE

Alligators, who bask in the sun for hours, appear to be ---- creatures, yet they are quite capable of sudden movement.

(A) active

(B) violent

(C) stern

(D) content

(E) sluggish

Read the sentence carefully, looking for clue words. *Yet* is a major clue. It tells you that the sentence switches direction midstream. The word in the blank must be the opposite of *sudden*.

Predict the word that goes in the blank. You can guess that alligators seem like lazy or idle creatures.

Compare your prediction with each answer choice, and pick the best match. (A), *active*, has nothing to do with being lazy or idle. Neither does (B), *violent*. Neither does (C), *stern*. Neither does (D), *content*. But (E), *sluggish*, means inactive or slow moving, so pick (E).

Check your answer by plugging it into the sentence. Let's check: "Alligators, who bask in the sun for hours, appear to be sluggish creatures, yet they are quite capable of sudden movement." Sounds okay. Finally, scan the other choices to make sure this is the best choice. None of the other choices works in the sentence, so (E) is correct.

EXAMPLE

The king's ---- decisions as a diplomat and administrator led to his legendary reputation as a just and ---- ruler.

(A) quick . . capricious

(B) equitable . . wise

(C) immoral . . perceptive

(D) generous . . witty

(E) clever . . uneducated

Get Charged

Look for word charges, the positive or negative connotations that a word may have, to help you make your prediction about what to put in the blanks.

See the Vocabulary chapter for more on word charges.

Read the sentence carefully, looking for clue words. A big clue here is the phrase *led to*. You know that the kind of decisions the king made led to his reputation as a just and ---- ruler. So whatever goes in both blanks must be consistent with *just*.

Predict the word that goes in the blank. Notice that both blanks must be similar in meaning. Because of his ---- decisions, the king is viewed a certain way, as a just and ---- ruler. So if the king's decisions were good, he'd be remembered as a good ruler, and if his decisions were bad, he'd be remembered as a bad ruler. *Just*, which means "fair," is a positive-sounding word; you can predict that both blanks will be similar in meaning, and that both will be positive words. Write a "+" in the blanks or over the columns of answer choices to remind you.

Compare your prediction with each answer choice, and pick the best match. One way to do this is to determine which answers are positive and which are negative.

Teacher Tip

"The hardest part of Sentence Completions for most students is finding the logic in the sentence. Once the structure is revealed through the structural clues, the rest is cake."

—Serineh Baghdasarian
  Kaplan Teacher
  Los Angeles, CA

In (A), *quick* and *capricious* aren't similar. (*Capricious* means "erratic or fickle.")

In (B), *equitable* means "fair." *Equitable* and *wise* are similar and they're both positive. When you plug them in, they make sense, so (B)'s right.

In (C), *immoral* and *perceptive* aren't similar at all. *Perceptive* is positive but *immoral* isn't.

In (D), *generous* and *witty* are both positive qualities, but they aren't really similar and they don't make sense in the sentence.

In (E), *clever* and *uneducated* aren't similar. *Clever* is positive but *uneducated* isn't.

Check your answer by plugging it into the sentence. "The king's equitable decisions as a diplomat and administrator led to his legendary reputation as a just and wise ruler." (B) makes sense in the sentence. Finally, a scan of the other choices reveals that none works as well. So (B) is our answer.

EXAMPLE

Charlie Parker was ---- artist, inspiring a generation of modern jazz musicians with his brilliant improvisations and experiments in bebop style.

(A) an arbitrary

(B) a benign

(C) a seminal

(D) an emphatic

(E) a candid

Impulse Answer Buyer

Don't be an "impulse answer buyer." It's hard to know what to buy when you don't know what you're shopping for. The same thing is true of Sentence Completions. You should make a prediction of the answer you're looking for before you go to the answer choices. This way, you won't fall for a distractor. You'll find the answer you want rather than the answer the test maker wants you to find.

Read the sentence carefully, looking for clue words. The big clue is: Whatever goes in the blank must fit with the phrase *inspiring a generation*.

Predict the word that goes in the blank. The sentence tells you Parker inspired a generation of musicians, so you can predict that he was an influential artist.

Compare your prediction with each answer choice, and pick the best match.

(A) *arbitrary:* Too negative—you need a positive word.

(B) *benign: Benign* means "mild or gentle"—again, not what you want.

(C) *seminal:* Most closely matches your prediction—it means "containing the seeds of later development."

(D) *emphatic:* Might sound reasonable at first, but it means "expressive or forceful," which is not the same as "major or important."

(E) *candid: Candid* means "frank or open," which doesn't adequately describe how Parker influenced a generation.

Choice (C), *seminal*, is the answer. Notice that you could have found this answer by elimination, without actually knowing what the word means. Check your answer by plugging it into the sentence. "Charlie Parker was a seminal, or influential, artist inspiring a generation with his brilliant improvisations." Sounds fine.

PICKING UP ON CLUES

To do well on Sentence Completions, you need to see how a sentence fits together. Clue words help you do that. The more clues you get, the clearer the sentence becomes, and the better you can predict what goes in the blanks.

What do we mean by clue words? Take a look at this example:

Get a Clue

Clue words help you get to the right answer. Look for the following types of words:

Contrasts:

- but
- however
- although

Continuations:

- ; (a semicolon)
- also
- and
- because
- due to
- notably

EXAMPLE

Though some have derided it as ----, the search for extraterrestrial intelligence has actually become a respectable scientific endeavor.

Here, *though* is an important clue. *Though* contrasts the way some have derided, belittled, or ridiculed the search for extraterrestrial intelligence with the fact that that search has become respectable. Another clue is *actually*. *Actually* completes the contrast—though some see the search one way, it has actually become respectable.

You know that whatever goes in the blank must complete the contrast implied by the word *though*. So for the blank, you need something that describes the opposite of a *respectable scientific endeavor*. A word such as *useless* or *trivial* would be a good prediction for the blank.

Try using clue words to predict the answers to the questions below. First, look at the sentences without the answer choices and:

- Circle clue words.
- Think of a word or phrase that might go in each blank.
- Write your prediction below each sentence.

1. One striking aspect of Caribbean music is its ---- of many African musical ----, such as call-and-response singing and polyrhythms.

   <u>adaption</u>   <u>styles</u>

2. Although Cézanne was inspired by the Impressionists, he ---- their emphasis on the effects of light and ---- an independent approach to painting that emphasized form.

   <u>disregarded</u>   <u>developed</u>

3. They ---- until there was no recourse but to ---- a desperate, last-minute solution to the problem.

   <u>waited</u>   <u>chance</u>

4. Her normally ---- complexion lost its usual glow when she heard the news of her brother's accident.

   <u>rosy</u>

Here are the same questions with their answer choices. Now find the right answer to each question, referring to the predictions you just made. See page 52 for the answers.

1. One striking aspect of Caribbean music is its ---- of many African musical ----, such as call-and-response singing and polyrhythms.

   (A) recruitment . . groups
   (B) proficiency . . events
   (C) expectation . . ideas
   (D) absorption . . forms
   (E) condescension . . priorities

   Ⓐ Ⓑ Ⓒ ⬤Ⓓ Ⓔ

2. Although Cézanne was inspired by the Impressionists, he ---- their emphasis on the effects of light and ---- an independent approach to painting that emphasized form.

   (A) accepted . . developed
   (B) rejected . . evolved
   (C) encouraged . . submerged
   (D dismissed . . aborted
   (E) nurtured . . founded

   Ⓐ ⬤Ⓑ Ⓒ Ⓓ Ⓔ

3. They ---- until there was no recourse but to ---- a desperate, last-minute solution to the problem.

   (A) compromised . . try
   (B) delayed . . envision
   (C) procrastinated . . implement
   (D debated . . maintain
   (E) filibustered . . reject

   Ⓐ Ⓑ ⬤Ⓒ Ⓓ Ⓔ

4. Her normally ---- complexion lost its usual glow when she heard the news of her brother's accident.

   (A) wan
   (B) pallid
   (C) sallow
   (D) ashen
   (E) sanguine

   Ⓐ Ⓑ Ⓒ Ⓓ ⬤Ⓔ

Answers and Explanations to Picking Up On Clues Exercises

1. (D) Clue: *aspect*. The only choice that could logically complete a description of Caribbean music is (D): Caribbean music is characterized by its *absorption* of many African musical *forms*.

2. (B) Clue: *Although*. *Although* indicates that Cézanne must have somehow differed from the Impressionists. So he must have (B) *rejected* or (D) *dismissed* their emphasis on the effects of light. For the second blank, there's no reason to say that Cézanne *aborted* an independent approach to painting. Only (B) works for both blanks.

3. (C) Clues: *until, desperate*. For the first blank, you can predict that they must have waited until only a "desperate solution" was possible. (C) and (D) fit this prediction. (C)'s *implement*, or carry out, makes more sense in the second blank.

4. (E) Clue: *usual glow*. If her complexion had a "usual glow" it must have been normally rosy. The only choice that means rosy is (E), *sanguine*.

TACKLING HARD QUESTIONS

The last few Sentence Completions in a set are usually difficult. If you're getting stuck, here are a few special techniques to pull you through:

- Avoid tricky wrong answers.

- Take apart tough sentences.

- Work around tough vocabulary.

Kaplan Rules

> Don't pick tough words just because they're tough—pick them because they work in the sentence.

Avoiding Tricky Wrong Answers

Towards the end of a set, watch out for tricky answer choices. Avoid:

- Opposites of the correct answer

- Words that sound right because they're hard

- Two-blankers in which one word fits but the other doesn't

HINT: *Questions go from easiest to hardest—the higher the question number, the harder the question.*

The following example would be the seventh question out of a ten-problem set.

EXAMPLE

Granted that Joyce is extremely ----, it is still
difficult to imagine her as a professional
comedian.

(A) dull

(B) garrulous

(C) effusive

(D) conservative

(E) witty

A Sentence Like This Might Show up Towards the End of a Set

Read this sentence carefully or you may get tricked. If you read too quickly, you might think,
"If Joyce is hard to imagine as a comedian, she's probably extremely dull or conservative. So
I'll pick either (A) or (D)." But the sentence is saying something else.

Pick Up the Clues

The key is the clue word *granted*. It's another way of saying *although*. So the sentence means,
"Sure Joyce is funny, but she's no professional comedian." Therefore, the word in the blank
must resemble funny. That means (E), *witty*, is correct.

Don't Pick an Answer Just Because It Sounds Hard

Garrulous means "talkative" and *effusive* means "overly expressive." You might be tempted to
pick one of these simply because they sound impressive. But they're put there to trick you.
Don't choose them without good reason.

Now let's look at a two-blank sentence. The following example is another seventh question
out of a ten-problem set.

Two-Blankers

Two-blank sentences can be
easier than one-blankers.

- Try the easier blank first.

- Eliminate all choices that
  won't work for that blank.

EXAMPLE

When the state government discovered that
thermal pollution was killing valuable fish,
legislation was passed to ---- the dumping of hot
liquid wastes into rivers and to ---- the fish
population.

(A) discourage . . decimate

(B) regulate . . quantify

(C) facilitate . . appease

(D) discontinue . . devastate

(E) prohibit . . protect

Look at All the Choices

Check out the first blank first. Legislation was not passed to *facilitate* dumping, so that eliminates choice (C). The other four are all possible.

Now check the second blanks. The legislature wouldn't pass a law to *decimate*, or *quantify*, or *devastate* the fish population, so (A), (B), and (D) are wrong. Only choice (E), *prohibit . . protect*, fits for both blanks. The legislature might well pass a law to *prohibit* dumping hot liquids and to *protect* fish.

HINT: *Don't jump at an answer choice because one blank fits. Check both blanks.*

Taking Apart Tough Sentences

Look at the following example, the seventh question of a nine-problem set.

Weird Words Don't Work

Listen to the part of the sentence around the blank. Rule out funny-sounding answer choices.

If you can rule out even one or two weird-sounding choices, you can profit by making an educated guess.

EXAMPLE

Although this small and selective publishing house is famous for its ---- standards, several of its recent novels have a mainly popular appeal.

(A) proletarian

(B) naturalistic

(C) discriminating

(D) imitative

(E) precarious

What if you were stumped, and had no idea which word to pick? Try this strategy.

The process might go like this:

(A) *Proletarian* standards? Hmmm . . . sounds funny.

(B) *Naturalistic* standards? Not great.

(C) *Discriminating* standards? That's got a familiar ring.

(D) *Imitative* standards? Weird-sounding

(E) *Precarious* standards? Nope.

(C) sounds best and, as it turns out, is correct. Although the small publishing house has *discriminating*, or picky, standards, several of its recent novels appeal to a general audience.

Now try a complex sentence with two blanks. Remember our rules:

• Try the easier blank first.

• Save time by eliminating all choices that won't work for one blank.

The following example is the fifth question out of a nine-problem set.

EXAMPLE

These latest employment statistics from the
present administration are so loosely
documented, carelessly explained, and
potentially misleading that even the most loyal
Senators will ---- the ---- of the presidential
appointees who produced them.

(A) perceive . . intelligence

(B) understand . . tenacity

(C) recognize . . incompetence

(D) praise . . rigor

(E) denounce . . loyalty

It's not so easy to see what goes in the first blank, so try the second blank. You need a word to describe presidential appointees who produced the "loosely documented," "carelessly explained," and "misleading" statistics. So it's got to be negative. The only second-word answer choice that's definitely negative is (C), *incompetence*, or inability to perform a task. Now try *recognize* in the first blank. It fits, too. (C) must be correct.

Working Around Tough Vocabulary

The following example is the second question out of a nine-problem set.

EXAMPLE

Despite her ---- of public speaking experience,
the student council member was surprisingly
cogent, and expressed the concerns of her
classmates persuasively.

(A) hope

(B) depth

(C) method

(D) lack

(E) union

Kaplan Rules

If you find a word you don't
understand, look in the sentence
for its definition.

If you don't know what *cogent* means, work around it.

From the sentence, especially the clue word *and*, you know that cogent goes with "expressed the concerns of her classmates persuasively." So you don't have to worry about what *cogent* means. All you need to know is that the student council member was persuasive despite a ---- of speaking experience. Only (D), *lack*, fits. "Despite her lack of public speaking experience, the student council member expressed the concerns of her classmates persuasively." (By the way, *cogent* means "convincing, believable," roughly the same as "expressing concern persuasively.")

Let's look at this Sentence Completion problem. This time the tough vocabulary is in the answer choices. This example is the sixth question out of nine questions.

A Valuable Resource

To help yourself earn extra points, study the vocabulary lists in the "SAT Study Aids" section.

EXAMPLE

Advances in technology occur at such a fast pace that dictionaries have difficulty incorporating the ---- that emerge as names for new inventions.

(A) colloquialisms

(B) euphemisms

(C) compensations

(D) neologisms

(E) clichés

Again, look at the sentence. Whatever goes in the blank has to describe "names for new inventions." If you don't know what the word *colloquialisms* or *euphemisms* means, don't give up. Rule out as many choices as you can, and guess among the remaining ones.

You can eliminate (C) and (E) right off the bat. They don't describe names for new inventions. Now you can make an educated guess. Again, educated guessing will help your score more than guessing blindly or skipping the question.

Or, if you studied your word roots, you might know that *neo-* means "new," so the word *neologisms* might be the best choice for names of new inventions. In fact, it's the right answer. *Neologisms* are newly coined words.

If All Else Fails

If you're really stumped, don't be afraid to guess. Eliminate all answer choices that seem wrong and guess from the remaining choices.

SENTENCE COMPLETIONS PRACTICE SET

1. In the years following World War II, almost all Canadian Inuits ---- their previously nomadic lifestyle; they now live in fixed settlements.

   (A) abandoned
   (B) continued
   (C) fashioned
   (D) preserved
   (E) rebuilt

2. A newborn infant's ---- skills are not fully ----, for it cannot discern images more than ten inches from its face.

    (A) perceptual . . stimulated
    (B) visual . . developed
    (C) descriptive . . ripened
    (D) olfactory . . shared
    (E) average . . familiar

    Ⓐ Ⓑ Ⓒ Ⓓ Ⓔ

3. Some geysers erupt regularly while others do so ----.

    (A) consistently
    (B) copiously
    (C) perennially
    (D) sporadically
    (E) violently

    Ⓐ Ⓑ Ⓒ Ⓓ Ⓔ

4. Because of the lead actor's ---- performance, the play received poor reviews from influential theater critics, and was canceled only one week after it opened.

    (A) erudite
    (B) corporeal
    (C) overwrought
    (D) fractious
    (E) resplendent

    Ⓐ Ⓑ Ⓒ Ⓓ Ⓔ

5. Sociologists have found that, paradoxically, many children of unorthodox, creative parents grow up to be rather tame ----.

    (A) idealists
    (B) conformists
    (C) individualists
    (D) alarmists
    (E) elitists

    Ⓐ Ⓑ Ⓒ Ⓓ Ⓔ

6. In Han mortuary art, the ---- and the ---- are combined; one tomb may contain eerie supernatural figures placed next to ordinary likenesses of government administrators at work.

    (A) fantastic . . mundane
    (B) inventive . . remorseful
    (C) illusory . . derivative
    (D) enlightened . . conservative
    (E) unique . . historical

    Ⓐ Ⓑ Ⓒ Ⓓ Ⓔ

Turn to the next page for answers and explanations.

Answers and Explanations to the Sentence Completions Practice Set

1. (A) *Nomadic* means "wandering, transient." If Inuit people now live in fixed settlements, we can predict that they rejected, or *abandoned*, "their previously nomadic lifestyle."

2. (B) If a newborn infant "cannot discern (or perceive) images more than 10 inches from its face," then the infant's ability to see things has not fully evolved. In other words, its visual skills are not fully developed. The word *olfactory*, choice (D), means "relating to sense of smell."

3. (D) The clue words *while others* indicate contrast. If some geysers "erupt regularly," we can predict that others do so irregularly. The best choice is (D), since *sporadically* means "infrequently or irregularly."

4. (C) If the play "received poor reviews" and was canceled because of something about the lead actor's performance, that performance must have been quite bad. The word *overwrought*, choice (C), means "overdone" or "excessively agitated." It is one of two negative words in the answer choices, and the only one that could logically describe a performance.

5. (B) Paradoxically (or contrary to what one would expect), children of creative and unorthodox parents grow up to be something other than creative and unorthodox. We need a word that contrasts with *creative* and *unorthodox* and goes along with *tame*. (B) is the best choice; *conformists* are people who follow established norms and customs without challenging anything or anyone.

6. (A) If "one tomb contains eerie supernatural figures" and "ordinary likenesses of government administrators," it's likely that Han mortuary art combines the unearthly or bizarre with the ordinary or mundane. The best answer is (A). In Han art, the *fantastic* (eerie supernatural figures) and the *mundane* (administrators) are combined.

Checklist

Once you've mastered a concept, check it off.

Sentence Completions:

❏ The format

❏ Kaplan's Four-Step Method

❏ Picking up on clues

❏ Tackling hard questions

❏ Practice set

7

Critical Reading: The Basics

HIGHLIGHTS

- Practice reading actively

- Apply the Kaplan Five-Step Method for Critical Reading questions

- Review Big Picture, Little Picture, and Vocabulary-in-Context question types

Improving your Critical Reading score means building the skills you have and applying them to the SAT. You don't need outside knowledge to answer the Critical Reading questions. And you don't need an amazing vocabulary, since unfamiliar words will be defined for you.

Doing well on the Critical Reading section isn't really that hard. Take this everyday situation as an example. If you bought a new VCR, as soon as you unpacked it you'd read the instruction manual to figure out how to hook it up and get it working. You probably wouldn't sit down and read the whole book, though. You'd skip the pages that contain step-by-step instructions on how to record programs from the TV until you'd gotten the VCR connected and plugged in. If the manual said, "connect the xygupts to terminal c," you'd probably figure out how to do that, even though you don't know the word *xygupts*.

In setting up your VCR, you'd have demonstrated that you know how to read with a purpose; know how and when to deal with details; and can figure out the meaning of unfamiliar words from context—all skills you'll be using in the Critical Reading section.

SAT Emergency

If you have two weeks or fewer to prep for the SAT, here's the best way to spend your time:

- Since Critical Reading makes up half of the Verbal section of the SAT, it's important that you read the whole chapter.

- Pay special attention to the practice questions beginning on pp. 63 and 68.

Critical Reading passages and questions are very predictable, since the test makers use a formula to write them. You'll be given four reading passages, 400 to 850 words each, drawn from the arts, humanities, social sciences, sciences, and fiction. One of these is a "paired passage" consisting of two related excerpts. You'll be asked about the overall tone and content of a passage, the details, and what the passage suggests. You'll also be asked to compare and contrast the related passages.

THE FORMAT

Critical Reading instructions tell you to answer questions based on what is stated or implied in the accompanying passage or passages. As with other question types, you should get familiar enough with the Critical Reading format that you don't waste time reading the directions again on the day of the test.

Each reading passage begins with a brief introduction. Related questions follow the passage. Don't skip the brief introductions. They'll help you focus your reading.

Critical Reading questions have a specific order: The first few questions ask about the beginning of the passage, the last few about the end.

Questions following "paired passages" are generally ordered. The first few questions relate to the first passage, the next few to the second passage, and the final questions ask about the passages as a pair—generally, but not always. You'll learn more about this on p. 70.

Critical Reading questions are not ordered by difficulty. Unlike the other kinds of questions on the SAT, the location of a Critical Reading question tells you nothing about its potential difficulty. So don't get bogged down on a hard Critical Reading question. The next one might be a lot easier.

How NOT to Read

DON'T wait for important information to jump out and hit you in the face. Search for important points.

DON'T read the passage thoroughly. It's a waste of time. Skim the passage to get the drift.

DON'T skim so quickly that you miss the passage's main point.

DON'T get caught up in details.

HOW TO READ A PASSAGE

Some students find Critical Reading passages dull or intimidating. Remember that each passage is written for a purpose: The author wants to make a point, describe a situation, or convince you of his or her ideas. As you're reading, ask yourself, "What's the point of this? What's this all about?" This is active reading, and it's the key to staying focused on the page.

Active reading doesn't mean reading the passage word-for-word. It means reading lightly, but with a focus—in other words, skimming. The questions will help you fill in the details by directing you back to important information in the passage.

Getting hung up on details is a major Critical Reading pitfall. You need to grasp the outline, but you don't need to get all the fine features.

The less time you spend on reading the passages, the more time you'll have to answer the questions—and that's where you score points.

Test Your Critical Reading Smarts

Test your reading skills on the following sample passage, keeping our tips in mind. Remember that active reading will make this difficult passage—and every passage—more doable.

EXAMPLE

In this essay, the author writes about her childhood on a Caribbean island that was an English colony for many years.

When I saw England for the first time, I was a child in school sitting at a desk. The England I was looking at was laid out on a map gently, beautifully, delicately, a very special jewel; it lay on a bed of sky blue, its yellow form
Line mysterious, because though it looked like a leg of mutton*, it could not
(5) really look like anything so familiar as a leg of mutton because it was England. England was a special jewel all right, and only special people got to wear it. The people who got to wear England were English people. They wore it well and they wore it everywhere: in jungles, in deserts, on plains, in places where they were not welcome, in places they should not have been. When my teacher had
(10) pinned this map up on the blackboard, she said, "This is England"—and she said it with authority, seriousness, and adoration, and we all sat up. We understood then—we were meant to understand then—that England was to be our source of myth and the source from which we got our sense of reality, our sense of what was meaningful, our sense of what was meaningless—and much
(15) about our own lives and much about the very idea of us headed that last list.

At the time I was a child sitting at my desk seeing England for the first time, I was already very familiar with the greatness of it. Each morning before I left for school, I ate a breakfast of half a grapefruit, a bowl of oat porridge, bread and butter and a slice of cheese, and a cup of cocoa. The can of cocoa was
(20) often left on the table in front of me. It had written on it the name of the company, the year the company was established, and the words "Made in England." Those words, "Made in England," were written on the box the oats came in too. The shoes I wore were made in England; so were my socks and cotton undergarments and the satin ribbons I wore tied at the end of two plaits of my hair. My father, who might have sat next to me at breakfast, was a
(25) carpenter and cabinet maker. The shoes he wore to work would have been made in England, as were his khaki shirt and trousers, his underpants and undershirt, his socks and brown felt hat. Felt was not the proper material from which a hat that was expected to provide shade from the hot sun should be made, but my father must have seen and admired a picture of an Englishman wearing such a hat in England. As we sat at breakfast a car might go by. The car, a Hillman or a
(30) Zephyr, was made in England. The very conception of the meal itself, breakfast, and its substantial quality and quantity was an idea from England; we somehow knew that in England they began the day with this meal called breakfast and a proper breakfast was a big breakfast.

At the time I saw this map—seeing England for the first time—I did not say to myself, "Ah, so that's what it looks like," because there was no longing in me to put a shape to those three
(35) words that ran through every part of my life, no matter how small; for me to have had such a longing would have meant that I lived in a certain atmosphere, an atmosphere in which those three words were felt as a burden. But I did not live in such an atmosphere. My father's brown felt hat would develop a hole in its crown, the lining would separate from the hat itself, and six weeks before he thought that he could not be seen wearing it—he was a very vain man—he
(40) would order another hat from England. And my mother taught me to eat my food in the English way: the knife in the right hand, the fork in the left, my elbows held still close to my side. When I had finally mastered it, I overheard her saying to a friend, "Did you see how nicely she can eat?" But I knew then that I enjoyed my food more when I ate it with my bare hands, and I continued to do so when she wasn't looking. And when my teacher showed us the map, she

Kaplan Rules

As you read the passage, ask yourself:

- What's this passage about?

- What's the point of this?

- Why did someone write this?

- What's the author trying to say?

- What are the two or three most important things in this passage?

(45)   asked us to study it carefully, because no test we would ever take would be complete without
         this statement: "Draw a map of England."
              I did not know then that the statement "Draw a map of England" was something far worse
         than a declaration of war. I did not know then that this statement was part of a process that
         would result in my erasure, not my physical erasure, but my erasure all the same. I did not know
(50)   then that this statement was meant to make me feel in awe and small whenever I heard the word
         "England": awe at its existence, small because I was not from it. I did not know very much of
         anything then—certainly not what a blessing it was that I was unable to draw a map of England
         correctly.

         *the flesh of a sheep

It's important to learn how to read the passage quickly and efficiently. Remember, though, that reading the passage won't earn you points—it's the questions that count.

KAPLAN'S FIVE-STEP METHOD

Here's Kaplan's proven approach to Critical Reading questions:

1. Read the question stem.
2. Locate the material you need.
3. Come up with an idea of the right answer.
4. Scan the answer choices.
5. Select your answer.

1. Read the Question Stem

This is the place to really read carefully. Take a second to make sure you understand what the question is asking.

Critical Reading Is Critical

The 38 to 40 Critical Reading questions count for about half your Verbal score. You need to do well on these questions.

2. Locate the Material You Need

If you are given a line reference, read the material surrounding the line mentioned. It will clarify exactly what the question is asking.

If you're not given a line reference, scan the text to find the place where the question applies, and quickly reread those few sentences. Keep the main point of the passage in mind.

3. Come up with an Idea of the Right Answer

Don't spend time making up a precise answer. You need only a general sense of what you're after, so you can recognize the correct answer quickly when you read the choices.

4. Scan the Answer Choices

Scan the choices, looking for one that fits your idea of the right answer. If you don't find an ideal answer, quickly eliminate wrong choices by checking back to the passage. Rule out choices that are too extreme or go against common sense. And get rid of answers that sound reasonable, but don't make sense in the context of the passage.

5. Select Your Answer

You've eliminated the obvious wrong answers. One of the remaining should fit your ideal. If you're left with more than one contender, consider the passage's main idea, and make an educated guess.

Now try the following Critical Reading practice questions. (Answers on p. 66.)

> **Having Trouble?**
>
> Unlike the other Verbal question types, Critical Reading questions are not ordered by difficulty. If you're having trouble answering a question, the next one might be easier.

1. According to the author, England could not really look like a leg of mutton (lines 4–5) because

    (A) maps generally don't give an accurate impression of what a place looks like
    (B) England was too grand and exotic a place for such a mundane image
    (C) England was an island not very different in appearance from her own island
    (D) the usual metaphor used to describe England was a precious jewel
    (E) mutton was one of the few foods familiar to her that did not come from England

2. The author's reference to felt as "not the proper material" (line 27) for her father's hat chiefly serves to emphasize her point about the

    (A) extremity of the local weather
    (B) arrogance of island laborers
    (C) informality of dress on the island
    (D) weakness of local industries
    (E) predominance of English culture

3. The word *conception* as used in line 30 means

    (A) beginning
    (B) image
    (C) origination
    (D) notion
    (E) plan

4. The word *substantial* in line 31 means

   (A) important
   (B) abundant
   (C) firm
   (D) down-to-earth
   (E) materialistic

   Ⓐ Ⓑ Ⓒ Ⓓ Ⓔ

5. In the third paragraph, the author implies that any longing to put a shape to the words *made in England* would have indicated

   (A) a resentment of England's predominance
   (B) an unhealthy desire to become English
   (C) an inability to understand England's authority
   (D) an excessive curiosity about England
   (E) an unfamiliarity with English customs

   Ⓐ Ⓑ Ⓒ Ⓓ Ⓔ

6. The author cites the anecdotes about her father and mother in lines 37–43 primarily to convey their

   (A) love for their children
   (B) belief in strict discipline
   (C) distaste for anything foreign
   (D) reverence for England
   (E) overemphasis on formal manners

   Ⓐ Ⓑ Ⓒ Ⓓ Ⓔ

7. The word *erasure* (line 49) as used by the author most nearly means

   (A) total annihilation
   (B) physical disappearance
   (C) sense of insignificance
   (D) enforced censorship
   (E) loss of freedom

   Ⓐ Ⓑ Ⓒ Ⓓ Ⓔ

8. The main purpose of the passage is to

   (A) advocate a change in the way a subject is taught in school
   (B) convey the personality of certain figures from the author's childhood
   (C) describe an overwhelming influence on the author's early life
   (D) analyze the importance of a sense of place to early education
   (E) relate a single formative episode in the author's life

   Ⓐ Ⓑ Ⓒ Ⓓ Ⓔ

9. For the author, the requirement to "Draw a map of England" (line 46) represented an attempt to

   (A) force students to put their studies to practical use
   (B) glorify one culture at the expense of another
   (C) promote an understanding of world affairs
   (D) encourage students to value their own heritage
   (E) impart outmoded and inappropriate knowledge

   Ⓐ Ⓑ Ⓒ Ⓓ Ⓔ

10. At the end of the passage, the author suggests that her inability "to draw a map of England correctly" indicated a

(A) heartfelt desire to see the country in person rather than through maps
(B) serious failure of the education she received
(C) conscious rejection of the prestige of a foreign power
(D) harmful preoccupation with local affairs and customs
(E) beneficial ignorance of her own supposed inferiority

Applying the Five-Step Method

Try Kaplan's Five-Step Method on question one from the sample reading passage above.

1. Read the Question Stem

In this case, the question is straightforward: Why couldn't England really look like a leg of mutton? (Notice that *mutton* is defined for you at the end of the passage—you aren't expected to know the meaning of unfamiliar terms.)

> **What's *Mutton*?**
>
> When a word is too obscure for the SAT, they'll define it at the bottom of the reading passage.

2. Locate the Material You Need

You're given a clue: The answer lies somewhere near the fourth or fifth line. But don't read just those lines—read the line or two before and after as well. By doing so, you learn that England was mysterious and special, so it couldn't look like something as familiar (to the author) as a leg of mutton.

3. Come up with an Idea of the Right Answer

After reading those couple of lines, you'd expect the answer to be something like, "England was too special to look like a familiar leg of mutton."

4. Scan the Answer Choices

Choice (B) comes close to the ideal—it should have popped out. But if you weren't sure, you could have quickly eliminated the other choices. Thinking of the main idea would have helped you eliminate (A) and (C). England was precious—like a jewel—but the author doesn't imply that England was usually compared to a jewel (D). And you never learn where mutton comes from (E).

> **Teacher Tip**
>
> "Mark up the passages! Have a system worked out where you use different symbols to mean different things. For example, circle names, box numbers and dates, underline key sentences, and draw arrows to lists of details. Once you know your system, you can find the facts you are looking for faster."
>
> —Laura Cunnington
> Kaplan Teacher
> Reno, NV

5. Select Your Answer

Choice (B) is the only one that works here. By reading the material surrounding the line reference and putting an answer into your own words, you should have been able to choose (B) with confidence.

Now try the Five-Step Method on the remaining questions for the passage.

HINT: *From the questions, you can "fill in" the information you don't get in a quick reading. It's a way of working backwards, to reconstruct the passage.*

BIG PICTURE, LITTLE PICTURE, AND VOCABULARY-IN-CONTEXT QUESTIONS

Most SAT Critical Reading questions fall into three basic types. "Big Picture" questions test your overall understanding of the passage's biggest points. "Little Picture" questions ask about localized bits of information. About 70 percent of Critical Reading questions are "Little Picture." Vocabulary-in-Context questions ask for the meaning of a single word.

In the passage above, question eight is an example of a Big Picture question. Question two is an example of a Little Picture question. Question three is a Vocabulary-in-Context question.

HINT: *Remember to skip around if you need to. You can tackle whichever passages you like in any order you like within the same section. But once you've read through the passage, try all the questions that go with it.*

Big Picture Questions

Big Picture questions test your overall understanding of a passage. They might ask about:

- The main point or purpose of a passage

- The author's attitude or tone

- The logic underlying the author's argument

- How ideas relate to each other

One way to see the Big Picture is to read actively. As you read, ask yourself, "What's this all about? What's the point of this?"

HINT: *Still stumped after reading the passage? Do the Little Picture questions first. They can help you fill in the Big Picture.*

Turn back to the passage you tried above. What did you get out of the first reading? Something like, "England was a profound influence on the author's early life, but not a completely positive influence"? That would have been enough.

Now look at question eight. It's a Big Picture question, asking for the main point of the passage. Use the Five-Step Method to find your answer.

1. Read the Question Stem

Simple enough: What's the main point of the passage?

2. Locate the Material You Need

In this case, you're asked about the overall point. You should have grasped a sense of that from reading the passage.

3. Get an Idea of the Right Answer

Again, you need just a rough statement. Here, something like this would do: "The purpose is to describe how England was a huge influence, but maybe not a completely positive one, in the author's young life."

Answers to Critical Reading Questions, pp. 63–65

1. (B)
2. (E)
3. (D)
4. (B)
5. (B)
6. (D)
7. (C)
8. (C)
9. (B)
10. (E)

4. Scan the Answer Choices

(C) should have popped out. But (D) might have looked good, too, if you focused on the words "sense of place." So put those two aside as contenders. How a subject was taught in school (A), figures in the author's childhood (B), and a single formative episode (E) are too narrow.

5. Select Your Answer

You've crossed off the poor choices, and you're down to two possibilities. Which matches your ideal? (C) comes closer. Look closely at (D) and you'll see that it's too general. Go with the best choice.

Little Picture Questions

More than two-thirds of Critical Reading questions ask about the Little Picture. Little Picture questions usually give you a line reference or refer you to a particular paragraph—a strong clue to where in the passage you'll find your answer.

> **Avoid the Farfetched**
>
> Don't pick farfetched inferences. SAT inferences tend to be strongly implied in the passage.

Little Picture questions might:

- Test whether you understand significant information that's stated in the passage

- Ask you to make inferences or draw conclusions based on a part of the passage

- Ask you to relate parts of the passage to one another

Question two is a Little Picture question. You're asked about the felt hat of the author's father—what does this point emphasize? Applying Kaplan's Step Two, locate the material you'll need. You're given a clue—a line reference—to help you here. Reread that, and the lines before and after it as well.

So why did the father wear a felt hat, which was probably quite hot in the tropical sun? Because it was English. That's what correct choice (E) says. Rereading that bit of the passage should have led you right to that answer. (A) comes close, but doesn't fit the main point of the passage. Even with Little Picture questions, grasping the main point of the passage can help you find the correct answer.

> **Kaplan Rules**
>
> Once you find the tested word in the passage, you can treat a Vocabulary-in-Context question like a Sentence Completion.
>
> Pretend the word is a blank in the sentence. Read a line or two around the "blank," if you need to. Then predict a word for the "blank." Check the answer choices for a word that comes close to your prediction.

HINT: *Beware of answer choices that provide a reasonable answer to the stem, but don't make sense in the context of the passage.*

Vocabulary-in-Context Questions

Vocabulary-in-Context questions ask about an even smaller part of the passage than other Little Picture questions do. They ask about the usage of a single word. These questions do not test your ability to define hard words such as *archipelago* and *garrulous*. They do test your ability to infer the meaning of a word from context.

In fact, the words tested in these questions will probably be familiar to you—they are usually fairly common words with more than one definition. Many of the answer choices will be definitions of the tested word, but only one will work in context. Vocabulary-in-Context questions always have a line reference, and you should always use it!

HINT: *CONTEXT is the most important part of Vocabulary-in-CONTEXT questions.*

Sometimes one of the answer choices will jump out at you. It'll be the most common meaning of the word in question—but it's rarely right! We call this the "obvious" choice. For example, say *curious* is the word being tested. The obvious choice is *inquisitive*. But *curious* also means "odd," and that's more likely to be the answer. Using context to find the answer will help prevent you from falling for this trap. You can use these choices to your advantage, though. If you get stuck on a Vocabulary-in-Context question, you can eliminate the "obvious" choice and guess.

HINT: *If a question has an "obvious" choice, steer clear of it.*

Vocabulary-in-Context Practice

(Answers on p. 70.)

1. Embodied and given life in the social realities of her own period, Jane Austen's satire still has currency in ours.

   In the lines above, *currency* most nearly means
   (A) usualness
   (B) stylishness
   (C) prevalence
   (D) funds
   (E) relevance

2. A perpetual doubting and a perpetual questioning of the truth of what we have learned is not the temper of science.

   In the lines above, *temper* most nearly means
   (A) disposition
   (B) nature
   (C) anger
   (D) mood
   (E) mixture

3. Captain Wentworth had no fortune. He had been lucky in his profession, but, spending freely what had come freely, had realized nothing.

   Which most nearly captures the meaning of the word *realized* in the sentence above?
   (A) understood
   (B) accomplished
   (C) learned
   (D) accumulated
   (E) fulfilled

4. Anyone with more than a superficial knowledge of Shakespeare's plays must necessarily entertain some doubt concerning their true authorship.

   In the lines above, *entertain* most nearly means
   (A) amuse
   (B) harbor
   (C) occupy
   (D) cherish
   (E) engage

   Ⓐ ⬤Ⓑ Ⓒ Ⓓ Ⓔ

5. Many people who invested in the booming art market of the 1980s were disappointed; few of the works appreciated in value.

   In the lines above, *appreciated* most nearly means
   (A) admired
   (B) applauded
   (C) spiraled
   (D) increased
   (E) acknowledged

   Ⓐ Ⓑ Ⓒ ⬤Ⓓ Ⓔ

6. Charles de Gaulle's independence of mind can be seen by the fact that he negotiated with Algerian nationalists, although he was pressed by his advisors, French colonists, and the army itself to continue the war.

   Which most nearly captures the meaning of the word *pressed* in the sentence above?
   (A) squeezed
   (B) urged
   (C) troubled
   (D) required
   (E) compelled

   Ⓐ ⬤Ⓑ Ⓒ Ⓓ Ⓔ

7. Today some would say that those struggles are all over—that all the horizons have been explored—that all the battles have been won—that there is no longer an American frontier. But I trust that no one in this vast assemblage will agree with those sentiments.

   In the lines above, *sentiments* most nearly means
   (A) beliefs
   (B) results
   (C) loyalties
   (D) challenges
   (E) emotions

   ⬤Ⓐ Ⓑ Ⓒ Ⓓ Ⓔ

8. The convicts made their escape by scaling the prison walls and stealing away under the cover of darkness.

   Which most nearly captures the meaning of the word *stealing* in the line above?
   (A) seizing
   (B) taking
   (C) slipping
   (D) grabbing
   (E) abducting

   Ⓐ Ⓑ ⬤Ⓒ Ⓓ Ⓔ

PAIRED PASSAGES—A (NOT-SO) SPECIAL CASE

Don't let the paired passages worry you—they're not twice as hard as the single reading selections. In fact, students often find the paired passages the most interesting on the test. With paired passages, focus as you read on the relationship between the two passages. Just as with single passages, the questions following paired passages can help fill in the picture.

Questions following paired passages tend to be ordered, with the first few questions relating to the first passage, the next few to the second passage, and the final questions asking about the passages as a pair. This is the best way to tackle the questions in any case, even if the test makers mix in a question about both passages amidst questions on the first passage (it's been known to happen).

To do paired passages:

1. Skim the first passage, looking for the drift (as you would with a single passage).

2. Do the questions that relate to the first passage.

3. Skim the second passage, looking for the drift and thinking about how the second passage relates to the first.

4. Do the questions that relate to the second passage.

5. Now you're ready to do the questions that ask about the relationship between the two passages.

Alternately skimming passages and answering questions is especially important if you're short of time. You'll be able to answer at least some of the questions before time runs out. By the time you've looked at both passages and answered the questions about each passage, you'll have a firm sense of the relationship between the pair. That will help you to answer the last group of questions.

Active reading can help you answer these questions, too. Remember to ask yourself, "What are these passages about? What is each author's point? What is similar about the two passages? What is different?"

Answers to Vocabulary-in-Context Questions, pp. 68–69

1. (E)
2. (B)
3. (D)
4. (B)
5. (D)
6. (B)
7. (A)
8. (C)

WHAT TO DO WHEN TIME IS RUNNING OUT

It's always best to skim the passage before you hit the questions. But if you only have a few minutes left, here's how to score points even while time is running out.

You can answer Vocabulary-in-Context questions and many Little Picture questions without reading the passage. If the question has a line reference, locate the material you need to find your answer and follow the five-step method as usual. You won't have the overall picture to guide you, but you might be able to reach the correct answer just by understanding the "little picture."

Checklist

Once you've mastered a concept, check it off.

The Basics of Critical Reading:

❏ How to read a passage

❏ Kaplan's Five-Step Method for Critical Reading questions

❏ Paired passages—a (not-so) special case

❏ What to do when time is running out

How to Do Specific Question Types:

❏ Big picture questions

❏ Little picture questions

❏ Vocabulary-in-context questions

8

Critical Reading Skills

- Learn to skim passages effectively and efficiently

- Use the Kaplan Four-Step Paraphrasing Method

- Strengthen your ability to draw inferences

In the previous chapter, you learned the basics of Critical Reading—what it looks like, what to expect, how to read the passages, how to tackle the questions. This chapter will help you improve the Critical Reading skills tested on the SAT—skimming, paraphrasing, and drawing inferences. You already have these skills.

- *Skimming* means reading quickly and lightly. You do this when you look information up in a phone book, or glance at a newspaper article only long enough to get the gist of the story.

- When you restate something in your own words, that's *paraphrasing*. You do it all the time in daily life—when you give a phone message, or retell a story.

- When you deduce information from a statement or situation, you're *making inferences*. You do it every day. If your best friend stopped talking to you, you'd probably infer that your friend was mad at you, even if your friend didn't actually say so.

SAT Emergency

If you have just a few weeks to prep for the SAT, here's the best way to spend your time:

- Read the section on skimming.

- Hold off on the rest of the chapter until you've covered all the basics in this book. If you have time to come back, work on the paraphrasing and inference sections.

SKIMMING

Skimming is a specific reading style in which you read quickly and in less detail than usual. These two characteristics are what make skimming the best way to read SAT passages. You want to read quickly because time is limited, and you want to read lightly because the questions direct you to the details you need. Spending a lot of time with the passage before you see the questions just doesn't make sense. So skimming works well—as long as you read with three things in mind:

- The content of the passage
- The organization of the passage
- The author's purpose or point of view

If you have a general idea of these three things when you're done skimming, then you're ready for the questions.

Read This Quickly

Joe stood at the edge of town, a cigarette in his left hand, a bottle of bourbon in his right. He'd had tough ones before, but this was gonna be the end of him. He looked back towards the light of the city below him. "If only I could get Martinez to talk," he thought to himself. In a flash, Joe was back in the Mustang racing towards town. . . .

What was this little story about? Chances are, even with a quick read, you took away some information that helped you piece it together. That's because you've already developed your reading skills (you're reading this, right?).

Your challenge on the SAT is to apply these skills in a peculiar context and not to be intimidated by the passages they throw at you.

In order to be an effective skimmer, you need to practice. Treat your practice sessions as an opportunity to learn. In time, you'll notice improvement.

- Practice frequently, in short sessions.
- Use these methods every time you read.

How to Skim

To improve your reading speed, get your eyes to move quickly and lightly along each line of type. Think about the way you usually read. Do you dwell on each word, as if you were plodding through a field of mud? Or do your eyes move quickly over the page, as if you were walking on hard, dry ground?

The way your eyes habitually move across each line of type and return to the beginning of the next line is your tracking style. That's what you'll work on here. The object is to make it light and swift, rather than heavy and deliberate. Don't read each word separately. Move your eyes lightly over the page, grouping words. Improving your tracking style will help you perform your best when under pressure.

Here are some skimming tips:

Don't Subvocalize

Subvocalizing is "sounding out" words as you read. Even if you don't move your lips, you're probably subvocalizing if you read one word at a time. Subvocalizing costs you time—because you can't read faster than you speak. If you group words, you won't subvocalize.

Keep Asking Yourself Where the Author's Going

Stay alert for the author's signals. Each SAT passage takes you on a journey, and every passage contains phrases or paragraph breaks that signal the next phase of this journey. As you skim, notice where each passage changes course.

Keep Your "Footsteps" Light

Don't read a passage slowly and deliberately. On the other hand, don't race as fast as you can. The idea is to increase your reading rate slightly while remaining comfortable.

Skimming Exercises

Now try a few exercises to see how skimming works. Read the following paragraph word by word.

> The prohibitive prices of some exhibits, as well as the continued depression of the local economy, prevented the 1939 World's Fair from being a great financial success. In a cultural sense, however, the Fair was enormously successful, and a landmark event of the era. As one historian noted, the Fair became "a cultural document of American values and aspirations at a crucial crossroads." After a decade of hardship, many Americans were ready to embrace a vision of social harmony, prosperity, and a bright future.

Now read the same paragraph, concentrating phrase by phrase.

> The prohibitive prices/ of some exhibits, /as well as/ the continued depression/ of the local economy, /prevented/ the 1939 World's Fair/ from being/ a great financial success. /In a /cultural sense,/ however,/ the Fair/ was enormously successful,/ and a landmark event/ of the era./ As one historian noted,/ the Fair became / "a cultural document/ of American values and aspirations/ at a crucial crossroads." /After a decade /of hardship,/ many Americans/ were ready to embrace/ a vision of social harmony,/ prosperity,/ and a bright future.

Here's another paragraph. Put in the slash marks yourself, phrase by phrase.

> The theme of the 1939 World's Fair was "Building the World of Tomorrow." Indeed, the modern and the futuristic were everywhere apparent. The main symbols of the Fair were the Trylon and the Perisphere, a huge pyramid and orb which were lit up at night in a dazzling display. The most popular exhibit, sponsored by General Motors, was the Futurama, which claimed to provide visitors with a glimpse of

Kaplan Rules

Don't put slash marks in your test booklet on the real SAT. You're allowed to, but it's a waste of time.

The point is to make "mental" slash marks so that you get in the habit of moving briskly through the passage.

automotive America in 1960. Patrons were carried by individual moving chairs on a simulated cross-country voyage, along a superhighway which would allow drivers to reach speeds up to 100 miles an hour.

No two readers will mark up this paragraph the same way, because each person sees phrases differently. That's okay. What's important is to begin working phrase-by-phrase, instead of word-by-word.

Now try another method. Read the following paragraphs, letting your eyes move down the page, and coming to rest at only two places per line:

The Catcher in the Rye, published in 1951, is the only novel written by J.D. Salinger in a career that lasted less than twenty years. It is the story of Holden Caulfield, a sensitive, rebellious New York City teen-ager taking his first hesitant steps into adulthood. Holden flees the confines of his snobbish Eastern prep school, searching for innocence and truth, but finds only "phoniness." Filled with humor and pathos, *The Catcher in the Rye* won wide critical acclaim at the time of its publication. In the four decades since then, however, it has become a true phenomenon, selling hundreds of thousands of copies each year, and Holden Caulfield has gained the status of a cultural icon. What accounts for this book's remarkable hold on generation after generation of American youth?

Holden Caulfield is the narrator of *The Catcher in the Rye*, and his narration is a stylistic tour de force, revealing Salinger's masterful ear for the linguistic idioms and rhythms of adolescent speech. Slang evolves continuously, of course, and yesterday's "in" expressions are usually passé by tomorrow. But Holden's characteristic means of expression—the vernacular of a teen-age social misfit, desperately trying to find his niche—transcends the particulars of time and place. Like another 1950s icon, James Dean in *Rebel Without a Cause*, Holden Caulfield has "outlived" his era and become an enduring symbol of sensitive youth, threatened by an indifferent society.

Teacher Tip

"Ordinary reading is too slow to find things and too fast to analyze text. Good test takers scan quickly to find what they need and then analyze intensely."

—Eirik Johnson
Kaplan Teacher
Chicago, IL

See how your eye takes in whole phrases, though you haven't read every word? That's another skimming method.

Remember, skim the passage before you turn to the questions. When you tackle the questions, you'll focus more tightly on parts of the passage. Many questions will direct you back to specific lines or paragraphs, so you won't be desperately searching for relevant information.

PARAPHRASING

What happens when your best friend misses a day of school? You probably tell her or him what went on that night on the phone, or the next day before class. If you did, you'd be paraphrasing—condensing a day's worth of events into a few minutes, highlighting the most important things. Critical Reading questions often ask you to do a similar thing. They ask what a passage, or part of it, says. The right answer accurately paraphrases the meaning of the passage or excerpt, that is, it restates the meaning without losing any important points. Let's see how this works. Here are a few sentences from a Critical Reading passage:

EXAMPLE

No doubt because it painted a less than flattering picture of American life in America for Asian immigrants, *East Goes West* was not well received by contemporary literary critics. According to them, Kang's book displayed a curious lack of insight regarding the American effort to accommodate those who had come over from Korea. The facet of the novel reviewers did find praiseworthy was Han's perseverance and sustained optimism in the face of adversity.

The passage indicates that the response of critics to *East Goes West* was one of

(A) irony regarding the difference between Han's expectations and reality

(B) admiration of the courage and creativity Kang showed in breaking from literary tradition

(C) confusion about the motivation of the protagonist

(D) qualified disapproval of Kang's perception of his adopted homeland

(E) anger that Kang had so viciously attacked American society

A Good Paraphrase

A good paraphrase accurately restates the meaning of the original, without adding or losing important points.

There's a lot going on in the passage, but don't let it confuse you. Follow our advice:

Kaplan's Four-Step Paraphrasing Method

1. Read the question stem. That's the partial sentence leading into the answer choices.

2. Read the lines you're referred to, searching for the relevant phrases. (If a question gives you a line reference, be sure to read a line or two before and after the keyed line.)

3. Predict a good paraphrase for what's being asked.

4. Find a similar answer choice.

Now apply Kaplan's method to the reading question above:

1–2. After reading the stem and relevant lines of the passage (in this case, we found them for you), the key phrases should have popped out: *not well received, a curious lack of insight,* and *the facet reviewers did find praiseworthy.*

3. Predicted paraphrase: The critics were displeased with Kang's view of the immigrant's experience, but approved of the hero's persistence.

4. Look for the answer choice that means the same as your paraphrase.

Choice (D) comes closest. *Qualified* means "modified" or "limited," so *qualified disapproval* captures both the negative and the positive reaction the reviewers had.

Notice that Choice (E) is too negative, and choice (B) is too positive. Choices (A) and (C) don't reflect what the excerpt says. So (D) is the answer.

Paraphrasing Practice

The excerpts on the following page will help you recognize a good paraphrase quickly. Follow the method you've just learned. Notice as you go if your paraphrase includes too much or too little information, or if it has the wrong focus. If so, adjust it.

Each excerpt is followed by a space in which you can write your own paraphrase. Compare your paraphrase with the answer choices and pick the best approximation. You'll find the answers on page 84.

1. He was not in love with Margaret, and he believed, though one could never be sure, that she was not in love with him—that her preference was for the handsome young clergyman who read Browning with her every Tuesday afternoon. But he was aware also that she would marry him if he asked her; he knew that the hearts of four formidable parents were set on the match; and in his past experience his mother's heart had invariably triumphed over his less intrepid resolves.

The protagonist believes that Margaret will marry him because (give the reason in your own words):

_____

_____

Now find the best paraphrase:

(A) she wouldn't have the resolve to refuse him

(B) they are in love with each other

(C) they both feel parental pressure

(D) she knows the clergyman won't marry her

(E) his mother will talk her into accepting him

2. Only with effort can the camera be forced to lie: basically it is an honest medium; so the photographer is much more likely to approach nature in a spirit of inquiry, of communion, instead of with the saucy swagger of self-dubbed "artists."

The distinction made in the passage between a photographer and an "artist" can best be summarized as which of the following (summarize the distinction in your own words):

_____

_____

Now find the best paraphrase:

(A) The photographer's job is to record the world, and the artist's is to embellish it.
(B) The photographer's work is realistic, while the artist's is impressionistic.
(C) The artist finds his inspiration in the urban environment, the photographer in nature.
(D) The photographer has a more open and unassuming attitude toward the natural world than the artist does.
(E) Photographers are more pretentious than artists are. Ⓐ Ⓑ Ⓒ ● Ⓔ

3. The following excerpt is from a speech given by Frederick Douglass.

"What to the American slave is your Fourth of July? I answer, a day that reveals more to him than all other days of the year, the gross injustice and cruelty to which he is the constant victim. To him your celebration is a sham; your boasted liberty an unholy license; your national greatness, swelling vanity . . . ."

According to Douglass, for slaves, the Fourth of July (complete the sentence in your own words):

_____

_____

Now find the best paraphrase:

(A) highlights the hypocrisy of stated American ideals
(B) reveals the injustice of not being invited to participate
(C) is a reminder of the greatness of their homeland
(D) shows the depravity of the celebrants
(E) is a completely meaningless day ● Ⓑ Ⓒ Ⓓ Ⓔ

MAKING INFERENCES

Inferences are conclusions you reach that are hinted at, but not directly stated, in the reading passage. When you infer, you're "reading between the lines." In Critical Reading:

- If you're given a line reference, be sure to read a line or two around it.

- Always look for evidence in the passage to support an inference.

Many SAT questions test your power to make accurate inferences.

EXAMPLE

My father was a justice of the peace, and I supposed that he possessed the power of life and death over all men and could hang anybody that offended him. This distinction was enough for me as a general thing; but the desire to become a steamboat man kept intruding, nevertheless. I first wanted to be a cabin boy, so that I could come out with a white apron on and shake a tablecloth over the side, where all my old comrades could see me. Later I thought I would rather be the deck hand who stood on the end of the stage plank with a coil of rope in his hand, because he was particularly conspicuous.

The author makes the statement that "I supposed he possessed the power of life and death over all men and could hang anybody that offended him" primarily to suggest the

(A) power held by a justice of the peace in a frontier town

(B) naive view that he held of his father's importance

(C) respect that the townspeople had for his father

(D) possibility of miscarriages of justice on the American frontier

(E) harsh environment in which he was brought up

The answer is implied here. The author doesn't say "my view of my father's importance at the time was naive." But the idea is implicit in the excerpt.

KAPLAN

As the author explains it, he supposed at the time that his father was all powerful and that he could kill almost anyone. On a first reading, that probably struck you as odd. You also probably wondered why the son was proud of it. But read the passage carefully and you'll realize the tone is ironic. The author is making fun of his youthful ideas. So the correct answer has to be (B).

Don't Go Too Far with Inferences

SAT inferences tend to be straightforward and consistent with the overall idea of the passage. They are not extreme, complex, or subtle. In fact, they're incredibly predictable. (You can use this to your advantage.) That's why choices (A) and (E) go too far.

- Is it realistic that the author's father could hang anyone he wanted? Even if he could, would the author be proud of it? Very unlikely.

- Do the boy's early assumptions about his father's power indicate anything about the environment he grew up in? Not a thing.

Look at another question about the same excerpt:

> EXAMPLE
>
> The author decides that he would rather become a deck hand than a cabin boy because
>
> (A) the job offers higher wages
>
> (B) he believes that the work is easier
>
> (C) he wants to avoid seeing his older friends
>
> (D) deck hands often go on to become pilots
>
> (E) the job is more visible to passersby

The author never says, "I decided to become a deck hand because the job was more visible to passersby." He does say he wanted to become a cabin boy so his old comrades could see him. And he adds the deck hand job would make him conspicuous. Between the lines, the correct answer, (E), is strongly implied.

Teacher Tip

"Once you've finished a reading passage or question, put it out of your mind. There's no connection at all between passages, so don't carry your stress or doubt to the next. Approach each passage as if it were the only one. Stay active and confident!"

—Marilyn Engle
Kaplan Teacher
Encino, CA

Inference Practice

To sharpen your ability to deal with all kinds of inferences, do the following exercise. (Answers on p. 84.)

1. The graduating classes were the nobility of the school. Like travelers with exotic destinations on their minds, the graduates were remarkably forgetful. They came to school without their books, or tablets, or even pencils. Volunteers fell over themselves to secure replacements for the missing equipment. Even the teachers were respectful of the now quiet and aging seniors, and tended to speak to them, if not as equals, as beings only slightly lower than themselves.

   In the lines above, the author most likely mentions the eagerness of the "volunteers" in order to

   (A) indicate the ambition of younger school members
   (B) explain a double standard in teachers' attitudes
   (C) underline the respect with which seniors were treated
   (D) emphasize how careless seniors were with their equipment
   (E) point out a shortage in school supplies

2. Without knowing exactly what he'd done, Marc realized that he'd really done it now, and he felt the silence incriminating him. "Now wait just a minute. Hold on there," he said, producing a laugh from somewhere. Marc was the statesman of the class. People joked about how much money he was going to make coming out of law school. But he was groping for his words now, his eyes flickering over the countertop as if the words he was looking for were visible there.

   In the lines above, Marc's reputation as "the statesman of the class" is most likely mentioned in order to indicate that

   (A) he is noted for his diplomacy
   (B) many people resent his success
   (C) he is generally an articulate speaker
   (D) he is a popular student on campus
   (E) his ambitions are not realistic

3. Everyone seems to agree that there is something wrong with the way science is being taught these days. But no one is at all clear about what went wrong or what is to be done about it. The term "scientific illiteracy" has become almost a cliché in educational circles. Graduate schools blame the colleges, colleges blame the high schools, the high schools blame the elementary schools, which, in turn, blame the family. I suggest that the scientific community is partly, perhaps largely, to blame.

   In the lines above, the phrase "almost a cliché in educational circles" is used to indicate

   (A) the lack of unity between different sectors of education
   (B) the widespread concern about the way science is being taught
   (C) the inability of many scientists to communicate effectively
   (D) the ignorance displayed by the scientific community about literature
   (E) the extent of agreement over specific educational reforms

Checklist

Once you've mastered a concept, check it off.

Building Reading Skills:

❏ Skimming

❏ Paraphrasing

❏ Making inferences

Answers to Paraphrasing and Inference Questions

Paraphrasing:

1. (C) Their parents want them to get married.

2. (D) A photographer is more open to nature and less pretentious than an "artist" is.

3. (A) The Fourth of July is a sham because the holiday celebrates freedom and they are not free.

Inferences:

1. (C)

2. (C)

3. (B)

Math Skills Workout

9

Introducing SAT Math

- Understand the breakdown and setup of the Math section

- Study traditional Math strategies as well as picking numbers and backsolving

Mathematics is many things. It is linear algebra and complex analysis. It is topology and trigonometry. It is number theory and multivariable calculus. Mathematics is a huge and daunting field, which requires years of study to master. But SAT Math is different. To ace the SAT, you need only a small body of mathematical knowledge covering basic concepts in arithmetic, algebra, and geometry. These concepts have been distilled into 100 principles that you'll find in the "SAT Study Aids" section of this book.

A solid grasp of these principles will get you a good SAT score. Understanding the ways in which these principles are tested—the twists and turns that the test makers throw into many SAT problems—can get you a great score.

This chapter explains:

- The SAT Math sections

- The SAT Math question types

- How to approach SAT Math problems

- Picking numbers

- Backsolving

SAT Emergency

This chapter will help you get a handle on the SAT Math section. You should read this chapter even if you have two weeks or fewer to prepare.

Then, in chapters 10 through 15, you'll learn:

- When to use your calculator
- Specific strategies for solving Regular Math questions, Quantitative Comparisons (QCs), and Grid-ins
- How to avoid math traps the test makers have set
- How to make educated guesses on difficult math problems

HOW SAT MATH IS SET UP

There are three scored Math sections on the SAT:

- One 30-minute section with 25 Regular Math questions
- One 30-minute section with a set of 15 QCs and a set of ten Grid-ins
- One 15-minute section with ten Regular Math questions

Difficulty Level

All sets of SAT Math questions are designed to start off basic and gradually increase in difficulty.

The ten Regular Math questions in the 15-minute section also get more difficult.

Always be aware of the difficulty level as you go through a question set. Easy problems call for different strategies. The harder the questions, the more traps you will encounter. If you know you're dealing with a hard question (even though it may look easy), you'll be prepared.

Know What to Expect

You'll save a lot of time on the SAT Math by knowing the directions. They take a fair amount of time to plow through and are the same for every test. With just a little prior experience, you'll know what to do with each question type so that you can skip the directions and go straight to the first question.

At the start of each Math section you will find the following information:

Note (2) means you won't have to deal with imaginary numbers, such as i (the square root of –1).

Note (3) tells you diagrams are drawn to scale, which means you can use these diagrams to estimate measurements. However, if the diagrams are labeled "Figure not drawn to scale," you can't do this.

Saying the figures "lie in a plane" simply means you are dealing with flat figures, like rectangles or circles, unless the question says otherwise.

The math information you're given includes many basic geometry formulas. By the day of the test you should know all these formulas by heart. But if you forget one at the last minute, you'll find them in the directions.

The Grid-ins and QCs have slightly different instructions, which we'll discuss in detail in chapter 11 and chapter 12.

HOW TO APPROACH SAT MATH

To maximize your Math score, you need to learn to use your time efficiently. Then you won't get bogged down on a single hard question and miss other problems you could have solved if you'd had more time.

The key to working systematically is: Think about the question before you look for the answer. A few seconds spent up front looking for traps, thinking about your approach, and deciding whether to tackle the problem now or come back to it later will pay off in SAT points. On basic problems, you may know what to do right away. But on hard problems, the few extra seconds are time well spent.

Now apply it to the problem below:

EXAMPLE

12. At a certain diner, Joe orders three doughnuts and a cup of coffee and is charged $2.25. Stella ordered two doughnuts and a cup of coffee and is charged $1.70. What is the price of two doughnuts?

(A) $0.55

(B) $0.60

(C) $1.10

(D) $1.30

(E) $1.80

Read Through the Question

This means the whole question. If you try to start solving the problem before reading it all the way through, you may end up doing unnecessary work.

Decide whether the question is basic, medium, or hard. All SAT Math questions are arranged in order of difficulty. Within a set, the first questions are basic, the middle ones moderately difficult, and the last ones are hard. Question 12 above is a moderately difficult word problem.

On difficult questions, watch out for Math Traps. Hard questions are often misleadingly worded to trip up careless readers. (For more on Math Traps, see chapter 14, Top Ten SAT Math Traps.)

Make sure you know what's being asked. Question 12 looks straightforward, but read through it carefully and you'll see a slight twist. You're asked to find the cost of two doughnuts, not one. Many people will find the price of a single doughnut and forget to double it.

What to Do When You Skip a Question

Circle it in your test booklet and make sure you skip it on your answer grid.

Decide Whether to Do the Problem or Skip It for Now

- If you have no idea what to do, skip the problem and circle it in your test booklet. Spend your time on the problems you can solve.

- If you think you can solve it, but it will take a lot of time, circle the question number in your test booklet and make a note to come back to it later if you have time.

- If you can eliminate one or more answer choices, do so and make an educated guess. Mark that you guessed in your test booklet, and try solving later if time permits. (For details on educated guessing, see the Math Guessing chapter.)

If You Do Tackle the Problem, Look for the Fastest Approach

Helpful Hint

When you skip a question, make a note in your test booklet to come back to it later, if you have time.

Look for hidden information. On an easy question, all the information you need to solve the problem may be given up front, in the stem, or in a diagram. But in a harder question, you may need to look for hidden information that will help you solve the problem. Since questions are arranged in order of difficulty, you should be a little wary of question 12. If you get the answer too easily, you may have missed something. In this case, you're asked to find the price of two doughnuts, not one. For more on Hidden Instructions, see chapter 14, Top Ten SAT Math Traps.

Look for shortcuts. Sometimes the obvious way of doing a problem is the long way. If the method you choose involves lots of calculating, look for another route. There's usually a shortcut you can use that won't involve tons of arithmetic.

In question 12, for example, the cost of doughnuts and coffee could be translated into two distinct equations using the variables d and c. You could find c in terms of d, then plug this into the other equation. But if you think carefully, you'll see there's a quicker way: The difference in price between three doughnuts and a cup of coffee and two doughnuts and a cup of coffee is the price of one doughnut. So one doughnut costs $2.25 – $1.70 = $0.55. (Remember, you have to find the price of *two* doughnuts. Twice $0.55 is $1.10.)

Use a variety of strategies. Chapter 13, Classic Problem-Solving Techniques, reviews many strategies for specific problem types that will help you get to the answer faster. You can also use special Kaplan methods, such as Picking Numbers and Backsolving. (For more on these methods, see pp. 92–96 in this chapter.)

Make an Educated Guess

If you're not sure what to do, or if you've tried solving a problem but got stuck, cut your losses. Eliminate any answer choices you can, and make an educated guess.

Let's say it's taking too long to solve the doughnut problem. Can you eliminate any answer choices? The price of two doughnuts and a cup of coffee is $1.70. That means the cost of two doughnuts alone can't be $1.80, which eliminates choice (E). Now you can choose between the remaining choices, and your odds of guessing correctly have improved. (See chapter 15, Math Guessing.)

If you practice using this approach to the Math problems on the SAT, you will save time and avoid mistakes on the day of the test.

WHEN YOU'RE STUCK

The great thing about math, even if you hate it, is that there are usually a lot of different ways to get to the right answer. On the SAT, there are two methods in particular that are really useful when you don't see the straightforward way to solve the problem—picking numbers and backsolving. These strategies can take longer than traditional methods, but they're worth trying if you have enough time.

Picking Numbers

Sometimes you can get stuck on a math question just because it's too general or abstract. A good way to get a handle on such a question is to bring it down to earth and make it more explicit by temporarily substituting particular numbers. This "picking numbers" strategy works especially well with even/odd questions.

EXAMPLE

If a is an odd integer and b is an even integer, which of the following must be odd?

(A) $2a + b$

(B) $a + 2b$

(C) ab

(D) a^2b

(E) ab^2

Rather than try to think this one through abstractly, it's easier for most people simply to pick numbers for a and b. There are rules that predict the evenness or oddness of sums, differences, and products, but there's no need to memorize these rules. When it comes to adding, subtracting, and multiplying evens and odds, what happens with one pair of numbers generally happens with all similar pairs.

Just say, for the time being, that $a = 3$ and $b = 2$. Plug those values into the answer choices, and there's a good chance that only one choice will be odd:

(A) $2a + b = 2(3) + 2 = 8$

(B) $a + 2b = 3 + 2(2) = 7$

(C) $ab = (3)(2) = 6$

(D) $a^2b = (3^2)(2) = 18$

(E) $ab^2 = (3)(2^2) = 12$

Choice (B) is the only odd one for $a = 3$ and $b = 2$, so it must be the one that's odd no matter what odd number a and even number b actually stand for. The answer is (B).

Another good situation for using the "picking numbers" strategy is when the answer choices to a percent problem are all percents.

EXAMPLE

From 1985 to 1990, the population of City *X* increased by 20 percent. From 1990 to 1995, the population increased by 30 percent. What was the percent increase in the population over the entire ten-year period 1985–1995?

(A) 10%

(B) 25%

(C) 50%

(D) 56%

(E) 60%

Instead of trying to solve this problem in the abstract, pick a number for the original 1985 population and see what happens. There's no need to pick a realistic number. You're better off picking a number that's easy to work with. And in percent problems the number that's easiest to work with is almost always 100. Say the 1985 population was 100, then what would the 1990 population be? Twenty percent more than 100 is 120. Now, if the 1990 population was 120, what would the 1995 population be? What's 30 percent more than 120? Be careful. Don't just add 30 to 120. You need to find 30 percent of 120 and add that on. Thirty percent of 120 is $(.30)(120) = 36$. Add 36 to 120 and you get a 1995 population of 156. What percent greater is 156 than 100? That's easy—that's why we picked 100 to start with. It's a 56 percent increase. The answer is (D).

A third good situation for using the "picking numbers" strategy is when the answer choices to a word problem are not numbers, but algebraic expressions.

EXAMPLE

If *n* apples cost *p* dollars, then how many dollars would *q* apples cost?

(A) $\dfrac{np}{q}$

(B) $\dfrac{nq}{p}$

(C) $\dfrac{pq}{n}$

(D) $\dfrac{n}{pq}$

(E) $\dfrac{p}{nq}$

Kaplan Rules

Avoid picking weird numbers like 0 and 1, as these often give several "possibly correct" answers.

The only thing that's hard about this question is that it uses variables instead of numbers. So, make it real. Pick numbers for the variables. Pick numbers that are easy to work with. Say $n = 2$, $p = 4$, and $q = 3$. Then the question becomes: "If two apples cost $4.00, how many dollars would three apples cost?" That's easy—$6.00. When $n = 2$, $p = 4$, and $q = 3$, the correct answer should equal 6. Plug those values into the answer choices and see which ones yield 6:

(A) $\dfrac{np}{q} = \dfrac{(2)(4)}{3} = \dfrac{8}{3}$

(B) $\dfrac{nq}{q} = \dfrac{(2)(3)}{3} = \dfrac{6}{3} = 2$

(C) $\dfrac{pq}{n} = \dfrac{(4)(3)}{2} = \dfrac{12}{2} = 6$

(D) $\dfrac{n}{pq} = \dfrac{2}{(4)(3)} = \dfrac{2}{12} = \dfrac{1}{6}$

(E) $\dfrac{p}{nq} = \dfrac{4}{(2)(3)} = \dfrac{4}{6} = \dfrac{2}{3}$

Choice (C) is the only one that yields 6, so it must be the correct answer.

When picking numbers for an abstract word problem like this one, it's important to try all five answer choices. Sometimes more than one choice will yield the correct result, in which case one or more choices work coincidentally with the numbers you picked. When that happens, pick another set of numbers to weed out the coincidences. Avoid picking weird numbers such as 0 and 1, as these often give several "possibly correct" answers.

Backsolving

On some Math questions, when you can't figure out the question, you can try working backwards from the answer choices. Plug the choices back into the question until you find the one that works.

Backsolving works best:

- When the question is a complex word problem and the answer choices are numbers
- When the alternative is setting up multiple algebraic equations

Don't backsolve:

- If the answer choices include variables
- On algebra questions or word problems that have ugly answer choices such as radicals and fractions (plugging them in takes too much time)

Complex Question, Simple Answer Choices

EXAMPLE

An office has 27 employees. If there are seven more women than men in the office, how many employees are women?

(A) 8

(B) 10

(C) 14

(D) 17

(E) 20

Speed Tip

To speed things up, start with the middle-range number. Since answer choices are always listed in increasing or decreasing order, you should start with choice (C). If it's too small, move to the bigger ones.

Sometimes backsolving is faster than setting up an equation.

The five answer choices represent the possible number of women in the office, so try them in the question stem. The choice that gives a total of 27 employees, with seven more women than men, will be the correct answer.

Plugging in choice (C) gives you 14 women in the office. Since there are seven more women than men, there are seven men in the office. But $14 + 7 < 27$. The sum is too small, so there must be more than 14 women. Eliminate answer choices (A), (B), and (C).

Either (D) or (E) will be correct. Plugging in (D) gives you 17 women in the office and $17 - 7$, or 10 men. $17 + 10 = 27$ employees total. Answer choice (D) is correct.

Algebra Problems for Which You Need to Solve Multiple Equations

EXAMPLE

If $a + b + c = 110$, $a = 4b$, and $3a = 2c$, then $b =$

(A) 6

(B) 8

(C) 9

(D) 10

(E) 14

You're looking for b, so plug in the answer choices for b in the question and see what happens. The choice that gives us 110 for the sum $a + b + c$ must be correct.

Start with the midrange number, 9, choice (C):

If $b = 9$, then $a = 4 \times 9 = 36$.

$2c = 3a = 3 \times 36 = 108$

$c = 54$

$a + b + c = 36 + 9 + 54 = 99$

Since this is a smaller sum than 110, the correct value for b must be greater. Therefore, eliminate answer choices (A), (B), and (C).

Now plug in either (D) or (E) and see if it works. If it doesn't, the remaining choice must be correct.

Short of time? Try guessing between (D) and (E). But guess intelligently. Since (C) wasn't far wrong, you want a number just slightly bigger. That's choice (D).

Now work through the remaining chapters in the Math Skills Workout section to master other strategies that will help you to ace your test.

Calculators and the SAT

- Practice with the calculator you'll bring to the test

- Use your calculator selectively

- Know the most common calculator mistakes and how to avoid them

You are allowed to use a calculator on the SAT. That's a mixed blessing. The good news is you can do computation faster. The bad news is you may be tempted to waste time using a calculator on questions that shouldn't involve lengthy computation.

Remember, you never *need* a calculator to solve an SAT problem. If you ever find yourself doing extensive calculation on the SAT—elaborate long division or long, drawn-out multiplication—stop and look again, because you probably missed a shortcut.

SHOULD I BRING A CALCULATOR?

You definitely want to bring your calculator on the day of the test. The fact is, there are some problems for which using the calculator will really come in handy. By using your calculator on particular problem types and by zeroing in on the parts of problems that need calculation, you can increase your score and save yourself time on the SAT.

SAT Emergency

If you have a week or two to prep for the SAT, be sure to read the section on common calculator mistakes.

WHAT KIND OF CALCULATOR SHOULD I BRING?

The best calculator to bring is one you're comfortable with. The most important thing is not how fancy your calculator is, but how good you are at using it. Remember, you won't be doing logs, trig functions, or preprogrammed formulas on the SAT. Most of the time you'll be multiplying and dividing.

You can use the following calculators on the SAT:

- A four-function calculator (that adds, subtracts, multiplies, divides)

- A scientific calculator (that also does radicals, exponents, etc.)

- A graphing calculator (that displays the graph of an equation in a coordinate plane)

But the following are not allowed:

- A calculator that prints out your calculations

- A hand-held minicomputer or a laptop computer

- Any calculator with a typewriter keypad

- A calculator that "speaks," makes strange noises, or requires an electrical outlet for use

The More You Know about the SAT . . .

. . . the less you'll use your calculator.

Using a calculator too much could actually hurt your score. The better you are at the SAT, the less you'll need your calculator.

WHEN SHOULD I USE A CALCULATOR?

Calculators help the most on Grid-ins and the least on QCs.

The reason for this is that QCs are designed to be done very quickly, and rarely involve much computation—if you think you need a calculator on them, then you're probably missing something. Both Grid-ins and Regular Math will sometimes involve computation—never as the most important part of the question, but often as a final step.

Since Grid-ins don't give you answer choices to choose from, it's especially important to be sure of your work. Calculators can help you avoid careless errors.

Remember, a calculator can be useful when used selectively. Not all parts of a problem are necessarily easier on a calculator. Consider this problem:

EXAMPLE

If four grams of cadmium yellow pigment can make 3 kilograms of cadmium yellow oil paint, how many kilograms of paint could be produced from 86 grams of pigment?

This word problem has two steps. Step one is to set up the following proportion:

$$\frac{4 \text{ gms}}{3 \text{ kgs}} = \frac{86 \text{ gms}}{x \text{ kgs}}$$

A little algebraic engineering tells you that:

$$x \text{ kgs} = \frac{3 \text{ kgs} \times 86 \text{ gms}}{4 \text{ gms}}$$

Here's where you whip out that calculator. This problem has now been reduced down to pure calculation: $(3 \times 86) \div 4 = 64.5$.

Your calculator will also be especially useful for picking numbers and backsolving.

When You Pick Numbers

When you plug in real numbers to replace variables in complex equations, your calculator can speed things up. (See Picking Numbers in chapter 9, Introducing SAT Math.)

When You Backsolve

When you plug multiple-choice answers into a problem to see which answer is right, your calculator can speed up the process. (See Backsolving, in chapter 9.)

WHEN SHOULDN'T I USE A CALCULATOR?

Don't be fooled. On most SAT problems you may be tempted to use your calculator, but many questions will be easier without a calculator. That's particularly true on QCs.

Consider this problem:

> **Check Your Batteries**
>
> The best calculator in the world won't help if the batteries are dead or if you forget to put them in. Make sure you have fresh batteries in your machine on the day of the test.

EXAMPLE

Column A	Column B

The ratio of b to 7 is equal to the ratio of 143 to 188.

b	7

Sure, you could set up the proportion $\frac{b}{7} = \frac{143}{188}$, grab your calculator, and cross multiply to find that $b = 5.324468085$. But why bother doing the calculation? Once you've set up the proportion, you can make a quick comparison without any further calculation. Your task is to compare b to 7. If $b = 7$, then $\frac{b}{7} = 1$. However, $\frac{b}{7}$ must be less than 1 since $\frac{143}{188} < 1$. Therefore, $b < 7$. Column B must be greater.

Be careful on non-QC questions, too. Consider this:

> EXAMPLE
>
> If $x^2 \times 8^2 = 49 \times 64 \times 81$, $x^2 =$
>
> (A) 49^2
>
> (B) 56^2
>
> (C) 63^2
>
> (D) 72^2
>
> (E) 81^2

Now if you punch in $49 \times 64 \times 81$ you'll get 254,016. But that won't be too helpful. Look at the answer choices! Instead realize that:

$$(x^2) \times 8^2 = (49 \times 81) \times 64$$

8^2 is the same as 64, so get rid of the 64s on both sides. You get:

$$x^2 = 49 \times 81$$

So that's $x^2 = 7^2 \times 9^2$ or $x^2 = 7 \times 7 \times 9 \times 9$, which is 63×63 or 63^2.

No calculator required.

COMMON MISTAKE #1: CALCULATING BEFORE YOU THINK

On the Grid-in problem below, how should you use your calculator?

Calculator Abuse: The Warning Signs

- Punching in numbers before you've read the question.

- Hand cramps from punching in too many numbers.

- Repeatedly spelling *hello* or *Shell Oil* on your calculator rather than answering the question.

> EXAMPLE
>
> The sum of all the integers from 1 to 44, inclusive, is subtracted from the sum of all the integers from 7 to 50, inclusive. What is the result?

The Wrong Approach:

- Grab calculator.

- Punch in all the numbers.

- Put down an answer and hope you didn't hit any wrong buttons.

The wrong approach is to punch in all the numbers from 1 to 44, find their sum, then do the same for numbers 7 through 50, and subtract the first sum from the second. Doing that means punching 252 keys. The odds are you'll slip up somewhere, hit the wrong key, and get the wrong answer. Even if you don't, punching in all those numbers takes too much time.

The Kaplan Method

- Think first.

- Decide on the best way to solve it.

- Only then, use your calculator.

The right approach is to *think first*. The amount of computation involved in solving this directly tells you that there *must* be an easier way. You'll see this if you realize that both sums are of the same number of consecutive integers. Each integer in the first sum has a corresponding integer six units greater than it in the second sum, like so:

$$
\begin{array}{cc}
1 & 7 \\
+2 & +8 \\
+3 & +9 \\
\cdot & \cdot \\
\cdot & \cdot \\
\cdot & \cdot \\
+42 & +48 \\
+43 & +49 \\
+44 & +50 \\
= & = \\
\end{array}
$$

> ### Teacher Tip
>
> "I often tell students not to rely on their calculators too much. They are excellent tools, but when we begin to use them to do every operation, they are no longer tools that we are using to augment our abilities, but tools we are using to replace them."
>
> —Jaelithe Russ
> Kaplan Teacher
> Akron, OH

There are 44 pairs of integers that are six units apart. So the total difference between the two sums will be the difference between each pair of integers times the number of pairs.

Now take out your calculator, multiply 6 by 44, and get the correct answer of 264, with little or no time wasted.

HINT: *If you're punching buttons for long stretches at a time, you're approaching the problem the wrong way.*

COMMON MISTAKE #2: FORGETTING THE ORDER OF OPERATIONS

Watch out. Even when you use your calculator, you can't just enter numbers in the order they appear on the page—you've got to follow the order of operations. This is a very simple error but it can cost you lots of points.

The order of operations, or PEMDAS, means you do whatever is in:

> ### Kaplan Rules
>
> Different calculators do chain calculations different ways. Make sure you know how your calculator does chains so you don't miscalculate.

Parentheses first, then deal with

Exponents, then

Multiplication and

Division, and finally

Addition and

Subtraction

For example, say you want to find the value of the expression:

$$\frac{x^2 + 1}{x + 3} \quad \text{when } x = 7$$

If you just punched in "7 $\times$ 7 + 1 $\div$ 7 + 3 =" you would get the wrong answer. The correct way to work it out is:

$$(7^2 + 1) \div (7 + 3) = (7 \times 7 + 1) \div (7 + 3) = (49 + 1) \div 10 = 50 \div 10 = 5$$

Combining a calculator with an understanding of when and how to use it can help you boost your score.

Checklist

Once you've mastered a concept, check it off.

Calculators and the SAT:

❏ What kind of calculator should I bring?

❏ When should I use a calculator?

❏ When shouldn't I use a calculator?

❏ Common mistakes

11

Grid-Ins

- Familiarize yourself with grid formats, techniques, and rules
- Practice gridding in answers with fractions, mixed numbers, and decimals

In high school math class, you usually don't get five answer choices to choose from on a test. And you don't lose a quarter of a point for a wrong answer. Instead, you're given a problem and asked to find the answer.

The Grid-in section on the SAT is a lot like the math tests you're already used to taking. Unlike other questions on the SAT, Grid-ins have no multiple-choice answers and there's no penalty for wrong answers. You have to figure out your own answer and fill it in on a special grid. Note that some Grid-ins have only one correct answer, while others have several, or even a range of correct answers.

SAT Emergency

If you have two weeks or fewer to prep for the SAT, here's the best way to spend your time:

- Read this entire chapter. It's pretty short and the gridding tips that we discuss can help prevent you from making careless mistakes that can make a big difference in your score.

- Do the gridding drills at the end of the chapter.

THE FORMAT

You'll get ten Grid-ins, following the QCs, in one of the Math sections. To get an idea of what the instructions will look like on the day of the test, check out the example below.

For each question, you'll see a grid with four boxes and a column of ovals beneath each. First write your numerical answer in the boxes, one digit, decimal point, or fraction bar per box. Then fill in the corresponding ovals below.

Warning:

- The computer cannot scan the numerical answer in the boxes; you must fill in the corresponding ovals.

- Fill in no more than one oval per column.

- Make the oval you grid match your number above that oval.

For each of the questions below (16–25), solve the problem and indicate your answer by darkening the ovals in the special grid. For example:

Answer: 1.25 or $\frac{5}{4}$ or 5/4

Write answer in boxes.

Grid in result

Fraction line

Decimal point

You may start your answers in any column, space permitting. Columns not needed should be left blank.

Either position is correct.

- It is recommended, though not required, that you write your answer in the boxes at the top of the columns. However, you will receive credit only for darkening the ovals correctly.

- Grid only one answer to a question, even though some problems have more than one correct answer.

- Darken no more than one oval in a column.

- No answers are negative.

- Mixed numbers cannot be gridded. For example: the number $1\frac{1}{4}$ must be gridded as 1.25 or 5/4.

(If ⟨1 1/4⟩ is gridded, it will be interpreted as $\frac{11}{4}$ not $1\frac{1}{4}$.)

- <u>Decimal Accuracy:</u> Decimal answers must be entered as accurately as possible. For example, if you obtain an answer such as 0.1666. . ., you should record the result as .166 or .167. **Less accurate values such as .16 or .17 are not acceptable.**

Acceptable ways to grid $\frac{1}{6}$ =.1666. . .

Grid instructions

FILLING IN THE GRID

The grid cannot accommodate:

- Negative answers

- Answers with variables

- Answers greater than 9,999

- Answers with commas

- Mixed numbers

Recommendation: Start your answer in the first column box. Do this even if your answer has only one or two figures. If you always start with the first column, your answers will always fit. Since there is no oval for 0 in the first column, grid an answer of 0 in any other column. (Technically, you can start in any column, but follow this rule to avoid mistakes.)

In a fractional answer, grid (/) in the correct column. The sign (/) separates the numerator from the denominator. It appears only in columns two and three.

Example: If you get an answer of $\frac{5}{8}$. Grid (/) in col. two.

Example: If you get an answer of $\frac{11}{9}$. Grid (/) in col. three.

WARNING: *A fractional answer with four digits won't fit.*

Change mixed numbers to decimals or fractions before you grid. If you try to grid a mixed number, it will be read as a fraction, and be counted wrong. For example, $4\frac{1}{2}$ will be read as the fraction $\frac{41}{2}$, which is $20\frac{1}{2}$.

Kaplan Rules

Always use the most accurate answer that fits. For example, 1.4 is not a substitute for 1.43.

So first change mixed numbers to fractions or decimals, then grid in. In this case:

- Change $4\frac{1}{2}$ to $\frac{9}{2}$ and grid in as shown below.

- Or change $4\frac{1}{2}$ to 4.5 and grid in the decimal.

HINT: *Watch where you put your decimal points.*

- For a decimal less than 1, such as .127, enter the decimal point in the first box as shown in the figure above.

- Put a zero before the decimal point only if it's part of the answer—don't just put one there to make your answer look more accurate.

- Never grid a decimal point in the last column.

With long or repeating decimals, grid the first three digits only and plug in the decimal point where it belongs. Say three answers are .45454545, 82.452312, and 1.428743. Grid .454, 82.4, and 1.42, respectively.

You could round 1.428743 up to the nearest hundredth (1.43), but it's not required. So don't bother, since you could make a mistake. Shorter, less accurate answers—such as 1.4—are wrong.

On Grid-ins with more than one right answer, choose one, and enter it. Say you're asked for a two-digit integer that is a multiple of 2, 3, and 5. You might answer 30, 60, or 90. Whichever you grid would be right.

Some Grid-ins have a range of possible answers. Suppose you're asked to grid a value of m, given that $1 - 2m < m$ and $5m - 2 < m$. Solving for m in the first inequality, you find that $\frac{1}{3} < m$. Solving for m in the second inequality, you find that $m < \frac{1}{2}$. So $\frac{1}{3} < m < \frac{1}{2}$. Grid in any value between $\frac{1}{3}$ and $\frac{1}{2}$. (Gridding in $\frac{1}{3}$ or $\frac{1}{2}$ would be wrong.) When the answer is a range of values, it's often easier to work with decimals: $.333 < m < .5$. Then you can quickly grid .4 (or .35 or .45, etc.) as your answer.

Write your answers in the number boxes. You will make fewer mistakes if you write your answers in the number boxes. You may think that gridding directly will save time, but writing first and then gridding ensures accuracy, which means more points.

PRACTICE GRIDDING

With just a little practice, you can master the gridding-in process. Complete the Grid-ins below, following our instructions. After you finish, check your work against the grids on p. 110.

126    $\frac{3}{8}$ 85.9   2,143 $5\frac{1}{2}$

0   .141414 $\frac{14}{5}$ $1\frac{2}{3}$ 8.175

Checklist

Once you've mastered a concept, check it off.

Grid-Ins:

❏ The format

❏ Filling in the grid

❏ Practice gridding

Gridding Answers

126      $\frac{3}{8}$ 85.9   2,143 $5\frac{1}{2}$

Or .375

Omit the comma.

Convert $5\frac{1}{2}$ to $\frac{11}{2}$ (or 5.5); "5 1/2" is incorrect.

0   .141414 $\frac{14}{5}$ $1\frac{2}{3}$ 8.175

Place the decimal point in the first column and grid as many digits as possible.

Convert $1\frac{2}{3}$ to $\frac{5}{3}$ (or 1.66 or 1.67); "12/3" is incorrect.

Or 8.18. Start in the left column and grid as many digits as possible.

12

Quantitative Comparisons

- Understand the answer choices and the rules for choice (D)

- Master Kaplan's six strategies for tackling QCs

- Complete the Quantitative Comparisons Practice Set

In Quantitative Comparisons, instead of solving for a particular value, you need to compare two quantities. At first, QCs may appear really difficult because of their unfamiliar format. However, once you become used to them, they can be quicker and easier than the other types of math questions.

THE FORMAT

Where They Appear

The 15 QCs appear in the Math section that also contains the ten Grid-in questions. They are arranged in order of increasing difficulty.

The Questions

In each question, you'll see two mathematical expressions. They are boxed, one in Column A, the other in Column B. Your job is to compare them.

SAT Emergency

If you don't have much time to prep for the SAT, here's the best way to spend your time:

- Read p. 112.

- Learn the two rules for choice (D) on p. 112.

- Do the practice problems on pp. 121–122. If you miss an answer, review the strategy before continuing.

Some questions include additional information about one or both quantities. This information is centered, unboxed, and essential to making the comparison.

HINT: *To score high on QCs, learn what the answer choices stand for.*

The Directions

The directions you'll see will look something like this. Familiarize yourself with them now.

WARNING: *Never pick choice (E) as the answer to a QC.*

Two Rules for Answer Choice (D)

Choices (A), (B), and (C) all represent definite relationships between the quantities in Column A and Column B. But choice (D) represents a relationship that cannot be determined. Here are two things to remember about choice (D) that will help you decide when to pick it:

1. Choice (D) is never correct if both columns contain only numbers. The relationship between numbers is unchanging, but choice (D) means more than one relationship is possible.

2. Choice (D) is correct if you can demonstrate two different relationships between the columns. Suppose you ran across the following QC:

Column A	Column B
$2x$	$3x$

If x is a positive number, Column B is greater than Column A. If $x = 0$, the columns are equal. If x equals any negative number, Column B is less than Column A. Since more than one relationship is possible, the answer is (D). In fact, as soon as you find a second possibility, stop work and pick choice (D).

COMPARE, DON'T CALCULATE: KAPLAN'S SIX STRATEGIES

Kaplan Rules

Usually there's a simpler way to solve a QC than using your calculator.

Here are six Kaplan strategies that will enable you to make quick comparisons. In the rest of this chapter you'll learn how they work and you'll try them on practice problems.

Strategy 1: Compare Piece by Piece

This works on QCs that compare two sums or two products.

Strategy 2: Make One Column Look Like the Other

This is a great approach when the columns look so different that you can't compare them directly.

Strategy 3: Do the Same Thing to Both Columns

Change both columns by adding, subtracting, multiplying, or dividing by the same amount on both sides in order to make the comparison more apparent.

Strategy 4: Pick Numbers

Use this to get a handle on abstract algebra QCs.

Strategy 5: Redraw the Diagram

Redrawing a diagram can clarify the relationships between measurements.

Strategy 6: Avoid QC Traps

Stay alert for questions designed to fool you by leading you to the obvious, wrong answer.

Now learn how these strategies work.

STRATEGY 1: COMPARE PIECE BY PIECE

EXAMPLE

Column A	Column B

$$w > x > 0 > y > z$$

Column A	Column B
$w + y$	$x + z$

In the problem above, there are four variables—w, x, y, and z. Compare the value of each "piece" in each column. If every "piece" in one column is greater than a corresponding "piece" in the other column and the only operation involved is addition, the column with the greater individual values will have the greater total value.

Kaplan Rules

Lengths and areas are always greater than zero.

From the given information we know that $w > x$ and $y > z$. Therefore, the first term in Column A, w, is greater than the first term in Column B, x. Similarly, the second term in Column A, y, is greater than the second term in Column B, z. Since each piece in Column A is greater than the corresponding piece in Column B, Column A must be greater; the answer is (A).

STRATEGY 2: MAKE ONE COLUMN LOOK LIKE THE OTHER

When the quantities in Columns A and B are expressed differently, you can often make the comparison easier by changing one column to look like the other. For example, if one column is a percent and the other a fraction, try converting the percent to a fraction.

EXAMPLE

Column A	Column B
$x(x-1)$	$x^2 - x$

Here Column A has parentheses, and Column B doesn't. So make Column A look more like Column B: Get rid of those parentheses. You end up with $x^2 - x$ in both columns, which means they are equal and the answer is (C).

Try another example, this time involving geometry.

EXAMPLE

Column A	Column B

The diameter of circle O is d and the area is a.

$$\frac{\pi d^2}{2} \qquad a$$

Make Column B look more like Column A by rewriting a, the area of the circle, in terms of the diameter, d. The area of any circle equals πr^2, with r as the radius.

Since the radius is half the diameter, we can plug in $\frac{d}{2}$ for r in the area formula to get $\pi\left(\frac{d}{2}\right)^2$ in Column B. Simplifying, we get $\frac{\pi d^2}{4}$. Since both columns contain π, we can simply compare $\frac{d^2}{2}$ with $\frac{d^2}{4}$. Since $\frac{d^2}{4}$ is half as much as $\frac{d^2}{2}$, and d^2 must be positive, Column A is greater.

Choice (A) is correct.

STRATEGY 3: DO THE SAME THING TO BOTH COLUMNS

Some QC questions become much clearer if you change not just the appearances, but the values of both columns. Treat them like two sides of an inequality, with the sign temporarily hidden.

You can add or subtract the same amount from both columns and multiply or divide by the same positive amount without altering the relationship. You can also square both columns if you're sure they're both positive. But watch out. Multiplying or dividing an inequality by a negative number reverses the direction of the inequality sign. Since it alters the relationship between the columns, avoid multiplying or dividing by a negative number.

> **Kaplan Rules**
>
> There are a number of traps to watch out for in QCs. QC traps may appear anywhere in the QC section, but they occur most often near the end because QCs are arranged in order of difficulty.
>
> For more on traps, see the Top Ten SAT Math Traps.

HINT: *Don't multiply or divide both QC columns by a negative number.*

In the QC below, what could you do to both columns?

| EXAMPLE |

Column A	Column B

$$4a + 3 = 7b$$

$20a + 10$	$35b - 5$

All the terms in the two columns are multiples of 5, so divide both columns by 5 to simplify. You're left with $4a + 2$ in Column A and $7b - 1$ in Column B. This resembles the equation given in the centered information. In fact, if you add 1 to both columns, you have $4a + 3$ in Column A and $7b$ in Column B. The centered equation tells us they are equal. Thus choice (C) is correct.

In the next QC, what could you do to both columns?

| EXAMPLE |

Column A	Column B

$$y > 0$$

$1 + \dfrac{y}{(y + 1)}$	$1 + \dfrac{1}{(1 + y)}$

Solution: First subtract 1 from both sides. That gives you $\dfrac{y}{(1 + y)}$ in Column A, and $\dfrac{1}{(1 + y)}$ in Column B. Then multiply both sides by $(1 + y)$, which must be positive since y is positive.

You're left comparing y with 1.

Kaplan Rules

Some surprising things can happen when you play around with negative numbers and fractions. Keep things like this in mind:

- When you square a positive fraction less than 1, the result is smaller than the original fraction.

- When you square a negative number, the result is a positive number.

- When you square 0 and 1, they stay the same.

You know y is greater than 0, but it could be a fraction less than 1, so it could be greater or less than 1. Since you can't say for sure which column is greater, the answer is (D).

STRATEGY 4: PICK NUMBERS

If a QC involves variables, try picking numbers to make the relationship clearer. Here's what you do:

- Pick numbers that are easy to work with.

- Plug in the numbers and calculate the values. Note the relationship between the columns.

- Pick another number for each variable and calculate the values again.

EXAMPLE

Column A	Column B
$r > s > t > w > 0$	
$\dfrac{r}{t}$	$\dfrac{s}{w}$

Try $r = 4$, $s = 3$, $t = 2$, and $w = 1$. Then Column A $= \dfrac{r}{t} = \dfrac{4}{2} = 2$. And Column B $= \dfrac{s}{w} = \dfrac{3}{1} = 3$. So in this case Column B is greater than Column A.

Always Pick Another Number and Calculate Again

In the example above, we first found Column B was bigger. But that doesn't mean Column B is always bigger and that the answer is (B). It *does* mean the answer is not (A) or (C). But the answer could still be (D)—not enough information to decide.

If time is short, guess between (B) and (D). But whenever you can, pick another set of numbers and calculate again.

As best you can, make a special effort to find a second set of numbers that will alter the relationship. Here for example, try making r a lot larger. Pick $r = 30$ and keep the other variables as they were. Now Column A $= \dfrac{30}{2} = 15$. This time, Column A is greater than Column B, so answer choice (D) is correct.

HINT: *If the relationship between Columns A and B changes when you pick other numbers, (D) must be the answer.*

Pick Different Kinds of Numbers

Don't assume all variables represent positive integers. Unless you're told otherwise, variables can represent zero, negative numbers, or fractions. Since different kinds of numbers behave differently, always pick a different kind of number the second time around. In the example above, we plugged in a small positive number the first time and a larger number the second.

In the next three examples, we pick different numbers and get different results. Since we can't find constant relationships between Columns A and B, in all these cases the answer is (D).

Speed Tip

If you're pressed for time, picking just one set of numbers will narrow it down to two choices. Guess from these.

EXAMPLE

Column A	Column B
w	$-w$

If $w = 5$, Column A = 5 and Column B = -5, so Column A is greater.

If $w = -5$, Column A = -5 and Column B = 5, so Column B is greater.

EXAMPLE

Column A	Column B

$$x \neq 0$$

Column A	Column B
x	$\dfrac{1}{x}$

If $x = 3$, Column A = 3 and Column B = $\dfrac{1}{3}$, so Column A is greater.

If $x = \dfrac{1}{3}$, Column A = $\dfrac{1}{3}$ and Column B = $\dfrac{1}{\frac{1}{3}} = 3$, so Column B is greater.

EXAMPLE

Column A	Column B
x	x^2

If $x = \dfrac{1}{2}$, Column A = $\dfrac{1}{2}$ and Column B = $\dfrac{1}{4}$, so Column A is greater.

If $x = 2$, Column A = 2 and Column B = 4, so Column B is greater.

STRATEGY 5: REDRAW THE DIAGRAM

- Redraw a diagram if the one that's given misleads you.

- Redraw scale diagrams to exaggerate crucial differences.

Don't Over (D) It

Choice (D) doesn't mean you can't determine which is greater—it means no one can.

If you frequently find (D) is your answer, double-check your work.

Kaplan Rules

Remember:

- Not all numbers are positive.
- Not all numbers are integers.

Some geometry diagrams may be misleading. Two angles or lengths may look equal as drawn in the diagram, but the given information tells you that there is a slight difference in their measures. The best strategy is to redraw the diagram so that their relationship can be clearly seen.

EXAMPLE

Column A   Column B

ABCD is a rectangle

a   b

Redraw this diagram to exaggerate the difference between the 89-degree angle and the 91-degree angle. In other words, make the larger angle much larger, and the smaller angle much smaller. The new rectangle that results is much wider than it is tall.

In the new diagram, where the crucial difference jumps out, *a* is clearly greater than *b*.

STRATEGY 6: AVOID QC TRAPS

To avoid QC traps, always be alert. Don't assume anything. Be especially cautious near the end of the question set.

Don't Be Tricked by Misleading Information

EXAMPLE

Column A   Column B

John is taller than Bob.

John's weight in pounds   Bob's weight in pounds

The test makers hope you think, "If John is taller, he must weigh more." But there's no guaranteed relationship between height and weight, so you don't have enough information. The answer is (D). Fortunately, problems like this are easy to spot if you stay alert.

Don't Assume

A common QC mistake is to assume that variables represent positive integers. As we saw in using the Picking Numbers strategy, fractions or negative numbers often show another relationship between the columns.

> EXAMPLE

Column A	Column B

When 1 is added to the square of x the result is 37.

x	6

It is easy to assume that x must be 6, since the square of x is 36. That would make choice (C) correct. However, it is possible that $x = -6$. Since x could be either 6 or -6, the answer is (D).

HINT: *Be aware of negative numbers!*

Don't Forget to Consider Other Possibilities

The following question appears at the end of the QC section.

> EXAMPLE

Column A	Column B

$$\begin{array}{r} R \\ S \\ T \\ \hline 1W \end{array}$$

In the addition problem above, R, S, and T are different digits that are multiples of 3, and W is a digit.

W	8

Since you're told that R, S, and T are digits and different multiples of 3, most people will think of 3, 6, and 9, which add up to 18. That makes W equal to 8, and Columns A and B equal. But that's too obvious for a QC at the end of the section.

There's another possibility. Zero is also a multiple of 3. So the three digits could be 0, 3, and 9, or 0, 6, and 9, which give totals of 12 and 15, respectively. That means W could be 8, 2, or 5. Since the columns could be equal, or Column B could be greater, answer choice (D) must be correct.

Don't Fall for Look-Alikes

EXAMPLE

Column A	Column B
$\sqrt{5} + \sqrt{5}$	$\sqrt{10}$

At first glance, forgetting the rules of radicals, you might think these quantities are equal and that the answer is (C). But use some common sense to see this isn't the case. Each $\sqrt{5}$ in Column A is bigger than $\sqrt{4}$, so Column A is more than 4. The $\sqrt{10}$ in Column B is less than another familiar number, $\sqrt{16}$, so Column B is less than 4. The answer is (A).

Now use Kaplan's six strategies to solve nine typical QC questions. Then check your work against our solutions on page 123.

TEST YOUR QC SMARTS

Column A | Column B

1. $x^2 + 2x - 2$ $x^2 + 2x - 1$ Ⓐ Ⓑ Ⓒ Ⓓ Ⓔ

....

$$x = 2y$$
$$y > 0$$

2. 4^{2y} 2^x Ⓐ Ⓑ Ⓒ Ⓓ Ⓔ

....

$$\frac{x}{y} = \frac{z}{4}$$

x, y, and z are positive

3. $6x$ $2yz$ Ⓐ Ⓑ Ⓒ Ⓓ Ⓔ

....

q, r, and s are positive integers
$$qrs > 12$$

4. $\dfrac{qr}{5}$ $\dfrac{3}{s}$ Ⓐ Ⓑ Ⓒ Ⓓ Ⓔ

....

$$x > 1$$
$$y > 0$$

5. y^x $y^{(x+1)}$ Ⓐ Ⓑ Ⓒ Ⓓ Ⓔ

....

$$7p + 3 = r$$
$$3p + 7 = s$$

6. r s Ⓐ Ⓑ Ⓒ Ⓓ Ⓔ

Column A   Column B

In triangle *XYZ*, the measure of angle *X* equals the measure of angle *Y*.

7.   The degree measure   The degree measure
     of angle *Z*   of angle *X* plus the
                               degree measure of
                               angle *Y*

Ⓐ Ⓑ Ⓒ **Ⓓ** Ⓔ

....

$$h > 1$$

8.   The number of $\dfrac{60}{h}$
     minutes in *h*
     hours

Ⓐ Ⓑ Ⓒ Ⓓ Ⓔ

....

Square *A*   Square *B*

Note: Figures not drawn to scale.

9. $\dfrac{\text{Perimeter of square } A}{\text{Perimeter of square } B}$ $\dfrac{\text{Length of } WY}{\text{Length of } PR}$

Ⓐ Ⓑ **Ⓒ** Ⓓ Ⓔ

Answers to QC Practice Set

1. (B) Comparing the respective pieces of the two columns, the only difference is the third piece: -2 in Column A and -1 in Column B. We don't know the value of x, but whatever it is, x^2 in Column A must have the same value as x^2 in Column B, and $2x$ in Column A must have the same value as $2x$ in Column B. Since any quantity minus 2 must be less than that quantity minus 1, Column B is greater than Column A.

2. (A) Replacing the x exponent in Column B with the equivalent value given in the problem, we're comparing 4^{2y} to 2^{2y}. Since y is greater than 0, raising 4 to the $2y$ power will result in a greater value than raising 2 to the $2y$ power.

3. (B) Do the same thing to both columns until they resemble the centered information. When we divide both columns by $6y$ we get $\frac{6x}{6y}$, or $\frac{x}{y}$ in Column A, and $\frac{2yz}{6y}$, or $\frac{z}{3}$ in Column B. Since $\frac{x}{y} = \frac{z}{4}$, and $\frac{z}{3} > \frac{z}{4}$ (because z is positive), $\frac{z}{3} > \frac{x}{y}$.

4. (D) Do the same thing to both columns to make them look like the centered information. When we multiply both columns by $5s$ we get qrs in Column A and 15 in Column B. Since qrs could be any integer greater than 12, it could be greater than, equal to, or less than 15.

5. (D) Try $x = y = 2$. Then Column A $= y^x = 2^2 = 4$. Column B $= y^{x+1} = 2^3 = 8$, making Column B greater. But if $x = 2$ and $y = \frac{1}{2}$, Column A $= \left(\frac{1}{2}\right)^2 = \frac{1}{4}$ and Column B $= \left(\frac{1}{2}\right)^3 = \frac{1}{8}$. In this case, Column A is greater than Column B, so the answer is (D).

6. (D) Pick a value for p, and see what effect this has on r and s. If $p = 1$, $r = (7 \times 1) + 3 = 10$, and $s = (3 \times 1) + 7 = 10$, and the two columns are equal. But if $p = 0$, $r = (7 \times 0) + 3 = 3$, and $s = (3 \times 0) + 7 = 7$, and Column A is smaller than Column B. Since there are at least two different possible relationships, the answer is choice (D).

7. (D) Since angle X = angle Y, this is an isosceles triangle. We can draw two diagrams with X and Y as the base angles of an isosceles triangle. In one diagram, make the triangle tall and narrow, so that angle X and angle Y are very large, and angle Z is very small. In this case, column B is greater. In the second diagram, make the triangle short and wide, so that angle Z is much larger than angle X and angle Y. In this case, Column A is greater. Since more than one relationship between the columns is possible, the correct answer is choice (D).

8. (A) The "obvious" answer here is choice (C), because there are 60 minutes in an hour, and 60 appears in Column B. But the number of minutes in h hours would equal 60 times h, not 60 divided by h. Since h is greater than 1, the number in Column B will be less than the actual number of minutes in h hours, so Column A is greater. (A) is correct.

9. (C) We don't know the exact relationship between Square A and Square B, but it doesn't matter. The problem is actually just comparing the ratios of corresponding parts of two squares. Whatever the relationship between them is for one specific length in both squares, the same relationship will exist between them for any other corresponding length. If a side of one square is twice the length of a side of the second square, the diagonal will also be twice as long. The ratio of the perimeters of the two squares is the same as the ratio of the sides. Therefore, the columns are equal. (C) is correct.

Checklist

Once you've mastered a concept, check it off.

Quantitative Comparisons:

❏ Compare piece by piece

❏ Make one column look like the other

❏ Do the same thing to both columns

❏ Pick numbers

❏ Redraw the diagram

❏ Avoid QC traps

13

Classic Problem-Solving Techniques

Review ten popular question types and methods to solve each:

- Remainders

- Averages

- Ratios

- Rates

- Percents

- Combinations

- Simultaneous equations

- Symbolism

- Special triangles

- Multiple and oddball figures

SAT Emergency

If you have just a few weeks to prep for the SAT, here's how you should spend your time:

- In each of the ten sections, try the sample problems.

- Review any section where you have trouble.

The test makers are not paid to be creative. In fact, there are certain types of problems that they like to use again and again on the SAT. This chapter gives you ten of their favorite problem types, along with Kaplan's classic techniques for solving them.

REMAINDERS

Remainder questions can be easier than they look. You might think you have to solve for a certain value, but often you don't.

EXAMPLE

When n is divided by 7, the remainder is 4.
What is the remainder when $2n$ is divided by 7?

(A) 0

(B) 1

(C) 2

(D) 3

(E) 4

The question above doesn't depend on knowing the value of n. In fact, n has an infinite number of possible values.

HINT: *Pick a number for* n.

Which number should you pick? Since the remainder when n is divided by 7 is 4, pick any multiple of 7 and add 4. The easiest multiple to work with is 7. So, $7 + 4 = 11$. Use 11 for n.

Plug 11 into the question and see what happens.

What is the remainder when $2n$ is divided by 7?

$$2(11) \div 7 =$$

$$22 \div 7 =$$

$$\frac{22}{7} = 3 \text{ remainder } 1$$

The remainder is 1 when $n = 11$. So the answer is (B). The remainder will also be 1 when $n = 18, 25,$ or 46.

QC Remainders

| EXAMPLE |

Column A   Column B

When p is divided by 5, the remainder is 3.

When q is divided by 5, the remainder is 4.

p q

The centered information tells you that p can be any of the integers 3, 8, 13, 18, 23, . . . ; and that q can be any of the integers 4, 9, 14, 19, 24, and so forth. So how do p and q compare? You can't tell; p could be small and q big, or the other way around. The answer is (D), not enough information to decide.

Practice Problems: Remainders

| REGULAR MATH |

1. When z is divided by 8, the remainder is 5. What is the remainder when $4z$ is divided by 8?

    (A) 1
    (B) 3
    (C) 4
    (D) 5
    (E) 7

    Ⓐ Ⓑ ● Ⓓ Ⓔ

| QC |

Column A   Column B

When x is divided by 6 the remainder is 3.
When y is divided by 6 the remainder is 4.

2. x y Ⓐ Ⓑ Ⓒ ● Ⓔ

When m is divided by 5 the remainder is 2.
When n is divided by 5 the remainder is 1.

3. The remainder when $m + n$ is divided by 5   The remainder when mn is divided by 5   ● Ⓑ Ⓒ Ⓓ Ⓔ

Answers to Remainders Problems

1. (C) Let $z = 13$ and plug in $4z = 4(13) = 52$, which leaves a remainder of 4 when divided by 8.

2. (D) We determine that x can be any of the integers 3, 9, 15, 21, . . . , and y can be any of the integers 4, 10, 16, 22, ... Since x could be greater than or less than y, the correct answer must be choice (D).

3. (A) The variable m can be any integer that ends in either a 2 or a 7; n can be any integer that ends in either a 1 or a 6. Plugging in will show that in any case, $m + n$ will leave a remainder of 3 when divided by 5, and mn will leave a remainder of 2 when divided by 5, so Column A is greater.

AVERAGES

Use Your Head

Use common sense to learn about the size of the value you're asked to find. If all the terms listed are less than the given average, then the unknown term must be greater than the average to balance it out.

Likewise, if adding a new value, x, to a group of numbers raises the average value of the group, then x must be greater than the average of the original numbers.

| EXAMPLE |

The average weight of five dogs in a certain kennel is 32 pounds. If four of the dogs weigh 25, 27, 19, and 35 pounds, what is the weight of the fifth dog?

(A) 28

(B) 32

(C) 49

(D) 54

(E) 69

Instead of giving you a list of values to plug into the average formula, SAT average questions often put a slight spin on the problem. They tell you the average of a group of terms and ask you to find the value of the missing term.

HINT: *Work with the sum.*

Let x = the weight of the fifth dog. Plug this into the average formula:

$$32 = \frac{25 + 27 + 19 + 35 + x}{5}$$

$$32 \times 5 = 25 + 27 + 19 + 35 + x$$

So the average weight of the dogs, times the number of dogs, equals the total weight of the dogs, or, mathematically:

$$\text{Average} \times \text{Number of Terms} = \text{Sum of Terms}$$

Remember this manipulation of the average formula so that whenever you know the average of a group of terms and the number of terms, you can find the total sum.

Now you can solve for the weight of the fifth dog:

$$32 \times 5 = 25 + 27 + 19 + 35 + x$$
$$160 = 106 + x$$
$$54 = x$$

So the weight of the fifth dog is 54 pounds, choice (D).

Practice Problems: Averages

REGULAR MATH

1. The average (arithmetic mean) of six numbers is 16. If five of the numbers are 15, 37, 16, 9, and 23, what is the sixth number?

    (A) −20
    (B) −4
    (C) 0
    (D) 6
    (E) 16

    16+6 = 15+37+16+9+23+x
    96 = 100 + x
    x = −4

2. Bart needs to buy five gifts with $80. If two of the gifts cost a total of $35, what is the average (arithmetic mean) amount Bart can spend on each of the remaining three gifts?

    (A) $45
    (B) $17
    (C) $16
    (D) $15
    (E) $10

3. The average (arithmetic mean) of five numbers is 8. If the average of two of these numbers is −6, what is the sum of the other three numbers?

    (A) 28
    (B) 34
    (C) 46
    (D) 52
    (E) 60

    8×5 = 2×−6 + 3x
    40 = −12 + 3x
    3x = 52

    Ⓐ Ⓑ Ⓒ Ⓓ Ⓔ

Answers to Averages Problems

1. (B) Average × Number of Terms = Sum of Terms

    $$16 \times 6 = 15 + 37 + 16 + 9 + 23 + x$$

    $$96 = 100 + x$$

    $$-4 = x$$

2. (D) Bart has $80 and spent $35 on two gifts; therefore he has $45 left to spend on the remaining three. So,

    $$x = \frac{\$45}{3}$$

    $$x = \$15$$

3. (D) Average × Number of Terms = Sum of Terms

    The sum of all five numbers is

    $$8 \times 5 = 40$$

    The sum of two of these numbers is

    $$(-6) \times 2 = -12$$

    So, the difference of these two sums, $40 - (-12) = 52$, is the sum of the other numbers.

RATIOS

Train Your Brain

Use common sense to check your math on this example to the right. Most of the chips are nondefective, so the ratio must be greater than 1. If you reversed the terms and thought (C) was the answer, that would tell you that you did something wrong.

EXAMPLE

Out of every 50 chips produced in a certain factory, 20 are defective. What is the ratio of nondefective chips produced to defective chips produced?

(A) 2:5

(B) 3:5

(C) 2:3

(D) 3:2

(E) 5:2

HINT: *Identify the parts and the whole in the problem.*

Find the parts and the whole in the problem. In this case the total number of chips is the whole, and the number of nondefective chips and the number of defective chips are the parts that make up this whole.

You're given a part-to-whole ratio—the ratio of defective chips to all chips, and asked to find a part-to-part ratio—the ratio of nondefective chips to defective chips.

If 20 chips out of every 50 are defective, the remaining 30 chips must be non-defective. So the part-to-part ratio of nondefective to defective chips is 30/20, or 3/2, which is equivalent to 3:2—answer choice (D).

If you hadn't identified the part and the whole first, it would be easy to get confused and compare a part to the whole, like the ratios in answer choices (A) and (B).

This approach also works for ratio questions that ask you to find actual quantities. For example:

> Out of every five chips produced in a certain factory, two are defective. If 2,200 chips were produced, how many were defective?

Here you need to find a quantity—the number of defective chips.

HINT: *If you're looking for the actual quantities in a ratio, set up and solve a proportion.*

You're given a part-to-whole ratio (the ratio of defective chips to all chips), and the total number of chips produced. You can find the answer by setting up and solving a proportion.

$$\frac{\text{Number of defective chips}}{\text{Total number of chips}} = \frac{2}{5} = \frac{x}{2,200}$$

$$x = \text{Number of defective chips}$$

$$5x = 4,400$$

$$x = 880$$

HINT: *Remember that ratios compare only relative size—they don't tell you the actual quantities involved.*

Kaplan Rules

When you look at a ratio, make sure you know if you're dealing with *parts* to *parts* or *parts* to *whole*.

You also need to see if the parts that you're given add up to the whole. For example, the number of male and female students in a classroom must add up to the whole. The number of students with blond hair and the number of students with brown hair are parts, but do not necessarily add up to the whole.

Practice Problems: Ratios

REGULAR MATH

1. The ratio of right-handed pitchers to left-handed pitchers in a certain baseball league is 11:7. What fractional part of the pitchers in the league are left-handed?

    (A) $\dfrac{6}{7}$

    (B) $\dfrac{6}{11}$

    (C) $\dfrac{7}{11}$

    (D) $\dfrac{7}{18}$

    (E) $\dfrac{11}{18}$

2. In a group of 24 people who are either homeowners or renters, the ratio of homeowners to renters is 5:3. How many homeowners are in the group?

    (A) 15
    (B) 14
    (C) 12
    (D) 9
    (E) 8

3. Magazine *A* has a total of 28 pages, 16 of which are advertisements and 12 of which are articles. Magazine *B* has a total of 35 pages, all of them either advertisements or articles. If the ratio of the number of pages of advertisements to the number of pages of articles is the same for both magazines, then Magazine *B* has how many more pages of advertisements than Magazine *A*?

    (A) 2
    (B) 3
    (C) 4
    (D) 5
    (E) 6

Answers to Ratios Problems

1. (D) The parts are the number of right-handed (11) and the number of left-handed pitchers (7). The whole is the total number of pitchers (right-handed + left-handed), which is 11 + 7, or 18. So:

$$\frac{\text{part}}{\text{whole}} = \frac{\text{left-handed}}{\text{total}} = \frac{7}{11 + 7} = \frac{7}{18}$$

2. (A) The parts are the number of homeowners (5) and the number of renters (3). The whole is the total (homeowners + renters). So:

$$\frac{\text{part}}{\text{whole}} = \frac{\text{homeowners}}{\text{homeowners} + \text{renters}} = \frac{5}{5 + 3} = \frac{5}{8}$$

Since we are trying to find an actual quantity, set up a proportion:

$$\frac{\text{Homeowners}}{\text{Total people}} = \frac{5}{8} = \frac{x}{24}$$

$$8x = 120$$

$$x = 15$$

Time Trouble

Use logic to narrow your choices. Most are homeowners, so the answer must be more than half of 24, or 12. Either (A) or (B) is the right answer.

3. (C) The $\frac{\text{part}}{\text{whole}}$ ratio of advertisements (16) to total pages (28) in Magazine A is $\frac{16}{28}$, or $\frac{4}{7}$. Magazine B has the same ratio, so if there are 35 pages in Magazine B, $\frac{4}{7} \times 35$—or 20 pages—are advertisements. Therefore, there are four more pages of advertisements in Magazine B than in Magazine A.

RATES

EXAMPLE

If eight oranges cost a dollars, b oranges would cost how many dollars?

(A) $8ab$

(B) $\dfrac{8a}{b}$

(C) $\dfrac{8}{ab}$

(D) $\dfrac{a}{8b}$

(E) $\dfrac{ab}{8}$

A rate is a ratio that compares quantities that are measured in different units. In the problem above the units are oranges and dollars.

What makes the rate problem above difficult is the presence of variables. It's hard to get a clear picture of the relationship between the units.

HINT: *Pick numbers for the variables to make the relationship between the units clearer.*

Pick numbers for a and b that are easy to work with in the problem. Let $a = 16$. Then eight oranges cost $16.00. So the cost per orange at this rate is $\dfrac{16 \text{ dollars}}{8 \text{ oranges}}$ = $2 per orange. Let $b = 5$. So the cost of five oranges at this rate is five oranges $\times$ $2.00 per orange = $10.00.

Now plug in $a = 16$ and $b = 5$ into the answer choices to see which one gives you a value of 10.

Choice (A): $8 \times 16 \times 5 = 640$. Eliminate.

Choice (B): $\dfrac{8 \times 16}{5} = \dfrac{128}{5}$. Eliminate.

Choice (C): $\dfrac{8}{16 \times 5} = \dfrac{1}{10}$. Eliminate.

Choice (D): $\dfrac{16}{8 \times 5} = \dfrac{2}{5}$. Eliminate.

Choice (E): $\dfrac{16 \times 5}{8} = 10$.

Since (E) is the only one that gives the correct value, it is correct.

Practice Problems: Rates

REGULAR MATH

1. If David paints at the rate of h houses per day, how many houses does he paint in d days, in terms of h and d ?

   (A) $\dfrac{h}{d}$

   (B) hd

   (C) $h + \dfrac{d}{2}$

   (D) $h - d$

   (E) $\dfrac{d}{h}$

2. Bill has to type a paper that is p pages long, with each page containing w words. If Bill types an average of x words per minute, how many hours will it take him to finish the paper?

   (A) $60\ wpx$

   (B) $\dfrac{wx}{60p}$

   (C) $\dfrac{60wp}{x}$

   (D) $\dfrac{wpx}{60}$

   (E) $\dfrac{wp}{60x}$

3. If Seymour drove 120 miles in x hours at constant speed, how many miles did he travel in the first 20 minutes of his trip?

   (A) $60x$

   (B) $3x$

   (C) $\dfrac{120}{x}$

   (D) $\dfrac{40}{x}$

   (E) $\dfrac{6}{x}$

Answers to Rates Problems

1. (B) Pick numbers for h and d. Let $h = 2$ and $d = 3$; that is, suppose he paints two houses per day and he paints for three days, so in three days he can paint six houses. You multiply the rate (h) by the number of days (d). The only answer choice that equals 6 when $h = 2$ and $d = 3$ is choice (B).

2. (E) Pick numbers for p, w, and x that work well in the problem. Let $p = 3$ and let $w = 100$. So there are three pages with 100 words per page, or 300 words total. Say he types five words a minute, so $x = 5$. So he types 5×60, or 300 words an hour. Therefore, it takes him one hour to type the paper. The only answer choice that equals 1 when $p = 3$, $w = 100$, and $x = 5$ is choice (E).

3. (D) Let $x = 4$. That means that he drove 120 miles in four hours, so his speed was $\dfrac{120 \text{ miles}}{4 \text{ hours}}$, or 30 miles per hour. Since 20 minutes $= \dfrac{1}{3}$ of an hour, the distance he traveled in the first 20 minutes is $\dfrac{1}{3}$ hours $\times$ 30 miles per hour $= 10$ miles. The only answer choice that equals 10 when $x = 4$ is choice (D).

PERCENTS

Memorize These

When you need to, you can figure out a percent equivalent on your calculator by dividing the numerator by the denominator. You'll save time by knowing some common percent equivalents.

$\dfrac{1}{5} = 20\%$

$\dfrac{1}{4} = 25\%$

$\dfrac{1}{3} = 33\dfrac{1}{3}\%$

$\dfrac{1}{2} = 50\%$

$\dfrac{2}{3} = 66\dfrac{2}{3}\%$

$\dfrac{3}{4} = 75\%$

EXAMPLE

Last year Julie's annual salary was $20,000. This year's raise brings her to an annual salary of $25,000. If she gets the same percent raise every year, what will her salary be next year?

(A) $27,500

(B) $30,000

(C) $31,250

(D) $32,500

(E) $35,000

In percent problems, you're usually given two pieces of information and asked to find the third. When you see a percent problem, remember:

- If you are solving for a percent:

$$\text{Percent} = \frac{\text{Part}}{\text{Whole}}$$

- If you need to solve for a part:

$$\text{Percent} \times \text{Whole} = \text{Part}$$

This problem asks for Julie's projected salary for next year—that is, her current salary plus her next raise.

You know last year's salary ($20,000) and you know this year's salary ($25,000), so you can find the difference between the two salaries:

$$\$25,000 - \$20,000 = \$5,000 = \text{her raise}$$

Now find the percent of her raise, by using the formula

$$\text{Percent} = \frac{\text{Part}}{\text{Whole}}$$

Since Julie's raise was calculated on last year's salary, divide by $20,000.

HINT: *Be sure you know which Whole to plug in. Here you're looking for a percent of $20,000, not $25,000.*

$$\text{Percent raise} = \frac{\$5,000}{\$20,000} = \frac{1}{4} = 25\%$$

You know she will get the same percent raise next year, so solve for the part. Use the formula Percent × Whole = Part. Her raise next year will be

$$25\% \times \$25,000 = \frac{1}{4} \times 25,000 = \$6,250$$

Add that sum to this year's salary and you have her projected salary: $25,000 + $6,250 = $31,250, or answer choice (C).

Make sure that you change the percent to either a fraction or a decimal before beginning calculations.

> **Mirror Image**
>
> x percent of y = y percent of x
>
> 20% of 50 = 50% of 20
>
> $\frac{1}{5} \times 50 = \frac{1}{2} \times 20$
>
> $10 = 10$

Practice Problems: Percents

QC

	Column A	Column B	
1.	5% of 3% of 45	6.75	Ⓐ Ⓑ Ⓒ Ⓓ Ⓔ

....

GRID-IN

2. Eighty-five percent of the members of a student organization registered to attend a certain field trip. If 16 of the members who registered were unable to attend, resulting in only 65 percent of the members making the trip, how many members are in the organization?

$16 = 20\%$
$\times 5$
$\overline{80}$

....

REGULAR MATH

3. If a sweater sells for $48 after a 25 percent markdown, what was its original price?

(A) $56
(B) $60
(C) $64
(D) $68
(E) $72

$\dfrac{48}{x} = \dfrac{75}{100}$

Ⓐ Ⓑ Ⓒ Ⓓ Ⓔ

Answers to Percents Problems

1.   (B) Percent $\times$ Whole = Part. Five percent of (3 percent of 45) = .05 $\times$ (.03 $\times$ 45) = .05 $\times$ 1.35 = .0675, which is less than 6.75 in Column B.

2.   (80) You need to solve for the Whole, so identify the Part and the Percent. If 85 percent planned to attend and only 65 percent did, 20 percent failed to attend, and you know that 16 students failed to attend.

Percent $\times$ Whole = Part

$$\frac{20}{100} \times \text{Whole} = 16$$

$$\text{Whole} = 16 \times \frac{100}{20}$$

$$\text{Whole} = 80$$

3.   (C) We want to solve for the original price, the Whole. The percent markdown is 25 percent, so $48 is 75 percent of the whole.

Percent $\times$ Whole = Part

75 percent $\times$ Original Price = $48

$$\text{Original Price} = \frac{\$48}{0.75} = \$64$$

COMBINATIONS

| EXAMPLE |

If Alice, Betty, and Carlos sit in three adjacent empty seats in a movie house, how many different seating arrangements are possible?

(A) 3

(B) 4

(C) 5

(D) 6

(E) 8

Combination problems ask you to find the different possibilities that can occur in a given situation.

HINT: *Simply count the number of possibilities by listing them in a quick but systematic way.*

To solve this problem, let the first letter of each name stand for that person. First, find all the combinations with Alice in the first seat:

ABC

ACB

Using the same system, try Betty in the first seat, and then Carlos:

BAC

BCA

CAB

CBA

At this point we've exhausted every possibility. So there are six possible arrangements, and that's answer choice (D).

Some problems set up conditions that limit the possibilities somewhat. Some may ask for the number of distinct possibilities, meaning that if the same combination shows up twice in different forms, you should count it only once. Consider the following problem.

EXAMPLE

Set I: {2, 3, 4, 5}

Set II: {1, 2, 3}

If x is a number generated by multiplying a number from Set I by a number from Set II, how many possible values of x are greater than 5?

(A) 3

(B) 4

(C) 5

(D) 6

(E) 7

Warning

Don't use complex formulas to solve combinations problems. SAT combinations questions are simple enough that you can write down the possibilities and count them.

Again, list the possibilities in a systematic way, pairing off each number in the first set with each number in the second set, so every combination is included:

$$2 \times 1 = 2 \qquad 4 \times 1 = 4$$
$$2 \times 2 = 4 \qquad 4 \times 2 = 8$$
$$2 \times 3 = 6 \qquad 4 \times 3 = 12$$
$$3 \times 1 = 3 \qquad 5 \times 1 = 5$$
$$3 \times 2 = 6 \qquad 5 \times 2 = 10$$
$$3 \times 3 = 9 \qquad 5 \times 3 = 15$$

How many of these values are greater than 5? Going down the list: 6, 6, 9, 8, 12, 10, and 15. Although there are seven answers for x that are greater than 5, two of them are the same. So there are six different values of x greater than 5, not seven. The answer is (D).

HINT: *Always write down the possibilities as you organize them, so you can count them accurately, and so you don't count the same combination twice.*

Practice Problems: Combinations

1. A three-digit code is made up of three different digits from the set {2,4,6,8}. If 2 is always the first digit in the code, how many three-digit codes can be formed?

(A) 16
(B) 12
(C) 10
(D) 8
(E) 6

Ⓐ Ⓑ Ⓒ Ⓓ Ⓔ

....

Column A   Column B

Five people attend a meeting. Each person shakes hands once with every other person at the meeting.

2. The total number   15
    of handshakes that
    take place

Ⓐ Ⓑ Ⓒ Ⓓ Ⓔ

....

3. Three people stop for lunch at a hot dog stand. If each person orders one item and there are three items to choose from, how many different combinations of food could be purchased? (Assume that order doesn't matter; e.g., a hot dog and two sodas are considered the same as two sodas and a hot dog.)

(A) 6
(B) 9
(C) 10
(D) 18
(E) 27

Ⓐ Ⓑ Ⓒ Ⓓ Ⓔ

Answers to Combinations Problems

1. (E) Every code starts with 2, so the last two digits determine the number of possibilities. The last two digits could be: 46, 48, 64, 68, 84, and 86. That makes six combinations that fit the conditions.

2. (B) Be careful not to count each handshake twice. Call the five people A, B, C, D, and E. We can pair them off like this:

   A with B, C, D, and E (four handshakes)

   B with C, D, and E (three more—note that we leave out A, since the handshake between A and B is already counted)

   C with D and E (two more)

   D with E (one more)

   The total is 4 + 3 + 2 + 1, or 10 handshakes.

3. (C) To find the number, let's call the three items they can purchase A, B, and C. The possibilities:

   All three order the same thing: AAA, BBB, CCC

   Two order the same thing: AAB, AAC, BBA, BBC, CCA, CCB

   All three order something different: ABC

   So there are ten different ways the three items could be ordered.

SIMULTANEOUS EQUATIONS

Kaplan Rules

When subtracting one equation from another, be sure to distribute the minus sign to each term. In the example to the left,

$$-p - 2q = -14$$

EXAMPLE

If $p + 2q = 14$ and $3p + q = 12$, then $p =$

(A) -2

(B) -1

(C) 1

(D) 2

(E) 3

In order to get a numerical value for each variable, you need as many different equations as there are variables to solve for. So, if you have two variables, you need two independent equations.

You could tackle this problem by solving for one variable in terms of the other, and then plugging this expression into the other equation. But the simultaneous equations that appear on the SAT can usually be handled in an easier way.

HINT: *Combine the equations—by adding or subtracting them—to cancel out all but one of the variables.*

You can't eliminate p or q by adding or subtracting the equations in their present form. But if you multiply the second equation by 2:

$$2(3p + q) = 2(12)$$
$$6p + 2q = 24$$

Now when you subtract the first equation from the second, the qs will cancel out so you can solve for p:

$$6p + 2q = 24$$
$$\underline{-[p + 2q = 14]}$$
$$5p + 0 = 10$$

If $5p = 10$, $p = 2$.

Practice Problems: Simultaneous Equations

REGULAR MATH

1. If $x + y = 8$ and $y - x = -2$, then $y =$

   (A) −2
   (B) 3
   (C) 5
   (D) 8
   (E) 10

   $x + y = 8$
   $-x + y = -2$
   _____
   $2y = 6$
   $y = 3$

   Ⓐ ⬤ Ⓒ Ⓓ Ⓔ

GRID-IN

2. If $4a + 3b = 19$ and $a + 2b = 6$, then $a + b =$

   $(a + 2b = 6) 4$
   $-(4a + 8b = 24)$
   _____
   $-5b = -5$
   $b = 1$

   $a + 2 = 6$
   $a = 4$

REGULAR MATH

3. If $m - n = 5$ and $2m + 3n = 15$, then $m + n =$

   (A) 1
   (B) 6
   (C) 7
   (D) 10
   (E) 15

   $2(m - n = 5)$
   $2m + 3n = 15$
   $-(2m - 2n = 10)$
   _____
   $5n = 5$
   $n = 1$
   $m = 6$

   Ⓐ Ⓑ ⬤ Ⓓ Ⓔ

Answers to Simultaneous Equations Problems

1. (B) When you add the two equations, the xs cancel out and you find that $2y = 6$, so $y = 3$.

2. (5) Adding the two equations, you find that $5a + 5b = 25$. Dividing by 5 shows that $a + b = 5$.

3. (C) Multiply the first equation by 2, then subtract the first equation from the second to eliminate the ms and find that $5n = 5$, or $n = 1$:

$$2m + 3n = 15$$
$$\underline{-2m + 2n = -10}$$
$$5n = 5$$
$$n = 1$$

Plugging this value for n into the first equation shows that $m = 6$:

$$m - n = 5$$
$$m - 1 = 5$$
$$m = 6$$

So $m + n = 7$:

$$m + n = 6 + 1 = 7$$

Choice (C) is correct.

SYMBOLISM

You should be quite familiar with the arithmetic symbols $+$, $-$, $\times$, $\div$, and %. Finding the value of $10 + 2$, $18 - 4$, 4×9, or $96 \div 16$ is easy.

However, on the SAT, you may come across bizarre symbols. You may even be asked to find the value of $10 \bigstar 2$, $5 \maltese 7$, $10 \maltese 6$, or $65 \heartsuit 2$.

The SAT test makers put strange symbols in questions to confuse or unnerve you. Don't let them. The question stem always tells you what the strange symbol means. Although this type of question may look difficult, it is really an exercise in plugging in. Look at the following example:

EXAMPLE

If $a \bigstar b = \sqrt{a + b}$ for all non-negative numbers, what is the value of $10 \bigstar 6$?

(A) 0

(B) 2

(C) 4

(D) 8

(E) 16

To solve, just plug in 10 for a and 6 for b into the expression $\sqrt{a + b}$. That equals $\sqrt{10 + 6}$ or $\sqrt{16}$ or 4, choice (C).

How about a more involved symbolism question?

EXAMPLE

If a ▲ means to multiply by 3 and a ✳ means to divide by –2, what is the value of $((8 ✳)▲)✳$?

(A) –6

(B) 0

(C) 2

(D) 3

(E) 6

HINT: *When a symbolism problem includes parentheses, do the operations inside the parentheses first.*

First find 8✳. This means to divide 8 by –2, which is –4. Working out to the next set of parentheses, we have (–4)▲, which means to multiply –4 by 3, which is –12. Lastly, we find (–12) ✳, which means to divide –12 by –2, which is 6, choice (E).

HINT: *When two or three questions include the same symbol, expect the last question to be the most difficult, and be extra careful.*

Practice Problems: Symbolism

QC

Column A	Column B

If $x \neq 0$, let ♠ x be defined by ♠ $x = x - \dfrac{1}{x}$

1.   –3   ♠ –3 $-3 - \frac{1}{(-3)}$ Ⓐ Ⓑ Ⓒ Ⓓ Ⓔ

REGULAR MATH

2. If $r \heartsuit s = r (r - s)$ for all integers r and s, then $4 \heartsuit (3 \heartsuit 5)$ equals

(A) –8

(B) –2 $3(3-5)$

(C) 2 $4[4-(-6)]$

(D) 20   40

(E) 40   Ⓐ Ⓑ Ⓒ Ⓓ Ⓔ

Questions 3 and 4 refer to the following definition:

$$c \star d = \frac{(c - d)}{c}, \text{ where } c \neq 0.$$

3. $12 \star 3 =$

(A) –3

(B) $\dfrac{1}{4}$

(C) $\dfrac{2}{3}$

(D) $\dfrac{3}{4}$

(E) 3   Ⓐ Ⓑ Ⓒ Ⓓ Ⓔ

4. If $9 \bigstar 4 = 15 \bigstar k$, then $k =$

(A) 3

(B) 6

(C) $\dfrac{20}{3}$

(D) $\dfrac{25}{3}$

(E) 9

Ⓐ Ⓑ ⬤ Ⓓ Ⓔ

Answers to Symbolism Problems

1. (B) Plug in -3 for x: $\spadesuit x = -3 - \dfrac{1}{-3} = -3 + \dfrac{1}{3} = -2\dfrac{2}{3}$, which is greater than -3 in Column A.

2. (E) Start in the parentheses and work out: $(3 \heartsuit 5) = 3(3 - 5) = 3(-2) = -6; 4 \heartsuit (-6) = 4[4 - (-6)] = 4(10) = 40.$

3. (D) Plug in 12 for c and 3 for d: $\dfrac{12 - 3}{12} = \dfrac{9}{12} = \dfrac{3}{4}.$

4. (C) Plug in on both sides of the equation:

$$\frac{9 - 4}{9} = \frac{15 - k}{15}$$

$$\frac{5}{9} = \frac{15 - k}{15}$$

Cross-multiply and solve for k:

$$75 = 135 - 9k$$

$$-60 = -9k$$

$$\frac{-60}{-9} = k$$

$$\frac{20}{3} = k$$

SPECIAL TRIANGLES

The Specials

The test makers often put triangles on the SAT to test your knowledge of special triangles.

Note: Figure not drawn to scale.

EXAMPLE

In the triangle above, what is the length of side *BC*?

(A) 4

(B) 5

(C) 4 $\sqrt{2}$

(D) 6

(E) 5 $\sqrt{2}$

HINT: *Look for the special triangles in geometry problems.*

Special triangles contain a lot of information. For instance, if you know the length of one side of a 30-60-90 triangle, you can easily work out the lengths of the others. Special triangles allow you to transfer one piece of information around the whole figure.

The following are the special triangles you should look for on the SAT.

Speed Tip

Popular right triangles:

• 3-4-5

• 5-12-13

Or multiples of these, such as:

• 6-8-10

• 10-24-26

Equilateral Triangles

All interior angles are 60° and all sides are of the same length.

Isosceles Triangles

Two sides are of the same length and the angles facing these sides are equal.

Right Triangles

Contain a 90° angle. The sides are related by the Pythagorean theorem. $a^2 + b^2 = c^2$ where a and b are the legs and c is the hypotenuse.

The "Special" Right Triangles

Many triangle problems contain "special" right triangles, whose side lengths always come in predictable ratios. If you recognize them, you won't have to use the Pythagorean theorem to find the value of a missing side length.

The 3-4-5 Right Triangle

(Be on the lookout for multiples of 3-4-5 as well.)

The Isosceles Right Triangle

(Note the side ratio—1:1:$\sqrt{2}$.)

The 30-60-90 Right Triangle

(Note the side ratio—1:$\sqrt{3}$:2, and which side is opposite which angle.)

Getting back to our example, you can drop a vertical line from *B* to line *AC*. This divides the triangle into two right triangles.

That means you know two of the angles in the triangle on the left: 90° and 45°. So this is an isosceles right triangle, with sides in the ratio of 1:1:$\sqrt{2}$. The hypotenuse here is 4$\sqrt{2}$, so both legs have length 4. Filling this in, you have:

Now you can see that the legs of the smaller triangle on the right must be 4 and 3, making this a 3-4-5 right triangle, and the length of hypotenuse *BC* is 5.

Practice Problems: Special Triangles

REGULAR MATH

Note: Figure not drawn to scale.

1. In triangle *ABC* above, if *AB* = 4, then *AC* =

   (A) 10
   (B) 9
   (C) 8
   (D) 7
   (E) 6

   Ⓐ Ⓑ Ⓒ Ⓓ Ⓔ

....

QC

Column A	Column B

In the coordinate plane, point *R* has coordinates (0, 0) and point *S* has coordinates (9, 12).

2. The distance from   16
        R to *S*

   Ⓐ Ⓑ Ⓒ Ⓓ Ⓔ

....

REGULAR MATH

3. If the perimeter of triangle *ABC* above is 16, what is its area?

   (A) 8
   (B) 9
   (C) 10
   (D) 12
   (E) 15

   Ⓐ Ⓑ Ⓒ Ⓓ Ⓔ

Answers to Special Triangles Problems

1. (C) Angle *BCA* is supplementary to the angle marked 150°, so angle *BCA* = 180° − 150° = 30°. Since the sum of interior angles of a triangle is 180°, angle *A* + angle *B* + angle *BCA* = 180°, so angle *B* = 180° − 60° − 30° = 90°. So triangle *ABC* is a 30-60-90 right triangle, and its sides are in the ratio 1: $\sqrt{3}$: 2. The side opposite the 30°, *AB*, which we know has length 4, must be half the length of the hypotenuse, *AC*. Therefore *AC* = 8, and that's answer choice (C).

2. (B) Draw a diagram. Since *RS* isn't parallel to either axis, the way to compute its length is to create a right triangle with legs that are parallel to the axes, so their lengths are easy to find. If the triangle formed is not a special triangle, we can then use the Pythagorean theorem to find the length of *RS*.

Since *S* has a *y*-coordinate of 12, it's 12 units above the *x*-axis, so the length of *ST* must be 12. And since *T* is the same number of units to the right of the *y*-axis as *S*, given by the *x*-coordinate of 9, the distance from the origin to *T* must be 9. So we have a right triangle with legs of 9 and 12. You should recognize this as a multiple of the 3-4-5 triangle. 9 = 3 × 3; 12 = 3 × 4; so the hypotenuse *RS* must be 3 × 5, or 15. That's the value of Column A, so Column B is greater.

3. (D) To find the area you need to know the base and height. If the perimeter is 16, then *AB* + *BC* + *AC* = 16; that is, *AB* = 16 − 5 − 6 = 5. Since *AB* = *BC*, this is an isosceles triangle. If you drop a line from vertex *B* to *AC*, it will divide the base in half. This divides up the triangle into two smaller right triangles:

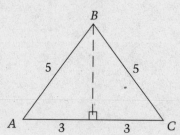

These right triangles each have one leg of 3 and a hypotenuse of 5; therefore they are 3-4-5 right triangles. So the missing leg (which is also the height of triangle *ABC*) must have length 4. We now know that the base of *ABC* is 6 and the height is 4, so the area is $\frac{1}{2}$ × 6 × 4, or 12, answer choice (D).

MULTIPLE AND ODDBALL FIGURES

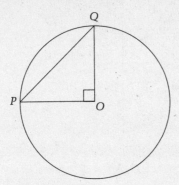

EXAMPLE

In the figure above, if the area of the circle with center O is 9π, what is the area of triangle POQ ?

(A) 4.5

(B) 6

(C) 9

(D) 3.5π

(E) 4.5π

Breaking Up Is Easy

When you see a shape that isn't a triangle, rectangle, or circle, try breaking it into familiar figures.

In a problem that combines figures, you have to look for the relationship between the figures.

HINT: *Look for pieces the figures have in common.*

For instance, if two figures share a side, information about that side will probably be the key.

In this case the figures don't share a side, but the triangle's legs are important features of the circle—they are radii. You can see that $PO = OQ =$ the radius of circle O.

The area of the circle is 9π. The area of a circle is πr^2, where $r =$ the radius. So $9\pi = \pi r^2$, $9 = r^2$, and the radius $= 3$. The area of a triangle is $\frac{1}{2}$ base times height. Therefore, the area of

ΔPOQ is $\frac{1}{2}$ (leg$_1$ $\times$ leg$_2$) $= \frac{1}{2}$ (3 $\times$ 3) $= \frac{9}{2} = 4.5$, answer choice (A).

But what if, instead of a number of familiar shapes, you are given something like this?

EXAMPLE

Kaplan Rules

Multiple figures are almost always made up of either several familiar shapes put together, or one familiar shape with a recognizable piece shaded or cut out of it.

What is the perimeter of quadrilateral *WXYZ* ?

(A) 680

(B) 760

(C) 840

(D) 920

(E) 1,000

Try breaking the unfamiliar shape into familiar ones. Once this is done, you can use the same techniques that you would for multiple figures. Perimeter is the sum of the lengths of the sides of a figure, so you need to find the length of *WZ*. Drawing a perpendicular line from point *X* to side *YZ* will divide the figure into a right triangle and a rectangle. Call the point of intersection *A*.

Opposite sides of a rectangle have equal length, so $WZ = XA$ and $WX = ZA$. *WX* is labeled as 180, so $ZA = 180$. Since *YZ* measures 300, *AY* is $300 - 180 = 120$. In right triangle *XYA*, hypotenuse $XY = 200$ and leg $AY = 120$; you should recognize this as a multiple of a 3-4-5 right triangle. The hypotenuse is 5×40, one leg is 3×40, so *XA* must be 4×40 or 160. (If you didn't recognize this special right triangle you could have used the Pythagorean theorem to find the length of *XA*.) Since $WZ = XA = 160$, the perimeter of the figure is $180 + 200 + 300 + 160 = 840$, answer choice (C).

Practice Problems: Multiple and Oddball Figures

REGULAR MATH

1. What is the value of x in the figure above?

   (A) 4
   (B) $3\sqrt{3}$
   (C) $3\sqrt{5}$
   (D) $5\sqrt{3}$
   (E) 9

Ⓐ Ⓑ Ⓒ Ⓓ Ⓔ

2. In the figure above, square *PQRS* is inscribed in a circle. If the area of square *PQRS* is 4, what is the radius of the circle?

   (A) 1
   (B) $\sqrt{2}$
   (C) 2
   (D) $2\sqrt{2}$
   (E) $4\sqrt{2}$

Ⓐ Ⓑ Ⓒ Ⓓ Ⓔ

Note: Figure not drawn to scale.

3. In the figure above, the quarter circle with center *D* has a radius of 4 and rectangle *ABCD* has a perimeter of 20. What is the perimeter of the shaded region?

(A) $20 - 8\pi$

(B) $10 + 2\pi$

(C) $12 + 2\pi$

(D) $12 + 4\pi$

(E) $4 + 8\pi$

Ⓐ Ⓑ Ⓒ Ⓓ Ⓔ

Answers to Multiple and Oddball Figures Problems

1. (D) Draw a straight line from point *H* to point *F*, to divide the figure into two right triangles.

ΔEFH is a 3-4-5 right triangle with a hypotenuse of length 10. Use the Pythagorean theorem in ΔFGH to find *x*:

$$x^2 + 5^2 = 10^2$$

$$x^2 + 5^2 = 100$$

$$x^2 = 75$$

$$x = \sqrt{75}$$

$$x = \sqrt{25}\sqrt{3}$$

$$x = 5\sqrt{3}$$

2. (B) Draw in diagonal *QS* and you will notice that it is also a diameter of the circle.

Since the area of the square is 4 its sides must each be 2. Think of the diagonal as dividing the square into two isosceles right triangles. Therefore, the diagonal = $2\sqrt{2}$ = the diameter; the radius is half this amount, or $\sqrt{2}$.

3. (C) The perimeter of the shaded region is *BC* + *AB* + *AE* + arc *EC*. The quarter circle has its center at *D*, and point *C* lies on the circle, so side *DC* is a radius of the circle and equals 4.

Opposite sides of a rectangle are equal, so *AB* is also 4. The perimeter of the rectangle is 20, and since the two short sides account for 8, the two longer sides must account for 12, making *BC* and *AD* each 6. To find *AE*, subtract the length of *ED*, another radius of length 4, from the length of *AD*, which is 6; *AE* = 2.

Since arc *EC* is a quarter circle, the length of the arc *EC* is $\frac{1}{4}$ of the circumference of a whole circle with radius 4: $\frac{1}{4} \times 2\pi r = \frac{1}{4} \times 8\pi = 2\pi$.

So the perimeter of the shaded region is $6 + 4 + 2 + 2\pi = 12 + 2\pi$.

Checklist

Once you've mastered a concept, check it off.

Classic Problem-Solving Techniques:

❑ Remainders

❑ Averages

❑ Ratios

❑ Rates

❑ Percents

❑ Combinations

❑ Simultaneous equations

❑ Symbolism

❑ Special triangles

❑ Multiple and oddball figures

14

Top Ten SAT Math Traps

HIGHLIGHTS

- Study the most common SAT Math traps and how to avoid them

- Train yourself to recognize wrong and tricky answer choices

- Pick up tips and hints on how to solve problems

- Complete the Math Traps Practice Sets

It's time for us to let you in on a little secret that will allow you to breeze through the entire SAT, get into any college you want, succeed in life, and find eternal happiness.

If you believed a word of the preceding paragraph, you need to pay special attention to this chapter. This chapter presents ten common SAT traps. Traps lure you into one answer, usually one that's easy to get to. But they conceal the correct answer, which requires some thought. If you're not wary of traps on the SAT, they may trip you up. Learn to recognize common traps and you'll gain more points.

HINT: *If you see what appears to be a basic problem late in a question set, there is probably a trap.*

SAT Emergency

If you have only a week or two to prep for the SAT, here's the best way to spend your time:

- Skim the chapter, paying special attention to the "Top Ten Trap" sidebars.

- Do the first practice set on p. 164. If you miss an answer, identify the trap that caught you and study that section.

- Do the second practice set on p. 178. Identify any trap that caught you and study that section. If you get all the answers right, you're strong at avoiding traps.

Kaplan's Favorite Trap

When the hands of your watch show 12:30, how many degrees separate the hour hand from the minute hand?

The obvious answer is 180 degrees. That's a trap. (At 12:30 the hour hand doesn't point directly at the 12; it's halfway between the 12 and the 1.) The test makers hoped that you would jump to the obvious answer, without taking the time to think it through.

Over the years, the SAT has had plenty of problems like this one. Traps catch unwary students who forget to think through the problem before they answer it. How do you prevent yourself from falling for other SAT Math traps? Read this chapter.

WATCH OUT FOR TRAPS

The following ten questions have one thing in common—they all have traps. Take 12 minutes to try to work through all of them. Then check your answers on p. 168.

1. Jackie purchased a new car in 1990. Three years later she sold it to a dealer for 40 percent less than she paid for it in 1990. The dealer then added 20 percent onto the price he paid and resold it to another customer. The price the final customer paid for the car was what percent of the original price Jackie paid in 1990?

    (A) 40 percent
    (B) 60 percent
    (C) 72 percent
    (D) 80 percent
    (E) 88 percent

2. In a class of 27 students, the average (arithmetic mean) score of the boys on the final exam was 83. If the average score of the 15 girls in the class was 92, what was the average of the whole class?

    (A) 86.2   12 : 15 = 4 : 5
    (B) 87.0   83 : 92
    (C) 87.5
    (D) 88.0
    (E) 88.2

3. Mike's coin collection consists of quarters, dimes, and nickels. If the ratio of the number of quarters to the number of dimes is 5:2, and the ratio of the number of dimes to the number of nickels is 3:4, what is the ratio of the number of quarters to the number of nickels?

    (A) 5 to 4   Q : D : N
    (B) 7 to 5   5 : 2   3 : 4
    (C) 10 to 6   15 : 6   6 : 8
    (D) 12 to 7
    (E) 15 to 8

    Ⓐ Ⓑ Ⓒ Ⓓ Ⓔ

Column A	Column B

$$p > q > 1$$

4. $p^2 - q^2$ $(p - q)^2$ Ⓐ Ⓑ Ⓒ Ⓓ Ⓔ

A, *B*, and *C* are points on a line such that point *A* is 12 units away from point *B* and point *B* is four units away from point *C*.

5. The distance from   16
    point *A* to point *C*   Ⓐ Ⓑ Ⓒ Ⓓ Ⓔ

6. | The area of a | Twice the area of a |
    | square with a | square with a |
    | perimeter of 14 | perimeter of 7 |

7. If $n \neq 0$, then which of the following must be true?

    I. $n^2 > n$
    II. $2n > n$
    III. $n + 1 > n$

    (A) I only
    (B) II only
    (C) III only
    (D) I and III only
    (E) I, II, and III

8. At a certain restaurant, the hourly wage for a waiter is 20 percent greater than the hourly wage for a dishwasher, and the hourly wage for a dishwasher is half as much as the hourly wage for a cook's assistant. If a cook's assistant earns $8.50 an hour, how much less than a cook's assistant does a waiter earn each hour?

    (A) $2.55
    (B) $3.40
    (C) $4.25
    (D) $5.10
    (E) $5.95

    (handwritten: CA = 8.5, D = 4.25, W = 5.1, 8.5 − 5.1 = 3.4)

9. A car traveled from A to B at an average speed of 40 miles per hour and then immediately traveled back from B to A at an average speed of 60 miles per hour. What was the car's average speed for the round-trip, in miles per hour?

    (A) 45
    (B) 48
    (C) 50
    (D) 52
    (E) 54

10. The tickets for a certain raffle are consecutively numbered. If Louis sold the tickets numbered from 75 to 148 inclusive, how many raffle tickets did he sell?

    (A) 71
    (B) 72
    (C) 73
    (D) 74
    (E) 75

HOW MATH TRAPS WORK AND HOW TO AVOID THEM

How did you do? If you got any wrong answers, unless you calculated incorrectly, chances are you got caught in a trap. The same traps occur again and again on the SAT. Learn how they work and how to avoid them. Once you can deal with traps, you'll do much better on the harder math questions.

To see how they work, let's take another look at the ten sample questions. Each contains one of the Top Ten Math Traps.

Trap 1: Percent Increase/Decrease

> EXAMPLE
>
> Jackie purchased a new car in 1990. Three years later she sold it to a dealer for 40 percent less than she paid for it in 1990. The dealer then added 20 percent onto the price he paid and resold it to another customer. The price the final customer paid for the car was what percent of the original price Jackie paid in 1990?
>
> (A) 40 percent
> (B) 60 percent
> (C) 72 percent
> (D) 80 percent
> (E) 88 percent

The Wrong Answer

The increase/decrease percentage problem usually appears at the end of a section and invariably contains a trap. Most students will figure that taking away 40 percent, and then adding 20 percent gives you an overall loss of 20 percent, and pick choice (D), 80 percent, as the correct answer.

The Trap

When a quantity is increased or decreased by a percent more than once, you cannot simply add and subtract the percents to get the answer.

In this kind of percent problem:

- The first percent change is a percent of the starting amount.

- The second change is a percent of the new amount.

Avoiding the Trap

Percents can be added and subtracted only when they are percents of the same amount.

Finding the Right Answer

We know:

- The 40 percent less that Jackie got for the car is 40 percent of her original price.

- The 20 percent the dealer adds on is 20 percent of what the dealer paid, a much smaller amount.

- Adding on 20 percent of that smaller amount is not the same thing as adding back 20 percent of the original price.

So We Can Solve the Problem

- Use 100 for a starting quantity, whether or not it makes sense in the real situation. The problem asks for the relative amount of change. So you can take any starting number, and compare it with the final result. Because you're dealing with percents, 100 is the easiest number to work with.

HINT: *Pick 100 as the starting quantity and see what happens.*

- If Jackie paid $100.00 for the car, what is 40 percent less?

- In the case of $100.00, each percent equals $1.00, so she sold it for $60.00.

- If the dealer charges 20 percent more than his purchase price, he's raising the price by 20 percent of $60.00, which is $12.00 (not 20 percent of $100.00, which is $20.00).

- Therefore the dealer sold the car again for $60.00 + $12.00, or $72.00.

- Finally, what percent of the starting price ($100.00) is $72.00? It's 72 percent. So the correct answer here is choice (C).

Trap 2: Weighted Averages

Top Ten Trap #2
Don't just average the averages.

EXAMPLE

In a class of 27 students, the average (arithmetic mean) score of the boys on the final exam was 83. If the average score of the 15 girls in the class was 92, what was the average of the whole class?

(A) 86.2

(B) 87.0

(C) 87.5

(D) 88.0

(E) 88.2

The Wrong Answer

If you simply average 83 and 92 to come up with 87.5 as the class average, you fell for the trap.

The Trap

You cannot combine averages of different quantities by taking the average of those averages.

In an average problem, if one value occurs more frequently than others it is "weighted" more. Remember that the average formula calls for the sum of all the terms, divided by the total number of terms.

Avoiding the Trap

Work with the sums, not the averages.

Finding the Right Answer

If 15 of the 27 students are girls, the remaining 12 must be boys. We can't just add 83 to 92 and divide by two. In this class there are more girls than boys, and therefore the girls' test scores are "weighted" more—they contribute more to the class average. So the answer must be either (D) or (E). To find each sum, multiply each average by the number of terms it represents. After you have found the sums of the different terms, find the combined average by plugging the sums into the average formula.

$$\text{Total class average} = \frac{\text{Sum of girls' scores} + \text{Sum of boys' scores}}{\text{Total number of students}}$$

$$= \frac{(\text{\# of girls} \times \text{girls' average score}) + (\text{\# of boys} \times \text{boys' average score})}{\text{Total number of students}}$$

$$= \frac{15(92) + 12(83)}{27} = \frac{1{,}380 + 996}{27} = 88$$

So the class average is 88, answer choice (D).

Stumped?

Use logic. There are more girls than boys, so the average would be closer to the girls' average—92. The only choices that are closer to 92 than 83 are (D) and (E).

Answer Key for Trap Exercise on pp. 164–165

1. (C)
2. (D)
3. (E)
4. (A)
5. (D)
6. (A)
7. (C)
8. (B)
9. (B)
10. (D)

Trap 3: Ratio:Ratio:Ratio

Money, Money, Money

Don't be distracted by money. In the example here, we care only about the *number* of coins, not their value.

EXAMPLE

Mike's coin collection consists of quarters, dimes, and nickels. If the ratio of the number of quarters to the number of dimes is 5:2, and the ratio of the number of dimes to the number of nickels is 3:4, what is the ratio of the number of quarters to the number of nickels?

(A) 5:4

(B) 7:5

(C) 10:6

(D 12:7

(E) 15:8

The Wrong Answer

If you chose 5:4 as the correct answer, you fell for the classic ratio trap.

The Trap

Parts of different ratios don't always refer to the same whole.

In the classic ratio trap, two different ratios each share a common part that is represented by two different numbers. The two ratios do not refer to the same whole, however, so they are not in proportion to each other. To solve this type of problem, restate both ratios so that the numbers representing the common part (in this case "dimes") are the same. Then all the parts will be in proportion and can be compared to each other.

Avoiding the Trap

Make sure parts of ratios refer to the same whole.

Finding the Right Answer

To find the ratio of quarters to nickels, restate both ratios so that the number of dimes is the same in both. We are given two ratios:

Quarters:dimes = 5:2   Dimes:nickels = 3:4

The number corresponding to dimes in the first ratio is 2.
The number corresponding to dimes in the second ratio is 3.
To restate the ratios, find the least common multiple of 2 and 3.
The least common multiple of 2 and 3 is 6.

Restate the ratios with the number of dimes as 6:

Quarters:dimes = 15:6   Dimes:nickels = 6:8

Top Ten Trap #3

Don't take one number from one ratio and compare it to another number from another ratio.

The ratios are still in their original proportions, but now they're in proportion to each other and they refer to the same whole.

The ratio of quarters to dimes to nickels is 15:6:8, so the ratio of quarters to nickels is 15:8, which is answer choice (E).

Trap 4: Expressions That Look Equal—But Aren't

EXAMPLE

Column A	Column B
$p > q > 1$	
$p^2 - q^2$	$(p - q)^2$

Top Ten Trap #4

Don't be fooled by appearances.

The Wrong Answer

If you said the expressions were equal, you'd be wrong.

The Trap

At first glance the expressions look like they're equal—but they're not.

This common SAT trap happens most often in QCs. Problems like this trap students who are too hasty, who answer on the basis of appearance, without considering the mathematical rules involved.

Avoiding the Trap

If two quantities seem obviously equal, double-check your answer, using your math knowledge and the techniques discussed in chapter 12, Quantitative Comparisons.

This is an example of the general rule that whenever an answer to a question late in a section looks obviously correct, it probably isn't.

Finding the Right Answer

In this case you can use the make-one-column-look-more-like-the-other technique discussed in chapter 12.

Factor Column A and rewrite Column B:

Column A	Column B
$(p-q)(p+q)$	$(p-q)(p-q)$

Now use the do-the-same-thing-to-both-columns technique. Both columns contain $(p-q)$. You know than $p > q$, so $p-q$ is a positive number. Therefore, you can divide both columns by $p-q$:

Column A	Column B
$p+q$	$p-q$

Since q is positive, adding q in Column A will get you more than subtracting q in Column B. Column A is greater, so the answer is (A).

This trap does not apply only to quadratics. Below are some other quantities that the hasty student might mistake as equal. Go through this list and make sure you can tell why these expressions are not equal except for special cases.

Stumped?

Pick numbers.

If $p = 3$ and $q = 2$, then

$p^2 - q^2 = 5$ and $(p - q)^2 = 1$.

Column A is bigger, so you know the answer must be either (A) or (D).

- $(x + y)^2$ does NOT equal $x^2 + y^2$

- $(2x)^2$ does NOT equal $2x^2$

- $x^{20} - x^{18}$ does NOT equal x^2

- $x^3 + x^3$ does NOT equal x^6

- $\sqrt{x} + \sqrt{x}$ does NOT equal $\sqrt{2x}$

- $\sqrt{x} - \sqrt{y}$ does NOT equal $\sqrt{x - y}$

- $\dfrac{1}{x} + \dfrac{1}{y}$ does NOT equal $\dfrac{1}{x + y}$

You could prove that any of these quantities need not be equal using the Picking Numbers technique.

Trap 5: Unspecified Order

EXAMPLE

Column A   Column B

A, B, and C are points on a line such that point A is 12 units away from point B and point B is 4 units away from point C.

The distance from   16
point A to point C

Top Ten Trap #5

Don't assume that there's just one way to draw the diagram.

The Wrong Answer

First you should always draw a diagram to help you visualize the relationship between the points.

A 12 B 4 C

In this diagram, the distance from A to C is 16, which is the same as Column B. But choice (C) is not the right answer.

The Trap

Don't assume that there is only one arrangement of the points—in this case, alphabetical order. We are not told what the relationship between A and C is. In fact C could lie to the left of B, like so:

Avoiding the Trap

Don't assume points lie in the order they are given or in alphabetical order. Look for alternatives.

Finding the Right Answer

In this case, the distance from A to C is 8, which is less than Column B. Since we have two possible relationships between the columns, the answer must be (D)—you can't be certain from the data given.

Trap 6: Length:Area Ratios

Top Ten Trap #6

The ratio of areas is not the same as the ratio of lengths.

Column A | Column B

The area of a square with a perimeter of 14 | Twice the area of a square with a perimeter of 7

The Wrong Answer

Twice the perimeter doesn't mean twice the area. Choice (C) is wrong.

The Trap

In proportional figures, the ratio of the areas is not the same as the ratio of the lengths.

Avoiding the Trap

Understand that the ratio of the areas of proportional figures is the square of the ratio of corresponding linear measures.

s $2s$

Finding the Right Answer

One way to solve this QC would be to actually compute the respective areas.

A square of perimeter 14 has side length $\frac{14}{4} = 3.5$. Its area then is $(3.5)^2 = 12.25$. On the other hand, the area of the square in Column B is $\left(\frac{7}{4}\right)^2 = (1.75)^2 = 3.0625$. Even twice that area is still less than the 12.25 in Column A. The answer is (A).

A quicker and more clever way to dodge this trap is to understand the relationship between the linear ratio and the area ratio of proportional figures. In proportional figures, the area ratio is the square of the linear ratio.

In the example above, we are given two squares with sides in a ratio of 14:7 or 2:1.

Using the rule above, we square the linear 4:1 ratio. The areas of the two figures will be in a four-to-one ratio.

The same goes for circles:

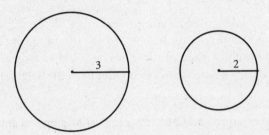

In the figure above, we are given two circles with radii in a 3:2 ratio. Using the rule above, we square the linear 3:2 ratio. The areas of the two circles will be in a 9:4 ratio.

Trap 7: Not All Numbers Are Positive Integers

EXAMPLE

If $n \neq 0$, then which of the following must be true?

    I. $n^2 > n$

    II. $2n > n$

    III. $n + 1 > n$

(A) I only

(B) II only

(C) III only

(D) I and III only

(E) I, II, and III

Top Ten Trap #7

Not all numbers are positive integers. Don't forget to consider 0, fractions, and negative numbers.

The Wrong Answer

In the example above, if you considered only positive integers greater than 1 for the value of n, you would assume that all three statements are true. However, that is not the case.

The Trap

Not all numbers are positive integers. Don't forget there are negative numbers and fractions as well. This is important because negative numbers and fractions between 0 and 1 behave very differently from positive integers.

Avoiding the Trap

When picking numbers for variables, consider fractions and negative numbers.

Finding the Right Answer

Looking at statement I, you may assume that when you square a number, you end up with a larger number as a result. For example, $4^2 = 16$, or $10^2 = 100$. However, when you square a fraction between 0 and 1, the result is quite different: $\left(\frac{1}{2}\right)^2 = \frac{1}{4} \cdot \left(\frac{1}{10}\right)^2 = \frac{1}{100}$, so you get a smaller number.

In statement II, what happens when you multiply a number by 2? $7 \times 2 = 14$; $25 \times 2 = 50$. Multiplying any positive number by 2 doubles that number, so you get a larger result. However, if you multiply a negative number by 2, your result is smaller than the original number. For example, $-3 \times 2 = -6$.

Finally, look at statement III. What happens when you add 1 to any number? Adding 1 to any number gives you a larger number as a result. For example, $5 + 1 = 6$; $\frac{1}{2} + 1 = 1\frac{1}{2}$; and $-7 + 1 = -6$.

Therefore, only statement III must be true, so choice (C) is correct. If you didn't consider fractions or negative numbers, you would have fallen into the trap and answered the question incorrectly.

HINT: *This trap appears most often in QC problems, so watch out.*

Trap 8: Hidden Instructions

| EXAMPLE |

Top Ten Trap #8

Make sure you're answering the question that's asked. Hint: underline the last phrase in the question.

At a certain restaurant, the hourly wage for a waiter is 20 percent greater than the hourly wage for a dishwasher, and the hourly wage for a dishwasher is half as much as the hourly wage for a cook's assistant. If a cook's assistant earns $8.50 an hour, how much less than a cook's assistant does a waiter earn each hour?

(A) $2.55

(B) $3.40

(C) $4.25

(D) $5.10

(E) $5.95

The Wrong Answer

To solve this problem, you must find the hourly wage of the waiter.

The cook's assistant earns $8.50 an hour. The dishwasher earns half of this—$4.25 an hour. The waiter earns 20 percent more than the dishwasher—$4.25 × 1.2 = $5.10.

So the waiter earns $5.10 an hour, and you might reach automatically to fill in answer choice (D). But (D) is the wrong answer.

The Trap

A small step, easily overlooked, can mean the difference between a right and wrong answer.

In this case the word is *less*. After spending all this time finding the waiter's hourly wage, in their moment of triumph many students skip right over the vital last step. They overlook that the question asks not what the waiter earns, but how much less than the cook's assistant the waiter earns.

Avoiding the Trap

Make sure you answer the question that's being asked. Watch out for hidden instructions.

Finding the Right Answer

You have figured out that the waiter earns $5.10 an hour. And the cook's assistant earns $8.50 an hour. To find out how much less than the cook's assistant the waiter earns, subtract the waiter's hourly wage from the cook's assistant's hourly wage.

The correct answer is (B).

Peek-a-Boo

Hidden instructions come in many forms. Watch out for questions that give all the information in one unit (say, minutes) and ask you for the answer in another unit (say, seconds or hours). Read carefully and solve for the correct quantity.

Trap 9: Average Rates

EXAMPLE

A car traveled from *A* to *B* at an average speed of 40 miles per hour and then immediately traveled back from *B* to *A* at an average speed of 60 miles per hour. What was the car's average speed for the round-trip, in miles per hour?

(A) 45

(B) 48

(C) 50

(D) 52

(E) 54

Top Ten Trap #9

Any time it says "average rate" in the question, be alert: You usually can't just average the rates to get the right answer.

The Wrong Answer

Do you see which answer choice looks too good to be true? The temptation is simply to average 40 and 60. The answer is "obviously" 50 (C). But 50 is wrong.

The Trap

To get an average speed, you can't just average the rates.

Why is the average speed not 50 mph? Because the car spent more time traveling at 40 mph than at 60 mph. Each leg of the round trip was the same distance, but the first leg, at the slower speed, took more time.

Avoiding the Trap

You can solve almost any Average Rate problem with this general formula:

$$\text{Average Rate} = \frac{\text{Total Distance}}{\text{Total Time}}$$

Use the given information to figure out the total distance and the total time. But how can you do that when many problems don't specify the distances?

Stumped?

Use common sense. The car spent more time at 40 mph so the answer will be less than 50—i.e., weighted more heavily towards 40 (remember weighted averages, trap #2).

If you saw this much but couldn't get the answer, you could guess between (A) and (B). (More on guessing in chapter 15.)

Finding the Right Answer

In our sample above, we are told that a car went from *A* to *B* at 40 miles per hour and back from *B* to *A* at 60 miles per hour. In other words, it went half the total distance at 40 mph and half the total distance at 60 mph.

How do you use the formula:

$$\text{Average Rate} = \frac{\text{Total Distance}}{\text{Total Time}}$$

if you don't know the total distance?

HINT: *Pick a number! Pick any number you want for the total distance.*

Divide that total distance into half distances. Calculate the time needed to travel each half distance at the different rates.

HINT: *Pick a number that's easy to work with.*

A good number to pick here would be 240 miles for the total distance, because you can figure in your head the times for two 120-mile legs at 40 mph and 60 mph:

A to *B*: $\dfrac{120 \text{ miles}}{40 \text{ miles per hour}} = 3$ hours

B to *A*: $\dfrac{120 \text{ miles}}{60 \text{ miles per hour}} = 2$ hours

Total time = 5 hours

Now plug "total distance = 240 miles" and "total time = 5 hours" into the general formula:

$$\text{Average Rate} = \frac{\text{Total Distance}}{\text{Total Time}} = \frac{240 \text{ miles}}{5 \text{ hours}} = 48 \text{ miles per hour}$$

Correct answer choice: (B).

Trap 10: Counting Numbers

You just can't subtract the first number from the last number; you have to add one.

EXAMPLE

The tickets for a certain raffle are consecutively numbered. If Louis sold the tickets numbered from 75 to 148 inclusive, how many raffle tickets did he sell?

(A) 71

(B) 72

(C) 73

(D) 74

(E) 75

The Wrong Answer

If you subtract 75 from 148 and get 73 as the answer, you are wrong.

The Trap

Subtracting the first and last integers in a range will give you the difference of the two numbers. It won't give you the number of integers in that range.

Avoiding the Trap

To count the number of integers in a range, subtract and then add 1.

If you forget the rule, pick two small numbers that are close together, such as 1 and 4. Obviously, there are four integers from 1 to 4, inclusive. But if you had subtracted 1 from 4, you would have gotten 3.

In the diagram below, you can see that 3 is actually the distance between the integers, if the integers were on a number line or a ruler.

Finding the Right Answer

In the problem above, subtract 75 from 148. The result is 73. Add 1 to this difference to get the number of integers. That gives you 74. The correct answer choice is (D).

The word "inclusive" tells you to include the first and last numbers given. So, for example, "the integers from 5 to 15 inclusive" would include 5 and 15. Questions always make it clear whether you should include the outer numbers or not, since the correct answer hinges on this point.

MORE PRACTICE

Now that you can recognize the Top Ten Traps, try the following test. This time, try to identify the trap in each problem. Check your answers on page 182.

<u>Column A</u>   <u>Column B</u>

A car traveled the first half of a 100-kilometer distance at an average speed of 120 kilometers per hour, and it traveled the remaining distance at an average speed of 80 kilometers per hour.

1. The car's average speed,   100
   in kilometers per hour,
   for the 100 kilometers

Ⓐ ⬤ Ⓒ Ⓓ Ⓔ

·········

The ratio of $\frac{1}{4}$ to $\frac{2}{5}$ is equal to the ratio of $\frac{2}{5}$ to x.

2. x $\frac{3}{5}$

Ⓧ ⬤ Ⓒ Ⓓ Ⓔ

·········

3. $14 - 6$ $\sqrt{14^2 - 6^2}$

Ⓐ ⬤ Ⓒ Ⓓ Ⓔ

·········

4. $\dfrac{a+b}{3}$ $a + b$

Ⓐ Ⓑ Ⓒ ⬤ Ⓔ

·········

John buys 34 books at $6.00 each, and 17 at $12.00 each.

$\dfrac{34(6) + 17(12)}{51} = \dfrac{288}{51}$

5.   The average price $9.00
       John pays per book

Ⓐ ⬤ Ⓒ Ⓓ Ⓔ

·········

On a certain highway Town X lies 50 miles away from Town Y, and Town Z lies 80 miles from Town X.

6. The number of minutes   30
   a car traveling at an
   average speed of 60
   miles per hour takes
   to travel from Town Y
      to Town Z

Ⓐ Ⓑ Ⓒ ⬤ Ⓔ

·········

a, b, and c are positive numbers; $b < c$

7. $(a+b)^2$ $a^2 + c^2$

Ⓐ ⬤ Ⓒ Ⓓ Ⓔ

	Column A	Column B	

8. The area of a circle with a diameter of 3 — The sum of the areas of three circles each with a diameter of 1

Ⓐ Ⓑ Ⓒ Ⓓ Ⓔ

....

Jane invests her savings in a fund that adds 10 percent interest to her savings at the end of every year.

9. The percent by which her money has increased after three years — 31 percent

Ⓐ Ⓑ Ⓒ Ⓓ Ⓔ

....

$$x > 1$$

10. $7^{2x} - 7^x$ — 7^x

Ⓐ Ⓑ Ⓒ Ⓓ Ⓔ

....

11. Pump 1 can drain a 400-gallon water tank in 1.2 hours. Pump 2 can drain the same tank in 1.8 hours. How many minutes longer than pump 1 would it take pump 2 to drain a 100-gallon tank?

(A) 0.15
(B) 1.2
(C) 6
(D) 9
(E) 18

Ⓐ Ⓑ Ⓒ Ⓓ Ⓔ

....

12. Volumes 12 through 30 of a certain encyclopedia are located on the bottom shelf of a bookcase. If the volumes of the encyclopedia are numbered consecutively, how many volumes of the encyclopedia are on the bottom shelf?

(A) 17
(B) 18
(C) 19
(D) 29
(E) 30

Ⓐ Ⓑ Ⓒ Ⓓ Ⓔ

....

13. A reservoir is at full capacity at the beginning of summer. By the first day of fall, the level in the reservoir is 30 percent below full capacity. Then during the fall a period of heavy rains raises the level by 30 percent. After the rains, the reservoir is at what percent of its full capacity?

(A) 100 percent
(B) 95 percent
(C) 91 percent
(D) 85 percent
(E) 60 percent

Ⓐ Ⓑ Ⓒ Ⓓ Ⓔ

14. Two classes, one with 50 students, the other with 30, take the same exam. The combined average of both classes is 84.5. If the larger class averages 80, what is the average of the smaller class?

(A) 87.2

(B) 89.0

(C) 92.0

(D) 93.3

(E) 94.5

$$\frac{50(80) + 30(x)}{80} = 84.5$$

$4000 + 30x = 6760$

$30x = 2760$

$x = 92$

15. In a pet shop, the ratio of puppies to kittens is 7:6 and the ratio of kittens to guinea pigs is 5:3. What is the ratio of puppies to guinea pigs?

(A) 7:3

(B) 6:5

(C) 13:8

(D) 21:11

(E) 35:18

35. 30 : 18

16. A typist typed the first *n* pages of a book, where *n* > 0, at an average rate of 12 pages per hour and typed the remaining *n* pages at an average rate of 20 pages per hour. What was the typist's average rate, in pages per hour, for the entire book?

(A) $14\frac{2}{3}$

(B) 15

(C) 16

(D) 17

(E) 18

17. In triangle *DGH* above, *DE* = *EG*, *EF* ∥ *GH*, and the area of triangle *DGH* is 30. What is the area of triangle *DEF* ?

(A) 7.5

(B) 15

(C) 22.5

(D) 60

(E) It cannot be determined from the information given.

Checklist

Once you've mastered a concept, check it off.

How Traps Work and How to Avoid Them:

❏ The wrong way to answer the questions

❏ Avoiding the traps

❏ Finding the right answers

Kaplan's Top Ten SAT Math Traps:

❏ Percent increase/decrease

❏ Weighted averages integers

❏ Ratio:ratio:ratio

❏ Expressions that look equal—but aren't

❏ Unspecified order

❏ Length:area ratios

❏ Not all numbers are positive

❏ Hidden instructions

❏ Average rates

❏ Counting numbers

Did You Fall for the Traps?

How did you do on the practice questions? Did you spot the trap in each problem? Use the answers below to see what your weaknesses are. Each wrong answer represents one trap you need to work on. Go back and reread the section on that trap. Then try the problems again, until you answer correctly.

1. (B) Trap 9: Average rates
2. (A) Trap 3: Ratio:ratio:ratio
3. (B) Trap 4: Expressions that look equal—but aren't
4. (D) Trap 7: Not all numbers are positive integers
5. (B) Trap 2: Weighted averages
6. (D) Trap 5: Unspecified order
7. (D) Trap 4 : Expressions that look equal—but aren't
8. (A) Trap 6: Length:area ratio
9. (A) Trap 1: Percent increase/decrease
10. (A) Trap 4: Expressions that look equal—but aren't
11. (D) Trap 8: Hidden instructions
12. (C) Trap 10: Counting numbers
13. (C) Trap 1: Percent increase/decrease
14. (C) Trap 2: Weighted averages
15. (E) Trap 3: Ratio:ratio:ratio
16. (B) Trap 9: Average rates
17. (A) Trap 6: Length:area ratios

Math Guessing

- Master the five strategies for making educated guesses
- See when to eliminate unreasonable or obvious choices
- Practice eyeballing geometry diagrams
- Learn to guess with confidence on Grid-ins

Obviously, the best way to find the answer is to actually solve the problem. But if you're stuck or running out of time, guessing can be a good alternative.

The Regular Math and QC sections, like the Verbal sections, are scored to discourage random guessing. For every question you get right you earn a whole point. For every question you get wrong, you lose a fraction of a point. So if you guess at random on a number of questions, the points you gain from correct guesses are canceled out by the points you lose on incorrect guesses, for no overall gain or loss.

But you can make *educated guesses*. This raises the odds of guessing correctly, so the fractional points you lose no longer cancel out all the whole points you gain. You have just raised your score..

To make an educated guess, eliminate answer choices you know to be wrong, and guess from what's left. Of course, the more answer choices you can eliminate, the better chance you have of guessing the correct answer from what's left over.

SAT Emergency

Guessing is an important strategy for scoring points, so read this chapter carefully, even if you only have a week or two to prep for the SAT. It's a short chapter, and there are no shortcuts to learning how to guess accurately.

FIVE STRATEGIES

In the pages that follow, you'll find five strategies for guessing intelligently on all types of math problems.

Eliminate Unreasonable Answer Choices

Before you guess, think about the problem, and decide which answers don't make sense. Take as an example the following problem:

Guessing Is Easy

Quick. Guess the right answer. William H. Harrison's middle name was:

- Hazel
- Hello
- Henry
- Hal
- Herbert

Except for the class clown who said Hazel, most people can safely eliminate two of the five choices. That means you've got a one-in-three chance of guessing Henry.

If you went into the SAT determined not to guess, you would have missed this great opportunity to score a point. If you can eliminate at least one answer, you should guess.

EXAMPLE

The ratio of men to women in a certain room is 13:11. If there are 429 men in the room, how many women are there?

(A)   143

(B)   363

(C)   433

(D)   507

(E)   792

Solution:

- The ratio of men to women is 13:11, so there are more men than women.
- Since there are 429 men, there must be fewer than 429 women.
- So you can eliminate choices (C), (D), and (E).
- The answer must be either (A) or (B), so guess. The correct answer is (B).

Eliminate the Obvious on Hard Questions

On the hard questions late in a set, obvious answers are usually wrong. So eliminate them when you guess. That doesn't hold true for early, easy questions, when the obvious answer could be right.

Now apply the rule. In the following difficult problem, which obvious answer should you eliminate?

EXAMPLE

A number x is increased by 30 percent and then the result is decreased by 20 percent. What is the final result of these changes?

(A) x is increased by 10 percent

(B) x is increased by 6 percent

(C) x is increased by 4 percent

(D) x is decreased by 5 percent

(E) x is decreased by 10 percent

If you picked (A) as the obvious choice to eliminate, you'd be right. Most people would combine the decrease of 20 percent with the increase of 30 percent, getting a net increase of 10 percent. That's the easy, obvious answer, but not the correct answer. If you must guess, avoid (A). The correct answer is (C).

Eyeball Lengths, Angles, and Areas on Geometry Problems

Use diagrams that accompany geometry problems to help you eliminate wrong answer choices. First make sure that the diagram is drawn to scale. Diagrams are always drawn to scale unless there's a note like this: "Note: Figure not drawn to scale." If it's not, don't use this strategy. If it is, estimate quantities or eyeball the diagram. Then eliminate answer choices that are way too large or too small.

Length

When a geometry question asks for a length, use the given lengths to estimate the unknown length. Measure off the given length by making a nick in your pencil with your thumbnail. Then hold the pencil against the unknown length on the diagram to see how the lengths compare.

In the following problem, which answer choices can you eliminate by eyeballing?

Stuck?

- Stuck on a QC or Regular Math question? Eliminate at least one answer choice and guess.

- Stuck on a Grid-in? You won't lose points for guessing wrong on Grid-ins. So go ahead and guess.

EXAMPLE

In the figure above, what is the length of *BC*?

(A) $\sqrt{2}$

(B) 2

(C) $2\sqrt{2}$

(D) 4

(E) $4\sqrt{2}$

Teacher Tip

"Many students struggle with more difficult math questions not because they don't know the math, but because they don't know where to start. That's no excuse! Don't spend forever on a single problem, but do something! Every SAT math problem is accessible—you can always do something small as a first step."

—Ed Cottrell
 Kaplan Teacher
 Houston, TX

Solution:

- *AB* is 2, so measure off this length on your pencil.

- Compare *BC* with this length.

- *BC* appears almost twice as long as *AB*, so *BC* is about 4.

- Since $\sqrt{2}$ is about 1.4, and *BC* is clearly longer than *AB*, choices (A) and (B) are too small.

- Choice (E) is much greater than 4, so eliminate that.

- Now guess between (C) and (D). The correct answer is (C).

Angles

You can also eyeball angles. To eyeball an angle, compare the angle with a familiar angle, such as a straight angle (180°), a right angle (90°), or half a right angle (45°). The corner of a piece of paper is a right angle, so use that to see if an angle is greater or less than 90°.

EXAMPLE

In the figure above, if $\ell_1 \parallel \ell_2$, what is the value of x ?

(A) 130

(B) 100

(C) 80

(D) 50

(E) 40

Solution:

- You see that x is less than 90 degrees, so eliminate choices (A) and (B).

- Since x appears to be much less than 90 degrees, eliminate choice (C).

- Now pick between (D) and (E). In fact, the correct answer is (E).

Areas

Eyeballing an area is similar to eyeballing a length. You compare an unknown area in a diagram to an area that you do know.

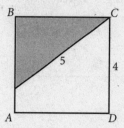

EXAMPLE

In square *ABCD* above, what is the area of the shaded region?

(A) 10

(B) 9

(C) 8

(D) 6

(E) 4

Solution:

- Since *ABCD* is a square, it has area 4^2, or 16.

- The shaded area is less than one-half the size of the square, so its area must be less than 8.

- Eliminate answer choices (A), (B), and (C). The correct answer is (D).

Eliminate Choice (D) on Some QCs

If both columns of a QC contain only concrete numbers, choice (D)—"the relationship cannot be determined"—can't be right. With no variables in either column, there must be one consistent relationship, even if you can't find it. If you don't know the answer, eliminate (D) as unreasonable and guess.

EXAMPLE

Column A	Column B
The largest prime factor of 1,224	18

Each column contains only numbers—so eliminate choice (D) and guess. If you were extra clever, you may also have seen that since 18 isn't prime, and Column A contains a prime number, the answer cannot be (C) either. The correct answer is (B).

Find the Range on Grid-Ins—then Guess

On Grid-ins, there are no answer choices to eliminate, but you won't lose points for guessing. So if you are stuck, try to estimate the general range of the answer, and guess.

Here are some examples of hard Grid-in questions.

EXAMPLE

1. If the three-digit number $11Q$ is a prime number, what digit is represented by Q?

2. The sum of five consecutive odd integers is 425. What is the greatest of these integers?

3. A triangle has one side of length 3 and another of length 7. If the length of the third side is a solution to the equation $x^2 - 2x = 63$, what is the length of the third side?

Solutions:

1. Since Q is a digit, it must be one of the integers 0 through 9. Eliminate all the even digits, since they are divisible by 2. And eliminate 5, since any number ending with 5 is divisible by 5. You can also eliminate 1 and 7, because they are divisible by 3 (the digits add up to a multiple of 3). You are left with 3 and 9 to pick between. The correct answer is 3.

2. Since the integers are consecutive, they are all about the same size. So the number we are looking for is an odd number around $425 \div 5$, which is 85. The right answer is 89.

3. Even if you can't solve that quadratic, you know that one side of a triangle has to be less than the sum and greater than the difference of the other two sides. So the third side is less than $7 + 3$, or 10, and greater than $7 - 3$, or 4. Since solutions to SAT quadratics are usually integers, pick an integer from 5 to 9. If you picked 9, you'd be right.

HINT: *Read "SAT Math in a Nutshell" in the "SAT Study Aids" section.*

Teacher Tip

"Many students are intimidated by math problems at the end of a section because they don't know how to approach them, so they often skip them. Take your time and figure out what you can, even if you're not sure how it may lead to the correct answer. You'll be surprised at how far you get."

—Serineh Baghdasarian
Kaplan Teacher
Los Angeles, CA

Checklist

Once you've mastered a concept, check it off.

Math Guessing:

❏ Eliminate unreasonable answer choices

❏ Eliminate the obvious on hard questions

❏ Eyeball lengths, angles, and areas on geometry problems

❏ Eliminate choice (D) on some QCs

❏ Find the range on Grid-ins—then guess

Ready, Set, Go!

16

Stress Management

HIGHLIGHTS

- Unearth your sources of stress and learn how to manage them

- Take stock of your strengths and weaknesses

- Imagine yourself succeeding

- Practice proper breathing and exercise techniques

- Prepare for the final countdown

The countdown has begun. Your date with THE TEST is looming on the horizon. Anxiety is on the rise. The butterflies in your stomach have gone ballistic. Perhaps you feel as if the last thing you ate has turned into a lead ball. Your thinking is getting cloudy. Maybe you think you won't be ready. Maybe you already know your stuff, but you're going into panic mode anyway. Worst of all, you're not sure of what to do about it.

Don't freak! It is possible to tame that anxiety and stress—before and during the test. We'll show you how. You won't believe how quickly and easily you can deal with that killer anxiety.

Lack of control is one of the prime causes of stress. A ton of research shows that if you don't have a sense of control over what's happening in your life you can easily end up feeling helpless and hopeless. So, just having concrete things to do and to think about—taking control—will help reduce your stress. This section shows you how to take control during the days leading up to taking the test.

SAT Emergency

If you have only a week or two to prep for the SAT, you may just want to skim this chapter. If you're feeling stressed out, take the time to read it carefully. It will help you relax!

IDENTIFY THE SOURCES OF STRESS

In the space provided, jot down (in pencil) anything you identify as a source of your test-related stress. The idea is to pin down that free-floating anxiety so that you can take control of it. Here are some common examples to get you started:

- I always freeze up on tests.

- I'm nervous about the math (or the vocabulary or reading, etc.).

- I need a good/great score to go to Acme College.

- My older brother/sister/best friend/girl- or boyfriend did really well. I *must* match their scores or do better.

Avoid Must-y Thinking
Let go of "must-y" thoughts, those notions that you must do something in a certain way—for example, "I must get a great score, or else!" or "I must meet Mom and Dad's expectations!"

- My parents, who are paying for school, will be really disappointed if I don't test well.

- I'm afraid of losing my focus and concentration.

- I'm afraid I'm not spending enough time preparing.

- I study like crazy but nothing seems to stick in my mind.

- I always run out of time and get panicky.

- I feel as though thinking is becoming like wading through thick mud.

Sources of Stress:

_____

_____

_____

_____

_____

_____

_____

_____

_____

Take a few minutes to think about the things you've just written down. Then rewrite them in some sort of order. List the statements you most associate with your stress and anxiety first, and put the least disturbing items last. Chances are, the top of the list is a fairly accurate description of exactly how you react to test anxiety, both physically and mentally. The later items usually describe your fears (disappointing Mom and Dad, looking bad, etc.). As you write the list, you're forming a hierarchy of items so you can deal first with the anxiety provokers that bug you most. Very often, taking care of the major items from the top of the list goes a long way towards relieving overall testing anxiety. You probably won't have to bother with the stuff you placed last.

TAKE STOCK OF YOUR STRENGTHS AND WEAKNESSES

Take one minute to list the areas of the test that you are good at. They can be general ("algebra") or specific ("quadratic equations"). Put down as many as you can think of, and if possible, time yourself. Write for the entire time; don't stop writing until you've reached the one-minute stopping point.

Strong Test Subjects:

_____

_____

_____

_____

_____

_____

_____

Next, take one minute to list areas of the test you're not so good at, just plain bad at, have failed at, or keep failing at. Again, keep it to one minute, and continue writing until you reach the cutoff. Don't be afraid to identify and write down your weak spots! In all probability, as you do both lists you'll find you are strong in some areas and not so strong in others. Taking stock of your assets *and* liabilities lets you know the areas you don't have to worry about, and the ones that will demand extra attention and effort.

Weak Test Subjects:

_____

_____

_____

_____

_____

_____

_____

Facing your weak spots gives you some distinct advantages. It helps a lot to find out where you need to spend extra effort. Increased exposure to tough material makes it more familiar and less intimidating. (After all, we mostly fear what we don't know and are probably afraid to face.) You'll feel better about yourself because you're dealing directly with areas of the test that bring on your anxiety. You can't help feeling more confident when you know you're actively strengthening your chances of earning a higher overall test score.

Very Superstitious

Stress expert Stephen Sideroff, Ph.D., tells of a client who always stressed out before, during, and even after taking tests. Yet, she always got outstanding scores. It became obvious that she was thinking superstitiously—subconsciously believing that the great scores were a result of her worrying. She also didn't trust herself, and believed that if she didn't worry she wouldn't study hard enough. Sideroff convinced her to take a risk and work on relaxing before her next test. She did, and her test results were still as good as ever—which broke her cycle of superstitious thinking.

Now, go back to the "good" list, and expand it for two minutes. Take the general items on that first list and make them more specific; take the specific items and expand them into more general conclusions. Naturally, if anything new comes to mind, jot it down. Focus all of your attention and effort on your strengths. Don't underestimate yourself or your abilities. Give yourself full credit. At the same time, don't list strengths you don't really have; you'll only be fooling yourself.

Expanding from general to specific might go as follows. If you listed "Verbal" as a broad topic you feel strong in, you would then narrow your focus to include areas of this subject about which you are particularly knowledgeable. Your areas of strength might include analogies, ability to decipher unfamiliar words through knowledge of Latin, ability to recognize vocabulary bridges, etc.

Whatever you know comfortably (that is, almost as well as you know the back of your hand) goes on your "good" list. Okay. You've got the picture. Now, get ready, check your starting time, and start writing down items on your expanded "good" list.

Strong Test Subjects: An Expanded List:

_____

_____

_____

_____

_____

_____

_____

_____

_____

_____

_____

_____

_____

_____

_____

_____

Stress Tip

Don't work in a messy or cramped area. Before you sit down to study, clear yourself a nice, open space. And, make sure you have books, paper, pencils—whatever tools you will need—within easy reach before you sit down to study.

After you've stopped, check your time. Did you find yourself going beyond the two minutes allotted? Did you write down more things than you thought you knew? Is it possible you know more than you've given yourself credit for? Could that mean you've found a number of areas in which you feel strong?

You just took an active step towards helping yourself. Notice any increased feelings of confidence? Enjoy them.

Here's another way to think about your writing exercise. Every area of strength and confidence you can identify is much like having a reserve of solid gold at Fort Knox. You'll be able to draw on your reserves as you need them. You can use your reserves to solve difficult questions, maintain confidence, and keep test stress and anxiety at a distance. The encouraging thing is that every time you recognize another area of strength, succeed at coming up with a solution, or get a good score on a test, you increase your reserves. And, there is absolutely no limit to how much self-confidence you can have or how good you can feel about yourself.

IMAGINE YOURSELF SUCCEEDING

This next little group of exercises is both physical and mental. It's a natural follow-up to what you've just accomplished with your lists.

First, get yourself into a comfortable sitting position in a quiet setting. Wear loose clothes. If you wear glasses, take them off. Then, close your eyes and breathe in a deep, satisfying breath of air. Really fill your lungs until your rib cage is fully expanded and you can't take in any more. Then, exhale the air completely. Imagine you're blowing out a candle with your last little puff of air. Do this two or three more times, filling your lungs to their maximum and emptying them totally. Keep your eyes closed, comfortably but not tightly. Let your body sink deeper into the chair as you become even more comfortable.

With your eyes shut you can notice something very interesting. You're no longer dealing with the worrisome stuff going on in the world *outside* of you. Now you can concentrate on what happens *inside* you. The more you recognize your own physical reactions to stress and anxiety, the more you can do about them. You may not realize it, but you've begun to regain a sense of being in control.

Let images begin to form on the "viewing screens" on the back of your eyelids. You're experiencing visualizations from the place in your mind that makes pictures. Allow the images to come easily and naturally; don't force them. Imagine yourself in a relaxing situation. It might be in a special place you've visited before or one you've read about. It can be a fictional location that you create in your imagination, but a real-life memory of a place or situation you know is usually better. Make it as detailed as possible and notice as much as you can.

Stay focused on the images as you sink farther back into your chair. Breathe easily and naturally. You might have the sensations of any stress or tension draining from your muscles and flowing downward, out your feet and away from you.

Take a moment to check how you're feeling. Notice how comfortable you've become. Imagine how much easier it would be if you could take the test feeling this relaxed and in this state of ease. You've coupled the images of your special place with sensations of comfort and relaxation. You've also found a way to become relaxed simply by visualizing your own safe, special place.

Teacher Tip

"I always tell my students that the best gift that Kaplan can give them is to eliminate the element of surprise, which can spell disaster. With Kaplan, students know what to expect; they always know what's coming. Remember, you are in control of the test. The test makers can dictate the questions themselves, but not how you handle them."

—Fran Longo
Kaplan Teacher
Boston, MA

Stress Tip

If you want to play music, keep it low and in the background. Music with a regular, mathematical rhythm—reggae, for example—aids the learning process. A recording of ocean waves is also soothing.

Now, close your eyes and start remembering a real-life situation in which you did well on a test. If you can't come up with one, remember a situation in which you did something (academic or otherwise) that you were really proud of—a genuine accomplishment. Make the memory as detailed as possible. Think about the sights, the sounds, the smells, even the tastes associated with this remembered experience. Remember how confident you felt as you accomplished your goal. Now start thinking about the upcoming test. Keep your thoughts and feelings in line with that successful experience. Don't make comparisons between them. Just imagine taking the upcoming test with the same feelings of confidence and relaxed control.

This exercise is a great way to bring the test down to earth. You should practice this exercise often, especially when the prospect of taking the exam starts to bum you out. The more you practice it, the more effective the exercise will be for you.

EXERCISE YOUR FRUSTRATIONS AWAY

Whether it is jogging, walking, biking, mild aerobics, pushups, or a pickup basketball game, physical exercise is a very effective way to stimulate both your mind and body and to improve your ability to think and concentrate. A surprising number of students get out of the habit of regular exercise, ironically because they're spending so much time prepping for exams. Also, sedentary people—this is a medical fact—get less oxygen to the blood and hence to the head than active people. You can live fine with a little less oxygen; you just can't think as well.

Any big test is a bit like a race. Thinking clearly at the end is just as important as having a quick mind early on. If you can't sustain your energy level in the last sections of the exam, there's too good a chance you could blow it. You need a fit body that can weather the demands any big exam puts on you. Along with a good diet and adequate sleep, exercise is an important part of keeping yourself in fighting shape and thinking clearly for the long haul.

Take a Hike, Pal

When you're in the middle of studying and hit a wall, take a short, brisk walk. Breathe deeply and swing your arms as you walk. Clear your mind. (And, don't forget to look for flowers that grow in the cracks of the sidewalk.)

There's another thing that happens when students don't make exercise an integral part of their test preparation. Like any organism in nature, you operate best if all your "energy systems" are in balance. Studying uses a lot of energy, but it's all mental. When you take a study break, do something active instead of raiding the fridge or vegging out in front of the TV. Take a five- to ten-minute activity break for every 50 or 60 minutes that you study. The physical exertion gets your body into the act, which helps to keep your mind and body in sync. Then, when you finish studying for the night and hit the sack, you won't lie there, tense and unable to sleep because your head is overtired and your body wants to pump iron or run a marathon.

One warning about exercise, however: It's not a good idea to exercise vigorously right before you go to bed. This could easily cause sleep onset problems. For the same reason, it's also not a good idea to study right up to bedtime. Make time for a "buffer period" before you go to bed: For 30 to 60 minutes, just take a hot shower, meditate, simply veg out.

THE DANGERS OF DRUGS

Using drugs (prescription or recreational) specifically to prepare for and take a big test is definitely self-defeating. (And if they're illegal drugs, you may end up with a bigger problem than the SAT on your hands.) Except for the drugs that occur naturally in your brain, every drug has major drawbacks—and a false sense of security is only one of them.

You may have heard that popping uppers helps you study by keeping you alert. If they're illegal, definitely forget about it. They wouldn't really work anyway, since amphetamines make it hard to retain information. Mild stimulants, such as coffee, cola, or over-the-counter caffeine pills can sometimes help as you study, since they keep you alert. On the down side, they can also lead to agitation, restlessness, and insomnia. Some people can drink a pot of high-octane coffee and sleep like a baby. Others have one cup and start to vibrate. It all depends on your tolerance for caffeine. Remember, a little anxiety is a good thing. The adrenaline that gets pumped into your bloodstream helps you stay alert and think more clearly. But, too much anxiety and you can't think straight at all.

Instead, go for endorphins—the "natural morphine." Endorphins have no side effects and they're free—you've already got them in your brain. It just takes some exercise to release them. Running around on the basketball court, bicycling, swimming, aerobics, power walking—these activities cause endorphins to occupy certain spots in your brain's neural synapses. In addition, exercise develops staying power and increases the oxygen transfer to your brain. Go into the test naturally.

Nutrition and Stress: The Dos and Don'ts

Do eat:

- Fruits and vegetables (raw is best, or just lightly steamed or nuked)
- Low-fat protein such as fish, skinless poultry, beans, and legumes
- Whole grains such as brown rice, whole wheat bread, and pasta

Don't eat:

- Refined sugar; sweet, high-fat snacks (simple carbohydrates like sugar make stress worse and fatty foods lower your immunity)
- Salty foods (they deplete potassium, which you need for nerve functions)

TAKE A DEEP BREATH . . .

Here's another natural route to relaxation and invigoration. It's a classic isometric exercise that you can do whenever you get stressed out—just before the test begins, even *during* the test. It's very simple and takes just a few minutes.

Close your eyes. Starting with your eyes and—*without holding your breath*—gradually tighten every muscle in your body (but not to the point of pain) in the following sequence:

1. Close your eyes tightly.
2. Squeeze your nose and mouth together so that your whole face is scrunched up. (If it makes you self-conscious to do this in the test room, skip the face-scrunching part.)
3. Pull your chin into your chest, and pull your shoulders together.
4. Tighten your arms to your body, then clench your hands into tight fists.
5. Pull in your stomach.
6. Squeeze your thighs and buttocks together, and tighten your calves.
7. Stretch your feet, then curl your toes (watch out for cramping in this part).

At this point, every muscle should be tightened. Now, relax your body, one part at a time, in *reverse order*, starting with your toes. Let the tension drop out of each muscle. The entire process might take five minutes from start to finish (maybe a couple of minutes during the test). This clenching and unclenching exercise should help you to feel very relaxed.

AND KEEP BREATHING

The Relaxation Paradox

Forcing relaxation is like asking yourself to flap your arms and fly. You can't do it, and every push and prod only gets you more frustrated. Relaxation is something you don't work at. You simply let it happen. Think about it. When was the last time you tried to force yourself to go to sleep, and it worked?

Conscious attention to breathing is an excellent way of managing test stress (or any stress, for that matter). The majority of people who get into trouble during tests take shallow breaths. They breathe using only their upper chests and shoulder muscles, and may even hold their breath for long periods of time. Conversely, the test taker who by accident or design keeps breathing normally and rhythmically is likely to be more relaxed and in better control during the entire test experience.

So, now is the time to get into the habit of relaxed breathing. Do the next exercise to learn to breathe in a natural, easy rhythm. By the way, this is another technique you can use during the test to collect your thoughts and ward off excess stress. The entire exercise should take no more than three to five minutes.

With your eyes still closed, breathe in slowly and deeply through your nose. Hold the breath for a bit, and then release it through your mouth. The key is to breathe slowly and deeply by using your diaphragm (the big band of muscle that spans your body just above your waist) to draw air in and out naturally and effortlessly. Breathing with your diaphragm encourages relaxation and helps minimize tension. Try it and notice how relaxed and comfortable you feel.

QUICK TIPS FOR THE DAYS JUST BEFORE THE EXAM

- The best test takers do less and less as the test approaches. Taper off your study schedule and take it easy on yourself. You want to be relaxed and ready on the day of the test. Give yourself time off, especially the evening before the exam. By that time, if you've studied well, everything you need to know is firmly stored in your memory banks.

- Positive self-talk can be extremely liberating and invigorating, especially as the test looms closer. Tell yourself things such as, "I choose to take this test" rather than "I have to"; "I will do well" rather than "I hope things go well"; "I can" rather than "I cannot." Be aware of negative, self-defeating thoughts and images and immediately counter any you become aware of. Replace them with affirming statements that encourage your self-esteem and confidence. Create and practice doing visualizations that build on your positive statements.

- Get your act together sooner rather than later. Have everything (including choice of clothing) laid out days in advance. Most important, know where the test will be held and the easiest, quickest way to get there. You will gain great peace of mind if you know that all the little details—gas in the car, directions, etc.—are firmly in your control before the day of the test.

- Experience the test site a few days in advance. This is very helpful if you are especially anxious. If at all possible, find out what room your part of the alphabet is assigned to, and try to sit there (by yourself) for a while. Better yet, bring some practice material and do at least a section or two, if not an entire practice test, in that room. In this case, familiarity doesn't breed contempt, it generates comfort and confidence.

- Forego any practice on the day before the test. It's in your best interest to marshal your physical and psychological resources for 24 hours or so. Even race horses are kept in the paddock and treated like princes the day before a race. Keep the upcoming test out of your consciousness; go to a movie, take a pleasant hike, or just relax. Don't eat junk food or tons of sugar. And—of course—get plenty of rest the night before. Just don't go to bed too early. It's hard to fall asleep earlier than you're used to, and you don't want to lie there thinking about the test.

HANDLING STRESS DURING THE TEST

The biggest stress monster will be the test itself. Fear not; there are methods of quelling your stress during the test.

- Keep moving forward instead of getting bogged down in a difficult question or passage. You don't have to get everything right to achieve a fine score. So, don't linger out of desperation on a question that is going nowhere even after you've spent considerable time on it. The best test takers skip difficult material temporarily in search of the easier stuff. They mark the ones that require extra time and thought. This strategy buys time and builds confidence so you can handle the tough stuff later.

- Don't be thrown if other test takers seem to be working more busily and furiously than you are. Continue to spend your time patiently but doggedly thinking through your answers; it's going to lead to higher-quality test taking and better results. Don't mistake the other people's sheer activity as signs of progress and higher scores.

- *Keep breathing!* Weak test takers tend to share one major trait: They forget to breathe properly as the test proceeds. They start holding their breath without realizing it, or they breathe erratically or arrhythmically. Improper breathing hurts confidence and accuracy. Just as important, it interferes with clear thinking.

- Some quick isometrics during the test—especially if concentration is wandering or energy is waning—can help. Try this: Put your palms together and press intensely for a few seconds. Concentrate on the tension you feel through your palms, wrists, forearms, and up into your biceps and shoulders. Then, quickly release the pressure. Feel the difference as you let go. Focus on the warm relaxation that floods through the muscles. Now you're ready to return to the task.

> ### What Are "Signs of a Winner," Alex?
>
> Here's some advice from a Kaplan instructor who won big on *Jeopardy!*™ In the green room before the show, he noticed that the contestants who were quiet and "within themselves" were the ones who did great on the show. The contestants who did not perform as well were the ones who were fact-cramming, talking a lot, and generally being manic before the show. Lesson: Spend the final hours leading up to the test getting sleep, meditating, and generally relaxing.

• Here's another isometric that will relieve tension in both your neck and eye muscles. Slowly rotate your head from side to side, turning your head and eyes to look as far back over each shoulder as you can. Feel the muscles stretch on one side of your neck as they contract on the other. Repeat five times in each direction.

With what you've just learned here, you're armed and ready to do battle with the test. This book and your studies will give you the information you'll need to answer the questions. It's all firmly planted in your mind. You also know how to deal with any excess tension that might come along, both when you're studying for and taking the exam. You've experienced everything you need to tame your test anxiety and stress. You're going to get a great score.

17

What Do I Do Now?

- Find out what to do in the time before, during, and after the test
- Improve your test mentality with confidence and the right attitude

Is it starting to feel like your whole life is a build-up to the SAT? You've known about it for years, worried about it for months, and now spent at least a few hours in solid preparation for it. As the test gets closer, you may find your anxiety is on the rise. You shouldn't worry. After the preparation you've received from this book, you're in good shape for the test.

ITINERARY

To calm any pretest jitters you may have, this chapter leads you through a sane itinerary for the last week.

SAT Emergency

Even if you're short on time, read this entire chapter. It tells you how to use your time wisely before, during, and after the test.

The Week Before the Test

Review the checklists in the chapters. Are there major holes in your preparation? If there are, choose a few of these areas to work on—but don't overload. You can't cram for the SAT.

Take a full-length SAT. If you haven't done so already, take one or more of the practice tests in this book. Actual SATs released by ETS are available in libraries and bookstores. You could also pick up from your guidance counselor a copy of *Taking the SAT I*, a College Board publication with a practice test. All of these are good practice for the real thing.

Two Days Before the Test

Do your last studying—a few more practice problems, a few more vocabulary words, and call it quits.

The Night Before the Test

Don't study. Get together the following items:

- A calculator with fresh batteries
- A watch
- A few No. 2 pencils
- Erasers
- Photo ID card
- Your admission ticket from ETS
- A snack—there are two breaks and you'll probably get hungry

Know exactly where you're going and exactly how you're getting there.

Relax the night before the test. Read a good book, take a bubble bath, watch TV. Get a good night's sleep. Go to bed at a reasonable hour and leave yourself extra time in the morning.

The Morning of the Test

Eat breakfast. Make it something substantial, but not anything too heavy or greasy. Don't drink a lot of coffee if you're not used to it; bathroom breaks cut into your time.

Dress in layers so that you can adjust to the temperature of the test room.

Read something. Warm up your brain with a newspaper or a magazine. You shouldn't let the SAT be the first thing you read that day.

Be sure to get there early.

During the Test

Don't be shaken. If you find your confidence slipping, remind yourself how well you've prepared. You know the structure of the test; you know the instructions; you've studied for every question type.

Even if something goes really wrong, don't panic. If the test booklet is defective—two pages are stuck together or the ink has run—try to stay calm. Raise your hand, tell the proctor you need a new book. If you accidentally misgrid your answer page or put the answers in the wrong section, again don't panic. Raise your hand, tell the proctor. He or she might be able to arrange for you to regrid your test after it's over, when it won't cost you any time.

Things Not to Do the Night Before the Test

- Try to copy the dictionary onto your fingernails.
- Stay up all night watching all the *Friday the 13th* movies.
- Eat a large double anchovy, sausage, and pepper pizza with a case of chocolate soda.
- Send away for brochures from vocational schools.
- Start making flashcards.
- Tattoo yourself.

Teacher Tip

"A skill that's absolutely necessary for all sections of the test is concentration. Being easily distracted diminishes your ability to pick up on every subtle and not-so-subtle component of the text. Everything from construction or traffic outside to a proctor's noisy watch can distract on test day. You can train to get into the test 'zone' by practicing with a radio on, or in a busy coffee shop. This is a valuable skill not only in every section of the test, but in school as well."

—Antonette Brigidi
Kaplan Teacher
Baltimore, MD

Don't think about which section is experimental. Remember, you never know for sure which section won't count. Besides, you can't work on any other section during that section's designated time slot.

After the Test

Once the test is over, put it out of your mind. If you don't plan to take the test again, give this book away and start thinking about more interesting things.

You might walk out of the SAT thinking that you blew it. You probably didn't.
You tend to remember the questions that stumped you, not the many that you knew. If you're really concerned, you can call ETS within 24 hours to find out about canceling your score. But there is usually no good reason to do so. Remember, you can retake the test as many times as you want, and most colleges consider only your highest scores.

If you want more help, or just want to know more about the SAT, college admissions, or Kaplan prep courses for the PSAT, SAT, and ACT, give us a call at 1-800-KAP-TEST. We're here to answer your questions and to help you in any way that we can.

Good luck!

> **Need More Help?**
>
> Call 1-800-KAP-TEST if you have any questions about the SAT or want more information about our other books or courses. You can also check out our website at www.kaptest.com.

The PSAT

Changes Ahead for the PSAT/NMSQT

A new version of the PSAT/NMSQT will be administered beginning with the October 2004 test. Much of the test will remain the same, but there are important changes.

Why Is the Test Changing?

The PSAT, which has always been promoted as a means to prepare for the SAT, is changing because of changes being made to the SAT that will take effect in March 2005. The changes planned for the SAT will be mirrored to a large extent in the PSAT. However, there will be two ways in which the new PSAT will be different from the new SAT: There will be no written essay on the PSAT, and the math on the PSAT will not cover math topics normally covered in algebra II that are being added to the SAT (simply because most PSAT test-takers have not yet taken algebra II).

What is Changing?

The changes will include both the type of questions used on the test and the content that will be tested. The content is being changed in an attempt to align the test more closely to the high school curricula and to the skills needed for academic success in college. The result is that the content—-primarily the math section—-will become more difficult. At the same time, two question types are being discontinued entirely—-Analogies and Quantitative Comparisons. Instead, there will be more traditional multiple choice questions and a couple more Student-Produced Response Questions ("Grid-ins").

Finally, the new PSAT/NMSQT will have a different time allocation than the old version. The College Board has announced that the new test will be two hours and five minutes in length—-five minutes shorter than the current one!

Changes in the Verbal Section

First, this section will no longer be called the Verbal section; in the new test, it will be labeled Critical Reading. Plans now call for this section to continue to be divided into two 25-minute subsections.

The Analogies questions, which require test takers to understand the meanings of specific words and analyze the relationship between them (see page 29 for examples) are being dropped. Instead, there will be short reading passages added with two to three questions after each passage.

Changes in the Math Section

Although the PSAT will not cover the topics associated with algebra II that will be added to the SAT, the Mathematical section of the PSAT will still become more difficult. According the College Board, the higher-level math content to be added to the PSAT includes the following:

Number and Operations
- Sequences and series involving exponential growth

- Sets (union, intersection, elements)

Algebra and Functions
- Operation on algebraic expressions

- Absolute value

- Rational equations and inequalities

- Radical Equations

- Manipulation with integer and rational exponents

- Direct and inverse variation

- Functions as models

- Linear functions: equations and graphs

Geometry and Measurement
- Geometric notation

- Triangles

- Properties of tangent lines

- Coordinate geometry

Data Analysis, Statistics, and Probability

- Data interpretation including scatterplots

- Geometric probability

- Median and mode

Although the test will include harder math questions, keep in mind that the PSAT/NMSQT is a norm-referenced test and your score is determined by how you compare with others taking the test. So if you can do a little better than most others taking the test on the new higher-level math content, your score will go up as a result of the addition of harder math content. The mean score of all test takers will remain the same on the new and the old test even though the new test will be more difficult. The new PSAT will be scored on a scale of 6—24, the same as the current test.

Both the new and the current versions of the PSAT/NMSQT include two 25-minute Mathematical sections. But, as mentioned above, one type of question, the Quantitative Comparison (see page 60 for examples) is being eliminated entirely. No longer will you have to compare the quantity in column A to the quantity in column B and try to figure out which is larger. Instead, there will be more regular multiple-choice questions and more Grid-ins (see page 62), for which you must determine the correct number and then grid it in on your answer sheet (rather than simply selecting which answer choice—a, b, c, d, or e—is best).

Changes in the Writing Section

The PSAT/NMSQT already has a writing section similar to that expected to be added to the new SAT making its debut in 2005. However, the PSAT Writing test does not include writing an essay, and this will not change even though an essay is being added to the new SAT. The College Board says the reason no essay will be added to the PSAT is that the amount of time and money required to score 2.5 million student essays would result in the delay of PSAT score reports and an increase in test administration costs.

One minor change will affect the Writing section. The PSAT currently includes one 30-minute Writing section; under the new test being administered in 2004, this section will be only 25 minutes in length.

This Book and the Upcoming Changes in the PSAT/NMSQT

This book will specifically prepare you for the October 2003 PSAT/NMSQT. It will also provide general preparation for the October 2004 test because the basic test content, except for the addition of some more difficult math questions, will stay the same. However, at press time, the exact character of the new test had not been completely finalized. Watch for the next edition of Kaplan's PSAT expected in bookstores in summer 2004 for test-preparation materials specific to the October 2004 PSAT/NMSQT.

18

Inside the PSAT:
Writing Skills

- Familiarize yourself with the breakdown and setup of the PSAT

- Review strategies for Usage, Sentence Correction, and Revision-in-Context question types

- Study the Kaplan Three-Step Method for Writing Skills questions

- Learn to spot and correct classic errors that appear on the test

You've learned a lot about the SAT as you've worked through this book. But what if you're taking the PSAT? Here's the good news: If you're taking the PSAT, you're already in great shape, because virtually all of the techniques and strategies that apply to the SAT also apply to the PSAT.

The one major difference between the SAT and PSAT is that since October 1997, students taking the PSAT have also had to complete a Writing Skills section. To meet the needs of today's high-school curriculum, and to address allegations that the PSAT unfairly discriminates against women, the College Board introduced the multiple-choice Writing Skills section to test proficiency in standard written English. We'll focus on the Writing Skills section in this chapter, reviewing the grammar rules, skills, and strategies you need for success on this section.

P Is for Practice

Don't be misled into thinking that the PSAT is not important. The PSAT contains the same math and verbal question types as the SAT—so studying for the PSAT gives you a head start in preparing for the SAT.

WHAT IS THE PSAT?

The PSAT (formally known as the PSAT/NMSQT or Preliminary Scholastic Assessment Test/National Merit Scholarship Qualifying Test) has two main functions. First, the PSAT serves as valuable practice for the SAT. Although shorter in duration than the actual SAT, the PSAT contains the same variety of math and verbal question types as the SAT and seeks to measure the same skills. And because your PSAT scores are not sent to colleges, you can use the PSAT to practice the skills you'll need for the SAT.

The National Merit Program

The PSAT/NMSQT also provides students with a chance to qualify for National Merit Scholarship Corporation programs. If you're one of the highest scorers in your state (typically this means scoring above the ninety-ninth percentile) you may be one of 50,000 juniors chosen to enter the competition for National Merit scholarships and recognition letters.

Qualifying for the program can be the first stepping stone to academic success, increasing your chances of acceptance at top-tier universities and helping you meet the financial demands of college life. Through the National Merit program, approximately 25,000 students every year receive letters of commendation and nearly 8,500 students receive scholarships ranging from $250 to $2,000 a year.

STRUCTURE OF THE TEST

There are five sections on the PSAT: two 25-minute-long Math sections, two 25-minute-long Verbal sections, and one 30-minute-long Writing section.

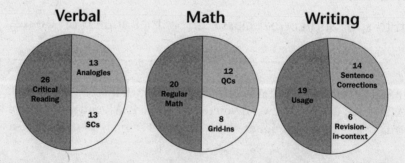

Students will receive scaled scores for Math, Verbal, and Writing in the 20–80 range. To calculate your National Merit qualifying score, simply add your Math, Verbal, and Writing scaled scores (M + V + W). The maximum score on the PSAT is 240.

WRITING SKILLS: FORMAT AND INSTRUCTIONS

The key phrase to focus on here is *multiple choice*. In spite of its name, this Writing Skills section doesn't actually *test* your writing ability. You're not required to produce a writing sample. Instead, you're asked to demonstrate your knowledge of the elements of good writing: correct grammar, accurate sentence structure, and paragraph construction.

Here's a great way to make the Writing Skills section easier: get familiar with the directions. Since the instructions are always the same from test to test, there is no reason to waste time reading them on the day of the test. By learning them ahead of time, you will save yourself some time on Test Day, and time is everything. Every second that you save while taking the test is a second that you can use to recheck your work and tackle the questions that you saved for last. So spend some time going over the test instructions that we provide and explain here.

> ### A Writing Test That Doesn't Test Writing
>
> In spite of its name, the Writing Skills section doesn't actually require you to do any writing. Instead, it tests your knowledge of the elements of good writing: correct grammar, accurate sentence structure, and paragraph construction.

Usage Questions

You'll encounter 19 Usage questions on the Writing Skills section. The directions for Usage questions look like this:

> DIRECTIONS: Choose the one underlined part that must be changed to make the sentence correct and fill in the corresponding oval on your answer grid. If there is no error, fill in oval E.

1. For <u>a number of years</u>, Gauguin was a friend
          A
    of the <u>painter</u> van Gogh; <u>they</u> met at <u>his</u> exhibition
           B   C   D
    in Paris. <u>No error</u>
              E

Usage questions require you to "spot the mistake." You're given a sentence like the one above in which certain words or phrases are underlined. Your job is to look at the underlined portions of the sentence, and to figure out which part is grammatically incorrect. For those sentences that contain no errors—and there will be some—choose choice (E), or "No error," as your answer.

Usage questions test your ability to catch words or phrases that are frequently used *incorrectly* in students' essays. If you are able to spot errors in word and phrase usage, the test makers assume that you are capable of using appropriate words and phrases in your own writing. In the example above, the correct answer is (D), since the ambiguous pronoun *his* doesn't indicate at whose exhibition the two painters met.

Sentence Correction Questions

There are 14 Sentence Correction questions on the Writing Skills section of the PSAT. The directions for them like this:

Don't Be Afraid of "No Error"

On each test, a certain number of questions will contain no error. Pick (E) on Usage questions, and (A) on Sentence Completions.

DIRECTIONS: Select the choice that best expresses the meaning of the original sentence. If the original sentence is better than any of the alternative phrasings, choose A; otherwise, select one of the alternatives.

2. To the surprise of the school's staff, the new freshman class at Ravenswood High being larger than last year's.

(A) being larger than last year's

(B) is large more so than last year

(C) which is larger than the one last year

(D) is larger than last year's

(E) by far larger than the last

In Sentence Correction questions, your job is to figure out whether the underlined portion of the sentence is grammatically correct. If the sentence is correct, pick answer choice (A), which will always be identical to the original sentence. If the sentence is grammatically flawed, you will need to pick the answer choice that best corrects the error.

Sentence Correction questions test your ability to identify and correct sentence-structure problems that often appear in students' essays. Again, the test makers assume that if you are able to *spot* poorly constructed sentences and fix them, then you can probably write good sentences on your own. In the question above, the correct answer is choice (D). The verb *being* is in the wrong form, creating a run-on sentence. Choice (D) solves the problem in straightforward fashion.

Revision-in-Context Questions

Here are the directions for the Revision-in-Context questions. There is only one Revision-in-Context passage on the test, accompanied by six questions.

DIRECTIONS: Read the essay and answer the questions that follow it. Pick the answer that most effectively conveys the author's meaning and follows the rules of standard written English.

(1) The school board recently took a controversial vote to allow advertising at Midville High. (2) Many disagree with this decision. (3) I do not. (4) As a member of the student council, it is important to make up for the shortfall in our school budget. (5) And we cannot afford the luxury of worrying about where the money is coming from.

3. Which of the following is the best way to revise and combine sentences 2 and 3 (reproduced below)?

    Many disagree with this decision. I do not.

    (A) Many disagreeing with this decision, I am not.

    (B) In contrast to the case that many that are disagreeing with this decision, I do not.

    (C) Although many disagree with this decision, I do not.

    (D) Even though many disagree with this decision, I am agreeing.

    (E) Many disagree with this decision, but not me.

You'll have noticed that Usage questions focus on words or phrases, and Sentence Corrections focus on whole sentences. In contrast, Revision-in-Context questions ask you to focus on whole *paragraphs*. In this section of the test, you will be given a passage whose individual sentences are numbered. You are then asked a series of questions about the passage. Some of the questions ask you to correct the structure or style of a particular sentence, to make it better fit into the passage as a whole. Other questions will ask you to make the passage clearer or more logical in development.

Usage and Sentence Correction questions test your ability to write accurate sentences. But good writing involves more than that. To write well, you need to be able to develop an idea or a thought into a well-constructed paragraph. Revision-in-Context questions test your ability to spot and correct logical flaws in a passage that contains errors commonly found in students' essays. If you can fix this sample passage, the test makers assume you can probably do the same thing to your own writing.

In the question above, the correct answer is (C). Sentences 2 and 3 sound choppy in their original form. Choice (C) neatly combines them together while remaining grammatically accurate and retaining the author's meaning.

THE KAPLAN THREE-STEP METHOD

Now that you are clear on the format and directions, you'll want to spend some time learning more about how to answer each question type. As with the Math and Verbal sections, the first thing you should realize about Writing questions is that you don't want to dive head first into the answer choices. Instead, you want to be systematic, and use a consistent, strategic method for each question. Without this book, you could spend hours trying to figure out the right methods to use. Chances are, you don't have that kind of time. Don't worry. We at Kaplan have already figured out what you need to do:

1. **Read the sentence, "listening" for a mistake.**

2. **Identify the error.**

3. **Check the answer choices.**

Where the Errors *Aren't*

Remember, if there is an error in the sentence, it will be in one of the underlined parts. Don't bother looking for errors in the nonunderlined parts; just read them to get the overall meaning of the sentence.

Now let's take a look at how you would use the Kaplan Three-Step Method when dealing with the different types of questions you'll find in the PSAT Writing Skills section.

Usage Questions

How do you listen for an error? If English is your native language, you already have an innate sense of grammar. No doubt you've often heard someone say something that didn't sound right; you could tell that the speaker used the wrong word, or used it in the wrong way. That's the approach you should take to Usage questions. By listening to the sentence in your mind as you read, you will be able to hear the error, if there is one.

Read the following question, applying the Kaplan Three-Step Method.

4. Early <u>experience</u> of racial discrimination <u>made</u> an
              A   B
    <u>indelible</u> <u>impression for</u> the late Supreme Court
           C   D
    Justice Thurgood Marshall. <u>No error</u>
                                    E

When you read the question, did you hear a mistake? If so, you are done with the question. On the test, you would just fill in the corresponding oval and move on. If you didn't hear the mistake, just go back and read each underlined part again. The word *experience* sounds fine. The word *made* seems fine in terms of subject verb agreement. And the word *indelible* also sounds fine. However, the phrase *impression for* sounds wrong. The correct phrase to use would be *impression on*, making choice (D) the correct answer.

This question was a classic example of an incorrect preposition. Let's take a look at some of the classic errors that appear on the Usage section.

Verb Tense Errors

In English grammar, verb tense indicates *when* an action is taking place—past, present, or future. You don't need to know the names of different tenses for the PSAT, but you do need to know how to use them. Take a look at the following sentence:

Because I was in the shower, I was missing your call.

Sounds awkward doesn't it? That's because *was missing* is in the wrong tense. Take a look at the following sentence:

Because I was in the shower, I <u>missed</u> your call.

That sounds much better doesn't it? By changing *was missing* to *missed*, the sentence was easily fixed. A number of Usage questions on the PSAT will require you to spot mistakes in verb tense. Try the following question:

Teacher Tip

"Students have to become aware of all the common mistakes that can be made on a question. If they do this, they will be more careful not to make these errors."

—Derek Veazey
Kaplan Teacher
Fort Worth, TX

5. The first woman aviator <u>to cross</u> the English
                            A
    Channel, Harriet Quimby <u>flown</u> <u>by monoplane</u>
                              B   C
    from Dover, England, to Hardelot, France <u>in</u> 1912.
                                               D

    <u>No error</u>
    E

When you read through the sentence, did you hear a mistake? If so, mark it down on this page. If not, read through the question again, eliminating answer choices as you go. To *cross* should sound fine to you. But *flown* probably sounds awkward. In fact, the sentence should read, "Harriet Quimby flew . . . ." Choice (B) contains the error in this sentence, making (B) the correct answer.

Subject-Verb Agreement Errors

Another common mistake on the PSAT has to do with subject-verb agreement. In standard written English, the subject and verb in each sentence must "agree" in person and in number. In other words, if the subject is singular, it must take the singular form of the verb; likewise for the plural forms. Also, the correct verb form is based on whether the subject is in the first-, second-, or third-person form. Take a look at the following sentence:

> Coming from a rural community, Orville were not
> accustomed to the pace of the big city.

The name Orville aside, this sentence sounds pretty strange, doesn't it? That's because the verb *were* does not agree with the subject *Orville*. Now look at the following:

> Coming from a rural community, Orville <u>was</u> not
> accustomed to the pace of the big city.

The sentence sounds much better after *were* is replaced with *was*. Now try the following Usage question, keeping the Kaplan Three-Step Method in mind.

6. The sailors <u>aboard</u> the cruiser Nimitz <u>was</u> <u>unsettled</u>
                 A   B   C
    by the bright lights that appeared <u>in the sky</u>.
                                        D

    <u>No error</u>
    E

Did you hear the error as you read through this sentence? The subject here is *sailors* and the verb is *was*. The problem here is that the subject of the sentence is plural, but the verb is singular. In other words, the verb *was* should really be *were*. The correct answer is therefore choice (B). Try reading the sentence again with the correct form of the verb and see if you hear the difference.

Pronoun Errors

Another very common error that is tested on the PSAT is the misuse of pronouns. In English grammar, pronouns must agree with their antecedents (the nouns that precede them) in both case and number. Try reading the following sentence:

> A person who spends all their money may be in danger of financial ruin.

This sentence is a good example of a very common error. In an effort to be "gender neutral" a lot of people use the pronoun *they* or *their* to refer to a person of unknown gender. Unfortunately, this creates grammatical problems, since *their* is plural and *a person* is singular. The sentence should read as follows:

> A person who spends all <u>his</u> money may be in danger of financial ruin.
>
> OR
>
> A person who spends all <u>her</u> money may be in danger of financial ruin.

Pronouns and Antecedents

A pronoun refers to a noun, or another pronoun. That noun, or other pronoun, is called an *antecedent*. In the sentences, "My cat is black and she likes to cross in people's paths," *cat* is the antecedent and *she* is the pronoun.

Case and Number Errors

The case of a pronoun is the form in which it appears—for example, *he* as opposed to *him*. The number of a pronoun is exactly what it sounds like—singular or plural. *She* is a singular pronoun; *they* is plural.

Give this question a try:

7. Mr. Jones <u>was</u> notorious <u>for failing</u> students <u>who</u>
       A   B   C
   skipped <u>his</u> classes. <u>No error</u>
           D   E

Did you hear an error as you read this sentence? If you did, you might want to read it again. That's right—there is no error in this sentence! Remember, a certain percentage of questions will not have an error. We threw in this question to remind you of that fact.

Try this question next (we promise that this one does have an error):

8. There <u>was</u> a huge public outcry <u>over</u> the cruel
        A   B

    methods <u>employed</u> at the animal pound, but in the
                    C

    end, nothing came of <u>them</u>. <u>No error</u>
                            D   E

Did you hear the error here? This sentence is a little tricky. You might think that *them* refers to the *methods*, and that the sentence contains no error (even though we told you that it did). But actually, *them* refers to *outcry*. Since *outcry* is singular and *them* is plural, you have a situation in which the pronoun does not agree with its antecedent. The correct answer is choice (D). If you replace *them* with *it*, then the sentence becomes correct.

Preposition and Connective Errors

The Usage section often tests your ability to choose the right preposition. Prepositions are the little words that connect sentences together. Often, if you choose the wrong preposition in a sentence, then the meaning of the sentence becomes vague or illogical. Take a look at the following sentence:

> I don't like to argue between my friends.

This sounds a little strange doesn't it? That's because *with* is the preposition most commonly used with the verb *to argue* in English. To argue with someone is to be engaged in an argument with that person. Read the following:

> I don't like to argue <u>with</u> my friends.

This sounds much better, doesn't it? As you can see, just a small word can drastically change a sentence. The PSAT will include questions that test your ability to spot the incorrect use of these small words. Try the following question, making sure that you use the Kaplan Three-Step Method:

9. The reproductive behavior of sea horses <u>is notable</u>
                                                 A

    <u>in respect of</u> the male <u>who</u>, <u>instead of</u> the female,
        B   C   D

    carries the fertilized eggs. <u>No error</u>
                          E

Get Your Idioms in Order

Idioms are word combinations that are correct for no apparent reason. There is no reason why *with respect to* is more correct than *in respect of*—it's just an idiom. If English is your native language, then you will naturally have a sense of idioms. If you have difficulty with idioms, you will want to familiarize yourself with them before the day of the test.

Did you hear the error? You probably noticed that *in respect of* sounded a little strange. In fact, *in respect of* should be replaced with *with respect to*, making (B) the correct answer here.

Comparison Errors

Here's something that you may not have known about standard written English. When you compare two or more parts of speech (for example, nouns or verb phrases) you should make sure you're comparing the same parts of speech in the same form. Take this example:

> The technician agreed that fixing a television is easier than computer repair.

Even though you can understand what this sentence is trying to communicate, it should sound a bit labored and clumsy. That's because the two elements that are being compared, *fixing a television* and *computer repair*, are not in the same form. The first half of the sentence includes a verb, and the second half does not. The sentence would be better if it were written as follows:

> The technician agreed that fixing a television is easier than <u>repairing computers</u>.

In this case, *fixing a television* and *repairing computers* are both in the same form—that is, they both have verbs that are in the same form. See if you can spot the mistake in this next question.

10. The work of Byron <u>has been underrated</u> more
                                        A
     often by <u>so-called</u> modernists in the field of
                       B
     literary criticism <u>than</u> <u>any other Romantic poet</u>.
                          C   D
     <u>No error</u>
        E

Did you spot the error here? If you had a hard time, here's a clue. What two things are being compared here? You have *the work of Byron* on the one hand, and *any other Romantic poet* on the other. Are these two things in the same form? As you can see, *the work of Byron* contains a preposition while *any other Romantic poet* does not. In other words, the two things being compared are not in the same form. You couldn't change *the work of Byron* because it isn't underlined. However, *any other Romantic poet* is underlined, making (D) the answer. To correct the sentence, you would want to replace *any other Romantic poet* with *the work of any other Romantic poet*.

Adjective and Adverb Errors

Adjectives are words that modify or describe nouns and pronouns. Adverbs are words that modify verbs, adjectives, or other adverbs. In the phrase *the ugly dog,* the word *ugly* is an adjective. In the phrase *he drove fast,* the word *fast* is an adverb. On the PSAT, the test makers like to find out whether you can identify commonly confused adjectives and adverbs. Take a look at the following sentence:

> Sam studied hard for the test, so he did good.

This sentence is a good example of a commonly misused adjective. In this sentence, *good* is used to modify the verb *did*. But the word *good* is an adjective, not an adverb. The sentence should read as follows:

Sam studied hard for the test, so he did well.

In this sentence, the error has been corrected. The word *well* is an adverb, and can be used to modify the verb *did*.

Take a look at the following question:

11. Increasing numbers of people are investing in the
        A   B
     stock market, according to a recent published
                     C   D
     newspaper article. No error
                         E

Did you hear the error? The word *recent* is an adjective, and should be used to modify a noun. But in the sentence above, *recent* is used to modify the adjective *published*. (*Published* is an adjective because it modifies *newspaper article*.) The word *recent* should be *recently*, making the answer choice (D).

Double Negatives

If a sentence contains two negatives (words such as *not* or *without*) they create a double negative and cancel each other out. It's sort of like math, in which two negatives make a positive. Read the following sentence:

Peggy can't have none of that food because she's allergic to it.

> **Tricky Negatives**
>
> Watch out for tricky negatives such as *hardly, barely, scarcely,* and *cannot.*

In this sentence, there are two negatives—*can't* and *none*. Because these two negatives are in the same sentence, they cancel each other out. In other words, the sentence is saying that Peggy cannot have none of that food, meaning that she must have that food. This conveys a meaning that is the opposite of the meaning that the sentence was trying to convey. Even though you can understand the meaning of the sentence, this redundancy contradicts the rules of standard written English and therefore is incorrect. The sentence should read as follows:

Peggy can't have any of that food because she's allergic to it.

Try the following question:

12. Sheila hasn't hardly any money left after her
                     A   B C
     shopping trip to the new outlet. No error
              D   E

Did you hear the error? By saying that Sheila hasn't *hardly any money*, the sentence is implying that Sheila does have money. But that is not what the sentence means. The sentence is trying to say that Sheila has very little money left. So, the words *hardly any* should be changed, making choice (A) correct. The sentence should read as follows:

Sheila hasn't <u>much</u> money left after her shopping trip to the new outlet.

Sentence Correction Questions

As was the case with Usage questions, you should also approach Sentence Correction questions as strategically as possible. The most effective way to do this is to follow the Kaplan Three-Step Method for Sentence Corrections:

1. **Read the sentence, listening for a mistake.**

2. **Predict a correction.**

3. **Select the answer choice that matches your prediction, while eliminating clearly wrong answer choices.**

Try reading through the following question, applying the Kaplan Three-Step Method.

The Importance of Listening

As was the case with Usage questions, you should "listen" for mistakes on Sentence Corrections. This will be particularly easy for you if English is your native language.

13. In the Middle Ages, when astronomical phenomena were poorly understood, the <u>comets that seemed to portend</u> military conflicts or other social crises.

(A) the comets that seemed to portend

(B) the comets that seeming to portend

(C) the comets seemed to portend

(D) the comets apparently portending

(E) and when the comets seemed to portend

When you read through the question, did you hear a mistake? You probably noticed that *the comets that seemed to portend* sounded strange; the sentence just sort of ended without really completing a thought. Now that you have found the error, you should try to fix it. How could you make the sentence sound more complete? The word *that* is unnecessary, isn't it? Now that you have corrected the question, find the answer choice which best matches your prediction. You can eliminate choice (A) because that just restates what is already in the passage. The correct choice is choice (C), which matches your prediction.

Classic Sentence Correction Errors

The next few pages list the most common types of errors found in Sentence Correction questions. You should work through this section, making sure that you understand what is wrong with each question.

Sentence Fragments A sentence fragment is exactly what it sounds like—a fragment of a sentence. To put it another way, a sentence fragment is an incomplete sentence. It may look like a sentence, but it is either grammatically incomplete because it lacks a main subject or a verb, or logically incomplete because it lacks the necessary elements to express a complete thought. Take a look at the following sentence:

Eggs and fresh vegetables on sale at the farmer's market.

It doesn't sound complete, does it? It sounds strange because it's missing a verb. If you read the following out loud, it will sound much better.

Eggs and fresh vegetables <u>are</u> on sale at the farmer's market.

By including the verb *are* the sentence becomes complete.

Now take a look at the following Sentence Correction question. See if you can answer it by using the Kaplan Three-Step Method.

14. The government, under pressure to satisfy the needs of consumers, <u>and loosening its</u> control of the economy.

   (A) and loosening its

   (B) by loosening its

   (C) is loosening their

   (D) but loosening their

   (E) is loosening its

The phrase *and loosening its* makes the sentence sound awkward. Like the previous example, you change the form of the verb to make the sentence sound complete. Can you predict what would make the sentence sound more complete? If you predicted *is loosening its*—choice (E)—then you are correct.

Run-On Sentences Run-on sentences occur when two complete sentences that should be separate are joined together. Here are two examples:

Winston Churchill is one of the twentieth century's most admired politicians, his speeches are still quoted today.

Winston Churchill is one of the twentieth century's most admired politicians his speeches are still quoted today.

You can tell that the above two examples are run-on sentences because they sound like they should be two sentences. Once again, your ear will be crucial to helping you in this section. There are three ways that you can fix a run-on sentence:

1. Use a period:

Winston Churchill is one of the twentieth century's most admired politicians. His speeches are still quoted today.

2. Use a conjunction/make one sentence dependent:

> Because Winston Churchill is one of the twentieth century's most admired politicians, his speeches are still quoted today.

3. Use a semicolon:

> Winston Churchill is one of the twentieth century's most admired politicians; his speeches are still quoted today.

You need to be aware of these three ways to fix run-on sentences as you work through Sentence Corrections. See if you can apply the Kaplan Three-Step Method and the information you just learned to correctly solve the following question:

15. <u>Amelia Earhart was born in Kansas the first person to fly from Hawaii to California.</u>

    (A) Amelia Earhart was born in Kansas the first person to fly from Hawaii to California.

    (B) Amelia Earhart being the first person to fly from Hawaii to California and was born in Kansas.

    (C) Being the first person to fly from Hawaii to California, Amelia Earhart was born in Kansas.

    (D) Amelia Earhart was the first person to fly from Hawaii to California and was born in Kansas.

    (E) Amelia Earhart, who was born in Kansas, was the first person to fly from Hawaii to California.

Notice that the entire sentence was underlined. This means that either the entire sentence needs to be changed, or that it is fine the way it is. Hopefully, you noticed that the sentence sounded strange. In fact, this is another example of a run-on sentence. To fix it, you need to find an answer choice that corrects the problem in one of the three ways discussed above. Only answer choice (E) corrects the problem.

Coordination/Subordination Errors Coordination and subordination errors are those in which clauses are joined together incorrectly. Faulty coordination and subordination are closely related to each other, but they require separate explanations.

- *Faulty Coordination.* Faulty coordination occurs when the word (or words) joining two sentences together does not express the right logical relationship. Here's an example:

> Wrong: Because he was very unhappy, he smiled all the time.

> Correct: <u>Although</u> he was very unhappy, he smiled all the time.

In these examples, it made no sense to say that "because he was unhappy, he smiled." But the second sentence corrects this problem by switching the word *because* with the word *although*.

- *Faulty Subordination.* Faulty subordination is similar to a sentence fragment. When a group of words contains two or more dependent clauses, but no independent clause, you have faulty subordination. To look at it another way, faulty subordination occurs when a group of words is not anchored to a complete thought. Take a look at the following sentence:

> Walking into the kitchen in my sleep and opening the refrigerator.

This sounds awkward, doesn't it? Now read the following:

> I walked into the kitchen in my sleep and opened the refrigerator.

See the difference? In the first example, the verbs *walking* and *opening* made the sentence incomplete. By changing *walking* to *I walked* and *opening* to *opened* in the second example, the sentence becomes a complete sentence.

See if you can answer the following question:

16. Unusual numbers of playwrights and artists <u>flourishing in the England of Shakespeare's time,</u> and the Italy of Michelangelo's day, when cultural conditions combined to promote creativity.

   (A) flourishing in the England of Shakespeare's time

   (B) by flourishing in the England of Shakespeare's time

   (C) while flourishing in Shakespeare's England

   (D) flourished in the England of Shakespeare's time

   (E) having flourished in Shakespeare's England

Exercising Your Independence

Clauses are groups of words that contain a subject and a verb. There are two kinds of clauses—dependent clauses and independent clauses. Dependent clauses do not express a complete thought; they are sentence fragments. Dependent clauses need to be tied to an independent clause to express a complete thought. Independent clauses express complete thoughts—they are independent because they can stand alone.

As you read through this sentence, you probably noticed that it sounded incomplete. Did you predict ahead of time how to fix the problem? The verb flourishing made the sentence sound strange; it needed to be changed to flourished, as in choice (D). Coordination and subordination occur frequently in Sentence Correction questions, so make sure that you understand them clearly before the day of the test.

Modifier Errors Modifiers are phrases that provide extra information about nouns and verbs in a sentence. The tricky thing about a modifier is that it must appear next to the word or words that it is modifying. Take a look at the following example:

> Designed for small children, Ed had to stoop to reach the water fountain.

The sentence sounds funny, doesn't it? You know what the sentence is trying to say. But the way in which it is written makes it sound like Ed was designed for small children (a scary thought, whoever Ed is). Notice how different the sentence sounds now:

> Ed had to stoop to reach the water fountain, which was designed for small children.

By moving the modifier "designed for small children" to the end of the sentence, we were able to make the meaning of this sentence totally clear. Try the following question and see if you can spot the answer:

17. Night shift workers lead a strange life, <u>working while the rest of us are sleeping</u>, then sleeping while the rest of us are working.

    (A) working while the rest of us are sleeping

    (B) and they work while the rest of us sleep

    (C) working while the rest of us sleep

    (D) they work while the rest of us sleep

    (E) working while the rest of us remain in our sleep

Did you hear the error? Are you sure? Sorry, we did it to you again. That's right; there is no error in this sentence. Remember, a fraction of Sentence Correction questions will have letter (A) as the correct answer. Now try the following question, which we promise does contain an error:

18. <u>The young couple eventually returned to the grassy spot where they had left their sandwiches, strolling hand in hand.</u>

    (A) The young couple eventually returned to the grassy spot where they had left their sandwiches, strolling hand in hand.

    (B) Eventually, the young couple returned to the grassy spot where they had left their sandwiches, strolling hand in hand.

    (C) Strolling hand in hand, the grassy spot where they had left their sandwiches was eventually returned to by the young couple.

    (D) The young couple, returning to the grassy spot where they had left their sandwiches, while strolling hand in hand.

    (E) Strolling hand in hand, the young couple eventually returned to the grassy spot where they had left their sandwiches.

Did you hear the error? The way that the sentence originally appears makes it sound as though the sandwiches were strolling hand in hand. We know that sandwiches are not capable of doing this. To fix the sentence, you need to make it clear that the young couple was strolling hand in hand. Choice (E) accomplishes this.

Parallelism Errors Parallelism is a lot like the comparisons that appeared earlier in this chapter. Parallelism refers to the rule that when you list items, they should be in the same form. Take a look at the following sentence:

> To conserve calories, to promote digestion, or so that they are less vulnerable to predators, wild animals rest during many of their waking hours.

Although you can understand the meaning of this sentence, it sounds a little awkward. This is because the items listed, "to conserve calories, to promote digestion or so that they are less vulnerable," are not parallel. Two of the items start with the word to while the third item does not. The sentence should read:

> To conserve calories, to promote digestion, or to be less vulnerable to predators, wild animals rest during many of their waking hours.

Can you hear the difference between the two sentences? Now try the following question and see how you do:

19. For success in school, it is important not only <u>being smart but also to do</u> your homework.

   (A) being smart but also to do

   (B) to be smart but also to do

   (C) to be smart but also doing

   (D) being smart but also doing

   (E) that you be smart but also that you do

The original version of this sentence probably sounded pretty strange to you. This is because the two items, *being smart* and *to do your homework*, were not in the same form. To correct this problem, you need both items to either start with *to* or to start with verbs that ended in *-ing*. Only choice (B) corrects the problem.

Revision-in-Context Questions

Don't let the fact that you have to read a whole paragraph to answer Revision-in-Context questions scare you. This portion of the test is actually not that hard. If you can do Usage questions and Sentence Correction questions, you will be in fine shape to tackle Revision-in-Context questions.

There are two things to keep in mind as you tackle Revision-in-Context questions. The first thing is that you should understand the point of these questions. The test makers want you to be able to write a concise, stylistically smooth, and logical essay. Every question that they ask you will be geared towards this purpose. The second thing you should keep in mind as you work is Kaplan's Three-Step Method:

1. **Read the essay.**
    As in Critical Reading, you need to get a sense of the essay's overall main idea and the main idea of each paragraph.

2. **Read the question stem.**
    Understand what the question wants you to do. Questions that require you to revise or combine sentences will supply the sentence numbers to you. Questions that ask about the entire essay generally won't refer to specific sentences.

3. **Reread the relevant portion of the essay.**
    Reread the sentences before and after the affected sentence(s). Rereading the lines around the affected sentence(s) will provide you with a sense of context, which will help you to choose the best construction from the answer choices.

Let's try applying the Kaplan Three-Step Method. As Step One, take a look at the passage below, and try to figure out what the author's main idea is.

(1) While watching skateboarders in a shopping mall, people sometimes shake their heads. (2) They shake their heads since because they think that skateboarders are bad kids and that the sport should be banned. (3) I think that skateboarding is a great sport. (4) It allows young people to be physically active, without doing something harmful to him. (5) Kids have a lot of energy that needs to be burned off. (6) All you have to do is to read the paper. (7) And if you did that, you would see that kids are getting into serious trouble everywhere, sometimes even killing people. (8) But skateboarders have found a way to burn off their energy in a way that is fun and in something that is challenging because it is physically hard. (9) A lot of adults worry that skateboarders are bad because they tend to mark up civic property, scuff buildings and even tear chunks out of staircases. (10) This is true sometimes. (11) Similarly I believe that that the best solution to this problem would be if the city acknowledged the positive aspects of skateboarding, and built more skateboard parks. (12) Then kids would have a place to go and skate, and adults wouldn't have to worry about parks and private property.

Did you figure out what the point of the passage was as you read? The author is trying to explain why he believes that skateboarding is worthwhile and healthy, in spite of the negative view that some people have of the sport.

You may even have noticed a few errors while you were reading. But don't bother trying to correct anything yet. You can make a small mark to note errors if you want to, but don't spend too much time on those errors. The purpose of your first read-through should be just to get you acquainted with the passage.

There are three types of Revision-in-Context questions.

- Sentence revision

- Sentence combination

- Logic and clarity

Now that you have read the passage, let's take a look at the first of these three question types.

Sentence Revision

Step Two of the Kaplan Three-Step Method is to read the question stem. Here is a typical Sentence Revision question:

20. Which of the following is the best way to revise the underlined portion of sentence 3?

I think that skateboarding is a great sport.

(A) Believing that, I

(B) Because of this, I

(C) However, I

(D) Unfortunately, I

(E) Furthermore, I

Kaplan Rules

Remember Kaplan's Three-Step Method for answering Writing Skills questions:

1. Read the essay.

2. Read the question stem.

3. Reread the relevant portion of the essay.

This question asks you to revise a sentence in the passage. Notice that the sentence is reprinted below the question itself. After you have read the question stem, and understand what it wants you to do, you should apply Step Three of the Three-Step Method—reread the relevant portion of the essay. You should read just enough of the passage to figure out the context in which this sentence fits. The author starts out the passage by explaining that some people do not like skateboarding. He then goes on to say that he likes the sport. However, the author did not make a smooth transition between these two opposing ideas. He needed to do something to make the paragraph flow better. Can you see which answer choice would make this transition? If you picked choice (C), you are right. Starting sentence 3 with the word *however* would make the paragraph stylistically much better.

The test makers believe that one of the most important aspects of writing involves clear and accurate sentence structure. Keep in mind the grammatical errors that we discussed in the sections on Usage and Sentence Correction questions, and you should do fine on this question type.

Sentence Combination

Now take a look at this question:

21. Which of the following is the best way to combine sentences 1 and 2 (reproduced below)?

While watching skateboarders in a shopping mall, people sometimes shake their heads. They shake their heads since because they think that skateboarders are bad kids and that the sport should be banned.

(A) While watching skateboarders in a shopping mall, people sometimes shake their heads: they shake their heads because they think that skateboarders are bad kids and that the sport should be banned.

(B) While watching skateboarders in a shopping mall, people sometimes shake their heads, because they think that skateboarders are bad kids and that the sport should be banned.

(C) While watching skateboarders in a shopping mall, people sometimes shake their heads because they skateboarders are bad kids and the sport should be banned.

(D) While watching skateboarders in a shopping mall, people sometimes shake their heads and they think that skateboarders are bad kids and that the sport should be banned.

(E) While watching skateboarders in a shopping mall, people sometimes shake their heads thinking that skateboarders are bad kids and that the sport should be banned.

This question asks you to combine two sentences together. Can you see why? These two sentences sound choppy and uneven. Also, the author repeats the phrase *shake their heads*. Can you see which answer choice fixes this problem? If you chose choice (B), you were right. Choice (B) combines the sentences together, by including the word *because*.

Remember that the test makers believe that a well-written essay avoids wordiness and redundancy. Also remember that correct answers will always be grammatically and logically correct.

Logic and Clarity

Another kind of question tests your ability to spot gaps in the author's logic and clarity. Take a look at the following question.

22. The writer of the passage could best improve sentence 10 by

    (A) acknowledging the weakness of his argument

    (B) providing a specific example

    (C) highlighting his opinion

    (D) discussing an example that is counter to his thesis

    (E) mentioning the other youth activities

The question asks you how sentence 10 could be improved. To figure out the answer to this question, you need to remember to do Step Three of the Kaplan Three-Step Method. Go back and read the portion of the passage that this sentence appeared in.

Now that you have reread the passage, can you see the flaw in the sentence? The author starts to say in sentence 9 that some people believe that skateboarders are destructive to private property. In sentence 10, the author says that this is true sometimes. In sentence 11, the author starts to discuss "the city." The problem is that the author moves to abruptly from one point to another. Furthermore, since this is an essay about the author's personal opinion, he needs to back up his opinion when he can. The problem with sentence 10 is that the author does not fully explain what he means, making choice (B) the correct answer.

GETTING READY FOR THE PSAT

If you were easily able to work through this material, then you should do fine on the PSAT's Writing Skills section. But if you feel that you need a little more practice, you might want to check out Kaplan's *PSAT* book for a targeted review and plenty of practice, or our *SAT II: Writing* book, which contains a wealth of grammar material, with detailed explanations and drills. But whether or not you choose to supplement your preparation, you should realize that by preparing as much as you have, you're in much better shape for the day of the test!

Practice Tests and Explanations

Practice Test One

HOW TO TAKE THIS PRACTICE TEST

Before taking this practice test, find a quiet room where you can work uninterrupted for two and a half hours. Make sure you have a comfortable desk, your calculator, and several No. 2 pencils.

Use the answer sheet provided to record your answers. (You can cut it out or photocopy it.)

Once you start this practice test, don't stop until you've finished. Remember—you can review any questions within a section, but you may not go back or forward a section.

You'll find an answer key, score conversion charts, and explanations following the test.

Good luck.

SAT Practice Test One
Answer Sheet

Remove (or photocopy) this answer sheet and use it to complete the practice test.
(See answer key following the test when finished.)

Start with number 1 for each section. If a section has fewer questions than answer spaces, leave the extra spaces blank.

SECTION 1

1 Ⓐ Ⓑ Ⓒ Ⓓ Ⓔ	11 Ⓐ Ⓑ Ⓒ Ⓓ Ⓔ	21 Ⓐ Ⓑ Ⓒ Ⓓ Ⓔ	31 Ⓐ Ⓑ Ⓒ Ⓓ Ⓔ
2 Ⓐ Ⓑ Ⓒ Ⓓ Ⓔ	12 Ⓐ Ⓑ Ⓒ Ⓓ Ⓔ	22 Ⓐ Ⓑ Ⓒ Ⓓ Ⓔ	32 Ⓐ Ⓑ Ⓒ Ⓓ Ⓔ
3 Ⓐ Ⓑ Ⓒ Ⓓ Ⓔ	13 Ⓐ Ⓑ Ⓒ Ⓓ Ⓔ	23 Ⓐ Ⓑ Ⓒ Ⓓ Ⓔ	33 Ⓐ Ⓑ Ⓒ Ⓓ Ⓔ
4 Ⓐ Ⓑ Ⓒ Ⓓ Ⓔ	14 Ⓐ Ⓑ Ⓒ Ⓓ Ⓔ	24 Ⓐ Ⓑ Ⓒ Ⓓ Ⓔ	34 Ⓐ Ⓑ Ⓒ Ⓓ Ⓔ
5 Ⓐ Ⓑ Ⓒ Ⓓ Ⓔ	15 Ⓐ Ⓑ Ⓒ Ⓓ Ⓔ	25 Ⓐ Ⓑ Ⓒ Ⓓ Ⓔ	35 Ⓐ Ⓑ Ⓒ Ⓓ Ⓔ
6 Ⓐ Ⓑ Ⓒ Ⓓ Ⓔ	16 Ⓐ Ⓑ Ⓒ Ⓓ Ⓔ	26 Ⓐ Ⓑ Ⓒ Ⓓ Ⓔ	36 Ⓐ Ⓑ Ⓒ Ⓓ Ⓔ
7 Ⓐ Ⓑ Ⓒ Ⓓ Ⓔ	17 Ⓐ Ⓑ Ⓒ Ⓓ Ⓔ	27 Ⓐ Ⓑ Ⓒ Ⓓ Ⓔ	37 Ⓐ Ⓑ Ⓒ Ⓓ Ⓔ
8 Ⓐ Ⓑ Ⓒ Ⓓ Ⓔ	18 Ⓐ Ⓑ Ⓒ Ⓓ Ⓔ	28 Ⓐ Ⓑ Ⓒ Ⓓ Ⓔ	38 Ⓐ Ⓑ Ⓒ Ⓓ Ⓔ
9 Ⓐ Ⓑ Ⓒ Ⓓ Ⓔ	19 Ⓐ Ⓑ Ⓒ Ⓓ Ⓔ	29 Ⓐ Ⓑ Ⓒ Ⓓ Ⓔ	39 Ⓐ Ⓑ Ⓒ Ⓓ Ⓔ
10 Ⓐ Ⓑ Ⓒ Ⓓ Ⓔ	20 Ⓐ Ⓑ Ⓒ Ⓓ Ⓔ	30 Ⓐ Ⓑ Ⓒ Ⓓ Ⓔ	40 Ⓐ Ⓑ Ⓒ Ⓓ Ⓔ

☐ # right in section 1

☐ # wrong in section 1

SECTION 2

1 Ⓐ Ⓑ Ⓒ Ⓓ Ⓔ	11 Ⓐ Ⓑ Ⓒ Ⓓ Ⓔ	21 Ⓐ Ⓑ Ⓒ Ⓓ Ⓔ	31 Ⓐ Ⓑ Ⓒ Ⓓ Ⓔ
2 Ⓐ Ⓑ Ⓒ Ⓓ Ⓔ	12 Ⓐ Ⓑ Ⓒ Ⓓ Ⓔ	22 Ⓐ Ⓑ Ⓒ Ⓓ Ⓔ	32 Ⓐ Ⓑ Ⓒ Ⓓ Ⓔ
3 Ⓐ Ⓑ Ⓒ Ⓓ Ⓔ	13 Ⓐ Ⓑ Ⓒ Ⓓ Ⓔ	23 Ⓐ Ⓑ Ⓒ Ⓓ Ⓔ	33 Ⓐ Ⓑ Ⓒ Ⓓ Ⓔ
4 Ⓐ Ⓑ Ⓒ Ⓓ Ⓔ	14 Ⓐ Ⓑ Ⓒ Ⓓ Ⓔ	24 Ⓐ Ⓑ Ⓒ Ⓓ Ⓔ	34 Ⓐ Ⓑ Ⓒ Ⓓ Ⓔ
5 Ⓐ Ⓑ Ⓒ Ⓓ Ⓔ	15 Ⓐ Ⓑ Ⓒ Ⓓ Ⓔ	25 Ⓐ Ⓑ Ⓒ Ⓓ Ⓔ	35 Ⓐ Ⓑ Ⓒ Ⓓ Ⓔ
6 Ⓐ Ⓑ Ⓒ Ⓓ Ⓔ	16 Ⓐ Ⓑ Ⓒ Ⓓ Ⓔ	26 Ⓐ Ⓑ Ⓒ Ⓓ Ⓔ	36 Ⓐ Ⓑ Ⓒ Ⓓ Ⓔ
7 Ⓐ Ⓑ Ⓒ Ⓓ Ⓔ	17 Ⓐ Ⓑ Ⓒ Ⓓ Ⓔ	27 Ⓐ Ⓑ Ⓒ Ⓓ Ⓔ	37 Ⓐ Ⓑ Ⓒ Ⓓ Ⓔ
8 Ⓐ Ⓑ Ⓒ Ⓓ Ⓔ	18 Ⓐ Ⓑ Ⓒ Ⓓ Ⓔ	28 Ⓐ Ⓑ Ⓒ Ⓓ Ⓔ	38 Ⓐ Ⓑ Ⓒ Ⓓ Ⓔ
9 Ⓐ Ⓑ Ⓒ Ⓓ Ⓔ	19 Ⓐ Ⓑ Ⓒ Ⓓ Ⓔ	29 Ⓐ Ⓑ Ⓒ Ⓓ Ⓔ	39 Ⓐ Ⓑ Ⓒ Ⓓ Ⓔ
10 Ⓐ Ⓑ Ⓒ Ⓓ Ⓔ	20 Ⓐ Ⓑ Ⓒ Ⓓ Ⓔ	30 Ⓐ Ⓑ Ⓒ Ⓓ Ⓔ	40 Ⓐ Ⓑ Ⓒ Ⓓ Ⓔ

☐ # right in section 2

☐ # wrong in section 2

SECTION 3

1 Ⓐ Ⓑ Ⓒ Ⓓ Ⓔ	11 Ⓐ Ⓑ Ⓒ Ⓓ Ⓔ	21 Ⓐ Ⓑ Ⓒ Ⓓ Ⓔ	31 Ⓐ Ⓑ Ⓒ Ⓓ Ⓔ
2 Ⓐ Ⓑ Ⓒ Ⓓ Ⓔ	12 Ⓐ Ⓑ Ⓒ Ⓓ Ⓔ	22 Ⓐ Ⓑ Ⓒ Ⓓ Ⓔ	32 Ⓐ Ⓑ Ⓒ Ⓓ Ⓔ
3 Ⓐ Ⓑ Ⓒ Ⓓ Ⓔ	13 Ⓐ Ⓑ Ⓒ Ⓓ Ⓔ	23 Ⓐ Ⓑ Ⓒ Ⓓ Ⓔ	33 Ⓐ Ⓑ Ⓒ Ⓓ Ⓔ
4 Ⓐ Ⓑ Ⓒ Ⓓ Ⓔ	14 Ⓐ Ⓑ Ⓒ Ⓓ Ⓔ	24 Ⓐ Ⓑ Ⓒ Ⓓ Ⓔ	34 Ⓐ Ⓑ Ⓒ Ⓓ Ⓔ
5 Ⓐ Ⓑ Ⓒ Ⓓ Ⓔ	15 Ⓐ Ⓑ Ⓒ Ⓓ Ⓔ	25 Ⓐ Ⓑ Ⓒ Ⓓ Ⓔ	35 Ⓐ Ⓑ Ⓒ Ⓓ Ⓔ
6 Ⓐ Ⓑ Ⓒ Ⓓ Ⓔ	16 Ⓐ Ⓑ Ⓒ Ⓓ Ⓔ	26 Ⓐ Ⓑ Ⓒ Ⓓ Ⓔ	36 Ⓐ Ⓑ Ⓒ Ⓓ Ⓔ
7 Ⓐ Ⓑ Ⓒ Ⓓ Ⓔ	17 Ⓐ Ⓑ Ⓒ Ⓓ Ⓔ	27 Ⓐ Ⓑ Ⓒ Ⓓ Ⓔ	37 Ⓐ Ⓑ Ⓒ Ⓓ Ⓔ
8 Ⓐ Ⓑ Ⓒ Ⓓ Ⓔ	18 Ⓐ Ⓑ Ⓒ Ⓓ Ⓔ	28 Ⓐ Ⓑ Ⓒ Ⓓ Ⓔ	38 Ⓐ Ⓑ Ⓒ Ⓓ Ⓔ
9 Ⓐ Ⓑ Ⓒ Ⓓ Ⓔ	19 Ⓐ Ⓑ Ⓒ Ⓓ Ⓔ	29 Ⓐ Ⓑ Ⓒ Ⓓ Ⓔ	39 Ⓐ Ⓑ Ⓒ Ⓓ Ⓔ
10 Ⓐ Ⓑ Ⓒ Ⓓ Ⓔ	20 Ⓐ Ⓑ Ⓒ Ⓓ Ⓔ	30 Ⓐ Ⓑ Ⓒ Ⓓ Ⓔ	40 Ⓐ Ⓑ Ⓒ Ⓓ Ⓔ

☐ # right in section 3

☐ # wrong in section 3

SECTION 4

right in section 4

wrong in section 4

If section 4 of your test book contains math questions that are not multiple choice, continue to item 16 below. Otherwise, continue to item 16 above.

SECTION 5

right in section 5

wrong in section 5

SECTION 6

right in section 6

wrong in section 6

Time—30 Minutes   For each of the following questions, choose the best answer and darken the
30 Questions   corresponding oval on the answer sheet.*

Select the lettered word or set of words that best completes the sentence.

Example:

Today's small, portable computers contrast markedly with the earliest electronic computers, which were ----.

(A) effective
(B) invented
(C) useful
(D) destructive
(E) enormous

1   More insurers are limiting the sale of property insurance in coastal areas and other regions ---- natural disasters.

(A) safe from
(B) according to
(C) despite
(D) which include
(E) prone to

2   Roman legions ---- the mountain ---- of Masada for three years before they were able to seize it.

(A) dissembled . . bastion
(B) assailed . . symbol
(C) besieged . . citadel
(D) surmounted . . dwelling
(E) honed . . stronghold

3   Unlike his calmer, more easygoing colleagues, the senator was ----, ready to quarrel at the slightest provocation.

(A) whimsical
(B) irascible
(C) gregarious
(D) ineffectual
(E) benign

4   Although historians have long thought of Genghis Khan as a ---- potentate, new research has shown he was ---- by many of his subjects.

(A) tyrannical . . abhorred
(B) despotic . . revered
(C) redundant . . venerated
(D) jocular . . esteemed
(E) peremptory . . invoked

5   Jill was ---- by her employees because she often ---- them for not working hard enough.

(A) deified . . goaded
(B) loathed . . berated
(C) disregarded . . eulogized
(D) cherished . . derided
(E) execrated . . lauded

6   Reconstructing the skeletons of extinct species like dinosaurs is ---- process that requires much patience and effort by paleontologists.

(A) a nascent
(B) an aberrant
(C) a disheveled
(D) a worthless
(E) an exacting

7   Nearly ---- by disease and the destruction of their habitat, koalas are now found only in isolated parts of eucalyptus forests.

(A) dispersed
(B) compiled
(C) decimated
(D) infuriated
(E) averted

8   Deep ideological ---- and internal power struggles ---- the government.

(A) disputes . . facilitated
(B) similarities . . protracted
(C) distortions . . accelerated
(D) agreements . . stymied
(E) divisions . . paralyzed

9   Medical experts have viewed high doses of vitamins as a popular remedy whose value is, as yet, ----.

(A) medicinal
(B) prescribed
(C) recommended
(D) unproven
(E) beneficial

GO ON TO THE NEXT PAGE ➡

*The directions on the actual SAT will vary slightly.

Choose the lettered pair of words that is related in the same way as the pair in capital letters.

Example:

FLAKE : SNOW ::

(A) storm : hail
(B) drop : rain
(C) field : wheat
(D) stack : hay
(E) cloud : fog

10 TROUT : FISH ::

(A) grain : sand
(B) human : mammal
(C) river : stream
(D) chicken : egg
(E) frog : toad

11 INHALE : LUNGS ::

(A) swallow : stomach
(B) attack : heart
(C) ache : head
(D) pump : blood
(E) travel : foot

12 BRAGGART : BOAST ::

(A) laggard : tarry
(B) hypocrite : speak
(C) extrovert : brood
(D) mendicant : compromise
(E) boor : gratify

13 ALLEVIATE : PAIN ::

(A) soothe : antidote
(B) depreciate : value
(C) contract : job
(D) deviate : standard
(E) officiate : safety

14 INFURIATE : ANNOY ::

(A) admire : respect
(B) indulge : lure
(C) terrify : frighten
(D) satiate : deprive
(E) vex : startle

15 MISERLY : MAGNANIMITY ::

(A) greedy : mirth
(B) transient : stupefaction
(C) admirable : fastidiousness
(D) innocent : culpability
(E) offensive : avarice

GO ON TO THE NEXT PAGE ➡

Answer the questions below based on the information in the accompanying passages.

Questions 16–23 are based on the following passage.

In this excerpt, a Nobel Prize–winning scientist discusses ways of thinking about extremely long periods of time.

There is one fact about the origin of life which is reasonably certain. Whenever and wherever it happened, it started a very long time ago, so long
Line ago that it is extremely difficult to form any
(5) realistic idea of such vast stretches of time. The shortness of human life necessarily limits the span of direct personal recollection.

Human culture has given us the illusion that our memories go further back than that. Before
(10) writing was invented, the experience of earlier generations, embodied in stories, myths, and moral precepts to guide behavior, was passed down verbally or, to a lesser extent, in pictures, carvings, and statues. Writing has made more precise and
(15) more extensive the transmission of such information and, in recent times, photography has sharpened our images of the immediate past. Even so, we have difficulty in contemplating steadily the march of history, from the beginnings of
(20) civilization to the present day, in such a way that we can truly experience the slow passage of time. Our minds are not built to deal comfortably with periods as long as hundreds or thousands of years.

Yet when we come to consider the origin of life,
(25) the time scales we must deal with make the whole span of human history seem but the blink of an eyelid. There is no simple way to adjust one's thinking to such vast stretches of time. The immensity of time passed is beyond our ready
(30) comprehension. One can only construct an impression of it from indirect and incomplete descriptions, just as a blind man laboriously builds up, by touch and sound, a picture of his immediate surroundings.

(35) The customary way to provide a convenient framework for one's thoughts is to compare the age of the universe with the length of a single earthly day. Perhaps a better comparison, along the same lines, would be to equate the age of our earth with
(40) a single week. On such a scale the age of the universe, since the Big Bang, would be about two or three weeks. The oldest macroscopic fossils (those from the start of the Cambrian Period*) would have been alive just one day ago. Modern
(45) man would have appeared in the last 10 seconds and agriculture in the last one or two. Odysseus** would have lived only half a second before the present time.

Even this comparison hardly makes the longer
(50) time scale comprehensible to us. Another alternative is to draw a linear map of time, with the different events marked on it. The problem here is to make the line long enough to show our own experience on a reasonable scale, and yet short
(55) enough for convenient reproduction and examination. But perhaps the most vivid method is to compare time to the lines of print themselves. Let us make a 200-page book equal in length to the time from the start of the Cambrian to the present;
(60) that is, about 600 million years. Then each full page will represent roughly three million years, each line about ninety thousand years and each letter or small space about fifteen hundred years. The origin of the earth would be about seven books ago and the
(65) origin of the universe (which has been dated only approximately) ten or so books before that. Almost the whole of recorded human history would be covered by the last two or three letters of the book.

If you now turn back the pages of the book, slowly
(70) reading *one letter at a time*—remember, each letter is fifteen hundred years—then this may convey to you something of the immense stretches of time we shall have to consider. On this scale the span of your own life would be less than the width of a comma.

*Cambrian: the earliest period in the Paleozoic era, beginning about 600 million years ago.
**Odysseus: the most famous Greek hero of antiquity; he is the hero of Homer's *The Odyssey*, which describes the aftermath of the Trojan War (ca. 1200 B.C.).

16 The word *span* in line 6 most nearly means

(A) rate of increase
(B) value
(C) bridge
(D) extent
(E) accuracy

GO ON TO THE NEXT PAGE ➡

17 The phrase *to a lesser extent* in line 13, indicates that, before the invention of writing, the wisdom of earlier generations was

(A) rejected by recent generations when portrayed in pictures, carvings, or statues
(B) passed down orally, or not at all
(C) transmitted more effectively by spoken word than by other means
(D) based on illusory memories that turned fact into fiction
(E) more strongly grounded in science than in the arts

18 The author most likely describes the impact of writing (lines 14–17) in order to

(A) illustrate the limitations of the human memory
(B) provide an example of how cultures transmit information
(C) indicate how primitive preliterate cultures were
(D) refute an opinion about the origin of human civilization
(E) explain the difference between historical facts and myth

19 The word *ready* in line 29 most nearly means

(A) set
(B) agreeable
(C) immediate
(D) apt
(E) willing

20 The analogy of the "blind man" (line 32) is presented primarily to show that

(A) humans are unable to comprehend long periods of time
(B) myths and legends fail to give an accurate picture of the past
(C) human history is only a fraction of the time since life began
(D) humans refuse to learn the lessons of the past
(E) long periods of time can only be understood indirectly

21 In lines 40–44, the author mentions the Big Bang and the Cambrian Period in order to demonstrate which point?

(A) The age of the earth is best understood using the time scale of a week.
(B) Agriculture was a relatively late development in human history.
(C) No fossil record exists before the Cambrian Period.
(D) Convenient time scales do not adequately represent the age of the earth.
(E) The customary framework for thinking about the age of the universe should be discarded permanently.

22 According to lines 52–56, one difficulty of using a linear representation of time is that

(A) linear representations of time do not meet accepted scientific standards of accuracy
(B) prehistoric eras overlap each other, making linear representation deceptive
(C) the more accurate the scale, the more difficult the map is to copy and study
(D) there are too many events to represent on a single line
(E) our knowledge of pre-Cambrian time is insufficient to construct an accurate linear map

23 The author of this passage discusses several kinds of time scales primarily in order to illustrate the

(A) difficulty of assigning precise dates to past events
(B) variety of choices faced by scientists investigating the origin of life
(C) evolution of efforts to comprehend the passage of history
(D) immensity of time since life began on earth
(E) development of the technology of communication

GO ON TO THE NEXT PAGE ➡

Questions 24–30 are based on the following passage.

The following excerpt is from a speech delivered in 1873 by Susan B. Anthony, a leader in the women's rights movement of the 19th century.

Friends and fellow-citizens: I stand before you tonight under indictment for the alleged crime of having voted at the last Presidential election, without having a lawful right to vote. It shall be
(5) my work this evening to prove to you that in thus voting, I not only committed no crime, but, instead, simply exercised my citizen's rights, guaranteed to me and all United States citizens by the National Constitution, beyond the power of
(10) any State to deny.

The preamble of the Federal Constitution says: "We, the people of the United States, in order to form a more perfect union, establish justice, insure domestic tranquillity, provide for the common
(15) defense, promote the general welfare, and secure the blessings of liberty to ourselves and our posterity, do ordain and establish this Constitution for the United States of America."

It was we, the people; not we, the white male
(20) citizens; nor yet we, the male citizens; but we, the whole people, who formed the Union. And we formed it, not to give the blessings of liberty, but to secure them; not to the half of ourselves and the half of our posterity, but to the whole people—
(25) women as well as men. And it is a downright mockery to talk to women of their enjoyment of the blessings of liberty while they are denied the use of the only means of securing them provided by this democratic-republican government—the
(30) ballot.

For any State to make sex a qualification that must ever result in the disfranchisement* of one entire half of the people is a violation of the supreme law of the land. By it the blessings of
(35) liberty are forever withheld from women and their female posterity. To them this government had no just powers derived from the consent of the governed. To them this government is not a democracy. It is not a republic. It is an odious
(40) aristocracy; a hateful oligarchy of sex; this oligarchy of sex, which makes father, brothers, husband, sons, the oligarchs over the mother and sisters, the wife and daughters of every household —which ordains all men sovereigns, all women
(45) subjects, carries dissension, discord and rebellion into every home of the nation.

Webster, Worcester and Bouvier all define a citizen to be a person in the United States, entitled to vote and hold office.

(50) The one question left to be settled now is: Are women persons? And I hardly believe any of our opponents will have the hardihood to say they are not. Being persons, then, women are citizens; and no State has a right to make any law, or to enforce
(55) any old law, that shall abridge their privileges or immunities. Hence, every discrimination against women in the constitutions and laws of the several States is today null and void, precisely as is every one against Negroes.

*disfranchisement: to deprive of the right to vote.

24 In the first paragraph, Anthony states that her action in voting was

(A) illegal, but morally justified
(B) the result of her keen interest in national politics
(C) legal, if the Constitution is interpreted correctly
(D) an illustration of the need for a women's rights movement
(E) illegal, but worthy of leniency

25 Which best captures the meaning of the word *promote* in line 15?

(A) further
(B) organize
(C) publicize
(D) commend
(E) motivate

26 By saying "we, the people . . . the whole people, who formed the Union" (lines 19–21), Anthony means that

(A) the founders of the nation conspired to deprive women of their rights
(B) some male citizens are still being denied basic rights
(C) the role of women in the founding of the nation is generally ignored
(D) society is endangered when women are deprived of basic rights
(E) all people deserve to enjoy the rights guaranteed by the Constitution

GO ON TO THE NEXT PAGE ➡

27 By "the half of our posterity" (lines 23–24),
    Anthony means

    (A) the political legacy passed down from her era
    (B) future generations of male United States
        citizens
    (C) those who wish to enjoy the blessings of
        liberty
    (D) current and future opponents of the women's
        rights movement
    (E) future members of the democratic-republican
        government

28 In the fifth paragraph, lines 31–46, Anthony's
    argument rests mainly on the strategy of
    convincing her audience that

    (A) any state which denies women the vote
        undermines its status as a democracy
    (B) women deprived of the vote will eventually
        raise a rebellion
    (C) the nation will remain an aristocracy if the
        status of women does not change
    (D) women's rights issues should be debated in
        every home
    (E) even an aristocracy cannot survive without the
        consent of the governed

29 The word *hardihood* in line 52 could best be
    replaced by

    (A) endurance
    (B) vitality
    (C) nerve
    (D) opportunity
    (E) stupidity

30 When Anthony warns that "no State . . . shall
    abridge their privileges" (lines 54–55), she means
    that

    (A) women should be allowed to live a life of
        privilege
    (B) women on trial cannot be forced to give up
        their immunity
    (C) every state should repeal its outdated laws
    (D) governments may not deprive citizens of their
        rights
    (E) the rights granted to women must be decided
        by the people, not the state

**IF YOU FINISH BEFORE TIME IS CALLED, YOU MAY CHECK YOUR WORK ON
THIS SECTION ONLY. DO NOT TURN TO ANY OTHER SECTION IN THE TEST.** **STOP**

Time—30 Minutes
25 Questions

Solve each of the following problems, decide which is the best answer choice, and darken the corresponding oval on the answer sheet. Use available space in the test booklet for scratchwork.*

Notes:

(1) Calculator use is permitted.

(2) All numbers used are real numbers.

(3) Figures are provided for some problems. All figures are drawn to scale and lie in a plane UNLESS otherwise indicated.

Reference Information

$A = \frac{1}{2}bh$ $c^2 = a^2 + b^2$ Special Right Triangles $A = \pi r^2$ $C = 2\pi r$ $V = \ell wh$ $V = \pi r^2 h$ $A = \ell w$

The sum of the degree measures of the angles of a triangle is 180.
The number of degrees of arc in a circle is 360.
A straight angle has a degree measure of 180.

1 Which of the following must be equal to 30 percent of x?

(A) $30x$

(B) $3x$

(C) $\frac{3x}{10}$

(D) $\frac{3x}{100}$

(E) $\frac{3x}{1000}$

2 $(2 \times 10^4) + (5 \times 10^3) + (6 \times 10^2) + (4 \times 10^1) =$

(A)   2,564
(B)   20,564
(C)   25,064
(D)   25,604
(E)   25,640

3 On the number line shown above, the length of YZ is how much greater than the length of XY?

(A) 3
(B) 4
(C) 5
(D) 6
(E) 7

4 If $2^{x+1} = 16$, what is the value of x?

(A) 2
(B) 3
(C) 4
(D) 5
(E) 6

$(x+1)\log 2 = \log 16$

$x + 1 =$

Note: Figure not drawn to scale.

5 In the figure above, what is the value of a ?

(A) 50
(B) 55
(C) 60
(D) 65
(E) 70

6 A machine labels 150 bottles in 20 minutes. At this rate, how many minutes does it take to label 60 bottles?

(A) 2
(B) 4
(C) 6
(D) 8
(E) 10

7 If $x - 1$ is a multiple of 3, which of the following must be the next greater multiple of 3?

(A) x
(B) $x + 2$
(C) $x + 3$
(D) $3x$
(E) $3x - 3$

8 When x is divided by 5, the remainder is 4. When x is divided by 9, the remainder is 0. Which of the following is a possible value for x ?

(A) 24
(B) 45
(C) 59
(D) 109
(E) 144

9 In triangle ABC, $AB = 6$, $BC = 12$, and $AC = x$. Which of the following cannot be a value of x ?

(A) 6
(B) 7
(C) 8
(D) 9
(E) 10

10 The average of 20, 70, and x is 40. If the average of 20, 70, x, and y is 50, then $y =$

(A) 100
(B) 80
(C) 70
(D) 60
(E) 30

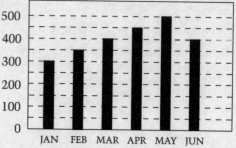

NUMBER OF BOOKS BORROWED
FROM MIDVILLE LIBRARY

11 According to the graph above, the number of books borrowed during the month of January was what fraction of the total number of books borrowed during the first six months of the year?

(A) $\frac{1}{8}$

(B) $\frac{1}{7}$

(C) $\frac{1}{6}$

(D) $\frac{3}{16}$

(E) $\frac{5}{12}$

12 If 40 percent of r is equal to s, then which of the following is equal to 10 percent of r ?

(A) $4s$

(B) $2s$

(C) $\frac{s}{2}$

(D) $\frac{s}{4}$

(E) $\frac{s}{8}$

GO ON TO THE NEXT PAGE ➡

13 In the figure above, which of the following must be true?

(A) $x + r = z + y$
(B) $x + r = z - y$
(C) $x - y = z + r$
(D) $x - r = y - z$
(E) $x + y = z + r$

14 If a *prifact number* is a nonprime integer such that each factor of the integer other than 1 and the integer itself is a prime number, which of the following is a *prifact number*?

(A) 12
(B) 18
(C) 21
(D) 24
(E) 28

15 If $3x + y = 14$, and x and y are positive integers, each of the following could be the value of $x + y$ EXCEPT

(A) 12
(B) 10
(C) 8
(D) 6
(E) 4

16 A certain deck of cards contains r cards. After the cards are distributed evenly among s people, 8 cards are left over. In terms of r and s, how many cards did each person receive?

(A) $\dfrac{s}{8 - r}$

(B) $\dfrac{r - s}{8}$

(C) $\dfrac{r - 8}{s}$

(D) $s - 8r$

(E) $rs - 8$

17 If d is an integer, which of the following CANNOT be an integer?

(A) $\dfrac{d}{2}$

(B) $\dfrac{\sqrt{d}}{2}$

(C) $2d$

(D) $d\sqrt{2}$

(E) $d + 2$

18 In the figure above, the area of triangle ABC is 6. If $BC = CD$, what is the area of triangle ACD ?

(A) 6
(B) 8
(C) 9
(D) 10
(E) 12

19 The ratio of x to y to z is 3 to 6 to 8. If $y = 24$, what is the value of $x + z$?

(A) 11
(B) 33
(C) 44
(D) 66
(E) 88

20 What is the minimum number of rectangular tiles, each 12 centimeters by 18 centimeters, needed to completely cover five flat rectangular surfaces, each 60 centimeters by 180 centimeters?

(A) 50
(B) 100
(C) 150
(D) 200
(E) 250

GO ON TO THE NEXT PAGE ➡

21 If $x + y = 11$, $y + z = 14$, and $x + z = 13$, what is the value of $x + y + z$?

(A) 16
(B) 17
(C) 18
(D) 19
(E) 20

22 In the figure above, side AB of square $ABDE$ is extended to point C. If $BC = 8$ and $CD = 10$, what is the perimeter of triangle ACD ?

(A) $18 + 6\sqrt{2}$
(B) $24 + 6\sqrt{2}$
(C) $26 + 6\sqrt{2}$
(D) 30
(E) 36

23 If $r < 0$ and $(4r - 4)^2 = 36$, what is the value of r ?

(A) -2
(B) -1
(C) $-\frac{1}{2}$
(D) $-\frac{1}{4}$
(E) $-\frac{1}{8}$

$4r - 4 = \pm 6$

$4r = 10 \quad -2$

$r = -\frac{1}{2}$

24 Five liters of water were poured from tank A into tank B, and 10 liters of water were then poured from tank A into tank C. If tank A originally had 10 more liters of water than tank C, how many more liters of water does tank C now have than tank A ?

(A) 0
(B) 5
(C) 10
(D) 15
(E) 20

25 If a cube has a surface area of $36n^2$ square feet, what is its volume in cubic feet, in terms of n ?

(A) $n^3\sqrt{6}$
(B) $6n^3\sqrt{6}$
(C) $36n^3$
(D) $36n^3\sqrt{6}$
(E) $216n^3$

$6 \cdot 6n^2 \quad \ell \cdot w$

$h = \sqrt{6n^2}$

IF YOU FINISH BEFORE TIME IS CALLED, YOU MAY CHECK YOUR WORK ON THIS SECTION ONLY. DO NOT TURN TO ANY OTHER SECTION IN THE TEST. **STOP**

250 **KAPLAN**

Time—30 Minutes   For each of the following questions, choose the best answer and darken the
35 Questions   corresponding oval on the answer sheet.

Select the lettered word or set of words that best completes the sentence.

Example:

Today's small, portable computers contrast markedly with the earliest electronic computers, which were ----.

(A) effective
(B) invented
(C) useful
(D) destructive
(E) enormous

1 The rain is so rare and the land is so ---- that few of the men who work there see much ---- in farming.

(A) plentiful . . hope
(B) barren . . difficulty
(C) productive . . profit
(D) infertile . . future
(E) dry . . danger

2 The principal declared that the students were not simply ignoring the rules, but openly ---- them.

(A) accepting
(B) redressing
(C) reviewing
(D) flouting
(E) discussing

3 Some critics believe that the ---- of modern art came with dadaism, while others insist that the movement was a ----.

(A) zenith . . sham
(B) pinnacle . . triumph
(C) decline . . disaster
(D) acceptance . . success
(E) originality . . fiasco

4 She would never have believed that her article was so ---- were it not for the ---- of correspondence that followed its publication.

(A) interesting . . dearth
(B) inflammatory . . lack
(C) controversial . . spate
(D) commonplace . . influx
(E) insignificant . . volume

5 The writings of the philosopher Descartes are ----; many readers have difficulty following his complex, intricately woven arguments.

(A) generic
(B) trenchant
(C) reflective
(D) elongated
(E) abstruse

6 The prisoner was ---- even though he presented evidence clearly proving that he was nowhere near the scene of the crime.

(A) abandoned
(B) indicted
(C) exculpated
(D) exhumed
(E) rescinded

7 Many biologists are critical of the film's ---- premise that dinosaurs might one day return.

(A) scientific
(B) tacit
(C) speculative
(D) unwitting
(E) ambiguous

8 Mozart composed music with exceptional ----; he left no rough drafts because he was able to write out his compositions in ---- form.

(A) audacity . . original
(B) facility . . finished
(C) incompetence . . ideal
(D) prestige . . orchestral
(E) independence . . concise

9 Known for their devotion, dogs were often used as symbols of ---- in Medieval and Renaissance art.

(A) resistance
(B) benevolence
(C) generosity
(D) fidelity
(E) antagonism

10 It is ---- that a people so capable of treachery and brutality should also exhibit such a tremendous capacity for heroism.

(A) unfortunate
(B) explicable
(C) paradoxical
(D) distressing
(E) appalling

GO ON TO THE NEXT PAGE ➡

Choose the lettered pair of words that is related in the same way as the pair in capital letters.

Example:

FLAKE : SNOW ::
(A) storm : hail
(B) drop : rain
(C) field : wheat
(D) stack : hay
(E) cloud : fog

11 CHARLATAN : SCRUPULOUS ::

(A) confidant : virtuous
(B) laborer : stalwart
(C) officer : mutinous
(D) dullard : irritable
(E) tyrant : just

12 GREED : ACQUIRE ::

(A) fear : disguise
(B) inertia : persuade
(C) gluttony : eat
(D) conformity : agree
(E) ignorance : speak

13 PARRY : BLOW ::

(A) counter : argument
(B) sidestep : offense
(C) defer : ruling
(D) stumble : pitfall
(E) shine : light

14 MALIGN : SLURS ::

(A) satisfy : treaties
(B) persecute : complaints
(C) torment : whispers
(D) court : debates
(E) flatter : compliments

15 LENTIL : LEGUME ::

(A) rice : cereal
(B) nutrition : food
(C) horseshoe : pony
(D) husk : corn
(E) baker : cake

16 INDULGE : APPETITE ::

(A) filter : impurity
(B) infuriate : anger
(C) coddle : emotion
(D) humor : whim
(E) liberate : freedom

17 MELLIFLUOUS : SOUND ::

(A) musical : entertainment
(B) fragrant : smell
(C) pale : color
(D) raucous : discussion
(E) auspicious : occasion

18 GUFFAW : LAUGH ::

(A) sniffle : sneeze
(B) whoop : cough
(C) yell : talk
(D) snore : sleep
(E) chuckle : sigh

19 CELESTIAL : HEAVENS ::

(A) planetary : orbit
(B) scientific : experiment
(C) nautical : ships
(D) solar : heat
(E) viscous : matter

20 ENERVATE : VITALITY ::

(A) consolidate : power
(B) energize : action
(C) daunt : courage
(D) estimate : worth
(E) admit : guilt

21 OLIGARCHY : FEW ::

(A) government : majority
(B) authority : consent
(C) constitution : country
(D) monarchy : one
(E) discrimination : minority

22 UNTRUTHFUL : MENDACIOUSNESS ::

(A) circumspect : caution
(B) timid : behavior
(C) agile : physique
(D) sensitive : patient
(E) trusting : honesty

23 INEXCUSABLE : JUSTIFY ::

(A) isolated : abandon
(B) unassailable : attack
(C) affable : like
(D) famous : admire
(E) splendid : revere

GO ON TO THE NEXT PAGE ➡

Answer the questions below based on the information in the accompanying passages.

Questions 24–35 are based on the following passage.

In the following passage, a 19th-century American writer recalls his boyhood in a small town along the Mississippi River.

My father was a justice of the peace, and I supposed he possessed the power of life and death over all men and could hang anybody that offended (5) him. This was distinction enough for me as a general thing; but the desire to be a steamboatman kept intruding, nevertheless. I first wanted to be a cabin boy, so that I could come out with a white apron on and shake a tablecloth over the side, where all my old comrades could see me. Later I (10) thought I would rather be the deck hand who stood on the end of the stage plank with a coil of rope in his hand, because he was particularly conspicuous.

But these were only daydreams—too heavenly to be contemplated as real possibilities. By and by (15) one of the boys went away. He was not heard of for a long time. At last he turned up as an apprentice engineer or "striker" on a steamboat. This thing shook the bottom out of all my Sunday-school teachings. That boy had been notoriously worldly (20) and I had been just the reverse—yet he was exalted to this eminence, and I was left in obscurity and misery. There was nothing generous about this fellow in his greatness. He would always manage to have a rusty bolt to scrub while (25) his boat was docked at our town, and he would sit on the inside guard and scrub it, where we could all see him and envy him and loathe him.

He used all sorts of steamboat technicalities in his talk, as if he were so used to them that he forgot (30) common people could not understand them. He would speak of the "labboard" side of a horse in an easy, natural way that would make you wish he was dead. And he was always talking about "St. Looy" like an old citizen. Two or three of the boys had long (35) been persons of consideration among us because they had been to St. Louis once and had a vague general knowledge of its wonders, but the day of their glory was over now. They lapsed into a humble silence, and learned to disappear when the (40) ruthless "cub" engineer approached. This fellow had money, too, and hair oil, and he wore a showy brass watch chain, a leather belt, and used no suspenders. No girl could withstand his charms. He "cut out" every boy in the village. When his boat blew up at (45) last, it diffused a tranquil contentment among us such as we had not known for months. But when he came home the next week, alive, renowned, and appeared in church all battered up and bandaged, a shining hero, stared at and wondered over by (50) everybody, it seemed to us that the partiality of

Providence for an undeserving reptile had reached a point where it was open to criticism.

This creature's career could produce but one result, and it speedily followed. Boy after boy (55) managed to get on the river. Four sons of the chief merchant, and two sons of the county judge became pilots, the grandest position of all. But some of us could not get on the river—at least our parents would not let us.

(60) So by and by I ran away. I said I would never come home again till I was a pilot and could return in glory. But somehow I could not manage it. I went meekly aboard a few of the boats that lay packed together like sardines at the long St. Louis (65) wharf, and very humbly inquired for the pilots, but got only a cold shoulder and short words from mates and clerks. I had to make the best of this sort of treatment for the time being, but I had comforting daydreams of a future when I should be a great and (70) honored pilot, with plenty of money, and could kill some of these mates and clerks and pay for them.

24 The author makes the statement that "I supposed he . . . offended him" (lines 1–4) primarily to suggest the

(A) power held by a justice of the peace in a frontier town
(B) naive view that he held of his father's importance
(C) respect in which the townspeople held his father
(D) possibility of miscarriages of justice on the American frontier
(E) harsh environment in which he was brought up

25 As used in line 4, the word *distinction* most nearly means

(A) difference
(B) variation
(C) prestige
(D) desperation
(E) clarity

26 The author decides that he would rather become a deck hand than a cabin boy (lines 6–12) because

(A) the job offers higher wages
(B) he believes that the work is easier
(C) he wants to avoid seeing his older friends
(D) deck hands often go on to become pilots
(E) the job is more visible to passersby

GO ON TO THE NEXT PAGE ➡

27 The author most likely mentions his "Sunday-school teachings" in lines 18–19 in order to emphasize

(A) the influence of his early education in later life
(B) his sense of injustice at the engineer's success
(C) his disillusionment with longstanding religious beliefs
(D) his determination to become an engineer at all costs
(E) the unscrupulous nature of the engineer's character

28 The author most likely concludes that the engineer is not "generous" (line 22) because he

(A) has no respect for religious beliefs
(B) refuses to share his wages with friends
(C) flaunts his new position in public
(D) takes a pride in material possessions
(E) ignores the disappointment of other people's ambitions

29 The author most probably mentions the use of "steamboat technicalities" (lines 28–30) in order to emphasize the engineer's

(A) expertise after a few months on the job
(B) fascination for trivial information
(C) ignorance on most other subjects
(D) desire to appear sophisticated
(E) inability to communicate effectively

30 The word *consideration* in line 35 most nearly means

(A) generosity
(B) deliberation
(C) contemplation
(D) unselfishness
(E) reputation

31 According to the passage, the "glory" of having visited St. Louis (lines 36–38) was over because

(A) the boys' knowledge of St. Louis was much less detailed than the engineer's
(B) St. Louis had changed so much that the boys' stories were no longer accurate
(C) the boys realized that traveling to St. Louis was not a mark of sophistication
(D) the engineer's account revealed that the boys' stories were lies
(E) travel to St. Louis had become too commonplace to be envied

32 The author describes the engineer's appearance (lines 41–42) primarily in order to

(A) suggest one reason why many people found the engineer impressive
(B) convey the way steamboatmen typically dressed
(C) emphasize the inadequacy of his own wardrobe
(D) contrast the engineer's behavior with his appearance
(E) indicate his admiration for fashionable clothes

33 In lines 50–52, the author's response to the engineer's survival is one of

(A) thankfulness for what he believes is God's providence
(B) astonishment at the engineer's miraculous escape
(C) reflection on the occupational hazards of a steamboating career
(D) outrage at his rival's undeserved good fortune
(E) sympathy for the extent of the engineer's wounds

34 The major purpose of the passage is to

(A) sketch the peaceful life of a frontier town
(B) relate the events that led to a boy's first success in life
(C) portray the unsophisticated ambitions of a boy
(D) describe the characteristics of a small-town boaster
(E) give a humorous portrayal of a boy's conflicts with his parents

35 At the end of the passage, the author reflects on

(A) his new ambition to become either a mate or a clerk
(B) the wisdom of seeking a job in which advancement is easier
(C) the prospect of abandoning a hopeless search for fame
(D) the impossibility of returning home and asking his parents' pardon
(E) his determination to keep striving for success in a glorious career

IF YOU FINISH BEFORE TIME IS CALLED, YOU MAY CHECK YOUR WORK ON THIS SECTION ONLY. DO NOT TURN TO ANY OTHER SECTION IN THE TEST.   **STOP**

Time—30 Minutes
25 Questions

Solve each of the following problems, decide which is the best answer choice, and darken the corresponding oval on the answer sheet. Use available space in the test booklet for scratchwork.*

Notes:

(1) Calculator use is permitted.

(2) All numbers used are real numbers.

(3) Figures are provided for some problems. All figures are drawn to scale and lie in a plane UNLESS otherwise indicated.

Reference Information

$A = \frac{1}{2} bh$ $c^2 = a^2 + b^2$ Special Right Triangles $A = \pi r^2$ $V = \ell wh$ $V = \pi r^2 h$ $A = \ell w$
$C = 2\pi r$

The sum of the degree measures of the angles of a triangle is 180.
The number of degrees of arc in a circle is 360.
A straight angle has a degree measure of 180.

DIRECTIONS FOR QUANTITATIVE COMPARISON QUESTIONS

Compare the boxed quantity in Column A with the boxed quantity in Column B. Select answer choice

  A if Column A is greater;
  B if Column B is greater;
  C if the columns are equal; or
  D if more information is needed to determine the relationship.

An E response will be treated as an omission.

Notes:

1. Some questions include information about one or both quantities. That information is centered and unboxed.
2. A symbol that appears in both Column A and Column B stands for the same thing in both columns.
3. All numbers used are real numbers.

EXAMPLES

	Column A	Column B	Answers
E1	3×4	$3 + 4$	● Ⓑ Ⓒ Ⓓ Ⓔ
E2	x	160	Ⓐ Ⓑ ● Ⓓ Ⓔ
E3	$x + 1$	$y - 1$	Ⓐ Ⓑ Ⓒ ● Ⓔ

(E2: *x*° / 20°)

x and *y* are positive

GO ON TO THE NEXT PAGE ➡

	Column A	**Column B**
1	$\dfrac{3}{8} + \dfrac{2}{5}$	1

	Column A	**Column B**
2	The cost of six pens at two for 22 cents	The cost of five pens at 22 cents each

$$2a + b = 17$$
$$b - 3 = 2$$

b - 5

	Column A	**Column B**
3	a	b

	Column A	**Column B**
4	$x - 2(y + z)$	$x - 2y - 2z$

a, b, and c are positive integers such that $a + b + c = 150$.

	Column A	**Column B**
5	The mean of a, b, and c	The median of a, b, and c

For all numbers x and y, let $x \ast y = (x + y)^3$.

	Column A	**Column B**
6	$4 \ast 5$	$0 \ast 9$

Column A   **Column B**

	Column A	**Column B**
7	The circumference of circle O	30

Jimmy owns a plant he waters every other day.

	Column A	**Column B**
8	The number of times Jimmy waters the plant during a certain week	The number of times Jimmy waters the plant during the following week

A certain line in the rectangular coordinate plane contains the points $(1, 1)$, $(3, r)$, $(s, 9)$, and $(6, 11)$.

5   4

	Column A	**Column B**
9	r	s

$$r^2 + 4 = 21$$

	Column A	**Column B**
10	r	4

GO ON TO THE NEXT PAGE ➡

Column A	**Column B**	**Column A**	**Column B**

In right triangle *RST*,
$RT = US = 6$ and $RU < 2$.

Note: Figure not drawn to scale.

11

The perimeter of *RST*	24

14

The length of *AB*	4

At a science fair, five students are semifinalists for first- and second-place prizes.

t is a positive integer.

12

The total number of ways to select the two science fair prize winners	10

15

The number of distinct prime factors of 2*t*	The number of distinct prime factors of 8*t*

$x > 0$
$0 < x^2 < 1$

13

$1 - x^2$	$1 - x$

GO ON TO THE NEXT PAGE ➡

DIRECTIONS FOR STUDENT-PRODUCED RESPONSE QUESTIONS

For each of the questions below (16–25), solve the problem and indicate your answer by darkening the ovals in the special grid. For example:

Answer: 1.25 or $\frac{5}{4}$ or 5/4

Write answer in boxes. →

Grid-in → result

Fraction line →

Decimal point →

You may start your answers in any column, space permitting. Columns not needed should be left blank.

Either position is correct.

- It is recommended, though not required, that you write your answer in the boxes at the top of the columns. However, you will receive credit only for darkening the ovals correctly.

- Grid only one answer to a question, even though some problems have more than one correct answer.

- Darken no more than one oval in a column.

- No answers are negative.

- Mixed numbers cannot be gridded. For example: the number $1\frac{1}{4}$ must be gridded as 1.25 or 5/4.

  (If $\boxed{1\,1\,/\,4}$ is gridded, it will be interpreted as $\frac{11}{4}$, not $1\frac{1}{4}$.)

- Decimal Accuracy: Decimal answers must be entered as accurately as possible. For example, if you obtain an answer such as 0.1666..., you should record the result as .166 or .167. **Less accurate values such as .16 or .17 are not acceptable.**

  Acceptable ways to grid $\frac{1}{6}$ = .1666...

---

16 If $A = 2.54$ and $20B = A$, what is the value of B ?

$B = \frac{2.54}{20} = 0.127$

$1\frac{1}{3}$ $1\frac{1}{2}$

2    $1\frac{2}{3}$ $= 9\frac{1}{2} = \frac{19}{2}$

3

17 What is the perimeter of the figure shown above?

GO ON TO THE NEXT PAGE ➡

18 If $\frac{h}{3}$ and $\frac{h}{4}$ are integers, and if $75 < h < 100$, what is one possible value of h ?

19 A retailer buys 16 shirts at \$4.50 each, and she sells all 16 shirts for \$6.75 each. If the retailer purchases more of these shirts at \$4.50 each, what is the greatest number of these shirts that she can buy with the profit she made on the 16 shirts?

16 × 4.5 = 72
16 × 6.75 = 108 − 72 = 36 ÷ 4.5

8

23 What is the area of $\triangle ABC$ shown above?

24 If x is a factor of $8,100$ and if x is an odd integer, what is the greatest possible value of x ?

20 Lines ℓ and m intersect at a point to form four angles. If one of the angles formed is 15 times as large as an adjacent angle, what is the measure, in degrees, of the smaller angle?

150/6

① = 11.25

25 In a certain class, $\frac{1}{2}$ of the male students and $\frac{2}{3}$ of the female students speak French. If there are $\frac{3}{4}$ as many girls as boys in the class, what fraction of the entire class speaks French?

$\frac{1}{2}m$ $\frac{2}{3}f$

4 boys — 8 girls

2 + 2 = 4

21 If $x = -4$ when $x^2 + 2xr + r^2 = 0$, what is the value of r ?

$(-4)^2 + 2(-4)r + r^2 = 0$

$16 + -8r + r^2 = 0$

$8r - r^2 = 16$ $r = 8, 16$

$r(8-r) = 16$

22 Let $n* = n^2 - n$ for all positive numbers n.

What is the value of $\frac{1}{4}* - \frac{1}{2}*$?

$\left[\left(\frac{1}{4}\right)^2 - \frac{1}{4}\right] - \left[\left(\frac{1}{2}\right)^2 - \frac{1}{2}\right]$

$-\frac{3}{16} - -\frac{1}{4} = \frac{1}{16}$

IF YOU FINISH BEFORE TIME IS CALLED, YOU MAY CHECK YOUR WORK ON THIS SECTION ONLY. DO NOT TURN TO ANY OTHER SECTION IN THE TEST.   **STOP**

Time—15 Minutes
13 Questions   Answer the questions below based on the information in the accompanying passages.

Questions 1–13 are based on the following passages.

The controversy over the authorship of Shakespeare's plays began in the 18th century and continues to this day. Here, the author of Passage 1 embraces the proposal that Francis Bacon actually wrote the plays, while the author of Passage 2 defends the traditional attribution to Shakespeare himself.

Passage 1

Anyone with more than a superficial knowledge of Shakespeare's plays must necessarily entertain some doubt concerning their true authorship. Can
Line scholars honestly accept the idea that such
(5) masterworks were written by a shadowy actor with limited formal education and a social position that can most charitably be called "humble"? Obviously, the author of the plays must have traveled widely, yet there is no record that Shakespeare ever left his
(10) native England. Even more obviously, the real author had to have intimate knowledge of life within royal courts and palaces, yet Shakespeare was a commoner, with little firsthand experience of the aristocracy. No, common sense tells us that the
(15) plays must have been written by someone with substantial expertise in the law, the sciences, classics, foreign languages, and the fine arts— someone, in other words, like Shakespeare's eminent contemporary, Sir Francis Bacon.
(20) The first person to suggest that Bacon was the actual author of the plays was Reverend James Wilmot. Writing in 1785, Wilmot argued that someone of Shakespeare's educational background could hardly have produced works of such erudition
(25) and insight. But a figure like Bacon, a scientist and polymath* of legendary stature, would certainly have known about, for instance, the circulation of the blood as alluded to in *Coriolanus*. And as an aristocrat, Bacon would have possessed the
(30) familiarity with court life required to produce a *Love's Labour's Lost*.
Delia Bacon (no relation to Sir Francis) was next to make the case for Francis Bacon's authorship. In 1856, in collaboration with Nathaniel Hawthorne,
(35) she insisted that it was ridiculous to look for the creator of Hamlet among "that dirty, doggish group of players, who come into the scene [of the play Hamlet] summoned like a pack of hounds to his service." Ultimately, she concluded that the plays
(40) were actually composed by a committee consisting of Bacon, Edmund Spenser, Walter Raleigh, and several others.
Still, some might wonder why Bacon, if indeed the plays were wholly or partly his work, would
(45) not put his own name on them. But consider the political climate of England in Elizabethan times. Given that it would have been politically and personally damaging for a man of Bacon's position to associate himself with such controversial plays,
(50) it is quite understandable that Bacon would hire a lowly actor to take the credit—and the consequences.
But perhaps the most convincing evidence of all comes from the postscript of a 1624 letter sent to
(55) Bacon by Sir Tobie Matthew. "The most prodigious wit that I ever knew . . . is your lordship's name," Matthew wrote, "though he be known by another." That name, of course, was William Shakespeare.

*polymath—a person of wide and varied learning

Passage 2

Over the years, there have been an astonishing
(60) number of persons put forth as the "true author" of Shakespeare's plays. Some critics have even gone so far as to claim that only a "committee" could have possessed the abundance of talent and energy necessary to produce Shakespeare's thirty-seven
(65) plays. Among the individual figures most seriously promoted as "the real Shakespeare" is Sir Francis Bacon. Apparently, the fact that Bacon wrote most of his own work in academic Latin does nothing to deter those who would crown him the premier
(70) stylist in the English language.
Although the entire controversy reeks of scholarly gamesplaying, the issue underlying it is worth considering: how could an uneducated actor create such exquisite works? But the answer to that
(75) is easy. Shakespeare's dramatic gifts had little to do with encyclopedic knowledge, complex ideas, or a fluency with great systems of thought. Rather, Shakespeare's genius was one of common sense and perceptive intuition—a genius that grows not out of
(80) book-learning, but out of a deep understanding of human nature and a keen grasp of basic emotions, passions, and jealousies.
One of the most common arguments advanced by skeptics is that the degree of familiarity with the
(85) law exhibited in a *Hamlet* or a *Merchant of Venice* can only have been achieved by a lawyer or other man of affairs. The grasp of law evidenced in these plays, however, is not a detailed knowledge of formal law, but a more general understanding of so-
(90) called "country law." Shakespeare was a landowner —an extraordinary achievement in itself for an ill-paid Elizabethan actor—and so would have been

GO ON TO THE NEXT PAGE ➡

knowledgeable about legal matters related to the buying, selling, and renting of real estate. Evidence

(95) of such a common understanding of land regulations can be found, for instance, in the gravedigging scene of *Hamlet*.

So no elaborate theories of intrigue and secret identity are necessary to explain the

(100) accomplishment of William Shakespeare. Scholars who have made a career of ferreting out "alternative bards" may be reluctant to admit it, but literary genius can flower in any socioeconomic bracket. Shakespeare, in short, was Shakespeare—an

(105) observation that one would have thought was obvious to everyone.

1   In line 2, *entertain* most nearly means

(A) amuse
(B) harbor
(C) occupy
(D) cherish
(E) engage

2   In Passage 1, the author draws attention to Shakespeare's social standing as a "commoner" (line 13) in order to cast doubt on the Elizabethan actor's

(A) aptitude for writing poetically
(B) knowledge of foreign places and habits
(C) ability to support himself by playwriting
(D) familiarity with life among persons of high rank
(E) understanding of the problems of government

3   *Coriolanus* and *Love's Labour's Lost* are mentioned in lines 28–31 as examples of works that

(A) only Francis Bacon could have written
(B) exhibit a deep understanding of human nature
(C) resemble works written by Francis Bacon under his own name
(D) portray a broad spectrum of Elizabethan society
(E) reveal expertise more likely held by Bacon than Shakespeare

4   In Passage 1, the quotation from Delia Bacon (lines 36–39) conveys a sense of

(A) disdain for the disreputable vulgarity of Elizabethan actors
(B) resentment at the way Shakespeare's characters were portrayed
(C) regret that conditions for Elizabethan actors were not better
(D) doubt that Shakespeare could actually have created such unsavory characters
(E) disappointment at the incompetence of Elizabethan actors

5   The author of Passage 1 maintains that Bacon did not put his own name on the plays attributed to Shakespeare because he

(A) regarded writing as an unsuitable occupation for an aristocrat
(B) wished to protect himself from the effects of controversy
(C) preferred being known as a scientist and politician rather than as a writer
(D) did not want to associate himself with lowly actors
(E) sought to avoid the attention that fame brings

6   In the first paragraph of Passage 2, the author calls into question Bacon's likely ability to

(A) write in a language with which he was unfamiliar
(B) make the transition between scientific writing and playwriting
(C) produce the poetic language evident in the plays
(D) cooperate with other members of a committee
(E) single-handedly create thirty-seven plays

7   The word *premier* in line 69 most nearly means

(A) earliest
(B) influential
(C) inaugural
(D) greatest
(E) original

GO ON TO THE NEXT PAGE ➡

8 In line 76, the word *encyclopedic* most nearly means

(A) technical
(B) comprehensive
(C) abridged
(D) disciplined
(E) specialized

9 The author of Passage 2 cites Shakespeare's status as a landowner in order to

(A) prove that Shakespeare was a success as a playwright
(B) refute the claim that Shakespeare had little knowledge of aristocratic life
(C) prove that Shakespeare didn't depend solely on acting for his living
(D) dispute the notion that Shakespeare was a commoner
(E) account for Shakespeare's apparent knowledge of the law

10 In lines 100–103, the author maintains that literary genius

(A) is not dependent on a writer's external circumstances
(B) must be based on an inborn comprehension of human nature
(C) is enhanced by the suffering that poverty brings
(D) frequently goes unrecognized among those of modest means and position
(E) can be stifled by too much book-learning and academic training

11 The author of Passage 2 would probably respond to the speculation in the fourth paragraph of Passage 1 by pointing out that

(A) Shakespeare's plays would not have seemed particularly controversial to Elizabethan audiences
(B) The extent and range of Bacon's learning has been generally exaggerated
(C) such scenarios are farfetched and unnecessary if one correctly understands Shakespeare's genius
(D) Bacon would not have had the knowledge of the lower classes required to produce the plays
(E) the claim implies that Shakespeare was disreputable when in fact he was a respectable landowner

12 The author of Passage 1 would probably respond to the skepticism expressed in lines 67–70 by making which of the following statements?

(A) The similarities between English and Latin make it plausible that one person could write well in both languages.
(B) Plays written in Latin would not have been likely to attract a wide audience in Elizabethan England.
(C) The premier stylist in the English language is more likely to have been an eminent scholar than an uneducated actor.
(D) Writing the plays in Latin would have shielded Bacon from much of the political damage he wanted to avoid.
(E) The style of the plays is notable mostly for the clarity of thought behind the lines rather than their musicality or beauty.

13 In line 105, "observation" most nearly means

(A) inspection
(B) measurement
(C) research
(D) comment
(E) memorandum

IF YOU FINISH BEFORE TIME IS CALLED, YOU MAY CHECK YOUR WORK ON THIS SECTION ONLY. DO NOT TURN TO ANY OTHER SECTION IN THE TEST. **STOP**

Time—15 Minutes

10 Questions

Solve each of the following problems, decide which is the best answer choice, and darken the corresponding oval on the answer sheet. Use available space in the test booklet for scratchwork.

Notes:

(1)   Calculator use is permitted.

(2)   All numbers used are real numbers.

(3)   Figures are provided for some problems. All figures are drawn to scale and lie in a plane UNLESS otherwise indicated.

$A=\frac{1}{2}bh$ $\qquad$ $c^2 = a^2 + b^2$ $\qquad$ Special Right Triangles $\qquad$ $A=\pi r^2$ $\quad$ $C=2\pi r$ $\qquad$ $V=\ell wh$ $\qquad$ $V=\pi r^2 h$ $\qquad$ $A=\ell w$

The sum of the degree measures of the angles of a triangle is 180.
The number of degrees of arc in a circle is 360.
A straight angle has a degree measure of 180.

1   If $p = -2$ and $q = 3$, then $p^3q^2 + p^2q =$

(A) -84
(B) -60
(C) 36
(D) 60
(E) 84

$(-2)^3(3)^2 + (-2)^2(3) =$

$72 + 12 =$

N	P
2	7
4	13
6	19
8	25

3   Which of the following equations describes the relationship of each pair of numbers (N, P) in the table above?

(A) $P = N + 5$
(B) $P = 2N + 3$
(C) $P = 2N + 5$
(D) $P = 3N + 1$
(E) $P = 3N - 1$

$A \quad B \quad C \; D \; E$

Note: Figure not drawn to scale.

2   In the figure above, B is the midpoint of AC and D is the midpoint of CE. If $AB = 5$ and $BD = 8$, what is the length of DE ?

(A)   8
(B)   6
(C)   5
(D)   4
(E)   3

GO ON TO THE NEXT PAGE ➡

Note: Figure not drawn to scale.

4 In the figure above, *MQ* is a straight line. If *PM* = *PN*, what is the value of *x* ?

(A) 30
(B) 45
(C) 60
(D) 75
(E) 90

5 Marty has exactly five blue pens, six black pens, and four red pens in his knapsack. If he pulls out one pen at random from his knapsack, what is the probability that the pen is either red or black?

(A) $\frac{11}{15}$

(B) $\frac{2}{3}$

(C) $\frac{1}{2}$

(D) $\frac{1}{3}$

(E) $\frac{1}{5}$

6 Two hot dogs and a soda cost $3.25. If three hot dogs and a soda cost $4.50, what is the cost of two sodas?

(A) $0.75
(B) $1.25
(C) $1.50
(D) $2.50
(E) $3.00

7 In the figure above, if *ℓ* ‖ *m*, which of the following must be equal to *a* ?

(A) *b* + *c*
(B) *b* + *e*
(C) *c* + *d*
(D) *d* + *e*
(E) *d* + *f*

8 A certain phone call costs 75 cents for the first three minutes plus 15 cents for each additional minute. If the call lasted *x* minutes and *x* is an integer greater than 3, which of the following expresses the cost of the call, in dollars?

(A) 0.75(3) + 0.15*x*
(B) 0.75(3) + 0.15(*x* + 3)
(C) 0.75 + 0.15(3 − *x*)
(D) 0.75 + 0.15(*x* − 3)
(E) 0.75 + 0.15*x*

9 The figure above shows a piece of wire in the shape of a semicircle. If the piece of wire is bent to form a circle without any of the wire overlapping, what is the area of the circle?

(A) 6π
(B) 9π
(C) 12π
(D) 18π
(E) 36π

10 If $a^2 - a = 72$, and *b* and *n* are integers such that $b^n = a$, which of the following cannot be a value for *b* ?

(A) −8
(B) −2
(C) 2
(D) 3
(E) 9

IF YOU FINISH BEFORE TIME IS CALLED, YOU MAY CHECK YOUR WORK ON THIS SECTION ONLY. DO NOT TURN TO ANY OTHER SECTION IN THE TEST. **STOP**

ANSWER KEY ON FOLLOWING PAGE ➡

Answer Key

Section 1	Section 2	Section 3	Section 4	Section 5	Section 6
1. E	1. C	1. D	1. B	1. B	1. B
2. C	2. E	2. D	2. B	2. D	2. E
3. B	3. A	3. A	3. A	3. E	3. D
4. B	4. B	4. C	4. C	4. A	4. A
5. B	5. E	5. E	5. D	5. B	5. B
6. E	6. D	6. B	6. C	6. C	6. C
7. C	7. B	7. C	7. A	7. D	7. C
8. E	8. E	8. B	8. D	8. B	8. D
9. D	9. A	9. D	9. C	9. E	9. B
10. B	10. B	10. C	10. D	10. A	10. C
11. A	11. A	11. E	11. B	11. C	
12. A	12. D	12. C	12. A	12. C	
13. B	13. D	13. A	13. A	13. D	
14. C	14. C	14. E	14. D		
15. D	15. E	15. A	15. C		
16. D	16. C	16. D	16. .127		
17. C	17. D	17. B	17. 9.5 or 19/2		
18. B	18. A	18. C	18. 84 or 96		
19. C	19. C	19. C	19. 8		
20. E	20. E	20. C	20. 45/4, 11.2, or		
21. A	21. D	21. D	11.3		
22. C	22. B	22. A	21. 4		
23. D	23. C	23. B	22. 1/16, .062, or		
24. C	24. D	24. B	.063		
25. A	25. B	25. C	23. 1/8 or .125		
26. E		26. E	24. 2025		
27. B		27. B	25. 4/7 or .571		
28. A		28. C			
29. C		29. D			
30. D		30. E			
		31. A			
		32. A			
		33. D			
		34. C			
		35. E			

KAPLAN

Compute Your Raw Score

First, check your answers against the answer key on the previous page, and count up the number right and the number wrong for each section (there are boxes on your answer sheet to record these numbers). Remember not to count omissions as wrong.

Then figure out your raw scores using the table below. The Verbal raw score is equal to the total right in the three Verbal sections minus one-fourth of the number wrong in those sections. The Math raw score is equal to the total right in the three Math sections minus one-fourth of the number wrong in the two Regular Math sections and minus one-third the number wrong in the QCs. (Remember: There is no deduction for wrong answers in the Grid-ins.) Round each raw score to the nearest whole number.

Finally, use the tables on the next page to convert each raw score to a range of scaled scores.

	NUMBER RIGHT		NUMBER WRONG		RAW SCORE
SECTION 1:	☐	−[.25 x	☐]	=	☐
SECTION 3:	☐	−[.25 x	☐]	=	☐
SECTION 5:	☐	−[.25 x	☐]	=	☐
			VERBAL RAW SCORE:		☐ (ROUNDED)
SECTION 4A: (Questions 1 to 15)	☐	−[.33 x	☐]	=	☐
SECTION 4B: (Questions 16 to 25)	☐	(No wrong - answer penalty)		=	☐
SECTION 2:	☐	−[.25 x	☐]	=	☐
SECTION 6:	☐	−[.25 x	☐]	=	☐
			MATH RAW SCORE:		☐ (ROUNDED)

Convert Your Score

Verbal						Math					
Raw	Scaled	Raw	Scaled	Raw	Scaled	Raw	Scaled	Raw	Scaled	Raw	Scaled
−3 or		22	450	48	620	−1 or		19	440	40	600
less	200	23	460	49	630	less	200	20	450	41	610
−2	230	24	470	50	640	0	220	21	460	42	620
−1	270	25	470	51	640	1	240	22	470	43	630
0	290	26	480	52	650	2	260	23	480	44	640
1	300	27	490	53	660	3	280	24	480	45	650
2	310	28	490	54	670	4	300	25	490	46	650
3	320	29	500	55	670	5	310	26	500	47	660
4	330	30	510	56	670	6	330	27	510	48	670
5	330	31	510	57	680	7	340	28	520	49	680
6	340	32	520	58	690	8	350	29	520	50	690
7	350	33	530	59	690	9	360	30	530	51	700
8	360	34	530	60	700	10	370	31	530	52	720
9	370	35	540	61	710	11	380	32	540	53	730
10	370	36	550	62	720	12	390	33	550	54	740
11	380	37	550	63	730	13	400	34	560	55	760
12	390	38	560	64	730	14	410	35	560	56	770
13	390	39	570	65	740	15	420	36	570	57	780
14	400	40	570	66	750	16	430	37	580	58	790
15	410	41	580	67	760	17	430	38	590	59	800
16	410	42	590	68	770	18	440	39	600	60	800
17	420	43	590	69	780						
18	430	44	600	70	790						
19	430	45	600	71 or							
20	440	46	610	more	800						
21	450	47	610								

Don't take these scores too literally. Practice test conditions cannot precisely mirror real test conditions. Your actual SAT scores will almost certainly vary from your practice test scores.

Your score on the practice test gives you a rough idea of your range on the actual exam. If you don't like your score, it's not too late to do something about it. Work your way way through this book again, and turn to Kaplan's *SAT Verbal Workbook* and *SAT Math Workbook* for even more help.

Practice Test One Answers and Explanations

SECTION 1

1. E

It's easy enough to understand that insurers don't like to insure property in places where natural disasters are likely to happen. The term **prone to** in (E) means "having a tendency to," so it is correct.

2. C

If it took Roman legions three years to seize Masada, we can predict that they spent a long time "surrounding or isolating" the mountain "fortress or stronghold" of Masada before they were finally able to take it. (C) is the best choice. (B) **assailed**, meaning "attacked," would make sense in the first blank, and (E) **stronghold** and (A) **bastion** would fit, too. But (A), (B), and (E)'s first-position words don't make sense when plugged in.

> *besieged: surrounded with armed forces*
> *citadel: fortress*
> *assailed: attacked*
> *bastion: fortified area*
> *dissembled: concealed*
> *honed: sharpened*

3. B

If the senator was **unlike** "his calmer, more easygoing colleagues" and "ready to quarrel at the slightest provocation," it's fair to infer that the senator was short-tempered or extremely irritable. The best choice is (B)—**irascible**.

> *irascible: easily angered*
> *whimsical: fanciful, erratic, or*
>   *unpredictable*
> *gregarious: sociable, friendly*
> *ineffectual: futile, unproductive*
> *benign: harmless or gentle*

4. B

You don't have to know that Genghis Khan was a violent dictator to get this question right. What's important to know is that the first word of the sentence, *although*, implies that the two blanks have to contain words that contrast with each other. (B) is the best choice—although historians had thought that Genghis Khan was a **despotic** potentate, new research shows that many of his subjects nevertheless **revered** him. Although (A) **tyrannical** is synonymous with *despotic*, (A)'s second-blank choice, **abhorred**, doesn't provide the predicted contrast. Choice (C) **venerated** doesn't really contrast with **redundant**. And in (E), it doesn't make sense to say that Khan's subjects **invoked** him despite his **peremptory** reputation.

> *despotic: oppressive, dictatorial*
> *potentate: dictator*
> *revered: worshiped, adored*
> *abhorred: hated*
> *venerated: highly respected*
> *redundant: repetitive*
> *jocular: jolly*
> *peremptory: putting an end to debate*
> *invoke: call upon for help*

5. B

The word *because* in the middle of the sentence lets us know that the words in the blanks will be consistent in meaning, which means that they will share the same type of charge. We can predict two positive words, like "Jill was appreciated by her employees because she often forgave" the fact that they were lazy, or two negative words like "Jill was disliked by her employees because she often scolded them" for being lazy. (B) matches the latter prediction—Jill was **loathed** by her employees because she often **berated** them for not working hard enough. No other choice besides (B) contains two like charges.

---

loathed: hated
berated: scolded
deified: made godlike
lauded: praised or celebrated
derided: made fun of
execrated: condemned, cursed

---

6. E

If "reconstructing the skeletons of extinct species like dinosaurs . . . requires much patience and effort by paleontologists," we can predict that such an activity is a "painstaking or tough, demanding process." (E) **exacting** is our best choice.

---

exacting: requiring lots of attention and
   extreme accuracy
nascent: introductory or starting
aberrant: abnormal

---

7. C

Because of disease and the destruction of their habitat, koalas are now found only in isolated parts of eucalyptus forests. The word in the blank must mean something like "killed off" or "destroyed," since things like "disease and habitat destruction" are destructive processes. (C) is our best choice—"nearly **decimated** or wiped out by disease and habitat destruction," koalas are now found only in isolated parts of eucalyptus forests. (A) **dispersed,** meaning "scattered," may have been a little tempting, but there's no reason to assume that the koalas were scattered around the forests due to "disease and habitat destruction."

dispersed: scattered
compiled: categorized, collected,
   arranged
averted: avoided

---

8. E

Looking at the first blank first, if there were "internal power struggles" in the government, then it's likely that the government had something like "deep ideological differences or conflicts." For the second blank, we can predict that these conflicts and power struggles harmed or crippled the government. Although choice (C)'s first-blank choice, **distortions,** sounds negative, like "differences or conflicts," choices (A) and (E) make *more* sense. We can easily imagine "deep ideological **disputes**" or "deep ideological **divisions**" going hand in hand with "internal power struggles," but it's hard to imagine ideological **distortions.**

Now we can turn to (A) and (E)'s second-blank choices. (A) doesn't make sense given the context of the sentence—why would "deep ideological **disputes** and internal power struggles **facilitate** the government"? (E) is the best choice—"deep ideological **divisions** and internal power struggles **paralyzed** the government."

---

distortions: perversions, twisted
   versions
facilitate: assist
stymied: frustrated, impeded

---

9. D

The terms *popular remedy* and *as yet* are key in this sentence. Large doses of vitamins are popularly thought to be good, but their effectiveness has not been proven at this time. (D) **unproven** is the correct answer. Answer choices (A), (B), (C), and (E) are wrong because they imply that medical experts understand and approve of large doses, which clearly contradicts the sentence.

10. B

A **TROUT** is a type of **FISH**, just as a **human** is a type of **mammal.**

11. A

Bridge: If you **INHALE** something, it goes into your **LUNGS.** If you **swallow** something, it goes into your **stomach.**

12. A

A **BRAGGART** is, by definition, someone who **BOAST**s. A **laggard** is, by definition, someone who **tarries.** A speaker, not a **hypocrite,** is someone who, by definition, **speaks,** so (B) is wrong.

> *laggard: lingerer, one who lags behind*
> *extrovert: someone very outgoing*
> *tarry: to dawdle, be late, delay*
> *hypocrite: someone who pretends to be what he or she is not*

13. B

To **ALLEVIATE** is to reduce **PAIN,** just as to **depreciate** is to reduce **value.** In choice (D), to **deviate** is to move away from some set **standard.** That's not the same as lowering a **standard.**

14. C

Bridge: To **INFURIATE** someone is to **ANNOY** him or her a great deal. In correct choice (C), to **terrify** someone is to **frighten** him or her a great deal.

> *satiate: to satisfy*

15. D

Someone **MISERLY** is not characterized by **MAGNANIMITY,** or generousness. Similarly, someone **innocent** is not characterized by **culpability.**

> *transient: wandering from place to place*
> *stupefaction: overwhelming amazement*
> *fastidiousness: the quality of being painstaking or particular*
> *avarice: greed*
> *magnanimity: generosity*
> *culpability: guilt*

The Time Passage

Next up is a fairly abstract science passage. This particular passage is perhaps a little bit harder than the ones you're going to encounter on the test—but don't be intimidated by the subject matter. Even if your passage is written by a Nobel Prize winner, it's going to contain ideas that you can relate to, and probably some ideas that you've seen before.

The topic of the passage is how difficult it is to comprehend long stretches of time. Paragraph two tells us that our minds aren't built to handle the idea of thousands of years passing. We have *some* conception of the past through the art, writing, and photography of previous generations, but the scale of longer time periods eludes us. Paragraphs four and five attempt to bridge this gap by providing a few everyday yardsticks; the time the human race has been around is compared to a few seconds in a week, or a few letters in a book. Essentially, that's all you need to take from your first reading of the passage; the details you can come back to later.

16. D

Here, in paragraph one, the author's talking about why we find it difficult to understand vast stretches of time. We're told that the "span" of what we can remember is limited because our lives are relatively short. So *span* in this context means the *amount* of time we're able to recollect—the (D) **extent.**

(A) **rate of increase,** (B) **value,** and (E) **accuracy** are all correct definitions of *span,* but they're not aspects of memory as discussed in the passage. And (C) **bridge,** the most common definition, doesn't fit at all.

HINT: *The golden rule about vocabulary questions on the Critical Reading section is that they test vocabulary IN CONTEXT. You're being asked how a particular word is used in the passage, not how it's usually defined.*

17. C

Before writing, we're told, the wisdom of generations was passed down in two ways—verbally, and "to a lesser extent," in pictures, carvings, and statues. This means that the wisdom of the past was transmitted less effectively by nonverbal means, and thus (C) **more effectively by the spoken word than by other means.**

Choices (A) and (B) *distort* this idea. Nowhere are we told that wisdom was rejected. And since spoken words *and* pictures were both used, it was obviously not an all or nothing proposition. (E) doesn't make much sense. How could there be an emphasis on science before writing existed? (D), finally, makes no sense at all—the author never says that all ancient wisdom was fiction.

18. B

This is a Little Picture question asking about the purpose of a detail. The question asks why the author discusses the impact of writing. Looking at the lines around the line reference given, we're told that writing has made the transmission of information about the past a lot more precise and extensive. Pictures and photography are also mentioned as ways in which the experience of the past has been passed down. So choice (B)'s correct here—writing is mentioned as an **example** of how cultures record knowledge about the past.

(A) is a distortion—the author is showing us something about the past, not why we remember hardly anything. He never implies any criticism of preliterate cultures, so choice (C) is out too. Choices (D) and (E) are wrong because the author never mentions them in the context referred to or in the whole passage.

19. C

Another Vocabulary-in-Context question. The word *ready* can mean several things—choices (A), (C), (D), and (E) are all possible meanings. In this context, however, it most nearly means **immediate,** choice (C). In the sentence before the cited line, the author says

"there is no simple way" to understand vast stretches of time. And in the sentence following the cited line, the author compares the way we understand time to the way a blind man "laboriously" constructs a picture of his surroundings. This implies that our understanding of time is a difficult and time-consuming task, not something we can do *readily* or **immediately.**

20. E

Another question asking about the *purpose behind* part of the author is argument. Give the context a quick scan. Once again, the author's talking about how difficult it is to understand vast stretches of time. We're told that it's like a blind man building up a sensory picture of his surroundings. This is an **indirect** process, so choice (E) is right.

Choice (C) is dealt with later in paragraph four, so you can eliminate it right away.

Choice (A) is too sweeping. The author never says that human beings are *completely* **unable to comprehend time.** (B) and (D) have nothing to do with the passage.

21. A

Inference skills are required here. What is the author's underlying point in mentioning the Big Bang and the Cambrian Period? The author *introduces* this discussion in the cited passage by saying that **a week** provides a better yardstick for the age of the earth than a day. The Big Bang and the Cambrian Period are used as examples to support this point. So (A) is right—it's the point about the time scale that the author's trying to demonstrate.

Choices (D) and (E) both distort the point in different ways. The author is not suggesting that the time scale of a day should be totally abandoned—just that the week is a better scale. The development of (B) **agriculture** is another supporting example like the Big Bang and the Cambrian Period, but it's not the author's central point here. Finally, **fossils** have nothing to do with the question at hand, so (C) is easily eliminated.

22. C

A more straightforward comprehension question this time. When we go back to the lines referred to, we're told about the problem with linear maps: When you produce one that's big enough to show us on it, the map becomes too big to study and reproduce conveniently. (C) gets the right paraphrase here. Notice especially the match up in synonyms for "convenient reproduction" and "examination."

(A), (B), and (E) aren't supported here—there's nothing about **overlapping** periods, **scientific standards,** or ignorance about **pre-Cambrian times** in the passage. (D) doesn't address the problem. The question is about getting our human experience on the map.

23. D

What's the overall point the author is trying to prove?

The Big Picture is that life started on earth so long ago that it is difficult for us to comprehend. Everything that follows is meant to illustrate this point, including the time scales. Don't let the material confuse you. The point is (D)—**the immensity of time** since the origin of **life.**

(C) is tricky to reject because it's an aspect of the larger argument, but it's not the whole point. The other wrong choices mention issues that the author hardly touches on. In paragraphs four to six, the author's *not* concerned with getting dates right (A), the question of how life actually began (B), or the (E) **development of communication.**

The Susan B. Anthony Passage

This humanities passage is from a speech by Susan B. Anthony, a 19th-century women's rights leader. Anthony admits at the outset that she was recently charged with the "crime" of voting. Her intention is to prove that her vote was no crime, but rather the exercise of her Constitutional rights, which no state should be allowed to impinge upon. This generates the passage's big idea: that Anthony—and by extension all women—should be allowed to vote. You may have found Anthony's style a little dated or confusing. Don't worry; the questions will help you focus on specific details.

24. C

The important thing here is to see what exactly Anthony is saying. The question stem is keyed to the first paragraph. In the second sentence she states that she "not only committed no crime, but . . . simply exercised my citizen's rights, guaranteed me . . . by the National Constitution." The words *no crime* are the first important clue. You can immediately rule out (A) and (E) because they say she believes the act was illegal. The second part of the line discusses the Constitution, so (C) is clearly a restatement of her argument.

(B) and (D) both make sense, but she does not state these points in the first paragraph. Therefore, they are wrong.

25. A

The most common meaning of "promote" is to move up—to a higher position, rank, or job. This doesn't make sense, though, in the phrase "promote the general welfare." "General welfare" means the good of all people, so to (A) **further** it, makes the most sense.

(B) **organize** and (C) **publicize** both could apply to the general welfare, but not as well as (A). They refer more to promotion as you would do with a concert or sports event. (D) **commend** means "praise," which seems silly in the context given, as does (E) **motivate.**

HINT: *In Vocabulary-in-Context questions, the right answer is usually not the most common meaning of the given word. Be sure to reread the context.*

26. E

Anthony points out that no subgroup was excluded by the wording of the preamble of the Constitution. " . . . we formed it . . . to secure [the blessings of liberty,] not to the half of ourselves . . . but to . . . women as well as men." Therefore (E) is correct. **All people deserve to enjoy the rights** of **the Constitution.**

Anthony never claims that the Founding Fathers plotted to deny women their rights (A). (B) is incorrect because the author's concern is women's rights and not rights of any other group. Though **some male citizens may still be denied basic rights,** (B) goes against the gist of what is being said. (C) is like (A) in that it's a claim Anthony never makes. Finally, though (D) is a point that Anthony does make, she doesn't make it until the next paragraph.

27. B

We're still looking at the same part of the passage.

Look at the structure of the quoted sentence: "We didn't do it only for X, but for X *and* Y." *Posterity* means "future generations," which would include men and women. So the X, the "half of our posterity," refers to the posterity of those who already enjoy the blessings of liberty. In other words, men. (B) is the right choice.

(A) has nothing to do with what Anthony is discussing. Since the construction of the sentence makes it clear that the "half of our posterity" is not the whole of those who want to vote, (C) is out. There's no way of saying that one-half of the people are and will be opponents of women's rights, so (D) is wrong. And (E) wrongly suggests that in the future, one half of the country's population will be members of government.

28. A

Reread the keyed paragraph. Anthony is saying that a state that prohibits women from voting violates federal law—the Constitution. Therefore it becomes "an odious aristocracy, a hateful oligarchy." Neither of these things is a democracy. (A) is the correct answer.

Anthony mentions rebellion, but she doesn't mean the kind of violent rebellion (B) talks about. (C) is wrong because of the word *remain*. The nation is not and never has been an aristocracy. (D) plays off the same sentence as (B) does, but instead of going too far, it doesn't go far enough. Anthony wants the laws against women voting repealed; she doesn't want them merely discussed. (E) is totally wrong because at no point is Anthony arguing that an aristocracy should be preserved.

29. C

You might readily associate *hardihood* with (A) **endurance** and (B) **vitality,** but a quick check back in context shows you these aren't correct. Anthony says she doesn't believe her opponents would have the ---- to say women aren't "persons." Saying such an offensive thing would take a lot of **nerve,** choice (C). It might also take a lot of **stupidity** (E), but that's too strong a word, considering Anthony's diplomatic tone.

30. D

The stem keys you to the second to last sentence of the passage. *Abridge* means "deprive," so Anthony is saying that no state can deprive citizens of their rights. (D) states exactly this.

In (A), *privilege* means "luxury," but voting is a basic right, not a luxury. (B) comes out of nowhere; there's no discussion of courts in this passage. (C) plays off Anthony's reference to "any old law." She's not talking about *any* outdated laws in this passage; she means any law *that prohibits women from voting*. Anthony never addresses how the laws will be changed, only that they must be changed, so (E) is out.

---

antagonism: hostility

SECTION 2

1. C

Use the formula Percent × Whole = Part.

30 percent is $\frac{30}{100}$, or $\frac{3}{10}$. So $\frac{3}{10} \times x$ = part, and choice (C) is correct.

2. E

$2 \times 10^4 = 20,000$. $5 \times 10^3 = 5,000$. $6 \times 10^2 = 600$. $4 \times 10^1 = 40$. So the sum is 25,640.

3. A

Find the length of each segment, and then subtract the length of XY from the length of YZ. Y is at 3 on the number line and Z is at 8, so the length of YZ is $8 - 3 = 5$. X is at 1 on the number line and Y is at 3, so the length of XY is $3 - 1 = 2$. So the length of YZ is $5 - 2 = 3$ greater than the length of XY.

4. B

To find the value of x, you need to change 16 into a power of 2: $16 = 2^4$. Therefore, $2^{x+1} = 2^4$. So $x + 1 = 4$, or $x = 3$.

5. E

The number of degrees around a point is 360. Therefore:

$$90 + 30 + 2a + 30 + a = 360$$
$$150 + 3a = 360$$
$$3a = 210$$
$$a = 70$$

6. D

If a machine labels 150 bottles in 20 minutes, it labels 15 bottles every 2 minutes. To label 60, or 4×15, bottles would take 4×2, or 8 minutes.

7. B

To find the next multiple of 3, simply add 3 to the expression: $x - 1 + 3 = x + 2$, choice (B).

If this is unclear, pick a number for x. If $x = 4$, $4 - 1 = 3$; the next greatest multiple of 3 is 6. Plugging 4 for x into each answer choice, we find that only choice (B) gives us 6.

8. E

Since x leaves a remainder of 4 when divided by 5, it must end in either a 4 or a 9, so choice (B) can be eliminated. Since x leaves no remainder when divided by 9, it is evenly divisible by 9. Of the remaining choices only 144 is divisible by 9.

9. A

The sum of the lengths of any two sides of a triangle must be greater than the length of the third side. So $AB + AC$ must be greater than BC; $6 + x > 12$. If $x = 6$, $6 + 6 = 12$ is not greater than 12, so x cannot equal 6.

10. B

Number of terms × average = sum of the terms. For the first group, $3 \times 40 = 120$, so the sum of 20, 70, and x is 120. For the second group, $4 \times 50 = 200$, so $20 + 70 + x + y = 200$. Since the sum of the first three terms is 120, $120 + y = 200$, $y = 80$.

11. A

Looking at the graph, you can see that the number of books borrowed in January was 300. To find the total number of books borrowed during the first six months of the year, add the values of each bar: $300 + 350 + 400 + 450 + 500 + 400 = 2,400$ books. So the number of books borrowed in January is $\frac{300}{2400}$ or $\frac{1}{8}$ of the total number of books borrowed during the first six months of the year.

12. D

We're told that 40% of $r = s$. The value of 40% of r is 4 times the value of 10% of r, so 10% of $r = \frac{1}{4} \times s = \frac{s}{4}$.

An alternative method is to pick numbers. Since you're dealing with percents, let $r = 100$. 40% of $r = s$, so 40% of $100 = 40 = s$. You're asked which answer choice is equal to 10% of r; 10% of $100 = 10$. Now plug the value for s into the answer choices to see which ones give you 10:

(A) $4s = 4 \times 40 = 160$. Eliminate.

(B) $2s = 2 \times 40 = 80$. Eliminate.

(C) $\frac{s}{2} = \frac{40}{2} = 20$. Eliminate.

(D) $\frac{s}{4} = \frac{40}{4} = 10$. Works!

(E) $\frac{s}{8} = \frac{40}{8} = 5$. Eliminate.

Since (D) is the only choice that produces the desired result, it is the correct answer. But remember, when picking numbers you need to check all the answer choices; if more than one works, pick new numbers and plug them in until only one answer choice works.

13. D

The two overlapping triangles share a common angle, which we can label $p°$. Since the interior angles of any triangle add up to 180°, we have two equations: $x + z + p = 180$ and $y + r + p = 180$. Subtracting p from both sides of each equation, we have $x + z = 180 - p$ and $y + r = 180 - p$. Since $x + z$ and $y + r$ both equal the same quantity, $x + z$ and $y + r$ must be equal to each other. Rearranging $x + z = y + r$, we get $x - r = y - z$, which matches choice (D).

14. C

Check the answer choices. If a number has even one factor (not including 1 and itself) that is not a prime number, eliminate that choice:

(A) 12: 4 is not prime. Eliminate.

(B) 18: 6 is not prime. Eliminate.

(C) 21: 3 and 7 are its only other factors, and both are prime. Correct!

(D) 24: 6 is not prime. Eliminate.

(E) 28: 4 is not prime. Eliminate.

15. E

Try different possible values for x and y, eliminating the incorrect answer choices. Since x is multiplied by 3, let's begin with the smallest positive integer value for x: 1. If $3(1) + y = 14$, then $y = 11$, and $x + y = 12$. So choice (A) is out.

If $3(2) + y = 14$, then $y = 8$, and $x + y = 10$. So choice (B) is out. If $3(3) + y = 14$, then $y = 5$, and $x + y = 8$. So choice (C) is also out. If you're really clever, you'll see at this point that answer choice (E) is impossible (which makes it the right choice). After all, the next smallest possible value of x is 4, and since x and y must both be positive integers, neither one can equal 0. (Zero is *not* positive—or negative.) So the sum of x and y must be greater than 4. (Sure enough, if $x = 4$, then $y = 2$, and $x + y = 6$, eliminating choice (D) as well.)

16. C

When the r cards are distributed, there are 8 left over, so the number of cards distributed is $r - 8$. Divide the number of cards distributed by the number of people. Since there are s people, each person gets $\frac{r - 8}{s}$ cards.

Another approach is to pick numbers. Let $r = 58$ and $s = 10$; if $58 - 8$ or 50 cards were distributed evenly among 10 people, each would receive 5 cards. Plug the values you picked for r and s into the answer choices to see which ones give you 5:

(A) $\frac{s}{8 - r} = \frac{10}{8 - 58} = -\frac{1}{5}$. Eliminate.

(B) $\frac{r - s}{8} = \frac{58 - 10}{8} = 6$. Eliminate.

(C) $\frac{r - 8}{s} = \frac{58 - 8}{10} = 5$. Works!

(D) $s - 8r = 10 - (8 \times 58) = -454$. Eliminate.

(E) $rs - 8 = (58 \times 10) - 8 = 572$. Eliminate.

Since (C) is the only answer choice that gives you 5, it is the correct answer. But be sure to check all the answer choices when picking numbers.

17. D

Check each answer choice to see which doesn't work:

(A) $\dfrac{d}{2}$: If d is an even integer, say 2, then $\dfrac{d}{2} = \dfrac{2}{2} = 1$ is an integer. Eliminate.

(B) $\dfrac{\sqrt{d}}{2}$: If d is a perfect square with an even square root, say $d = 4$, then $\dfrac{\sqrt{4}}{2} = \dfrac{2}{2} = 1$ is an integer. Eliminate.

(C) $2d$: This will always produce an even integer; if $d = 3$, $2d = 2 \times 3 = 6$ is an integer. Eliminate.

(D) $d\sqrt{2}$ CANNOT produce an integer. An integer would result if $\sqrt{2}$ is multiplied by another multiple of $\sqrt{2}$, which is impossible because d must be an integer. So (D) is correct.

Let's check (E) just to make sure.

(E) $d + 2$: This will always produce an integer; if $d = 5$, $d + 2 = 5 + 2 = 7$ is an integer. Eliminate.

18. A

The area of a triangle $= \dfrac{1}{2}$(base $\times$ height). Since the area of $\triangle ABC$ is 6, $\dfrac{1}{2}(AB \times BC) = 6$. If you consider CD as the base of $\triangle ACD$, you will notice that its height is represented by altitude AB. So the area of $\triangle ACD = \dfrac{1}{2}(CD \times AB)$. Since $CD = BC$, the area of $\triangle ACD$ can be expressed as $\dfrac{1}{2}(BC \times AB)$, which you know equals 6.

19. C

Since the ratio of x to y to z is 3:6:8, if $y = 24$ or 4×6, x and z must also be multiplied by 4 for the ratio to hold. So $x = 4 \times 3 = 12$ and $z = 4 \times 8 = 32$, and $x + z = 44$.

20. E

Each of the five surfaces is 60 by 180 centimeters, so tiles measuring 12 by 18 centimeters can be laid down in 5 rows of 10 to exactly cover one surface. There are 5 surfaces so $5 \times 5 \times 10 = 250$ tiles are needed.

21. D

If you add the 3 equations together, you find that $2x + 2y + 2z = 38$; dividing both sides by 2 shows that $x + y + z = 19$, answer choice (D).

22. B

The perimeter of triangle $ACD = AD + AB + BC + CD$. You are given the lengths of BC and CD, so you need to find the lengths of AD and AB. Angle DBC is a right angle because it is supplementary to $\angle DBA$, one of the 4 right angles of square $ABDE$. Since right triangle DBC has sides of length 8 and 10, you should recognize it as a 6-8-10 right triangle (a multiple of the 3-4-5 right triangle) and realize that $BD = 6$. (If you didn't recognize this, you could have used the Pythagorean theorem to find the length of BD.) BD is also a side of the square and since all sides of a square are equal, $AB = 6$.

So triangle DBA is an isosceles right triangle with sides in the ratio of $1:1:\sqrt{2}$. That means hypotenuse AD is equal to the length of a side times $\sqrt{2}$, so $AD = 6\sqrt{2}$. Now you can find the perimeter of triangle ACD: $6\sqrt{2} + 6 + 8 + 10 = 24 + 6\sqrt{2}$.

23. C

$(4r - 4)^2 = 36$, so $4r - 4$ could equal 6 or -6, since the result is 36 when each of these integers is squared. But the problem states that $r < 0$, so try -6. $4r - 4 = -6$, $4r = -2$, and $r = -\dfrac{2}{4} = -\dfrac{1}{2}$, answer choice (C). (If you try $4r - 4 = 6$ you'll find $r = 2\frac{1}{2}$, which cannot be correct for this question since $r < 0$.)

24. D

Tank A originally contained 10 more liters of water than tank C, so represent the initial number of liters in each tank in terms of tank A:

tank $A = a$

tank $C = a - 10$

5 liters of water are poured from A to B, and an additional 10 liters are poured from A to C. A total of 15 liters are removed from tank A so it now contains $a - 15$ liters of water. 10 liters are added to tank C so it now contains $a - 10 + 10 = a$ liters. So tank C contains 15 more liters of water than tank A.

25. B

The surface area of a cube is $6e^2$, where $e =$ the length of an edge of the cube. Since the surface area is $36n^2$:

$$6e^2 = 36n^2$$
$$e^2 = 6n^2$$
$$e = n\sqrt{6}$$

The volume of a cube is e^3. To solve for the volume in terms of n, plug in the value for an edge that you just found: Volume $= e^3 = (n\sqrt{6})^3 = 6n^3\sqrt{6}$, answer choice (B).

SECTION 3

1. D

This is not a difficult question. The use of the word *and* tells us that we're looking for a word to fill the first blank which is consistent with "scarcity of rain"—a word like *dry*. We can, therefore, eliminate (A) and (C) at once. Since farming conditions are "bad," our second blank should express the idea that there's no point in trying to work there. By that criterion, choices (B) and (E) can be eliminated. This leaves us with (D) **future.** (D)'s first word, **infertile,** also fits perfectly, so (D) is the correct answer.

barren: not productive

2. D

The structural clue in this sentence is *not only . . . but,* which suggests that the students were doing something even worse than ignoring the rules. The only word that fits here is **flouting,** choice (D).

flouting: mocking, treating with
  contempt

3. A

The word *while* following the comma in the second part of the sentence tells us that there will be a contrast between what some critics believe about dadaism and what *others* "insist the movement was." The best choice is (A)—"some critics believe that the **zenith** of modern art came with dadaism, while others insist the movement was a **sham.**" Other choices have single words that would make sense in one of the blanks, but none of the pairs except (A) expresses the contrast that is implied by the sentence.

zenith: highest point
sham: hoax

4. C

In this question you are asked to make a logical connection between two parts of a sentence. It is clear that the content of the journalist's article either had no impact, in which case there was little or no response from the public, or it attracted a great deal of attention and was followed by a lot of correspondence. (C) is the correct answer. The author would never have thought her article was **controversial** were it not for the **spate** of correspondence. The other answer choices are wrong because they sound contradictory when plugged into the sentence. For example, in choice (A), if the article were **interesting,** one would expect it to be followed by a lot of correspondence—not by a **dearth,** or lack of it. In choice (D), if the article were **commonplace** (ordinary), why would an **influx** of letters follow its publication?

> spate: a sudden flood or rush
> dearth: lack
> inflammatory: likely to arouse strong
>   feeling or anger
> influx: flow coming in

5. E

If many readers have difficulty following Descartes's complex, intricately woven arguments, then it's likely that his writings are something like *complicated, esoteric,* or *obscure.* The best choice is (E) **abstruse.**

> abstruse: difficult to understand
> generic: common, general
> trenchant: extremely perceptive,
>   insightful

6. B

The phrase *even though* indicates contrast. So, *even though* the prisoner "presented evidence clearly proving that he was nowhere near the scene of the crime," he was **indicted** or formally charged with committing the crime.

> exculpated: absolved, proved to be
>   innocent
> exhumed: removed from a grave
> rescinded: cancelled, taken back

7. C

A *premise* is a proposition which is used as the basis for an argument—or a story. If scientists are critical of the premise for a movie, we can infer that they are so because they consider it to be unscientific, without basis in fact, or **speculative.** (C) is therefore the correct answer. (A) is wrong, because if the premise, or underlying argument, were **scientific** then it would hardly be open to criticism by scientists. (B) is wrong because there's no reason to think that the theme of the return of the dinosaurs is unexpressed in the movie.

> tacit: silent; understood but
>   unexpressed

8. B

Looking at the second blank first, if Mozart "left no rough drafts," it's probably "because he was able to write out his compositions in a complete, unrevised form." So, for the second blank, (B) **finished** looks best. (E) **concise** is also possible, so let's try (B) and (E) in the first blank. We've already seen that Mozart didn't need to revise his compositions—therefore, it makes sense to say that he "composed music with exceptional *ease* or **facility.**" (E) **independence** is just too ambiguous to fit in to the context of the sentence.

> concise: using as few words as possible,
>   to the point

9. D

If dogs are "known for their devotion," then it's likely that they "were often used as symbols of *faithfulness, loyalty,* or **fidelity**" in Medieval and Renaissance art. (A) **resistance** and (E) **antagonism** are not what we're looking for, and choices (B) and (C), while positive, don't relate to the idea of *devotion.*

> antagonism: hostility

10. C

In this sentence we find a description of two contra-dictory characteristics which exist in the same group of people. On the one hand, they are brutal; on the other, they are heroic. Such an occurrence is termed a *para-dox* and therefore (C) **paradoxical** is the correct an-swer. Choices (A), (D), and (E) are wrong; it is **unfortunate, distressing,** and **appalling** that they are brutal—but not that they are heroic.

> *paradoxical: like a riddle; opposed to common sense but true*
> *explicable: able to be explained*

11. E

A **CHARLATAN** is, by definition, not **SCRUPULOUS.** A **tyrant** is a ruler who uses power oppressively and unjustly. So a **tyrant** is, by definition, not **just.**

> *charlatan: a fraud or a quack, someone who pretends to have more knowledge or skill than he or she possesses*

12. C

GREED is the desire to **ACQUIRE** large amounts of things. **Gluttony** is the desire to **eat** large amounts, so (C) is the best answer.

(A) won't work; someone who experiences **fear** may or may not want to **disguise** himself or herself. In (B), it may be hard to **persuade** someone characterized by **inertia,** but **inertia** isn't the desire to **persuade** large amounts.

> *inertia: apathy, inactivity*

13. A

The word **BLOW** is being used to mean "a swipe or punch." To **PARRY** means "to deflect, ward off," so our bridge is "to **PARRY** a **BLOW** is to deflect it." (A) shares the same bridge—to **counter** an **argument** is to deflect it.

In choice (B), you might **sidestep** or avoid an argu-ment or issue, but there isn't really any clear connec-tion between **sidestep** and **offense.** In (C), to **defer** isn't to deflect or ward off a **ruling.**

> *pitfall: a trap or hidden danger*
> *defer: put off or delay*

14. E

By definition, **SLURS** are words that **MALIGN,** just as **compliments** are words that **flatter.** The other choices don't fit this bridge. For instance, in (C), **whispers** aren't necessarily words that **torment.**

15. A

A **LENTIL** is classified as a **LEGUME,** a bean or pea, in the same way that **rice** is classified as a **cereal.**

Even if you didn't know that a **LENTIL** is a **LEGUME,** you might have been able to arrive at the answer by eliminating all choices with no good bridges. For example, in (B) **food** may or may not provide **nutri-tion,** or nourishment.

> *husk: the outer covering of a kernel or seed*

16. D

To **INDULGE** an **APPETITE** is to satisfy it. Similarly, to **humor** a **whim** is to satisfy it.

In (A), you can **filter** out an **impurity,** but it doesn't make sense to say that to **filter** out an **impurity** is to satisfy it. (C) might have been a tempting choice, since the word **coddle** is similar to **indulge.** But **coddle** doesn't have a necessary connection to **emotion.**

> *coddle: to overindulge, pamper*

17. B

Bridge: **MELLIFLUOUS** means "sweet **SOUND**ing." **Fragrant** means "sweet **smell**ing."

In (D), a **raucous discussion** would be a harsh-sounding, noisy debate.

> *mellifluous: sweet sounding, melodious*
> *fragrant: sweet smelling*
> *raucous: harsh or grating*

18. C

By definition, a **GUFFAW** is loud, unrestrained **LAUGH**ing. In the same way, a **yell** is loud, unrestrained **talk**ing.

19. C

The word **CELESTIAL** means "having to do with the **HEAVENS**." The word **nautical** means "having to do with **ships**."

> *celestial: having to do with the heavens*
> *nautical: having to do with ships*
> *viscous: thick and gluey*

20. C

To **ENERVATE** is to lessen or decrease **VITALITY**. In (C), to **daunt** is to lessen **courage**.

You could have worked backwards by eliminating answer choices with inappropriate or weak bridges. For example, in (A), one can **consolidate power** by securing and strengthening one's position, but that bridge doesn't work with the stem words. Choice (B) has a weak bridge, too: To **energize** is to fill with energy, but that doesn't always result in **action**. If you plug the stem words into (D)'s bridge, you get, "To enervate is to assess the vitality of something." It doesn't sound sensible, so (D) is out, too. In (E) to **admit guilt** is to confess. That couldn't be true of the stem as well. By process of elimination, (C) is correct.

> *enervate: to lessen or decrease vitality*
> *daunt: to subdue or dismay*
> *energize: to fill with energy*
> *estimate: to assess the worth of something*

21. D

An **OLIGARCHY** is, by definition, a form of government in which power is held by a **FEW** people. Answer choice (D) is analogous to this: A **monarchy** is a form of government in which power is held by **one** person.

If the definition of **OLIGARCHY** posed a problem, you could again eliminate wrong answers. For instance, in choice (A), the terms **government** and **majority** are not always linked. Similarly, in (B), **authority** and **consent** don't necessarily go together. In (C), a **country** may or may not have a **constitution**.

> *oligarchy: a form of government in*
> *   which power is held by a few people*
> *monarchy: a form of government in*
> *   which power is held by one person*
> *constitution: a set of principles according*
> *   to which a nation is governed*

22. A

Bridge: Someone who is **UNTRUTHFUL** is characterized by **MENDACIOUSNESS**. Choice (A) is correct: Someone who is **circumspect** is characterized by **caution**.

What if you don't know what *mendaciousness* or *circumspect* mean? You must try to eliminate wrong answers. Remember that the stem words and the correct answer choice will have the same strong bridge. Work backwards. Does (B) have a strong bridge? A person who is **timid** exhibits a certain type of **behavior**—that's not a strong connection. Similarly, (C)'s bridge is weak: Everyone has a **physique** of some kind, not just **agile** people. Answer choices (D) and (E) can also be eliminated because they have weak bridges. That leaves us with (A).

> *mendaciousness: lying*
> *circumspect: cautious or watchful*

23. B

The bridge can be stated as: Something that is **INEX-CUSABLE** is impossible to **JUSTIFY.** Likewise, in (B), something that is **unassailable** is impossible to **attack.**

> *unassailable: not open to attack or question*
> *affable: friendly and polite*
> *revere: to feel deep respect or awe for*

The Twain Passage

This excerpt from Mark Twain's *Life on the Mississippi* should be amusing and easy to read. All the humor comes from the same technique—using deadpan, matter-of-fact language to describe the exaggerated daydreams and jealousies of a boy's life.

The central point here is the author's envy of the engineer, and many of the questions focus on this. The author starts with his own glamorous ideas about steamboating, then spends most of the passage on the show-off engineer. The passage finishes with the author's own failure to find work as a pilot. The slightly old-fashioned style isn't hard to follow, but several questions focus on the author's figurative use of words.

24. B

The key word in the sentence is *supposed.* Of course, a justice of the peace *doesn't* possess unlimited power, but because of inexperience the author "supposed" he did. (B) accurately uses *naive* (inexperienced, gullible) to characterize the author's misconception. Three of the wrong choices assume that the father really *did* have unlimited powers and explain this in different ways—frontier justice (A, D), public support (C). (E) mistakenly views the boy's description of his father as an indication that the boy's childhood environment was harsh.

25. C

Distinction has several meanings, including those in (A), (B), (C), and (E). The key to its use here is context: In the previous sentence the author is talking about his naive ideas of his father's great power. **Prestige,** (C), suggesting high status and honor, fits this context; the other three don't. (D) is not a meaning of *distinction* at all.

26. E

This question asks about the literal meaning of the sentence, but inference and context help, too. The sentence explains that the author wanted the job because a deck hand was "conspicuous," or easily seen. The previous sentence stresses standing "where all my old comrades could see me," so you can deduce that the author wants to be seen and admired in what he imagines is a glamorous profession (E).

(A) and (B) invent advantages that are not mentioned, and miss the humor by suggesting common-sense economic motivations. (C) assumes that if the author could be seen by his "old comrades" in the first job, he must want *not* to be seen by them in a different job; but this is false, since he'd be "conspicuous" in the second job, too. (D) brings in an ambition—becoming a pilot—that the author doesn't develop until the end of the passage.

27. B

Again, context helps you to figure out the answer to the question. The **Sunday-school** reference is explained in the next sentence. The engineer had been "worldly"—which is what Sunday-school probably taught students not to be—and the author had been "just the reverse." In other words, the author followed his Sunday-school teachings and the engineer didn't—yet the engineer gets the glory. The underlying idea is that this was unjust, choice (B).

(A) is never mentioned. (C) takes the Sunday-school reference literally and misses the humorous tone. (D) invents an ambition that the author never mentions; his reaction is pure envy, not frustrated ambition. (E) misconstrues the reference to the engineer as "worldly"; it means he didn't take Sunday-school seriously, not that he was **unscrupulous** (dishonest or crooked).

28. C

To get this question, you need to read the sentence that follows. The engineer was not generous because he sat about where "we all could see him and envy him." The implication is that great people should be generous by not showing off or (C) **flaunting** their success.

(A) refers to the Sunday-school comment, but that was about undeserved greatness, not lack of generosity. (B) and (D) interpret *generous* in the literal sense of not caring for money, but the author is using the word figuratively. (E) relates to the author's unfulfilled desire to work on a steamboat, but the engineer is not thinking about the author, he is just showing off.

29. D

The engineer does everything for the purpose of showing off. He talks the jargon of the trade to make himself look knowledgeable, or (D) **sophisticated.**

Reading between the lines, we realize he's not an expert (A), and doesn't care about knowledge for its own sake (B). His (C) **ignorance** on other subjects is not mentioned; in fact, he has a working knowledge of St. Louis. (E) takes literally the phrase about how the engineer "forgot common people could not understand"—he couldn't **communicate effectively.** But the author says the engineer talked "as if" he forgot common people. In other words he didn't *fail* to communicate, he *chose not* to, to impress others.

30. E

The first four choices are all common meanings of *consideration,* but the context makes it clear that the figurative use in (E) is meant. The boys had "consideration" because they knew something about St. Louis, but their glory is over because the engineer knows much more. Prestige, respect, or (E) **reputation** supplies the meaning that fits. Boys are not likely to have the qualities of **generosity, deliberation, contemplation,** or **unselfishness** as a result of knowing a little about St. Louis.

31. A

The context makes it clear that the engineer had, or at least seemed to have, much more familiarity with St. Louis than the other boys with their "vague knowledge"; their "glory" is ended because he can talk rings around them about St. Louis (A).

There's no indication that (B) **St. Louis has changed,** or that the boys had been lying—their knowledge was "vague," not false (D). Reading between the lines, it's clear that travel to St. Louis was still rare enough to seem enviable (E). As for choice (C), the passage implies just the opposite.

32. A

With his "hair oil . . . showy brass watch chain, [and] leather belt," the engineer was obviously out to impress (A). The next sentence confirms that, telling us "no girl could withstand his charms."

The author never says the young man's dress is typical (B). (C) and (E) are both wrong; the emphasis here is on the engineer's charms, not the author's wardrobe or fashion ideas. (D) won't work because the engineer's behavior is as showy and superficial as his clothes.

33. D

As often in these questions, wrong choices give flat-footed, literal interpretations where the author is being humorous. (A) misunderstands the reference to Providence—the author is criticizing providence, not thanking it, because it has spared an "undeserving reptile," the engineer. So the author feels resentment, or (D) **outrage,** because the engineer's good luck seems **undeserved.**

Choice (B) sounds believable at first, but the passage doesn't emphasize the lucky escape—it focuses on people's sense that the engineer got better than he deserved. (C) and (E) are never mentioned.

34. C

The passage focuses on the author's ambition to work on a steamboat and his envy of the engineer. This makes (C) and (D) the strongest choices, so you need to decide between them. Looking at (D), the passage certainly emphasizes the engineer's **boastfulness,** but only within the framework of the author's dreams and ambitions (paragraphs one and five) and the author's reactions to the engineer. So (C) describes the *whole* passage whereas (D) describes only the long central paragraphs. In a *major purpose/major focus* question, the answer that sums up the *whole* passage will be correct.

The (A) **life** of the **town** is barely suggested. (B) is wrong because the passage's events don't end in **success**—although in reality, Mark Twain did go on to become a pilot. The author's (E) **conflict with his parents** is mentioned only briefly, toward the end of paragraph four.

35. E

The last paragraph discusses the author's failed attempts to become a pilot, and his daydreams that he will still become one, so (E) works best. Mates and clerks are mentioned as ignoring the author, but he never considers becoming either a (A) **mate or a clerk,** looking for some other job (B), giving up his aim of being a pilot (C), or asking his parents' forgiveness (D).

SECTION 4

1. B

You could find the answer by calculating the value of Column A, but there's a shortcut. You should see that both fractions in Column A are less than $\frac{1}{2}$. Therefore, their sum must be less than 1, and Column B is greater than Column A.

2. B

The cost of 6 pens at 2 for 22 cents is $\frac{22}{2}$ cents $\times$ 6, or $0.66, which is the value of Column A. The cost of 5 pens at 22 cents each is $1.10, and that's the value of Column B. So Column B is greater, and choice (B) is correct.

3. A

You can solve for b using the second equation: $b - 3 = 2$, so $b = 5$. Plug in 5 for b in the first equation and solve for a: $2a + 5 = 17$, $2a = 12$, $a = 6$. So Column A is greater than Column B, and choice (A) is correct.

4. C

Make one column look more like the other. Perform the multiplication in Column A: $x - 2(y + z)$ becomes $x - 2y - 2z$, which is the same expression as in Column B. Therefore, choice (C) is correct.

5. D

The mean (or average) of a group of terms is equal to the sum of the terms divided by the number of terms. You don't know the values of a, b, or c, but you do know that they sum to 150. So in Column A their mean is $\frac{150}{3} = 50$. The median is the middle term in a group of terms in numerical order. All you know about *a*, *b*, and *c* is that their sum is 150. It is possible that *a* = 1, *b* = 2, and *c* = 147; if so, the median would be 2 and in this case Column A would be greater. But what if *a* = *b* = *c* = 50? Then the median would be 50 and the columns would be equal. Since more than one relationship between the columns is possible, the answer must be choice (D).

6. C

Plug the values from each column into the given expression:

Column A = $(4 + 5)^3$ or $(9)^3$.

Column B = $(0 + 9)^3$ or $(9)^3$.

Since the values in both columns are equal, choice (C) is correct.

7. A

To find the circumference of circle *O*, you need to find the length of its radius. Draw a right triangle as shown below:

The lengths of the legs of the triangle are 4 and 3. You should recognize that this is a special 3-4-5 right triangle, so the length of the hypotenuse, which is also the radius of the circle, must be 5. Since circumference = $2\pi r$, the circumference of circle *O* = 10π. Since π is approximately 3.14, the circumference of circle *O* is greater than 30; Column A is greater than Column B.

8. D

If Jimmy waters his plant every other day, the number of times he waters it in one week depends upon whether he waters it the first day of the week or not. If he does, then he will water the plant the first, third, fifth, and seventh days for a total of 4 times that week. So Column A can be 4. Then the following week he will water it on the second, fourth, and sixth days for a total of 3 times. So Column B is 3, which makes Column A greater in this case. However, it's possible that in a given week he doesn't water the plant until the second day of the week. Then he will water it only 3 times that week and 4 times the following week. In this case, Column A is 3 and Column B is 4, making Column B greater. So Column A can be either greater than or less than Column B, and the answer must be choice (D).

9. C

To find the values of *r* and *s*, you need to find the slope of the line. Plug coordinates (1, 1) and (6, 11) into the slope formula:

$$\text{Slope} = \frac{y_2 - y_1}{x_2 - x_1}$$

$$= \frac{11 - 1}{6 - 1}$$

$$= \frac{10}{5}$$

$$= 2$$

So the slope of the line is 2.

Now find the value of *r* using coordinates (1, 1) and (3, *r*):

$$2 = \frac{r - 1}{3 - 1}$$

$$2 = \frac{r - 1}{2}$$

$$4 = r - 1$$

$$5 = r$$

Then find the value of *s* using coordinates (*s*, 9) and (6, 11):

$$2 = \frac{11 - 9}{6 - s}$$

$$2 = \frac{2}{6 - s}$$

$$12 - 2s = 2$$

$$-2s = -10$$

$$s = 5$$

The values in both columns are the same, and choice (C) is correct.

10. D

$r^2 + 4 = 21$, so $r^2 = 17$. You might think this means that r in Column A is greater than 4 in Column B, since $r^2 = 17$ while 4^2 equals only 16. But r can have a positive or negative value, since a negative squared also produces a positive. If r has a positive value, Column A is greater; if r has a negative value, Column B is greater. Since more than one relationship is possible, the answer is choice (D).

11. B

The perimeter of a triangle is equal to the sum of the lengths of its sides. You're given that $RT = US = 6$ and $RU < 2$. This means that RS must be less than 8. However, if $RS = 8$, then triangle RST would be a special right triangle with side lengths in a ratio of 3:4:5. So the length of ST would be 10, and the perimeter would be $6 + 8 + 10$, or 24. But RS is less than 8, which means the perimeter must be less than 24. Therefore, Column B is greater than Column A, and choice (B) is correct.

12. A

Think of the 5 students as A, B, C, D, and E and then systematically consider all the possible winning combinations. If A wins 1st place, then B, C, D, or E could win 2nd; if B wins 1st place, then A, C, D, or E could win 2nd; if C wins 1st place, then A, B, D, or E could win 2nd; if D wins 1st place, then A, B, C, or E could win 2nd; if E wins 1st place, then A, B, C, or D could win 2nd. This is a total of 20 different combinations, so Column A is greater than 10 in Column B.

13. A

Since x^2 is a positive fraction less than 1, its positive square root, x, must also be a fraction less than 1, which you are told is positive. When a positive fraction less than 1 is squared, the result is a positive fraction smaller than the original. Therefore, $x^2 < x$.

For example, $\left(\frac{1}{2}\right)^2 < \frac{1}{2}$, since $\left(\frac{1}{2}\right)^2 = \frac{1}{4}$. So in Column A you're subtracting a positive value from 1, and in Column B you're subtracting a larger positive value from 1, so Column A must be greater.

14. D

Do not assume that $ABCD$ is a square and that $AB = BC = AD = 4$. You know that triangle ACD is an isosceles right triangle and angle CAD is a 45° angle, which means that angle BAD is a right angle. However, no information is given about the lengths of AB and BC, or whether angles ABC and BCD are right angles. If necessary, redraw the diagram to see this. So the relationship cannot be determined and answer choice (D) is correct.

15. C

To determine the number of distinct prime factors of an integer, break the integer down into its prime factors and see how many different prime factors it has. Since you don't know the value of t, there is no way to determine how many distinct prime factors it has. This isn't a problem though—since t appears as a factor in both of the columns, we can eliminate it from each without affecting the relationship between the columns. So that leaves 2 in Column A and 8 in Column B. The only prime factor of 2 is 2, and the prime factorization of 8 is $2 \times 2 \times 2$. While 2 appears as a factor three times in Column B, there is still only one distinct prime factor in each, so the columns are equal.

16. .127

If $A = 2.54$ and $20B = A$, then $20B = 2.54$. So $B = \dfrac{2.54}{20}$ or .127.

17. 9.5 or 19/2

The perimeter of the figure is equal to the sum of the lengths of its sides: $2 + 1\dfrac{1}{3} + 1\dfrac{1}{2} + 1\dfrac{2}{3} + 3 = 9\dfrac{1}{2}$, which is $\dfrac{19}{2}$ expressed as an improper fraction, or 9.5 expressed as a decimal.

18. 84 or 96

If $\dfrac{h}{3}$ and $\dfrac{h}{4}$ are both integers, then h must be a multiple of 3×4, or 12. Since it's given that h is between 75 and 100, h must be 84 or 96.

19. 8

The profit made by the retailer on the shirts is equal to the difference between the selling price and the cost for each shirt, multiplied by the number of shirts: $(\$6.75 - \$4.50) \times 16 = \$2.25 \times 16 = \$36.00$ profit. To find the number of \$4.50 shirts that can be bought for \$36.00, you need to divide \$36.00 by \$4.50, and $\dfrac{36}{4.5} = 8$.

20. 45/4 or 11.2 or 11.3

Draw a diagram and label it according to the given information:

Let the smaller angle measure $x°$. Since the other angle formed is 15 times as large, label it $(15x)°$. Notice that these two angles are supplementary, that is, they add up to $180°$. Therefore:

$$x + 15x = 180$$
$$16x = 180$$
$$x = \frac{45}{4}$$

So the smaller angle is $\dfrac{45}{4}$ degrees, which can also be gridded in decimal form as 11.2 or 11.3.

21. 4

Before you plug in -4 for x, you should factor the given equation:

$$x^2 + 2xr + r^2 = 0$$
$$(x + r)(x + r) = 0$$
$$(x + r)^2 = 0$$

Now plug in -4 for x to solve for r: $(-4 + r)^2 = 0$, $-4 + r = 0$, and $r = 4$.

22. 1/16 or .062 or .063

Plug the values into the given definition:

$$\frac{1}{4} \ast = \left(\frac{1}{4}\right)^2 - \frac{1}{4}$$
$$= \frac{1}{16} - \frac{1}{4}$$
$$= \frac{1}{16} - \frac{4}{16}$$
$$= \frac{-3}{16}$$

$$\frac{1}{2} \ast = \left(\frac{1}{2}\right)^2 - \frac{1}{2}$$
$$= \frac{1}{4} - \frac{1}{2}$$
$$= \frac{-1}{4}$$

So:

$$\frac{1}{4} \ast - \frac{1}{2} \ast = \frac{-3}{16} - \left(\frac{-1}{4}\right)$$
$$= \frac{-3}{16} - \left(-\frac{4}{16}\right)$$
$$= \frac{1}{16}$$

This can also be gridded as .062 or .063.

23. 1/8 or .125

You should recognize that right $\triangle ABC$ is a 45-45-90 triangle, with side lengths in a ratio of $1:1:\sqrt{2}$. Therefore, the length of the two equal legs AB and AC is $\frac{1}{2}$.

To find the area of the triangle, plug the values of the base and height (the lengths of the two equal legs) into the area formula:

Area of a triangle $= \frac{1}{2}(\text{base} \times \text{height})$

$$= \frac{1}{2}\left(\frac{1}{2}\right)^2$$

$$= \frac{1}{2}\left(\frac{1}{4}\right)$$

$$= \frac{1}{8}, \text{ or } .125$$

24. 2025

You're given that x is a factor of 8,100 and it's an odd integer. To find the greatest possible value of x, begin factoring 8,100 by using its smallest prime factor, 2, as one of the factors. Continue factoring out a 2 from the remaining factors until you find an odd one as shown below:

8,100

2 × 4,050

2 × 2,025

Since 2,025 is odd, you can stop factoring; it is the greatest odd factor of 8,100.

25. 4/7 or .571

Translate the problem into math: Let b = number of boys; let g = number of girls. So $b + g$ = total number of students in the class.

$\frac{1}{2}$ of the boys speak French, so $\frac{1}{2}b$ = the number of boys who speak French.

$\frac{2}{3}$ of the girls speak French, so $\frac{2}{3}g$ = the number of girls who speak French.

Therefore, $\frac{1}{2}b + \frac{2}{3}g$ = total French speakers.

So the fraction of the class that speaks French

$$= \frac{\frac{1}{2}b + \frac{2}{3}\left(\frac{3}{4}b\right)}{b + g}$$

Since there are $\frac{3}{4}$ as many girls as boys in the class, $g = \frac{3}{4}b$. Plug in $\frac{3}{4}b$ for g into the fraction above.

Fraction of the class that speaks French:

$$= \frac{\frac{1}{2}b + \frac{2}{3}\left(\frac{3}{4}b\right)}{b + \frac{3}{4}b}$$

$$= \frac{\frac{1}{2}b + \frac{1}{2}b}{\frac{7}{4}b}$$

$$= \frac{b}{\frac{7}{4}b}$$

$$= \frac{4}{7}, \text{ or } .571$$

SECTION 5

The Shakespeare Pair

These paired passages present two opposing arguments on a single subject, the subject here being "Who Really Wrote Shakespeare's Plays?" The author of the first passage maintains that Francis Bacon actually wrote the plays, basing that conclusion on the assertion that Shakespeare didn't have the education and social experience necessary to create such sophisticated plays. The author of the second passage takes issue with that, claiming that Shakespeare's genius grew out of a deep understanding of human nature rather than any wide learning or arcane knowledge.

1. B

A Vocabulary-in-Context question. Here we're asked the definition of the word *entertain* in line 2, where it is used in the phrase "entertain some doubt." Well, when you entertain doubt, or entertain an idea, you are holding it in your head. You are **harboring** it, in the sense of **to harbor** as "to be host to." So choice (B) is correct.

The other choices are all acceptable dictionary definitions of the verb *entertain,* but none fits the context as well as choice (B) does. (A) **amuse** is a common synonym for *entertain,* but how does one amuse doubt? (C) **occupy** and (E) **engage** are closer, but they don't fit the sentence either. One's *mind* is occupied or engaged, but the doubt itself is not occupied or engaged. Meanwhile, (D) **cherish** adds a sense of valuing the entertained thing, as if it were something desirable.

2. D

The author claims that the person who actually wrote the plays must have had "intimate knowledge of life within royal courts and palaces," but that Shakespeare was just a commoner, without that kind of "firsthand experience" of the aristocracy. He wants to cast doubt on Shakespeare's **familiarity with the life of [aristocrats],** or choice (D).

Shakespeare's ability to (A) **write poetically** and his (C) **ability to support himself as a playwright** never come up in Passage 1. The **knowledge of foreign places** mentioned in (B) does come up, but being a commoner is not necessarily related to Shakespeare's apparent lack of travel. Choice (E) is the closest wrong choice, since the aristocracy was the **government** in Elizabethan England, but the issue is his knowledge of all aspects of aristocratic life.

3. E

Two Shakespearian plays—*Coriolanus* and *Love's Labour's Lost*—are mentioned in lines 28–31 in connection with the allegedly specialized knowledge they contain. They support the point that the educated aristocrat Bacon was a more likely author than was the undereducated commoner Shakespeare. So (E) answers the question best.

Choice (A) is a clever wrong choice, but it's too extreme. The author's not trying to prove that *only* Bacon could have written these plays, just that Bacon was far more likely than Shakespeare to have written them. The **deep understanding of human nature** mentioned in (B) is something brought up in Passage 2, not Passage 1. The author is not comparing the two plays to **works written by Bacon,** as (C) claims. And (D) is wrong since nothing about society is mentioned with regard to *Coriolanus.* Also, it's not the **broad spectrum of society** the author alludes to with regard to *Love's Labour's Lost,* but rather the knowledge of just the upper range of society.

4. A

It's clear that Ms. Bacon is looking down on actors, of which Shakespeare was one, regarding them with the **disdain** expressed in correct choice (A).

She's not **resentful** at how the **characters are portrayed,** choice (B), since she's talking about the characters themselves and what they tell us about real-life actors. Given her opinion of actors, she certainly doesn't **regret that their conditions weren't better,** choice (C). (D) is closer, but it's a distortion. She never doubts that anyone could **create such characters;** she doubts that the author of the plays could *be like* such a character. And finally, in (E), there's no evidence in the quote that Ms. Bacon thinks the actors are inept at their art, just that they are vulgar and lowly persons.

5. B

This question sends you back to paragraph 4 of Passage 1, where Bacon's preference for anonymity is explained. The author claims that, because the plays were "controversial," Bacon felt that associating himself with them would have been "politically and personally damaging." So **he wished to protect himself from the effects of controversy,** choice (B).

(A) is wrong, since Bacon did publish a lot of writing under his own name. (C) is plausible, but it's not the reason given in paragraph 4 or anywhere else in the first passage. (D) tries to confuse us by introducing the subject of **lowly actors** from the preceding paragraph. And (E) is a fabrication since we know that Bacon was already famous from his other writings.

6. C

This question takes us to the first paragraph of Passage 2, where the emphasis is on language ability. The author doubts that Bacon, a writer primarily of academic Latin, would have had the ability to produce the exalted English in which the plays were written. That makes (C) the best answer.

(A) is a distortion. Just because Bacon wrote most of his own work in another language doesn't mean that he was **unfamiliar** with English. (B)'s emphasis on the difficult switch from **scientific writing** to **writing plays** is close, but language rather than the type of writing is the focus. There's no reason to surmise that the author doubts Bacon's ability to **cooperate** on a **committee,** choice (D). Finally, (E) is wrong because there is no evidence in the first paragraph that the author has doubts about Bacon's ability to produce that amount of work.

7. D

Back to Vocabulary-in-Context. This question asks about *premier* as it is used in the phrase "premier stylist in the English language." The author definitely wants to indicate the sublime language of the plays here, so *premier* is being used in the sense of "of the first rank," or, as choice (D) has it, **greatest.** (A), (C), and (E) all play on the sense of premier as "first in sequence"(*inaugural,* by the way, means "marking the commencement or beginning"), but the author is not referring here to *when* Shakespeare wrote. He's writing about how *well*

Shakespeare wrote. On the other hand, (B) **influential** misses on two counts—first, it's not a definition of *premier* in any context, and second, the issue of influence on other writers is not brought up here.

8. B

The next Vocabulary-in-Context question concerns the adjective *encyclopedic* in line 76, where it's used to modify the noun "knowledge." The author says that Shakespeare's genius was one of common sense and perceptive intuition, not encyclopedic knowledge, which is related to great book-learning. So the knowledge described as "encyclopedic" is wide-ranging and in-depth—**comprehensive,** in other words, choice (B).

(A) **technical** is close to the sense of the context, but it's not a synonym of *encyclopedic,* so it really won't work here. (C) won't work either, since **abridged** (meaning "condensed") cannot describe the kind of exhaustive knowledge the author is describing here. And while it may take discipline to gain encyclopedic knowledge, *encyclopedic* itself cannot be defined as **disciplined,** so cut (D). Finally, (E) **specialized** isn't quite right, since it implies a narrowness of focus.

9. E

The reference to Shakespeare's status as a landowner comes in the third paragraph of Passage 2, where it is brought up to show that Shakespeare would have been "knowledgeable about legal matters related to . . . real estate." That makes (E) the best answer, "legal matters" being equivalent to **the law.**

(A) is interesting, since the author does say that owning land was quite an accomplishment for a playwright, but it has nothing to do with his knowledge of the law. (B) is off, since owning land doesn't make one automatically friendly with the highborn set. (C) is wrong, because Shakespeare's financial state is just a side issue; it's not the point of bringing up Shakespeare's landowning status. And (D) doesn't fit, since no one doubts that **Shakespeare was a commoner.**

10. A

This question directs us to lines 100–103, where the author claims that literary genius "can flower in any socioeconomic bracket." That implies that genius has little to do with a person's social and financial position—or, as correct choice (A) has it—genius doesn't depend **on a writer's external circumstances.**

(B) fails by bringing in the notion of **comprehension of human nature** from elsewhere in the passage. (C) is a common cliché, but there's no evidence here that the author felt that Shakespeare's genius was **enhanced by poverty.** In fact, this author implies that Shakespeare wasn't even all that poor. (D) may be a true statement, but recognition of genius isn't really under discussion here; it's the simple existence of genius. And (E) is a distortion; the author claims that at least one kind of genius does not *stem* from **book-learning and academic training,** but that doesn't mean that those things would **stifle** *literary genius.*

11. C

Go back to the fourth paragraph of Passage 1, where our first author claims that Bacon may have "hired a lowly actor" like Shakespeare to put his name to the plays and take the heat of controversy. How would our second author respond to this claim? The second author, remember, writes in the concluding paragraph of Passage 2 that "no elaborate theories of intrigue and secret identity are necessary to explain the accomplishment of William Shakespeare." Surely author 2 would regard the **scenario** described in Passage 1 as just this kind of **unnecessary** theory, so (C) is the best guess for how author 2 would react.

As for choice (A), author 2 may or may not agree that the plays were **controversial** in their time, so (A) won't work. (B) gets the thrust of author 2's argument wrong. Author 2 denigrates the notion that Bacon wrote the plays *not* by arguing that Bacon wasn't a great scholar, but by arguing that it didn't require a great scholar to write the plays. (D) tries to turn author 1's argument on its head. A nice idea, perhaps, but author 2 shows no hint of doing anything of the kind. And (E) brings up the notion of Shakespeare's social *respectability,* which really isn't of much concern to author 2.

12. C

What would be author 1's reaction to author 2's skepticism that Bacon, the author of Latin treatises, could be the "premier stylist in the English language"? Well, author 1's repeated assertions of Bacon's scholarly genius and Shakespeare's lack of education are both reflected in choice (C), which makes it a good bet as the correct answer.

(A)'s mention of the **similarities between Latin and English** is enough to kill this choice, since author 1 mentions no such similarities in the passage. (B) is a true statement, perhaps, but it doesn't really address the issue. (D) is fairly nonsensical, since it would weaken author 1's entire theory about why Bacon hired Shakespeare. Finally, (E) makes a good point, but again, there is no hint of this sentiment in author 1's statements.

13. D

Always check back to the passage to figure out the meaning of a Vocab-in-Context word. Here, the word "observation" refers to the phrase that "Shakespeare, in short, was Shakespeare"—a jokey comment on the author's part. None of the other choices fits the context of an informal remark, so (D) is correct here.

SECTION 6

1. B

Plug in −2 for p and 3 for q: $p^3q^2 + p^2q = (-2)^3 3^2 + (-2)^2 3 = (-8)(9) + 4(3)$, or $(-72) + 12 = -60$. (Note that a negative number raised to an *even* power becomes positive, but raised to an *odd* power stays negative.)

2. E

Keep track of the lengths you know on the diagram. B is the midpoint of AC so $AB = BC$. Since $AB = 5$, $BC = 5$. $BD = 8$, so $BC + CD = 8$. $BC = 5$, so $5 + CD = 8$, $CD = 3$. D is the midpoint of CE, so $CD = DE = 3$.

3. D

Try each answer choice until you find one that works for all of the pairs of numbers.

Choice (A), $P = N + 5$ works for 2 and 7, but not for 4 and 13.

Choice (B), $P = 2N + 3$ also works for 2 and 7, but not for 4 and 13.

Choice (C), $P = 2N + 5$, doesn't work for 2 and 7.

Choice (D), $P = 3N + 1$, works for all four pairs of numbers, so that's the answer.

4. A

$\angle PNM$ is supplementary to $\angle PNQ$, so $\angle PNM + 105° = 180°$, and $\angle PNM = 75°$. Since $PM = PN$, triangle MPN is an isosceles and $\angle PMN = \angle PNM = 75°$. The interior angles of a triangle sum to 180°, so $75 + 75 + x = 180$, and $x = 30$.

5. B

Probability is defined as the number of desired events divided by the total number of possible events. There are $5 + 6 + 4$, or 15 pens in the knapsack. If he pulls out 1 pen, there are 15 different pens he might pick, or 15 possible outcomes. The desired outcome is that the pen be either red or black.

The group of acceptable pens consists of $4 + 6$, or 10 pens. So the probability that one of these pens will be picked is 10 out of 15, or $\frac{10}{15}$, which we can reduce to $\frac{2}{3}$.

6. C

Pick variables for the two items and translate the given information into algebraic equations. Let h = the price of a hot dog and s = the price of a soda. The first statement is translated as $2h + s = \$3.25$, and the second as $3h + s = \$4.50$. If you subtract the first equation from the second, the s is eliminated so you can solve for h:

$$3h + s = \$4.50$$
$$\underline{-2h + s = \$3.25}$$
$$h \quad\ = \$1.25$$

Plug this value for h into the first equation to solve for s:

$$2(\$1.25) + s = \$3.25$$
$$\$2.50 + s = \$3.25$$
$$s = \$0.75$$

So two sodas would cost $2 \times \$0.75 = \$1.50$.

7. C

$a = f$, since all the obtuse angles formed when two parallel lines are cut by a transversal are equal. f is an exterior angle of the small triangle containing angles c, d, and e, so it is equal to the sum of the two nonadjacent interior angles, c and d. Since $a = f$ and $f = c + d$, $a = c + d$, answer choice (C).

8. D

The first 3 minutes of the phone call cost 75 cents or 0.75 dollars. If the entire call lasted x minutes, the rest of the call lasted $x - 3$ minutes. Each minute after the first 3 cost 15 cents or $\$0.15$, so the rest of the call cost $\$0.15(x - 3)$. So the cost of the entire call is $0.75 + 0.15(x - 3)$ dollars.

If this isn't clear, pick numbers. Let $x = 5$. The first 3 minutes cost $\$0.75$ and the additional $5 - 3 = 2$ minutes are $\$0.15$ each. So the entire call costs $\$0.75 + 2(\$0.15) = \$1.05$. Plug 5 for x into all the answer choices to see which ones give you 1.05:

(A) $0.75(3) + 0.15x = 2.25 + 0.15(5) = 2.25 + 0.75 = 3.00$. Eliminate.

(B) $0.75(3) + 0.15(x + 3) = 2.25 + 0.15(5 + 3) = 2.25 + 1.20 = 3.45$. Eliminate.

(C) $0.75 + 0.15(3 - x) = 0.75 + 0.15(3 - 5) = 0.75 - 0.30 = 0.45$. Eliminate.

(D) $0.75 + 0.15(x - 3) = 0.75 + 0.15(5 - 3) = 0.75 + 0.30 = 1.05$. Works!

(E) $0.75 + 0.15(5) = 0.75 + 0.75 = 1.50$. Eliminate.

The only choice that yields the desired result is (D), so it must be correct.

9. B

Before you can find the area of the circle, you need to find the length of the wire. The wire is in the shape of a semicircle with diameter 12. Since circumference = πd, the length of a semicircle is half of that, $\frac{\pi d}{2}$. So the length of the wire is $\frac{\pi(12)}{2}$, or 6π. When this wire is bent to form a circle, the circumference of this circle will equal 6π. So the length of the circle's diameter must equal 6, and the radius must be 3. Now you can find the area of the circle:

$$\text{Area} = \pi r^2$$
$$= \pi(3)^2$$
$$= 9\pi$$

10. C

If $a^2 - a = 72$, then $a^2 - a - 72 = 0$. Factoring this quadratic equation: $(a - 9)(a + 8) = 0$. So $a - 9 = 0$ or $a + 8 = 0$, and $a = 9$ or $a = -8$. b to the nth power equals a, so b must be a root of either 9 or -8. Look through the answer choices to find the choice that is not a root of either 9 or -8:

(A) -8: $(-8)1 = -8$, so this can be a value for b.

(B) -2: $(-2)3 = -8$, so this can be a value for b.

(C) 2: $23 = 8$, *not* -8, so this *cannot* be a value for b.

(D) 3: $32 = 9$, so this can be a value for b.

(E) 9: $91 = 9$, so this can be a value for b.

So (C) is the only answer choice that cannot be a value for b.

Practice Test Two

HOW TO TAKE THIS PRACTICE TEST

Before taking this practice test, find a quiet room where you can work uninterrupted for two and a half hours. Make sure you have a comfortable desk, your calculator, and several No. 2 pencils.

Use the answer sheet provided to record your answers. (You can cut it out or photocopy it.)

Once you start this practice test, don't stop until you've finished. Remember—you can review any questions within a section, but you may not go back or forward a section.

You'll find an answer key, score conversion charts, and explanations following the test.

Good luck.

SAT Practice Test Two
Answer Sheet

Remove (or photocopy) this answer sheet and use it to complete the practice test.
(See answer key following the test when finished.)

Start with number 1 for each section. If a section has fewer questions than answer spaces, leave the extra spaces blank.

SECTION 1

1 Ⓐ Ⓑ Ⓒ Ⓓ Ⓔ   11 Ⓐ Ⓑ Ⓒ Ⓓ Ⓔ   21 Ⓐ Ⓑ Ⓒ Ⓓ Ⓔ   31 Ⓐ Ⓑ Ⓒ Ⓓ Ⓔ
2 Ⓐ Ⓑ Ⓒ Ⓓ Ⓔ   12 Ⓐ Ⓑ Ⓒ Ⓓ Ⓔ   22 Ⓐ Ⓑ Ⓒ Ⓓ Ⓔ   32 Ⓐ Ⓑ Ⓒ Ⓓ Ⓔ
3 Ⓐ Ⓑ Ⓒ Ⓓ Ⓔ   13 Ⓐ Ⓑ Ⓒ Ⓓ Ⓔ   23 Ⓐ Ⓑ Ⓒ Ⓓ Ⓔ   33 Ⓐ Ⓑ Ⓒ Ⓓ Ⓔ
4 Ⓐ Ⓑ Ⓒ Ⓓ Ⓔ   14 Ⓐ Ⓑ Ⓒ Ⓓ Ⓔ   24 Ⓐ Ⓑ Ⓒ Ⓓ Ⓔ   34 Ⓐ Ⓑ Ⓒ Ⓓ Ⓔ
5 Ⓐ Ⓑ Ⓒ Ⓓ Ⓔ   15 Ⓐ Ⓑ Ⓒ Ⓓ Ⓔ   25 Ⓐ Ⓑ Ⓒ Ⓓ Ⓔ   35 Ⓐ Ⓑ Ⓒ Ⓓ Ⓔ
6 Ⓐ Ⓑ Ⓒ Ⓓ Ⓔ   16 Ⓐ Ⓑ Ⓒ Ⓓ Ⓔ   26 Ⓐ Ⓑ Ⓒ Ⓓ Ⓔ   36 Ⓐ Ⓑ Ⓒ Ⓓ Ⓔ
7 Ⓐ Ⓑ Ⓒ Ⓓ Ⓔ   17 Ⓐ Ⓑ Ⓒ Ⓓ Ⓔ   27 Ⓐ Ⓑ Ⓒ Ⓓ Ⓔ   37 Ⓐ Ⓑ Ⓒ Ⓓ Ⓔ
8 Ⓐ Ⓑ Ⓒ Ⓓ Ⓔ   18 Ⓐ Ⓑ Ⓒ Ⓓ Ⓔ   28 Ⓐ Ⓑ Ⓒ Ⓓ Ⓔ   38 Ⓐ Ⓑ Ⓒ Ⓓ Ⓔ
9 Ⓐ Ⓑ Ⓒ Ⓓ Ⓔ   19 Ⓐ Ⓑ Ⓒ Ⓓ Ⓔ   29 Ⓐ Ⓑ Ⓒ Ⓓ Ⓔ   39 Ⓐ Ⓑ Ⓒ Ⓓ Ⓔ
10 Ⓐ Ⓑ Ⓒ Ⓓ Ⓔ   20 Ⓐ Ⓑ Ⓒ Ⓓ Ⓔ   30 Ⓐ Ⓑ Ⓒ Ⓓ Ⓔ   40 Ⓐ Ⓑ Ⓒ Ⓓ Ⓔ

right in
section 1

wrong in
section 1

SECTION 2

1 Ⓐ Ⓑ Ⓒ Ⓓ Ⓔ   11 Ⓐ Ⓑ Ⓒ Ⓓ Ⓔ   21 Ⓐ Ⓑ Ⓒ Ⓓ Ⓔ   31 Ⓐ Ⓑ Ⓒ Ⓓ Ⓔ
2 Ⓐ Ⓑ Ⓒ Ⓓ Ⓔ   12 Ⓐ Ⓑ Ⓒ Ⓓ Ⓔ   22 Ⓐ Ⓑ Ⓒ Ⓓ Ⓔ   32 Ⓐ Ⓑ Ⓒ Ⓓ Ⓔ
3 Ⓐ Ⓑ Ⓒ Ⓓ Ⓔ   13 Ⓐ Ⓑ Ⓒ Ⓓ Ⓔ   23 Ⓐ Ⓑ Ⓒ Ⓓ Ⓔ   33 Ⓐ Ⓑ Ⓒ Ⓓ Ⓔ
4 Ⓐ Ⓑ Ⓒ Ⓓ Ⓔ   14 Ⓐ Ⓑ Ⓒ Ⓓ Ⓔ   24 Ⓐ Ⓑ Ⓒ Ⓓ Ⓔ   34 Ⓐ Ⓑ Ⓒ Ⓓ Ⓔ
5 Ⓐ Ⓑ Ⓒ Ⓓ Ⓔ   15 Ⓐ Ⓑ Ⓒ Ⓓ Ⓔ   25 Ⓐ Ⓑ Ⓒ Ⓓ Ⓔ   35 Ⓐ Ⓑ Ⓒ Ⓓ Ⓔ
6 Ⓐ Ⓑ Ⓒ Ⓓ Ⓔ   16 Ⓐ Ⓑ Ⓒ Ⓓ Ⓔ   26 Ⓐ Ⓑ Ⓒ Ⓓ Ⓔ   36 Ⓐ Ⓑ Ⓒ Ⓓ Ⓔ
7 Ⓐ Ⓑ Ⓒ Ⓓ Ⓔ   17 Ⓐ Ⓑ Ⓒ Ⓓ Ⓔ   27 Ⓐ Ⓑ Ⓒ Ⓓ Ⓔ   37 Ⓐ Ⓑ Ⓒ Ⓓ Ⓔ
8 Ⓐ Ⓑ Ⓒ Ⓓ Ⓔ   18 Ⓐ Ⓑ Ⓒ Ⓓ Ⓔ   28 Ⓐ Ⓑ Ⓒ Ⓓ Ⓔ   38 Ⓐ Ⓑ Ⓒ Ⓓ Ⓔ
9 Ⓐ Ⓑ Ⓒ Ⓓ Ⓔ   19 Ⓐ Ⓑ Ⓒ Ⓓ Ⓔ   29 Ⓐ Ⓑ Ⓒ Ⓓ Ⓔ   39 Ⓐ Ⓑ Ⓒ Ⓓ Ⓔ
10 Ⓐ Ⓑ Ⓒ Ⓓ Ⓔ   20 Ⓐ Ⓑ Ⓒ Ⓓ Ⓔ   30 Ⓐ Ⓑ Ⓒ Ⓓ Ⓔ   40 Ⓐ Ⓑ Ⓒ Ⓓ Ⓔ

right in
section 2

wrong in
section 2

Remove (or photocopy) this answer sheet and use it to complete the practice test.

Start with number 1 for each section. If a section has fewer questions than answer spaces, leave the extra spaces blank.

SECTION 3

1 Ⓐ Ⓑ Ⓒ Ⓓ Ⓔ   11 Ⓐ Ⓑ Ⓒ Ⓓ Ⓔ   21 Ⓐ Ⓑ Ⓒ Ⓓ Ⓔ   31 Ⓐ Ⓑ Ⓒ Ⓓ Ⓔ
2 Ⓐ Ⓑ Ⓒ Ⓓ Ⓔ   12 Ⓐ Ⓑ Ⓒ Ⓓ Ⓔ   22 Ⓐ Ⓑ Ⓒ Ⓓ Ⓔ   32 Ⓐ Ⓑ Ⓒ Ⓓ Ⓔ
3 Ⓐ Ⓑ Ⓒ Ⓓ Ⓔ   13 Ⓐ Ⓑ Ⓒ Ⓓ Ⓔ   23 Ⓐ Ⓑ Ⓒ Ⓓ Ⓔ   33 Ⓐ Ⓑ Ⓒ Ⓓ Ⓔ
4 Ⓐ Ⓑ Ⓒ Ⓓ Ⓔ   14 Ⓐ Ⓑ Ⓒ Ⓓ Ⓔ   24 Ⓐ Ⓑ Ⓒ Ⓓ Ⓔ   34 Ⓐ Ⓑ Ⓒ Ⓓ Ⓔ
5 Ⓐ Ⓑ Ⓒ Ⓓ Ⓔ   15 Ⓐ Ⓑ Ⓒ Ⓓ Ⓔ   25 Ⓐ Ⓑ Ⓒ Ⓓ Ⓔ   35 Ⓐ Ⓑ Ⓒ Ⓓ Ⓔ
6 Ⓐ Ⓑ Ⓒ Ⓓ Ⓔ   16 Ⓐ Ⓑ Ⓒ Ⓓ Ⓔ   26 Ⓐ Ⓑ Ⓒ Ⓓ Ⓔ   36 Ⓐ Ⓑ Ⓒ Ⓓ Ⓔ
7 Ⓐ Ⓑ Ⓒ Ⓓ Ⓔ   17 Ⓐ Ⓑ Ⓒ Ⓓ Ⓔ   27 Ⓐ Ⓑ Ⓒ Ⓓ Ⓔ   37 Ⓐ Ⓑ Ⓒ Ⓓ Ⓔ
8 Ⓐ Ⓑ Ⓒ Ⓓ Ⓔ   18 Ⓐ Ⓑ Ⓒ Ⓓ Ⓔ   28 Ⓐ Ⓑ Ⓒ Ⓓ Ⓔ   38 Ⓐ Ⓑ Ⓒ Ⓓ Ⓔ
9 Ⓐ Ⓑ Ⓒ Ⓓ Ⓔ   19 Ⓐ Ⓑ Ⓒ Ⓓ Ⓔ   29 Ⓐ Ⓑ Ⓒ Ⓓ Ⓔ   39 Ⓐ Ⓑ Ⓒ Ⓓ Ⓔ
10 Ⓐ Ⓑ Ⓒ Ⓓ Ⓔ   20 Ⓐ Ⓑ Ⓒ Ⓓ Ⓔ   30 Ⓐ Ⓑ Ⓒ Ⓓ Ⓔ   40 Ⓐ Ⓑ Ⓒ Ⓓ Ⓔ

right in section 3

wrong in section 3

If section 3 of your test book contains math questions that are not multiple choice, continue to item 16 below. Otherwise, continue to item 16 above.

16   17   18   19   20   21   22   23   24   25

[Grid-in answer boxes numbered 16 through 25, each with columns of digits 0–9]

SECTION 4

1 Ⓐ Ⓑ Ⓒ Ⓓ Ⓔ   11 Ⓐ Ⓑ Ⓒ Ⓓ Ⓔ   21 Ⓐ Ⓑ Ⓒ Ⓓ Ⓔ   31 Ⓐ Ⓑ Ⓒ Ⓓ Ⓔ
2 Ⓐ Ⓑ Ⓒ Ⓓ Ⓔ   12 Ⓐ Ⓑ Ⓒ Ⓓ Ⓔ   22 Ⓐ Ⓑ Ⓒ Ⓓ Ⓔ   32 Ⓐ Ⓑ Ⓒ Ⓓ Ⓔ
3 Ⓐ Ⓑ Ⓒ Ⓓ Ⓔ   13 Ⓐ Ⓑ Ⓒ Ⓓ Ⓔ   23 Ⓐ Ⓑ Ⓒ Ⓓ Ⓔ   33 Ⓐ Ⓑ Ⓒ Ⓓ Ⓔ
4 Ⓐ Ⓑ Ⓒ Ⓓ Ⓔ   14 Ⓐ Ⓑ Ⓒ Ⓓ Ⓔ   24 Ⓐ Ⓑ Ⓒ Ⓓ Ⓔ   34 Ⓐ Ⓑ Ⓒ Ⓓ Ⓔ
5 Ⓐ Ⓑ Ⓒ Ⓓ Ⓔ   15 Ⓐ Ⓑ Ⓒ Ⓓ Ⓔ   25 Ⓐ Ⓑ Ⓒ Ⓓ Ⓔ   35 Ⓐ Ⓑ Ⓒ Ⓓ Ⓔ
6 Ⓐ Ⓑ Ⓒ Ⓓ Ⓔ   16 Ⓐ Ⓑ Ⓒ Ⓓ Ⓔ   26 Ⓐ Ⓑ Ⓒ Ⓓ Ⓔ   36 Ⓐ Ⓑ Ⓒ Ⓓ Ⓔ
7 Ⓐ Ⓑ Ⓒ Ⓓ Ⓔ   17 Ⓐ Ⓑ Ⓒ Ⓓ Ⓔ   27 Ⓐ Ⓑ Ⓒ Ⓓ Ⓔ   37 Ⓐ Ⓑ Ⓒ Ⓓ Ⓔ
8 Ⓐ Ⓑ Ⓒ Ⓓ Ⓔ   18 Ⓐ Ⓑ Ⓒ Ⓓ Ⓔ   28 Ⓐ Ⓑ Ⓒ Ⓓ Ⓔ   38 Ⓐ Ⓑ Ⓒ Ⓓ Ⓔ
9 Ⓐ Ⓑ Ⓒ Ⓓ Ⓔ   19 Ⓐ Ⓑ Ⓒ Ⓓ Ⓔ   29 Ⓐ Ⓑ Ⓒ Ⓓ Ⓔ   39 Ⓐ Ⓑ Ⓒ Ⓓ Ⓔ
10 Ⓐ Ⓑ Ⓒ Ⓓ Ⓔ   20 Ⓐ Ⓑ Ⓒ Ⓓ Ⓔ   30 Ⓐ Ⓑ Ⓒ Ⓓ Ⓔ   40 Ⓐ Ⓑ Ⓒ Ⓓ Ⓔ

right in section 4

wrong in section 4

KAPLAN

Remove (or photocopy) this answer sheet and use it to complete the practive test.

Start with number 1 for each section. If a section has fewer questions than answer spaces, leave the extra spaces blank.

SECTION 5

1 Ⓐ Ⓑ Ⓒ Ⓓ Ⓔ   11 Ⓐ Ⓑ Ⓒ Ⓓ Ⓔ   21 Ⓐ Ⓑ Ⓒ Ⓓ Ⓔ   31 Ⓐ Ⓑ Ⓒ Ⓓ Ⓔ
2 Ⓐ Ⓑ Ⓒ Ⓓ Ⓔ   12 Ⓐ Ⓑ Ⓒ Ⓓ Ⓔ   22 Ⓐ Ⓑ Ⓒ Ⓓ Ⓔ   32 Ⓐ Ⓑ Ⓒ Ⓓ Ⓔ
3 Ⓐ Ⓑ Ⓒ Ⓓ Ⓔ   13 Ⓐ Ⓑ Ⓒ Ⓓ Ⓔ   23 Ⓐ Ⓑ Ⓒ Ⓓ Ⓔ   33 Ⓐ Ⓑ Ⓒ Ⓓ Ⓔ
4 Ⓐ Ⓑ Ⓒ Ⓓ Ⓔ   14 Ⓐ Ⓑ Ⓒ Ⓓ Ⓔ   24 Ⓐ Ⓑ Ⓒ Ⓓ Ⓔ   34 Ⓐ Ⓑ Ⓒ Ⓓ Ⓔ
5 Ⓐ Ⓑ Ⓒ Ⓓ Ⓔ   15 Ⓐ Ⓑ Ⓒ Ⓓ Ⓔ   25 Ⓐ Ⓑ Ⓒ Ⓓ Ⓔ   35 Ⓐ Ⓑ Ⓒ Ⓓ Ⓔ
6 Ⓐ Ⓑ Ⓒ Ⓓ Ⓔ   16 Ⓐ Ⓑ Ⓒ Ⓓ Ⓔ   26 Ⓐ Ⓑ Ⓒ Ⓓ Ⓔ   36 Ⓐ Ⓑ Ⓒ Ⓓ Ⓔ
7 Ⓐ Ⓑ Ⓒ Ⓓ Ⓔ   17 Ⓐ Ⓑ Ⓒ Ⓓ Ⓔ   27 Ⓐ Ⓑ Ⓒ Ⓓ Ⓔ   37 Ⓐ Ⓑ Ⓒ Ⓓ Ⓔ
8 Ⓐ Ⓑ Ⓒ Ⓓ Ⓔ   18 Ⓐ Ⓑ Ⓒ Ⓓ Ⓔ   28 Ⓐ Ⓑ Ⓒ Ⓓ Ⓔ   38 Ⓐ Ⓑ Ⓒ Ⓓ Ⓔ
9 Ⓐ Ⓑ Ⓒ Ⓓ Ⓔ   19 Ⓐ Ⓑ Ⓒ Ⓓ Ⓔ   29 Ⓐ Ⓑ Ⓒ Ⓓ Ⓔ   39 Ⓐ Ⓑ Ⓒ Ⓓ Ⓔ
10 Ⓐ Ⓑ Ⓒ Ⓓ Ⓔ   20 Ⓐ Ⓑ Ⓒ Ⓓ Ⓔ   30 Ⓐ Ⓑ Ⓒ Ⓓ Ⓔ   40 Ⓐ Ⓑ Ⓒ Ⓓ Ⓔ

right in section 5

wrong in section 5

SECTION 6

1 Ⓐ Ⓑ Ⓒ Ⓓ Ⓔ   11 Ⓐ Ⓑ Ⓒ Ⓓ Ⓔ   21 Ⓐ Ⓑ Ⓒ Ⓓ Ⓔ   31 Ⓐ Ⓑ Ⓒ Ⓓ Ⓔ
2 Ⓐ Ⓑ Ⓒ Ⓓ Ⓔ   12 Ⓐ Ⓑ Ⓒ Ⓓ Ⓔ   22 Ⓐ Ⓑ Ⓒ Ⓓ Ⓔ   32 Ⓐ Ⓑ Ⓒ Ⓓ Ⓔ
3 Ⓐ Ⓑ Ⓒ Ⓓ Ⓔ   13 Ⓐ Ⓑ Ⓒ Ⓓ Ⓔ   23 Ⓐ Ⓑ Ⓒ Ⓓ Ⓔ   33 Ⓐ Ⓑ Ⓒ Ⓓ Ⓔ
4 Ⓐ Ⓑ Ⓒ Ⓓ Ⓔ   14 Ⓐ Ⓑ Ⓒ Ⓓ Ⓔ   24 Ⓐ Ⓑ Ⓒ Ⓓ Ⓔ   34 Ⓐ Ⓑ Ⓒ Ⓓ Ⓔ
5 Ⓐ Ⓑ Ⓒ Ⓓ Ⓔ   15 Ⓐ Ⓑ Ⓒ Ⓓ Ⓔ   25 Ⓐ Ⓑ Ⓒ Ⓓ Ⓔ   35 Ⓐ Ⓑ Ⓒ Ⓓ Ⓔ
6 Ⓐ Ⓑ Ⓒ Ⓓ Ⓔ   16 Ⓐ Ⓑ Ⓒ Ⓓ Ⓔ   26 Ⓐ Ⓑ Ⓒ Ⓓ Ⓔ   36 Ⓐ Ⓑ Ⓒ Ⓓ Ⓔ
7 Ⓐ Ⓑ Ⓒ Ⓓ Ⓔ   17 Ⓐ Ⓑ Ⓒ Ⓓ Ⓔ   27 Ⓐ Ⓑ Ⓒ Ⓓ Ⓔ   37 Ⓐ Ⓑ Ⓒ Ⓓ Ⓔ
8 Ⓐ Ⓑ Ⓒ Ⓓ Ⓔ   18 Ⓐ Ⓑ Ⓒ Ⓓ Ⓔ   28 Ⓐ Ⓑ Ⓒ Ⓓ Ⓔ   38 Ⓐ Ⓑ Ⓒ Ⓓ Ⓔ
9 Ⓐ Ⓑ Ⓒ Ⓓ Ⓔ   19 Ⓐ Ⓑ Ⓒ Ⓓ Ⓔ   29 Ⓐ Ⓑ Ⓒ Ⓓ Ⓔ   39 Ⓐ Ⓑ Ⓒ Ⓓ Ⓔ
10 Ⓐ Ⓑ Ⓒ Ⓓ Ⓔ   20 Ⓐ Ⓑ Ⓒ Ⓓ Ⓔ   30 Ⓐ Ⓑ Ⓒ Ⓓ Ⓔ   40 Ⓐ Ⓑ Ⓒ Ⓓ Ⓔ

right in section 6

wrong in section 6

Time—30 Minutes	Solve each of the following problems, decide which is the best answer choice, and darken the corresponding oval on the answer sheet. Use available space in the test booklet for scratchwork.*
25 Questions	

Notes:

(1)   Calculator use is permitted.

(2)   All numbers used are real numbers.

(3)   Figures are provided for some problems. All figures are drawn to scale and lie in a plane UNLESS otherwise indicated.

Reference Information

$A=\frac{1}{2}bh$ $c^2 = a^2 + b^2$ Special Right Triangles $A=\pi r^2$ $C=2\pi r$ $V=\ell wh$ $V=\pi r^2 h$ $A=\ell w$

The sum of the degree measures of the angles of a triangle is 180.
The number of degrees of arc in a circle is 360.
A straight angle has a degree measure of 180.

---

1 $\left(\frac{1}{5} + \frac{1}{3}\right) \div \frac{1}{2} =$

(A) $\frac{1}{8}$

(B) $\frac{1}{4}$

(C) $\frac{4}{15}$

(D) $\frac{1}{2}$

(E) $\frac{16}{15}$

2   What is the value of $x^2 - 2x$ when $x = -2$?

(A)   −8
(B)   −4
(C)   0
(D)   4
(E)   8

3   Vito read 96 pages in 2 hours and 40 minutes. What was Vito's average rate of pages per hour?

(A)   24
(B)   30
(C)   36
(D)   42
(E)   48

4   For how many integer values of x will $\frac{7}{x}$ be greater than $\frac{1}{4}$ and less than $\frac{1}{3}$?

(A)   6
(B)   7
(C)   12
(D)   28
(E)   Infinitely many

5   What is the average (arithmetic mean) of $2x + 5$, $5x - 6$, and $-4x + 2$?

(A) $x + \frac{1}{3}$

(B) $x + 1$

(C) $3x + \frac{1}{3}$

(D) $3x + 3$

(E) $3x + 3\frac{1}{3}$

GO ON TO THE NEXT PAGE ➡

*The directions on the actual SAT will vary slightly.

6 In a group of 25 students, 16 are female. What percent of the group is female?

(A) 16%
(B) 40%
(C) 60%
(D) 64%
(E) 75%

7 In the triangle above, what is the degree measure of angle B ?

(A) 45
(B) 60
(C) 65
(D) 75
(E) 80

8 For all $x \neq 0$, $\dfrac{x^2 + x^2 + x^2}{x^2} =$

(A) 3
(B) 3x
(C) x^2
(D) x^3
(E) x^4

9 The equation $x^2 = 5x - 4$ has how many distinct real solutions?

(A) 0
(B) 1
(C) 2
(D) 3
(E) Infinitely many

10 Which of the following sets of numbers has the property that the sum of any two numbers in the set is also a number in the set?

   I. The set of even integers
   II. The set of odd integers
   III. The set of prime numbers

(A) I only
(B) III only
(C) I and II only
(D) I and III only
(E) I, II, and III

11 Martin's average (arithmetic mean) score after 4 tests is 89. What score on the 5th test would bring Martin's average up to exactly 90?

(A) 90
(B) 91
(C) 92
(D) 93
(E) 94

12 The price s of a sweater is reduced by 25% for a sale. After the sale, the reduced price is increased by 20%. Which of the following represents the final price of the sweater?

(A) 1.05s
(B) .95s
(C) .90s
(D) .85s
(E) .80s

13 How many distinct prime factors does the number 36 have?

(A) 2
(B) 3
(C) 4
(D) 5
(E) 6

14 If the area of a triangle is 36 and its base is 9, what is the length of the altitude to that base?

(A) 2
(B) 4
(C) 6
(D) 8
(E) 12

15 Let $a\clubsuit$ be defined for all positive integers a by the equation $a\clubsuit = \dfrac{a}{4} - \dfrac{a}{6}$. If $x\clubsuit = 3$, what is the value of x ?

(A) 18
(B) 28
(C) 36
(D) 40
(E) 54

16 Joan has q quarters, d dimes, n nickels, and no other coins in her pocket. Which of the following represents the total number of coins in Joan's pocket?

(A) $q + d + n$
(B) $5q + 2d + n$
(C) $.25q + .10d + .05n$
(D) $(25 + 10 + 5)(q + d + n)$
(E) $25q + 10d + 5n$

GO ON TO THE NEXT PAGE ➡

17 Which of the following is an equation for the graph above?

(A) $y = -2x + 1$
(B) $y = x + 1$
(C) $y = x + 2$
(D) $y = 2x + 1$
(E) $y = 2x + 2$

18 If an integer is divisible by 6 and by 9, then the integer must be divisible by which of the following?

    I. 12
    II. 18
    III. 36

(A) I only
(B) II only
(C) I and II only
(D) II and III only
(E) I, II, and III

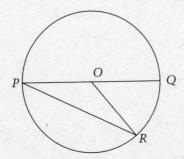

19 In the figure above, O is the center of the circle and P, O, and Q are collinear. If $\angle ROQ$ measures $50°$, what is the degree measure of $\angle RPQ$?

(A) 20
(B) 25
(C) 30
(D) 35
(E) 40

20 A wooden cube with volume 64 is sliced in half horizontally. The two halves are then glued together to form a rectangular solid which is not a cube. What is the surface area of this new solid?

(A) 128
(B) 112
(C) 96
(D) 56
(E) 48

21 A drawer contains 6 blue socks, 12 black socks, and 14 white socks. If one sock is chosen at random, what is the probability that it will be black?

(A) $\frac{1}{4}$

(B) $\frac{1}{3}$

(C) $\frac{3}{8}$

(D) $\frac{1}{2}$

(E) $\frac{5}{8}$

22 Danielle drives from her home to the store at an average speed of 40 miles per hour. She returns home along the same route at an average speed of 60 miles per hour. What is her average speed, in miles per hour, for her entire trip?

(A) 45
(B) 48
(C) 50
(D) 52
(E) 55

23 What is the area of a right triangle if the length of one leg is a and the length of the hypotenuse is c ?

(A) $\frac{ac}{2}$

(B) $\frac{ac - a^2}{2}$

(C) $\frac{a^2 + c^2}{2}$

(D) $\frac{a\sqrt{c^2 - a^2}}{2}$

(E) $\sqrt{a^2 + c^2}$

GO ON TO THE NEXT PAGE ➡

24 In △*PRS* above, *RT* is the altitude to side *PS* and *QS* is the altitude to side *PR*. If *RT* = 7, *PR* = 8, and *QS* = 9, what is the length of *PS* ?

(A) $5\frac{1}{7}$

(B) $6\frac{2}{9}$

(C) $7\frac{7}{8}$

(D) $10\frac{2}{7}$

(E) $13\frac{4}{9}$

25 There are 3 routes from Bay City to Riverville. There are 4 routes from Riverville to Straitstown. There are 3 routes from Straitstown to Frog Pond. If a driver must pass through Riverville and Straitstown exactly once, how many possible ways are there to go from Bay City to Frog Pond?

(A)   6
(B)   10
(C)   12
(D)   24
(E)   36

IF YOU FINISH BEFORE TIME IS CALLED, YOU MAY CHECK YOUR WORK ON THIS SECTION ONLY. DO NOT TURN TO ANY OTHER SECTION IN THE TEST.   **STOP**

KAPLAN

Time—30 Minutes
35 Questions

For each of the following questions, choose the best answer and darken the corresponding oval on the answer sheet.*

Select the lettered word or set of words that best completes the sentence.

Example:

Today's small, portable computers contrast markedly with the earliest electronic computers, which were ----.

(A) effective
(B) invented
(C) useful
(D) destructive
(E) enormous

 Ⓐ Ⓑ Ⓒ Ⓓ ●

1   Finding an old movie poster that is still ---- usually proves difficult because such posters were meant to be used and then ----.

(A) recognizable . . returned
(B) relevant . . discarded
(C) intact . . destroyed
(D) immaculate . . restored
(E) displayed . . maintained

2   The Kemp's Ridley turtle, long considered one of the most ---- creatures of the sea, finally appears to be making some headway in its battle against extinction.

(A) elusive
(B) prevalent
(C) combative
(D) voracious
(E) imperiled

3   Before the invention of the tape recorder, quotes from an interview were rarely ----; journalists usually paraphrased the words of their subject.

(A) verbatim
(B) misconstrued
(C) pragmatic
(D) extensive
(E) plagiarized

4   Batchelor's reputation as ---- novelist encouraged hopes that his political thriller would offer more ---- characterizations than are usually found in the genre.

(A) a serious . . subtle
(B) a maturing . . sweeping
(C) a prolific . . accurate
(D) an accomplished . . fictional
(E) a reclusive . . authentic

5   The governor commented on the disadvantages of political ----, saying that after his extended tenure in office the voters had grown used to blaming him for everything.

(A) acumen
(B) savvy
(C) longevity
(D) decorum
(E) celebrity

6   Although normally ----, the researcher was ---- by the news that her work had not been accepted for publication.

(A) introverted . . devastated
(B) imperious . . incensed
(C) melodramatic . . electrified
(D) buoyant . . subdued
(E) reserved . . bewildered

7   The agency's failure to ---- policies that it has acknowledged are flawed is a potent demonstration of its ---- approach to correcting its problems.

(A) support . . ambiguous
(B) institute . . earnest
(C) rescind . . lackadaisical
(D) amend . . devoted
(E) chasten . . meticulous

8   The inconsistency of the educational policies adopted by various schools across the state has been greatly ---- by the rapid turnover of school superintendents.

(A) counteracted
(B) stabilized
(C) criticized
(D) exacerbated
(E) understated

9   The journalist's claim of ---- is belied by her record of contributing to the campaign funds of only one party's candidates.

(A) innocence
(B) corruption
(C) impartiality
(D) affluence
(E) loyalty

GO ON TO THE NEXT PAGE ➡

*The directions on the actual SAT will vary slightly.

10 The repeated breakdown of negotiations only
---- the view that the two sides were not truly
committed to the goal of ---- a military
confrontation.

(A) established . . escalating
(B) undermined . . avoiding
(C) distorted . . financing
(D) strengthened . . initiating
(E) reinforced . . averting

11 These are times of national budgetary ---- now
that a long era of sustained growth has been
succeeded by a period of painful ----.

(A) turmoil . . acquisition
(B) stringency . . decline
(C) expansion . . stagnation
(D) indecision . . renewal
(E) prudence . . development

12 To the ---- of those who in bygone years tiptoed
their way past poinsettia displays for fear of
causing leaves to fall, breeders have developed
more ---- versions of the flower.

(A) consternation . . amorphous
(B) dismay . . fragrant
(C) surprise . . alluring
(D) disappointment . . diversified
(E) relief . . durable

13 Aristotle espoused a ---- biological model in which
all extant species are unchanging and eternal and
no new species ever come into existence.

(A) paradoxical
(B) morbid
(C) static
(D) holistic
(E) homogeneous

GO ON TO THE NEXT PAGE ➡

Choose the lettered pair of words that is related in the same way as the pair in capital letters.

Example:

FLAKE : SNOW ::
(A) storm : hail
(B) drop : rain
(C) field : wheat
(D) stack : hay
(E) cloud : fog

14 LABORATORY : EXPERIMENT ::

(A) garage : repair
(B) beach : sunbathe
(C) statement : formulate
(D) graveyard : inter
(E) invention : create

15 EXONERATE : BLAME ::

(A) disinfect : contamination
(B) divert : stream
(C) indict : guilt
(D) obey : order
(E) absolve : ministry

16 LOOK : SCRUTINIZE ::

(A) amble : scurry
(B) deliberate : propose
(C) read : peruse
(D) importune : plead
(E) flicker : shine

17 GULLIBLE : DUPE ::

(A) fallible : err
(B) foolhardy : confuse
(C) dejected : dishearten
(D) headstrong : coax
(E) submissive : control

18 CONVERSATION : INTERLOCUTOR ::

(A) speech : orator
(B) hearing : prosecutor
(C) game : player
(D) novel : publisher
(E) diagnosis : doctor

19 ENTOMOLOGY : INSECTS ::

(A) agriculture : cows
(B) pedagogy : education
(C) astronomy : telescope
(D) literature : character
(E) evolution : man

20 SKIRMISH : BATTLE ::

(A) misdemeanor : crime
(B) desertion : divorce
(C) fledgling : expert
(D) faculty : instructor
(E) estimate : measurement

21 FORENSIC : LITIGATION ::

(A) maritime : sea
(B) euphoria : feeling
(C) conjugal : bliss
(D) exemplary : example
(E) illusory : magic

22 FEIGN : IMPRESSION ::

(A) adapt : evolution
(B) perjure : testimony
(C) play : role
(D) impersonate : celebrity
(E) slander : reputation

23 POLEMIC : IMPARTIAL ::

(A) antidote : curative
(B) discipline : harsh
(C) heretic : persecuted
(D) defendant : guilty
(E) extrovert : retiring

GO ON TO THE NEXT PAGE ➡

Answer the questions below based on the information in the accompanying passage.

Questions 24–35 are based on the following passage.

The following passage is an excerpt from a book about wolves, written by a self-taught naturalist who studied them in the wild.

My precautions against disturbing the wolves were superfluous. It had required me a week to get their measure, but they must have taken mine at
Line our first meeting; and while there was nothing
(5) disdainful in their evident assessment of me, they managed to ignore my presence, and indeed my very existence, with a thoroughness which was somehow disconcerting.

Quite by accident I had pitched my tent within
(10) ten yards of one of the major paths used by the wolves when they were going to, or coming from, their hunting paths to the westward; and only a few hours after I had taken up my residence one of the wolves came back from a trip and discovered
(15) me and my tent.

He was at the end of a hard night's work and was clearly tired and anxious to go home to bed. He came over a small rise fifty yards from me with his head down, his eyes half-closed, and a preoccupied
(20) air about him. Far from being the preternaturally alert and suspicious beast of fiction, this wolf was so self-engrossed that he came straight on to within fifteen yards of me, and might have gone right past the tent without seeing it at all, had I not banged an
(25) elbow against the teakettle, making a resounding clank. The wolf's head came up and his eyes opened wide, but he did not stop or falter in his pace. One brief, sidelong glance was all he vouchsafed to me as he continued on his way.

(30) By the time this happened, I had learned a great deal about my wolfish neighbors, and one of the facts which had emerged was that they were not nomadic roamers, as is almost universally believed, but were settled beasts and the possessors of a large
(35) permanent estate with very definite boundaries. The territory owned by my wolf family comprised more than a hundred square miles, bounded on one side by a river but otherwise not delimited by geographical features. Nevertheless there were
(40) boundaries, clearly indicated in wolfish fashion.

Once a week, more or less, the clan made the rounds of the family lands and freshened up the boundary markers—a sort of lupine* beating of the bounds. This careful attention to property rights
(45) was perhaps made necessary by the presence of two other wolf families whose lands abutted on ours, although I never discovered any evidence of bickering or disagreements between the owners of the various adjoining estates. I suspect, therefore,
(50) that it was more of a ritual activity.

In any event, once I had become aware of this strong feeling of property among the wolves, I decided to use this knowledge to make them at least recognize my existence. One evening, after
(55) they had gone off for their regular nightly hunt, I staked out a property claim of my own, embracing perhaps three acres, with the tent at the middle, and including a hundred yard long section of the wolves' path. This took most of the night and
(60) required frequent returns to the tent to consume copious quantities of tea; but before dawn brought the hunters home the task was done and I retired, somewhat exhausted, to observe the results.

I had not long to wait. At 0814 hours, according
(65) to my wolf log, the leading male of the clan appeared over the ridge behind me, padding homeward with his usual air of preoccupation. As usual, he did not deign to look at the tent; but when he reached the point where my property line
(70) intersected the trail, he stopped as abruptly as if he had run into an invisible wall. His attitude of fatigue vanished and was replaced by one of bewilderment. Cautiously he extended his nose and sniffed at one of my marked bushes. After a minute
(75) of complete indecision he backed away a few yards and sat down. And then, finally, he looked directly at the tent and me. It was a long, considering sort of look.

Having achieved my object—that of forcing at
(80) least one of the wolves to take cognizance of my existence—I now began to wonder if, in my ignorance, I had transgressed some unknown wolf law of major importance and would have to pay for my temerity. I found myself regretting the absence
(85) of a weapon as the look I was getting became longer, more thoughtful, and still more intent. In an effort to break the impasse I loudly cleared my throat and turned my back on the wolf to indicate as clearly as possible that I found his continued
(90) scrutiny impolite, if not actually offensive.

He appeared to take the hint. Briskly, and with an air of decision, he turned his attention away from me and began a systematic tour of the area, sniffing each boundary marker once or twice, and
(95) carefully placing his mark on the outside of each clump of grass or stone. In fifteen minutes he rejoined the path at the point where it left my property and trotted off towards his home, leaving me with a good deal to occupy my thoughts.

lupine: relating to wolves

GO ON TO THE NEXT PAGE ➡

24 According to the author, why were his precautions against disturbing the wolves "superfluous" (line 2)?

(A) It was several weeks before he encountered his first wolf.
(B) Other wild animals posed a greater threat to his safety.
(C) The wolves noticed him, but were not interested in harming him.
(D) He was not bothered by the wolves until he started interfering with them.
(E) The wolves were unable to detect him due to their poor eyesight.

25 The author mentions the wolves' "assessment" of him (line 5) in order to

(A) account for their strange behavior towards him
(B) convey his initial fear of being attacked
(C) emphasize his ignorance on first encountering them
(D) indicate the need for precautions against disturbing them
(E) suggest his courage in an unfamiliar situation

26 In the third paragraph, the author is primarily surprised to find that the wolf

(A) is traveling alone
(B) lacks the energy to respond
(C) is hunting at night
(D) is not more on its guard
(E) does not attack him

27 In line 17, the word *anxious* most nearly means

(A) distressed
(B) afraid
(C) eager
(D) uneasy
(E) worried

28 In line 34, the word *settled* most nearly means

(A) decided
(B) resolute
(C) stable
(D) inflexible
(E) confident

29 Lines 30–35 provide

(A) a contradiction of popular myth
(B) an explanation of a paradox
(C) a rebuttal of established facts
(D) an exception to a general rule
(E) a summary of conclusions

30 The author suggests that boundary marking was a "ritual activity" (line 50) because

(A) the wolves marked their boundaries at regular intervals
(B) no disputes over territory ever seemed to occur
(C) the boundaries were marked by geographical features
(D) the boundaries were marked at the same time each week
(E) the whole family of wolves participated in the activity

31 Which of the following discoveries would most weaken the author's thesis concerning the wolves' "strong feeling of property" (line 52)?

(A) Disputes over boundaries are a frequent occurrence.
(B) Wolf territories are typically around one hundred square miles in area.
(C) Wolf families often wander from place to place to find food.
(D) Territorial conflicts between wolves and human beings are rare.
(E) Wolves are generally alert when encountering other animals.

32 The author most likely mentions an "invisible wall" (line 71) in order to emphasize

(A) his delight in attracting the wolf's attention
(B) the wolf's annoyance at encountering a challenge
(C) the high speed at which the wolf was traveling
(D) the sudden manner in which the wolf stopped
(E) the wolf's exhaustion after a night of hunting

GO ON TO THE NEXT PAGE ➡

33 The wolf's first reaction on encountering the
author's property marking is one of

(A) combativeness
(B) confusion
(C) anxiety
(D) wariness
(E) dread

34 In line 84, *temerity* means

(A) discourtesy
(B) rashness
(C) courage
(D) anger
(E) discretion

35 The author turns his back on the wolf
(lines 88–90) primarily in order to

(A) demonstrate his power over the wolf
(B) bring about some change in the situation
(C) compel the wolf to recognize his existence
(D) look for a suitable weapon
(E) avoid the wolf's hypnotic gaze

**IF YOU FINISH BEFORE TIME IS CALLED, YOU MAY CHECK YOUR WORK ON
THIS SECTION ONLY. DO NOT TURN TO ANY OTHER SECTION IN THE TEST.** **STOP**

Time—30 Minutes
25 Questions

Solve each of the following problems, decide which is the best answer choice, and darken the corresponding oval on the answer sheet. Use available space in the test booklet for scratchwork.*

Notes:

(1)   Calculator use is permitted.

(2)   All numbers used are real numbers.

(3)   Figures are provided for some problems. All figures are drawn to scale and lie in a plane UNLESS otherwise indicated.

Reference Information

$A = \frac{1}{2}bh$ $c^2 = a^2 + b^2$ Special Right Triangles $A = \pi r^2$
$C = 2\pi r$ $V = \ell wh$ $V = \pi r^2 h$ $A = \ell w$

The sum of the degree measures of the angles of a triangle is 180.
The number of degrees of arc in a circle is 360.
A straight angle has a degree measure of 180.

DIRECTIONS FOR QUANTITATIVE COMPARISON QUESTIONS

Compare the boxed quantity in Column A with the boxed quantity in Column B. Select answer choice

A   if Column A is greater;
B   if Column B is greater;
C   if the columns are equal; or
D   if more information is needed to determine the relationship.

An E response will be treated as an omission.

Notes:

1.   Some questions include information about one or both quantities. That information is centered and unboxed.
2.   A symbol that appears in both Column A and Column B stands for the same thing in both columns.
3.   All numbers used are real numbers.

EXAMPLES

	Column A	Column B	Answers
E1	3×4	$3 + 4$	● Ⓑ Ⓒ Ⓓ Ⓔ
E2	x	160	Ⓐ Ⓑ ● Ⓓ Ⓔ
E3	$x + 1$	$y - 1$	Ⓐ Ⓑ Ⓒ ● Ⓔ

E2: $x°$ / $20°$

E3: x and y are positive

GO ON TO THE NEXT PAGE ➡

*The directions on the actual SAT will vary slightly.

Column A	**Column B**

1 $\frac{1}{8} + \frac{1}{10}$ $\frac{1}{9} + \frac{1}{11}$

$x < 1$

2 x $\frac{1}{x}$

3 52% of 34   17

4 $3(x - 2)$ $3x - 4$

The product of two integers is 10.

5 6   The sum of the integers

x and y are nonzero integers.

6 $\frac{x^2}{y^2}$ $x^2 y^2$

Column A	**Column B**

$AC = BD$

7 AB BC

$x > 0$
$y > 1$

8 x xy

$x > 1$

9 x^5 $(x^3)^2$

$y \neq 0$

10 $\frac{1}{y}$ $\frac{y^2}{y}$

GO ON TO THE NEXT PAGE ➡

Column A	Column B	Column A	Column B

11

The number of square units in the area of a square with side 6	The number of units in the perimeter of a square with side 9

$y > 0$

14

$1 - \dfrac{y}{1 + y}$	$1 - \dfrac{1}{1 + y}$

Wilfredo's math test scores are the following:
88, 82, 94, 93, 85, 90, 93, 98

12

Wilfredo's mode test score	Wilfredo's median test score

$ABCD$ is a rectangle with perimeter 32.
$AB > BC$

15

The area of $ABCD$	The area of a square with perimeter 32

13

The area of the circle	The area of the rectangle

GO ON TO THE NEXT PAGE ➡

DIRECTIONS FOR STUDENT-PRODUCED RESPONSE QUESTIONS

For each of the questions below (16–25), solve the problem and indicate your answer by darkening the ovals in the special grid. For example:

Answer: 1.25 or $\frac{5}{4}$ or 5/4

Write answer in boxes. →

Grid-in result →

Fraction line ←

Decimal point ←

Either position is correct.

You may start your answers in any column, space permitting. Columns not needed should be left blank.

- It is recommended, though not required, that you write your answer in the boxes at the top of the columns. However, you will receive credit only for darkening the ovals correctly.

- Grid only one answer to a question, even though some problems have more than one correct answer.

- Darken no more than one oval in a column.

- No answers are negative.

- Mixed numbers cannot be gridded. For example: the number $1\frac{1}{4}$ must be gridded as 1.25 or 5/4.

(If $1\,1\,/\,4$ is gridded, it will be interpreted as $\frac{11}{4}$, not $1\frac{1}{4}$.)

- Decimal Accuracy: Decimal answers must be entered as accurately as possible. For example, if you obtain an answer such as 0.1666..., you should record the result as .166 or .167. **Less accurate values such as .16 or .17 are not acceptable.**

Acceptable ways to grid $\frac{1}{6}$ = .1666. . .

17 What is $\frac{1}{4}$ percent of 16?

16 In the figure above, if line p is parallel to line q, what is the value of y ?

GO ON TO THE NEXT PAGE ➡

18 Each of the fractions above is in its simplest
    reduced form and *a* is an integer greater than 1 and
    less than 50. Grid in one possible value of *a* .

19 If there are 36 men and 24 women in a group,
    women make up what fraction of the entire group?

23 What is the area of the triangle in the figure
    above?

20 What is the value of $\frac{3s+5}{4}$ when *s* = 9?

24 A square is divided in half to form two congruent
    rectangles, each with perimeter 24. What is the
    area of the original square?

21 If the positive integer *x* leaves a remainder of 2
    when divided by 6, what will the remainder be
    when *x* + 8 is divided by 6 ?

25 The formula for converting a Fahrenheit
    temperature reading to a Celsius temperature
    reading is $C = \frac{5}{9}(F - 32)$, where *C* is the reading in
    degrees Celsius and *F* is the reading in degrees
    Fahrenheit. What is the Fahrenheit equivalent to
    a reading of 95° Celsius?

22 Pat deposited 15% of last week's take-home pay
    into a savings account. If she deposited $37.50,
    what was last week's take-home pay?

**IF YOU FINISH BEFORE TIME IS CALLED, YOU MAY CHECK YOUR WORK ON
THIS SECTION ONLY. DO NOT TURN TO ANY OTHER SECTION IN THE TEST.**

STOP

Time—30 Minutes
31 Questions

For each of the following questions, choose the best answer and darken the corresponding oval on the answer sheet.

Select the lettered word or set of words that best completes the sentence.

Example:

Today's small, portable computers contrast markedly with the earliest electronic computers, which were ----.

(A) effective
(B) invented
(C) useful
(D) destructive
(E) enormous

1   The band has courted controversy before in order to get attention, and the ---- lyrics on their new album demonstrate that they found the strategy ----.

(A) sedate . . plausible
(B) vacuous . . rewarding
(C) belligerent . . counterproductive
(D) scandalous . . effective
(E) provocative . . comparable

2   James Joyce regarded ---- as central to the creative process, which is evident in the numerous scribbled edits that cover even his supposedly final drafts.

(A) contrivance
(B) revision
(C) inspiration
(D) obsession
(E) disavowal

3   Fans who believe that the players' motivations are not ---- would be ---- to learn that they now charge for their signatures.

(A) self-serving . . vindicated
(B) venal . . chagrined
(C) altruistic . . unsurprised
(D) atypical . . disillusioned
(E) tainted . . gratified

4   Though the film ostensibly deals with the theme of ----, the director seems to have been more interested in its absence—in isolation and the longing for connection.

(A) reliance
(B) fraternity
(C) socialism
(D) privation
(E) levity

5   Everything the candidate said publicly was ----; he manipulated the media in order to present the image he wanted.

(A) incendiary
(B) calculated
(C) facetious
(D) scrupulous
(E) impromptu

6   Most young artists struggle, producing works that have but ---- of future greatness, but Walt Whitman's transformation into a genius was ----.

(A) glimmers . . effortless
(B) shadows . . noteworthy
(C) features . . protracted
(D) critiques . . immediate
(E) aspirations . . unforeseeable

7   Although Sub-Saharan Africa encompasses a large number of ---- cultures, its music is often considered an essentially ---- mass.

(A) disparate . . homogeneous
(B) impoverished . . inimitable
(C) warring . . concrete
(D) interwoven . . distinctive
(E) proud . . languid

8   His face was ----, his features pulled downward by the weight of heavy thoughts.

(A) morose
(B) onerous
(C) contorted
(D) ossified
(E) inscrutable

9   The unfortunate demise of the protagonist in the final scene of the movie ---- all possibility of a sequel.

(A) entertained
(B) dissembled
(C) raised
(D) exacerbated
(E) precluded

GO ON TO THE NEXT PAGE ➡

Choose the lettered pair of words that is related in the same way as the pair in capital letters.

Example:

FLAKE : SNOW ::

- (A) storm : hail
- (B) drop : rain
- (C) field : wheat
- (D) stack : hay
- (E) cloud : fog

10 SCAR : INJURY ::

- (A) monument : marble
- (B) fever : illness
- (C) dent : collision
- (D) exhibition : painting
- (E) blood : fistfight

11 YAWN : BOREDOM ::

- (A) react : surprise
- (B) pout : displeasure
- (C) gasp : breath
- (D) repose : sleep
- (E) cheer : depression

12 ACTOR : AUDITION ::

- (A) singer : debut
- (B) judge : verdict
- (C) architect : plan
- (D) instrumentalist : solo
- (E) gymnast : tryout

13 ALIENATE : ESTRANGEMENT ::

- (A) discommode : inconvenience
- (B) sequester : monasticism
- (C) palliate : boredom
- (D) orchestrate : symphony
- (E) aspire : enthusiasm

14 PUNGENT : SNIFFED ::

- (A) itinerant : traveled
- (B) prickly : touched
- (C) venomous : bitten
- (D) acrid : burned
- (E) belligerent : feuded

15 DISCONCERT : CONFUSION ::

- (A) fear : superstition
- (B) daunt : discouragement
- (C) spend : extravagance
- (D) remonstrate : reward
- (E) stabilize : imbalance

GO ON TO THE NEXT PAGE ➡

Answer the questions below based on the information in the accompanying passages.

Questions 16–22 are based on the following passage.

The following passage is from a discussion of the origin of the Cold War between the United States and the Soviet Union.

Revisionist historians maintain that it was within the power of the United States, in the years during and immediately after the Second World
Line War, to prevent the Cold War with the Soviet
(5) Union. Revisionists suggest that the prospect of impending conflict with the Soviets could have been avoided in several ways. The U.S. could have officially recognized the new Soviet sphere of influence in Eastern Europe instead of continuing
(10) to call for self-determination in those countries. A much-needed reconstruction loan could have helped the Soviets recover from the war. The Americans could have sought to assuage Soviet fears by giving up the U.S. monopoly of the atomic
(15) bomb and turning the weapons over to an international agency (with the stipulation that future nuclear powers do the same).

This criticism of the post-war American course of action fails to take into account the political
(20) realities in America at the time, and unfairly condemns the American policy-makers who did consider each of these alternatives and found them to be unworkable. Recognition of a Soviet Eastern Europe was out of the question. Roosevelt had
(25) promised self-determination to the Eastern European countries, and the American people, having come to expect this, were furious when Stalin began to shape his spheres of influence in the region. The President was in particular acutely
(30) conscious of the millions of Polish-Americans who would be voting in the upcoming election.

Negotiations had indeed been conducted by the administration with the Soviets about a reconstruction loan, but the Congress refused to
(35) approve it unless the Soviets made enormous concessions tantamount to restructuring their system and withdrawing from Eastern Europe. This, of course, made Soviet rejection of the loan a foregone conclusion. As for giving up the bomb—
(40) the elected officials in Washington would have been in deep trouble with their constituents had that plan been carried out. Polls showed that 82 percent of the American people understood that other nations would develop bombs eventually, but that
(45) 85 percent thought that the U.S. should retain exclusive possession of the weapon. Policy-makers have to abide by certain constraints in deciding what is acceptable and what is not. They, and not historians, are in the best position to perceive those
(50) constraints and make the decisions.

Revisionist historians tend to eschew this type of political explanation of America's supposed failure to reach a peaceful settlement with the Soviets in favor of an economic reading of events.
(55) They point to the fact that in the early post-war years American businessmen and government officials cooperated to expand American foreign trade vigorously and to exploit investment opportunities in many foreign countries. In order to
(60) sustain the lucrative expansion, revisionists assert, American policy-makers were obliged to maintain an "Open Door" foreign policy, the object of which was to keep all potential trade opportunities open. Since the Soviets could jeopardize such
(65) opportunities in Eastern Europe and elsewhere, they had to be opposed. Hence, the Cold War. But if American policy-makers were simply pawns in an economic game of expansionist capitalism, as the revisionists seem to think, why do the revisionists
(70) hold them responsible for not attempting to reach an accord with the Soviets? The policy-makers, swept up by a tidal wave of capitalism, clearly had little control and little choice in the matter.

Even if American officials had been free and
(75) willing to make conciliatory gestures toward the Soviets, the Cold War would not have been prevented. Overtures of friendship would not have been reciprocated (as far as we can judge; information on the inner workings of the Kremlin
(80) during that time is scanty). Soviet expert George F. Kennan concluded that Russian hostility could not be dampened by any effort on the part of the United States. The political and ideological differences were too great, and the Soviets had too long a
(85) history of distrust of foreigners—exacerbated at the time by Stalin's rampant paranoia, which infected his government—to embark on a process of establishing trust and peace with the United States, though it was in their interest to do so.

16 The primary purpose of the passage is to

(A) explode a popular myth
(B) criticize historical figures
(C) refute an argument
(D) analyze an era
(E) reconcile opposing views

GO ON TO THE NEXT PAGE ➡

17 In line 8, the word *recognized* most nearly means

(A) identified
(B) noticed
(C) acknowledged
(D) distinguished
(E) remembered

18 The author refers to the Polish-Americans (lines 29–31) chiefly to illustrate that

(A) the president had an excellent rapport with ethnic minorities
(B) immigrants had fled from Eastern European countries to escape communism
(C) giving up the idea of East European self-determination would have been costly in political terms
(D) the Poles could enjoy self-determination only in America
(E) the political landscape of the United States had changed considerably since the President was elected

19 A fundamental assumption underlying the author's argument in the second and third paragraphs is that

(A) the Soviets were largely to blame for the failure of conciliatory U.S. initiatives
(B) the American public was very well-informed about the incipient Cold War situation
(C) none of the proposed alternatives would have had its intended effect
(D) the American public was overwhelmingly opposed to seeking peace with the Soviets
(E) the government could not have been expected to ignore public opinion

20 The phrase *certain constraints* in line 47 most likely refers to

(A) the etiquette of international diplomacy
(B) the danger of leaked information about atomic bombs
(C) the views of the electorate
(D) the potential reaction of the enemy
(E) the difficulty of carrying out a policy initiative

21 Which statement best summarizes the revisionist argument concerning the origin of the Cold War (lines 51–66)?

(A) The United States started the Cold War in order to have a military cover for illegal trading activities.
(B) The Soviets were oblivious to the negative impact they had on the American economy.
(C) The economic advantage of recognizing Soviet Europe outweighed the disadvantage of an angry public.
(D) America could trade and invest with foreign countries only if it agreed to oppose the Soviet Union.
(E) American economic interests abroad would have been threatened by any Soviet expansion.

22 The question at the end of the fourth paragraph (lines 66–71) serves to

(A) point out an inconsistency in a position
(B) outline an area that requires further research
(C) contrast two different historical interpretations
(D) sum up a cynical view of post-war economic activity
(E) restate the central issue of the passage

GO ON TO THE NEXT PAGE ➡

Questions 23–31 are based on the following passage.

James Weldon Johnson was a poet, diplomat, composer and historian of black culture who wrote around the turn of the century. In this narrative passage Johnson recalls his first experience of hearing rag-time jazz.

When I had somewhat collected my senses, I realized that in a large back room into which the main room opened, there was a young fellow
Line singing a song, accompanied on the piano by a
(5) short, thickset black man. After each verse he did some dance steps, which brought forth great applause and a shower of small coins at his feet. After the singer had responded to a rousing encore, the stout man at the piano began to run his fingers
(10) up and down the keyboard. This he did in a manner which indicated that he was a master of a good deal of technique. Then he began to play; and such playing! I stopped talking to listen. It was music of a kind I had never heard before. It was music that
(15) demanded physical response, patting of the feet, drumming of the fingers, or nodding of the head in time with the beat. The dissonant harmonies, the audacious resolutions, often consisting of an abrupt jump from one key to another, the intricate
(20) rhythms in which the accents fell in the most unexpected places, but in which the beat was never lost, produced a most curious effect . . .

This was rag-time music, then a novelty in New York, and just growing to be a rage, which has
(25) not yet subsided. It was originated in the questionable resorts about Memphis and St. Louis by Negro piano-players who knew no more of the theory of music than they did of the theory of the universe, but were guided by natural musical
(30) instinct and talent. It made its way to Chicago, where it was popular some time before it reached New York. These players often improvised simple and, at times, vulgar words to fit the melodies. This was the beginning of the rag-time song . . .
(35) American musicians, instead of investigating rag-time, attempt to ignore it, or dismiss it with a contemptuous word. But that has always been the course of scholasticism in every branch of art. Whatever new thing the *people* like is pooh-
(40) poohed; whatever is *popular* is spoken of as not worth the while. The fact is, nothing great or enduring, especially in music, has ever sprung full-fledged and unprecedented from the brain of any master; the best that he gives to the world he
(45) gathers from the hearts of the people, and runs it through the alembic* of his genius. In spite of the bans which musicians and music teachers have placed upon it, the people still demand and enjoy rag-time. One thing cannot be denied; it is music
(50) which possesses at least one strong element of greatness: it appeals universally; not only the American, but the English, the French, and even

the German people find delight in it. In fact, there is not a corner of the civilized world in which it is
(55) not known, and this proves its originality; for if it were an imitation, the people of Europe, anyhow, would not have found it a novelty . . .

I became so interested in both the music and the player that I left the table where I was sitting,
(60) and made my way through the hall into the back room, where I could see as well as hear. I talked to the piano player between the musical numbers and found out that he was just a natural musician, never having taken a lesson in his life. Not only
(65) could he play almost anything he heard, but he could accompany singers in songs he had never heard. He had, by ear alone, composed some pieces, several of which he played over for me; each of them was properly proportioned and
(70) balanced. I began to wonder what this man with such a lavish natural endowment would have done had he been trained. Perhaps he wouldn't have done anything at all; he might have become, at best, a mediocre imitator of the great masters in
(75) what they have already done to a finish, or one of the modern innovators who strive after originality by seeing how cleverly they can dodge about through the rules of harmony and at the same time avoid melody. It is certain that he would not have
(80) been so delightful as he was in rag-time.

*alembic: scientific apparatus used in the process of distillation

23 In relating his initial impression of rag-time music to the reader, the narrator makes use of

(A) comparison with the improvisations of classical music
(B) reference to the audience's appreciative applause
(C) description of the music's compelling rhythmic effect
(D) evocation of poignant visual images
(E) allusion to several popular contemporary tunes

24 In the first paragraph, the narrator portrays rag-time as a type of music that

(A) would be a challenge to play for even the most proficient musician
(B) satisfied the narrator's expectations regarding the genre
(C) violated all of the accepted rules governing musical composition
(D) made up for a lack of melody with a seductive rhythm
(E) contained several surprises for the discerning listener

GO ON TO THE NEXT PAGE ➡

25 In line 26, *questionable* most nearly means

(A) disreputable
(B) ambiguous
(C) doubtful
(D) approachable
(E) unconfirmed

26 The narrator's perspective during the second and third paragraphs is that of

(A) an impartial historian of events in the recent past
(B) a mesmerized spectator of a musical spectacle
(C) a knowledgeable critic of the contemporary musical scene
(D) a commentator reflecting on a unique experience
(E) an adult reminiscing fondly about his youth

27 In lines 28–29, the reference to "the theory of the universe" serves to

(A) emphasize that rag-time at its inception was an unconventional musical form
(B) show that the originators of rag-time were wholly engrossed in their own music
(C) imply that the attainment of musical proficiency should take priority over academic pursuits
(D) suggest that those who founded rag-time could not have imagined the extent of its future influence
(E) demonstrate that level of education is not commensurate with artistic success

28 The discussion in the third paragraph of the refusal of American musicians to investigate rag-time suggests that they

(A) have little or no interest in pleasing people with their music
(B) need to be made aware of the popularity of rag-time in Europe
(C) are misguided in their conservative and condescending attitude
(D) attack rag-time for being merely an imitation of an existing style
(E) know that it would be difficult to refine rag-time as a musical form

29 Which statement best summarizes the author's argument in the third paragraph?

(A) Any type of music that is extremely popular should be considered great.
(B) The two criteria for musical greatness are popularity and originality.
(C) Music that has become popular overseas cannot be ignored by American musicians.
(D) Rag-time must be taken up by a musical master and purified to earn critical acclaim.
(E) Mass appeal in music can be a sign of greatness rather than a stigma.

30 The statement in lines 72–73 ("Perhaps he wouldn't have done anything at all") is best interpreted as conveying

(A) doubt about the depth of the piano player's skill
(B) understanding that no amount of talent can compensate for a lack of discipline
(C) cynicism about the likelihood that a man can live up to his potential
(D) a recognition that the piano player might have wasted his talent
(E) frustration at the impossibility of knowing what might have been

31 The author's view (lines 72–80) about the rag-time piano player's lack of formal training can best be summarized as which of the following?

(A) The piano player's natural talent had allowed him to develop technically to the point where formal training would have been superfluous.
(B) Formal lessons would have impaired the piano player's native ability to play and compose by ear alone.
(C) More would have been lost than gained if the piano player had been given formal lessons.
(D) The piano player's potential to be a truly innovative rag-time artist had been squandered because he had not been formally trained.
(E) Although dazzling when improvising rag-time, the piano player could never have been more than mediocre as a classical pianist.

IF YOU FINISH BEFORE TIME IS CALLED, YOU MAY CHECK YOUR WORK ON THIS SECTION ONLY. DO NOT TURN TO ANY OTHER SECTION IN THE TEST.

STOP

Time—15 Minutes

10 Questions

Solve each of the following problems, decide which is the best answer choice, and darken the corresponding oval on the answer sheet. Use available space in the test booklet for scratchwork.

Notes:

(1)   Calculator use is permitted.

(2)   All numbers used are real numbers.

(3)   Figures are provided for some problems. All figures are drawn to scale and lie in a plane UNLESS otherwise indicated.

Reference Information

$A=\frac{1}{2}bh$ $c^2 = a^2 + b^2$ Special Right Triangles $A=\pi r^2$ $C=2\pi r$ $V=\ell wh$ $V=\pi r^2 h$ $A=\ell w$

The sum of the degree measures of the angles of a triangle is 180.
The number of degrees of arc in a circle is 360.
A straight angle has a degree measure of 180.

---

1   For all x, $(3x + 4)(4x - 3) =$

(A) $7x + 1$
(B) $7x - 12$
(C) $12x^2 - 12$
(D) $12x^2 - 25x - 12$
(E) $12x^2 + 7x - 12$

2   In a certain set of numbers, the ratio of integers to nonintegers is 2:3. What percent of the numbers in the set are integers?

(A)   20%

(B) $33\frac{1}{3}\%$

(C)   40%

(D)   60%

(E) $66\frac{2}{3}\%$

3   If $xyz \neq 0$, which of the following is equivalent to $\frac{x^2y^3z^4}{(xyz^2)^2}$?

(A) $\frac{1}{y}$

(B) $\frac{1}{z}$

(C) y

(D) $\frac{x}{yz}$

(E) xyz

4   When the positive integer p is divided by 7, the remainder is 5. What is the remainder when $5p$ is divided by 7?

(A)   0
(B)   1
(C)   2
(D)   3
(E)   4

GO ON TO THE NEXT PAGE ➡

5 What is the *y*-intercept of the line with the equation $2x - 3y = 18$?

(A) −9
(B) −6
(C) −3
(D) 6
(E) 9

6 Jan types at an average rate of 12 pages per hour. At that rate, how long will it take Jan to type 100 pages?

(A) 8 hours and 3 minutes

(B) 8 hours and 15 minutes

(C) 8 hours and 20 minutes

(D) 8 hours and 30 minutes

(E) 8 hours and $33\frac{1}{3}$ minutes

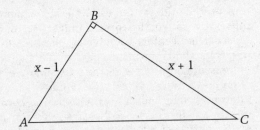

7 In the figure above, *AB* is perpendicular to *BC*. The lengths of *AB* and *BC* are given in terms of *x*. Which of the following represents the area of △*ABC* for all *x* > 1 ?

(A) *x*

(B) 2*x*

(C) x^2

(D) $x^2 - 1$

(E) $\frac{x^2 - 1}{2}$

8 If Jim and Bill have less than 15 dollars between them, and Bill has 4 dollars, which of the following could be the number of dollars that Jim has?

    I. 10
    II. 11
    III. 15

(A) I only
(B) II only
(C) I and II only
(D) II and III only
(E) I, II, and III

9 Angelo makes *x* dollars for *y* hours of work. Sarah makes the same amount of money for 1 less hour of work. Which of the following expressions represents the positive difference between the two people's hourly wage?

(A) $\frac{x}{y-1} - \frac{x}{y}$

(B) $\frac{x}{y} - \frac{x}{y-1}$

(C) $\frac{x}{y-1} + \frac{x}{y}$

(D) $\frac{y-1}{x} - \frac{y}{x}$

(E) $\frac{y}{x} - \frac{y-1}{x}$

10 Erica has 8 squares of felt, each with area 16. For a certain craft project she cuts the largest circle possible from each square of felt. What is the combined area of the excess felt left over after cutting out all the circles?

(A) $4(4 - \pi)$
(B) $8(4 - \pi)$
(C) $8(\pi - 2)$
(D) $32(4 - \pi)$
(E) $16(16 - \pi)$

IF YOU FINISH BEFORE TIME IS CALLED, YOU MAY CHECK YOUR WORK ON THIS SECTION ONLY. DO NOT TURN TO ANY OTHER SECTION IN THE TEST.

STOP

Time—15 Minutes
12 Questions   Answer the questions below based on the information in the accompanying passages.

Questions 1–12 are based on the following passages.

These passages present two critics' perspectives on the topic of design museums.

Passage 1

City museums are places where people can learn about various cultures by studying objects of particular historical or artistic value. The
(5) increasingly popular "design museums" that are opening today perform quite a different function. Unlike most city museums, the design museum displays and assesses objects that are readily available to the general public. These museums
(10) place ignored household appliances under spotlights, breaking down the barriers between commerce and creative invention.

Critics have argued that design museums are often manipulated to serve as advertisements for new industrial technology. But their role is not
(15) simply a matter of merchandising—it is the honoring of impressive, innovative products. The difference between the window of a department store and the showcase in a design museum is that the first tries to sell you something, while the
(20) second informs you of the success of the attempt.

One advantage that the design museum has over other civic museums is that design museums are places where people feel familiar with the exhibits. Unlike the average art gallery patron, design
(25) museum visitors rarely feel intimidated or disoriented. Partly this is because design museums clearly illustrate how and why mass-produced consumer objects work and look as they do, and show how design contributes to the quality of our
(30) lives. For example, an exhibit involving a particular design of chair would not simply explain how it functions as a chair. It would also demonstrate how its various features combine to produce an artistic effect or redefine our manner of performing the
(35) basic act of being seated. The purpose of such an exhibit would be to present these concepts in ways that challenge, stimulate and inform the viewer. An art gallery exhibit, on the other hand, would provide very little information about the chair and charge
(40) the visitor with understanding the exhibit on some abstract level.

Within the past decade, several new design museums have opened their doors. Each of these museums has responded in totally original ways to
(45) the public's growing interest in the field. London's Design Museum, for instance, displays a collection of mass-produced objects ranging from Zippo lighters to electric typewriters to a show of Norwegian sardine-tin labels. The options open to
(50) curators of design museums seem far less rigorous, conventionalized and pre-programmed than those applying to curators in charge of public galleries of paintings and sculpture. The humorous aspects of our society are better represented in the display of
(55) postmodern playthings or quirky Japanese vacuum cleaners in pastel colors than in an exhibition of Impressionist landscapes.

Passage 2

The short histories of some of the leading technical and design museums make clear an
(60) underlying difficulty in this area. The tendency everywhere today is to begin with present machines and technological processes and to show how they operate and the scientific principles on which they are based without paying much
(65) attention to their historical development, to say nothing of the society that produced them. Only a few of the oldest, largest and best-supported museums collect historical industrial objects. Most science centers put more emphasis on mock-
(70) ups, graphs and multimedia devices. This approach of "presentism" often leads the museum to drop all attempts at study and research; if industry is called upon to design and build the exhibits, curators may be entirely dispensed with, so that impartial
(75) and scientific study disappears, and emphasis is placed on the idea that progress automatically follows technology.

Industrialization and the machine have, of course, brought much progress; a large portion of
(80) humankind no longer works from sunup to sundown to obtain the bare necessities of life. But industrialization also creates problems—harm to the environment and ecology, neglect of social, cultural and humanistic values, depletion of
(85) resources, and even threats of human extinction. Thus progress needs to be considered critically— from a wider social and humanitarian point of view. Unfortunately, most museums of science and technology glorify machines. Displayed in
(90) pristine condition, elegantly painted or polished, they can make the observer forget the noise, dirt, danger and frustration of machine-tending. Mines, whether coal, iron or salt, are a favorite museum display but only infrequently is there even a hint of
(95) the dirt, the damp, the smell, the low headroom, or the crippling and destructive accidents that sometimes occur in industry.

GO ON TO THE NEXT PAGE ➡

Machinery also ought to be operated to be meaningful. Consequently, it should not be shown (100) in sculptured repose but in full, often clattering, action. This kind of operation is difficult to obtain, and few museums can command the imagination, ingenuity, and manual dexterity it requires. Problems also arise in providing adequate safety (105) devices for both the public and the machine operators. These, then, are some of the underlying problems of the technical museum—problems not solved by the usual push buttons, cranks or multimedia gimmicks. Yet attendance figures show (110) that technical museums outdraw all the others; the public possesses lively curiosity and a real desire to understand science and technology.

1 In line 7, the word *readily* most nearly means

(A) easily
(B) willingly
(C) instantly
(D) cheaply
(E) constantly

2 In lines 14–20, the author of Passage 1 suggests that design museums are different from store windows in that

(A) design museums display more technologically advanced products
(B) store window displays are not created with as much concern to the visual quality of the display
(C) design museums are not concerned with the commercial aspects of a successful product
(D) design museums focus on highlighting the artistic qualities that help sell products
(E) the objects in store displays are more commercially successful than those in design museums

3 From lines 21–30, it can be inferred that the author believes that most museum visitors

(A) are hostile towards the concept of abstract art
(B) prefer to have a context in which to understand museum exhibits
(C) are confused when faced with complex technological exhibits
(D) are unfamiliar with the exhibits in design museums
(E) undervalue the artistic worth of household items

4 The third paragraph of Passage 1 suggests that one important difference between design museums and the art galleries is

(A) the low price of admission at design museums
(B) the amount of information presented with design museum exhibits
(C) the intelligence of the average museum visitor
(D) that art galleries feature exhibits that have artistic merit
(E) the contribution that design museums make to our quality of life

5 In line 49, the word *options* most likely refers to the ability of curators of design museums to

(A) afford large collections of exhibits
(B) attract a wide range of visitors
(C) put together unconventional collections
(D) feature rare objects that interest the public
(E) satisfy their own personal whims in planning exhibitions

6 In line 57, the author most likely mentions "Impressionist landscapes" in order to

(A) provide an example of a typical design museum exhibit
(B) compare postmodern exhibits to nineteenth-century art
(C) point out a decline in the sophistication of the museum-going public
(D) refute the notion that postmodern art is whimsical
(E) emphasize the contrast between two different types of exhibits

7 Which of the following best describes the "underlying difficulty" mentioned in line 60 of Passage 2?

(A) Design museums rarely mention the historical origin of objects they display.
(B) Industrial involvement often forces curators out of their jobs.
(C) Design museums appropriate technology that is essential for study and research.
(D) Technology almost never leads to progress.
(E) Industry places too much emphasis on impartial research.

GO ON TO THE NEXT PAGE ➡

8 The author of Passage 2 most likely mentions "harm to the environment and ecology" (lines 82–83) in order to

(A) encourage a critical response to the technological age
(B) discourage the reader from visiting technology museums
(C) describe the hazardous conditions in coal, iron and salt mines
(D) dissuade museum visitors from operating the machinery on display
(E) praise museums that present an accurate depiction of technology

9 The author uses the phrase "sculptured repose" (line 100) in order to

(A) condemn the curators of design museums for poor planning
(B) illustrate the greatest problem inherent in design museums
(C) present an idealized vision of a type of exhibit
(D) describe the unrealistic way in which machinery is generally displayed
(E) compare the shape of a machine to a work of art

10 The word *command* (line 102) most nearly means:

(A) oversee
(B) direct
(C) control
(D) summon
(E) order

11 The author of Passage 2 would probably object to the statement that design "contributes to the quality of our lives" (lines 29–30) on the grounds that

(A) technical innovation has historically posed threats to our physical and social well-being
(B) the general public would benefit more from visiting art galleries
(C) machinery that is not shown in action is meaningless to the viewer
(D) industry has made a negligible contribution to human progress
(E) few people have a genuine interest in the impact of science and technology

12 The authors of both passages would probably agree that

(A) machinery is only enjoyable to watch when it is moving
(B) most people are curious about the factors behind the design of everyday objects
(C) the public places a higher value on packaging than it does on quality
(D) the very technology that is displayed in the museums is likely to cost curators their jobs
(E) design museums are flawed because they fail to accurately portray the environmental problems that technology sometimes causes

IF YOU FINISH BEFORE TIME IS CALLED, YOU MAY CHECK YOUR WORK ON THIS SECTION ONLY. DO NOT TURN TO ANY OTHER SECTION IN THE TEST.

STOP

ANSWER KEY ON FOLLOWING PAGE ➡

Answer Key

Section 1	Section 2	Section 3	Section 4	Section 5	Section 6
1. E	1. C	1. A	1. D	1. E	1. A
2. E	2. E	2. D	2. B	2. C	2. D
3. C	3. A	3. A	3. B	3. C	3. B
4. A	4. A	4. B	4. B	4. E	4. B
5. A	5. C	5. D	5. B	5. B	5. C
6. D	6. D	6. D	6. A	6. C	6. E
7. C	7. C	7. D	7. A	7. E	7. A
8. A	8. D	8. B	8. A	8. A	8. A
9. C	9. C	9. B	9. E	9. A	9. D
10. A	10. E	10. D	10. C	10. D	10. D
11. E	11. B	11. C	11. B		11. A
12. C	12. E	12. A	12. E		12. B
13. A	13. C	13. A	13. A		
14. D	14. D	14. D	14. B		
15. C	15. A	15. B	15. B		
16. A	16. C	16. 115	16. C		
17. E	17. E	17. .04	17. C		
18. B	18. C	18. 11, 13, 17,	18. C		
19. B	19. B	19, 23, 29,	19. E		
20. B	20. A	31, 37, 41,	20. C		
21. C	21. A	43, or 47	21. E		
22. B	22. B	19. 2/5 or .4	22. A		
23. D	23. E	20. 8	23. C		
24. D	24. C	21. 4	24. E		
25. E	25. A	22. 250	25. A		
	26. D	23. 9	26. C		
	27. C	24. 64	27. A		
	28. C	25. 203	28. C		
	29. A		29. E		
	30. B		30. D		
	31. C		31. C		
	32. D				
	33. B				
	34. B				
	35. B				

KAPLAN

Compute Your Raw Score

First, check your answers against the answer key on the previous page, and count up the number right and the number wrong for each section (there are boxes on your answer sheet to record these numbers). Remember not to count omissions as wrong.

Then figure out your raw scores using the table below. The Verbal raw score is equal to the total right in the three Verbal sections minus one-fourth of the number wrong in those sections. The Math raw score is equal to the total right in the three Math sections minus one-fourth of the number wrong in the two Regular Math sections and minus one-third the number wrong in the QCs. (Remember: There is no deduction for wrong answers in the Grid-ins.) Round each raw score to the nearest whole number.

Finally, use the tables on the next page to convert each raw score to a range of scaled scores.

	NUMBER RIGHT		NUMBER WRONG		RAW SCORE
SECTION 2:	☐	−[.25 x	☐]	=	☐
SECTION 4:	☐	−[.25 x	☐]	=	☐
SECTION 6:	☐	−[.25 x	☐]	=	☐
			VERBAL RAW SCORE:		☐ (ROUNDED)
SECTION 3A: (Questions 1 to 15)	☐	−[.33 x	☐]	=	☐
SECTION 3B: (Questions 16 to 25)	☐	(No. wrong − answer penalty)		=	☐
SECTION 1:	☐	−[.25 x	☐]	=	☐
SECTION 5:	☐	−[.25 x	☐]	=	☐
			MATH RAW SCORE:		☐ (ROUNDED)

Convert Your Score

Verbal						Math					
Raw	Scaled	Raw	Scaled	Raw	Scaled	Raw	Scaled	Raw	Scaled	Raw	Scaled
−3 or		22	450	48	620	−1 or		19	440	40	600
less	200	23	460	49	630	less	200	20	450	41	610
−2	230	24	470	50	640	0	220	21	460	42	620
−1	270	25	470	51	640	1	240	22	470	43	630
0	290	26	480	52	650	2	260	23	480	44	640
1	300	27	490	53	660	3	280	24	480	45	650
2	310	28	490	54	670	4	300	25	490	46	650
3	320	29	500	55	670	5	310	26	500	47	660
4	330	30	510	56	670	6	330	27	510	48	670
5	330	31	510	57	680	7	340	28	520	49	680
6	340	32	520	58	690	8	350	29	520	50	690
7	350	33	530	59	690	9	360	30	530	51	700
8	360	34	530	60	700	10	370	31	530	52	720
9	370	35	540	61	710	11	380	32	540	53	730
10	370	36	550	62	720	12	390	33	550	54	740
11	380	37	550	63	730	13	400	34	560	55	760
12	390	38	560	64	730	14	410	35	560	56	770
13	390	39	570	65	740	15	420	36	570	57	780
14	400	40	570	66	750	16	430	37	580	58	790
15	410	41	580	67	760	17	430	38	590	59	800
16	410	42	590	68	770	18	440	39	600	60	800
17	420	43	590	69	780						
18	430	44	600	70	790						
19	430	45	600	71 or							
20	440	46	610	more	800						
21	450	47	610								

Don't take these scores too literally. Practice test conditions cannot precisely mirror real test conditions. Your actual SAT scores will almost certainly vary from your practice test scores.

Your score on the practice test gives you a rough idea of your range on the actual exam. If you don't like your score, it's not too late to do something about it. Work your way way through this book again, and turn to Kaplan's *SAT Verbal Workbook* and *SAT Math Workbook* for even more help.

Practice Test Two Answers and Explanations

SECTION 1

1. E

Do what's in parentheses first:

$$\left(\frac{1}{5}+\frac{1}{3}\right)\div\frac{1}{2}=\left(\frac{3}{15}+\frac{5}{15}\right)\div\frac{1}{2}$$
$$=\frac{8}{15}\div\frac{1}{2}$$

Then, to divide fractions, invert the one after the division sign and multiply:

$$\frac{8}{15}\div\frac{1}{2}=\frac{8}{15}\times\frac{2}{1}=\frac{16}{15}$$

2. E

Plug in $x=-2$ and see what you get:

$$x^2-2x=(-2)^2-2(-2)$$
$$=4-(-4)$$
$$=4+4$$
$$=8$$

3. C

To get Vito's rate in pages per hour, take the 96 pages and divide by the time *in hours*. The time is given as "2 hours and 40 minutes." Forty minutes is $\frac{2}{3}$ of an hour, so you can express Vito's time as $2\frac{2}{3}$ hours, or $\frac{8}{3}$ hours:

$$\text{Pages per hour}=\frac{96\text{ pages}}{\frac{8}{3}\text{ hours}}$$
$$=96\times\frac{3}{8}=36$$

4. A

For $\frac{7}{x}$ to be greater than $\frac{1}{4}$, the denominator x has to be less than 4 times the numerator, or 28. And for $\frac{7}{x}$ to be less than $\frac{1}{3}$, the denominator x has to be greater than 3 times the numerator, or 21. Thus x could be any of the integers 22 through 27, of which there are 6.

5. A

To find the average of three numbers—even if they're algebraic expressions—add them up and divide by 3:

$$\text{Average}=\frac{(2x+5)+(5x-6)+(-4x+2)}{3}$$
$$=\frac{3x+1}{3}$$
$$=x+\frac{1}{3}$$

6. D

Percent times Whole equals Part:

$$(\text{Percent})\times25=16$$
$$\text{Percent}=\frac{16}{25}\times100\%=64\%$$

7. C

The measures of the interior angles of a triangle add up to 180, so add the two given measures and subtract the sum from 180. The difference will be the measure of the third angle:

$$45+70=115$$
$$180-115=65$$

8. A

$$\frac{x^2+x^2+x^2}{x^2}=\frac{3x^2}{x^2}=3$$

9. C

To solve a quadratic equation, put it in the "$ax^2 + bx + c = 0$" form, factor the left side (if you can), and set each factor equal to 0 separately to get the two solutions. To solve $x^2 = 5x - 4$, first rewrite it as $x^2 - 5x + 4 = 0$. Then factor the left side:

$$x^2 - 5x + 4 = 0$$
$$(x - 1)(x - 4) = 0$$
$$x = 1 \text{ or } 4$$

10. A

Picking numbers is the easiest, fastest way to do this problem. Choose a pair of numbers from each set and add them together. If you are unable to prove immediately that a set does not have the property described in the question stem, you may want to choose another pair. In set I, if we add 2 and 4, we get 6. Adding 12 and 8 gives us 20. Adding -2 and 8 gives us 6. Since each sum is a member of the set of even integers, set I seems to be true. For set II, adding 3 and 5 yields 8, which is not an odd integer. Therefore, II is not true. Finally, if we add two primes, say 2 and 3, we get 5. That example is true. If we add 3 and 5, however, we get 8, and 8 is not a prime number. Therefore, only set I has the property and the answer is (A).

11. E

The best way to deal with changing averages is to use the sum. Use the old average to figure out the total of the first 4 scores:

Sum of first 4 scores = $(4)(89) = 356$

Use the new average to figure out the total he needs after the 5th score:

Sum of 5 scores = $(5)(90) = 450$

To get his sum from 356 to 450, Martin needs to score $450 - 356 = 94$.

12. C

Don't fall for the trap choice (B): You can't add or subtract percents of different wholes. Let the original price $s = 100$. Reducing s by 25% gives you a sale price of 75. This price is then increased by 20%, so the final price

is 90. Since $s = 100$, it's easy to see that this is equal to choice (C), $.90s$.

13. A

The prime factorization of 36 is $2 \times 2 \times 3 \times 3$. That factorization includes 2 distinct prime factors, 2 and 3.

14. D

The area of a triangle is equal to one-half the base times the height:

$$\text{Area} = \frac{1}{2}(\text{base})(\text{height})$$
$$36 = \frac{1}{2}(9)(\text{height})$$
$$36 = \frac{9}{2}h$$
$$h = \frac{2}{9} \times 36 = 8$$

15. C

According to the definition, $x \clubsuit = \frac{x}{4} - \frac{x}{6}$. Set that equal to 3 and solve for x:

$$\frac{x}{4} - \frac{x}{6} = 3$$
$$12\left(\frac{x}{4} - \frac{x}{6}\right) = 12(3)$$
$$3x - 2x = 36$$
$$x = 36$$

16. A

Read carefully. This question's a lot easier than you might think at first. It's asking for the total *number* of coins, not the total value. q quarters, d dimes, and n nickels add up to a total of $q + d + n$ coins.

17. E

Use the points where the line crosses the axes—(–1, 0) and (0, 2)—to find the slope:

$$\text{Slope} = \frac{y_2 - y_1}{x_2 - x_1} = \frac{2 - 0}{0 - (-1)} = 2$$

The *y*-intercept is 2. Now plug $m = 2$ and $b = 2$ into the slope-intercept equation form:

$$y = mx + b$$
$$y = 2x + 2$$

18. B

An integer that's divisible by 6 has at least one 2 and one 3 in its prime factorization. An integer that's divisible by 9 has at least two 3's in its prime factorization. Therefore, an integer that's divisible by both 6 and 9 has at least one 2 and two 3's in its prime factorization. That means it's divisible by 2, 3, $2 \times 3 = 6$, $3 \times 3 = 9$, and $2 \times 3 \times 3 = 18$. It's *not* necessarily divisible by 12 or 36, each of which includes *two* 2's in its prime factorization.

You could also do this one by picking numbers. Think of a common multiple of 6 and 9 and use it to eliminate some options. $6 \times 9 = 54$ is an obvious common multiple—and it's not divisible by 12 or 36, but it is divisible by 18. The *least* common multiple of 6 and 9 is 18, which is also divisible by 18. It looks like every common multiple of 6 and 9 is also a multiple of 18.

19. B

Angles *POR* and *ROQ* are adjacent and supplementary, so the measure of ∠*ROP* is 180° – 50° = 130°. Now look at △*POR*:

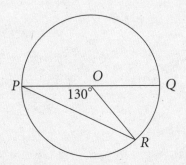

OP and *OR* are radii of the same circle, so they are equal and △*POR* is isosceles. That means ∠*P* and ∠*R*

are equal. The two of them need to add up to 50° so that the triangle's 3 interior angles will add up to 180°. If ∠*P* and ∠*R* are equal and add up to 50°, then they each measure 25°.

20. B

The volume of a cube is equal to an edge cubed, so $e^3 = 64$ and each edge of the cube has length 4. If the cube is sliced horizontally in two, each of the resulting solids will have two sides of length 4, and one of length 2. So when they are glued together, the resulting figure will have one edge of length 2, one of length 4, and one of length 4 + 4 or 8.

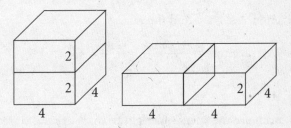

The surface area is the sum of the areas of the solid's six faces. The top and bottom each have area $8 \times 4 = 32$, the front and back each have area $8 \times 2 = 16$, and each side has area $4 \times 2 = 8$. So the surface area of the new solid is $2(32) + 2(16) + 2(8) = 64 + 32 + 16 = 112$.

21. C

Probability equals the number of favorable outcomes over the number of total outcomes. In this case, the favorable outcome is that the chosen sock will be black. Since there are 12 black socks, there are 12 favorable outcomes. The number of total outcomes is the total number of socks. $6 + 12 + 14 = 32$, so there are 32 total outcomes. The probability is $\frac{12}{32}$, which can be reduced to $\frac{3}{8}$.

22. B

This is an average rate problem, so don't just average the two rates. Instead, you have to use total distance and total time to find the average rate. First, pick a distance that is easy to use. For instance, since the speeds for the two halves of the trip are 40 and 60 miles per hour, 120 is an easy number to work with. Using 120 miles as the distance to the store, it would take $\frac{120}{40}$, or 3 hours to go to the store and $\frac{120}{60}$, or 2 hours to return. Thus, it takes 5 hours to complete a round trip of 240 miles. Now find the rate:

$$\text{Average rate} = \frac{\text{distance}}{\text{time}} = \frac{240}{5} = 48$$

23. D

You can use the 2 legs of a right triangle to get the area. Here one leg is a and you can use the Pythagorean theorem to get the other leg:

$$(\text{leg}_1)^2 + (\text{leg}_2)^2 = (\text{hypotenuse})^2$$
$$a^2 + b^2 = c^2$$
$$b^2 = c^2 - a^2$$
$$b = \sqrt{c^2 - a^2}$$

Now plug the legs a and $\sqrt{c^2 - a^2}$ into the triangle area formula:

$$\begin{aligned}
\text{Area} &= \frac{1}{2}(\text{base})(\text{height}) \\
&= \frac{1}{2}(\text{leg}_1)(\text{leg}_2) \\
&= \frac{1}{2}a\sqrt{c^2 - a^2} \\
&= \frac{a\sqrt{c^2 - a^2}}{2} \cdot
\end{aligned}$$

24. D

The area of a triangle is equal to one-half the base times the height. You can use any of the 3 sides of a triangle for the base—each side has a height to go along with it. It doesn't make any difference which base-height pair you use—a triangle has the same area no matter how you figure it. Thus one-half times PR times QS will be the same as one-half times PS times RT:

$$\frac{1}{2}(PR)(QS) = \frac{1}{2}(PS)(RT)$$
$$\frac{1}{2}(8)(9) = \frac{1}{2}(PS)(7)$$
$$(8)(9) = (PS)(7)$$
$$PS = \frac{72}{7} = 10\frac{2}{7}$$

25. E

In order to find the number of possibilities, multiply the number of possibilities in each step. In other words, there are 3 routes from Bay City to Riverville and 4 routes from Riverville to Straitstown. There are 3 more routes from Straitstown to Frogs Pond, so there are $12 \times 3 = 36$ total routes from Bay City to Frog Pond.

SECTION 2

1. C

The phrase "proves difficult" is a clue: the two missing words have to be nearly opposite in meaning. Choice (C) is correct, because few posters would be **intact** if they were meant to be **destroyed.** None of the other choices makes sense: being (A) **returned** would not stop something from being **recognizable,** being (B) **discarded** would not necessarily stop something from being **relevant,** and so on.

2. E

The phrases "long considered" and "finally" suggest contrast. The missing word is probably the opposite of "making some headway in its battle against extinction." (E) **imperiled,** "in danger," is the best answer. (A) **elusive** means "hard to find"; (B) **prevalent** means "common"; (C) **combative** means "eager to fight"; (D) **voracious** means "having a huge appetite."

3. A

The sentence sets up a contrast between the situation before the invention of the tape recorder, and the situation after. We need a word that's the opposite of "paraphrased," which means "expressed in different words." The answer is **verbatim,** "word-for-word."

4. A

The phrase "encouraged hopes" suggests that the two missing words will be somewhat related in meaning. Choice (A) is the best answer, because we expect **a serious** novelist to use **subtle** characterizations. The other choices make less sense; in fact, it's not clear what (C) **accurate** or (D) **fictional** or (E) **authentic** characterizations would be. (C) **prolific** means "highly productive"; (D) **accomplished** means "skillful, experienced"; (E) **reclusive** means "unsociable."

5. C

The missing word has to be related in meaning to "extended tenure." (C) **longevity** is the best choice. (A) **acumen** and (B) **savvy** both mean "skill" or "knowledge." (D) **decorum** means "proper behavior"; (E) **celebrity** means "fame."

6. D

The word *although* indicates contrast: the two missing words have to be opposite in meaning. This is the case with **buoyant,** "light-hearted, cheerful," and **subdued,** "quiet." In (A), **introverted** means "reserved, not outgoing." In (B), **imperious** means "commanding," and **incensed** means "angry."

7. C

The phrase "failure to" establishes the negative tone of the sentence. An agency ought to "fix" or "get rid of" flawed policies. Possible answers for the first blank are (C) **rescind** or "remove, cancel," and (D) **amend** or "fix." Failure to do this is a bad thing, so we need a negative word for the second blank. The best choice is **lackadaisical,** "careless, sloppy."

8. D

"Rapid turnover" would tend to increase "inconsistency," so we need a word that means "increased" or "worsened." **Exacerbated** means "made worse."

9. C

What claim would be "belied" or contradicted by a record of contributing to only one party? A claim of **impartiality,** of not favoring one side over the other.

10. E

"Repeated breakdown of negotiations" would tend to "support" or **reinforce** the view that the sides "were not truly committed to" "preventing" or **averting** a military confrontation. In (A) and (D), **established** and **strengthened** fit the first blank, but **escalating** and **initiating** are wrong for the second. In (B), **avoiding** fits the second blank, but **undermined** is wrong for the first.

11. B

The phrase "now that" suggests a similarity of tone between the two missing words, and the word "painful" tells us that the words will be negative. Only (B) provides a negative word for both blanks. A painful **decline** would indeed tend to cause budgetary **stringency** or tightness.

12. E

The word in the second blank has to relate in some logical way to "fear of causing leaves to fall," and the only word that does so is **durable,** "tough, not fragile." If the plant has become more **durable,** that should be a **relief** to those who were afraid of damaging it. In (A), **consternation** is "concern or worry," and **amorphous** means "shapeless."

13. C

Words like "unchanging" and "eternal" provide a definition of the missing word, (C) **static.** (D) **holistic** means "functioning as a whole," and (E) **homogeneous** means "all of one kind"; neither word implies species being unchanging and no new species coming into existence.

14. D

A **LABORATORY** is by definition a place where you **EXPERIMENT.** A **graveyard** is by definition a place where you **inter,** or bury, people. Choices (A) and (B) are wrong because you can do things in a **garage** besides **repair** things, and you can do things on a **beach** besides **sunbathe.**

15. A

To **EXONERATE** someone is to remove **BLAME** from him or her. To **disinfect** something is to remove **contamination** from it. To (B) **divert** a **stream** is to change its course; to (C) **indict** someone is to assert that person's **guilt.** Choice (E) is a bridgeless pair.

16. C

By definition, to **SCRUTINIZE** something is to **LOOK** at it very carefully. To **peruse** something is to **read** it very carefully. In (D), **importune** means the same thing as **plead.**

17. E

A **GULLIBLE** person is easy to **DUPE** or fool. A **submissive** person is easy to **control.** In (A), a **fallible** person has a tendency to **err;** this is a different bridge. Choice (B) is a bridgeless pair. In (C), a **dejected** person is already **disheartened.** In choice (D) a **headstrong** person is difficult to **coax.**

18. C

A **CONVERSATION** is carried on by two or more **INTERLOCUTOR**s, the people who participate in a conversation. A **game** is carried on by two or more **players.** The other choices have different bridges. An (A) **orator** makes a **speech** and an (E) **doctor** makes a **diagnosis.** Choices (B) and (D) have weak bridges: a **prosecutor** can take part in a **hearing,** and a **publisher** can publish a **novel.**

19. B

ENTOMOLOGY is, by definition, the study of **INSECTS. Pedagogy** is the study of **education.** In each of the other choices, there is a connection between the two words, but not the same connection as in the stem pair.

20. A

A **SKIRMISH** is, by definition, a minor **BATTLE.** A **misdemeanor** is a minor **crime.**

21. A

FORENSIC means "having to do with **LITIGATION,"** or legal procedure (you've probably heard of "forensic medicine," medical procedure used in the investigation of a crime). (A) **Maritime** means "having to do with the **sea."** Choice (D) may be tempting, but **exemplary** means "ideal," not "having to do with an **example."** Choice (C) simply combines two words that are often paired, but have no necessary relation. In (B), **euphoria** is an example of a **feeling.** In (E), something **illusory** does not necessarily have to do with **magic.**

22. B

By definition, to **FEIGN** is to give a false **IMPRESSION.** To **perjure** is to give false **testimony.** In (C),

(D), and (E), the first word has connotations of false-hood, but it does not specifically mean falsifying the second word.

23. E

A **POLEMIC** is a speech or piece of writing that advocates a particular point of view; by definition, it is not **IMPARTIAL**. Similarly, an **extrovert,** a sociable, outgoing person, is not **retiring** or shy and withdrawn. In (A), an **antidote** is **curative**. In the other choices, **discipline** may or may not be **harsh,** a **heretic** may or may not be **persecuted,** and a **defendant** may or may not be **guilty**.

The Wolves Passage

This Science passage is written by a naturalist who recounts how he went into the wilderness and, through trial and error experimentation and observation, learned some new and surprising things about the way wolves live. For example, wolves are a lot less suspicious and aggressive than people think they are, and contrary to popular belief, wolf families are not nomadic—they live and stay in territories with very definite boundaries.

24. C

In the first paragraph, the author explains how the wolves were aware of his presence but ignored him. That's why the author's precautions were superfluous. (C) basically paraphrases that idea: the author's precautions were unnecessary because the wolves weren't interested in him. (A) doesn't work because the author never really says how long it was before he encountered the wolves. (B) is out because the author never mentions any wild animals other than wolves. Contrary to (D), even after the author interfered with the wolves' boundaries, they never bothered him. (E) is out because it's never suggested that the wolves have poor eyesight.

25. A

The author's basic point in paragraph 1 is that he was surprised at the way the wolves behaved towards him: they sized him up quickly right at the beginning and, from then on, ignored him. He found this behavior disconcerting, or **strange**, as (A) puts it. (B) sounds exaggerated—the author never really suggests that he was fearful of attack. With (C), the author says that he took longer to assess the wolves than they took to assess him, but his basic point is not to emphasize his own ignorance. (D) doesn't work because the wolves left the author alone—precautions weren't necessary. (E), like (B), isn't suggested—that the author thinks he has a lot of courage.

26. D

In paragraph 3 the author describes how the wolf was so preoccupied that he came within 15 yards of his tent without seeing it. It wasn't until the author made noise that the wolf suddenly became aware of its surroundings. (D) paraphrases this idea: that the wolf was not **on its guard**—it was self-absorbed. The author expresses no surprise about the wolf traveling alone (A) or hunting at night (C). As for (B), the point is not that the wolf lacks energy—it does respond when the author startles it. (E) is out because the author doesn't really mention any fear of attack.

27. C

The first sentence of paragraph 3 describes the wolf as "anxious to go home to bed." The idea is that he was **eager** to get home (C). **Distressed** (A), **afraid** (B), **uneasy** (D), and **worried** (E) are other definitions of *anxious*, but they don't fit the idea in the sentence.

28. C

In paragraph 4, the author explains that one of the things he learned is that, contrary to popular belief, the wolves were "settled beasts" rather than "nomadic hunters." The idea, in other words, is that the wolves were **stable**—they had established homes. **Decided** (A) and **resolute** (B) are other meanings of *settled*, but they don't work in the sentence. Neither **inflexible** (D) nor **confident** (E) fits when plugged in.

29. A

The idea at the beginning of paragraph 4 is that the wolves, contrary to what people generally think, are not nomadic. (A) catches the idea: the author is countering a popular myth or belief about the behavior of wolves. (B) is tricky, but there's really no paradox or ambiguity: the idea is that the wolves are NOT nomadic. (C) is tricky too, but the passage never says that the idea that wolves are nomadic is an established fact. As for (D), there's no indication that what the author observed—that the wolves live in established territories—is an exception to a general rule. (E) doesn't work because there's really no summary of any conclusions in the quoted lines. (A) is the best choice.

30. B

In the middle of paragraph 5 the author describes how the wolf family regularly made the rounds of their lands and "freshened up the boundary markers." He guessed that this was done because there were other wolves living in adjacent areas, although he never saw any sign of trouble between the neighboring wolf families. Then you get the quoted idea: since he never witnessed any disputes, he figured that it was all basically a ritual activity. (B) catches the idea. The idea that the activity was a ritual isn't related to the fact that it was repeated (A), that the boundaries were marked by geographic features (C), that they were marked at the same time each week (D)—that's never suggested, or that the whole family participated (E). The wrong choices miss the point.

31. C

One of the author's discoveries is that the wolves live in territories with clearly marked boundaries. So, contrary to what most people think, they aren't nomadic—they don't travel endlessly from place to place looking for food and sleeping in new areas. The idea in (C), if it were true, would contradict or weaken that idea. The idea in (A) would strengthen the thesis—if there were disputes over boundaries, that would suggest that the wolves are protective of their territory. The idea in (B)—the particular size of the wolves' territory—is irrelevant—it doesn't really relate to the question. (D) is tricky, but it doesn't work: the author finds that the wolves are territorial even though they actually don't have conflicts with their neighbors. The idea in (E) is irrelevant: the passage never discusses whether or not wolves are alert when encountering other animals.

32. D

The phrase "invisible wall" occurs in paragraph 7, and the point is that the wolf, who was plodding home as preoccupied as usual, was suddenly stopped in its tracks when it encountered the spot where the author had left his own markings. So the idea about the invisible wall is that the wolf was stopped suddenly (D), as if it had suddenly banged up against it. The idea of an invisible wall has nothing to do with delight in getting the wolf's attention (A), annoyance on the part of the wolf (B), high speed (C)—the wolf was "padding," not running—or exhaustion after a night of hunting (E).

33. B

In the very same sentence in paragraph 7, the author says that the wolf, upon finding the author's marks, immediately became bewildered. (B) restates that. The passage says nothing about **combativeness** (A), **anxiety** (C), **wariness** (D), or **dread** (E).

34. B

Temerity is a tough vocabulary word—it means impetuousness or **rashness** (B). But you really didn't have to know that definition to pick the right answer. All you have to do with Vocab-in-Context questions is plug in each of the answer choices, and eliminate the ones that don't fit the sentence's meaning. If you do that here, none of the other choices works. With (A), it's not that the author's being discourteous. That sounds strange. Rather, he's being too bold—only (B) makes sense. Remember, if you're stumped with any hard question, work backwards by eliminating any wrong choices you can—and then guess.

35. B

At the end of paragraph 8, the author states that he turned his back on the wolf "in an effort to break the impasse." In other words, he did it to bring about a change in the situation (B). Nothing suggests that he did it to show his power over the wolf (A); make the wolf recognize his existence (C)—the wolf already did; look for a weapon (D); or avoid the wolf's "hypnotic" gaze (E).

SECTION 3

1. A

Don't calculate. Compare piece by piece. The first fraction in Column A is greater than the first fraction in Column B, and the second fraction in Column A is greater than the second fraction in Column B. Therefore the sum in Column A is also greater.

2. D

Try a few numbers. Plugging in $\frac{1}{2}$ for x, you get $\frac{1}{2}$ in Column A, but in Column B you get 1 over $\frac{1}{2}$, which is 1 divided by $\frac{1}{2}$, which is 2. Here Column B is greater. But when you plug in a negative number, things change. Plugging in $-\frac{1}{2}$ gives you $-\frac{1}{2}$ in Column A, and 1 over $-\frac{1}{2}$, which is the same as -2, in Column B. More than one relationship exists, so the answer is (D).

3. A

Don't calculate. Compare Column A to a percent of 34 that's easy to find. Think of 52% as just a bit more than 50%, or $\frac{1}{2}$. 52% of 34, then, is just a bit more than half of 34, so it's more than 17.

4. B

Expand Column A to make it look more like Column B. Distribute the 3 and you get $3x - 6$. No matter what x is, subtracting 6 from $3x$ will leave you with less than subtracting 4 from $3x$.

5. D

There are several pairs of integers that have a product of 10. You don't need to find every pair. Just try to find a pair that has a sum greater than 6 and another pair that has a sum less than 6. An example of the former is 5 and 2. An example of the latter is -5 and -2. The answer is (D).

6. D

We know that x and y are integers that do not equal zero, but that's all we know. First instinct may tell you that Column B is larger because the squares of x and y are both positive, and the product of two positive integers is usually greater than the quotient. However, what if $y = 1$? In this case, $\frac{x^2}{y^2} = x^2y^2$. Since there is more than one possible relationship between Column A and Column B, the answer is (D).

7. D

It looks at first glance like B and C divide the segment into three equal pieces. But check the mathematics of the situation to be sure. You're given that $AC = BD$:

What can you deduce from that? You can subtract BC from both equal lengths and you'll end up with another equality: $AB = CD$. But what about BC? Does it have to be the same as AB and CD? No. The diagram could be resketched like this:

Now you can see that it's possible for AC and BD to be equal but for BC to be longer than AB. It's also possible for BC to be shorter:

More than one relationship is possible, so the answer is (D).

8. B

If you try picking numbers, you'll find that Column B is always greater. It has to be, because $y > 1$, and multiplying a positive number x by something greater than 1 will result in something greater than x.

9. B

First figure out what the simplified form of Column B is. Since x^3 is squared, you must multiply the exponents, leaving you with x^6. Since x is greater than 1, the number gets larger as it is raised to higher powers. Since x^6 has a larger exponent than x^5, and since x is greater than 1, Column B must be greater.

10. D

First simplify Column B by dividing both the numerator and denominator by y. Thus you're left comparing $\dfrac{1}{y}$ in Column A to y in Column B. Don't jump to the conclusion that Column A is a fraction and Column B is an integer. It could be the other way around. If $y = 2$, then Column A is $\dfrac{1}{2}$ and Column B is 2. On the other hand, if $y = \dfrac{1}{2}$, then Column A is 2 and Column B is $\dfrac{1}{2}$. More than one possible relationship means that the answer is (D).

11. C

The first step in this problem is finding the values you must compare. Column A equals the area of a square with side 6, so plug 6 into the formula for the area of a square:

$A = s^2$

$A = 6^2$

$A = 36$

Now find the value of Column B by plugging 9 into the formula for the perimeter of a square:

$P = 4s$

$P = 4(9)$

$P = 36$

Since the columns are equal, the answer is (C).

12. A

The key to this problem is knowing how to find the median and mode of the scores. The mode is the value occurring most often, which is 93 for this set of scores. The median is the middle value, so the first thing you have to do is to rearrange the scores into numerical order:

82, 85, 88, 90, 93, 93, 94, 98

Now take the middle value. Since there is an even number of scores, you'll have to take the average of the two middle scores for the median. In this case, the two middle scores are 90 and 93. $90 + 93 = 183$, which when divided by 2 is 91.5. Therefore, the mode, 93, is greater than the median, 91.5, and Column A is greater than Column B.

13. A

The area of the circle is $\pi r^2 = \pi(3)^2 = 9\pi$. The area of the rectangle is 9×3. Don't think of it as 27; it's easier to compare in the form 9×3. π is more than 3, so 9π is more than 9×3.

14. D

Re-express both columns. In each case you can turn 1 into $\dfrac{1+y}{1+y}$. Column A, then, becomes $\dfrac{1+y}{1+y} - \dfrac{y}{1+y}$, which is equal to $\dfrac{1+y-y}{1+y}$, or $\dfrac{1}{1+y}$. Column B becomes $\dfrac{1+y}{1+y} - \dfrac{1}{1+y}$, which is equal to $\dfrac{1+y-1}{1+y}$, or $\dfrac{y}{1+y}$. Now both columns have the same positive denominator, so the larger quantity will be the one with the larger numerator. (You could think of it as multiplying both columns by the positive quantity $1 + y$.) All you have to do now is compare 1 to y. Which is bigger? You don't know. All you know is that y is positive, but because it could be less than, more than, or even equal to 1, the answer is (D).

15. B

First consider Column B. If a square has a perimeter of 32, the length of each side must be 8. Therefore the area is $8^2 = 64$. Now consider Column A. Since $AB > BC$, one dimension of the rectangle must be larger than the other. To get an idea of how the area of a rectangle changes as its dimensions change, pick numbers for the dimensions. Since the perimeter of $ABCD$ is 32, the sum of one length and one width is half of that, or 16. Pick numbers that add up to 16, but also give you a clear idea of how the area changes. To do this, pick one pair of numbers which represents something near a square and one pair which represents a very elongated rectangle. You could choose 9 and 7 for the first pair and 15 and 1 for the second, for instance. Now find the areas of the rectangles with your chosen dimensions. Multiplying the first pair gives you $9 \times 7 = 63$, while multiplying the second yields $15 \times 1 = 15$. As the dimensions get closer to the square, the area gets larger. However, a square with a certain perimeter has a greater area than any other rectangle with the same perimeter, so Column B is larger than Column A.

16. 115

Since lines p and q are parallel, we can use the rule about alternate interior angles to fill in the following:

Since the angle marked $y°$ is adjacent and supplementary to a 65° angle, $y = 180 - 65 = 115$.

17. .04

Be careful. The question is not asking: "What is $\frac{1}{4}$ of 16?" It's asking: "What is $\frac{1}{4}$ *percent* of 16?" One-fourth of 1 percent is 0.25%, or 0.0025:

$$\frac{1}{4}\% \text{ of } 16 = 0.0025 \times 16 = 0.04$$

18. 11, 13, 17, 19, 23, 29, 31, 37, 41, 43, or 47

In order for each of these fractions to be in its simplest form, a would have to be a number that has no prime factors in common with 3, 5, or 14. So just find a value between 2 and 50 that fits that description. Your best bet is to use a prime number, such as 11. That's one of 11 acceptable answers.

19. 2/5 or .4

If there are 36 men and 24 women in the group, then the total number of group members is 60. The women make up $\frac{24}{60}$ of the group. Since this fraction cannot be gridded, reduce it or turn it into a decimal. To reduce it, divide both the numerator and denominator by 12, and you end up with $\frac{2}{5}$. To turn it into a decimal, divide 60 into 24, and you end up with .4.

20. 8

To evaluate this expression when $s = 9$, simply plug 9 in for s. Substituting 9 into the expression yields:

$$\frac{3(9) + 5}{4} = \frac{27 + 5}{4} = \frac{32}{4} = 8$$

21. 4

The easiest way to get the answer here is to pick numbers. Pick a number for x that has a remainder of 2 when divided by 6, such as 8. Increase the number you picked by 8. In this case, $8 + 8 = 16$. Now divide 16 by 6, which gives you 2 remainder 4. Therefore, the answer is 4.

22. 250

Percent times Whole equals Part:

$$(15\%) \times (\text{take-home pay}) = \$37.50$$

$$(0.15) \times (\text{take-home pay}) = \$37.50$$

$$\text{take-home pay} = \frac{\$37.50}{0.15} = \$250.00$$

23. 9

The area of a triangle is equal to one-half the base times the height. Here the base (along the x-axis) is 6 and the height (perpendicular to the base—i.e., parallel to the y-axis) is 3, so the area is $\frac{1}{2}bh = \frac{1}{2}(6)(3) = 9$.

24. 64

You cannot find the area of the square without finding the length of a side, so use the information you are given about the rectangles to find the length of the square's sides. Since the rectangles have the same dimensions, we know that the side of the square must be twice the length of the shorter side of either rectangle. The side of the square must also be the longer side of either rectangle.

Call the length of a side of the square, which is also the length of a longer side of either rectangle, x. Then the shorter side of either rectangle is $\frac{x}{2}$. Now use the formula for the perimeter:

$$P = 2l + 2w$$

For either rectangle, you have

$$24 = 2x + 2\left(\frac{x}{2}\right)$$

$$24 = 2x + x$$

$$24 = 3x$$

$$8 = x$$

To find the area of the square, simply multiply 8 by 8. The answer is 64.

25. 203

This looks like a physics question, but in fact it's just a "plug-in-the-number-and-see-what-you-get" question. Be sure you plug 95 in for C (not F):

$$C = \frac{5}{9}(F - 32)$$

$$95 = \frac{5}{9}(F - 32)$$

$$\frac{9}{5} \times 95 = F - 32$$

$$F - 32 = 171$$

$$F = 171 + 32 = 203$$

SECTION 4

1. D

The word in the first blank has to be similar in meaning to "controversy": (C) **belligerent,** (D) **scandalous,** and (E) **provocative** would fit. The band wouldn't do this if they didn't find that the strategy worked, so (B) **rewarding** and (D) **effective** fit for the second blank. Only (D) fits for both blanks.

2. B

The correct answer is implied by "numerous scribbled edits that cover even his supposed final drafts." In other words, Joyce attached great importance to (B) **revision.**

3. B

The key is that the players "now charge for their signatures." Either the fans who believe that the players are not "greedy" would be "surprised" or "disappointed," or the fans who believe that the players are not "ungreedy" would be "confirmed." Choice (B) fits the former prediction.

4. B

The words *though* and *absence* indicate contrast, so the missing word has to be nearly opposite in meaning to "isolation and the longing for connection." **Fraternity**—brotherhood or fellowship—is the best choice. Choice (D) may be tempting, but the term **socialism** refers to a specific set of political and economic doctrines, not just to any sort of society.

5. B

The part of the sentence after the semicolon pretty basically defines the missing word. The word is **calculated,** consciously planned. (A) **incendiary** means "inflaming"; (C) **facetious** means "joking"; (D) **scrupulous** means "honest"; (E) **impromptu** means "unplanned."

6. A

The word *but* after the comma indicates that the word in the second blank contrasts with "struggle." (A) **effortless** and (D) **immediate** are possibilities. The word "but" before the first blank means something like "merely," so the word in the first blank has to suggest something small, like a faint prediction. **Glimmers** fits the meaning.

7. A

The word *although* indicates contrast, and the words "large number" and "mass" provide a clue to what's missing. We need something that means "different" for the first blank, and something that means "the same" for the second blank. This is basically what **disparate** and **homogeneous** mean.

8. A

We need something here that goes with "heavy thoughts." **Morose,** "gloomy," is the best choice.

9. E

The "demise" or death of the protagonist presumably "eliminated" all possibility of a sequel. That's what **precluded** means.

10. C

A **SCAR** is the mark left by an **INJURY**. A **dent** is the mark left by a **collision.** In (E), **blood** is not a permanent mark, and it is not always the result of a **fistfight.**

11. B

To **YAWN** to display **BOREDOM**. To **pout** is to display **displeasure.** One can **react** to any number of things; to **react** is not necessarily to show **surprise.**

12. E

An **ACTOR**'s tryout is called an **AUDITION**. A **gymnast**'s audition is called a **tryout.** In each of the other choices, there is a valid bridge, but not the stem bridge. In (A), a **debut** is a **singer**'s first performance.

13. A

To **ALIENATE** is to impose **ESTRANGEMENT,** making people aliens or strangers. To **discommode** is to impose **inconvenience.** In (B), **monasticism** is the life of monks and nuns; these people are usually **sequestered** or separated from other people, not everyone who is **sequestered** enters a life of **monasticism** (for example, juries are often sequestered). In (C), **palliate** is to relieve **boredom.**

14. B

Something **PUNGENT** or foul-smelling is, by definition, unpleasant to be **SNIFFED.** Something **prickly** is unpleasant to be **touched.** Something (C) **venomous** does not necessarily work by being **bitten.**

15. B

To **DISCONCERT** is to cause **CONFUSION.** To **daunt** is to cause **discouragement.** Note that (D) is a bridge-less pair.

The Cold War Passage

The author of this passage has one overarching strategy: Set up the arguments of the revisionist historians and then knock 'em down. Paragraph 1 explains the things that, according to the revisionists, could have been done to avoid the Cold War, which are 1) the U.S. could have just accepted Soviet domination in Eastern Europe, 2) the U.S. could have given them money for reconstruction, and 3) the U.S. could have given up its monopoly of the bomb. Paragraphs 2 and 3 outline the author's refutation of these arguments; he concentrates on the American political atmosphere as the main reason that the revisionists' ideas were not really workable at the time. Revisionists, he then asserts in paragraph 4, would reject this politics-based argument and claim instead that it was the economic situation that forced American policy makers to oppose the Soviets. The author of course then knocks down this new argument; it is contradictory, he says, to say that American officials were caught in an economic tide and then to blame them for not doing things differently. The author concludes in the final paragraph by stating that there was essentially no way, given the climate in the Soviet Union, that the Cold War could have been avoided.

16. C

As we noted above, the author of this passage is primarily engaged in setting up and knocking down the arguments of the revisionist historians of the Cold War. This makes (C) correct and (E) wrong (the author is definitely not interested in reconciling his view with that of the revisionists). (A) is wrong because the ideas of the revisionists are not, as far as we know, a popular myth. (B) is out because the author is defending historical figures—the policy makers—for what they did, not criticizing them. (D) is too neutral a choice for this passage; the author does engage in analysis of the era of the beginning of the Cold War, but his purpose is to do far more than just analyze events. He wants to poke holes in revisionist theories.

17. C

When revisionists say that the U.S. could have "recognized" the Soviet influence in Eastern Europe, they mean that the U.S. could have formally **acknowledged** this Soviet presence. (C) is correct.

18. C

Look back to the second half of the second paragraph. The author says there that Roosevelt could never have recognized a Soviet Eastern Europe because the American people did not like the idea of the Soviets holding sway in that region. In particular, the president would have lost the votes of the Polish Americans who, you can infer, did not want the Soviets controlling their "old country." (C) spells out this point. Each of the other choices is a misreading of the context of the sentence about the Polish American voters.

19. E

In the second and third paragraphs, the author refutes the suggestions of the revisionists primarily by saying that the policy-makers couldn't do what was necessary to avoid the Cold War because the American people were against it. The assumption the author makes is that the policy makers **could not have been expected to ignore public opinion** (E). The author never says in the second and third paragraphs that the Soviets were to blame for failed U.S. peace initiatives (A), or that none of the alternatives would work (C)—what he does say, in a later paragraph, is that if peace initiatives had not run aground due to American politics, then they would have run aground due to the Soviet climate. The author also does not say in the second and third paragraphs that the American public was **well-informed** (B) or **overwhelmingly opposed to seeking peace** (D); all we know is that they opposed Soviet influence in Eastern Europe as well as the idea of giving up the atom bomb monopoly.

20. C

This question is closely linked to the previous one. The author refers to the "certain constraints" at the end of the third paragraph, in the midst of the discussion on the impact of public opinion on the policy-makers. From context, then, you know that the constraints the author is talking about are the opinions of the people—in other words, **the views of the electorate** (C). If you didn't put the sentence about "constraints" in context, any of the other choices might have looked appealing.

21. E

This question centers on the fourth paragraph, which is where the author explains the revisionists' view that American policy makers decided to oppose the Soviet Union because Soviet expansion could jeopardize U.S. trade and investment opportunities in Eastern Europe and elsewhere. (E) captures this idea. The author says nothing about illegal trading activities (A), nor does he indicate whether or not the Soviets knew about the negative impact they could have on the American economy (B). (C) is out because the Soviet Union was not recognized by the United States, so this could not possibly have had anything to do with the origin of the Cold War. (D) is wrong because there is no evidence in the paragraph to support it.

22. A

The author poses the question in order to show that there is a problem with the revisionists' economic interpretation of the Cold War: you can't blame the policy-makers if they didn't have any control. Thus the question serves to **point out an inconsistency** (A) in the revisionists' position. (D) might be tempting since the revisionists' view is pretty cynical, but the author is questioning that view here, not summing it up.

The James Weldon Johnson Passage

Johnson, the author of this autobiographical piece, does not just describe the experience he had watching the piano-player playing rag-time; he also uses the scene as a jumping-off point from which to comment on the origin of rag-time (second paragraph), to disparage American musicians for refusing to accept rag-time (third paragraph), and to speculate on what the piano player could have amounted to under different circumstances (fourth paragraph).

23. C

The author's initial impression of rag-time can be found in the first paragraph. He emphasizes how the beat demanded a physical response and meshed with the "dissonant harmonies," etc. to produce a "curious effect." (C) is the correct answer. The only other choice that has anything to do with the first paragraph is (B). (B) is wrong because the audience is said to have applauded the singer's dance steps, not the rag-time music.

24. E

Let's go through the choices one-by-one, keeping in mind that we're focusing exclusively on the first paragraph. Although the piano player is "master of a good deal of technique," choice (A) is too extreme to be correct. We know nothing in the first paragraph of the author's expectations of rag-time, so (B) is out too. (C), (D), and (E) are different interpretations of the author's description of the piano player's playing. While it is certainly true that rag-time has dissonant harmonies and jumps from one key to another, you cannot infer from this that rag-time violates every rule of musical composition (C) or that it has no melody at all (D). (E) is correct since the narrator notes that "the accents fell in the most unexpected places."

25. A

In the context of the phrase "questionable resorts about Memphis and St. Louis," the word *questionable* means **disreputable** (A).

26. C

Choice (B) might have jumped right out at you since the narrator's perspective in paragraph 1 is that of a mesmerized spectator, but his perspective in paragraphs 2 and 3 changes. He steps back from the description of his first encounter with rag-time and begins to discuss rag-time's history, appeal, and impact on the contemporary musical scene. Therefore, (C) is the correct answer. (A) is wrong because the author is not impartial; he thinks highly of rag-time. Watching rag-time playing is not a "unique experience," which eliminates (D). As for (E), the narrator says nothing about his youth in the second and third paragraphs.

27. A

Put the reference to the "theory of the universe" in the context of the second paragraph. The author says that the players who first developed rag-time knew "no more of the theory of music than they did of the theory of the universe"—in other words, they had no formal music education—but their natural talent guided them. Since they had no conventional schooling in music, you can infer that their invention, rag-time, was **an unconventional musical form** (A).

(B) and (E) are the close wrong answers. (B) is out because the originators of rag-time could have been interested in other people's music even though they had no formal music education. (E) is wrong since it misunderstands the overall point of the paragraph; the author is not interested in making general statements about the relationship between education and artistic success. (C) is the sort of choice you can rule out by common sense; no SAT question is going to have a correct answer that downplays the importance of academics. Finally, there is no evidence that indicates (D) could be true.

28. C

The narrator argues in the third paragraph that rag-time should not be ignored or dismissed by American musicians just because it is popular. All great music, he states, comes from the hearts of the people. In other words, he is saying that the **conservative and condescending attitude** of the American musicians is misguided (C). There is no evidence in the third paragraph to support any of the other choices. (B) is perhaps the most tempting, since the author talks in the third paragraph about rag-time's popularity in Europe, but it

seems as though American musicians do know about rag-time's popularity and find it distasteful.

29. E

This question is a follow-up on the previous one. As we've said, the author's argument in the third paragraph is that music should not be dismissed by serious musicians just because it happens to be popular. (E) paraphrases this idea. (A) stretches the author's argument way too far. (B) is wrong because the author does not try to establish criteria for musical greatness. (C) focuses too narrowly on the author's mention of the fact that rag-time was popular abroad. (D) is clearly wrong since rag-time gained popularity even though it had not been "taken up by a musical master."

30. D

The narrator poses to himself the question about what might have become of the piano player had he been properly trained and then answers himself by saying "perhaps he wouldn't have done anything at all." The narrator goes on to say that even if the piano player achieved some success as an imitator of the greats or as an innovator, he still would not have been as "delightful" as he was playing rag-time. Thus the statement that "perhaps he wouldn't have done anything at all" can best be interpreted as a **recognition that the piano player might have wasted his talent** (D) had he been formally trained. (A) and (B) are wrong because the narrator thinks highly of the piano player's skill even if that skill is not genius-level or particularly disciplined. (C) and (E) are both far too broad and too negative to be the correct answer.

31. C

The correct answer here is going to be a paraphrase of the idea that no matter how far the piano player would have gone if trained, he would not have been as delightful as he was as a rag-time player. (C) is the choice you're looking for. (E) is the most tempting wrong answer since the author's statements at the end of the passage can easily be misconstrued to mean that the piano player could never have been more than mediocre as a classical artist. However, "never" is too strong a word here—the narrator is not, and cannot be, as sure as that—so this choice is wrong.

SECTION 5

1. E

Use FOIL:

$$(3x + 4)(4x - 3)$$
$$= (3x \times 4x) + [3x \times (-3)] + (4 \times 4x) + [4 \times (-3)]$$
$$= 12x^2 - 9x + 16x - 12$$
$$= 12x^2 + 7x - 12$$

2. C

When you know that the given parts add up to the whole, then you can turn a part-to-part ratio into 2 part-to-whole ratios—put each term of the ratio over the sum of the terms. In this case, since all the numbers in the set must be either integers or nonintegers, the parts do add up to the whole. The sum of the terms in the ratio 2:3 is 5, so the two part-to-whole ratios are 2:5 and 3:5.

$$\frac{\text{integers}}{\text{numbers}} = \frac{2}{5} = \frac{2}{5}(100\%) = \frac{200\%}{5} = 40\%$$

3. C

Get rid of the parentheses in the denominator, and then cancel factors the numerator and denominator have in common:

$$\frac{x^2 y^3 z^4}{(xyz^2)^2} = \frac{x^2 y^3 z^4}{x^2 y^2 z^4}$$
$$= \frac{x^2}{x^2} \times \frac{y^3}{y^2} \times \frac{z^4}{z^4}$$
$$= y$$

4. E

If p divided by 7 leaves a remainder of 5, you can say that $p = 7n + 5$, where n represents some integer. Multiply both sides by 5 to get $5p = 35n + 25$. The remainder when you divide 7 into $35n$ is 0. The reminder when you divide 7 into 25 is 4, so the remainder when you divide $5p$ by 7 is $0 + 4 = 4$.

For most people this one's a lot easier to do by picking numbers. Think of an example for p and try it out. p could be 12, for example, because when you divide 12

by 7, the remainder is 5. (p could also be 19, 26, 33, or any of infinitely many more possibilities.) Now multiply your chosen p by 5: $12 \times 5 = 60$. Divide 60 by 7 and see what the remainder is: $60 \div 7 = 8$, remainder 4.

5. B

To find the y-intercept of a line from its equation, put the equation in slope-intercept form:

$$2x - 3y = 18$$
$$-3y = -2x + 18$$
$$y = \frac{2}{3}x - 6$$

In this form, the y-intercept is what comes after the x—in this case it's -6.

6. C

Set up a proportion:

$$\frac{12 \text{ pages}}{1 \text{ hour}} = \frac{100 \text{ pages}}{x \text{ hours}}$$
$$12x = 100$$
$$x = \frac{100}{12} = 8\frac{1}{3}$$

One-third of an hour is $\frac{1}{3}$ of 60 minutes, or 20 minutes. So $8\frac{1}{3}$ hours is 8 hours and 20 minutes.

7. E

With a right triangle you can use the 2 legs as the base and the height to figure out the area. Here the leg lengths are expressed algebraically. Just plug the 2 expressions in for b and h in the triangle area formula:

$$\text{Area} = \frac{1}{2}(x - 1)(x + 1)$$
$$= \frac{1}{2}(x^2 - 1) = \frac{x^2 - 1}{2}$$

8. A

The easiest way to do this problem is to subtract Bill's money from the total of the money that Jim and Bill have. Doing this gives you $15 - 4 = 11$. However, the problem states that they have LESS THAN 15 dollars. Therefore, Jim must have less than 11 dollars. Of I, II, and III, the only value that is less than 11 is I, so the answer must be (A).

To solve this problem algebraically, set up an inequality where J is Jim's money and B is Bill's money:

$J + B < 15$ where $B = 4$

$J + 4 < 15$

$J < 11$

Again, be wary of the fact that this is an inequality, NOT an equation.

9. A

Pick numbers for x and y. For instance, say that Angelo makes 20 dollars for working 5 hours and Sarah makes 20 dollars for working 4 hours. In this case, Angelo makes \$4 per hour and Sarah makes \$5. The difference between their wages is \$1 per hour. Now plug 20 in for x and 5 in for y in each of the answer choices. Which ones give you a result of 1? Only (A), which is the answer.

10. D

A square with area 16 has sides of length 4. Therefore the largest circle that could possibly be cut from such a square would have a diameter of 4.

Such a circle would have a radius of 2, making its area 4π. So the amount of felt left after cutting such a circle from one of the squares of felt would be $16 - 4\pi$, or $4(4 - \pi)$. There are 8 such squares, so the total area of the left over felt is $8 \times 4(4 - \pi) = 32(4 - \pi)$.

SECTION 6

The Design Museums Passages

Passage 1   The position of the author of this passage starts to become clear in the second paragraph: she likes design museums and is willing to defend them against critics. She thinks design museums are not just advertisements for new technology but places where new products can be honored. Design museums, she asserts, are comfortable for visitors because the exhibits provide a lot of information about the objects displayed—information you wouldn't get in an art gallery. Another advantage of design museums, she says, is that their curators have more freedom than do the curators of public art galleries.

Passage 2   Author 2 does not hold technical and design museums in the same high regard as author 1 does, you soon find out in this passage. Author 2 complains about several things: 1) technical museums concentrate on present technology and ignore historical study and research; 2) they glorify machines and industrialization when these things do harm as well as good; and 3) they do not (and cannot safely and imaginatively) show machinery in action. Author 2 does admit at the very end, however, that the public has shown a healthy curiosity about science and technology.

1. A

To say that something is "readily available to the general public" is to say that it is **easily** available. (A) is the correct answer.

2. D

Author 1 says that department store windows try to sell you something whereas design exhibits try to give you an appreciation of the aesthetic value of something. (D) paraphrases this idea. (A), (B), and (E) can be readily eliminated. Be careful with (C), though. Even though design museums focus on the artistic qualities of products, it does not automatically follow from this that design museums are not concerned at all with the commercial aspects of a successful product. (C) is wrong.

3. B

In the third paragraph of Passage 1, the author argues that design museums make visitors feel comfortable because the exhibits illustrate the purpose behind the look and function of the displayed object; art gallery exhibits, by contrast, provide no such information. From this argument you can infer that author 1 thinks that visitors want to be informed about the object they are viewing. This makes (B) correct. There is no evidence to support any of the other choices, all of which are misreadings of paragraph 3. (A) can be eliminated as soon as you see "hostile towards . . . abstract art." (C) and (D) contradict the author, who says that visitors are not confused by technological exhibits since they are familiar and informative. (E) is an unwarranted inference based on the author's statement that design exhibits point out the artistic qualities of the displayed items; you cannot conclude from this that most museum visitors undervalue the artistic worth of household items.

4. B

Since you just reviewed paragraph 3 for the last question, the answer to this one should jump right out at you. The difference between a design museum exhibit and an art gallery exhibit is that a design museum exhibit provides you with information about the object being displayed, whereas the art gallery exhibit does not. (B) is correct. None of the other choices has any basis in the passage.

5. C

After mentioning the collection of Zippo lighters, etc., in London's Design Museum, author 1 says that curators of design museums have options that are far less rigorous, conventionalized and pre-programmed than those open to curators of art galleries. This is a fancy way of saying that the curators of design museums have more freedom to put together unconventional collections (C). (E) is the tempting wrong answer to this question. It's wrong because it goes too far: the design curators have freedom, but not, as far as we know, the freedom to satisfy "their own personal whims."

6. E

In the very last sentence of passage 1, the author says that design museums ("the display of postmodern playthings or quirky Japanese vacuum cleaners") are better able to represent humor than art galleries ("an exhibition of Impressionist landscapes"). The author is emphasizing the contrast between design museum and art gallery exhibits (E). (B) is the trickiest wrong answer. It misses the point of the last sentence because the author is not comparing "postmodern playthings" with Impressionist art; she is comparing the different ways these two things are exhibited.

7. A

The answer to this question will be the choice that summarizes paragraph 1. Since the author spends paragraph 1 complaining that design museums ignore the historical aspect of technology, choice (A) is the best answer. (B) focuses too narrowly on the last part of the paragraph, where the author says that since industry builds the exhibits, curators may be dispensed with. This is not the underlying difficulty referred to at the beginning of the paragraph. The other choices have nothing to do with the first paragraph.

8. A

Author 2's point in the second paragraph is that industrialization and "progress" have not been all good and should be considered critically, but technology museums just glorify them. He mentions industrialization's harm to the environment and ecology to support this point and to encourage **a critical response** to technology, so (A) is correct. (B) is wrong because it's too negative even for this author. (C) is a distortion of a detail at the end of the second paragraph, while (D) is a distorted idea from the third paragraph. (E) is out because author 2 doesn't do any praising in the second paragraph.

9. D

Put the phrase in context. Author 2 says that displayed machinery should be in action, not in "sculptured repose," as is the case with the machinery in technology museums. To author 2, you can infer, the "sculptured repose" is meaningless and **unrealistic** (D). (A) is out because the author is not condemning the curators for poor planning; in fact, the author admits that displaying operating machinery would be extremely difficult. (B) can be eliminated because it's too extreme. The author never says which—if any—of the problems he discusses is the "greatest problem." (C) and (E) miss the author's point and the context in which the phrase "sculptured repose" is found.

10. D

Choices (A), (B), (C), and (E) are common synonyms for "command," but none of them works in the context of the phrase "command the imagination, ingenuity and manual dexterity it requires." Only choice (D) can do the job.

11. A

Predict the answer to the question before you go looking through the choices. You know that author 2 thinks that technology has had a lot of negative consequences, so you can assume that he would point this out in response to author 1's optimistic statement. This makes (A) the best answer. We don't know what author 2's position on art galleries is, so (B) is out. (C) comes from passage 2 but is irrelevant to the question asked in the stem. (D) and (E) contradict specific things author 2 says in the course of his passage.

12. B

In questions like this one, wrong answer choices are often statements that one author, but not both, would agree with. For example, author 2 would probably agree with choice (A) and would definitely agree with (D) and (E), but author 1 would most likely not agree with any of these three. That narrows the field to (B) and (C). (C) is a very general statement that really has no basis in either passage. (B), on the other hand, is an idea that can be found in both passages, so it is the correct answer.

Practice Test Three

HOW TO TAKE THIS PRACTICE TEST

Before taking this practice test, find a quiet room where you can work uninterrupted for two and a half hours. Make sure you have a comfortable desk, your calculator, and several No. 2 pencils.

Use the answer sheet provided to record your answers. (You can cut it out or photocopy it.)

Once you start this practice test, don't stop until you've finished. Remember—you can review any questions within a section, but you may not go back or forward a section.

You'll find an answer key, score conversion charts, and explanations following the test.

Good luck.

SAT Practice Test Three
Answer Sheet

Remove (or photocopy) this answer sheet and use it to complete the practice test.
(See answer key following the test when finished.)

Start with number 1 for each section. If a section has fewer questions than answer spaces, leave the extra spaces blank.

SECTION 1

1 Ⓐ Ⓑ Ⓒ Ⓓ Ⓔ   11 Ⓐ Ⓑ Ⓒ Ⓓ Ⓔ   21 Ⓐ Ⓑ Ⓒ Ⓓ Ⓔ   31 Ⓐ Ⓑ Ⓒ Ⓓ Ⓔ
2 Ⓐ Ⓑ Ⓒ Ⓓ Ⓔ   12 Ⓐ Ⓑ Ⓒ Ⓓ Ⓔ   22 Ⓐ Ⓑ Ⓒ Ⓓ Ⓔ   32 Ⓐ Ⓑ Ⓒ Ⓓ Ⓔ
3 Ⓐ Ⓑ Ⓒ Ⓓ Ⓔ   13 Ⓐ Ⓑ Ⓒ Ⓓ Ⓔ   23 Ⓐ Ⓑ Ⓒ Ⓓ Ⓔ   33 Ⓐ Ⓑ Ⓒ Ⓓ Ⓔ
4 Ⓐ Ⓑ Ⓒ Ⓓ Ⓔ   14 Ⓐ Ⓑ Ⓒ Ⓓ Ⓔ   24 Ⓐ Ⓑ Ⓒ Ⓓ Ⓔ   34 Ⓐ Ⓑ Ⓒ Ⓓ Ⓔ
5 Ⓐ Ⓑ Ⓒ Ⓓ Ⓔ   15 Ⓐ Ⓑ Ⓒ Ⓓ Ⓔ   25 Ⓐ Ⓑ Ⓒ Ⓓ Ⓔ   35 Ⓐ Ⓑ Ⓒ Ⓓ Ⓔ
6 Ⓐ Ⓑ Ⓒ Ⓓ Ⓔ   16 Ⓐ Ⓑ Ⓒ Ⓓ Ⓔ   26 Ⓐ Ⓑ Ⓒ Ⓓ Ⓔ   36 Ⓐ Ⓑ Ⓒ Ⓓ Ⓔ
7 Ⓐ Ⓑ Ⓒ Ⓓ Ⓔ   17 Ⓐ Ⓑ Ⓒ Ⓓ Ⓔ   27 Ⓐ Ⓑ Ⓒ Ⓓ Ⓔ   37 Ⓐ Ⓑ Ⓒ Ⓓ Ⓔ
8 Ⓐ Ⓑ Ⓒ Ⓓ Ⓔ   18 Ⓐ Ⓑ Ⓒ Ⓓ Ⓔ   28 Ⓐ Ⓑ Ⓒ Ⓓ Ⓔ   38 Ⓐ Ⓑ Ⓒ Ⓓ Ⓔ
9 Ⓐ Ⓑ Ⓒ Ⓓ Ⓔ   19 Ⓐ Ⓑ Ⓒ Ⓓ Ⓔ   29 Ⓐ Ⓑ Ⓒ Ⓓ Ⓔ   39 Ⓐ Ⓑ Ⓒ Ⓓ Ⓔ
10 Ⓐ Ⓑ Ⓒ Ⓓ Ⓔ   20 Ⓐ Ⓑ Ⓒ Ⓓ Ⓔ   30 Ⓐ Ⓑ Ⓒ Ⓓ Ⓔ   40 Ⓐ Ⓑ Ⓒ Ⓓ Ⓔ

☐ # right in section 1

☐ # wrong in section 1

SECTION 2

1 Ⓐ Ⓑ Ⓒ Ⓓ Ⓔ   11 Ⓐ Ⓑ Ⓒ Ⓓ Ⓔ   21 Ⓐ Ⓑ Ⓒ Ⓓ Ⓔ   31 Ⓐ Ⓑ Ⓒ Ⓓ Ⓔ
2 Ⓐ Ⓑ Ⓒ Ⓓ Ⓔ   12 Ⓐ Ⓑ Ⓒ Ⓓ Ⓔ   22 Ⓐ Ⓑ Ⓒ Ⓓ Ⓔ   32 Ⓐ Ⓑ Ⓒ Ⓓ Ⓔ
3 Ⓐ Ⓑ Ⓒ Ⓓ Ⓔ   13 Ⓐ Ⓑ Ⓒ Ⓓ Ⓔ   23 Ⓐ Ⓑ Ⓒ Ⓓ Ⓔ   33 Ⓐ Ⓑ Ⓒ Ⓓ Ⓔ
4 Ⓐ Ⓑ Ⓒ Ⓓ Ⓔ   14 Ⓐ Ⓑ Ⓒ Ⓓ Ⓔ   24 Ⓐ Ⓑ Ⓒ Ⓓ Ⓔ   34 Ⓐ Ⓑ Ⓒ Ⓓ Ⓔ
5 Ⓐ Ⓑ Ⓒ Ⓓ Ⓔ   15 Ⓐ Ⓑ Ⓒ Ⓓ Ⓔ   25 Ⓐ Ⓑ Ⓒ Ⓓ Ⓔ   35 Ⓐ Ⓑ Ⓒ Ⓓ Ⓔ
6 Ⓐ Ⓑ Ⓒ Ⓓ Ⓔ   16 Ⓐ Ⓑ Ⓒ Ⓓ Ⓔ   26 Ⓐ Ⓑ Ⓒ Ⓓ Ⓔ   36 Ⓐ Ⓑ Ⓒ Ⓓ Ⓔ
7 Ⓐ Ⓑ Ⓒ Ⓓ Ⓔ   17 Ⓐ Ⓑ Ⓒ Ⓓ Ⓔ   27 Ⓐ Ⓑ Ⓒ Ⓓ Ⓔ   37 Ⓐ Ⓑ Ⓒ Ⓓ Ⓔ
8 Ⓐ Ⓑ Ⓒ Ⓓ Ⓔ   18 Ⓐ Ⓑ Ⓒ Ⓓ Ⓔ   28 Ⓐ Ⓑ Ⓒ Ⓓ Ⓔ   38 Ⓐ Ⓑ Ⓒ Ⓓ Ⓔ
9 Ⓐ Ⓑ Ⓒ Ⓓ Ⓔ   19 Ⓐ Ⓑ Ⓒ Ⓓ Ⓔ   29 Ⓐ Ⓑ Ⓒ Ⓓ Ⓔ   39 Ⓐ Ⓑ Ⓒ Ⓓ Ⓔ
10 Ⓐ Ⓑ Ⓒ Ⓓ Ⓔ   20 Ⓐ Ⓑ Ⓒ Ⓓ Ⓔ   30 Ⓐ Ⓑ Ⓒ Ⓓ Ⓔ   40 Ⓐ Ⓑ Ⓒ Ⓓ Ⓔ

☐ # right in section 2

☐ # wrong in section 2

SECTION 3

1 Ⓐ Ⓑ Ⓒ Ⓓ Ⓔ   11 Ⓐ Ⓑ Ⓒ Ⓓ Ⓔ   21 Ⓐ Ⓑ Ⓒ Ⓓ Ⓔ   31 Ⓐ Ⓑ Ⓒ Ⓓ Ⓔ
2 Ⓐ Ⓑ Ⓒ Ⓓ Ⓔ   12 Ⓐ Ⓑ Ⓒ Ⓓ Ⓔ   22 Ⓐ Ⓑ Ⓒ Ⓓ Ⓔ   32 Ⓐ Ⓑ Ⓒ Ⓓ Ⓔ
3 Ⓐ Ⓑ Ⓒ Ⓓ Ⓔ   13 Ⓐ Ⓑ Ⓒ Ⓓ Ⓔ   23 Ⓐ Ⓑ Ⓒ Ⓓ Ⓔ   33 Ⓐ Ⓑ Ⓒ Ⓓ Ⓔ
4 Ⓐ Ⓑ Ⓒ Ⓓ Ⓔ   14 Ⓐ Ⓑ Ⓒ Ⓓ Ⓔ   24 Ⓐ Ⓑ Ⓒ Ⓓ Ⓔ   34 Ⓐ Ⓑ Ⓒ Ⓓ Ⓔ
5 Ⓐ Ⓑ Ⓒ Ⓓ Ⓔ   15 Ⓐ Ⓑ Ⓒ Ⓓ Ⓔ   25 Ⓐ Ⓑ Ⓒ Ⓓ Ⓔ   35 Ⓐ Ⓑ Ⓒ Ⓓ Ⓔ
6 Ⓐ Ⓑ Ⓒ Ⓓ Ⓔ   16 Ⓐ Ⓑ Ⓒ Ⓓ Ⓔ   26 Ⓐ Ⓑ Ⓒ Ⓓ Ⓔ   36 Ⓐ Ⓑ Ⓒ Ⓓ Ⓔ
7 Ⓐ Ⓑ Ⓒ Ⓓ Ⓔ   17 Ⓐ Ⓑ Ⓒ Ⓓ Ⓔ   27 Ⓐ Ⓑ Ⓒ Ⓓ Ⓔ   37 Ⓐ Ⓑ Ⓒ Ⓓ Ⓔ
8 Ⓐ Ⓑ Ⓒ Ⓓ Ⓔ   18 Ⓐ Ⓑ Ⓒ Ⓓ Ⓔ   28 Ⓐ Ⓑ Ⓒ Ⓓ Ⓔ   38 Ⓐ Ⓑ Ⓒ Ⓓ Ⓔ
9 Ⓐ Ⓑ Ⓒ Ⓓ Ⓔ   19 Ⓐ Ⓑ Ⓒ Ⓓ Ⓔ   29 Ⓐ Ⓑ Ⓒ Ⓓ Ⓔ   39 Ⓐ Ⓑ Ⓒ Ⓓ Ⓔ
10 Ⓐ Ⓑ Ⓒ Ⓓ Ⓔ   20 Ⓐ Ⓑ Ⓒ Ⓓ Ⓔ   30 Ⓐ Ⓑ Ⓒ Ⓓ Ⓔ   40 Ⓐ Ⓑ Ⓒ Ⓓ Ⓔ

☐ # right in section 3

☐ # wrong in section 3

Remove (or photocopy) this answer sheet and use it to complete the practice test.

Start with number 1 for each section. If a section has fewer questions than answer spaces, leave the extra spaces blank.

SECTION 4

1 Ⓐ Ⓑ Ⓒ Ⓓ Ⓔ	11 Ⓐ Ⓑ Ⓒ Ⓓ Ⓔ	21 Ⓐ Ⓑ Ⓒ Ⓓ Ⓔ	31 Ⓐ Ⓑ Ⓒ Ⓓ Ⓔ
2 Ⓐ Ⓑ Ⓒ Ⓓ Ⓔ	12 Ⓐ Ⓑ Ⓒ Ⓓ Ⓔ	22 Ⓐ Ⓑ Ⓒ Ⓓ Ⓔ	32 Ⓐ Ⓑ Ⓒ Ⓓ Ⓔ
3 Ⓐ Ⓑ Ⓒ Ⓓ Ⓔ	13 Ⓐ Ⓑ Ⓒ Ⓓ Ⓔ	23 Ⓐ Ⓑ Ⓒ Ⓓ Ⓔ	33 Ⓐ Ⓑ Ⓒ Ⓓ Ⓔ
4 Ⓐ Ⓑ Ⓒ Ⓓ Ⓔ	14 Ⓐ Ⓑ Ⓒ Ⓓ Ⓔ	24 Ⓐ Ⓑ Ⓒ Ⓓ Ⓔ	34 Ⓐ Ⓑ Ⓒ Ⓓ Ⓔ
5 Ⓐ Ⓑ Ⓒ Ⓓ Ⓔ	15 Ⓐ Ⓑ Ⓒ Ⓓ Ⓔ	25 Ⓐ Ⓑ Ⓒ Ⓓ Ⓔ	35 Ⓐ Ⓑ Ⓒ Ⓓ Ⓔ
6 Ⓐ Ⓑ Ⓒ Ⓓ Ⓔ	16 Ⓐ Ⓑ Ⓒ Ⓓ Ⓔ	26 Ⓐ Ⓑ Ⓒ Ⓓ Ⓔ	36 Ⓐ Ⓑ Ⓒ Ⓓ Ⓔ
7 Ⓐ Ⓑ Ⓒ Ⓓ Ⓔ	17 Ⓐ Ⓑ Ⓒ Ⓓ Ⓔ	27 Ⓐ Ⓑ Ⓒ Ⓓ Ⓔ	37 Ⓐ Ⓑ Ⓒ Ⓓ Ⓔ
8 Ⓐ Ⓑ Ⓒ Ⓓ Ⓔ	18 Ⓐ Ⓑ Ⓒ Ⓓ Ⓔ	28 Ⓐ Ⓑ Ⓒ Ⓓ Ⓔ	38 Ⓐ Ⓑ Ⓒ Ⓓ Ⓔ
9 Ⓐ Ⓑ Ⓒ Ⓓ Ⓔ	19 Ⓐ Ⓑ Ⓒ Ⓓ Ⓔ	29 Ⓐ Ⓑ Ⓒ Ⓓ Ⓔ	39 Ⓐ Ⓑ Ⓒ Ⓓ Ⓔ
10 Ⓐ Ⓑ Ⓒ Ⓓ Ⓔ	20 Ⓐ Ⓑ Ⓒ Ⓓ Ⓔ	30 Ⓐ Ⓑ Ⓒ Ⓓ Ⓔ	40 Ⓐ Ⓑ Ⓒ Ⓓ Ⓔ

right in section 4

wrong in section 4

If section 4 of your test book contains math questions that are not multiple choice, continue to item 16 below. Otherwise, continue to item 16 above.

SECTION 5

1 Ⓐ Ⓑ Ⓒ Ⓓ Ⓔ	11 Ⓐ Ⓑ Ⓒ Ⓓ Ⓔ	21 Ⓐ Ⓑ Ⓒ Ⓓ Ⓔ	31 Ⓐ Ⓑ Ⓒ Ⓓ Ⓔ
2 Ⓐ Ⓑ Ⓒ Ⓓ Ⓔ	12 Ⓐ Ⓑ Ⓒ Ⓓ Ⓔ	22 Ⓐ Ⓑ Ⓒ Ⓓ Ⓔ	32 Ⓐ Ⓑ Ⓒ Ⓓ Ⓔ
3 Ⓐ Ⓑ Ⓒ Ⓓ Ⓔ	13 Ⓐ Ⓑ Ⓒ Ⓓ Ⓔ	23 Ⓐ Ⓑ Ⓒ Ⓓ Ⓔ	33 Ⓐ Ⓑ Ⓒ Ⓓ Ⓔ
4 Ⓐ Ⓑ Ⓒ Ⓓ Ⓔ	14 Ⓐ Ⓑ Ⓒ Ⓓ Ⓔ	24 Ⓐ Ⓑ Ⓒ Ⓓ Ⓔ	34 Ⓐ Ⓑ Ⓒ Ⓓ Ⓔ
5 Ⓐ Ⓑ Ⓒ Ⓓ Ⓔ	15 Ⓐ Ⓑ Ⓒ Ⓓ Ⓔ	25 Ⓐ Ⓑ Ⓒ Ⓓ Ⓔ	35 Ⓐ Ⓑ Ⓒ Ⓓ Ⓔ
6 Ⓐ Ⓑ Ⓒ Ⓓ Ⓔ	16 Ⓐ Ⓑ Ⓒ Ⓓ Ⓔ	26 Ⓐ Ⓑ Ⓒ Ⓓ Ⓔ	36 Ⓐ Ⓑ Ⓒ Ⓓ Ⓔ
7 Ⓐ Ⓑ Ⓒ Ⓓ Ⓔ	17 Ⓐ Ⓑ Ⓒ Ⓓ Ⓔ	27 Ⓐ Ⓑ Ⓒ Ⓓ Ⓔ	37 Ⓐ Ⓑ Ⓒ Ⓓ Ⓔ
8 Ⓐ Ⓑ Ⓒ Ⓓ Ⓔ	18 Ⓐ Ⓑ Ⓒ Ⓓ Ⓔ	28 Ⓐ Ⓑ Ⓒ Ⓓ Ⓔ	38 Ⓐ Ⓑ Ⓒ Ⓓ Ⓔ
9 Ⓐ Ⓑ Ⓒ Ⓓ Ⓔ	19 Ⓐ Ⓑ Ⓒ Ⓓ Ⓔ	29 Ⓐ Ⓑ Ⓒ Ⓓ Ⓔ	39 Ⓐ Ⓑ Ⓒ Ⓓ Ⓔ
10 Ⓐ Ⓑ Ⓒ Ⓓ Ⓔ	20 Ⓐ Ⓑ Ⓒ Ⓓ Ⓔ	30 Ⓐ Ⓑ Ⓒ Ⓓ Ⓔ	40 Ⓐ Ⓑ Ⓒ Ⓓ Ⓔ

right in section 5

wrong in section 5

SECTION 6

1 Ⓐ Ⓑ Ⓒ Ⓓ Ⓔ	11 Ⓐ Ⓑ Ⓒ Ⓓ Ⓔ	21 Ⓐ Ⓑ Ⓒ Ⓓ Ⓔ	31 Ⓐ Ⓑ Ⓒ Ⓓ Ⓔ
2 Ⓐ Ⓑ Ⓒ Ⓓ Ⓔ	12 Ⓐ Ⓑ Ⓒ Ⓓ Ⓔ	22 Ⓐ Ⓑ Ⓒ Ⓓ Ⓔ	32 Ⓐ Ⓑ Ⓒ Ⓓ Ⓔ
3 Ⓐ Ⓑ Ⓒ Ⓓ Ⓔ	13 Ⓐ Ⓑ Ⓒ Ⓓ Ⓔ	23 Ⓐ Ⓑ Ⓒ Ⓓ Ⓔ	33 Ⓐ Ⓑ Ⓒ Ⓓ Ⓔ
4 Ⓐ Ⓑ Ⓒ Ⓓ Ⓔ	14 Ⓐ Ⓑ Ⓒ Ⓓ Ⓔ	24 Ⓐ Ⓑ Ⓒ Ⓓ Ⓔ	34 Ⓐ Ⓑ Ⓒ Ⓓ Ⓔ
5 Ⓐ Ⓑ Ⓒ Ⓓ Ⓔ	15 Ⓐ Ⓑ Ⓒ Ⓓ Ⓔ	25 Ⓐ Ⓑ Ⓒ Ⓓ Ⓔ	35 Ⓐ Ⓑ Ⓒ Ⓓ Ⓔ
6 Ⓐ Ⓑ Ⓒ Ⓓ Ⓔ	16 Ⓐ Ⓑ Ⓒ Ⓓ Ⓔ	26 Ⓐ Ⓑ Ⓒ Ⓓ Ⓔ	36 Ⓐ Ⓑ Ⓒ Ⓓ Ⓔ
7 Ⓐ Ⓑ Ⓒ Ⓓ Ⓔ	17 Ⓐ Ⓑ Ⓒ Ⓓ Ⓔ	27 Ⓐ Ⓑ Ⓒ Ⓓ Ⓔ	37 Ⓐ Ⓑ Ⓒ Ⓓ Ⓔ
8 Ⓐ Ⓑ Ⓒ Ⓓ Ⓔ	18 Ⓐ Ⓑ Ⓒ Ⓓ Ⓔ	28 Ⓐ Ⓑ Ⓒ Ⓓ Ⓔ	38 Ⓐ Ⓑ Ⓒ Ⓓ Ⓔ
9 Ⓐ Ⓑ Ⓒ Ⓓ Ⓔ	19 Ⓐ Ⓑ Ⓒ Ⓓ Ⓔ	29 Ⓐ Ⓑ Ⓒ Ⓓ Ⓔ	39 Ⓐ Ⓑ Ⓒ Ⓓ Ⓔ
10 Ⓐ Ⓑ Ⓒ Ⓓ Ⓔ	20 Ⓐ Ⓑ Ⓒ Ⓓ Ⓔ	30 Ⓐ Ⓑ Ⓒ Ⓓ Ⓔ	40 Ⓐ Ⓑ Ⓒ Ⓓ Ⓔ

right in section 6

wrong in section 6

Time—30 Minutes   For each of the following questions, choose the best answer and darken the
30 Questions   corresponding oval on the answer sheet.*

Select the lettered word or set of words that best completes the sentence.

Example:

Today's small, portable computers contrast markedly with the earliest electronic computers, which were ----.

(A) effective
(B) invented
(C) useful
(D) destructive
(E) enormous

1 Despite their fierce appearance, caymans are rarely ----, and will not attack humans unless provoked.

(A) extinct
(B) timid
(C) domesticated
(D) amphibious
(E) aggressive

2 Some historians claim that the concept of courtly love is a ---- that dates from the age of chivalry, while others believe it has more ---- origins.

(A) relic . . simultaneous
(B) notion . . ancient
(C) memento . . discovered
(D) period . . documented
(E) doctrine . . amorous

3 In Shakespeare's day, ---- theater audiences would often throw fruits and vegetables at actors who failed to live up to their expectations.

(A) doting
(B) ravenous
(C) jingoistic
(D) boisterous
(E) stagnant

4 Although they physically resemble each other, the brothers could not be more ---- temperamentally; while the one is quiet and circumspect, the other is brash and ----.

(A) inimical . . timid
(B) passionate . . superficial
(C) dissimilar . . audacious
(D) different . . forgiving
(E) alike . . respectful

5 The retreat of Napoleon's army from Moscow quickly turned into a rout as French soldiers, already ---- in the snow, were ---- by Russian troops.

(A) replenishing . . ravaged
(B) pursuing . . joined
(C) sinking . . camouflaged
(D) floundering . . assaulted
(E) tottering . . upbraided

6 The Morgan Library in New York provides a ---- environment in which scholars work amidst costly tapestries, paintings, stained-glass windows, and hand-crafted furniture.

(A) realistic
(B) frugal
(C) sumptuous
(D) friendly
(E) practical

7 The lecturer's frustration was only ---- by the audience's ---- to talk during her presentation.

(A) compounded . . propensity
(B) alleviated . . invitation
(C) soothed . . authorization
(D) increased . . inability
(E) supplanted . . desire

8 The proposal to build a nuclear power plant was the most ---- issue ever to come up at a council meeting; it is astonishing, therefore, that the members' vote was unanimous.

(A) popular
(B) contentious
(C) concise
(D) exorbitant
(E) inconsequential

9 The itinerary set by their travel agent included so many stops in ---- amount of time that they received only the most ---- impressions of places visited.

(A) a limited . . lasting
(B) a brief . . cursory
(C) a generous . . favorable
(D) a sufficient . . fleeting
(E) an unnecessary . . preliminary

*The directions on the actual SAT will vary slightly.

GO ON TO THE NEXT PAGE ➡

Choose the lettered pair of words that is related in the same way as the pair in capital letters.

Example:

FLAKE : SNOW ::

(A) storm : hail
(B) drop : rain
(C) field : wheat
(D) stack : hay
(E) cloud : fog

10 STEEL : METAL ::

(A) coal : mine
(B) silk : fabric
(C) suit : card
(D) player : team
(E) carat : diamond

11 FUNNEL : CONICAL ::

(A) pipe : cylindrical
(B) solid : spherical
(C) hose : spiral
(D) line : parallel
(E) hive : hexagonal

12 FUTILE : USE ::

(A) expensive : value
(B) faint : light
(C) superficial : depth
(D) furtive : stealth
(E) educated : morals

13 SUBMISSION : KNEEL ::

(A) equilibrium : stand
(B) leisure : sit
(C) mutiny : lie
(D) disrespect : bow
(E) assent : nod

14 MOVEMENT : SYMPHONY ::

(A) note : piano
(B) projector : film
(C) act : play
(D) rhythm : poem
(E) canvas : painting

15 PURGATIVE : CLEANSING ::

(A) fixative : preparation
(B) vitamin : deficiency
(C) spice : aroma
(D) inoculation : reaction
(E) catalyst : change

GO ON TO THE NEXT PAGE ➡

Answer the questions below based on the information in the accompanying passages.

Questions 16–23 are based on the following passage.

The passage below is adopted from a short story set in the wilderness of Alaska.

Day had broken cold and gray, exceedingly cold
and gray, when the man turned away from the
main Yukon trail and climbed the high earth-bank,
Line where a dim and little-traveled trail led eastward
(5) through the spruce timberland. It was a steep bank,
and he paused for breath at the top, excusing the
act to himself by looking at his watch. It was nine
o'clock. There was no hint of sun, though there
was not a cloud in the sky. It was a clear day, and
(10) yet there seemed an intangible pall over the face of
things that made the day dark. This fact did not
worry the man.
In fact, all this—the dim trail, the absence of
sun from the sky, the tremendous cold, and the
(15) strangeness and weirdness of it all—made no
impression on the man. It was not because he was
used to it. He was a newcomer in the land, and this
was his first winter. The trouble was that he was
without imagination. He was young and quick and
(20) alert in the things of life, but only in the things,
and not in the significances. It was fifty degrees
below zero, he judged. That impressed him as
being cold and uncomfortable, but it did not lead
him to meditate upon his frailty as a creature of
(25) temperature, and upon human frailty in general,
able only to live within narrow limits of heat and
cold; and from there on it did not lead him to the
conjectural field of immortality and humanity's
place in the universe. Fifty degrees below zero
(30) stood for a bite of frost that hurt and that must be
guarded against. Nothing more than that entered
his head.
He plunged in among the trees with
determination. The trail was faint. A foot of snow
(35) had fallen since the last sled had passed, and he
was glad he was traveling light. In fact, he carried
nothing but the lunch wrapped in his
handkerchief. He was surprised, however, at the
cold. It certainly was cold, he concluded, as he
(40) rubbed his numb nose and cheekbones with his
mittened hand. He was bearded, but that did not
protect the high cheekbones and the eager nose
that thrust itself aggressively into the frosty air.
At his heels walked a dog, a big native husky,
(45) gray-coated, without any visible or temperamental
difference from its close relative, the wild wolf. The
animal was depressed by the tremendous cold. It
knew that it was no time for traveling. Its instinct
told it a truer tale than was told by the man's
(50) judgment. In reality, it was not merely colder than
fifty below zero; it was colder than sixty below, than
seventy below. It was seventy-five below zero. The
dog knew nothing of thermometers. Possibly in its
brain there was no sharp consciousness of a
(55) condition of very cold such as was in the human
brain. But the brute had its instinct. It experienced a
vague but menacing apprehension that subdued it
and made it slink along at the man's heels, and that
made it question every unusual movement of the
(60) man as if expecting him to go into camp or to seek
shelter somewhere and build a fire. The dog had
learned fire, and it wanted fire, or else to burrow
under the snow and cuddle its warmth away from
the air.

16   By using the phrase "excusing the act to
     himself" (lines 6–7), the author suggests that
     the man

     (A) is annoyed that it is already nine o'clock
         in the morning
     (B) distrusts his own intuitive reactions to
         things
     (C) finds fault with others more readily than
         with himself
     (D) doubts that the time of day has any real
         bearing on things
     (E) dislikes admitting to personal
         weaknesses

17   The author identifies the man as "a
     newcomer in the land" (line 17) most likely
     in order to suggest that the man was

     (A) excited at being in a new place with
         many opportunities
     (B) nervous about being alone in an
         unfamiliar place
     (C) lacking in knowledge and experience
         about the things around him
     (D) trying hard to forget something in his
         past
     (E) unsure about why he chose to come to
         the new place

GO ON TO THE NEXT PAGE ➡

18 In lines 24–25, the phrase "a creature of temperature" refers to

   (A) the man's preference for cold climates
   (B) the innate human ability to judge temperature
   (C) the fact that one's personality is shaped by the environment
   (D) the human body's physical vulnerability in extreme climates
   (E) the man's unfamiliarity with wilderness survival techniques

19 Judging from lines 18–29, the man does not see that

   (A) he should appreciate the immense beauty of nature
   (B) humans cannot survive in the Alaskan wilderness
   (C) there is no way to accurately judge the temperature
   (D) the extreme cold could potentially be fatal
   (E) he has undertaken to do something which most people could not

20 The man's opinion of the temperature (lines 29–32) reveals which aspect of his character?

   (A) determination to succeed against all odds
   (B) lack of concern about personal welfare
   (C) pragmatic approach to travel
   (D) absence of insight and understanding
   (E) apprehension about the extreme cold

21 In lines 46–56, by discussing the dog's reaction to the "tremendous cold," the author suggests that

   (A) animal instinct can prove to be superior to human intelligence
   (B) animals can judge temperature more accurately than humans can
   (C) humans are ill-equipped to survive in the wilderness
   (D) there is little difference between animal instinct and human judgment
   (E) animals and humans have different reactions to extreme temperatures

22 The statement "the dog knew nothing of thermometers" (lines 52–53) means that

   (A) dogs need not be as concerned about temperature as humans do
   (B) the dog's awareness of its environment is on a different level from the man's
   (C) a dog's mental faculties are not very well developed
   (D) the dog's experience of humans had been rather limited
   (E) the dog could not rely on the technological devices that the man could

23 Which of the following best explains why the dog would "question every unusual movement of the man" (lines 59–60)?

   (A) The dog senses that it cannot rely on the man for survival.
   (B) The man is beginning to be visibly affected by the cold.
   (C) The dog recognizes the need for protection from the cold.
   (D) The dog worries that the man intends to leave it behind.
   (E) The dog understands that the man does not realize how cold it is.

GO ON TO THE NEXT PAGE ➡

Questions 24–30 are based on the following passage.

The social science passage below was adapted from an article written by a health scientist.

Line
(5)

For people in Southeast Asian refugee families, the experience of aging in America is very different from what they had expected for their second half of life. Older Southeast Asian refugees must cope with their rapidly acculturating younger family members, while taking on new roles and expectations in a foreign culture.

(10)

Many Southeast Asian immigrants find that, by American standards, they are not even considered elderly. Migration to a new culture often changes the definition of life stages. In the traditional Hmong culture of Vietnam, one can become an elder at 35 years of age when one becomes a grandparent. With grandparent status, elder Hmong

(15)

can retire and expect their children to take financial responsibility for the family. Retiring at 35, of course, is not acceptable in the United States.

(20)

There is a strong influence of Confucianism in traditional Vietnamese society. Confucianism, an ancient system of moral and religious thought, fosters strong filial piety and respect for family elders. In many Southeast Asian societies, age roles are hierarchical, with strict rules for social interaction. In America, however, because older

(25)

refugees lack facility with the English language and knowledge of American culture, their credibility decreases when advising younger family members about important decisions. As younger family members take on primary roles as family mediators

(30)

with American institutions—schools, legal systems, and social service agencies, for example— the leadership position of elders within the family is gradually eroded.

(35)

Refugee elders must also cope with differences in gender role in the United States. Even before migration, traditional gender roles were changing in Southeast Asia. During the Vietnam War, when men of military age were away, women took responsibility for tasks normally divided along

(40)

gender lines. When Vietnamese families came to this country, changes in traditional gender roles became more pronounced. There were more employment opportunities for younger refugees and middle-aged refugee women because their

(45)

expectations often fit with the lower status jobs that were among the few opportunities open to refugees. Many middle-aged women and younger refugees of both sexes became family breadwinners. This was a radical change for

(50)

middle-aged men, who had been the major breadwinners of the family.

(55)

Although the pattern for long-term adaptation of middle-aged and older Southeast Asian refugees is still unknown, there are indications that the outlook for women is problematic. Many older women provide household and childcare services in order to allow younger family members to hold jobs or go to school. While these women are helping younger family members to succeed in

(60)

America, they themselves are often isolated at home and not learning English or other new skills, or becoming more familiar with American society. Thus, after the immigrant family passes through the early stages of meeting basic survival needs,

(65)

older women may find that they are strangers in their own families as well as their new country.

24 The major purpose of the passage is to discuss

(A) the reasons why Southeast Asian people move to the United States
(B) educational challenges facing young refugees in America today
(C) problems that elderly Southeast Asian people encounter in America
(D) the influence of Confucianism in Southeast Asian cultures
(E) changing gender relationships in Southeast Asian refugee families

25 The author mentions the "traditional Hmong culture" (lines 11–12) in order to

(A) show that social expectations may vary greatly from one country to another
(B) suggest the lessening importance of traditional values in Vietnamese society
(C) indicate that modern Vietnam encompasses a number of ancient cultures
(D) illustrate the growing influence of Confucianism in Vietnamese society
(E) compare the religious beliefs of the Vietnamese to those of other Southeast Asian peoples

GO ON TO THE NEXT PAGE ➡

26 The author uses the term *family mediators* (line 29) to mean the

   (A) traditional role of elders in Vietnamese families
   (B) responsibilities which young refugees assume in a new country
   (C) help that newly arrived refugees get from friends who migrated earlier
   (D) professional help available to refugee families in U.S. communities
   (E) benefits that American society derives from immigrant people

27 The word *pronounced* in line 42 most nearly means

   (A) delivered
   (B) noticeable
   (C) famous
   (D) acceptable
   (E) declared

28 The phrase *radical change* (line 49) refers to the fact that

   (A) older refugees find that retirement ages are very different in America
   (B) women filled men's jobs during the Vietnam War
   (C) education of their children is considered crucial by refugee parents
   (D) refugee men are often displaced as primary income earners in their families
   (E) it is difficult for young refugees of both sexes to find jobs in America

29 The author's point about the problematic long-term outlook for refugee women is made primarily through

   (A) personal recollection
   (B) historical discussion
   (C) case study analysis
   (D) philosophical commentary
   (E) informed speculation

30 The author mentions which of the following problems facing elderly Southeast Asian refugees?

   I. Southeast Asian women have greater employment opportunities in their own countries than in the United States.
   II. Southeast Asians respect their elders, while Americans do not.
   III. Americans and Southeast Asians differ in their definition of when one becomes elderly.

   (A) I only
   (B) II only
   (C) III only
   (D) II and III only
   (E) I, II, and III

IF YOU FINISH BEFORE TIME IS CALLED, YOU MAY CHECK YOUR WORK ON THIS SECTION ONLY. DO NOT TURN TO ANY OTHER SECTION IN THE TEST.   **STOP**

Time—30 Minutes

25 Questions

Solve each of the following problems, decide which is the best answer choice, and darken the corresponding oval on the answer sheet. Use available space in the test booklet for scratchwork.*

Notes:

(1) Calculator use is permitted.

(2) All numbers used are real numbers.

(3) Figures are provided for some problems. All figures are drawn to scale and lie in a plane UNLESS otherwise indicated.

Reference Information

$A=\frac{1}{2}bh$ $c^2 = a^2 + b^2$ Special Right Triangles $A=\pi r^2$ $C=2\pi r$ $V=\ell wh$ $V=\pi r^2 h$ $A=\ell w$

The sum of the degree measures of the angles of a triangle is 180.
The number of degrees of arc in a circle is 360.
A straight angle has a degree measure of 180.

---

1 If $2(x + y) = 8 + 2y$, then $x =$

(A) 1
(B) 2
(C) 3
(D) 4
(E) 8

2 On the number line above, what is the distance from point B to the midpoint of AC ?

(A) 1
(B) 2
(C) 3
(D) 4
(E) 5

3 A certain machine caps 5 bottles every 2 seconds. At this rate, how many bottles will be capped in 1 minute?

(A) 10
(B) 75
(C) 150
(D) 225
(E) 300

4 If $2n + 3 = 5$, then $4n =$

(A) 1
(B) 2
(C) 4
(D) 8
(E) 16

5 If $a + b < 5$, and $a - b > 6$, which of the following pairs could be the values of a and b ?

(A) (1, 3)
(B) (3, −2)
(C) (4, −2)
(D) (4, −3)
(E) (5, −1)

---

*The directions on the actual SAT will vary slightly.

GO ON TO THE NEXT PAGE ➡

Note: Figure not drawn to scale.

6 In the triangle above, if the measure of angle B is 60 degrees, then what is the value of y ?

(A) 24
(B) 26
(C) 28
(D) 30
(E) 32

7 In a certain building, there are 10 floors and the number of rooms on each floor is R. If each room has exactly C chairs, which of the following gives the total number of chairs in the building?

(A) $10R + C$

(B) $10R + 10C$

(C) $\frac{10}{RC}$

(D) $10RC$

(E) $100RC$

8 If a "sump" number is defined as one in which the sum of the digits of the number is greater than the product of the digits of the same number, which of the following is a "sump" number?

(A) 123
(B) 234
(C) 332
(D) 411
(E) 521

9 If 4 percent of r is 6.2, then 20 percent of r =

(A) 25
(B) 26
(C) 30
(D) 31
(E) 35

10 At a certain school, if the ratio of teachers to students is 1 to 10, which of the following could be the total number of teachers and students?

(A) 100
(B) 121
(C) 144
(D) 222
(E) 1,011

11 If $x \wedge y$ is defined by the expression $(x - y)^x + (x + y)^y$, what is the value of $4 \wedge 2$?

(A) 52
(B) 44
(C) 28
(D) 20
(E) 16

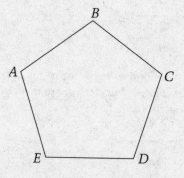

12 In pentagon $ABCDE$ shown above, each side is 1 centimeter. If a particle starts at point A and travels clockwise 723 centimeters along $ABCDE$, the particle will stop on which point?

(A) A
(B) B
(C) C
(D) D
(E) E

13 Which of the following values of s would yield the smallest value for $4 + \frac{1}{s}$?

(A) $\frac{1}{4}$

(B) $\frac{1}{2}$

(C) 1

(D) 2

(E) 4

GO ON TO THE NEXT PAGE ➡

14 The first and seventh terms in a sequence are 1 and 365 respectively. If each term after the first in the sequence is formed by multiplying the preceding term by 3 and subtracting 1, what is the sixth term?

(A) 40
(B) 41
(C) 121
(D) 122
(E) 123

15 If an integer is randomly chosen from the first 50 positive integers, what is the probability that an integer with a digit of 3 is selected?

(A) $\frac{7}{25}$

(B) $\frac{3}{10}$

(C) $\frac{8}{25}$

(D) $\frac{2}{5}$

(E) $\frac{3}{5}$

16 In a certain triangle, the measure of the largest angle is 40 degrees more than the measure of the middle-sized angle. If the measure of the smallest angle is 20 degrees, what is the degree measure of the largest angle?

(A) 60
(B) 80
(C) 100
(D) 120
(E) 160

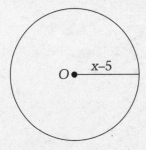

17 In the circle with center O above, for what value of x does the circle have a circumference of 20π ?

(A)   5
(B) 10
(C) 15
(D) 20
(E) 25

18 In a coordinate plane, if points $A(p, 3)$ and $B(6, p)$ lie on a line with a slope of 2, what is the value of p ?

(A) 1
(B) 2
(C) 3
(D) 4
(E) 5

19 At a fruit stand, the price of one pound of cherries is twice the price of one pound of grapes. If 32 pounds of cherries and 8 pounds of grapes were sold and sales totaled $90.00, how much more money was made on the cherries than on the grapes?

(A) $75.00
(B) $70.00
(C) $65.00
(D) $60.00
(E) $55.00

20 In the coordinate plane above, points $P(0, 6)$, $Q(1, 4)$, and $C(3, 0)$ are on line ℓ. What is the sum of the areas of the shaded triangular regions?

(A) $\frac{7}{2}$

(B) 4

(C) $\frac{9}{2}$

(D) 5

(E) $\frac{11}{2}$

GO ON TO THE NEXT PAGE ➡

21 The average (arithmetic mean) of two numbers is equal to twice the positive difference between the two numbers. If the larger number is 35, what is the small number?

(A)   3
(B)   9
(C)   15
(D)   21
(E)   27

23 In the figure above, if $BC = DC$, and $AD = AB$, what is the value of $\frac{AB}{CD}$?

(A) $\frac{\sqrt{2}}{2}$

(B) $\sqrt{2}$

(C) $\frac{\sqrt{3}}{3}$

(D) $\sqrt{3}$

(E)   2

n cubes

22 In the figure above, there is a total of *n* cubes, each with an edge of 1 inch, stacked directly on top of each other. If $n > 1$, what is the total surface area, in square inches, of the resulting solid, in terms of *n* ?

(A) $2n$
(B) $2n^2 + 2$
(C) $4n + 2$
(D) $4n^2$
(E) $5n$

24 If the sum of 5 different positive integers is 100, what is greatest possible value for the median of the 5 integers?

(A)   31
(B)   32
(C)   33
(D)   34
(E)   50

25 The lengths of two sides of a triangle are $(x - 2)$ and $(x + 2)$, where $x > 2$. Which of the following ranges includes all and only the possible values of the third side *y* ?

(A) $0 < y < x$
(B) $0 < y < 2x$
(C) $2 < y < x$
(D) $4 < y < x$
(E) $4 < y < 2x$

IF YOU FINISH BEFORE TIME IS CALLED, YOU MAY CHECK YOUR WORK ON THIS SECTION ONLY. DO NOT TURN TO ANY OTHER SECTION IN THE TEST.   **STOP**

Time—30 Minutes
35 Questions

For each of the following questions, choose the best answer and darken the corresponding oval on the answer sheet.

Select the lettered word or set of words that best completes the sentence.

Example:

Today's small, portable computers contrast markedly with the earliest electronic computers, which were ----.

(A) effective
(B) invented
(C) useful
(D) destructive
(E) enormous

1 Ozone in the upper layers of Earth's atmosphere is beneficial, ---- animal and plant life from dangerous ultraviolet radiation.

(A) reflecting
(B) withdrawing
(C) displacing
(D) thwarting
(E) protecting

2 While George Balanchine's choreography stayed within a classical context, he challenged convention by recombining ballet idioms in ---- ways.

(A) unexpected
(B) familiar
(C) redundant
(D) naive
(E) awkward

3 All of today's navel oranges are ---- of a single mutant tree that began bearing seedless fruit 200 years ago.

(A) progenitors
(B) combinations
(C) descendants
(D) conglomerations
(E) spores

4 Because he consumed ---- quantities of food and drink at feasts given in his honor, King Henry VIII was considered a ---- by his subjects.

(A) enormous . . glutton
(B) prodigious . . peer
(C) minute . . luminary
(D) unhealthy . . fraud
(E) unknown . . dolt

5 The prime minister ordered the cabinet to stay on as ----administration until a new government could be formed.

(A) an interim
(B) a political
(C) an invalid
(D) a premature
(E) a civilian

6 Many formerly ---- peoples have moved into ---- settlements as urban areas have encroached upon their land.

(A) roving . . vulnerable
(B) despondent . . stable
(C) transitory . . covert
(D) fervid . . enduring
(E) nomadic . . permanent

7 The ---- effect of the sleeping tablets was so ---- that she still felt groggy the next day.

(A) toxic . . erratic
(B) soporific . . pronounced
(C) salubrious . . dependable
(D) pharmaceutical . . peculiar
(E) stimulating . . unreliable

8 For many years Davis had difficulty in accepting those who were in positions of authority; in fact, when he was in high school his teachers described him as a ---- student.

(A) compliant
(B) slothful
(C) conscientious
(D) model
(E) recalcitrant

9 Although the actress had lived in a large city all her life, she was such a ---- performer that she became the virtual ---- of the humble farm girl she portrayed in the play.

(A) versatile . . opposite
(B) melodramatic . . understudy
(C) natural . . nemesis
(D) consummate . . incarnation
(E) drab . . caricature

10 The chairman ---- the decision of the board members, describing it as a ---- of every worthy ideal that the organization had hitherto upheld.

(A) defended . . denial
(B) lamented . . negation
(C) criticized . . fulfillment
(D) endorsed . . renunciation
(E) applauded . . repudiation

GO ON TO THE NEXT PAGE ➡

Choose the lettered pair of words that is related in the same way as the pair in capital letters.

Example:

FLAKE : SNOW ::
(A) storm : hail
(B) drop : rain
(C) field : wheat
(D) stack : hay
(E) cloud : fog

11 MILL : FLOUR ::

(A) paddock : horses
(B) stadium : ballgame
(C) pharmacy : prescription
(D) brewery : beer
(E) pantry : food

12 STETHOSCOPE : LISTEN ::

(A) microscope : record
(B) needle : inject
(C) bandage : cut
(D) scale : reduce
(E) cough : breathe

13 BOTANIST : PLANTS ::

(A) zoologist : animals
(B) linguist : verbs
(C) philologist : stamps
(D) physicist : experiments
(E) chemist : laboratories

14 ABUNDANT : ADEQUATE ::

(A) arid : moist
(B) peaceful : boisterous
(C) timid : illegitimate
(D) overflowing : full
(E) bold : anxious

15 DOUBLE-CROSSER : BETRAY ::

(A) slowpoke : lag
(B) watchdog : dread
(C) trendsetter : pace
(D) sweetheart : hug
(E) pessimist : cooperate

16 EVADE : STRAIGHTFORWARD ::

(A) leave : inviting
(B) enliven : animated
(C) flatten : smooth
(D) boast : modest
(E) assist : helpful

17 REPREHENSIBLE : BLAME ::

(A) incomprehensible : knowledge
(B) treasonable : invasion
(C) relevant : information
(D) difficult : failure
(E) commendable : praise

18 CONCORD : AGREEMENT ::

(A) insurrection : peace
(B) chaos : order
(C) promise : force
(D) revolution : army
(E) flux : change

19 FLORAL : FLOWERS ::

(A) perennial : plants
(B) morbid : cemeteries
(C) emotional : feelings
(D) moral : stories
(E) maniacal : men

20 CALM : COMPOSURE ::

(A) scared : trouble
(B) cold : sickness
(C) congested : traffic
(D) sad : melancholy
(E) bored : gladness

21 SEQUESTER : JUROR ::

(A) quarantine : patient
(B) cloister : convent
(C) parole : prisoner
(D) graduate : pupil
(E) elect : mayor

22 HACKNEYED : ORIGINALITY ::

(A) omnipotent : power
(B) debauched : virtue
(C) fictitious : objectivity
(D) correct : judgment
(E) stubborn : resolve

23 SLAKE : THIRST ::

(A) stoke : fire
(B) starve : hunger
(C) assuage : pain
(D) endure : discomfort
(E) induce : sleep

GO ON TO THE NEXT PAGE ➡

Answer the questions below based on the information in the accompanying passages.

Questions 24–35 are based on the following passage.

In the following passage, a famous zoologist discusses the origins of the domesticated animal.

Line
(5)

The relationship between humans and animals dates back to the misty morning of history. The caves of southern France and northern Spain are full of wonderful depictions of animals. Early African petroglyphs depict recognizable mammals and so does much American Indian art. But long before art, we have evidence of the closeness of humans and animals. The bones of dogs lie next to those of humans in the excavated villages of
(10) northern Israel and elsewhere. This unity of death is terribly appropriate. It marks a relationship that is the most ancient of all, one that dates back at least to the Mesolithic Era.* With the dog, the hunter acquired a companion and ally very early
(15) on, before agriculture, long before the horses and the cat. The companion animals were followed by food animals and then by those that provided enhanced speed and range, and those that worked for us.

(20) How did it all come about? A dog of some kind was almost inevitable. Consider its essence: a social carnivore, hunting larger animals across the broad plains it shared with our ancestors. Because of its pack structure it is susceptible to domination
(25) by, and attachment to, a pack leader—the top dog. Its young are born into the world dependent, rearable without too much skill, and best of all, they form bonds with the rearers. Dogs have a set of appeasement behaviors that elicit affective
(30) reactions from even the most hardened and unsophisticated humans. Puppies share with human babies the power to transform cynics into cooing softies. Furthermore, the animal has a sense of smell and hearing several times more acute than
(35) our own, great advantages to a hunting companion and intrusion detector. The dog's defense behavior makes it an instinctive guard animal.

No wonder the dog was first and remains so close to us. In general, however, something else
(40) was probably important in narrowing the list—the candidates had to be camp followers or cohabitants. When humankind ceased to be continually nomadic, when we put down roots and established semi-permanent habitations, hut
(45) clusters and finally villages, we created an instant, rich food supply for guilds of opportunistic feeders. Even today, many birds and mammals parasitize our wastes and feed from our stores. They do so because their wild behaviors provide the
(50) mechanisms for opportunistic exploitation. A striking example occurred in Britain during the

1940s and '50s. In those days, milk was delivered to the homeowners' doorstep in glass bottles with aluminum foil caps. Rich cream topped the milk,
(55) the paradise before homogenization. A chickadee known as the blue tit learned to puncture the cap and drink the cream. The behavior soon spread among the tits, and soon milk bottles were being raided in the early morning throughout Britain. If
(60) the birds had been so specialized that they only fed in deep forest, it never would have happened. But these were forest-edge opportunists, pioneers rather than conservatives. It is from animals of this ilk that we find our allies and our foes.

(65) Returning to the question of how it all came about, my instincts tell me that we first domesticated those individual animals that were orphaned by our hunting ancestors. In my years in the tropics, I have seen many wild animals raised
(70) by simple people in their houses. The animals were there, without thought of utility or gain, mainly because the hunter in the family had brought the orphaned baby back for his wife and children. In Panama it was often a beautiful small,
(75) spotted cat that bounced friskily out of a peasant's kitchen to play at my feet. The steps from the home-raised wolfling to the domestic dog probably took countless generations. I bet it started with affection and curiosity. Only later did it become
(80) useful.

When we consider that there are more than 55 million domestic cats and 50 million dogs in this country, and that they support an industry larger than the total economy of medieval Europe, we
(85) must recognize the strength of the ancient bond. Without the "aid" of goats, sheep, pigs, cattle and horses we would never have reached our present population densities. Our parasitization of some species and symbiosis with others made
(90) civilization possible. That civilization, in turn, is increasingly causing the extinction of many animals and plant species—an ironic paradox indeed.

*Mesolithic Era: also known as the Middle Stone Age, between 8,000 and 3,000 years B.C.

GO ON TO THE NEXT PAGE ➡

24 The author most likely describes the archeological discoveries mentioned in lines 8–10 as "terribly appropriate" because

(A) dogs were always buried next to their owners in the Mesolithic Era
(B) few animals were of religious significance in prehistoric cultures
(C) they illustrate the role of dogs on a typical hunting expedition
(D) our relationship with dogs goes back farther than with any other animal
(E) they indicate the terrible speed of natural disasters

25 According to the first paragraph, the first animals that humans had a close relationship with were those that

(A) acted as companions
(B) provided a source of food
(C) helped develop agriculture
(D) enabled humans to travel farther
(E) raided our food supply

26 According to the author, why was some kind of dog "inevitable" (line 21) as a companion animal for humans?

(A) It survived by maintaining its independence.
(B) It was stronger than other large animals.
(C) It shared its prey with our ancestors.
(D) It was friendly to other carnivores.
(E) It was suited for human domination.

27 In line 21, *essence* means

(A) history
(B) nature
(C) scent
(D) success
(E) aggression

28 Judging from lines 29–30, *affective reactions* most probably means

(A) callous decisions
(B) rational judgements
(C) emotional responses
(D) juvenile behavior
(E) cynical comments

29 The author most likely compares puppies with human babies in lines 31–33 in order to

(A) criticize an uncaring attitude towards animals
(B) point out ways in which animals dominate humans
(C) support the idea that dogs form bonds with their owners
(D) dispel some misconceptions about the innocence of puppies
(E) show how rewarding the ownership of a dog can be

30 In line 40, *the list* most likely refers to

(A) the types of birds that scavenge human food supplies
(B) the number of animals that developed relationships with humans
(C) the group of species that are able to communicate with dogs
(D) the variety of attributes that make dogs good hunters
(E) the range of animals depicted in cave paintings

31 The author most likely discusses the case of the British blue tit (lines 52–59) in order to

(A) highlight a waste of valuable food supplies
(B) indicate the quality of milk before homogenization
(C) explain how unpredictable animal behavior can be
(D) point out the disadvantages of living in rural areas
(E) provide one example of an opportunistic feeder

32 In lines 63–64, *animals of this ilk* refers to animals that are

(A) good companions
(B) forest inhabitants
(C) adaptable feeders
(D) efficient hunters
(E) persistent pests

GO ON TO THE NEXT PAGE ➡

33 The author most likely describes his experience in the tropics (lines 68–76) in order to

(A) portray the simple life led by a hunter's family
(B) show how useful animals can be in isolated places
(C) underline the effort involved in training a wild animal
(D) illustrate how the first domesticated animals were created
(E) indicate the curious nature of the domestic cat

34 In line 86, the use of "aid" in quotation marks emphasizes the point that

(A) the animals' help was involuntary
(B) population levels are dangerously high
(C) the contribution of animals is rarely recognized
(D) many animals benefited from the relationship
(E) livestock animals are not as loyal as dogs

35 Which of the following best describes the "ironic paradox" mentioned in line 92?

(A) More money is now spent on domestic animals than on animal livestock.
(B) Pet ownership will become impractical if population density continues to increase.
(C) The pet care industry in the U.S. today is larger than the total economy of medieval Europe.
(D) Many parasitical species have a beneficial effect on the human population.
(E) Human civilization is currently making extinct many of the other life forms that enabled it to grow.

IF YOU FINISH BEFORE TIME IS CALLED, YOU MAY CHECK YOUR WORK ON THIS SECTION ONLY. DO NOT TURN TO ANY OTHER SECTION IN THE TEST. **STOP**

KAPLAN   369

Time—30 Minutes

25 Questions

Solve each of the following problems, decide which is the best answer choice, and darken the corresponding oval on the answer sheet. Use available space in the test booklet for scratchwork.*

Notes:

(1) Calculator use is permitted.

(2) All numbers used are real numbers.

(3) Figures are provided for some problems. All figures are drawn to scale and lie in a plane UNLESS otherwise indicated.

Reference Information

$A=\frac{1}{2}bh$ $c^2 = a^2 + b^2$ Special Right Triangles $A=\pi r^2$
$C=2\pi r$ $V=\ell wh$ $V=\pi r^2 h$ $A=\ell w$

The sum of the degree measures of the angles of a triangle is 180.
The number of degrees of arc in a circle is 360.
A straight angle has a degree measure of 180.

DIRECTIONS FOR QUANTITATIVE COMPARISON QUESTIONS

Compare the boxed quantity in Column A with the boxed quantity in Column B. Select answer choice

A   if Column A is greater;
B   if Column B is greater;
C   if the columns are equal; or
D   if more information is needed to determine the relationship.

An E response will be treated as an omission.

Notes:

1. Some questions include information about one or both quantities. That information is centered and unboxed.
2. A symbol that appears in both Column A and Column B stands for the same thing in both columns.
3. All numbers used are real numbers.

EXAMPLES

Column A	Column B	Answers
E1 3×4	$3 + 4$	● Ⓑ Ⓒ Ⓓ Ⓔ

$x°$ $20°$

| E2 x | 160 | Ⓐ Ⓑ ● Ⓓ Ⓔ |

x and y are positive

| E3 $x + 1$ | $y - 1$ | Ⓐ Ⓑ Ⓒ ● Ⓔ |

*The directions on the actual SAT will vary slightly.

GO ON TO THE NEXT PAGE ➡

<u>Column A</u>	<u>Column B</u>

1

| 1,000 − 3.45002 | 1,000 − 3.45601 |

$$x + y > 11$$
$$x < 5.5$$

2

| x | y |

3

| $\dfrac{27}{17^{17}}$ | $\dfrac{27}{17^{18}}$ |

4

| The number of hours in 60 days | The number of seconds in 30 minutes |

$$a + b = 60$$
$$b + c = 40$$
$$a > b > c > 0$$

5

| The average (arithmetic mean) of a, b, and c. | 50 |

<u>Column A</u>	<u>Column B</u>

6

| The number of units of the perimeter triangle ABC | The number of square units of the area triangle ABC |

$$1, 2, -3, -4, 1, 2, -3, -4\ldots$$

The sequence above begins with 1 and repeats in the pattern 1, 2, −3, −4 indefinitely.

7

| The sum of the 49th and 51st terms | The sum of the 50th and 52nd terms |

Kearne is twice as old as Amanda.

8

| Kearne's age five years ago | Amanda's age five years from now |

$$2x + y = 2$$
$$4x + y = 3$$

9

| $3x$ | $2y$ |

$$x + y = -3$$
$$x = 2y$$

10

| x | y |

GO ON TO THE NEXT PAGE ➡

Column A	**Column B**

Note: Figure is not drawn to scale.

$BD > AC$

11

AB	CD

12

$b - a$	90

Each side of cube $ABCDEFGH$ has a length e.
M is the midpoint of segment CD.

13

The length of MH	$\dfrac{3}{2}e$

Column A	**Column B**

Note: Figure not drawn to scale.

C is the center of the circle.
AB is perpendicular to CD.

14

The x-coordinate of point D	The y-coordinate of point D

75% of 80 > 25% of x

15

x	200

GO ON TO THE NEXT PAGE ➡

KAPLAN

DIRECTIONS FOR STUDENT-PRODUCED RESPONSE QUESTIONS

For each of the questions below (16–25), solve the problem and indicate your answer by darkening the ovals in the special grid. For example:

Answer: 1.25 or $\frac{5}{4}$ or 5/4

Write answer in boxes.

Grid-in result

Fraction line

Decimal point

Either position is correct.

You may start your answers in any column, space permitting. Columns not needed should be left blank.

- It is recommended, though not required, that you write your answer in the boxes at the top of the columns. However, you will receive credit only for darkening the ovals correctly.

- Grid only one answer to a question, even though some problems have more than one correct answer.

- Darken no more than one oval in a column.

- No answers are negative.

- Mixed numbers cannot be gridded. For example: the number $1\frac{1}{4}$ must be gridded as 1.25 or 5/4.

  (If $\boxed{1\,1\,/\,4}$ is gridded, it will be interpreted as $\frac{11}{4}$, not $1\frac{1}{4}$.)

- **Decimal Accuracy:** Decimal answers must be entered as accurately as possible. For example, if you obtain an answer such as 0.1666..., you should record the result as .166 or .167. **Less accurate values such as .16 or .17 are not acceptable.**

Acceptable ways to grid $\frac{1}{6}$ = .1666. . .

---

16 If $y = 2$, then $(5 - y)(y + 3) =$

17 At a certain car rental company, the daily rental rate for a mid-size car is $18.99. If the weekly rental rate for the same car is $123.50, how much money, in dollars, is saved by renting this car by the week instead of renting daily for seven days? (Exclude the $ sign when gridding your answer.)

GO ON TO THE NEXT PAGE ➡

Note: Figure not drawn to scale.

18 In the figure above, $AB = 4$, $BC = 5$, and DC is 12. If point E lies somewhere between points A and B on line segment AB, what is one possible length of DE?

19 If $\frac{3}{4}$ of a cup of a certain drink mix is needed for every 2 quarts of water, how many cups of this drink mix is needed for 10 quarts of water?

20 In the figure above, what is the value of x?

Note: Figure not drawn to scale.

21 On the number line above, what is one possible value for y?

22 Melanie drove at an average rate of 40 miles per hour for two hours and then increased her average rate by 25% for the next 3 hours. Her average rate of speed for the 5 hours was t miles per hour. What is the value of t?

23 At a convention of 500 dealers, each dealer sold coins or stamps or both. If 127 dealers sold both coins and stamps, and 198 dealers sold *only* stamps, how many dealers sold only coins?

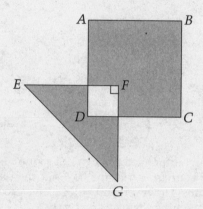

Note: Figure not drawn to scale.

24 In the figure above, square $ABCD$ and right triangle EFG overlap to form a smaller square of length 2. If $AB = EF = FG = 6$, what is the sum of the areas of the shaded regions?

$$\begin{array}{r} N R \\ + R N \\ \hline A B C \end{array}$$

25 The addition problem above is correct. If N, R, A, B, and C are different digits, what is the greatest possible value of $B + C$?

IF YOU FINISH BEFORE TIME IS CALLED, YOU MAY CHECK YOUR WORK ON THIS SECTION ONLY. DO NOT TURN TO ANY OTHER SECTION IN THE TEST. **STOP**

Time—15 Minutes
13 Questions   Answer the questions below based on the information in the accompanying passages.

Questions 1–13 are based on the following passages.

The two excerpts below are from speeches that were made by outstanding American leaders of the nineteenth century. The first excerpt is from Thomas Jefferson's first Inaugural Address in 1801; the second was delivered by Frederick Douglass during the Fourth of July celebration in Rochester, New York, in 1852.

Passage 1

Let us then, with courage and confidence, pursue our own federal and republican principles; our attachment to union and representative government.
Line Kindly separated by nature and a wide ocean from
(5) the exterminating havoc of one quarter of the globe; too high-minded to endure the degradation of others, possessing a chosen country, with room enough for our descendants to the thousandth and thousandth generation, entertaining a due sense of our equal
(10) right to the use of our own faculties, to the acquisition of our own industry, to honor and confidence from our fellow-citizens, resulting not from birth, but from our actions and their sense of them, enlightened by a benign religion, professed in
(15) deed and practiced in various forms, yet all of them inculcating honesty, truth, temperance, gratitude, and the love of man...Still one thing more, fellow citizens, a wise and frugal government, which shall restrain men from injuring one another, shall leave
(20) them otherwise free to regulate their own pursuits of industry and improvement, and shall not take from the mouth of labor the bread it has earned. This is the sum of good government; and this is necessary to close the circle of our felicities.
(25) About to enter, fellow citizens, upon the exercise of duties which comprehend everything dear and valuable to you, it is proper you should understand what I deem the essential principles of our government, and consequently, those which
(30) ought to shape its administration. I will compress them within the narrowest compass they will bear, stating the general principle, but not all its limitations. Equal and exact justice to all men, of whatever state or persuasion, religious or
(35) political...

Passage 2

I say it with a sad sense of disparity between us. I am not included within the pale of this glorious anniversary! Your high independence only reveals the immeasurable distance between us. The
(40) blessings in which you this day rejoice are not enjoyed in common. The rich inheritance of justice, liberty, prosperity, and independence bequeathed by your fathers is shared by you, not by me. The

(45) sunlight that brought life and healing to you has brought stripes and death to me. This Fourth of July is yours, not mine. You may rejoice, I must mourn. To drag a man in fetters into the grand illuminated temple of liberty, and call upon him to join you in
(50) joyous anthems, were inhuman mockery and sacrilegious irony. Do you mean, citizens, to mock me by asking me to speak today?
...Fellow citizens, above your national, tumultuous joy, I hear the mournful wail of
(55) millions, whose chains, heavy and grievous yesterday, are today rendered more intolerable by the jubilant shouts that reach them. If I do forget, if I do not remember those bleeding children of sorrow this day, "may my right hand forget her
(60) cunning, and may my tongue cleave to the roof of my mouth!" To forget them, to pass lightly over their wrongs, and to chime in with the popular theme, would be treason most scandalous and shocking, and would make me a reproach before
(65) God and the world. My subject, then, fellow citizens, is "American Slavery..."
...Would you have me argue that man is entitled to liberty? That he is the rightful owner of his own body? You have already declared it. Must I argue the
(70) wrongfulness of slavery? Is that a question for republicans? Is it to be settled by the rules of logic and argumentation, as a matter beset with great difficulty, involving a doubtful application of the principle of justice, hard to understand?...
(75) ...What to the American slave is your Fourth of July? I answer, a day that reveals more to him than all other days of the year, the gross injustice and cruelty to which he is the constant victim. To him your celebration is a sham; your boasted liberty an
(80) unholy license; your national greatness, swelling vanity; your sounds of rejoicing are empty and heartless; your denunciation of tyrants, brass-fronted impudence; your shouts of liberty and equality, hollow mockery; your prayers and hymns,
your sermons and thanksgivings, with all your
(85) religious parade and solemnity, are to him mere bombast, fraud, deception, impiety, and hypocrisy—a thin veil to cover up crimes which would disgrace a nation of savages. There is not a nation of the earth guilty of practices more
(90) shocking and bloody than are the people of the United States at this very hour.

GO ON TO THE NEXT PAGE ➡

1   By "our equal right . . . to honor and confidence from our fellow-citizens, resulting not from birth, but from our actions and their sense of them" (lines 9–14), Jefferson means that

   (A) members of all nations are welcome to come to America
   (B) citizens have the right to demand respect from each other
   (C) citizens should judge each other by their accomplishments rather than their ancestry
   (D) one can build trust by doing things for others
   (E) one should rely not only on one's family but also on other citizens

2   In line 26, the word *comprehend* most nearly means

   (A) include
   (B) understand
   (C) perceive
   (D) outline
   (E) realize

3   By "I will compress them within the narrowest compass they will bear" (lines 30–31), Jefferson means that

   (A) he intends to limit the role of government
   (B) those who oppose justice will be imprisoned
   (C) the general principles of government have boundaries
   (D) he will speak concisely about the principles of government
   (E) government bureaucracy has become too inflated

4   The word *persuasion* in line 34 most nearly means

   (A) enticement
   (B) influence
   (C) cajolery
   (D) authority
   (E) opinion

5   The statement "To drag a man . . . sacrilegious irony" (lines 47–50) conveys a sense of

   (A) indignation at the hypocrisy of Fourth of July celebrations
   (B) sorrow over the way the slaves had been treated
   (C) anger that slavery had not yet been abolished
   (D) disbelief that Fourth of July celebrations could even take place
   (E) amazement that slaves were being forced to join in the celebration

6   In Passage 2, the references to the "mournful wail" and the "jubilant shouts" (lines 53–56) serve to

   (A) remind the audience of difficulties in the past that have been overcome
   (B) indicate the importance of commemorating the Fourth of July
   (C) warn that the future of the country looks deceptively bright
   (D) emphasize the different outlooks of two groups in the country
   (E) suggest that some are faced with an unsolvable problem

7   In line 62, the author uses the word *treason* to refer to the act of

   (A) rebelling against authority
   (B) betraying the needs of a social group
   (C) renouncing one's own principles
   (D) expressing unpopular views
   (E) acting upon irrational impulses

8   The author of Passage 2 most likely describes "American Slavery" as "my subject" (lines 64–65) in order to

   (A) underline an unexpected new direction in his argument
   (B) indicate the broad historical scope of his address
   (C) emphasize his intent to discuss an apparent contradiction
   (D) highlight the answer to a problem facing the United States
   (E) underscore his eagerness to learn more about the topic of slavery

9   In lines 81–82 of Passage 2, the phrase *brass-fronted impudence* is primarily used to convey the author's

   (A) outrage at the contrast between political speeches and social reality
   (B) exasperation at the many obstacles to racial equality
   (C) resentment at the number of people excluded from July Fourth celebrations
   (D) belief that resistance to authority is ultimately futile
   (E) anger at the acts of tyrants throughout the world

GO ON TO THE NEXT PAGE ➡

10 The author of Passage 1 would most likely react to the questions at the beginning of the third paragraph of Passage 2 (lines 66–70) by commenting that

(A) a nation's political ideals are not always consistent with its actions

(B) the doctrine of equality is necessary for good government

(C) political views must be expressed through the proper democratic channels

(D) the goal of liberty for all may not be practical to attain

(E) the degradation of others must sometimes be endured

11 The author of Passage 2 would most likely react to the general principle of government in the last sentence of Passage 1 by pointing out that

(A) this general principle is hopelessly naive

(B) the real situation strongly contradicts this principle

(C) experience has proven this principle to be unattainable

(D) this principle is meaningless because it is vaguely worded

(E) the government never intended to adhere to this principle

12 Which statement is best supported by a comparison of the excerpts from the two speeches?

(A) Both excerpts denounce the degradation of some men and women in America.

(B) The purpose of both excerpts is to urge citizens to critically evaluate themselves.

(C) Both excerpts emphasize the necessity of justice for all citizens.

(D) Both excerpts argue that slavery is a violation of human rights.

(E) Both excerpts present a hopeful vision of the future.

13 The attitudes expressed in Passage 1 and Passage 2 towards equality in the United States might best be described as

(A) caution versus anger

(B) disappointment versus adulation

(C) optimism versus criticism

(D) hope versus promise

(E) indulgence versus prudence

IF YOU FINISH BEFORE TIME IS CALLED, YOU MAY CHECK YOUR WORK ON THIS SECTION ONLY. DO NOT TURN TO ANY OTHER SECTION IN THE TEST. **STOP**

KAPLAN 377

Time—15 Minutes
10 Questions

Solve each of the following problems, decide which is the best answer choice, and darken the corresponding oval on the answer sheet. Use available space in the test booklet for scratchwork.

Notes:

(1)   Calculator use is permitted.

(2)   All numbers used are real numbers.

(3)   Figures are provided for some problems. All figures are drawn to scale and lie in a plane UNLESS otherwise indicated.

Reference Information

$A=\frac{1}{2}bh$ $c^2 = a^2 + b^2$ Special Right Triangles $A=\pi r^2$ $C=2\pi r$ $V=\ell wh$ $V=\pi r^2 h$ $A=\ell w$

The sum of the degree measures of the angles of a triangle is 180.
The number of degrees of arc in a circle is 360.
A straight angle has a degree measure of 180.

Sales (in millions of dollars)

1   According to the graph above, April sales accounted for approximately what percent of the total 2nd-quarter sales?

(A) $12\frac{1}{2}$

(B)   25

(C) $37\frac{1}{2}$

(D)   50

(E)   60

2   If xy is negative, which of the following CANNOT be negative?

(A) $y - x$
(B) $x - y$
(C) $x^2 y$
(D) xy^2
(E) $x^2 y^2$

3   If a bora = 2 fedis and 1 fedi = 3 glecks, how many boras are equal to 48 glecks?

(A)   4
(B)   8
(C)   16
(D)   48
(E)   96

GO ON TO THE NEXT PAGE ➡

4 A college class is made up of f freshman and s sophomores. If 5 freshman drop this class, the number of sophomores in the class is 3 times the number of freshman. Which of the following equations represents s in terms of f ?

(A) $s = \dfrac{f-5}{3}$

(B) $s = \dfrac{f+5}{3}$

(C) $s = 3(f-5)$

(D) $s = 3(f+5)$

(E) $s = 5(f-3)$

5 If the perimeter of triangle ABC is 4 more than the perimeter of triangle ACD, what is the perimeter of quadrilateral $ABCD$?

(A) 20
(B) 22
(C) 24
(D) 25
(E) 26

6 The figure above shows a cubed-shaped stone with edges of 3 centimeters. Points A, B, and C are on three different edges of the cube, each 1 centimeter away from the same vertex. A jeweler slices off the corner with a straight cut through A, B, and C, as shown, and slices pieces of the same size off all the other corners of the stone. What is the total number of faces on the resulting stone?

(A) seven
(B) ten
(C) twelve
(D) fourteen
(E) sixteen

7 What is the average of the first 30 positive integers?

(A) 14
(B) 14.5
(C) 15
(D) 15.5
(E) 16

Note: Figure not drawn to scale.

8 What is the area of the figure above?

(A) 96
(B) 102
(C) 104
(D) 108
(E) 110

9 Sixty cookies were to be equally distributed to x campers. When 8 campers did not want the cookies, the other campers each received 2 more cookies. Which of the following equations could be used to find the number of campers x ?

(A) $x^2 - 8x - 240 = 0$
(B) $x^2 - 8x + 240 = 0$
(C) $x^2 + 8x - 240 = 0$
(D) $x^2 + 8x + 240 = 0$
(E) $x^2 - 4x - 120 = 0$

10 If six students are eligible for 2 scholarships worth $1,000 each how many different combinations of 2 students winning the 2 scholarships are possible?

(A) 6
(B) 9
(C) 12
(D) 15
(E) 30

IF YOU FINISH BEFORE TIME IS CALLED, YOU MAY CHECK YOUR WORK ON THIS SECTION ONLY. DO NOT TURN TO ANY OTHER SECTION IN THE TEST.

STOP

Answer Key

Section 1	Section 2	Section 3	Section 4	Section 5	Section 6
1. E	1. D	1. E	1. A	1. C	1. D
2. B	2. A	2. A	2. B	2. A	2. E
3. D	3. C	3. C	3. A	3. D	3. B
4. C	4. C	4. A	4. B	4. E	4. C
5. D	5. D	5. A	5. B	5. A	5. E
6. C	6. A	6. E	6. A	6. D	6. D
7. A	7. D	7. B	7. C	7. B	7. D
8. B	8. D	8. E	8. D	8. C	8. B
9. B	9. D	9. D	9. B	9. A	9. A
10. B	10. B	10. B	10. B	10. B	10. D
11. A	11. A	11. D	11. B	11. B	
12. C	12. D	12. B	12. C	12. C	
13. E	13. E	13. A	13. C	13. C	
14. C	14. D	14. D	14. C		
15. E	15. A	15. A	15. D		
16. E	16. C	16. D	16. 15		
17. C	17. C	17. E	17. 9.43		
18. D	18. E	18. E	18. $13 < \text{length} < 15$		
19. D	19. B	19. C	19. 15/4 or 3.75		
20. D	20. D	20. D	20. 166		
21. A	21. D	21. A	21. $0.5 < y < 0.625$		
22. B	22. C	22. B	22. 46		
23. C	23. B	23. C	23. 175		
24. C	24. A	24. D	24. 46		
25. A	25. E	25. A	25. 11		
26. B		26. E			
27. B		27. B			
28. D		28. C			
29. E		29. C			
30. C		30. B			
		31. E			
		32. C			
		33. D			
		34. A			
		35. E			

Compute Your Raw Score

First, check your answers against the answer key on the previous page, and count up the number right and the number wrong for each section (there are boxes on your answer sheet to record these numbers). Remember not to count omissions as wrong.

Then figure out your raw scores using the table below. The Verbal raw score is equal to the total right in the three Verbal sections minus one-fourth of the number wrong in those sections. The Math raw score is equal to the total right in the three Math sections minus one-fourth of the number wrong in the two Regular Math sections and minus one-third the number wrong in the QCs. (Remember: There is no deduction for wrong answers in the Grid-ins.) Round each raw score to the nearest whole number.

Finally, use the tables on the next page to convert each raw score to a range of scaled scores.

	NUMBER RIGHT		NUMBER WRONG		RAW SCORE
SECTION 1:	☐	−[.25 x	☐]	=	☐
SECTION 3:	☐	−[.25 x	☐]	=	☐
SECTION 5:	☐	−[.25 x	☐]	=	☐
VERBAL RAW SCORE:					☐ (ROUNDED)
SECTION 4A: (Questions 1 to 15)	☐	−[.33 x	☐]	=	☐
SECTION 4B: (Questions 16 to 25)	☐		(No wrong-answer penalty)	=	☐
SECTION 2:	☐	−[.25 x	☐]	=	☐
SECTION 6:	☐	−[.25 x	☐]	=	☐
MATH RAW SCORE:					☐ (ROUNDED)

Convert Your Score

Verbal

Raw	Scaled	Raw	Scaled	Raw	Scaled
−3 or less	200	22	450	48	620
−2	230	23	460	49	630
−1	270	24	470	50	640
0	290	25	470	51	640
1	300	26	480	52	650
2	310	27	490	53	660
3	320	28	490	54	670
4	330	29	500	55	670
5	330	30	510	56	670
6	340	31	510	57	680
7	350	32	520	58	690
8	360	33	530	59	690
9	370	34	530	60	700
10	370	35	540	61	710
11	380	36	550	62	720
12	390	37	550	63	730
13	390	38	560	64	730
14	400	39	570	65	740
15	410	40	570	66	750
16	410	41	580	67	760
17	420	42	590	68	770
18	430	43	590	69	780
19	430	44	600	70	790
20	440	45	600	71 or more	800
21	450	46	610		
		47	610		

Math

Raw	Scaled	Raw	Scaled	Raw	Scaled
−1 or less	200	19	440	40	600
0	220	20	450	41	610
1	240	21	460	42	620
2	260	22	470	43	630
3	280	23	480	44	640
4	300	24	480	45	650
5	310	25	490	46	650
6	330	26	500	47	660
7	340	27	510	48	670
8	350	28	520	49	680
9	360	29	520	50	690
10	370	30	530	51	700
11	380	31	530	52	720
12	390	32	540	53	730
13	400	33	550	54	740
14	410	34	560	55	760
15	420	35	560	56	770
16	430	36	570	57	780
17	430	37	580	58	790
18	440	38	590	59	800
		39	600	60	800

Don't take these scores too literally. Practice test conditions cannot precisely mirror real test conditions. Your actual SAT scores will almost certainly vary from your practice test scores.

Your score on the practice test gives you a rough idea of your range on the actual exam. If you don't like your score, it's not too late to do something about it. Work your way way through this book again, and turn to Kaplan's *SAT Verbal Workbook* and *SAT Math Workbook* for even more help.

Practice Test Three Answers and Explanations

SECTION 1

1. E

Despite is our first clue word, signaling a contrast coming up. Despite their fierce appearance, caymans are actually rarely ----, to the point at which they won't attack humans unless provoked. So for the blank we need a word that means the same as "fierce." The closest word here is choice (E), **aggressive.** Choice (B) was the exact opposite of what we wanted. Choice (C), **domesticated,** means tame, and usually refers to animals treated as house pets.

2. B

There are two different schools of thought competing in this sentence. One group believes one thing *while* another believes something else. So, clearly we want words that help create a sense of the opposition between these two viewpoints. Let's start with the second blank. One group argues that courtly love "dates from the age of chivalry." In other words, they think it's a fairly old idea, dating back from the days of knights and fair maidens. Another group thinks something else though, so they must feel it's either an even older idea or a more recent idea. A quick check through the answer choices for the second blank leads us to choice (B) **ancient. Notion,** or idea, fits quite nicely into the first blank, fitting with the word "concept" in the first half of the sentence.

3. D

Here we want a word that would describe the sort of people who might throw fruits and vegetables at those whose performance dissatisfied them. People like this are surely not **doting** (A), overindulgent or excessively fond, nor are they **ravenous** (B), or extremely hungry. If they were hungry, they'd eat the food instead of throwing it at the stage. There's nothing to imply that the audience is (C) **jingoistic,** or excessively national-

istic. However, the audience might certainly be described as (D) **boisterous,** or rowdy. (E) **stagnant** means dead or lifeless, which is illogical in the blank.

4. C

"Although" two brothers look alike, they could not be more ---- in terms of their personalities. "Not alike" or "different" or some such word must go into this first blank, something that helps convey that they look alike, but their behavior is not alike. The semicolon is our hint that the information following it will be more or less in line with what preceded it. So, *while* one is circumspect, or cautious, the other is brash, or the opposite of cautious. For this second blank, you should predict something that means the opposite of quiet, something that's sort of synonymous with brash. The best answer is choice (C), because **dissimilar** fits our prediction for the first blank, while **audacious** means bold—it's kind of a synonym for brash. (A) **inimical** is related to the word "enemy." **Inimical** means hostile.

5. D

Napoleon's army was hightailing it out of Moscow. The retreat "quickly turned into a rout," a state of wild confusion, a disastrous defeat. Why did it turn into an even bigger defeat? Probably because the French were stuck or struggling in the snow—if they were doing well traveling through snow, it's unlikely they'd end up being such big losers. Then, something was done to them by Russian troops. Well, if you know that Napoleon's army was routed by the opposing side, then it seems that we want a second-blank word that means something like "clobbered." Choices (A) and (D) come close to that prediction. **Ravage** means to violently destroy. Now, going back to the first blank, we know we want something that implies the troops were stuck or struggling in the snow. Only choice (D) fits both blanks: the retreat of Napoleon's army turned into a rout as French troops, already **floundering** in the snow, were **assaulted** by Russian soldiers. To flounder is to struggle awkwardly and stumble about. In (A), **replenishing** in the snow sounds a bit weird—**replenishing** means replacing something that was used up. In (E), **tottering** means walking unsteadily, and **upbraided** means scolded or reprimanded—a little mild-mannered for our purposes here.

6. C

The word that will fill in the blank is defined here in the sentence—we want a word that describes an environment composed of tapestries, paintings, stained glass windows, and hand-crafted furniture. A quick survey of the answer choices leads us to choice (C), because **sumptuous** means costly or lavish, particularly with regard to furnishings and decor. While you might have been tempted to think that **friendly** in choice (D) was a plausible answer, it's hard to say to sure that an environment filled with rich, arty items is a friendly environment. For some people, such surroundings might be quite intimidating. **Frugal,** in choice (B), means thrifty or careful with money, which is quite the opposite of what we wanted here.

7. A

In this question, a lecturer is frustrated by something her audience has done. This frustration was only ---- by some connection between the audience and talking. It sounds like the lecturer was frustrated by her audience's desire or tendency to talk during her presentation. Lecturers want to be heard; an audience's inability or lack of desire to talk would not frustrate a lecturer. So, for the second blank, we want something like desire—choice (A) **propensity,** or tendency, and choice (E) **desire** could work. (C) makes no sense. What's an "audience's **authorization**"? To choose between (A) and (E), let's look at the second blank. (E) **supplanted,** or replaced, is illogical. So (A)'s got to be correct. In fact, it makes the most sense: The lecturer's frustration was **compounded,** or increased, by the audience's **propensity,** or tendency, to talk.

8. B

There's something about the issue of the nuclear power plant that makes it surprising the council all voted in agreement. If it was shocking that there was

agreement, the issue must have been divisive or controversial. The answer here is (B), because **contentious** means causing controversy and disagreement. **Concise** in (C) means brief and to the point, while **exorbitant** in (D) means extravagant or excessive.

9. B

So many stops in some particular amount of time led to only the most ---- impression about the places the tour visited. There's a connection between the amount of time spent visiting, and the impression of the places visited. So the two words that will fill in the blanks here must be roughly synonymous. Only choice (B) works here. There were so many stops in such a **brief** amount of time that only a **cursory** (superficial or hasty) impression of places was gained. (D)'s second word fits the blank, but (D)'s first word, **sufficient,** isn't a rough synonym and doesn't fit. In (A), many stops probably wouldn't leave a **lasting** impression. Nor would a tour at breakneck speed necessarily leave (C) a **favorable** impression on travelers.

10. B

STEEL is a type of **METAL,** just as **silk** is a type of **fabric.** In choice (E), a **carat** is a measure of the weight of a precious stone. It is not a type of **diamond.**

11. A

By definition, all **FUNNEL**s have a **CONICAL** shape. Choice (A) is correct here because **pipes** have a **cylindrical** shape. **Solid**s are substances which have a definite size, shape and weight—in other words, **solid**s are substances which aren't liquids or gases. Not all solids are **spherical** or round in shape—there are many differently shaped **solid**s. In (C), a twisted **hose** might be **spiral** in shape, but not every **hose** is **spiral.** As for choice (D), **parallel** is not a shape of a **line,** it's the relationship between **line**s which never cross.

12. C

When something is **FUTILE,** it's hopeless; it has no **USE.** So, the answer here is (C), because something **superficial,** or shallow, has no **depth.** If you weren't quite sure what the link was, you still might have ruled out (B) and (E). After all, all **light** is not **faint.** And education and morals have little to do with each other; receiving an **education** doesn't mean you have **morals.** **Furtive,** in choice (D), means sneaky. Stealth describes the quality of secretive actions or movement, as in the Stealth Bomber, the radar-evading plane. Something or someone **furtive** is characterized by **stealth.**

13. E

KNEELing is a gesture of **SUBMISSION,** obedience or meekness. People may kneel in prayer, to show their reverence to a deity. Therefore, (E) is correct, because **nod**ding is a gesture of **assent,** or agreement. You need **equilibrium,** poise or balance, in order to **stand,** but **stand**ing isn't a gesture of **equilibrium.** A **mutiny,** in choice (C), is an uprising against the powers that be; this word is used most frequently to describe a mutiny of a crew on a ship against the captain or officers.

14. C

A **MOVEMENT** is, by definition, one part of a **SYMPHONY** as a whole. The right answer here is choice (C), because an **act** is one part of a **play.** If you didn't know this meaning of **MOVEMENT,** process of elimination could have led you to the right answer. A **projector,** in choice (B), is a machine you use to show a film. Could a **MOVEMENT** be a machine used to show a **SYMPHONY?** No, so (B) can be crossed out. In (E), a **canvas** might be the material that a **painting** is done on; might a **MOVEMENT** be the material a **SYMPHONY** is done on? No again; (E) can be crossed out, too. Finally, choices (A) and (D) can be eliminated because of their weak bridges. In (D), a **poem** may or may not have **rhythm.** In (A), a **note** is something you might play on a **piano;** then again, you might play it on a guitar, on a piccolo, or on many other instruments.

15. E

Perhaps the word **PURGATIVE** reminded you of the related word "purge." You may have heard "purge" in history class. Dictators are fond of purging their party or government of so-called traitors by, for example, killing them. To purge means to cleanse or rid of impurities or other undesirable elements. So, a **PURGATIVE** results in **CLEANSING.** Similarly, a **catalyst** results in **change,** so (E) is correct here. A **fixative,** in choice (A), is almost what it sounds like; it's a

substance that "fixes" something or holds it in place. Artists spray **fixative** on pastel or pencil drawings to prevent them from smearing. An **inoculation** is the injection of some sort of virus or serum meant to produce resistance to a disease.

To Build a Fire Passage

This fiction passage shouldn't pose too many problems: it's short, clear, and straightforward. If you enjoy reading fiction, be careful not to relax too much while reading the passage—you may slow down and lose time. Save pleasure reading for when you're not taking the SAT! The passage describes a man and a dog entering a little-traveled path in Alaska. A comparison is set up between the man, who "lacks imagination" and isn't alarmed by the extreme cold, and his dog who, going on instinct, is alarmed.

16. E

Review the beginning of the passage to see what "act" the man is "excusing to himself." It turns out he stopped because he was out of breath, but doesn't want to admit it (to himself, since he's alone), so he plays it off by looking at his watch. That makes choice (E) correct. He shows no reaction to what time it is (A). You may have been confused by choice (B) because the narrator (later in the passage) implies that the dog's instincts are more accurate than the man's. However, the man never shows distrust of himself (B). You're overinterpreting if you chose (C)—there's no evidence in the passage to support this inference. The point of the man's "excusing the act to himself" has nothing to do with "the time of day" (D); it has to do with him not admitting why he stopped in the first place.

17. C

Watch for the tone in the lines around the quote—it'll help you eliminate choices. For example, does the man seem at all "excited"? No, so (A) is out. He also doesn't seem "nervous" (B), although by the end of the passage there's an ominous feeling of danger in the air. (C) is right because it's a straightforward description of what's going on. There's no evidence in the passage to support choice (D). (E) is similarly wrong—there's no discussion of why the man is in the wilderness. Remember, most inferences (or "suggestions," as the question phrases it) are very mild, and are always supported by the passage.

18. D

Reread the lines the quote appears in. The man's being a "creature of temperature" is the same "frailty" that all humans have: we're "able only to live within narrow limits of heat and cold." In other words, if it's too cold, we'll freeze to death. Choice (D) is correct. "A creature of temperature" does not imply the man prefers cold climates (A), because "temperature" includes hot and cold. The author shows later in the passage how wrong the man's judgment of the temperature is, so (B) is unlikely. There's no discussion of "personality being shaped by the environment" (C). The man may or may not know wilderness survival techniques (E), but in any case, that's not what "a creature of temperature" refers to.

19. D

This question refers you to a big chunk of text, so save time by scanning the choices before you go to the passage. Choice (A) implies the wrong thing. This wilderness must be immensely beautiful, but whether the man notices it or not is not the point. The point is the judgment the man makes about the temperature. (B) overstates the case. The author isn't flatly declaring, "humans can't survive in the Alaskan wilderness." Instead, he's describing a man who is underestimating the potential danger. That makes (D) correct. Just because this character can't judge the temperature accurately doesn't mean "there's no way to accurately judge the temperature" (C). There's no evidence that "most people could not do" what this guy is doing, even though it's obviously a difficult thing (E).

20. D

All of paragraph 2 leads up to the four lines you're sent to for this question. After a discussion of the potential danger extreme temperatures pose to humans, the paragraph concludes by saying none of this entered the man's head. In other words, he lacks "insight and understanding" (D). The man thinks the cold "must be guarded against," so (B) can't be right. At the same time, (A) is too strong—the man doesn't even acknowledge that there are "odds" to succeed against.

(C) is too general. "Apprehension" in (E) means "fearfulness," which we've already seen the man lacks.

21. A

Again, you have a lot of lines to review, so save time by scanning the answer choices before you check the passage. It's in these lines that the author introduces the dog and its "instinct"—which tells it to take shelter from the cold. Correct choice (A) restates what's in lines 48–50. The dog isn't judging the temperature (B), it's just reacting to an instinct of danger. Choice (C) is an inference that goes too far—it's too general for these lines. (D) contradicts the point the author's making. (E) is partially true, but it captures only a small part of what the author suggests.

22. B

This question doesn't require too much interpretation, so don't go digging for difficult answers. The passage says that the dog "knew nothing of thermometers," but that it "had its instinct." In other words, it didn't read the temperature with a device as humans do, and it didn't need to—it knew instinctively how cold it was. The answer is (B)—the dog's awareness of its environment is different from the man's. Nothing implies that dogs "need not be concerned about temperature" (A); the point is that they perceive it differently than people do. (C) is too negative. Although the author calls the dog a "brute" at one point, it is done with respect, since the dog's instincts prove to be more valuable than the man's intelligence. (D) is too literal. And the point is not that the dog "could not rely on technological devices" (E), but that the dog has no need of them.

23. C

Reread the lines at the end of the passage to see what's going on. We've seen that the dog fears the cold, and the end of the passage describes the dog watching the man for a sign that they are heading for protection (C). Choices (A) and (E) miss the mark because the author never says that the dog recognizes the man's mistaken estimation of the cold. There is also no sign that the man is being visibly affected by the cold (B). Choice (D) invents something not found in the passage.

Elderly Asians Passage

Next you have a passage about Southeast Asian immigrants' experience of aging in America. This passage may be a little dry, but it's not complex. The discussion focuses on the problems older immigrants have when they come to America. These include: different standards of what's considered "elderly;" not getting the kind of respect they would in their homelands; dealing with different gender roles; and elderly women being isolated in the home and becoming estranged from their families. Don't worry about any more detail than this until you get to the questions.

24. C

Remember this strategy for dealing with main idea questions: look for an answer that's not too broad or too narrow, but that encompasses the whole passage. In this case, (A) is too broad. From the first paragraph, you know that the focus is more specific than "the reasons why Southeast Asian people move to the U.S." This helps you eliminate (B) as well: from the start you're told the passage is concerned with the problems of the elderly, not the young. (C) covers the whole passage, and is correct. (D) picks up on a detail—Confucianism—and expands it beyond the scope of the passage. And (E) is just one topic discussed in the passage, not the focus of it.

25. A

Review paragraph 2 to understand why the author mentions the "traditional Hmong culture." There, the author says that American and Asian cultures define "elderly" differently. In the Hmong culture, people become elders and retire at 35; obviously, in American culture, this is not the case. So Hmong culture is mentioned to illustrate the paragraph's main point—that "social expectations vary greatly from one country to another" (A). There's no mention of traditional values in Vietnamese society "lessening" (B). No other ancient cultures are mentioned in paragraph 2, so (C) is out. (D) is out because Confucianism isn't mentioned until paragraph 3. Likewise, no other Southeast Asian peoples are mentioned (E).

26. B

Go back to the line in which "family mediators" appears. This part of paragraph 3 says that younger members of immigrant families deal with schools and other institutions because they have better English language skills than older family members. So being a "family mediator" is a responsibility that young refugees assume in a new country (B). (A) might've confused you because a hasty reading of the passage makes it sound like this is a role older people used to fill—but in fact, it's not. The passage really says that in the traditional culture there are strict rules for social interaction based on age, which the new role of "family mediator" gradually erodes. The passage says nothing about getting help from friends (C) or professionals (D). The author doesn't write about the benefits American society derives from immigrant people anywhere (E).

27. B

After rereading the line that "pronounced" is in, the first thing you should do is eliminate the obvious choice. In this case, that's (E), "declared." The author uses "pronounced" to mean (B) "noticeable." Gender roles changed somewhat in Southeast Asia during the Vietnam War, but they changed even more drastically for families that emigrated to the United States. None of the other choices fits this context. The author doesn't imply that these changes became more "acceptable" (D); she implies that they happened out of necessity and says they were a "radical change."

28. D

As the discussion of question 27 touched on, the "radical change" the author refers to is the fact that women often become the main source of income in immigrant families in the U.S. This is a major change in gender roles, because in Asia men were usually the breadwinners. (D) is correct. (A) is an unlikely answer because retirement ages were discussed back in paragraph 2. (B) might've been tempting, because the Vietnam War is mentioned in paragraph 4, along with the answer. But the author says that while gender roles are changing in Southeast Asia due to the Vietnam War, the "radical change" occurs when families emigrate. Education (C) is not discussed in these lines. (E) is out because the author says there are more jobs for younger refugees, not that it's hard for young refugees to find them.

29. E

When you're not given a line reference, it makes sense to look in the passage where the previous question left off because Critical Reading questions are ordered sequentially. So that takes you to the last paragraph, which is indeed where the author makes a point about the "long-term outlook for refugee women." The author starts off by saying that although the long-term outlook is "unknown," there are "indications" about it. Now look at the choices. There's no evidence that this is a "personal recollection" (A), or a "historical discussion" (B). No specific "case" is mentioned or analyzed (C). The author isn't being "philosophical" (D); if anything, she's being as scientific as possible, given the lack of data. That leaves (E), "informed speculation." Since the author is knowledgeable about the subject matter, but has to go on "indications" to make her final point, (E) is the best answer.

30. C

Use the available combinations of Roman Numeral options to help you get through this oddball question type easily. Option I is false: the author never gives us a sense of Southeast Asian women's employment opportunities in Asia. All we know is that during the Vietnam war, women were forced to take on more traditionally male responsibilities. If anything, female refugees have greater access than do men to lower-paying jobs here. So if Option I is false, you can eliminate choices A and E. II is also false: you can't infer from the passage that Americans don't respect their elders. Since Option II is false, you can eliminate choices B and D. That leaves C—III only—as the correct choice. Double check to make sure, though, and you'll see from paragraph 2 that Americans and Asians have different notions of when one is considered old.

SECTION 2

1. D

We want the value of x. Let's begin by distributing the 2 over the terms inside the parentheses on the left side of the equation. This gives us $2x + 2y = 8 + 2y$. Subtracting $2y$ from both sides results in $2x = 8$. Dividing both sides by 2 gives us $x = 4$.

2. A

Since point A is at 1 on the number line and point C is on the 7, the distance between them is $7 - 1$, or 6. Half the distance from A to C is $\frac{1}{2}$ of 6, or 3, and 3 units from either point A or point C is 4, since $1 + 3 = 4$ and $7 - 3 = 4$. Therefore the point at 4 on the number line is the midpoint of AC, since a midpoint by definition divides a line in half. Point B is at 3 and the midpoint of AC is at 4, so the distance between them is 1, answer choice (A).

3. C

The machine caps 5 bottles every 2 seconds, and we want to know how many bottles it caps in 1 minute, or 60 seconds. Multiplying 2 seconds by 30 gives you 60 seconds. If the machine caps 5 bottles in 2 seconds, how many bottles does it cap in 30 times 2 seconds? Just 30×5, or 150 bottles, answer choice (C).

4. C

All you have to do here is solve the equation, but instead of solving it for n, you have to solve it for $4n$. If $2n + 3 = 5$, then you can subtract 3 from both sides of the equation to get $2n = 2$. Multiplying both sides of this equation by 2 gives you $4n = 4$, choice (C).

5. D

The easiest way to do this problem is just to backsolve. Since each pair of numbers in the answer choices represents possible values of a and b, just add up each a and b to see if $a + b < 5$, and subtract each b from each a to see if $a - b > 6$. If you do this, you'll find that in all 5 cases $a + b < 5$, but in only 1 case, in choice (D), is $a - b > 6$. In choice (D), $a + b = 4 + (-3) = 1$ and $a - b = 4 - (-3) = 7$.

If you think about the properties of negative and positive numbers (drawing a number line can help) you'll probably realize that the only way $a - b$ could be larger than $a + b$ is if b is a negative number, but that would only eliminate choice (A). In some problems your knowledge of math only helps you a little bit. In those cases you just have to play with the given answer choices in order to solve.

6. A

In the figure angle B is labeled $(2x - 4)°$ and in the question stem you're told that angle B measures 60°. So $2x - 4 = 60$, and $x = 32$. That means that angle A, which is labeled $(3x)°$, must measure 3×32, or 96°. Since the 3 angles of a triangle must add up to 180°, $60° + 96° + y° = 180°$, and $y = 24$.

7. D

This one is easier if you plug in numbers for C and R. Suppose R is 2. Then there would be 2 rooms on each floor, and since there are 10 floors in the building, there would be 2×10 or 20 rooms altogether. If $C = 3$, then there are 3 chairs in each room. Since there are 20 rooms and 3 chairs per room there are $20 \times 3 = 60$ chairs altogether. Which answer choices are 60 when R is 2 and C is 3? Only $10RC$, choice (D).

You don't have to plug in numbers here if you think about the units of each variable. There are 10 floors, R rooms per floor, and C chairs per room. If you multiply 10 floors by $R \dfrac{\text{rooms}}{\text{floor}}$, the unit "floors" will cancel out, leaving you with $10R$ rooms, and if you multiply $10R$ rooms by $C \dfrac{\text{chairs}}{\text{room}}$, the unit "rooms" will cancel out, leaving $10RC$ chairs in the building, again choice (D).

8. D

Here you have a strange word, *sump*, which describes a number that has a certain relationship between the sum and the product of its digits. To solve this one, just find the sum and the product of the digits for each answer choice. You're told that for a "sump" number, the sum should be greater than the product. Choice (D), 411, has a sum of 6 and a product of 4, so that's the one you're looking for.

9. D

In this question, if you think about the relationship between the information you're given and the information you have to find it becomes very easy. You're given 4% of a number and you have to find 20% of that same number. 4% of r is just a certain fraction, $\dfrac{4}{100}$ to be exact, times r; and 20% of r is just $\dfrac{20}{100}$ times r. That means that 20% of r is 5 times as great as 4% of r, since $\dfrac{4}{100}$ times 5 is $\dfrac{20}{100}$. So if you're given that 4% of r is 6.2, then 20% of r must be 5 times 6.2, or 31, choice (D).

You could also have figured out the value of r and then found 20% of that value, but this takes a bit longer. 4% of r is the same as 4% times r, or $.04r$. If $.04r = 6.2$, then $r = \dfrac{6.2}{.04} = 155$, and 20% of 155 is $.2 \times 155 = 31$, choice (D) again.

10. B

The ratio of teachers to students is 1 to 10, so there might be only 1 teacher and 10 students, or there might be 50 teachers and 500 students, or just about any number of teachers and students that are in the ratio 1 to 10. That means that the teachers and the students can be divided into groups of 11: one teacher and 10 students in each group. Think of it as a school with a large number of classrooms, all with 1 teacher and 10 students, for a total of 11 people in each room. So, the total number of teachers and students in the school must be a multiple of 11. If you look at the answer choices, you'll notice that 121, choice (B), is the only multiple of 11, so (B) must be correct.

11. A

Since x and y with a funny symbol between them is equal to $(x - y)^x + (x + y)^y$, to find 4 and 2 with a funny symbol between them just plug 4 in for x and 2 in for y. That gives you $(4 - 2)^4 + (4 + 2)^2$, or $2^4 + 6^2$, or $16 + 36$, or 52, answer choice (A).

12. D

If the particle travels from A to B to C to D to E and then back to A it has traveled 5 centimeters, since each side of the pentagon measures 1 centimeter. If it goes all the way around the pentagon again it's traveled another 5 centimeters, for a total of 10 centimeters. In fact, every time the particle makes a complete revolution around the pentagon (from point A back to point A again) it travels an additional 5 centimeters. So if the number of centimeters the particle has traveled is a multiple of 5, the particle must be at point A. The number 723 is 3 more than a multiple of 5. If the particle had gone 720 centimeters it would be at point A; since it has gone 3 more centimeters it must be at point D, answer choice (D).

13. E

When would $4 + \dfrac{1}{s}$ have the smallest possible value? Certainly if s, and its reciprocal $\dfrac{1}{s}$, were negative, $4 + \dfrac{1}{s}$ would be smaller than 4, since adding a negative number is like subtracting a positive number. However, none of the answer choices are negative, so $4 + \dfrac{1}{s}$ will be greater than 4. However, it will be as small as possible when $\dfrac{1}{s}$ is as small as possible. If you look at the answer choices, you can find the values for $\dfrac{1}{s}$. If $s = \dfrac{1}{4}$,

then $\dfrac{1}{s} = 4$, etc. If you do that you'll probably notice that as s gets larger its reciprocal gets smaller, so $\dfrac{1}{s}$ is smallest when s is largest, in this case when $s = 4$, choice (E).

14. D

Since you're looking for the sixth term of the sequence, let's call the sixth term x. Every term in this sequence is formed by multiplying the previous term by 3 and then subtracting 1, so the seventh term must be formed by multiplying the sixth term, x, by 3 and then subtracting 1; in other words, the seventh term is equal to $3x - 1$. Since the seventh term is 365, $365 = 3x - 1$, and you can solve for x to get $x = 122$, choice (D).

15. A

If an integer is chosen randomly from the first 50 integers the probability of choosing any particular number is 1 divided by 50, and the probability of choosing an integer with a digit of 3 is the number of integers with a digit of 3 divided by 50. The integers 3, 13, 23, 30, 31, 32, 33, 34, 35, 36, 37, 38, 39, and 43 are the only integers with 3's in them, for a total of 14 different integers, so the probability is $\dfrac{14}{50}$, or $\dfrac{7}{25}$, choice (A).

16. C

Let's call the degree measure of the largest angle x. Since the degree measure of the middle-sized angle is 40 degrees less than the degree measure of the largest angle, the degree measure of the middle-sized angle is $x - 40$. We also know that the smallest angle is 20 degrees. We know that the sum of the measures of the three interior angles of any triangle is 180 degrees. So we can write an equation for our triangle: $x + (x - 40) + 20 = 180$.

Now let's solve for x:

$$x + x - 40 + 20 = 180$$
$$2x - 20 = 180$$
$$2x = 200$$
$$x = 100$$

17. C

The diagram tells you that the radius of the circle is $x - 5$ and the question stem tells you that the circumference of the circle is 20π. Since the circumference of a circle is 2π times the radius, 20π must equal 2π times $(x - 5)$, which gives you the equation $20\pi = 2\pi(x - 5)$. Solving this equation gives you $x = 15$, answer choice (C).

18. E

The slope of a line is defined as the change in the y-coordinate divided by the change in the x-coordinate. As you go from point A to point B, the x-coordinate goes from p to 6 and the y-coordinate goes from 3 to p, so the change in the x-coordinate is $6 - p$ and the change in the y-coordinate is $p - 3$. You can make this into an equation: $\dfrac{p-3}{6-p} = 2$, and solve this equation for p. That would give you $p = 5$, choice (E). You could also plug the 5 possible values for p into the expression $\dfrac{p-3}{6-p}$ to see which one gives you 2 as a result. Either way, choice (E) is correct.

19. B

If C is the price of one pound of cherries and G is the price of one pound of grapes, then $C = 2G$. The total cost of 32 pounds of cherries and 8 pounds of grapes is $32C + 8G$, and is also equal to $90. You can use the equations $C = 2G$ and $32C + 8G = 90$ to solve for C and G. Plugging $2G$ for C into the equation $32C + 8G = 90$,

we have $32(2G) + 8G = 90$, $64G + 8G = 90$, $72G = 90$, and $G = \dfrac{90}{72} = \dfrac{5}{4} = 1.25$. $C = 2G$, so $C = 2(1.25) = 2.50$. Since 32 pounds of cherries and 8 pounds of grapes were sold, $2.50 \times 32 = 80$ were made on the cherries, and $1.25 \times 8 = 10$ were made on the grapes. That means that $80 - 10 = 70$ more was made on the cherries than on the grapes, answer choice (B).

20. D

In order to find the areas of the shaded triangles, you have to find the coordinates of all the vertices of the triangles. You know where points P, Q, and C are in the coordinate plane, but what about the rest of them? Well, first of all let's label all the other points that are vertices of the triangles. The triangle on top has 2 labeled vertices, P and Q. The third vertex of that triangle is on the y-axis between P and the origin. Let's call it point A. The other triangle has vertices Q, C, and an unlabeled point that is also the upper right-hand corner of the rectangle. Call that point B. Points A and B are both on the same horizontal line that point Q is on, so all 3 points must have the same y-coordinate of 4. The x-coordinate of point A is 0 since it is on the y-axis, and the x-coordinate of B must be 3, the same as point C's x-coordinate, since points B and C lie on the same vertical line. So point A's coordinates are $(0, 4)$ and point B's coordinates are $(3, 4)$. Since triangles PQA and QBC are right triangles, we just need to know the lengths of their legs in order to find their areas. In the coordinate plane, the length of a horizontal line segment is the difference of the x-coordinates of its endpoints and the length of a vertical line segment is the difference of the y-coordinates of its endpoints. So, the length of PA is $6 - 4$, or 2, and the length of AQ is $1 - 0$, or 1, so the area of triangle PQA is $\frac{1}{2} \times 2 \times 1 = 1$. The length of QB is $3 - 1$, or 2, and the length of BC is $4 - 0$, or 4, so the area of triangle QBC is $\frac{1}{2} \times 2 \times 4 = 4$. The sum of those areas is $1 + 4 = 5$, answer choice (D).

21. D

Here you're told about certain properties of two numbers and that the larger of the two numbers is 35, and you're asked to find the smaller number, which we'll of course call x. The positive difference of 2 numbers is simply the larger number minus the smaller number, or in this case $35 - x$. The average of 35 and x is equal to twice the positive difference, or twice $35 - x$, or $2(35 - x)$. The average of 35 and x is just $\frac{35 + x}{2}$, so all you have to do is solve the equation $\frac{35 + x}{2} = 2(35 - x)$, and if you do that, you'll get $x = 21$, choice (D).

You could also solve this by backsolving. Starting with choice (C), if the smaller number is 15, the positive difference is $35 - 15$, or 20, and twice the positive difference is 40. Is 40 the average of 35 and 15? No, it couldn't be, since 40 is larger than both 35 and 15. That means that the smaller number must be closer to 35 than 15 is, in order to make the positive difference smaller, so let's try 21. $35 - 21$ is 14, and twice 14 is 28. The average of 21 and 35 is half of $21 + 35$, or half of 56, which is indeed 28, so again choice (D) is correct.

22. C

No matter what the value of n is, this figure will be a rectangular solid. All rectangular solids have 6 faces. You just have to figure out the area of each of the 6 faces. The face on the bottom, which is the face up against the table or whatever this stack of cubes is sitting on, is a square, and it will have an area of 1 square

inch, since the edge of each cube has a length of 1 inch. The face on the top of the stack of cubes is also a square and it will also have a surface area of 1 square inch. The other 4 faces making up the stack are identical rectangles, each with dimensions of 1 inch by n inches. So the area of one of these rectangles is $1 \times n$ or n square inches and these four identical rectangular faces have a total area of $4 \times n$ or $4n$ square inches. So the total surface area of the solid is the sum of the areas of the square top, the square bottom, and the four identical rectangular faces, which is $1 + 1 + 4n$ or $4n + 2$ square inches.

If you found that confusing, it might be easier just to pick a value for n. Suppose $n = 4$ and there are 4 cubes, as in the figure shown. Then just add up the areas of the faces of the stack in the figure, but don't forget the faces that aren't shown in the drawing. Since each face of each cube has an area of 1, in square inches, the figure shown has an area of 4 in the front plus 4 on the right side plus 4 on the left side (not shown in the drawing) plus 4 in the back (not shown in the drawing) plus 1 on the top and finally 1 on the bottom (not shown in the drawing), for a total of 18. Only choice (C) has a value of 18 when $n = 4$, so choice (C) must be correct.

23. B

Since $BC = DC$, triangle BCD is an isosceles right triangle and angles BDC and DBC each equal 45°. Since $AD = AB$, angle ABD must equal angle ADB, which is 60°. Since 2 angles of triangle ADB measure 60°, the third must also measure 60°, and triangle ADB is equilateral. That means that all 3 sides are equal. One of those sides, BD, is also the hypotenuse of isosceles right triangle BCD. That means that you can figure out the relationship between all the line segments in this figure. If the length of CD is x, then the length of BC is also x and the length of BD is $x\sqrt{2}$, using the 1:1:$\sqrt{2}$ ratio of the sides of a 45–45–90 triangle. That means that AD and AB are also $x\sqrt{2}$. So $\frac{AB}{CD}$ is $\frac{x\sqrt{2}}{x}$, which reduces to $\sqrt{2}$, answer choice (B).

You could have eyeballed the diagram here. Since *AB* is clearly longer than *CD*, the ratio $\frac{AB}{CD}$ must be greater than 1, which eliminates choices (A) and (C). *AB* doesn't look anywhere near twice as large as *CD*, however, so choice (E) is also out. That narrows it down to only two answer choices, (B) and (D).

24. A

Here you're looking for the largest possible median of a group of 5 numbers, all of which are positive integers, and which sum to 100. The median of group of numbers is simply the one in the middle when the numbers are placed in ascending order. That means that 2 of the 5 numbers are greater than the median and 2 of the 5 numbers are less than the median. Since we're looking for the largest possible value for the median, let's start by looking at the largest of the 5 answer choices, choice (E). If 50 were the median, 2 other numbers would have to be greater than 50. The smallest values that those 2 numbers could have are 51 and 52. But if 3 of the 5 positive numbers are 50, 51, and 52, the sum of the 5 numbers will be greater than 100, so cross out choice (E). If choice (D), 34, is the median, then the 2 larger numbers have to be at least 35 and 36 so the sum is again too large (34 + 35 + 36 = 105). Choice (C), 33, doesn't work as the median either, since 33 + 34 + 35 = 102, so eliminate choices (D) and (C). Choice (B) looks like it might be okay, since 32 as the median gives you 33 and 34 as the smallest possible numbers larger than the median. However, the smallest possible values for the 2 numbers less than the median are 1 and 2, so if 32 is the median, the smallest values the 5 numbers could have would be 1, 2, 32, 33, and 34, which add up to 102, so forget choice (B). Choice (A) is the only one left, so it must be correct. Just to check, though, if 31 were the median, then 32 and 33 could be the larger numbers. They add up to 96, so the 2 smaller numbers could be 1 and 3, and the sum of the 5 would be 100. Choice (A) is correct.

25. E

In order to solve this problem, you have to know that the sum of the lengths of any 2 sides of a triangle must be greater than the length of the third side. If the 3 sides of a triangle have lengths $x + 2$, $x - 2$, and y, then adding up any 2 of those quantities should give you a greater value than the value of the third quantity. If you add together the 2 sides with the lengths involving x, you get $x + 2 + (x - 2) = 2x$. This value must be greater than the third side, which is y, so $2x > y$. Switching this around gives you $y < 2x$. So far we have one condition for y. The 2 sides with lengths $x + 2$ and y must add up to more than the third side, $x - 2$, so $x + 2 + y > x - 2$. Subtracting x from both sides of this inequality results in $2 + y > -2$, and subtracting 2 from both sides results in $y > -4$. The 2 sides with lengths $x - 2$ and y must add up to more than the third side, $x + 2$, so $x - 2 + y > x + 2$. Subtracting x from both sides of this inequality results in $-2 + y > 2$, and adding 2 to both sides results in $y > 4$. So the results of these 3 calculations are $y < 2x$, $y > -4$, and $y > 4$. The second result, $y > -4$, is irrelevant since if y is greater than 4, then it is automatically also greater than -4, so what is significant is that $y < 2x$ and $y > 4$. Another way of writing this is $4 < y < 2x$, answer choice (E).

SECTION 3

1. E

The key here is the word *beneficial*, or helpful. If you don't know *beneficial*, a knowledge of word roots would help you. *Beneficial* contains the root BENE, meaning good, which indicates to you that it's a positive word. Well, if in one breath we are told that the ozone layer is positive, and in the next, that it does something for plant and animal life relating to dangerous ultraviolet radiation, we know we need a fairly positive word in the blank. The only choice that fits this requirement is choice (E) **protecting**. (D), **thwarting,** means impeding or preventing.

2. A

"While" is our tip-off that this sentence will in some way contain a contrast. While George Balanchine's choreography stayed within a classical context, he challenged convention by recombining ballet idioms. (If you don't know exactly what this means, it doesn't matter—you just need to grasp that this is how he challenged convention.) He's challenging convention by recombining typical ballet moves or whatever in some ---- way. The word in the blank must mean something like unconventional. The best choice here is (A), **unexpected**. Choice (C), **redundant,** means needlessly repetitive or excessive.

3. C

All of today's navel oranges have some common relationship to a single mutant tree that produced seedless fruit 200 years ago. They must all be descended from this one mutant. So the word in the blank must mean "descended from." Choice (C), **descendants,** jumps out as the correct choice. **Progenitors,** in choice (A) is meant to fool you since it has something to do with genetics. If you break **progenitor** down, PRO means "for" or "before," while the GENUS root is related to the word "gene." So, **progenitors** are ancestors—people (or things) which are related but came before—like grandparents. **Progenitors** are the opposite of descendants. Choice (E) was another word trap—just because **spores** have something to do with plants doesn't mean this is right. A **spore** is a reproductive body found in

simpler forms of life. But you don't need to know biology to figure this one out. Just use your reasoning skills. While a seed could be a spore, it makes no sense to say that all of today's navel oranges are the actual **spores** of a 200-year-old tree. But it is more plausible that this one tree produced a number of seeds, which in turn produced more of their own seeds, and so on.

4. A

In this sentence, there's a relationship between the quantities of food and drink Henry VIII consumed, and the type of person he was seen as. Either he consumed minimal quantities of food and drink, and was considered a spartan of sorts, or he consumed large amounts, and was considered a pig. Well, choice (A) is the only one that fits either one of these predictions. A **glutton** is one who overindulges in the consumption of food and drink. This option is the only one that fits, where there's a connection between the type of person his subjects saw him as, and the amount of food and drink he scarfed up. (C)'s first word, **minute,** or very small, fits okay, but a **luminary,** a famous or important person, doesn't. Consuming small quantities of food wouldn't make someone famous. In (B), **prodigious** means either extraordinary or enormous, while a **peer** is an equal, or a member of nobility.

5. A

You want a vocabulary word that means something like "transition" or "temporary"—some word that describes a government that no longer is in power, but is staying in power just until a new government is ready to take over the reins. Choice (A), **interim,** means temporary or provisional, so this is the answer. INTER is a root you should know—it means between.

6. E

The peoples discussed in this sentence were formerly ----. But now they've lost their land. They're living in ---- settlements. So we need two adjectives that are roughly the opposite of each other. The answer here is (E). Peoples who were once **nomadic,** or roaming freely without a **permanent** home, have moved into permanent settlements as their land got swallowed up by growing cities. **Fervid,** in choice (D), means passionate.

7. B

For the first blank, we want something that describes sleeping tablets—I'd rule out (E) right away, since **stimulating** is the one word here that most definitely would not describe sleeping tablets, even those with little impact. For the second blank, we want a word that characterizes the effect of those sleeping tablets, an effect that resulted in a woman feeling groggy the day after taking them. Something like "strong" or "intense" would be good. The best choice here is (B), because **soporific** means sleep-inducing—what word could be better to describe sleeping pills? **Pronounced,** meaning unmistakable or obvious, fits closely with our prediction. **Salubrious** in choice (C) means healthful.

8. E

Here we want a vocabulary word meaning something like "unable to accept the authority of others." Choice (A), **compliant,** means the exact opposite of this; a **compliant** person is one who bends easily to the will of others. (B) **slothful** means lazy. In choice (C), **conscientious** means responsible, hardly a word to describe Davis. (E) is correct because **recalcitrant** describes someone who refuses to obey authority.

9. D

"Although" tells us that there will be some sort of contrast with the fact that the actress has lived in a large city her whole life. The contrast will be that, despite her upbringing in a city, she still manages to be successful at portraying a humble farm girl. Therefore, she must be quite a good performer—the first blank will be a positive word, describing what a good actress she is. The second blank must be a word that explains how successfully she portrays the farm girl. The best choice here is (D), because a **consummate** actress is very skilled, while an **incarnation** is the embodiment of something or someone—you'd have to be a pretty good actress to become the embodiment of the character you're playing. In choice (C), **nemesis** means enemy.

10. B

Notice the word *hitherto* in this sentence. It means "previously." The board members had previously upheld worthy ideals. This implies that they no longer

do. For the second blank, then, we need a word like *rejection*: the board's recent decision must be a rejection of the previous worthy ideals. In the first blank, we need a word to describe what the chairman was doing as he described the board's decision so negatively. So the first blank must mean something like "criticized." (C) fits in the first blank, but not in the second. Remember to try both words in the blanks! Choice (B) works with both blanks: to **lament** is to regret, while a **negation** is what it sounds like, a rejection. The chairman lamented the decision of the board, describing it as a **negation** of worthy ideals. This was the only choice with two negative words that fit the context. To **endorse,** in choice (D), is to offer one's support, while a **renunciation** is a giving up or casting off of something like values. Finally, in (E), a **repudiation** is similar to a **renunciation**—it is a denial or rejection of something or someone.

11. D

A **MILL** is, by definition, a place where **FLOUR** is made. A **brewery** is a place where **beer** is made. A **pharmacy** is a place where a **prescription** is filled; but the **prescription** itself is not made there. A pharmacist dispenses pills and other medicines; a pharmaceutical company makes the medicine.

12. B

A **STETHOSCOPE** is an instrument used for **LISTEN**ing. A **needle** is an instrument used for **inject**ing.

13. A

By definition, a **BOTANIST** is one who pursues the scientific study of **PLANTS**. And a **zoologist** is one who scientifically studies **animals.** A **philologist** is a scholar, someone who studies the role of speech in literature.

14. D

ABUNDANT means more than **ADEQUATE**. So we're looking at a question of extremes—the first word is a more extreme version of the second. **Arid,** in choice (A), describes a desert environment, not a more extreme version of **moist. Boisterous,** in (B) means loud and rowdy. The answer is (D): something **overflowing** is more than **full.**

15. A

A **DOUBLE-CROSSER** is one who **BETRAY**s, by definition. Similarly, a **slowpoke** is one who **lags,** moves slowly or falls behind.

16. D

When you **EVADE,** or avoid the truth, you are not being **STRAIGHTFORWARD.** When you **boast,** or brag, you are not being **modest,** so (D) is right here. To **enliven,** in choice (B), is what it sounds like—to put a little life or energy into something. **Animated** means spirited or lively.

17. E

A **REPREHENSIBLE** person is someone who's done something wrong. So someone **REPREHENSIBLE** deserves **BLAME.** (E) is the right answer because someone **commendable** deserves **praise.**

18. E

In this question, **CONCORD** is not referring to the site where the American Revolution began, but to a state of **AGREEMENT.** Remember, CON can mean together or with, while COR is a root you've seen in words like "discord," and means "heart." An **insurrection,** in choice (A), means an uprising, hardly a state of **peace.** The answer is (E), because **flux** is a state of **change.**

19. C

FLORAL means having to do with **FLOWERS.** (C) is right, because **emotional** means having to do with **feelings. Perennial,** in (A), means perpetual, permanent, lasting for several years. **Perennial**s are plants that bloom year after year without needing to be replanted. This was an SST, a wrong answer choice from the same subject category as the stem. But it doesn't have the same bridge. Be sure to pick an answer pair because it has the same bridge as the stem, not just because it reminds you of the stem. (B) **morbid** means gloomy.

20. D

A **CALM** person possesses **COMPOSURE.** You might be familiar with the phrase "calm and composed" which describes a relaxed and poised individual. (D) is

the best answer here because a **sad** person possesses **melancholy,** or sorrow. In choice (B), don't confuse the adjective **cold** with the noun. If you have a **cold** you sort of do "possess" **sickness,** but if you *feel* **cold,** which is what this choice is referring to, you don't necessarily possess **sickness.** As for (C), there's no necessary connection between **congested** and **traffic.** While a **congested** highway might possess **traffic,** a **congested** person probably possesses sinus problems.

21. A

By definition, to **SEQUESTER** a **JUROR** is to place him or her in isolation. During trials covered extensively by the media, **JUROR**s are often **SEQUESTER**ed to prevent them from being influenced by what the rest of the world thinks about the case they're working on. The right answer is (A) because to **quarantine** a **patient** is to place them in isolation, to prevent them from spreading whatever wildly contagious disease they have. To cloister can also mean to place in isolation; it generally describes what members of religious orders do, particularly nuns. They go into seclusion at a religious site. However, you don't **cloister** a **convent,** you're cloistered within a **convent.** Choice (C) was an SST, with its reference to the world of crime and punishment.

22. B

By definition, something **HACKNEYED** lacks **ORIGINALITY.** You know what **ORIGINALITY** means—if you at least knew that **HACKNEYED** was negative, you'd be in good shape. You could get a rough idea of the stem's bridge. **Debauched** means corrupted. Someone who's **debauched** is lacking in **virtue,** so (B)'s correct.

23. C

To **SLAKE** one's **THIRST** is to satisfy or ease it. **Stoke** sounds a little like **SLAKE,** but (A)'s bridge differs from the stem's. To stoke a **fire,** in (A), is to stir it up or feed it, to make it burn longer and stronger. (B) doesn't work here either. You don't satisfy or lessen **hunger** by **starv**ing it. (B)'s another SST. To **assuage pain** means to ease it, and so this is the right answer. To **induce sleep** is to cause it. Drinking warm milk before bed, or reading a long, boring book, may **induce** sleep.

Domesticated Animals Passage

If you're an animal lover you might enjoy this passage. Actually, it's not a bad passage, but it's long, so be sure to keep up a good pace. You should aim at getting the main points of paragraphs and moving on. Basically, the author says that the dog was the first domesticated animal, which makes sense because of the dog's nature (it comes from a pack and likes to have a leader; puppies are cute and trainable; and it has better senses of hearing and smell than humans do, which makes it a valuable hunting companion). Then the author wonders how domestication occurred, which sends him off on a tangent about animals that "parasitize" human wastes or food stores. He speculates that domestication began because baby animals were cute—only later did domesticated animals actually become useful. He concludes that it's ironic that human civilization is destroying many species, since our learning to live with them is what made civilization possible.

24. D

The "archaeological discoveries" mentioned in the question stem are human and dog bones lying next to each other in ancient burial sites. The reason the author feels it's "terribly appropriate" that these bones are found together comes a few lines later, when he says "it marks a relationship that is the most ancient of all." (D) paraphrases that idea. You can see from this how important it is to read a few lines before and after the line reference in the stem. The author says nothing about burial habits in the Mesolithic Era (A), or the religious significance of animals in prehistoric cultures (B). He says nothing about "natural disasters" (E) either. He does mention hunting (C), but the bone finds are not "appropriate" because they "illustrate the role of dogs in hunting expeditions." (D) is the only possibility.

25. A

The end of paragraph 1 provides the answer. The author says that the dog was the first domesticated animal because it served as "a companion and an ally" (A). Only *after* domesticating animals as companions did humans domesticate "food animals" (B) and then "those that provide enhanced speed and range" (D) and then those that helped us farm (C). The key thing is to see that all these other types of domesticated animals came after animals were domesticated as companions.

26. E

The line reference takes you to the beginning of paragraph 2. The author says that having a dog as a companion animal was almost "inevitable," and then lists several reasons why. One of these is that the dog "is susceptible to domination by, and attachment to, a pack leader—the top dog." The implication is that humans formed bonds with dogs because they could dominate them (E). None of the other choices gives characteristics that make sense in answer to the question.

27. B

As with all Vocabulary-in-Context questions, you should go back to the sentence to see how the word is used. The author asks us to consider the "essence" of the dog in order to understand why it became a companion. He then lists several of the dog's characteristics that made it easy to domesticate. In other words, we're looking at the dog's "nature" (B). The only other choice that might seem to make sense in this context is (A) "history"—but what follows the line "consider its essence" is not a history; rather, it's a list of characteristics that make up the dog's nature.

28. C

This is definitely a question you need to return to the passage to answer. You're back in the second paragraph, where the author lists the characteristics that made dogs "inevitable" companions for humans. In addition to being born dependent and forming bonds with their rearers, dogs "have a set of appeasement behaviors" that elicit "affective reactions" from even the most "hardened" humans. The author goes on to talk about puppies transforming "cynics" into "cooing softies." Even if you weren't sure what "appeasement behaviors" were, you can see the gist of the author's point here: humans form bonds with dogs largely because dogs are cute and loveable. So would it make sense if "affective reactions" were "callous" (A), "rational" (B), or "cynical" (E)? No. (D) goes too far. The author isn't saying humans become childish around dogs, but that dogs arouse human emotions. (C) is the best answer.

29. C

The easiest way to understand the point of a comparison is to understand the context. What's the author saying in these lines? He's trying to show why it was inevitable that dogs became human companions. One reason is that dogs form bonds with their owners (C). That's the only reason he compares puppies with babies—to show how emotional people get about dogs. The author's point has nothing to do with "criticizing an uncaring attitude" (A), so that can't be the point of his comparing puppies and babies. The same is true for the rest of the choices, so (C) is correct.

30. B

Again, go back to the passage. Notice that the start of paragraph 3 actually refers back to the end of the *first* paragraph. Paragraph 1 ended with the author listing the dog as the first domesticated animal, followed by food animals, work animals, etc. Paragraph 2 talks about *why* the dog came first. So when paragraph 3 begins with "no wonder the dog was first," it's referring to the dog's status as the first domesticated animal. Similarly, "the list" refers to other domesticated animals, or "the number of animals that developed relationships with humans" (B). The author hasn't yet mentioned "birds that scavenge human food supplies," and when he does, he only mentions one, not many "types" (A). The passage never mentions species that are able to communicate with dogs (C), or the variety of attributes that make dogs good hunters (D). Finally, if you chose (E), you were losing track of the author's main points. Read over the first three paragraphs to see what's going on, and give a closer reading next time.

31. E

This question might seem more complicated than it really is. If you were confused by the digression the author made to talk about the blue tit, taking a look at the choices first probably would've saved you time. (A), (B), and (D) are fairly easy to eliminate—they have nothing to do with any of the author's main points. Good—now that you've eliminated three choices, you can always guess. But first let's go back to the passage. In line 46 the author mentions "opportunistic feeders." He goes on, saying "even today, many birds . . . feed from our stores." So (E) must be right;

the blue tit is an example of an opportunistic feeder. The question doesn't go any more into depth than that, so you're done.

32. C

A clear reference question. Go back to the lines you're given to see what kind of animals are being referred to. You have to read above a little to find the answer. The author has just finished describing the blue tit as an example of an opportunistic feeder. He reinforces the idea that the tit is an animal that feeds when and where it can by saying, "If all birds had been so specialized that they only fed in deep forest, it never would have happened." In other words, they are *not* so specialized—they'll eat wherever they find a food source (C). The author isn't talking here about companion animals (A). Forest inhabitants (B) is too broad. (D) is out because the birds are not hunting, they're feeding. And the point about the tits is not to give an example of "persistent pests" (E).

33. D

Go back to the passage to see in what context the author discusses his experiences in the tropics. At the beginning of paragraph 4, the author says that he thinks that the very first domesticated animals were orphaned as a result of hunting. He then tells how, in the tropics, he saw many instances of wild animals raised in homes of hunters. So his experiences illustrate his theory about how "the first domesticated animals were created" (D). None of the other choices relate to the author's argument here (or anywhere in the passage).

34. A

This one's a little tricky—if you thought so, you should've jumped ahead and come back later if you had time. Remember, reading questions don't go from easy to hard, so the next one could be easier. Check out the line "aid" is in to see what's going on. The author says that without domesticated animals—goats, sheep, pigs, cattle, and horses—we never would've achieved civilization. These animals helped or "aided" us—but they didn't have much choice in the matter. We dominated them, and then used them for food or labor. That's why "aid" is in quotes, and (A) is correct. The

KAPLAN

passage never says "population levels are dangerously high" (B). (C) is a better possibility—but it's not a point the author makes; you're inferring too much if you chose (C). It's not clear that animals benefited at all from domestication (D). (E) is really far-out, not supported by the passage.

35. E

The "ironic paradox" is found in the last four lines of the passage. The author says our living with other species—using them for food and labor—is what made our civilization possible. It is ironic then, that our civilization is presently wiping out many plant and animal species (E). Nowhere does the author say anything about (A) or (B). With (C), the author does talk about the pet care industry in the final paragraph, but not to say its size is "ironic." His point is just to show how big it is. (D) twists the author's point. It's by being parasites on other species that humans benefit, not the other way around.

SECTION 4

1. A

3.45601 is greater than 3.45002, since 3.45601 has a 6 in the thousandths' place and 3.45002 has a 0 is the thousandths' place. The number that is being subtracted from 1000 is greater in Column B than in Column A, so the result will be smaller in Column B than in Column A and choice (A) is correct.

2. B

The centered information tells you that the sum of x and y is greater than 11, and that x is less than 5.5. If x is less than 5.5, but $x + y$ is greater than 11, then y must be greater than $11 - 5.5$, or $y > 5.5$. If you try a few values for x and y you'll see that this is true. Since x is less than 5.5 and y is greater than 5.5, y is greater than x and choice (B) is correct.

3. A

The numerators of the 2 fractions are the same, so the fraction with the smaller denominator is the larger number. Since $17^{17} < 17^{18}$, choice (A) is correct.

4. B

There are 24 hours in one day, so there are 24×60 hours in 60 days. There are 60 seconds in one minute, so there are 30×60 seconds in 30 minutes. 30×60 is greater than 24×60, so choice (B) is correct.

5. B

Since $a + b = 60$ and $b + c = 40$, $a + b + b + c = 100$. The 3 variables are all positive, so $a + b + b + c$ is greater than $a + b + c$. Therefore $a + b + c < 100$. The average of a, b, and c is just $\frac{a+b+c}{3}$, and since $a + b + c < 100$, $\frac{a + b + c}{3}$ must be less than $\frac{100}{3}$, which is also less than the 50 in Column B, so the correct answer choice is (B).

6. A

You should immediately recognize that this is a 3-4-5 right triangle, so AC must measure 3. Even if you didn't you could have plugged in 4 and 5 for b and c in the Pythagorean equation $(a^2 + b^2 = c^2)$, and you would have gotten 3 for the third side. Since the sides measure 3, 4, and 5, the perimeter of the triangle is $3 + 4 + 5 = 12$. The area of the triangle is $\frac{1}{2} \times 3 \times 4 = 6$, so Column A is greater and choice (A) is correct.

7. C

This is a sequence consisting of a cycle of 4 numbers that repeats forever. The first term is 1, the second term is 2, the third term is -3, and the fourth term is -4. When it repeats the first time, the fifth term is 1, the sixth term is 2, the seventh term is -3, and the eight term is -4. It will repeat again, and the ninth term will be 1, the tenth term will be 2, the eleventh term will be -3, and the twelfth term will be -4. Notice that the number -4 is so far the fourth, eighth, and twelfth term. Since it is the fourth term in a repeating cycle of 4 numbers, its position in the sequence will always be a multiple of 4. So -4 will be the fourth, eighth, twelfth, sixteenth, twentieth, etc., terms in the sequence. This means that -4 will be the 48th term in the sequence, since 48 is a multiple of 4. If -4 is the 48th term, then the 49th term is 1, the 50th term is 2, the 51st term is -3, and the 52nd term is -4. So the sum of the 49th and 51st terms is the sum of 1 and -3, or $1 - 3$, or -2, and the sum of the 50th and 52nd terms is the sum of 2 and -4, or $2 - 4$, or -2, so the 2 columns are the same and the correct answer is (C).

8. D

If K represents Kearne's age and A represents Amanda's age, then the centered information can be translated to $K = 2A$. Then Kearne's age 5 years ago is $K - 5$, or $2A - 5$. Amanda's age 5 years from now is $A + 5$. Now you're comparing $2A - 5$ with $A + 5$. You can't really tell which is greater without knowing more about A, so the correct answer is (D). If you're not convinced, try doing the same thing to both columns. If you add 5 and then subtract A from both columns, you get A in Column A and 10 in Column B. Since you don't have any way of knowing whether or not Amanda's age is greater than 10, choice (D) must be correct.

You could also use picking numbers here. If Kearne is 40 and Amanda is 20 you have 35 in Column A and 25 in Column B and Column A is greater. Now you know that the correct answer is either (A) or (D). If Kearne is 16 and Amanda is 8, then you have 11 in Column A and 13 in Column B. Since the relationship changes for different values of K and A, choice (D) is the correct answer.

9. B

We want to compare $3x$ with $2y$. To do this, we need the values of x and y which we can find by solving the two equations in the centered information. We could solve these two equations by first solving for one variable in terms of the other in one equation and then plugging the expression for the variable we solved for into the other equation, resulting in one equation with one variable. We would then solve for this variable and then we could use either of the two original equations and the value of the variable we found to solve for the value of the other variable. However, there is a much faster way to solve for x and y in this problem. Notice that there is a y being added in each equation, so if we subtract the first equation from the second, the y's will cancel each other out:

$$4x + y = 3$$
$$-(2x + y = 2)$$
$$\overline{\hspace{2em}}$$
$$2x = 1$$
$$x = \frac{1}{2}$$

Now plug $\frac{1}{2}$ for x into the first equation, $2x + y = 2$. We have $2\left(\frac{1}{2}\right) + y = 2$, $1 + y = 2$, and $y = 1$. Column A, $3x$, is $3\left(\frac{1}{2}\right) = \frac{3}{2}$, or $1\frac{1}{2}$. Column B, $2y$, is $2(1) = 2$. Column B is greater.

10. B

The second equation tells you that $x = 2y$, so substitute $2y$ for x in the first equation. Then $x + y = -3$ becomes $2y + y = -3$, or $3y = -3$, or $y = -1$. Since $x = 2y$, $x = 2 \times (-1)$, or -2. Since x is -2 and y is -1, y is greater and choice (B) is correct.

11. B

Line segment BD is the same as line segments BC and CD put together. In other words $BD = BC + CD$. For the same reason we can say that $AC = AB + BC$. Since $BD > AC$, $BC + CD > AB + BC$. You can subtract BC from both sides of that inequality to give you $CD > AB$, which tells you that Column B is greater.

12. C

Each angle of the larger triangle here measures $a° + a°$, or $2a°$. Since the sum of the angles of a triangle is 180°, $2a° + 2a° + 2a° = 180°$, and $6a = 180$. That means that $a = 30$. The smaller triangles each have 2 angles measuring $a°$ and 1 angle measuring $b°$. Since $a = 30$, $30 + 30 + b = 180$. Therefore $60 + b = 180$ and $b = 120$. That means that $b - a = 120 - 30 = 90$. The 2 columns are equal so choice (C) is correct.

13. C

This is a tough question, as you would expect for one of the last three QC's. If you draw the line MH in the figure, you'll probably notice that there are a number of points on the cube each of which together with M and H can be three vertices of a right triangle. Whenever you have to find the length of a line segment in a complicated figure you should look for right triangles—this is often the key to solving. There are several ways to proceed from here. Probably the easiest way is to draw a line from M to A and a line from M to H. This creates a right triangle, AMH, inside the cube with MH as hypotenuse, AH as one leg and AM as the other leg. The length of AH is e, since it is an edge of the cube, so if you can figure out the length of AM, the other leg, you can figure out the length of the hypotenuse, MH, which is what you're looking for.

In order to find the length of AM you'll have to use another right triangle, ADM, on top of the cube. AM is the hypotenuse of this right triangle and AD and DM are the legs. AD is an edge of the cube so it has length e, and since M is the midpoint of CD, DM has length $\frac{e}{2}$. You can find the length of the hypotenuse using the Pythagorean theorem: $e^2 + \left(\frac{e}{2}\right)^2 = (AM)^2$, so $(AM)^2 = e^2 + \frac{e^2}{4} = \frac{5e^2}{4}$ and $AM = \frac{e\sqrt{5}}{2}$. Now back to triangle AMH. The legs have lengths e and $\frac{e\sqrt{5}}{2}$, so again using the Pythagorean theorem, $(MH)^2 = e^2 + \left(\frac{e\sqrt{5}}{2}\right)^2 = e^2 + \frac{5e^2}{4} = \frac{9e^2}{4}$. MH is then $\frac{3e}{2}$, so both columns are the same and the correct answer is choice (C).

14. C

Since points A and B have the same y-coordinate, the line segment they are on must be parallel to the x-axis, or a horizontal line segment, so point C has the same y-coordinate as A and B, 7. This line segment is also a diameter of circle C. The length of a horizontal segment in a coordinate plane is the difference in the x-coordinates of the line's endpoints, or in this case $7 - 1 = 6$. That means that circle C has a diameter of 6 and therefore a radius of 3. Since C is the center of the circle, AC is a radius and the distance from A to C is 3, so the x-coordinate of C must be $1 + 3 = 4$. The coordinates of point C are $(4, 7)$. The line segment that C and D are on is perpendicular to AB, so it must be a vertical line segment, parallel to the y-axis. So, C and D have the same x-coordinate of 4. CD is a radius of the circle and so has length 3, so the y-coordinate of D is $7 - 3 = 4$. Point D has coordinates $(4, 4)$. That means that its x- and y-coordinates are the same, and the answer is (C).

15. D

75% of 80 is the same as $\frac{3}{4}$ of 80, or 60. 25% is the same as $\frac{1}{4}$, so 25% of x is $\frac{1}{4}$ of x. If 60 is greater than $\frac{1}{4}$ of x then 4 times 60, or 240, is greater than 4 times $\frac{1}{4}$ of x, or x. If 240 is greater than x, x could be less than 200, but it could also be greater than or equal to 200, so the correct answer is (D).

16. 15

This is a simple plug-in, but make sure you write out every step so as to avoid a careless error. This is especially important in the Grid-ins. If $y = 2$, the expression $(5 - y)(y + 3)$ becomes $(5 - 2)(2 + 3)$. Remember to do the calculations inside the parentheses first. $5 - 2$ is 3 and $2 + 3$ is 5 so $(5 - 2)(2 + 3) = 3 \times 5 = 15$, so put a 15 in the grid.

17. 9.43

If the daily rate is $18.99, then the price for a week, or 7 days, is $7 \times \$18.99 = \$132.93$. Since the weekly rate is less, only $123.50, you can save $\$132.93 - \$123.50 = \$9.43$ by renting at the weekly rate.

18. 13 < length < 15

The first thing to do is to put the numbers 4, 5, and 12 in the appropriate places in the figure. Now you should see that you have the lengths of 2 sides of triangle BCD. Since BCD is a right triangle, you can use the Pythagorean theorem to figure out the length of the hypotenuse, but if you've memorized the common Pythagorean triplets you don't have to do that—you'll immediately recognize that this is a 5-12-13 right triangle, and so the length of BD is 13. The length of AC is $4 + 5 = 9$, so the triangle ACD has legs of lengths 9 and 12. Again, you can use the Pythagorean theorem to find the length of the hypotenuse, but you should notice that ACD is a multiple of the 3-4-5 right triangle, and AD has length 15. If you draw in point E in the figure between A and B, you'll see that DE will be longer than BD but shorter than AD, or greater than 13 but less than 15. So, any number between 13 and 15, such as 14, is a possible answer.

19. 15/4 or 3.75

If you need $\frac{3}{4}$ of a cup of drink mix for 2 quarts of water, then you need more than $\frac{3}{4}$ of a cup of drink mix for 10 quarts of water. How much more? Since $2 \times 5 = 10$, you have 5 times as much water, so you also need 5 times as much drink mix. $5 \times \frac{3}{4} = \frac{15}{4}$, so grid in $\frac{15}{4}$ (in the form of 15/4).

20. 166

The sum of the 3 angles of the triangle must be 180°. One angle measures 31°, but you don't know the measures of the other 2 angles in the triangle. However, the interior angle of the triangle on top lies on a straight line with an angle measuring 45°, so that interior angle must measure $180° - 45° = 135°$. If 2 angles of a triangle measure 135° and 31°, then the third angle measures $180° - 135° - 31° = 14°$. The 14° angle lies on a straight line with the $x°$ angle, so $14° + x° = 180°$, and $x = 166$.

If you remembered that any exterior angle of a triangle has the same measure as the sum of the 2 opposite interior angles, you could have saved a few steps. Once you figure out that the top angle of the triangle is 135°, you know that $x° = 135° + 31°$, and therefore $x = 166$.

21. 0.5 < y < 0.625

The only thing you know about y is that it is between $\frac{1}{2}$ and $\frac{5}{8}$. $\frac{1}{2}$ is the same as $\frac{4}{8}$, so y is between $\frac{4}{8}$ and $\frac{5}{8}$. You can't grid a fraction like $\frac{4\frac{1}{2}}{8}$, but you can change $\frac{4}{8}$ to $\frac{8}{16}$ and $\frac{5}{8}$ to $\frac{10}{16}$. That gives you an obvious value for y; since y is between $\frac{8}{16}$ and $\frac{10}{16}$, it could be $\frac{9}{16}$, so that's one possible number to grid in. You could also solve this question by converting $\frac{1}{2}$ and $\frac{5}{8}$ to decimals.

If you convert $\frac{1}{2}$ to .5 and $\frac{5}{8}$ to .625, you can grid in

any number greater .5 and less than .625. For example,

you can grid in .6.

22. 46

The average rate of speed is the total distance traveled divided by the total hours traveled. Melanie drove at 40 miles per hour for 2 hours, for a total of 40×2 or 80 miles. If she increased her speed by 25%, then she increased her speed by 25% of 40, or 10, so her new speed was $40 + 10 = 50$. So, she drove at 50 miles per hour for the next 3 hours, for a total of $50 \times 3 = 150$ miles. She went 80 miles and then 150 miles, for a total of 230 miles, and she drove for 2 hours and then for 3 hours, for a total of 5 hours. Her average rate for the trip was therefore 230 miles divided by 5 hours, or 46 miles per hour.

23. 175

There are 3 types of dealers at this convention—dealers who sell only stamps, dealers who sell only coins, and dealers who sell both stamps and coins. The total number of dealers is 500. You're given the number of 2 out of the 3 types of dealers—there are 127 that sell both stamps and coins, and 198 that sell only stamps. Since there are only 3 types of dealers, $127 + 198 +$ the number of dealers who sell only coins $= 500$, and so the number of dealers who sell only coins is $500 - 198 - 127 = 175$.

24. 46

Since the small square has a side of length 2, the area of the square must be 2^2, or 4. The larger square has a side of length 6, so its area is 6^2, or 36. The shaded part of square $ABCD$ is then $36 - 4$, or 32. The triangle is a right triangle with both legs of length 6, so the area of

the triangle is $\frac{1}{2} \times 6 \times 6$, or 18. The shaded area of the triangle is then $18 - 4 = 14$. The total shaded area is 32 $+ 14$, or 46, so grid in a 46.

25. 11

If N and R added up to a number less than 10, the problem would look different, something like:

$$\begin{array}{r} NR \\ RN \\ \hline XX \end{array}$$

Since it doesn't look like that, $N + R$ must be greater than 10. The best way to proceed from here is to try different pairs of numbers for R and N, and see what you get for B and C (keeping in mind that N, R, A, B, and C are different digits.) If you try setting either N or R equal to 9, you'll notice that you won't get different digits for all 5 variables. For example, if $R = 9$ and $N = 7$:

$$\begin{array}{r} 79 \\ 97 \\ \hline 176 \end{array}$$

Since there is always a 1 carried over into the tens' place, if $R = 9$ then the tens' column will add up to 9 + $N + 1$, or $10 + N$. The sum $10 + N$ has the same units' digit as N, so B and N will be the same if $R = 9$. The same thing happens if $N = 9$, only R and B turn out to be the same. If you try the next largest combination of numbers for N and R, which is 7 and 8, B and C turn out to be 6 and 5, so $B + C = 11$. Any smaller values for N and R will result in smaller values for B and C, so the largest possible value of $B + C$ is 11.

SECTION 5

The Jefferson/Douglass Passages

These two passages may seem hard because of their old-fashioned language. But the main points should be clear on a quick read-through. Jefferson emphasizes the natural and social riches of the United States (paragraph 1), supports the idea of limited government (end of paragraph 1), and states the principle of equal justice for all (paragraph 2). Douglass, speaking as an escaped slave, stresses that slaves do not have the freedoms celebrated on the Fourth of July. (If you don't remember who Douglass was, you may not catch the point of his speech until the end of paragraph 2, where it is stated directly. Always be patient—the drift of a passage often becomes clearer as you go along.) In paragraph 2, Douglass says that the case against slavery should not have to be argued, because freedom and liberty are basic American principles. In paragraph 3, he concludes that as long as slavery exists, the Fourth of July is a "sham."

Before going to the questions it can be helpful to think for a second about how the two passages relate—an important paired-passage strategy. You should come up with something like: Jefferson is stating American principles, but Douglass is saying they haven't been applied in practice. In a double passage, you'll have several questions on passage 1, followed by several on passage 2, followed by some asking for comparisons. Since answering the questions is the priority, be sure to read the first passage, do the questions that relate to it, then read the second passage and answer the rest of the questions.

1. C

In the cited lines, Jefferson is saying that Americans feel entitled to respect, or "honor and confidence," on the basis of "actions" rather than "birth." (C) is a paraphrase of this idea. Remember that the United States didn't have a hereditary aristocracy like European countries—that's what Jefferson is talking about. (A), (D), and (E) bring in ideas not mentioned in the excerpt—immigration (A), mutual help (D), family (E). (B)'s idea of demanding respect is wrong; Jefferson feels respect has to be based on actions.

2. A

In this Vocabulary-in-Context question, choice (B) might've jumped out at you. *But remember, the correct answer is probably not going to be the most common or familiar definition of the word, so don't be too hasty. Find the word in the passage and see how it's used there.* In this case, Jefferson is talking about what his duties as president involve, or "include." Choices (A). (C) and (E) give you other common synonyms for "comprehend," but they don't fit the context. (D) does not mean "comprehend."

3. D

Again, look at the context. Read the rest of the sentence in question, and the sentence before it. This should clarify that Jefferson is about to state what he believes to be the essential principles of government. Further, he's going to state them in the briefest possible way, which is what correct choice (D) says. (A) and (C) refer to Jefferson's mention of "limitations," but all Jefferson says is that he won't mention "limitations" or exceptions to the general principles. (B) is wrong because "them" in Jefferson's sentence refers to the principles of government, not to people who oppose the principles. Finally, Jefferson never mentions bureaucracy, choice (E).

4. E

Ignore the choices for the moment and look at the context: Jefferson is talking about equal justice for all, regardless of something, religious or political. This suggests that Jefferson is talking about people's beliefs, creeds, opinions, or convictions. (E) gives you the word that fits this context. (A), (B), and (C) are all vocabulary-list meanings for "persuasion," but they don't fit the context. "Authority" (D) is often seen as the opposite of persuasion; it has nothing to do with Jefferson's meaning here.

5. A

The next two questions take us through the Douglass excerpt. This one asks about paragraph 1, in which Douglass is contrasting the American celebration of independence and liberty with the bondage of slaves. The overall idea is that the celebrations are a "mockery" and an "irony" (lines 49–50) because they don't apply to everyone. In other words, they are hypocritical (A). (B) and (C) refer to emotions Douglass undoubtedly feels, but is not expressing here. (D) is an idea he never expresses at all. (E) interprets "drag a man in fetters" (chains) literally—force a slave to attend. Don't go for a simple paraphrase like this. *Go back and get the meaning in context!* Douglass is speaking figuratively; he doesn't mean he's actually being dragged to the celebration in chains.

6. D

In the cited sentence, the "millions" who are wailing are the slaves, while the "shouts" come from Fourth of July celebrants. Douglass uses this contrast to emphasize the differences between the lives and attitudes of slaves and free Americans (D). (A) and (C) twist the meaning of Douglass's mention of "yesterday" and "today" in these lines. Choice (B) goes against Douglass's overall point, which is to point out the hypocrisy of Fourth of July celebrations. And while the problem of slavery is not yet solved, Douglass doesn't imply it is "unsolvable" (E).

7. B

Always put the detail in context by rereading the surrounding lines. Here, the author's referring to the "treason" of betraying the American slaves by failing to protest during July 4th celebrations. Douglass is saying that he'd be committing "treason" to them by not speaking out. So in this example, "treason" refers to acting against the needs of a social group, i.e., the slaves. (A) and (D) may have sounded tempting as common definitions of "treason," but they don't express what the author means in this context.

8. C

A tough Little Picture question. Rereading the context, you can see that Douglass is emphasizing throughout paragraph 2 the contradiction between July 4th celebrations and the condition of the slaves. When he describes "American Slavery" as "my subject," he's highlighting this paradox, and also describing what

he's about to talk about next—literally outlining what the subject of the rest of his speech is. (A)'s wrong because the topic of slavery is not unexpected—it's what Douglass has been discussing all along. (B)'s wrong because Douglass isn't talking about slavery through the ages. (D)'s wrong because Douglass suggests no immediate answer to the problem. Finally, there's no suggestion that Douglass has to (E) learn more about his topic.

9. A

Again, put the detail in context—who or what is "impudent" here? Douglass is contrasting political speeches with the actual conditions that slaves endured, making (A) the correct answer. (B) is too general; (C) is off the point. (D) actually contradicts Douglass's explicit point of view. Finally, (E) is a distortion—according to the passage, it's the hypocritical speeches of politicians that railed against tyrants.

10. B

A tricky Compare and Contrast question. In passage 1, Jefferson deals with the themes of liberty and equality as the necessary principles of good government—he's describing these qualities as the bedrock of the Constitution. Based on passage 1, you can infer that he would respond to Douglass's questions about liberty in a similar manner—by agreeing that these are staples in any democracy. None of the other choices are consistent with any statement made in passage 1—remember, you've always got to find evidence for your answer in the passage.

11. B

The last two questions ask for comparisons. In this one, you're asked how Douglass would respond to Jefferson's stated principle, "equal and exact justice to all men." Douglass gives the answer when he says slaves do not enjoy the liberties of other Americans (paragraph 1). So he would respond that the principle is not being carried out in reality (B). (A), (C), and (E) all imply that the principle is invalid. But Douglass's argument is that a principle that is valid in general isn't being followed for African Americans. (E) is a possible response, but (B) sums up Douglass's overall point better.

12. C

Since each of the answer choices uses the word "both," you should be looking for a similarity between the speeches. Jefferson states a general principle; Douglass points out how it has been violated. The only point that both agree on is that equal justice is desirable, choice (C). Choices (A) and (D) describe Douglass's speech as a whole; (B) is implied in Douglass's final sentence—but Jefferson's speech never discusses these topics. (E), on the other hand, is true of Jefferson's speech but not Douglass's.

13. C

Summarizing each passage's point of view, you'd probably argue that Jefferson was optimistic about equality in the United States (having just established the Constitution), but that Douglass was critical of United States standards on equality 50 years later. Choice (C) picks up this contrast. None of the other choices captures the appropriate positive/negative answer required.

SECTION 6

1. D

The graph shows you the sales of all the toys for each month of the second quarter of a certain year, which is the months April, May, and June. If you look at the sales for those 3 months, you'll see that the bar for April goes up to 40, the bar for May goes up to 10, and the bar for June goes up to 30. The title on the vertical axis says "Sales (in millions of dollars)" so that's what those numbers represent: $40 million in sales for April, $10 million for May, and $30 million for June, for a total of $40 + 10 + 30 = 80$ million dollars total in sales for the 2nd quarter. The total sales were $80 million and the April sales were $40 million, and you want to know what percent of the total the April sales were. Since it says "of the total," the total, or $80 million is the whole and the $40 million is the part, so using the formula PERCENT × WHOLE = PART you get PERCENT × 80 = 40, or PERCENT $= \frac{40}{80} = \frac{1}{2} = 50\%$, answer choice (D).

2. E

If you remembered that any number squared is positive, a quick look at the answer choices would tell you that choice (E), x^2y^2, will be positive for any nonzero values of x and y. If you didn't remember that you should make a note of it, since it's a very important concept. You can also solve this one by picking numbers. If xy is negative, then either x or y is negative and the other is positive since a negative times a positive equals a negative. Picking a couple of pairs of numbers for x and y will tell you that both $x - y$ and $y - x$ can be either positive or negative depending on the exact values of x and y. x^2y can be negative if y is negative and

xy^2 can be negative if x is negative. However, any values you pick for x and y will give you a positive number for x^2y^2, so again choice (E) is correct.

3. B

Don't get confused by the strange words! They're just symbols for an unknown quantity, the same as the letters x and y, which we usually use as symbols for unknown quantities. If 1 fedi = 3 glecks, then multiplying both sides by 2 tells you that 2 fedis = 6 glecks. You're given that 1 bora = 2 fedis, so 1 bora must be equal to 6 glecks. Now that we know the relationship between boras and glecks (whatever they are), the rest is easy. 1 bora is equal to 6 glecks, so how many boras equal 48 glecks? Since $6 \times 8 = 48$, just multiply both sides of the equation 1 bora = 6 glecks by 8 to get 8 boras = 48 glecks. So, the correct answer is 8, answer choice (B).

4. C

If algebra confuses you, try picking numbers. If $f = 10$ then there are 10 freshmen in the class. If 5 freshmen drop the class then there are $10 - 5$, or 5 freshmen left in the class. The number of sophomores is 3 times the number of freshmen left, or 3 times 5, or 15. So there are 15 sophomores in the class and $s = 15$. Which of the answer choices work with $f = 10$ and $s = 15$? All you have to do is plug those numbers into the 5 choices and you'll find that only choice (C) works and is therefore correct.

To do it algebraically, just translate one step at a time. There are f freshmen in the class, but if 5 freshmen drop the class there are $f - 5$ freshmen left. The number of sophomores is 3 times the number of freshmen left, or 3 times $f - 5$, or $3(f - 5)$. So $s = 3(f - 5)$, answer choice (C).

5. E

The perimeter of triangle ABC is $AC + AB + 7$, and the perimeter of triangle ACD is $AC + 5 + 6$. You can combine that with the given information that the perimeter of triangle ABC is 4 more than the perimeter of triangle ACD to get $AC + AB + 7 = AC + 5 + 6 + 4$. Adding the numbers on the right side of the equation gives you $AC + AB + 7 = AC + 15$ and subtracting 7 from both sides gives you $AC + AB = AC + 8$. If you subtract AC from both sides you get $AB = 8$. That's all you need to find the perimeter of $ABCD$, which is $5 + 6 + 7 + 8$, or 26, answer choice (E).

6. D

Notice that at each corner of the cube, a triangular face like triangular face ABC is being made. How many corners are there? There are 8 corners; 4 of the corners are on the top and 4 of them are on the bottom. After all 8 triangular faces are made, a part of each of the original 6 faces of the cube remains. The total number of faces of the resulting stone must be $6 + 8$, or 14.

7. D

We want the average of the first 30 positive integers. Whenever we want the average of a group of evenly spaced numbers, we just have to take the average of the smallest number and the largest number. If you have difficulty seeing this, consider a simpler problem. Consider the average of 1, 2, 3, and 4. The average of 1, 2, 3, and 4 is $\frac{1+2+3+4}{4} = \frac{10}{4} = \frac{5}{2} = 2\frac{1}{2}$, using the average formula: Average $= \frac{\text{Sum of the terms}}{\text{Number of terms}}$. What happens if we just take the average of the smallest number, 1, and the largest number, 4? We get $\frac{1+4}{2} = \frac{5}{2} = 2\frac{1}{2}$, which is what we got by finding the average the other way. So the average of the first 30 positive integers is just the average of 1 and 30, which is $\frac{1+30}{2} = \frac{31}{2} = 15\frac{1}{2}$. None of the answer choices is $15\frac{1}{2}$, but $15\frac{1}{2}$ is 15.5. The average is 15.5.

8. B

You may notice that the figure looks like a rectangle with a quadrilateral piece hanging off of it. That means that you can find the area of the figure by adding the area of the rectangle and the area of the quadrilateral. The quadrilateral piece can be divided into a rectangle and a triangle. It may help to draw in some dotted lines to represent this:

The larger rectangle on the top has length 10 and width 9. Since the vertical line segment on the right is labeled 12, the length of the part of that line that is not part of the larger rectangle must be 12 – 9, or 3, so write that on your figure. The short horizontal line in the middle of the figure has length 4, the small rectangle on the bottom has length 2, and the entire figure has a top horizontal length of 10, so the dotted horizontal line that is a leg of the right triangle must have length 10 – 4 – 2, or 4. Now we've got the lengths of all the pieces of the figure:

The rectangle on the top has an area of $9 \times 10 = 90$. The small rectangle on the bottom right has length 3 and width 2, so its area is 6, and the triangle has legs 4 and 3, so its area is also 6. The total area of the figure is $90 + 6 + 6 = 102$, answer choice (B).

9. A

If 60 cookies are distributed among x campers, then each camper gets $\frac{60}{x}$ cookies. When the same number of cookies is divided among less campers, then each camper gets 2 more than $\frac{60}{x}$ cookies, or $\frac{60}{x} + 2$. This number of cookies per camper is also equal to 60 cookies divided by 8 less than the original number of campers, or $\frac{60}{x-8}$. This gives us the equation $\frac{60}{x} + 2 = \frac{60}{x-8}$. Unfortunately, this equation is not in the same form as the equations in the answer choices, so you'll have to do some algebra:

$$\frac{60}{x} + 2 = \frac{60}{x-8}$$
$$\frac{60 + 2x}{x} = \frac{60}{x-8}$$
$$(60 + 2x)(x - 8) = 60x$$
$$60x - 480 + 2x^2 - 16x = 60x$$
$$2x^2 - 16x - 480 = 0$$
$$x^2 - 8x - 240 = 0, \text{ answer choice (A).}$$

10. D

All they're asking here is—how many different pairs can you make from a group of 6? Let's call the 6 students $A, B, C, D, E,$ and F. A can be joined with the others to make the 5 pairs $AB, AC, AD, AE,$ and AF. Since you've already paired A and B you don't have to do it again, so just pair B up with the rest of the group to get $BC, BD, BE,$ and BF. That's 4 new pairs. C has already been matched up with A and B, so the new pairs that involve C are $CD, CE,$ and CF, for 3 new pairs. There are only 2 new pairs left for $D, DE,$ and DF, and finally 1 more, EF. So there's a total of $5 + 4 + 3 + 2 + 1 = 15$, choice (D).

SAT
Study Aids

SAT Word List

This Word List can boost your knowledge of SAT-level words, and that can help you get more questions right. No one can predict exactly which words will show up on your SAT test. But there are certain words that the test makers favor. The more of these you know, the better.

MEMORIZING SAT WORDS

In general, the very best way to improve your vocabulary is to read. Choose challenging, college-level material. If you encounter an unknown word, put it on a flashcard or in your vocabulary notebook. If you are mainly concerned with honing your knowledge of SAT words, memorizing the words on the following list can help. Here are some techniques for memorizing words.

1. Learn words in groups. You can group words by a common root they contain (see the Root List for some examples), or you can group words together if they are related in meaning (i.e., Word Families). Memorizing words this way may help you to remember them.

2. Use flashcards. Write down new words or word groups and run through them when you have a few minutes to spare. Put one new word or word group on one side of a 3 × 5 card and put a short definition or definitions on the back.

SAT Emergency

If you're short on time, you may want to just skim through this Word List to familiarize yourself with the types of words the SAT often tests.

3. Make a vocabulary notebook. List words in one column and their definitions in another. Test yourself. Cover up the meanings, and see which words you can define from memory. Make a sample sentence using each word in context.

4. Think of hooks that lodge a new word in your mind—create visual images of words.

5. Use rhymes, pictures, songs, and any other devices that help you remember words.

To get the most out of your remaining study time, use the techniques that work for you, and stick with them.

A

❑ ABANDON (n.)—total lack of inhibition

With her strict parents out of the way, Kelly danced all night with *abandon*.

❑ ABASE—to humble; disgrace

After his immature behavior, John was *abased* in my eyes.

❑ ABATE—decrease, reduce

As the hurricane's force *abated*, the winds dropped and the sea became calm.

❑ ABDICATE—to give up a position, right, or power

With the angry mob clamoring outside the palace, the king *abdicated* his throne and fled.

❑ ABERRATION—something different from the usual

Due to the bizarre *aberrations* in the author's behavior, her publicist decided that the less the public saw of her, the better.

❑ ABET—to aid; act as accomplice

While Derwin robbed the bank, Marvin *abetted* his friend by pulling up the getaway car.

❑ ABEYANCE—temporary suppression or suspension

Michelle held her excitement in *abeyance* while the college review board considered her application.

❑ ABHOR—to loathe, detest

After she repeatedly failed to learn the Pythagorean theorem, Susan began to *abhor* geometry.

❑ ABJECT—miserable, pitiful

When we found the *abject* creature lying on the ground, we took it inside and tended to its broken leg.

❑ ABJURE—to reject, abandon formally

Claiming he had changed, the president *abjured* his old beliefs during his speech.

❑ ABLUTION—act of cleansing

Taking off her makeup was the last step in Minnie's evening *ablutions*.

❑ ABNEGATE—to deny; renounce

The monks had dedicated themselves to a humble and self-*abnegating* lifestyle, refusing all comforts.

❑ ABOLITIONIST—one who opposes the practice of slavery

Harriet Beecher Stowe, a known *abolitionist*, portrayed the evils of slavery in her novel *Uncle Tom's Cabin*.

❑ ABORTIVE—interrupted while incomplete

Her attempt at reaching the other side of the lake was *abortive*—her sailboat capsized halfway across.

❑ ABRIDGE—to condense, shorten

The teacher assigned an *abridged* version of *Tristram Shandy* to her class, as the original was very long.

❑ ABROGATE—to put an end to, abolish by authority

The immigration authorities agreed to *abrogate* their original decision to deport Juan after evidence was submitted that he was in fact a political refugee, as he had claimed.

❑ ABSCOND—to depart secretly

After being fired, the disgruntled ex-employee *absconded* with six company computers in the middle of the night.

❑ ABSOLVE—to forgive, free from blame

The queen *absolved* the general from blame for the disastrous military campaign, much to his relief.

❑ ABSTAIN—to choose not to do something

During Lent, practicing Catholics *abstain* from eating meat.

❑ ABSTRACT (adj.)—theoretical; complex, difficult

The theory was too *abstract* for the students to comprehend.

❑ ABSTRUSE—difficult to comprehend

The philosopher's elucidation was so clear that he turned an *abstruse* subject into one his audience could grasp.

❑ ACCEDE—to express approval; agree to

When the mayor proposed lower taxes, the people readily *acceded*.

❑ ACCESSIBLE—attainable, available; approachable

Preeti was surprised that the famous professor was so *accessible*, inviting students to visit him at all hours.

❑ ACCOLADE—praise, distinction

The winner of the spelling bee beamed as *accolades* were heaped upon her from all sides.

❑ ACCOST—to approach and speak to someone

Furious, Maria *accosted* the man who had trampled her flower bed and demanded that he apologize.

❑ ACCRETION—growth in size or increase in amount

The committee's strong fund-raising efforts resulted in an *accretion* in available scholarship money.

❑ ACCRUE—to accumulate, grow by additions

Before he knew it, Cliff had *accrued* an overwhelmingly large debt.

❑ ACERBIC—bitter, sharp in taste or temper

Gina's *acerbic* wit and sarcasm were feared around the office.

❑ ACME—highest point; summit

The dictator was assassinated just as he reached the *acme* of his power.

❑ ACQUIESCE—to agree; comply quietly

The princess *acquiesced* to demands that she marry a nobleman, but she was not happy about it.

❑ ACQUITTAL—release from blame

The public was astonished at the jury's *acquittal* of the serial killer—how could they let a man like that go?

❑ ACRID—harsh, bitter

The *acrid* smell of vinegar drove the children out of the kitchen.

❑ ACRIMONY—bitterness, animosity

The *acrimony* the newly divorced couple showed towards each other made everyone feel uncomfortable.

❑ ACUITY—sharpness

Although Dr. Patel is in her mid-eighties, her mental *acuity* is still impressive.

❑ ACUMEN—sharpness of insight

The portfolio manager's financial *acumen* helped him to select high-yield stocks for his clients.

❑ ACUTE—sharp, pointed, severe

There is an *acute* shortage of food in the city, and people will starve if food is not brought in soon.

❑ ADAGE—old saying or proverb

"A penny saved is a penny earned" is a popular *adage*.

❑ ADAMANT—uncompromising, unyielding

The lawyer was *adamant* in his tireless defense of the death penalty.

❑ ADAPT—to accommodate; adjust

Although it may be difficult at first, we all have to *adapt* to the new computer system.

❑ ADHERE—to cling or follow without deviation

He was a strict Catholic who *adhered* to all the teachings of the Church.

❑ ADJACENT—next to

The photocopier is down the hall, *adjacent* to the water cooler.

❑ ADJUNCT—something added, attached, or joined

An *adjunct* professor is one not given the same full-time status as other faculty members.

❑ ADMONISH—to caution or reprimand

My mother began to *admonish* me about my poor grades.

❑ ADROIT—skillful, accomplished, highly competent

The *adroit* athlete completed even the most difficult obstacle course with ease.

❑ ADULATION—high praise

After Ana's piano recital, the audience lavished her with *adulation*.

❑ ADULTERATE—to corrupt or make impure

The restaurateur made his ketchup last longer by *adulterating* it with water.

❑ ADUMBRATE—to sketch, outline in a shadowy way

There was only time to *adumbrate* an escape plan before the cyclone hit.

❑ ADVANTAGEOUS—favorable, useful

Derek found his Spanish-speaking skills to be *advantageous* in his travels in Mexico.

❑ ADVERSARIAL—antagonistic, competitive

The brothers' *adversarial* relationship made it impossible for them to support each other in times of need.

❑ ADVERSE—unfavorable, unlucky; harmful

They canceled the baseball game due to *adverse* weather conditions.

❑ AERIAL—having to do with the air

From the plane, we took several *aerial* pictures of the mountain tops.

❑ AERIE—nook or nest built high in the air

The eagle's *aerie*, filled with eggs, was perched high in the trees.

❑ AERODYNAMIC—relating to objects moving through the air

We made the paper airplane more *aerodynamic* by folding the wings at an angle.

❑ AESTHETIC—pertaining to beauty or art

The museum curator, with her fine *aesthetic* sense, created an exhibit that was a joy to behold.

❑ AFFABLE—friendly, easy to approach

The *affable* postman was on good terms with everyone on his route.

❑ AFFECTED (adj.)—pretentious, phony

The *affected* hairdresser spouted French phrases continually, even though she had never been to France.

❑ AFFINITY—fondness, liking; similarity

George felt an instant *affinity* for his new neighbor when he realized that he, too, was a Broncos fan.

❑ AFFLUENT—rich, abundant

An *affluent* woman, Enid was able to give large sums of money to charity.

❑ AFFRONT (n.)—personal offense, insult

Clyde took the waiter's insulting remark as an *affront* to his whole family.

❑ AGENDA—plan, schedule

The board put the urgent issue at the top of the *agenda* for their next meeting.

❑ AGGRANDIZE—to make larger or greater in power

All the millionaire really wanted was to *aggrandize* his personal wealth as much as possible.

❑ AGGREGATE (n.)—collective mass or sum; total

An *aggregate* of panic-stricken customers mobbed the bank, demanding their life savings.

❑ AGGRIEVE—to afflict, distress

Elizabeth, the chambermaid, felt *aggrieved* at the harsh treatment she received from her mistress.

❑ AGILE—well coordinated, nimble

The *agile* monkey leapt onto the table and snatched the boy's banana away in the blink of an eye.

❑ AGITATION—commotion, excitement; uneasiness

The patient's *agitation* was obvious; she was terrified at the thought of undergoing the operation.

❑ AGNOSTIC—one who doubts that God exists

When she could find no evidence to affirm the existence of God, she proclaimed herself an *agnostic*.

❑ AGRARIAN—relating to farming or rural matters

She took a course in *agrarian* accounting in order to help her family run the farm after college.

❑ ALACRITY—cheerful willingness, eagerness; speed

The eager dog fetched with *alacrity* the stick that had been tossed for him.

❑ ALCHEMY—medieval chemical philosophy aimed at trying to change metal into gold

Scientists of old struggled to master the secrets of *alchemy*, but could never change metal to gold.

❑ ALGORITHM—mechanical problem-solving procedure

Sara's new computer used *algorithms* to solve equations.

❑ ALIAS—assumed name

The criminal who goes by the *alias* "Big Bad Bobby" was just arrested.

❑ ALIENATED—distanced, estranged

Anthony made an effort to make the new student feel less *alienated* by inviting her out with the group.

❑ ALIGNED—precisely adjusted; committed to one side

Jackie always made sure her pens were perfectly *aligned* in her drawer.

❑ ALLAY—to lessen, ease, or soothe

The nurse tried to *allay* the couple's fears that their son's health had deteriorated.

❑ ALLEGORY—symbolic representation

The novelist used the stormy ocean as an *allegory* for her life's struggles.

❑ ALLEVIATE—to relieve, improve partially

This medicine will help to *alleviate* the pain.

❑ ALLITERATION—repetition of the beginning sounds of words

The poet was fond of using *alliteration* in her work, as in her poem "Preening Pigeons Perch Prettily."

❑ ALLOCATION—allowance, portion, share

The treasurer will be in charge of the *allocation* of funds during the campaign.

❑ ALLURE (v.)—to entice by charm; attract

The video arcade owner *allured* teenage customers by installing the coolest, most desirable new games.

❑ ALLUSION—indirect reference

He was sometimes referred to as "the Slugger," an *allusion* to his ability to hit the baseball very hard.

❑ ALLUSIVENESS—quality of making many indirect references

Joyce found Michael's *allusiveness* increasingly irritating—sometimes she wished he'd just get to the point.

❑ ALOOF—detached, indifferent

The newcomer remained *aloof* from all our activities and therefore made no new friends.

❏ ALTERCATION—noisy dispute

When the drunken cowboy knocked someone's beer bottle off the table, a serious *altercation* ensued.

❏ ALTRUISM—unselfish concern for others' welfare

The woman's *altruism* revealed itself in the way she gave out money to all who seemed needy.

❏ AMALGAMATE—to mix, combine

Giant Industries *amalgamated* with Mega Products to form Giant-Mega Products Incorporated.

❏ AMBIDEXTROUS—able to use both hands equally well

The *ambidextrous* man was able to chop vegetables with both hands simultaneously, making him one of the fastest short-order cooks in the business.

❏ AMBIGUOUS—uncertain; subject to multiple interpretations

The directions he gave were so *ambiguous* that we disagreed on which way to turn.

❏ AMBIVALENCE—attitude of uncertainty; conflicting emotions

Jane was filled with *ambivalence*—on the one hand, switching jobs would get her away from her tyrannical boss, but on the other hand, she'd lose her high salary and corner office.

❏ AMELIORATE—to make better, improve

Conditions in the hospital were *ameliorated* by the hiring of dozens of expertly trained nurses.

❏ AMENABLE—agreeable, cooperative

Although the new director seemed rigid at first, the cast soon found her to be *amenable* to change.

❏ AMEND—to improve or correct flaws in

Congress must *amend* the bill before the president will agree to sign it.

❏ AMENITY—pleasantness; something increasing comfort

The star was overjoyed to have access to all the *amenities* of civilized society after her stint in the jungle.

❏ AMIABLE—friendly, pleasant, likable

The new boss was an *amiable* young man with a smile for everyone.

❏ AMICABLE—friendly, agreeable

Despite their former arguments, the team was able to form an *amicable* working relationship.

❏ AMITY—friendship

Correspondence over the years contributed to a lasting *amity* between the women.

❏ AMORAL—unprincipled, unethical

The preacher ranted about the *amoral* nature of modern values.

❏ AMOROUS—strongly attracted to love; showing love

The love-sick young poet wrote many *amorous* poems about his girlfriend.

❏ AMORPHOUS—having no definite form

The movie *The Blob* featured an *amorphous* creature that was constantly changing shape.

❏ AMORTIZE—to diminish by installment payments

She was able to *amortize* her debts by paying a small amount each month.

❏ AMPHIBIAN—creature equally at home on land or in water

The frog's ability to live both on land and in the water classifies it as an *amphibian*.

❏ AMPHITHEATER—arena theater with rising tiers around a central open space

The *amphitheater* in the park is the perfect place for a summer concert.

❏ AMPLE—abundant, plentiful

Though our backpacks were small, we had *ample* food for the hike.

❏ AMPLIFY—increase, intensify

We will need to *amplify* the music at the wedding so that everyone can dance.

❏ AMULET—ornament worn as a charm against evil spirits

Though she claimed it was not due to superstition, Vivian always wore an *amulet* around her neck.

❏ ANACHRONISM—something chronologically inappropriate

The aged hippie used *anachronisms* like "groovy" and "far out" that had not been popular for years.

❏ ANACHRONISTIC—outdated

The hippie's clothes, with their beads and dangling tassles, were *anachronistic* in style.

❏ ANALOGOUS—comparable, parallel

In a famous argument for the existence of God, the universe is *analogous* to a mechanical watch, the creation of a divinely intelligent "clockmaker."

❏ ANARCHY—absence of government or law; chaos

Some believe that without a strong police force to keep society in order, *anarchy* would soon prevail.

❏ ANATHEMA—ban, curse; something shunned or disliked

Sweaty, soiled clothing was *anathema* to the elegant Madeleine.

❏ ANCILLARY—accessory; subordinate; helping

Reforms were instituted at the main factory, but not at its *ancillary* plants, so defects continued to occur.

❏ ANECDOTE—short, usually funny account of an event

The child's grandparents entertained him for hours with *anecdotes* from their younger days.

❏ ANGULAR—characterized by sharp angles; lean and gaunt

Her *angular* frame contrasted sharply with that of her overweight sister.

❏ ANIMATION—enthusiasm, excitement

Ben's face filled with *animation* as he described his wonderful, exciting trip to Venice.

❏ ANIMOSITY—hatred, hostility

The deep-rooted *animosity* between them made it difficult for the cousins to work together.

❏ ANNUL—to cancel, nullify, declare void, or make legally invalid

The couple asked the court to *annul* their marriage, as they had made a mistake in wedding each other.

❏ ANODYNE—something that calms or soothes pain

The skittish patient asked the dentist for an *anodyne* to dull the pain.

❏ ANOINT—to apply oil to, especially as a sacred rite

The ceremony required the woman to *anoint* her child's head with oil.

❏ ANOMALY—irregularity or deviation from the norm

Albino animals may display too great an *anomaly* in their coloring to attract normally colored mates.

❏ ANONYMITY—condition of having no name or an unknown name

After abandoning her movie career at a relatively youthful age, Garbo retreated into relative *anonymity*.

❏ ANTAGONIST—foe, opponent, adversary

The child and the cat became bitter *antagonists* after the child pulled the cat's tail.

❏ ANTECEDENT (adj.)—coming before in place or time

Though the war appeared to be over, the *antecedent* events made the soldiers wary of retreating.

❏ ANTEDILUVIAN—prehistoric, ancient beyond measure

The *antediluvian* fossils were displayed in the museum.

❏ ANTEPENULTIMATE—third from last

In the word "ultimate," the spoken stress is on the *antepenultimate* syllable, "ul."

❏ ANTERIOR—preceding, previous, before, prior (to)

Following tradition, the couple's wedding was *anterior* to the honeymoon.

❏ ANTHOLOGY—collection of literary works

Whenever the student needed a quotation, she consulted her *anthology*.

❏ ANTHROPOMORPHIC—attributing human qualities to nonhumans

Milo's *anthropomorphic* behavior towards his computer was evident when he called it "Fred."

❏ ANTIPATHY—dislike, hostility; extreme opposition or aversion

The *antipathy* between the French and the English regularly erupted into open warfare.

❏ ANTIQUATED—outdated, obsolete

The old man's typewriter was completely *antiquated*, especially when compared to his son's computer.

❏ ANTIQUITY—ancient times; the quality of being old

It was obviously a castle of great *antiquity*, unchanged since before the Middle Ages.

❏ ANTITHESIS—exact opposite or direct contrast

The ill-mannered boy was often described as the *antithesis* of his sweet sister.

❏ APATHETIC—indifferent, unconcerned

The author seemed *apathetic*, going along with all the editor's proposed changes without an argument.

❏ APATHY—lack of feeling or emotion

The *apathy* of voters is so great that less than half the people who are eligible to vote bother to do so.

❏ APHASIA—inability to speak or use words

Stroke victims often suffer from *aphasia*, making it difficult for them to communicate with others.

❏ APHELION—point in a planet's orbit that is farthest from the sun

When the Earth is at its *aphelion*, it has reached its greatest distance from the sun.

❏ APHORISM—old saying or short, pithy statement

The country doctor was given to *aphorisms* such as "Still waters run deep."

❏ APOCRYPHAL—not genuine; fictional

Sharon suspected that the stories she was hearing about alligators in the sewer were *apocryphal*.

❏ APOSTATE—one who renounces a religious faith

The king declared himself an *apostate* before flouting the Church's doctrines to divorce his wife.

❏ APOSTROPHE—an address to the reader or someone not present

The author often used *apostrophe* to present a viewpoint directly to the reader.

❏ APOTHEOSIS—glorification; glorified ideal

In her heyday, many people considered Jackie Kennedy to be the *apotheosis* of stylishness.

❏ APPEASE—to satisfy, placate, calm, pacify

We all sang lullabies to try to *appease* the bawling infant.

❏ APPROBATION—praise; official approval

Billy was sure he had gained the *approbation* of his teacher when he received a glowing report card.

❏ APPROPRIATE (v.)—to take possession of

Lucia came up with the great idea to *appropriate* the abandoned building for storage.

❏ AQUATIC—belonging or living in water

The heaviest *aquatic* creature, the whale, dwarfs heavy land animals, as its weight is supported by water.

❏ ARABLE—suitable for cultivation

The overpopulated country desperately needed more *arable* land to grow food for its starving people.

❏ ARBITRARY—depending solely on individual will; inconsistent

Nancy won a prize, but not Fred, making the judges' decisions seem completely *arbitrary*.

❏ ARBITRATE—mediate, negotiate

Since the couple could not come to agreement, a judge was forced to *arbitrate* their divorce proceedings.

❏ ARBOREAL—relating to trees; living in trees

The squirrel is an *arboreal* mammal, spending much of its time running up and down trees.

❏ ARBORETUM—place where trees are displayed and studied

The botanist spent many hours in the *arboretum* doing research.

❏ ARCANE—secret, obscure, known only to a few

The *arcane* rituals of the sect were passed down through many generations.

❏ ARCHAIC—antiquated, from an earlier time; outdated

Her *archaic* Commodore computer could not run the latest software.

❏ ARCHIPELAGO—large group of islands

Boat taxis are the only form of transportation between villages in the Stockholm *archipelago*.

❏ ARDENT—passionate, enthusiastic, fervent

After a 25-game losing streak, even the Mets' most *ardent* fans realized the team wouldn't finish first.

❏ ARDOR—great emotion or passion

Bishop's *ardor* for landscape was evident when he passionately described the beauty of the Hudson Valley.

❏ ARDUOUS—extremely difficult, laborious

Amy thought she would pass out after completing the *arduous* climb up the mountain.

❏ ARID—extremely dry or deathly boring

The *arid* farmland produced no crops.

❏ ARRAIGN—to call to court to answer an indictment

The conman was *arraigned* yesterday, but failed to show up in court.

❏ ARROGATE—to demand, claim arrogantly

Lynn watched in astonishment as her boss *arrogated* all the credit for Lynn's brilliant work on the project.

❏ ARSENAL—ammunition storehouse

The soldiers rushed to the *arsenal* to fetch more cannonballs.

❏ ARTICULATE (adj.)—well spoken, expressing oneself clearly

She is such an *articulate* defender of labor that unions are among her strongest supporters.

❏ ARTIFACT—historical relic, item made by human craft

The archaeologist discovered hundreds of interesting *artifacts* in the ruins of the mansion.

❏ ARTISAN—craftsperson; expert

Artisans were among the most valued citizens of the kingdom for their skills in tool-making.

❏ ASCEND—to rise or climb

As Mr. Boggs *ascended* the stairs, he panted heavily.

❏ ASCENDANCY—state of rising, ascending; power or control

The devious politician's *ascendancy* to the top ranks of government seemed inevitable.

❏ ASCERTAIN—to determine, discover, make certain of

Try as he might, the archaeologist couldn't *ascertain* the correct age of the Piltdown man's skeleton.

❏ ASCETIC—self-denying, abstinent, austere

The monk lived an *ascetic* life deep in the wilderness, denying himself all forms of luxury.

❏ ASCRIBE—to attribute to, assign

Aunt Fran was shocked when she heard about the negative qualities her family *ascribed* to her.

❏ ASHEN—resembling ashes; deathly pale

The *ashen* look on Jesse's face made it clear he had already heard the bad news.

❏ ASKEW—crooked, tilted

I was so late for work that I rushed out of the house with my hair uncombed and my hat *askew*.

❏ ASPERSION—false rumor, damaging report, slander

It is unfair to cast *aspersions* on someone behind his or her back.

❏ ASPIRE—to have great hopes; to aim at a goal

Although Sid started out in the mailroom, he *aspired* to owning the company someday.

❏ ASSAIL—to attack, assault

The foreign army *assailed* the fort for days, but did not manage to take it.

❏ ASSENT—to express agreement

I want to make money, but I would never *assent* to doing anything illegal.

❏ ASSERT—to affirm, attest

Some people look favorably on politicians who are willing to *assert* their views boldly.

❏ ASSIDUOUS—diligent, persistent, hard-working

The chauffeur scrubbed the limousine *assiduously*, hoping to make a good impression on his employer.

❏ ASSIGNATION—appointment for lovers' meeting; assignment

Romeo and Juliet made an *assignation* to meet at her balcony.

❏ ASSIMILATION—act of blending in, becoming similar

Language classes were offered to aid in the *assimilation* of the immigrants with the native citizens.

❏ ASSONANCE—resemblance in sound, especially in vowel sounds; partial rhyme

The professor pointed out how *assonance* among the words contributed to the flow of the poem.

❏ ASSUAGE—to make less severe, ease, relieve

Like many people, Philip Larkin used alcohol to *assuage* his sense of meaninglessness and despair.

❏ ASTRINGENT—harsh, severe, stern

The principal's punishments seemed overly *astringent*, but the students did not dare to complain.

❏ ASTUTE—having good judgment

The novelist Judy Blume is an *astute* judge of human nature; her characters ring true.

❏ ASUNDER (adv.)—into different parts

Though the boat was strong, the violent storm tore it *asunder*.

❏ ASYMMETRICAL—not corresponding in size, shape, position, etcetera

The hairstylist was shocked to find that the two sides of his customer's hair were *asymmetrical*.

❏ ATONE—to make amends for a wrong

Many people go to church to *atone* for their wrongdoings and seek forgiveness.

❏ ATROCIOUS—monstrous, shockingly bad, wicked

The British officer committed the *atrocious* act of slaughtering a large group of peaceful Indian villagers.

❑ ATROPHY—to waste away, wither from disuse

When Mimi stopped exercising, her muscles began to *atrophy*.

❑ ATTAIN—to accomplish, gain

It is clear that Clem's hard work will help him *attain* that raise he's been hoping for.

❑ ATTENUATE—to make thin or slender; weaken

The Bill of Rights *attenuated* the traditional power of government to change laws at will.

❑ ATTEST—to testify, stand as proof of, bear witness

Once her husband had *attested* to the fact that Mrs. Martin was with him on the night of the murder, the jury had no choice but to acquit her of the crime.

❑ AUDACIOUS—bold, daring, fearless

"And you, your majesty, may kiss my bum!" replied the *audacious* peasant.

❑ AUDIBLE—capable of being heard

The shy boy's voice was barely *audible* as he answered the teacher's questions.

❑ AUDIT—formal examination of financial records

The grocer cursed the IRS's decision to *audit* him, as he couldn't pay all the back taxes they demanded.

❑ AUDITORY—having to do with hearing

Sometimes, people's *auditory* canals become blocked by large quantities of wax.

❑ AUGMENT—to expand, extend

Ben *augmented* his salary with overtime hours as much as possible.

❑ AUGURY—prophecy, prediction of events

Troy hoped the rainbow was an *augury* of good things to come.

❑ AUGUST—dignified, awe inspiring, venerable

The *august* view of the summit of the Grand Teton filled the climbers with awe.

❑ AUSPICIOUS—having favorable prospects, promising

Tamika thought that having lunch with the boss was an *auspicious* start to her new job.

❑ AUSTERE—stern, strict, unadorned

The lack of decoration makes Zen temples seem *austere* to the untrained eye.

❑ AUTHORITARIAN—extremely strict, bossy

The *authoritarian* manager alienated his employees with his bossy manner.

❑ AUTOCRAT—dictator

Mussolini has been described as an *autocrat* who did not tolerate opposition.

❑ AUTONOMOUS—separate, independent

There is a movement underway to make Scotland an independent country, *autonomous* from England.

❑ AUXILIARY—supplementary, reserve

Gasping for air, the astronaut was forced to open his *auxiliary* canister of oxygen.

❑ AVARICE—greed

Rebecca's *avarice* motivated her to stuff the $100 bill in her pocket instead of returning it to the man who had dropped it.

❑ AVENGE—to retaliate, take revenge for an injury or crime

"You'll regret humiliating me! Someday, I will *avenge* this insult!" shouted the furious count.

❑ AVER—to declare to be true, affirm

The witness *averred* that the man had in fact been holding a gun.

❑ AVERSION—intense dislike

Laura took an instant *aversion* to Mike because of his obnoxious personality.

❑ AVERT—to turn (something) away; prevent, hinder

The queasy medical school student had to *avert* her eyes when the operation began.

❑ AVIARY—large enclosure housing birds

The tourists brought their cameras to the city's famous *aviary*, hoping to capture its exotic birds on film.

❑ AVOW—to state openly or declare

The groom *avowed* his love for his bride to the rabbi.

❑ AWRY—crooked, askew, amiss

Something must have gone *awry* in the computer system, because some of my files are missing.

❑ AXIOM—premise, postulate, self-evident truth

Halle lived her life based on the *axioms* her grandmother had passed on to her.

B

❑ BALEFUL—harmful, with evil intentions

The sullen teenager gave his nagging mother a *baleful* look.

❑ BALK—to refuse, shirk; prevent

The horse *balked* at jumping over the high fence and instead threw his rider off.

❑ BALLAD—folk song, narrative poem

We heard the singer perform many romantic *ballads* at the country inn.

❑ BALM—soothing, healing influence

"Let me give you some lip *balm* for your chapped lips," said Donna.

❑ BAN—to forbid, outlaw

After getting drunk one night and smashing dozens of bottles, Joe was *banned* from the bar for life.

❑ BANAL—trite, overly common

He used *banal* phrases like "Have a nice day" or "Another day, another dollar."

❑ BANE—something causing death, destruction, or ruin

Speeches were the *bane* of Jenny's existence; she hated having to stand up in front of a crowd.

❑ BANTER—playful conversation

The eligible young man's cheerful *banter* was misinterpreted as flirtation by the woman who adored him.

❑ BASTION—fortification, stronghold

The club was well known as a *bastion* of conservative values in the liberal city.

❑ BAY (v.)—to bark, especially in a deep, prolonged way

The dog *bayed* all night, much to the annoyance of the neighbors.

❑ BECALM—to make calm or still; keep motionless by lack of wind

Most of the sailors fell prey to scurvy as the *becalmed* ship made little or no progress for weeks on end.

❑ BECLOUD—to confuse; darken with clouds

The ink of the squid *beclouded* the water.

❑ BEGUILE—to deceive, mislead; charm

Beguiled by the songs of the Sirens, Odysseus wanted to abandon all his men and forget his family.

❑ BEHEMOTH—huge creature

Titanic's budget became such a *behemoth* that observers predicted that the film would never make a profit.

❑ BELABOR—to insist repeatedly or harp on

I understand completely; you do not need to *belabor* the point.

❑ BELEAGUER—to harass, plague

Mickey's *beleaguered* parents finally gave in to his request for a Nintendo.

❑ BELFRY—bell tower, room in which a bell is hung

The town was shocked when a bag of money was found stashed in the old *belfry* of the church.

❑ BELIE—to misrepresent; expose as false

The first lady's carefree appearance *belied* rumors that she was on the verge of divorcing her husband.

❑ BELITTLE—to represent as unimportant, make light of

Carla's parents scolded her for constantly *belittling* her younger sister's views.

❑ BELLICOSE—warlike, aggressive

Immediately after defeating one of his enemies, the *bellicose* chieftain declared war on another.

❑ BELLIGERENT—hostile, tending to fight

The bartender realized that it would be fruitless to try to subdue the *belligerent* drunk by himself.

❑ BELLOW—to roar, shout

The poor acoustics of the lecture hall required the professor to *bellow* as loud as she could.

❏ BEMUSE—to confuse, stupefy; plunge deep into thought

The computer technician, continually *bemused* by the complex problems he had to deal with each day, decided to quit and find an easier job.

❏ BENCHMARK—standard of measure

The average scores of the previous year's students are used as a *benchmark* against which new applicants are measured.

❏ BENEFACTOR—someone giving aid or money

A mysterious *benefactor* paid off all Robin's bills, making it possible for her to send her children to college.

❏ BENEFICENT—kindly, charitable; doing good deeds; producing good effects

Despite his tough reputation, Kirk was a *beneficent* man, donating millions of dollars to worthy charities.

❏ BENIGHTED—unenlightened

Ben scoffed at the crowd, as he believed it consisted entirely of *benighted* individuals.

❏ BENIGN—kindly, gentle, or harmless

Suraj was relieved to discover that his tumor was *benign* and he did not have cancer after all.

❏ BEQUEATH—to give or leave through a will; to hand down

Grandpa *bequeathed* the house to his daughter and the car to his son.

❏ BERATE—to scold harshly

Andy was embarrassed when his mother *berated* him in public for smashing the family car.

❏ BESEECH—to beg, plead, implore

She *beseeched* him to give her a second chance, but he refused.

❏ BESTIAL—beastly, animal-like

The *bestial* nature of the growl in the dark made the campers shake with fright.

❏ BESTOW—to give as a gift

The students *bestowed* gifts upon the teacher, attempting to procure better grades.

❏ BETOKEN—to indicate, signify, give evidence of

She turned her back to us, *betokening* her hostility.

❏ BEVY—group

As predicted, a *bevy* of teenagers surrounded the rock star's limousine.

❏ BIAS—prejudice, slant

Racial *bias* in employment is illegal in the United States.

❏ BIBLIOGRAPHY—list of books

Please include a *bibliography* at the end of your paper so I can identify your sources.

❏ BIBLIOPHILE—book lover

The librarian was a real *bibliophile*; she knew every author we mentioned.

❏ BILATERAL—two-sided

The battle finally came to a halt when the two sides signed a *bilateral* treaty.

❏ BILK—to cheat, defraud

Though the lawyer seemed honest, the woman feared he would try to *bilk* her out of her money.

❏ BILLET—board and lodging for troops

The old cabins served as the soldiers' *billets* for two months.

❏ BIPED—two-footed animal

Human beings are *bipeds*, whereas horses are quadrupeds.

❏ BISECT—to cut into two (usually equal) parts

We were so hungry that we *bisected* the cake and each ate half.

❏ BLANCH—to pale; take the color out of

The murderess *blanched* when the man she thought she had killed walked into the room.

❏ BLANDISH—to coax with flattery

We *blandished* the bouncer with compliments until he finally let us into the club.

❏ BLASPHEMOUS—cursing, profane, irreverent

The protesters found the politician's offhanded biblical references *blasphemous* and inappropriate.

❏ BLATANT—glaring, obvious, showy

That movie was a *blatant* ripoff of *Star Wars*; they didn't even change the name of the villain!

❏ BLIGHT (v.)—to afflict, destroy

The farmers feared that the previous night's frost had *blighted* the potato crops entirely.

❏ BLITHE—joyful, cheerful, or without appropriate thought

She *blithely* assumed that no one would care if she took the only printer in the office home with her.

❏ BLUDGEON—to hit as with a short, heavy club

Rudy was horrified to discover that vandals had *bludgeoned* his car with a baseball bat.

❏ BOISTEROUS—rowdy, loud, unrestrained

The *boisterous* football fans ran riot in the streets until the police restrained them.

❏ BOMBASTIC—using high-sounding but meaningless language

Mussolini's speeches were mostly *bombastic*; his boasting and outrageous claims had no basis in fact.

❏ BONANZA—extremely large amount; something profitable

Judi was overjoyed at the unexpected *bonanza* of winning the lottery.

❏ BONHOMIE—good-natured geniality; atmosphere of good cheer

The general *bonhomie* that characterized the party made it a joy to attend.

❏ BOON—blessing, something to be thankful for

Dirk realized that his new coworker's computer skills would be a real *boon* to the company.

❏ BOOR—crude person, one lacking manners or taste

"That utter *boor* ruined my recital with his constant guffawing!" wailed the pianist.

❏ BOTANIST—scientist who studies plants

The *botanist* spent endless hours studying the orchids that fascinated her.

❏ BOUNTIFUL—plentiful

Food is *bountiful* in the United States, yet some people are still hungry.

❏ BOURGEOIS—middle-class

The *bourgeois* family was horrified when the lower-class family moved in next door.

❏ BOVINE—cowlike; relating to cows

An epidemic commonly known as "mad cow disease" devastated Britain's *bovine* population not long ago.

❏ BRAZEN—bold, shameless, impudent; of or like brass

"I can't believe Hayward was *brazen* enough to quit during busy season!" fumed his boss.

❏ BREACH—act of breaking, violation

The record company sued the singer for *breach* of contract when he recorded for another company without permission.

❏ BRIGAND—bandit, outlaw

Brigands held up the bank and made off with the contents of the safe.

❏ BROACH (v.)—to mention or suggest for the first time

Polly was nervous about *broaching* the subject of a raise to her boss.

❏ BRUSQUE—rough and abrupt in manner

The bank teller's *brusque* treatment of his customers soon evoked several complaints.

❏ BUFFET (v.)—to toss about

The swing, *buffeted* by the wind, smashed into the tree and broke.

❏ BUFFOON—clown or fool

The boy was known as the school *buffoon*, so he wasn't taken seriously as a candidate for class president.

❏ BULWARK—defense wall; anything serving as defense

The villagers used logs to construct a *bulwark* against the invading army.

❏ BURGEON—to sprout or flourish

We will need major subway expansion to accommodate the *burgeoning* population of the city.

❏ BURLY—brawny, husky

Freddy was a bit intimidated by the tall, *burly* man standing by the bar.

❏ BURNISH—to polish, make smooth and bright

Mr. Frumpkin loved to stand in the sun and *burnish* his luxury car until it gleamed.

❏ BURSAR—treasurer

For billing concerns, please contact the *bursar* via telephone or e-mail.

❏ BUSTLE—commotion, energetic activity

The *bustle* of the crowd made Andrea remember how much she hated Christmas shopping.

❏ BUTT—person or thing that is object of ridicule

Chip's unusual haircut made him the *butt* of jokes at the high school prom.

❏ BUTTRESS (v.)—to reinforce or support

The construction workers attempted to *buttress* the ceiling with pillars.

❏ BYWAY—back road

During rush hour, it is wise to use the *byway* and avoid the traffic.

C

❏ CACOPHONY—jarring, unpleasant noise

The junior high orchestra created an almost unbearable *cacophony* as they tried to tune their instruments.

❏ CADENCE—rhythmic flow of poetry; marching beat

Pierre spoke with a lovely *cadence*, charming all those who heard him.

❏ CAJOLE—to flatter, coax, persuade

The spoiled girl could *cajole* her father into buying her anything.

❏ CALAMITOUS—disastrous, catastrophic

Everyone hoped this year's event would be less *calamitous* than last year's fiasco.

❏ CALLOUS—thick-skinned, insensitive

Mrs. Meriwether *callously* ignored the pathetic whining of the injured puppy.

❏ CALLOW—immature, lacking sophistication

The young and *callow* fans hung on every word the talk show host said.

❏ CALUMNY—false and malicious accusation, misrepresentation, slander

The unscrupulous politician used *calumny* to bring down his opponent in the senatorial race.

❏ CANDOR—honesty of expression

The *candor* of his confession impressed his parents, and they gave him a light punishment as a result.

❏ CANNY—smart; founded on common sense

The executive's *canny* business sense saved the company from bankruptcy.

❏ CANONIZE—to declare a person a saint; raise to highest honors

Discrimination may be the reason certain authors have not been *canonized* by the literary establishment.

❑ CANVASS—to examine thoroughly; conduct a poll

After *canvassing* people for months, the market researchers finally tabulated the results.

❑ CAPACIOUS—large, roomy; extensive

We wondered how many hundreds of stores occupied the *capacious* mall.

❑ CAPITULATE—to submit completely, surrender

After atom bombs devastated Hiroshima and Nagasaki, the Japanese had little choice but to *capitulate*.

❑ CAPRICIOUS—impulsive, whimsical, without much thought

Queen Elizabeth I was quite *capricious*; her courtiers could never be sure who would catch her fancy.

❑ CARDIOLOGIST—physician specializing in diseases of the heart

Although a famous *cardiologist* performed the operation, Kevin's heart transplant was unsuccessful.

❑ CARICATURE—exaggerated portrait, cartoon

The star was extremely upset by the unflattering *caricature* of him that appeared in the magazine.

❑ CARNAL—of the flesh

Although nothing of a truly intimate, *carnal* nature had occurred between the senator and his intern, he was forced to resign when the scandal broke out.

❑ CARNIVOROUS—meat-eating

Dogs, as *carnivorous* animals, generally do not do well on purely vegetarian diets.

❑ CARP (v.)—to find fault, complain constantly

If the new employee hadn't *carped* all the time, she might not have been fired.

❑ CARTOGRAPHY—science or art of making maps

Shawn's interest in *cartography* may stem from the extensive traveling he did as a child.

❑ CAST (n.)—copy, replica

The proud parents made a *cast* of their infant's first pair of shoes.

❑ CAST (v.)—to fling, to throw

Embarrassed, the fisherman *cast* his empty line back into the water.

❑ CASTIGATE—to punish, chastise, criticize severely

Authorities in Singapore harshly *castigate* perpetrators of what would be considered minor crimes in the United States.

❑ CATALYST—something causing change without being changed

The imposition of harsh taxes was the *catalyst* that finally brought on the revolution.

❑ CATEGORICAL—absolute, without exception

Annette *categorically* denied any involvement in the crime that led to her husband's arrest.

❑ CATHARSIS—purification, cleansing

Plays can be more satisfying if they end in some sort of emotional *catharsis* for the characters involved.

❏ CATHOLIC—universal; broad and comprehensive

Hot tea with honey is a *catholic* remedy for a sore throat.

❏ CAUCUS—smaller group within an organization; a meeting of such a group

The president met with the delegated *caucus* to discuss the national crisis.

❏ CAULK—to make watertight

As a precaution, the sailors *caulked* the ship's windows with fiberglass.

❏ CAUSALITY—cause-and-effect relationship

There was definite *causality* between the dog's shedding fur and the humid weather.

❏ CAUSTIC—biting, sarcastic; able to burn

Dorothy Parker gained her reputation for *caustic* wit from her cutting, yet clever, insults.

❏ CAVALIER—carefree, happy; with lordly disdain

The nobleman's *cavalier* attitude towards the suffering of the peasants made them hate him.

❏ CAVORT—to frolic, frisk

The puppies looked adorable as they *cavorted* in the grass.

❏ CEDE—to surrender possession of something

Argentina *ceded* the Falkland Islands to Britain after a brief war in which it was soundly defeated.

❏ CENSORIOUS—severely critical

Saddam, unconcerned by the *censorious* attitude of the U.N., continued his nuclear weapons testing.

❏ CENTRIPETAL—directed or moving towards the center

It is *centripetal* force that keeps trains from derailing as they round curves.

❏ CERTITUDE—assurance, freedom from doubt

According to Oliver Wendell Holmes, *certitude* is not the test of certainty.

❏ CESSATION—temporary or complete halt

The *cessation* of hostilities ensured that soldiers were able to spend the holidays with their families.

❏ CESSION—act of surrendering something

After the *cession* of his crown to his younger brother, the former king felt extremely depressed.

❏ CHAGRIN—shame, embarrassment, humiliation

No doubt, the president felt a good deal of *chagrin* after vomiting on his neighbor at the state banquet.

❏ CHALICE—goblet, cup

The knight drank from the jewel-encrusted *chalice* with great enjoyment.

❏ CHAMPION (v.)—to defend or support

Ursula continued to *champion* the rights of the prisoner, even after it was proven beyond a doubt that he was guilty.

❏ CHAOTIC—extremely disorderly

His office was so *chaotic* that he couldn't find the proposal he was supposed to present.

❑ CHARLATAN—quack, fake

"That *charlatan* of a doctor prescribed the wrong medicine for me!" complained the patient.

❑ CHARY—watchful, cautious, extremely shy

Mindful of the fate of the Titanic, the captain was *chary* of navigating the iceberg-filled sea.

❑ CHASTISE—to punish, discipline, scold

The little girl was *chastised* for breaking the priceless vase.

❑ CHERUBIC—sweet, innocent, resembling a cherub angel

Her *cherubic* appearance made people think her personality was also sweet, when the opposite was true.

❑ CHICANERY—trickery, fraud, deception

Dishonest used car salesmen often use *chicanery* to sell their beat-up old cars.

❑ CHIDE—to scold, express disapproval

Florence *chided* her poodle for eating the birthday cake she had baked for her friend.

❑ CHIMERICAL—fanciful, imaginary, visionary, impossible

The inventor's plans seemed *chimerical* to the conservative businessman from whom he was asking for financial support.

❑ CHOLERIC—easily angered, short-tempered

The *choleric* principal raged at the students who had come late to school.

❑ CHOICE (adj.)—specially selected, preferred

Wendell took the *choicest* cut of beef for himself, annoying the others at the dinner.

❑ CHORTLE—to chuckle

The jolly old man *chortled* as he watched the amusing sitcom.

❑ CHROMATIC—relating to color

Because he was color blind, his *chromatic* senses were different from those of other people.

❑ CHRONICLER—one who keeps records of historical events

The court *chronicler* wrote a description of the battle, so that future generations could read about the king's heroic exploits.

❑ CIRCUITOUS—roundabout

The cab driver took a *circuitous* route to the airport, making me miss my plane.

❑ CIRCUMFERENCE—boundary or distance around a circle or sphere

The space shuttle set a course around the *circumference* of the Earth.

❑ CIRCUMLOCUTION—roundabout, lengthy way of saying something

He avoided discussing the real issues with endless *circumlocutions*.

❑ CIRCUMNAVIGATE—to sail completely around

The explorer discovered many new lands in his attempt to *circumnavigate* the globe.

❑ CIRCUMSCRIBE—to encircle; set limits on, confine

Diego Buenaventura's country estate is *circumscribed* by rolling hills.

❑ CIRCUMSPECT—cautious, wary

His failures have made Jack far more *circumspect* in his exploits than he used to be.

❑ CIRCUMVENT—to go around; avoid

Laura *circumvented* the hospital's visiting schedule, slipping into her boyfriend's room long after visiting hours were over.

❑ CISTERN—tank for rainwater

When their water supply was cut off, the Rileys had to rely on the rainwater captured by their *cistern*.

❑ CITADEL—fortress or stronghold

The nobleman retreated to his mountain *citadel* to protect himself from a counterattack.

❑ CIVIL—polite; relating to citizens

Police officers are instructed to be *civil* to the general public, although cases of police brutality do occur.

❑ CIVILITY—courtesy, politeness

The subway ticket seller treated his customers with the utmost *civility*, which they appreciated.

❑ CLAIRVOYANT (adj.)—having ESP, psychic

The *clairvoyant* fortuneteller claimed to have communicated with the ghost of Abraham Lincoln.

❑ CLAMOR (v.)—to make a noisy outcry

The chicks *clamored* for worms from their mother's beak.

❑ CLAMOR (n.)—noisy outcry

The *clamor* of children playing outside made it impossible for me to study.

❑ CLANDESTINE—secretive, concealed for a darker purpose

The double agent paid many *clandestine* visits to the president's office in the dead of night.

❑ CLARITY—clearness; clear understanding

Henrietta explained the plan to Greg with the utmost *clarity*, but he still failed to understand.

❑ CLAUSTROPHOBIA—fear of small, confined places

Isaac's *claustrophobia* made it impossible for him to join his friends in exploring the cave.

❑ CLEAVE—to split or separate or to stick, cling, adhere

Brent *cleaved* the log in two in one mighty blow.

❑ CLEMENCY—merciful leniency

Kyle begged for *clemency*, explaining that he had been under the influence of hallucinogens when he robbed the bank.

❑ CLOISTER (v.)—to confine, seclude

The Montagues *cloistered* their wayward daughter in a convent, hoping to keep her out of trouble.

❑ COAGULATE—to clot or change from a liquid to a solid

Hemophiliacs can bleed to death because their blood is incapable of *coagulating*.

❑ COALESCE—to grow together or cause to unite as one

The different factions of the organization *coalesced* to form one united front against their opponents.

❑ CODDLE—to baby, treat indulgently

The strict grandmother frowned disapprovingly as her daughter *coddled* the spoiled, whining infant.

❑ COERCE—to compel by force or intimidation

The thief *coerced* the cashier into handing over all the money in her cash register.

❑ COFFER—strongbox, large chest for money

The taxman chuckled gleefully as he stuffed huge quantities of money into his *coffer*.

❑ COGENT—logically forceful, compelling, convincing

Swayed by the *cogent* argument of the defense, the jury had no choice but to acquit the defendant.

❑ COGNATE—related, similar, akin

The young man was *cognate* to several royal families, making him a hot prospect on the marriage market.

❑ COGNITION—mental process by which knowledge is acquired

If scientists completely understood the processes of *cognition*, the ways in which people learn could be mapped out and education could be revolutionized.

❑ COGNOMEN—family name; any name, especially a nickname

The gambler went by the *cognomen* "Lucky Luke."

❑ COHABIT—to live together

The couple *cohabited* for years before finally deciding to get married.

❑ COHERENT—intelligible, lucid, understandable

Cathy was so tired that her speech was barely *coherent*.

❑ COLLATERAL—accompanying

"Let's try to stick to the main issue here and not get into all the *collateral* questions," urged the CEO.

❑ COLLOQUIAL—characteristic of informal speech

The book was written in a *colloquial* style so that the information in it would be more user-friendly.

❑ COLLOQUY—dialogue or conversation, conference

The congressmen held a *colloquy* to determine how to proceed with the environmental legislation.

❑ COLLUSION—collaboration, complicity, conspiracy

It came to light that the police chief and the mafia were in *collusion* in running the numbers racket.

❑ COMELINESS—physical grace and beauty

Ann's *comeliness* made her perfect for the role of Sleeping Beauty.

❑ COMMEND—to compliment, praise

The teacher *commended* Yumi on her brilliant performance on the exam.

❑ COMMENSURATE—proportional

Steve was given a salary *commensurate* with his experience.

❑ COMMISSION—fee payable to an agent; authorization

The realtor earned a hefty *commission* on every property he sold.

❑ COMMODIOUS—roomy, spacious

Raqiyah was able to stretch out fully in the *commodious* bathtub.

❑ COMMONPLACE—ordinary, found every day

Computers are *commonplace* in modern offices.

❑ COMMUNICABLE—transmittable

Nurses must wear surgical masks as a precaution when treating people with *communicable* diseases.

❑ COMMUTE—to change a penalty to a less severe one

His death sentence was *commuted* when it was discovered that he was in fact innocent of the crime.

❑ COMPATRIOT—fellow countryman

Halfway across the world from home, Jeff felt most comfortable in the company of his *compatriots*.

❑ COMPELLING (adj.)—having a powerful and irresistible effect

The defense lawyer's *compelling* arguments made the jurors sympathize with the cold-blooded killer.

❑ COMPENSATE—to repay or reimburse

The moving company *compensated* me for the furniture it broke while moving my stuff to the new house.

❑ COMPLACENT—self-satisfied, smug

Philip smiled *complacently* as he was showered with compliments for his handling of the Buckman deal.

❑ COMPLEMENT—to complete, perfect

Gina's pink sweater *complemented* her red hair perfectly.

❑ COMPLIANT—submissive and yielding

Lowell used to fight with his stubborn ex-wife, but his new girlfriend has a more *compliant* personality.

❑ COMPLICITY—knowing partnership in wrongdoing

The two boys exchanged a look of sly *complicity* when their father shouted "Who broke the window?"

❑ COMPOUND (adj.)—complex; composed of several parts

A *compound* word is one containing components that are words in themselves.

❑ COMPRESS—to reduce, squeeze

The campers *compressed* the six-man tent into a tiny package.

❑ COMPULSIVE—obsessive, fanatic

A *compulsive* liar, Reggie told his boss that he had once climbed Mount Everest with a yak on his back.

❑ COMPUNCTION—feeling of uneasiness caused by guilt or regret

It is often said that psychopaths have no consciences, suffering little *compunction* for the pain they cause.

❑ CONCAVE—curving inward

The *concave* shape of the inside of a bowl makes it ideal for holding food.

❑ CONCEDE—to yield, admit

Ralph *conceded* that he should have checked that he had enough gas before driving into the wilderness.

❑ CONCEPTUALIZE—to envision, imagine

It was difficult for me to *conceptualize* how Bert's crackpot scheme could possibly work.

❑ CONCERTO—musical composition for orchestra and one or more soloists

The orchestra performed the *concerto* every night for weeks.

❑ CONCILIATORY—overcoming distrust or hostility

Fred made the *conciliatory* gesture of buying Abby flowers after their big fight.

❑ CONCORD—agreement

The manager and her employees were in *concord* over the necessity of improving the product.

❑ CONCUR—to agree

When Jamal proposed that the staff devote more time to quality control, everyone *concurred*, and the change was made.

❑ CONDONE—to pardon or forgive; overlook, justify, or excuse a fault

"We cannot *condone* your behavior," said Raj's parents after he missed his curfew. "You're grounded."

❑ CONDUIT—tube, pipe, or similar passage

The *conduit* carried excess rainwater down to the ocean, preventing flooding.

❑ CONFECTION—something sweet to eat

The children begged for a taste of the delicious *confection*.

❑ CONFISCATE—to appropriate, seize

The FBI agents *confiscated* the heroin shipment and arrested the drug dealers.

❑ CONFLAGRATION—big, destructive fire

After the *conflagration* had finally died down, the city center was nothing but a mass of blackened embers.

❑ CONFLUENCE—meeting place; meeting of two streams

The town of Harper's Ferry, Virginia, was built at the *confluence* of two rivers.

❑ CONFOUND—to baffle, perplex

Vince, *confounded* by the difficult algebra problems, threw his math book at the wall in frustration.

❑ CONGEAL—to become thick or solid, as a liquid freezing

The melted butter *congealed* on the floor, forming a sticky mass.

❏ CONGENIAL—similar in tastes and habits

Couples with *congenial* personalities stay together longer than couples who are polar opposites.

❏ CONGENITAL—existing since birth

The infant's *congenital* deformity was corrected through surgery.

❏ CONGLOMERATE—collected group of varied things

The Acme *conglomerate* manufactured everything from diapers to trucks.

❏ CONGRESS—formal meeting or assembly

The *congress* debated the thorny issues long into the night, but could not reach a compromise.

❏ CONGRUITY—correspondence, harmony, agreement

There was an obvious *congruity* between Mark's pleasant personality and his kind actions towards others.

❏ CONJECTURE—speculation, prediction

The actor refused to comment, forcing gossip columnists to make *conjectures* on his love life.

❏ CONJUGAL—pertaining to marriage

Larry terminated all *conjugal* relations with his wife after he discovered that she was having an affair.

❏ CONJURE—to evoke a spirit, cast a spell

The cotton candy *conjured* up the image of the fairgrounds he used to visit as a child in Arthur's mind.

❏ CONNIVE—to conspire, scheme

The customs officials were not above *conniving* with criminals in smuggling drugs into the country.

❏ CONSANGUINEOUS—of the same origin; related by blood

The geologist discovered that the rocks of the two sides of the canyon were *consanguineous*, indicating that at one point in time they had been joined together.

❏ CONSCIENTIOUS—governed by conscience; careful and thorough

Harrison wrote *conscientiously* in his diary, never missing a day if he could help it.

❏ CONSECRATE—to declare sacred; dedicate to a goal

The priest *consecrated* the clothing of the saint, and it was placed in the church to be worshiped.

❏ CONSENSUS—unanimity, agreement of opinion or attitude

The jurors finally reached a *consensus* and declared the defendant guilty as charged.

❏ CONSIGN—to commit, entrust

Gertrude *consigned* her cat to the care of her neighbor while she vacationed in Costa Rica.

❏ CONSOLATION—something providing comfort or solace for a loss or hardship

The millions she inherited were little *consolation* to the grief-stricken widow.

❏ CONSOLIDATE—to combine, incorporate

The author *consolidated* various articles she had previously published into one book.

❑ CONSONANT (adj.)—consistent with, in agreement with

The pitiful raise Ingrid received was *consonant* with the low opinion her manager had of her performance.

❑ CONSTITUENT—component, part; citizen, voter

A machine will not function properly if one of its *constituents* is defective.

❑ CONSTRAINED—forced, compelled; confined, restrained

Oscar, *constrained* by the limitations his editor imposed upon him, had to cut 2,000 pages from his book.

❑ CONSTRAINT—something that forces or compels; something that restrains or confines

The madman was put in a strait jacket, but this *constraint* was insufficient to prevent him from injuring five orderlies.

❑ CONSTRUE—to explain or interpret

"I wasn't sure how to *construe* that last remark he made," said Delia, "but I suspect it was an insult."

❑ CONSUMMATE (adj.)—accomplished, complete, perfect

The skater delivered a *consummate* performance, perfect in every aspect.

❑ CONSUMMATE (v.)—to complete, fulfill

Since the marriage was never *consummated*, the couple was able to legally annul it.

❑ CONTEND—to battle, clash; compete

No boxer, past or present, would have been able to *contend* with Muhammad Ali in his prime.

❑ CONTENTIOUS—quarrelsome, disagreeable, belligerent

The *contentious* gentleman in the bar angrily ridiculed whatever anyone said.

❑ CONTINENCE—self-control, self-restraint

Lucy exhibited impressive *continence* in steering clear of fattening foods, and she lost 50 pounds.

❑ CONTRAVENE—to contradict, deny, act contrary to

The watchman *contravened* his official instructions by leaving his post for an hour.

❑ CONTRITE—deeply sorrowful and repentant for a wrong

After three residents were mugged in the lobby while the watchman was away from his post, he felt very *contrite*.

❑ CONTUSION—bruise

The boxer had ugly *contusions* all over his face after the fight.

❑ CONUNDRUM—riddle, puzzle or problem with no solution

The old man puzzled over the *conundrum* for hours, but eventually gave up in disgust.

❑ CONVALESCENCE—gradual recovery after an illness

During her *convalescence* from the malaria attack, Tatiana read dozens of novels.

❑ CONVENE—to meet, come together, assemble

The members of the board *convene* at least once a week.

❑ CONVENTIONAL—typical, customary, commonplace

Conventional wisdom today says that a good job requires a college education.

❑ CONVEX—curved outward

The *convex* shape of his pot belly contrasted sharply with his wife's tautly concave stomach.

❑ CONVIVIAL—sociable; fond of eating, drinking, and people

The restaurant's *convivial* atmosphere contrasted starkly with the gloom of Maureen's empty apartment.

❑ CONVOKE—to call together, summon

The president *convoked* a group of experts to advise him on how to deal with the crisis.

❑ CONVOLUTED—twisted, complicated, involved

Although many people bought *A Brief History of Time*, few could follow its *convoluted* ideas and theories.

❑ COPIOUS—abundant, plentiful

The hostess had prepared *copious* amounts of food for the banquet.

❑ COQUETTE—woman who flirts

The *coquette* flirted shamelessly with all the married men in the room.

❑ CORPOREAL—having to do with the body; tangible, material

Makiko realized that the supposed ghost was *corporeal* in nature when it bumped into a chair.

❑ CORPULENCE—obesity, fatness, bulkiness

Egbert's *corpulence* increased as he spent several hours each day eating and drinking.

❑ CORRELATION—association, mutual relation of two or more things

All too often, there is little *correlation* between the amount of money someone makes and her intelligence.

❑ CORROBORATE—to confirm, verify

Fingerprints *corroborated* the witness's testimony that he saw the defendant in the victim's apartment.

❑ CORRUGATE—to mold in a shape with parallel grooves and ridges

The *corrugated* tin roofs of the shanty town glinted in the haze.

❑ COSMETIC (adj.)—relating to beauty; affecting the surface of something

Cosmetic surgery such as a nose job is generally not covered by insurance.

❑ COSMOGRAPHY—science that deals with the nature of the universe

The scientist's bizarre claims about the universe were not accepted by leading experts in *cosmography*.

❑ COSMOPOLITAN—sophisticated, free from local prejudices

Diplomats are usually more *cosmopolitan* than farmers who have never left the towns they were born in.

❑ COSSET—to pamper, treat with great care

Mimi *cosseted* her toy poodle, feeding it gourmet meals and buying it a silk pillow to sleep on.

❑ COTERIE—small group of persons with a similar purpose

Judith invited a *coterie* of fellow stamp enthusiasts to a stamp-trading party.

❑ COUNTENANCE (n.)—facial expression; look of approval or support

Jeremy was afraid of the new Music Appreciation instructor because she had such an evil *countenance*.

❑ COUNTENANCE (v.)—to favor, support

When the girls started a pillow fight, the baby-sitter warned them, "I will not *countenance* such behavior."

❑ COUNTERMAND—to annul, cancel, make a contrary order

Protestants were relieved when the king *countermanded* his decree that they should be burned at the stake as heretics.

❑ COUNTERVAIL—to counteract, to exert force against

The guerrillas *countervailed* the army offensive by hiding in the jungle and picking off the soldiers one by one.

❑ COVEN—group of witches

The *coven* of witches cackled evilly as they brewed a potion that would turn the prince into a frog.

❑ COVERT—hidden; secret

Spies typically engage in *covert* operations.

❑ COVET—to desire strongly something possessed by another

Harold *coveted* his neighbor's new Mercedes Benz, but he did not have enough money to buy his own.

❑ CRASS—crude, unrefined

Miss Manner watched in horror as her *crass* date belched loudly and snapped his fingers at the waiter.

❑ CRAVEN—cowardly

The *craven* lion cringed in the corner of his cage, terrified of the mouse.

❑ CREDENCE—acceptance of something as true or real

Mr. Biggles couldn't give any *credence* to the charge that his darling son had cheated on his test.

❑ CREDIBLE—plausible, believable

With such a *credible* witness testifying against his client, the lawyer's chances of winning the case were small.

❑ CREDULOUS—gullible, trusting

Although some 4-year-olds believe in the Easter Bunny, only the most *credulous* 9-year-olds do.

❑ CREED—statement of belief or principle

It was a basic tenet of the old man's *creed* that killing was indefensible.

❑ CRESCENDO—gradual increase in volume of sound

The *crescendo* of tension became unbearable as Evel Knievel prepared to jump his motorcycle over the school buses.

❑ CRITERION—standard for judging, rule for testing

Only recently has intelligence become an important *criterion* in the judging of beauty pageants.

❏ CRYPTIC—puzzling

Sherlock Holmes was baffled by the *cryptic* message left on his doorstep.

❏ CUISINE—characteristic style of cooking

French *cuisine* is delicious, yet fattening.

❏ CULMINATION—climax, final stage

Fireworks marked the *culmination* of the festivities.

❏ CULPABLE—guilty, responsible for wrong

The CEO is *culpable* for the bankruptcy of the company; he was, after all, in charge of it.

❏ CULPRIT—guilty person

The police caught the *culprit* eating a doughnut he had stolen in the street outside the burglarized deli.

❏ CUMULATIVE—resulting from gradual increase

"The *cumulative* effect of all this downsizing will be that one day, there won't be enough staff to do the work around here!" exclaimed the exasperated manager.

❏ CUPIDITY—greed

The poverty-stricken man stared at the shining jewels with *cupidity* in his gleaming eyes.

❏ CURATOR—caretaker and overseer of an exhibition, especially in a museum

The *curator* resigned when he could no longer bear begging for donations to keep his museum open.

❏ CURMUDGEON—cranky person

The old man was a notorious *curmudgeon* who snapped at anyone who disturbed him for any reason.

❏ CURSORY—hastily done, superficial

The copy editor gave the article a *cursory* once-over, missing dozens of errors.

❏ CURT—abrupt, blunt

The grouchy shop assistant was curt with one of her customers, and she was reprimanded by her manager.

❏ CURTAIL—to shorten

I had to *curtail* my vacation in the Bahamas after I ran out of money.

❏ CUTLERY—cutting instruments; tableware

The restaurant was notorious for not washing its *cutlery* properly.

❏ CYGNET—young swan

Cygnets may look like ugly, clumsy ducklings, but they grow up to be graceful swans.

❏ CYNIC—person who distrusts the motives of others

Have we become a nation of *cynics* who have lost faith in our own system of government?

D

❑ DAINTY—delicate, sweet

The slim, *dainty* girl made a perfect ballerina.

❑ DAUNT—to discourage, intimidate

She was *daunted* by the enormity of the task before her.

❑ DEARTH—lack, scarcity, insufficiency

The *dearth* of supplies in our city made it difficult to hold out for long against the attack of the aliens.

❑ DEBASE—to degrade or lower in quality or stature

The president's deceitful actions *debased* the stature of his office.

❑ DEBAUCH—to corrupt, seduce from virtue or duty; indulge

After the unscrupulous count *debauched* the innocent girl, she was shunned by her fellow villagers.

❑ DEBILITATE—to weaken, enfeeble

Debilitated by the flu, the postman was barely able to finish his rounds.

❑ DEBUNK—to discredit, disprove

It was the teacher's mission in life to *debunk* the myth that girls are bad at math.

❑ DEBUTANTE—young woman making debut in high society

The *debutante* spent hours dressing for her very first ball, hoping to catch the eye of an eligible bachelor.

❑ DECAPITATE—to behead

In late 18th-century France, the guillotine was used to *decapitate* the enemies of the revolution.

❑ DECATHLON—athletic contest with ten events

Only the most versatile athletes can do well on an event like the *decathlon*.

❑ DECIDUOUS—losing leaves in the fall; short-lived, temporary

Deciduous trees are bare in winter, which is why coniferous trees such as evergreens are used as Christmas trees.

❑ DECLIVITY—downward slope

Because the village was situated on the *declivity* of a hill, it never flooded.

❑ DECOROUS—proper, tasteful, socially correct

The countess trained her daughters in the finer points of *decorous* behavior, hoping they would make a good impression when she presented them at Court.

❑ DECORUM—proper behavior, etiquette

The duke complained that the vulgar peasants lacked the *decorum* appropriate for a visit to the palace.

❑ DECRY—to belittle, openly condemn

Governments all over the world *decried* the dictator's vicious massacre of the helpless peasants.

❑ DEFACE—to mar the appearance of, vandalize

After the wall was torn down, statues of Communist leaders were *defaced* all over the former Eastern bloc.

❑ DEFAMATORY—slanderous, injurious to the reputation

The tabloid was sued for making *defamatory* statements about the celebrity.

❑ DEFERENTIAL—respectful and polite in a submissive way

The respectful young law clerk treated the Supreme Court justice very *deferentially*.

❑ DEFILE—to dirty, spoil; to disgrace, dishonor

The natives became enraged after the insensitive explorer spat in their temple, *defiling* it.

❑ DEFINITIVE—clear-cut, explicit or decisive

The brilliant 1949 production has been hailed as the *definitive* version of *A Doll's House*.

❑ DEFLATION—decrease, depreciation

The *deflation* of the currency resulted in financial disaster for many ordinary Russians.

❑ DEFORM—to disfigure, distort

Betty shrieked at the sight of the *deformed* features of the circus freak.

❑ DEFT—skillful, dexterous

It was a pleasure to watch the *deft* carpenter as he repaired the furniture.

❑ DEFUNCT—no longer existing, dead, extinct

That factory, which used to produce bowler hats, has been *defunct* for many years.

❑ DELECTABLE—appetizing, delicious

"That cake was simply *delectable*!" cooed Mrs. Vanderbilt, congratulating the chef.

❑ DELEGATE (v.)—to give powers to another

After learning to *delegate* more work to his assistants, the manager reduced his stress level significantly.

❑ DELETERIOUS—harmful, destructive, detrimental

If we put these defective clocks on the market, it could be quite *deleterious* to our reputation.

❑ DELINEATION—depiction, representation

Mrs. Baxter was very satisfied with the artist's *delineation* of her new mansion.

❑ DELTA—tidal deposit at the mouth of a river

The *delta* of the Nile river is a very impressive sight from the air.

❑ DELUGE (n.)—flood

The president's veto of the housing bill brought a *deluge* of angry calls from people all over America.

❑ DELUGE (v.)—to submerge, overwhelm

The popular actor was *deluged* with fan mail.

❑ DEMAGOGUE—leader, rabble-rouser, usually using appeals to emotion or prejudice

Hitler began his political career as a *demagogue*, giving fiery speeches in the beerhalls of Munich.

❑ DEMARCATION—borderline; act of defining or marking a boundary or distinction

The Berlin Wall formed a clear *demarcation* between East and West Berlin.

❑ DEMEAN—to degrade, humiliate, humble

The editor felt that it would *demean* the newspaper to publish letters containing obscenities.

❑ DEMOGRAPHICS—data relating to study of human population

Demographics seem to indicate that the population of the world will double within the foreseeable future.

❑ DEMOTE—to reduce to a lower grade or rank

The army will *demote* any soldier who disobeys orders.

❑ DEMOTION—lowering in rank or grade

Disgruntled by his *demotion*, the accountant planned to search for a new job.

❑ DEMUR—to express doubts or objections

When scientific authorities claimed that all the planets revolved around the Earth, Galileo, with his superior understanding of the situation, was forced to *demur*.

❑ DEMYSTIFY—to remove mystery from, clarify

The process by which traits are inherited was *demystified* by the discovery of the gene.

❑ DENIGRATE—to slur or blacken someone's reputation

The people still loved the president, despite his enemies' attempts to *denigrate* his character.

❑ DENOUNCE—to accuse, blame

After Stella *denounced* her coworkers for stealing pencils from the office, she was promoted.

❑ DENUDE—to make bare, uncover, undress

The mountain was completely *denuded* by uncontrolled logging.

❑ DENUNCIATION—public condemnation

The church staged a public *denunciation* of Galileo for his controversial beliefs.

❑ DEPICT—to describe, represent

Official royal portraits generally *depict* their subjects in a flattering light.

❑ DEPLETE—to use up, exhaust

The ozone layer is gradually being *depleted* by pollution.

❑ DEPLORE—to express or feel disapproval of; regret strongly

"I simply *deplore* your table manners," she told him, as he stuck his head into the bowl to lick up the last of the oatmeal.

❑ DEPLOY—to spread out strategically over an area

The general *deployed* his troops all over the region, overwhelming the enemy through sheer numbers.

❑ DEPOSE—to remove from a high position, as from a throne

After being *deposed* from his throne, the king spent the rest of his life in exile.

❏ DEPRAVITY—sinfulness, moral corruption

The *depravity* of the actor's Hollywood lifestyle shocked his traditional parents.

❏ DEPRECATE—to belittle, disparage

Ernest *deprecated* his own contribution, instead praising the efforts of his coworkers.

❏ DEPRECIATE—to lose value gradually

The Barrettas sold their house, fearful that its value would *depreciate* due to the nuclear reactor being built around the corner.

❏ DERIDE—to mock, ridicule, make fun of

The awkward child was often *derided* by his "cooler" peers.

❏ DERIVATIVE—copied or adapted; not original

The TV show was so obviously *derivative* of *Seinfeld* that viewers who prize originality were not interested in watching it.

❏ DERIVE—to originate; take from a certain source

Maple syrup is *derived* from the sap of maple trees.

❏ DEROGATE—to belittle, disparage

The sarcastic old man never stopped *derogating* the efforts of his daughter, even after she won the Nobel Prize.

❏ DESECRATE—to abuse something sacred

The archaeologist tried to explain to the explorer that he had *desecrated* the temple by spitting in it, but to no avail.

❏ DESICCATE—to dry completely, dehydrate

After a few weeks of lying on the desert's baking sands, the cow's carcass became completely *desiccated*.

❏ DESIST—to stop doing something

The old man was ordered to *desist* from breeding rats in his apartment by the manager.

❏ DESPONDENT—feeling discouraged and dejected

Mr. Baker was lonely and *despondent* after his wife's death.

❏ DESPOT—tyrannical ruler

The *despot* executed half the nobles in his court on a whim.

❏ DESTITUTE—very poor, poverty-stricken

After the stock market crash, Jeanette was *destitute*, forced to beg on the streets in order to survive.

❏ DESULTORY—at random, rambling, unmethodical

Diane had a *desultory* academic record; she had changed majors 12 times in 3 years.

❏ DETER—to discourage; prevent from happening

Some sociologists claim that the death penalty does not really *deter* criminals from committing crimes.

❏ DETERMINATE—having defined limits; conclusive

The sweeper violated the *determinate* rules of his caste by shaking hands with the Brahmin priest.

❑ DETRIMENTAL—causing harm or injury

It is generally acknowledged that cigarette smoking can be *detrimental* to your health.

❑ DEVIATE—to stray, wander

As long as you don't *deviate* from the trail, you should be fine out there in the wilderness.

❑ DEVIATION—departure, exception, anomaly

The supervisor would not tolerate any *deviation* from his established way of doing things.

❑ DEVOID—totally lacking

Roger is utterly *devoid* of tact; did you hear him tell that off-color joke at the funeral?

❑ DEVOUT—deeply religious

Priests and nuns are known to be *devout* people.

❑ DEXTEROUS—skilled physically or mentally

The gymnast who won the contest was far more *dexterous* than the other competitors.

❑ DIABOLICAL—fiendish; wicked

Sherlock Holmes's archenemy is the *diabolical* Professor Moriarty.

❑ DIALECT—regional style of speaking

Jay has lost his original southern *dialect* completely; he sounds like he was born in New York City.

❑ DIAPHANOUS—allowing light to show through; delicate

Ginny's *diaphanous* gown failed to disguise the fact that she was wearing ripped panty hose.

❑ DIATRIBE—bitter verbal attack

During the CEO's lengthy *diatribe*, the board members managed to remain calm and self-controlled.

❑ DICHOTOMY—division into two parts

Westerns often feature a simple *dichotomy* between good guys and bad guys.

❑ DICTUM—authoritative statement; popular saying

Chris tried to live his life in accordance with the *dictum* "Two wrongs don't make a right."

❑ DIDACTIC—excessively instructive

The father was overly *didactic* with his children, turning every activity into a lesson.

❑ DIFFERENTIATE—to distinguish between two items

Ned hoped that his fiancée would not be able to *differentiate* between a real diamond ring and the ring he had bought her.

❑ DIFFIDENCE—shyness, lack of confidence

Steve's *diffidence* during the job interview stemmed from his nervous nature and lack of experience.

❑ DIFFRACT—to cause to separate into parts, especially light

The crystal *diffracted* the ray of sunlight, separating it into beams of all the colors of the spectrum.

❑ DIFFUSE—widely spread out

The smoke was *diffuse*, spreading instead of concentrating in the room in which the fire had started.

❑ DIGRESS—to turn aside; to stray from the main point

The professor *digressed* repeatedly from the subject of the lecture, boring his students.

❑ DILAPIDATED—in disrepair, run down, neglected

It was amazing that the *dilapidated* jalopy could still be driven.

❑ DILATE—to enlarge, swell, extend

When you enter a darkened room, the pupils of your eyes *dilate* to let in more light.

❑ DILATORY—slow, tending to delay

The congressman used *dilatory* measures to delay the passage of the bill.

❑ DILUVIAL—relating to a flood

Mandy came home after the flood to find her basement filled with *diluvial* deposits.

❑ DIMINUTIVE—small

Napoleon made up for his *diminutive* stature with his aggressive personality, terrifying his courtiers.

❑ DIPLOMACY—discretion, tact

Ambassadors need to be skilled in the art of *diplomacy* in order to deal with erratic foreign governments.

❑ DIRGE—funeral hymn

The deceased's relatives wept as the mournful *dirge* was played on the funeral home's organ.

❑ DISAFFECTED—discontented and disloyal

The *disaffected* employee spent most of his time at work surfing the Web for job opportunities and sending out résumés.

❑ DISARRAY—clutter, disorder

Johnny's room fell into *disarray* after his mother decided to stop cleaning it up for him.

❑ DISBAND—to break up

The rock group decided to *disband* after their record sold fewer than 100 copies.

❑ DISBAR—to expel from legal profession

The lawyer was *disbarred* after he was accused of bribing a juror.

❑ DISBURSE—to pay out

The government *disbursed* millions of dollars to reform elementary schools.

❑ DISCERN—to perceive something obscure

It is easy to *discern* the difference between real butter and butter-flavored topping.

❑ DISCLAIM—to deny, disavow

Francine's statement was so silly that she later *disclaimed* it, pretending she had never made it.

❑ DISCLOSE—to confess, divulge

The CIA agent *disclosed* that he had been selling top secret information to the enemy for years.

❑ DISCONCERTING—bewildering, perplexing, slightly disturbing

Brad found his mother-in-law's hostile manner so *disconcerting* that he acted like a fool in her presence.

❑ DISCORDANT—harsh-sounding, badly out of tune

The harpsichord sounded completely *discordant* after not having been played for 50 years.

❑ DISCREDIT—to dishonor or disgrace

The war hero was *discredited* after it was revealed that he had fled in terror from the scene of the battle.

❑ DISCREDITED—disbelieved, discounted; disgraced, dishonored

The *discredited* evangelist struggled to win back his flock, begging their forgiveness for his sins.

❑ DISCREPANCY—difference between

The obvious *discrepancy* between the appearance of the man and the photo in his passport led officials to believe that the passport was a fake.

❑ DISCRETIONARY—subject to one's own judgment

Ambassadors have some *discretionary* powers, though they must bow to the authority of the secretary of state.

❑ DISCURSIVE—wandering from topic to topic

The professor, known for his *discursive* speaking style, covered everything from armadillos to zebras in his zoology lecture.

❑ DISDAIN—to regard with scorn and contempt

The gorgeous contestant *disdained* her competitors, certain that she would win the Miss America crown.

❑ DISDAINFUL—contemptuous, scornful

The interior designer's face took on a *disdainful* expression as he inspected the tacky, vulgar apartment.

❑ DISENGAGED—disconnected, disassociated

Disengaged from the proceedings, the aged senator didn't notice when the fire drill went off.

❑ DISGORGE—to vomit, discharge violently

The drunken man *disgorged* huge quantities of beer, then passed out.

❑ DISHEVELED—untidy, disarranged, unkempt

After his car broke down and he had to walk to work through the rain, Pete showed up at work *disheveled*.

❑ DISINCLINED—averse, unwilling, lacking desire

Harry was *disinclined* to put a lot of effort into his homework, since the teacher never checked it.

❑ DISPARAGE—to belittle, speak disrespectfully about

Gregorio loved to *disparage* his brother's dancing skills, pointing out every mistake he made on the floor.

❑ DISPARATE—dissimilar, different in kind

Although the twins appear to be identical physically, their personalities are *disparate*.

❑ DISPARITY—contrast, dissimilarity

There was a marked *disparity* between his high opinion of himself and the low opinion others had of him.

- ❑ DISPASSIONATE—free from emotion; impartial, unbiased

  Judges should be as *dispassionate* as possible when adjudicating a court case.

- ❑ DISPEL—to drive out or scatter

  Arnie's heroic rescue of the family from the flames *dispelled* any doubts that he could be a good fireman.

- ❑ DISPENSE—to distribute, administer

  Pharmacists will only *dispense* medicine to customers with doctors' prescriptions.

- ❑ DISPENSE WITH—to suspend the operation of, do without

  "I think we can *dispense with* the formalities, now that we know each other so well," said Mr. Rollins.

- ❑ DISPERSE—to break up, scatter

  The workers *dispersed* after receiving their paychecks, many of them heading for the local bar.

- ❑ DISPIRIT—to dishearten, make dejected

  "Henry's been looking *dispirited* since the failure of his business. I'm worried about him," sighed his wife.

- ❑ DISREPUTE—disgrace, dishonor

  The law firm fell into *disrepute* after it was revealed that one of its lawyers was guilty of jury tampering.

- ❑ DISSEMBLE—to pretend, disguise one's motives

  The villain could *dissemble* to the police no longer—he finally had to confess to the forgery.

- ❑ DISSEMINATE—to spread far and wide

  The wire service *disseminates* information so rapidly that events get reported shortly after they happen.

- ❑ DISSENSION—difference of opinion

  The government was forced to abandon the extensive reforms it had planned, due to continued *dissension* within its party ranks about the form these reforms should take.

- ❑ DISSIPATE—to scatter; to pursue pleasure to excess

  The fog gradually *dissipated*, revealing all the ships docked in the harbor.

- ❑ DISSOCIATE—to separate; remove from an association

  Yun-fat *dissociated* himself from the project when he realized how badly it would turn out.

- ❑ DISSONANT—harsh and unpleasant sounding

  The screeching of the opera singer was completely *dissonant* to the ears of her audience.

- ❑ DISSUADE—to persuade someone to alter original intentions

  I tried to *dissuade* him from climbing Everest without an oxygen tank, but he refused to listen.

- ❑ DISTEND—to swell, inflate, bloat

  Her stomach was *distended* after she gorged on the six-course meal.

❑ DISTRAUGHT—very worried and distressed

The *distraught* mother searched desperately for her missing children.

❑ DITHER—to move or act confusedly or without clear purpose

Ellen *dithered* around her apartment, uncertain how to tackle the family crisis.

❑ DIURNAL—daily

Diurnal creatures tend to become inactive during the night.

❑ DIVINE (v.)—to foretell or know by inspiration

The fortune-teller *divined* from the pattern of the tea leaves that her customer would marry five times.

❑ DIVISIVE—creating disunity or conflict

The leader used *divisive* tactics to pit his enemies against each other.

❑ DOCILE—tame, willing to be taught

Wolves are not as *docile* as dogs, which is why they are not recommended as house pets.

❑ DOCTRINAIRE—rigidly devoted to theories

The professor was *doctrinaire* in his devotion to the theories of Ayn Rand.

❑ DOGMATIC—rigidly fixed in opinion, opinionated

The dictator was *dogmatic*—he, and only he, was right.

❑ DOLEFUL—sad, mournful

Looking into the *doleful* eyes of the lonely pony, the girl decided to take him home with her.

❑ DOLT—idiot, dimwit, foolish person

"You *dolt*," she yelled, spitting out her coffee, "you put salt in the sugar bowl!"

❑ DOMINEER—to rule over something in a tyrannical way

The powerful man *domineered* over his timid wife and children.

❑ DORMANT—at rest, inactive, in suspended animation

The volcano seemed *dormant*, but a devastating eruption was brewing deep in the earth beneath it.

❑ DOTARD—senile old person

The *dotard*, unable to care for himself any longer, was sent to a nursing home.

❑ DOTING—excessively fond, loving to excess

Tony's *doting* father let him get away with all sorts of bad behavior.

❑ DOUR—sullen and gloomy; stern and severe

The *dour* hotel concierge demanded payment for the room in advance.

❑ DOWRY—money or property given by a bride to her husband

Because her parents could offer a large *dowry*, Sonal had her pick of husbands.

❑ DRAFT (v.)—to plan, outline; to recruit, conscript

The boys were *drafted* into the army on their 18th birthday.

☐ DRIVEL—stupid talk; slobber

"I don't want to hear any more of that *drivel*," the impatient wife shouted at her whining husband.

☐ DROLL—amusing in a wry, subtle way

Although the play couldn't be described as hilarious, it was certainly *droll*.

☐ DROSS—waste produced during metal smelting; garbage

The steel mill tried to come up with ways to dispose of *dross* in an environmentally friendly manner.

☐ DULCET—pleasant sounding, soothing to the ear

The *dulcet* tone of her voice lulled me to sleep.

☐ DUPE (v.)—to deceive, trick

Bugs Bunny was able to *dupe* Elmer Fudd by dressing up as a lady rabbit.

☐ DUPE (n.)—fool, pawn

One day, Elmer Fudd decided that he would be Bugs Bunny's *dupe* no longer; he tried to pull off the lady rabbit's wig, only to discover that she was in fact a lady rabbit after all.

☐ DUPLICITY—deception, dishonesty, double-dealing

Diplomatic relations between the two superpowers were outwardly friendly, yet characterized by *duplicity*.

☐ DURABILITY—strength, sturdiness

The all-terrain pickup truck was built for *durability*.

☐ DURATION—period of time that something lasts

Doreen was seasick in her cabin for the entire *duration* of the voyage.

☐ DURESS—threat of force or intimidation; imprisonment

Under *duress*, the political dissident revealed the names of others in his organization to the secret police.

☐ DYSPEPTIC—suffering from indigestion; gloomy and irritable

The *dyspeptic* young man cast a gloom over the party the minute he walked in.

E

☐ EBB—to fade away, recede

Melissa enjoyed watching the *ebb* and flow of the tide from her beachside balcony.

☐ EBULLIENT—exhilarated, full of enthusiasm and high spirits

The *ebullient* child exhausted the baby-sitter, who lacked the energy to keep up with her.

☐ ECLECTIC—selecting from various sources

Budapest's architecture is an *eclectic* mix of eastern and western styles.

☐ ECSTATIC—joyful

Mortimer's parents were *ecstatic* when they learned of his 1600 SAT score.

❑ EDDY—air or wind current

When water gets pulled down a drain, it forms a small *eddy*.

❑ EDICT—law, command, official public order

Pedestrians often disobey the *edict* that they should not jaywalk.

❑ EDIFICE—building

The towering *edifice* dominated the city skyline.

❑ EDIFY—to instruct morally and spiritually

The guru was paid to *edify* the actress in the ways of Buddhism.

❑ EDITORIALIZE—to express an opinion on an issue

Most of the papers in the country *editorialized* on the subject of the president's impeachment.

❑ EFFACE—to erase or make illegible

Benjamin attempted to *efface* all traces of his troubled past by assuming a completely new identity.

❑ EFFERVESCENT—bubbly, lively

Tina's *effervescent* personality made her perfect for the job of game show host.

❑ EFFICACIOUS—effective, efficient

Penicillin was one of the most *efficacious* drugs on the market when it was first introduced; the drug completely eliminated almost all bacterial infections for which it was administered.

❑ EFFIGY—stuffed doll; likeness of a person

The anti-American militants burned Uncle Sam in *effigy* during their demonstration.

❑ EFFLUVIA—outpouring of gases or vapors

Poisonous *effluvia* from the factory contaminated the surrounding countryside.

❑ EFFRONTERY—impudent boldness; audacity

The receptionist had the *effrontery* to laugh out loud when the CEO tripped over a computer wire and fell flat on his face.

❑ EFFULGENT—brilliantly shining

The *effulgent* angel hovering in the dark evening sky dazzled the sharecroppers.

❑ EFFUSIVE—expressing emotion without restraint

The teacher praised Brian *effusively* for his brilliant essay.

❑ EGOCENTRIC—acting as if things are centered around oneself

Craig was so *egocentric* that he didn't even notice that his comments were hurting Pat's feelings.

❑ EGREGIOUS—conspicuously bad

The English text book contained several *egregious* errors; for example, "grammar" was misspelled as "gramer" throughout.

❑ EGRESS—exit

Airplanes should have points of convenient *egress* so that passengers can escape in the event of a crash.

❏ ELATION—exhilaration, joy

The actress was filled with *elation* when she heard that she had been awarded the Emmy.

❏ ELEGY—mournful poem, usually about the dead

Although Thomas Gray's *Elegy Written in a Country Churchyard* is about death and loss, it urges its readers to endure this life, and to trust in spirituality.

❏ ELICIT—to draw out, provoke

The tough policeman was not able to *elicit* the confession he wanted from the murder suspect.

❏ ELOQUENCE—fluent and effective speech

The Gettysburg Address is moving because of its lofty sentiments as well as its *eloquence*.

❏ ELUCIDATE—to explain, clarify

The teacher *elucidated* the reasons why she had failed the student to his upset parents.

❏ EMACIATED—skinny, scrawny, gaunt, especially from hunger

The *emaciated* stray dog begged for scraps from the picnickers.

❏ EMANCIPATE—to set free, liberate

After the slaves were *emancipated*, many of them moved to eastern cities in search of new opportunities.

❏ EMBELLISH—to ornament; make attractive with decoration or details; add details to a statement

Sanjev's story is too short: It needs to be *embellished* with more details about life among the penguins.

❏ EMBEZZLE—to steal money in violation of a trust

The accountant *embezzled* millions of dollars from the company before management discovered what he was up to.

❏ EMBROIL—to involve in; cause to fall into disorder

Lawyers became *embroiled* in the dispute when it became obvious that no compromise could be reached without them.

❏ EMEND—to correct a text

The catalog was *emended* so that correct prices were given for the products on sale.

❏ EMINENT—celebrated, distinguished; outstanding, towering

They were amazed that such an *eminent* scholar could have made such an obvious error.

❏ EMOLLIENT—having soothing qualities, especially for skin

After using the *emollient* lotion for a couple of weeks, Donna's skin changed from scaly to smooth.

❏ EMOTIVE—appealing to or expressing emotion

The film had a strong *emotive* appeal, reducing the audience to tears.

❏ EMPATHY—identification with another's feelings

Having taught English herself, Julie felt a strong *empathy* for the troubled English teacher in the film.

❏ EMULATE—to copy, imitate

The graduate student sought to *emulate* the professor he admired in every way.

❑ ENCIPHER—to translate a message into code

The spy *enciphered* the top-secret document before sending it to headquarters via radio transmitter.

❑ ENCORE—additional performance, often demanded by audience

The soprano performed three *encores*, much to the delight of the enthusiastic audience.

❑ ENCUMBER—to hinder, burden, restrict motion

Encumbered by her huge backpack, Luisa could not run fast enough to catch the bus.

❑ ENDEMIC—belonging to a particular area, inherent

The health department determined that the outbreak was *endemic* to the small village, so they quarantined the inhabitants before the virus could spread.

❑ ENDURANCE—ability to withstand hardships

To prepare for the marathon, Becky built up her *endurance* by running ten miles every day.

❑ ENERVATE—to weaken, sap strength from

The guerrillas hoped that a series of surprise attacks would *enervate* the regular army.

❑ ENGENDER—to produce, cause, bring about

His fear of clowns was *engendered* when he witnessed the death of his father at the hands of a clown.

❑ ENIGMATIC—puzzling, inexplicable

Because he spoke in riddles and dressed in robes, his peers considered the artist's behavior *enigmatic*.

❑ ENJOIN—to urge, order, command; forbid or prohibit, as by judicial order

The stalker was *enjoined* from coming within 100 yards of the woman with whom he was obsessed.

❑ ENMITY—hostility, antagonism, ill-will

After Adams was killed by Bell, the *enmity* between their families continued for hundreds of years.

❑ ENNUI—boredom, lack of interest and energy

Joe tried to alleviate the *ennui* he felt while doing his tedious job by flirting with all his coworkers.

❑ ENORMITY—state of being gigantic or terrible

The manager underestimated the *enormity* of the problem and did not act quickly to solve it, which resulted in disaster.

❑ ENSCONCE—to settle comfortably into a place

Wayne sold the big, old family house and *ensconced* his aged mother in a cozy little cottage.

❑ ENSHROUD—to cover, enclose with a dark cover

The Chinese *enshroud* themselves in white cloths at funerals, since white is the color of mourning.

❑ ENTAIL—to involve as a necessary result, necessitate

The reforms you are suggesting would *entail* massive changes in the way we do things around here.

❑ ENTHRALL—to captivate, enchant, enslave

The children were *enthralled* by the spectacular circus show.

❑ ENTITY—something with its own existence or form

Attempts have been made to preserve Hong Kong as a territorial *entity*, separate from China.

❑ ENTOMOLOGIST—scientist who studies insects

Entomologists protested when several animated movies were released in which ants were given the wrong number of legs.

❑ ENTREAT—to plead, beg

I *entreated* him to just tell me what the problem was instead of bottling it up inside, but he refused.

❑ ENUMERATE—to count, list, itemize

Moses returned from the mountain with tablets on which the commandments were *enumerated*.

❑ ENUNCIATE—to pronounce clearly

Airport announcers must learn to *enunciate* clearly so that international passengers can understand them.

❑ EPHEMERAL—momentary, transient, fleeting

The lives of mayflies seem *ephemeral* to us, since the flies' average life span is a matter of hours.

❑ EPICURE—person with refined taste in food and wine

Restaurant critics should be *epicures*, as people rely on their judgments in choosing where to eat.

❑ EPIGRAM—short, witty saying or poem

The poet was renowned for his skill in making up amusing *epigrams*.

❑ EPIGRAPH—quotation at the beginning of a literary work

The *epigraph* of the book didn't seem to have a connection to the content that followed it.

❑ EPILOGUE—concluding section of a literary work

In the *epilogue* of the novel, the author described the ultimate fate of its characters.

❑ EPITOME—representative of an entire group; summary

The host was the *epitome* of graciousness, making all of his guests feel perfectly comfortable.

❑ EPOCHAL—very significant or influential; defining an epoch or time period

Martin Luther King's "I Have a Dream" speech was *epochal* for the Civil Rights era.

❑ EQUANIMITY—calmness, composure

Kelly took the news that she had been fired with outward *equanimity*, though she was crying inside.

❑ EQUESTRIAN—one who rides on horseback

The *equestrian* visited a horse show to select a new mare for her personal use.

❑ EQUINE—relating to horses

Many donkeys have *equine* characteristics, although they are not horses.

❑ EQUIVOCAL—ambiguous, open to more than one interpretation

Poems are inherently *equivocal*, and there is no point in trying to assign a definitive meaning to them.

❑ EQUIVOCATE—to use vague or ambiguous language intentionally

When faced with criticism of his policies, the politician *equivocated* and left all parties thinking he agreed with them.

❏ ERADICATE—to erase or wipe out

It is unlikely that poverty will ever be completely *eradicated* in this country, though the general standard of living has significantly improved in recent decades.

❏ ERRANT—straying, mistaken, roving

The *errant* elephant was eventually caught and sent back to the zoo.

❏ ERUDITE—learned, scholarly

The annual meeting of professors brought together the most *erudite*, respected individuals in the field.

❏ ESCHEW—to abstain from, avoid

Models generally *eschew* rich desserts because such desserts are fattening.

❏ ESOTERIC—understood by only a learned few

Only a handful of experts are knowledgeable about the *esoteric* world of particle physics.

❏ ESPOUSE—to support or advocate; to marry

Due to his religious beliefs, the preacher could not *espouse* the practice of abortion.

❏ ESTRANGE—to alienate, keep at a distance

Estranged from his family for many years, Alan had not heard that his both his parents had died.

❏ ETHEREAL—not earthly, spiritual, delicate

Her delicate, *ethereal* beauty made her a popular model for pre-Raphaelite artists.

❏ ETHOS—beliefs or character of a group

In accordance with the *ethos* of his people, the teenage boy underwent a series of initiation rituals to become a man.

❏ ETYMOLOGY—origin and history of a word; study of words

The professor devoted himself to an ambitious study of the *etymology* of all words beginning with "E."

❏ EULOGY—high praise, often in a public speech

His best friend gave the *eulogy*, outlining his many achievements and talents.

❏ EUPHEMISM—use of an inoffensive word or phrase in place of a more distasteful one

The funeral director preferred to use the *euphemism* "passed away" instead of the word "dead."

❏ EUPHONY—pleasant, harmonious sound

To their loving parents, the children's orchestra performance sounded like *euphony*, although an outside observer probably would have called it a cacophony of hideous sounds.

❏ EUPHORIA—feeling of well-being or happiness

Euphoria overwhelmed her when she discovered that she had scored a perfect 1600 on her SAT.

❏ EURYTHMICS—art of harmonious bodily movement

Ballerinas must be skilled in the art of *eurythmics*.

❏ EUTHANASIA—mercy killing; intentional, easy, and painless death

The widow claimed that she had committed *euthanasia*, not murder, when she gave her terminally ill husband an overdose of morphine.

❑ EVADE—to avoid, dodge

He *evaded* answering my question by pretending not to hear me and changing the subject.

❑ EVANESCENT—momentary, transitory, short-lived

It is lucky that eclipses are *evanescent*, or the world would never see sunlight.

❑ EVICT—to put out or force out

Mrs. Rose was *evicted* from the apartment when she failed to pay rent for three months in a row.

❑ EVINCE—to show clearly, display, signify

The new secretary *evinced* impressive typing and filing skills.

❑ EVOKE—to inspire memories; to produce a reaction

The sight of the old elm tree *evoked* memories of the treehouse she had built as a little girl.

❑ EXACERBATE—to aggravate, intensify the bad qualities of

It is unwise to take aspirin to relieve heartburn; instead of providing relief, the drug will only *exacerbate* the problem.

❑ EXASPERATION—irritation

The catcher couldn't hide his *exasperation* when the pitcher refused to listen to his advice, throwing a series of pitches that resulted in home runs for the opposing team.

❑ EXCERPT (n.)—selection from a book or play

If you want to reprint an *excerpt* from that play, you'll have to get permission from the author.

❑ EXCOMMUNICATE—to bar from membership in the church

The king was *excommunicated* from the Church when he decided to divorce his wife and remarry.

❑ EXCRUCIATING—agonizing, intensely painful

Although it's a minor injury, stubbing your toe can be *excruciatingly* painful.

❑ EXCULPATE—to clear of blame or fault, vindicate

The adversarial legal system is intended to convict those who are guilty and to *exculpate* those who are innocent.

❑ EXECRABLE—utterly detestable, abhorrent

The stew tasted utterly *execrable* after the cook accidentally dumped a pound of salt into it.

❑ EXHILARATION—state of being energetic or filled with happiness

Fred was filled with *exhilaration* after he learned that he had won the lottery.

❑ EXHORT—to urge or incite by strong appeals

Rob's friends *exhorted* him to beware of ice on the roads when he insisted on driving home in the middle of a snowstorm.

❑ EXHUME—to remove from a grave; uncover a secret

The murder victim's corpse was *exhumed*, but no new evidence was discovered and it was reburied the following day.

❑ EXIGENT—urgent; excessively demanding

The patient was losing blood so rapidly that it was *exigent* to stop the source of the bleeding.

❏ EXONERATE—to clear of blame, absolve

The fugitive was *exonerated* when another criminal confessed to committing the crime.

❏ EXORBITANT—extravagant, greater than reasonable

After the harvest was destroyed by freezing temperatures, shops charged *exorbitant* prices for oranges.

❏ EXORCISE—to expel evil spirits

The priest struggled to *exorcise* the spirit of the Devil from the body of the little girl.

❏ EXOTIC—foreign; romantic, excitingly strange

The atmosphere of the restaurant was *exotic*, but the food was ordinary.

❏ EXPANSIVE—sweeping, comprehensive; tending to expand

"Soon, all this will be mine!" declared the evil emperor, indicating the city below him with an *expansive* sweep of his arm.

❏ EXPATRIATE (n.)—one who lives outside one's native land

He spent much of his adult life as an *expatriate*, only returning to his own country for his retirement.

❏ EXPATRIATE (v.)—to drive someone from his/her native land

Imelda Marcos was *expatriated* from the Phillipines after her husband was deposed.

❏ EXPEDIENT (adj.)—convenient, efficient, practical

It was considered more *expedient* to send the fruit directly to the retailer instead of through a middleman.

❏ EXPIATE—to atone for, make amends for

The nun *expiated* her sins by scrubbing the floor of the convent on her hands and knees.

❏ EXPIRE—to come to an end; die; breathe out

Since her driver's license was about to *expire*, she had to go and exchange it for a new one.

❏ EXPLICABLE—capable of being explained

"I'm sure that all these bizarre events are completely *explicable*," said Nancy, trying to reassure her family that the terrifying sounds coming from the haunted house were nothing to worry about.

❏ EXPLICIT—clearly defined, specific; forthright in expression

The owners of the house left a list of *explicit* instructions detailing their house-sitters' duties.

❏ EXPONENT—one who champions or advocates

The vice president was an enthusiastic *exponent* of computer technology.

❏ EXPOUND—to elaborate; to expand or increase

The teacher *expounded* on the theory of relativity for hours, boring his students.

❏ EXPUNGE—to erase, eliminate completely

The censor wanted to *expunge* all the parts of Joyce's *Ulysses* he thought were obscene.

❏ EXPURGATE—to censor

Government propagandists *expurgated* all negative references to the dictator from the film.

❑ EXTEMPORANEOUS—unrehearsed, on the spur of the moment

Jan gave an *extemporaneous* performance of a Monty Python skit at her surprise birthday party.

❑ EXTENUATE—to lessen the seriousness, strength, or effect of

The fact that the man whom Ronnie shot was trying to strangle him at the time was considered an *extenuating* circumstance, and the judge gave him a fairly light sentence.

❑ EXTINCTION—end of a living thing or species

The dodo was hunted to *extinction* by man many years ago.

❑ EXTOL—to praise

The salesman *extolled* the virtues of the used car he was trying to convince the customer to buy.

❑ EXTORT—to obtain something by threats

The president's ex-lover *extorted* a cushy job from him, threatening to reveal their affair if he did not do as she wished.

❑ EXTRANEOUS—irrelevant, unrelated, unnecessary

When none of the committee members acknowledged that she had even spoken, June realized that her presence at the meeting was completely *extraneous*.

❑ EXTREMITY—outermost or farthest point

The *extremities* of the body, such as toes, are vulnerable to frostbite in extreme cold weather.

❑ EXTRICATE—to free from, disentangle

The fly was unable to *extricate* itself from the flypaper.

❑ EXTRINSIC—not inherent or essential, coming from without

"While it's a cute idea, I'd say that the espresso machine accessory is *extrinsic* to our basic concept of a good, functional car," said the Ford executive.

❑ EXUBERANT—lively, happy, and full of good spirits

The *exuberant* puppy jumped up and licked the face of its master, happy to see him home again.

❑ EXUDE—to give off, ooze

The job candidate *exuded* an aura of self-confidence, impressing his interviewers.

❑ EXULT—to rejoice

The investor *exulted* as the price of the stocks he had bought skyrocketed.

F

❑ FABRICATE—to make or devise; construct

A prefab house is one that is *fabricated* before it is transported to a plot of land.

❑ FABRICATED—constructed, invented; faked, falsified

The reporter was disgraced when it was uncovered that the stories he'd published were largely *fabricated*.

❑ FACADE—face, front; mask, superficial appearance

The drug dealers conducted business from a small bodega in order to maintain a *facade* of respectability.

❑ FACILE—very easy

She was alarmingly *facile* when it came to telling lies; they seemed to roll off her tongue.

❑ FACILITATE—to aid, assist

The organizers tried to *facilitate* the social interaction of the delegates by giving everyone name tags.

❑ FACILITY—aptitude, ease in doing something

Bob had a *facility* for trigonometry problems, although he could not do algebra at all.

❑ FALLACIOUS—wrong, unsound, illogical

We now know that the statement "the Earth is flat" is *fallacious*.

❑ FALLOW—uncultivated, unused

This field should lie *fallow* for a year so that the soil does not become completely depleted.

❑ FANATICISM—extreme devotion to a cause

The stormtroopers' *fanaticism* in their devotion to the Emperor was so great that they would readily have sacrificed their lives for him.

❑ FARCICAL—absurd, ludicrous

"The idea that I would burn down my own house is completely *farcical*," sneered the arson suspect.

❑ FASTIDIOUS—careful with details

Brett was normally so *fastidious* that Rachel was astonished to find his desk littered with clutter.

❑ FATHOM (v.)—to measure the depth of, gauge

The marine scientists used their sophisticated equipment to attempt to *fathom* the depth of the underwater canyon.

❑ FATUOUS—stupid; foolishly self-satisfied

Ted's *fatuous* comments always embarrassed his keen-witted wife at parties.

❑ FAULT—break in a rock formation; mistake or error

The San Andreas *fault* runs under several major urban areas in California, making earthquakes a frequent occurrence.

❑ FAWN (v.)—to flatter excessively, seek the favor of

The understudy *fawned* over the director in hopes of being cast in the part on a permanent basis.

❑ FAZE—to bother, upset, or disconcert

Strangely, the news that his car had been stolen did not *faze* Nathan, although his wife was hysterical.

❑ FEASIBLE—possible, capable of being done

It was decided that the idea of giving away free fur coats was not *feasible*, and it was abandoned.

❑ FECKLESS—ineffective, careless, irresponsible

Anja took on the responsibility of caring for her aged mother, realizing that her *feckless* sister was not up to the task.

❑ FECUND—fertile, fruitful, productive

The *fecund* housewife gave birth to a total of twenty children.

❑ FEDERATION—union of organizations; union of several states, each of which retains local power

The states formed a *federation* in order to put together a united army to resist the attacking foreign power.

❑ FEIGN—to pretend, give a false impression; to invent falsely

Although Sean *feigned* indifference, he was very much interested in the contents of the envelope.

❑ FEISTY—excitable, easily drawn into quarrels

The *feisty* old lady alienated her neighbors with her habit of picking fights with anyone who crossed her.

❑ FELICITOUS—suitable, appropriate; well-spoken

The father of bride made a *felicitous* speech at the wedding, contributing to the success of the event.

❑ FELL (v.)—to chop, cut down

The muscular logger *felled* the tree in one powerful blow.

❑ FERVID—passionate, intense, zealous

The fans of Maria Callas were particularly *fervid*, doing anything to catch a glimpse of the great singer.

❑ FETID—foul-smelling, putrid

The *fetid* stench from the outhouse caused Laura to wrinkle her nose in disgust.

❑ FETTER—to bind, chain, confine

The chain gang, *fettered* together in a long line, trudged slowly through the mud.

❑ FIASCO—disaster, utter failure

After the soloist turned up drunk, it was hardly surprising that the concert proved to be an utter *fiasco*.

❑ FICTIVE—fictional, imaginary

The boy had a *fictive* friend who kept him company during the long hours he had to spend alone.

❑ FIDELITY—loyalty

A traitor is someone whose *fidelity* is questioned.

❑ FILCH—to steal

The pickpocket managed to *filch* ten wallets in the rush hour crowd.

❑ FILIBUSTER—use of obstructive tactics in a legislative assembly to prevent adoption of a measure

Democrats *filibustered* for hours, desperately trying to prevent the adoption of the Republican measure.

❑ FINICKY—fussy, difficult to please

The *finicky* child rejected every dish on the menu, to the exasperation of his parents.

❑ FISSION—process of splitting into two parts

The discovery of the process of nuclear *fission* enabled scientists to construct the atom bomb.

❑ FITFUL—intermittent, irregular

The water came through the tap in *fitful* spurts at first, then began to pour in a steady flow.

❑ FLACCID—limp, flabby, weak

The woman jiggled her *flaccid* arms in disgust, resolving to begin lifting weights as soon as possible.

❑ FLAGRANT—outrageous, shameless

His *flagrant* disregard for the rules has resulted in his dismissal from the job.

❑ FLAMBOYANT—flashy, garish; exciting, dazzling

Reginald's *flamboyant* clothing made him stick out like a sore thumb at his conservative office.

❑ FLAUNT—to show off

Rhonda *flaunted* her engagement ring all over the office.

❑ FLEDGLING—young bird just learning to fly; beginner, novice

The *fledgling* eagle clung to the edge of the cliff, afraid to take its first plunge into the open air.

❑ FLORA—plants

The local *flora* of the Kenyan savannah includes the baobab tree.

❑ FLORID—gaudy, extremely ornate; ruddy, flushed

The palace had been decorated in an excessively *florid* style; every surface had been carved and gilded.

❑ FLOUNDER—to falter, waver; to muddle, struggle

The previously glib defendant began to *flounder* when the prosecutor found a hole in his story.

❑ FLOUT—to treat contemptuously, scorn

The motorist *flouted* the traffic cop's instructions, cutting several cars off to barrel across the intersection.

❑ FLUCTUATE—to alternate, waver

Certain stock prices *fluctuate* so much that it is risky to invest in them.

❑ FODDER—raw material; feed for animals

The gossip columnist chatted with as many celebrities as possible, seeking *fodder* for her articles.

❑ FOIBLE—minor weakness or character flaw

Her habit of licking out the centers of Oreo cookies is a *foible*, not a serious character flaw.

❑ FOIL (v.)—to defeat, frustrate

James Bond *foiled* the villain's evil plot to take over the world.

❑ FOLIATE—to grow, sprout leaves

The plant looked dead, so Victor was astonished when it began to *foliate*.

❑ FOMENT—to arouse or incite

The protesters tried to *foment* feeling against the war through their speeches and demonstrations.

❑ FORBEARANCE—patience, restraint, leniency

In light of the fact that he was new on the job, Collette decided to exercise *forbearance* with her assistant's numerous errors.

❑ FORECLOSE—to rule out; to seize debtor's property for lack of payments

The bank *foreclosed* on the Okie family farm, forcing them to drive to California to look for work.

❑ FORD (v.)—to cross a body of water at a shallow place

Because of the recent torrential rains, the cowboys were unable to *ford* the swollen river.

❑ FOREBODING—dark sense of evil to come

Carrie felt an acute sense of *foreboding* when she thought about the upcoming high school prom.

❑ FORENSIC—relating to legal proceedings; relating to debates

The law school offered an excellent program in *forensics*.

❑ FORESTALL—to prevent, delay; anticipate

The landlord *forestalled* Bob's attempt to avoid paying the rent by waiting for him outside his door.

❑ FORETHOUGHT—anticipation, foresight

If you had given a little *forethought* to your presentation, I'm sure it would have turned out better.

❑ FORGO—to go without, refrain from

In an effort to lose weight, Lisa decided to *forgo* dessert for the next month or so.

❑ FORLORN—dreary, deserted; unhappy; hopeless, despairing

Ying felt *forlorn* at the prospect of moving out of the house in which she had been born.

❑ FORMULATE—to conceive, devise; to draft, plan; to express, state

The marketers *formulated* an advertising strategy to launch the new product on the market.

❑ FORSAKE—to abandon, withdraw from

It is common for criminals on Death Row to feel that everyone they know has *forsaken* them.

❑ FORSWEAR—to repudiate, renounce, disclaim, reject

I was forced to *forswear* french fries after the doctor told me that my cholesterol was too high.

❑ FORTE—strong point, something a person does well

Since math was Dan's *forte*, his friends always asked him to calculate the bill whenever they went out to dinner together.

❑ FORTUITOUS—happening by luck, fortunate

Rochelle got her start in the music industry when a powerful agent happened, *fortuitously*, to attend one of her gigs.

❑ FOSTER—to nourish, cultivate, promote

The record agent *fostered* the development of his clients by sending them to singing lessons.

❑ FOUNDATION—groundwork, support; institution established by donation to aid a certain cause

The claim that the sun revolves around the Earth has no *foundation*; scientific evidence disproves it.

❑ FOUNDER (v.)—to fall helplessly; sink

After colliding with the jagged rock, the ship *foundered*, forcing the crew to abandon it.

❑ FRACAS—noisy dispute

When the bandits discovered that the gambler was cheating them at cards, a violent *fracas* ensued.

❑ FRACTIOUS—unruly, rebellious

The general had a hard time maintaining discipline among his *fractious* troops.

❑ FRAGMENTATION—division, separation into parts, disorganization

After the *fragmentation* of the former India into India, Pakistan, and Bangladesh, ethnic violence erupted.

❑ FRANK—honest and straightforward

"Let me be *frank*: there's no way I would ever hire you," said the recruiter to the job applicant.

❑ FRAUD—deception, hoax

The salesman was arrested for *fraud* after selling 500 acres of mosquito-infested swamp, which he claimed was choice beachside property, to the senior citizens.

❑ FRAUDULENT—deceitful, dishonest, unethical

The factory engaged in *fraudulent* practices, producing radios with no internal components.

❑ FRAUGHT—full of, accompanied by

The sea voyage was *fraught* with peril; the crew had to contend with storms, sharks, and scurvy on board.

❑ FRENETIC—wildly frantic, frenzied, hectic

The *frenetic* manager worked insane hours, trying desperately to finish the important project on time.

❑ FRENZIED—feverishly fast, hectic, and confused

The family made a *frenzied* dash through the airport, arriving at their gate just before their plane took off.

❑ FRIVOLOUS—petty, trivial; flippant, silly

The biggest problem in the world for the *frivolous* debutante was that her ribbon was the wrong color.

❑ FROND—leaf

The fern *fronds* made a beautiful pattern against the window.

❑ FULSOME—sickeningly excessive; repulsive

Diana felt nauseous at the sight of the rich, *fulsome* dishes weighing down the table at the banquet.

❑ FUNEREAL—mournful, appropriate to a funeral

Depressed by the party's *funereal* atmosphere, Suzanne decided to leave early.

❑ FURTIVE—secret, stealthy

Glenn *furtively* peered out of the corner of his eye at the stunningly beautiful model.

❑ FUSION—process of merging things into one

Cement is a *fusion* formed from a combination of shale and limestone.

G

❏ GALL (n.)—bitterness; careless nerve

I cannot believe she had the *gall* to show up late her first day of work.

❏ GALL (v.)—to exasperate and irritate

My uncle constantly *galls* my aunt by putting his feet up on the coffee table.

❏ GAMBOL—to dance or skip around playfully

The parents gathered to watch the children *gambol* about the yard.

❏ GAMELY—courageously

Though Xena lacked sufficient weapons, she *gamely* faced her opponent.

❏ GARGANTUAN—giant, tremendous

Cleaning a teenager's room can often be a *gargantuan* task.

❏ GARNER—to gather and store

The director managed to *garner* financial backing from several different sources for his next project.

❏ GARRULOUS—very talkative

The *garrulous* parakeet distracted its owner with its continuous talking.

❏ GAUNT—thin and bony

The actress's *gaunt* frame led the press to speculate that she was anorexic.

❏ GAVEL—mallet used for commanding attention

The judge pounded the desk with his *gavel* to silence the crowd.

❏ GENRE—type, class, category

My sister loves mysteries, but I can't stand that *genre* of books.

❏ GERMINATE—to begin to grow (as with a seed or idea)

Three weeks after planting, the seeds will *germinate*.

❏ GESTATION—growth process from conception to birth

The longer the *gestation* period of an organism is, the more developed the baby is at birth.

❏ GIBE—to make heckling, taunting remarks

Tina *gibed* at her brothers mercilessly as they clumsily attempted to pitch the tent.

❏ GIRTH—distance around something

The young boy marvelled at the *girth* of his pregnant cat's stomach.

❏ GLIB—fluent in an insincere manner; offhand, casual

The slimy politician managed to continue gaining supporters because he was a *glib* speaker.

❏ GLOBAL—involving the entire world; relating to a whole

People all over the world are finally realizing that pollution is a *global* problem.

❑ GLOWER—to glare, stare angrily and intensely

The cranky waitress *glowered* at the indecisive customer.

❑ GLUTTONY—eating and drinking to excess

It took days for the guests to recover their appetites after the *gluttony* that had taken place at the party.

❑ GNARL—to make knotted, deform

The old oak was extremely *gnarled* after withstanding the force of powerful winds for centuries.

❑ GNOSTIC—having to do with knowledge

The *gnostics* were distrusted by the Church because of their preference for knowledge over faith.

❑ GOAD—to prod or urge

Denise *goaded* her sister Leigh into running the marathon with her.

❑ GRADATION—process occurring by regular degrees or stages; variation in color

The paint store offers so many different *gradations* of red that it's impossible to choose among them.

❑ GRANDILOQUENCE—pompous talk, fancy but meaningless language

The pompous headmistress was notorious for her *grandiloquence* as well as for her ostentatious clothes.

❑ GRANDIOSE—magnificent and imposing; exaggerated and pretentious

The house had a *grandiose* facade that disguised its humble and simple interior.

❑ GRANULAR—having a grainy texture

The chemist poured the *granular* substance into the test tube.

❑ GRASP (v.)—to perceive and understand; to hold securely

Peggy could not *grasp* the concept that Dwight had dumped her, and she continued to call him every day.

❑ GRATIS—free, costing nothing

The college students swarmed around the *gratis* buffet in the lobby.

❑ GRATUITOUS—free, voluntary; unnecessary and unjustified

Matt's snubbing of his old friend seemed *gratuitous*, as there had been no bad blood between the two of them previously.

❑ GRATUITY—something given voluntarily, tip

At many restaurants, an 18 percent *gratuity* is added to the bill when the dining party is large enough.

❑ GREGARIOUS—outgoing, sociable

She was so *gregarious* that when she found herself alone she felt quite sad.

❑ GRIEVOUS—causing grief or sorrow; serious and distressing

Maude and Bertha sobbed loudly throughout the *grievous* event.

❑ GRIMACE—facial expression showing pain or disgust

The count *grimaced* when his wife, drunk as usual, spilled a carafe of wine on the king.

❑ GRIMY—dirty, filthy

Beth was displeased when her date, Spike, showed up in a *grimy* t-shirt and torn jeans.

❑ GROSS (adj.)—obscene; blatant, flagrant

Spike's comment that he liked the "casual" look was a *gross* understatement.

❑ GROSS (n.)—total before deductions

The company's *gross* earnings exceeded their predictions.

❑ GROVEL—to humble oneself in a demeaning way

The dog *groveled* at his owner's feet, hoping for a few table scraps.

❑ GUILE—trickery, deception

Greg used considerable *guile* to acquire his rent-controlled apartment, even claiming to be a Vietnam Vet.

❑ GULLIBLE—easily deceived

The *gullible* landlord believed Rich's story that he was only going away for a few days, despite the moving boxes that littered the apartment.

❑ GUSTATORY—relating to sense of taste

Murdock claimed that he loved cooking because he enjoyed the *gustatory* pleasures in life.

H

❑ HABITAT—dwelling place

A rabbit's *habitat* should be a large, dry area with plenty of food, water, and hay available.

❑ HACKNEYED—worn out by overuse

We always mock my father for his *hackneyed* expressions and dated hairstyle.

❑ HALLOWED—holy; treated as sacred

The Constitution is a *hallowed* document in the United States.

❑ HAMLET—small village

Did you know her husband grew up in a *hamlet* in Sweden? No wonder he can't adjust to New York City.

❑ HAPLESS—unfortunate, having bad luck

I wish someone would give that poor, *hapless* soul some food and shelter.

❑ HARBINGER—precursor, sign of something to come

The groundhog's appearance on February 2 is a *harbinger* of spring.

❑ HARDY—robust, vigorous

Heidi was a strong, *hardy* girl who beat up her older brothers on a daily basis.

❑ HARROWING—extremely distressing, terrifying

We stayed up all night listening to Dave and Will talk about their *harrowing* adventures on the sea.

❑ HASTEN—to hurry, to speed up

Juanita *hastened* to the post office to send off her presents in time for Christmas.

❑ HAUGHTY—arrogant and condescending

The teacher resented Sally's *haughty* attitude and gave her a D for the semester.

❑ HEADSTRONG—reckless; insisting on one's own way

Sally was *headstrong* and brought her teacher up before the school board for unfair grading.

❑ HEATHEN—pagan; uncivilized and irreligious

The missionaries considered it their duty to convert as many of the *heathen* natives as possible.

❑ HECTIC—hasty, hurried, confused

Breakfast at their house was always a *hectic* affair, with ten children running around and screaming.

❑ HEDONISM—pursuit of pleasure as a goal

Michelle lay on the couch eating cookies all day, claiming *hedonism* was her philosophy of life.

❑ HEGEMONY—leadership, domination, usually by a country

When Germany claimed *hegemony* over Russia, Stalin was outraged.

❑ HEIGHTEN—to raise

In the past decade, doctors have worked to *heighten* women's awareness of breast cancer.

❑ HEINOUS—shocking, wicked, terrible

Nobody could believe the *heinous* crime the baby-sitter had committed.

❑ HEMICYCLE—semicircular form or structure

The architect sketched the building in the shape of a *hemicycle*.

❑ HEMORRHAGE (n.)—heavy bleeding

The wounded soldiers worried they would have *hemorrhages* as they awaited the doctor's return.

❑ HEMORRHAGE (v.)—to bleed heavily

The girl applied a bandage to her wound to keep from *hemorrhaging* and losing too much blood.

❑ HERETICAL—opposed to an established religious orthodoxy

After the onset of the Inquisition, the *heretical* priest was forced to flee the country to escape the Church's punishment.

❑ HERMETIC—tightly sealed

The *hermetic* seal of the jar proved impossible to break.

❑ HETERODOX—unorthodox, not widely accepted

After the preacher had delivered his *heterodox* sermon, the congregation was speechless.

❑ HETEROGENEOUS—composed of unlike parts, different, diverse

The United Nations is by nature a *heterogenous* body.

❑ HEW—to cut with an ax

Vlad *hewed* down the trees in order to build himself a cabin.

❏ HIATUS—break, interruption, vacation

Julia Roberts returned to acting after a lengthy *hiatus*.

❏ HIDEBOUND—excessively rigid; dry and stiff

The *hidebound* old patriarch would not tolerate any opposition to his orders.

❏ HINDSIGHT—perception of events after they happen

In *hindsight*, Hank realized that eating the entire box of chocolates himself was probably not a wise idea.

❏ HINTERLAND—wilderness

The anthropologists noticed that the people had moved out of the cities and into the *hinterland*.

❏ HOARY—very old; whitish or gray from age

The old man's *hoary* beard contrasted starkly to the new stubble of his teenage grandson.

❏ HOLISTIC—emphasizing importance of the whole and interdependence of its parts

Angie is studying internal medicine and believes in a *holistic* approach to healing.

❏ HOLOCAUST—widespread destruction, usually by fire

The city was desolate, utterly destroyed by a *holocaust*.

❏ HOMAGE—public honor and respect

Upon arriving at the village, the warriors paid *homage* to its chief.

❏ HOMOGENEOUS—composed of identical parts

Finland was a very *homogenous* country until immigrants began to settle there several decades ago.

❏ HOMONYM—word identical in pronunciation and spelling but different in meaning

"Right" as in the direction and "right" meaning "correct" are *homonyms*.

❏ HONE—to sharpen

You might want to *hone* your writing skills before filling out college applications.

❏ HUMANE—merciful, kindly

A *humane* man, the camp commander made sure to treat all the prisoners of war fairly.

❏ HUSBAND (v.)—to farm; manage carefully and thriftily

The farmer's wife *husbanded* the money she had made from her strawberry preserves all year.

❏ HUTCH—pen or coop for animals; shack, shanty

The rabbits bred so rapidly that soon their *hutch* could not contain them all.

❏ HYDRATE—to add water to

You'll need to *hydrate* these powdered eggs in order to make an omelet from them.

❏ HYGIENIC—clean, sanitary

A century or two ago, it was realized that surgery should be performed under *hygienic* conditions.

❏ HYMN—religious song, usually of praise or thanks

The churchgoers sang a number of *hymns* together in the course of the service.

❏ HYPERBOLE—purposeful exaggeration for effect .

When the mayor claimed his town was one of the seven wonders of the world, outsiders classified his statement as *hyperbole*.

❏ HYPERVENTILATE—to breathe abnormally fast

During her anxiety attack, Joan *hyperventilated* and sweated profusely.

❏ HYPOCHONDRIA—unfounded belief that one is often ill

Dr. Pradesh groaned when he saw Mr. Crupp on his appointment list yet again; the man was a classic victim of *hypochondria*.

❏ HYPOCRITE—person claiming beliefs or virtues he or she doesn't really possess

The prudish evangelist was accused of being a *hypocrite* when he was discovered with a prostitute.

❏ HYPOTHERMIA—abnormally low body temperature

The Arctic explorer, suffering from *hypothermia*, was wrapped in thick blankets by his companions.

❏ HYPOTHESIS—assumption subject to proof

It's an interesting *hypothesis*, but I'll need proof before I'll believe that Pluto is made of cheese.

❏ HYPOTHETICAL—theoretical, speculative

The official claimed that his radical proposal to close half the city hospitals was only *hypothetical*.

I

❏ ICONOCLAST—one who attacks traditional beliefs

His lack of regard for traditional beliefs soon established him as an *iconoclast*.

❏ IDEALISM—pursuit of noble goals

"I admire his *idealism*, but how does Bola think he can support ten orphans?" complained his sister.

❏ IDIOSYNCRASY—peculiarity of temperament, eccentricity

His numerous *idiosyncrasies* included a fondness for wearing bright green shoes with mauve socks.

❏ IGNOBLE—dishonorable, not noble in character

The *ignoble* grocer took pleasure in selling his customers flour that was laced with dust.

❏ IGNOMINIOUS—disgraceful and dishonorable

He was humiliated by his *ignominious* dismissal.

❏ ILK—type or kind

"I try not to associate with men of his *ilk*," sniffed the respectable old lady.

❏ ILLICIT—illegal, improper

The mafia is heavily involved in *illicit* activities such as racketeering and drugs.

❏ ILLIMITABLE—limitless

The universe is considered *illimitable*, or in any case so large that humans cannot fathom its end.

❑ ILLUSORY—unreal, deceptive

The desert explorer was devastated to discover that the lake he had seen in the distance was in fact *illusory*.

❑ ILLUSTRIOUS—famous, renowned

The *illustrious* composer produced masterpiece after masterpiece, entrancing her fans.

❑ IMBUE—to infuse; dye, wet, moisten

Marcia struggled to *imbue* her children with decent values, a difficult task in this day and age.

❑ IMMACULATE—spotless; free from error

After I cleaned my apartment for hours, it was finally *immaculate*.

❑ IMMATERIAL—extraneous, inconsequential, nonessential; not consisting of matter

"Where you get the money is *immaterial* to me; just pay up!" grumbled the loanshark.

❑ IMMENSE—enormous, huge

In the main hall of the museum, the *immense* dinosaur skeleton towered over the children.

❑ IMMERSE—to bathe, dip; to engross, preoccupy

The Japanese snow monkey *immersed* itself in the hot spring.

❑ IMMOBILE—not moveable; still

Although Gerald's legs have been *immobile* since the accident, he gets around pretty well with his crutches.

❑ IMMUNE—exempt; protected from harm or disease; unresponsive to

After you get chicken pox once, you are *immune* to the disease.

❑ IMMUNOLOGICAL—relating to immune system

Her *immunological* system was severely damaged by the onset of AIDS, making her vulnerable to illness.

❑ IMMUTABLE—unchangeable, invariable

Poverty was an *immutable* fact of life for the unfortunate Wood family; every moneymaking scheme they tried failed.

❑ IMPAIR—to damage, injure

After embroidering in poor light for decades, Doris's vision became *impaired*.

❑ IMPASSE—blocked path, dilemma with no solution

The rock slide produced an *impasse* so that we could proceed no further on the road.

❑ IMPASSIONED—with passion

The protesters made an *impassioned* plea for the life of the condemned man.

❑ IMPASSIVE—showing no emotion

The queen looked on *impassively* as the traitor argued desperately that his life should be spared.

❑ IMPEACH—to charge with misdeeds in public office; accuse

The senators debated whether or not the president should be *impeached* for his crimes.

❑ IMPECCABLE—flawless, without fault

The dress rehearsal was *impeccable*; nothing needed to be changed before the actual performance.

❑ IMPECUNIOUS—poor, having no money

After the stock market crashed, many former millionaires found themselves *impecunious*.

❑ IMPEDIMENT—barrier, obstacle; speech disorder

Ludmila's speech *impediment* made it difficult to understand what she was saying.

❑ IMPERATIVE—essential; mandatory

It's *imperative* that you follow the instructions of the crew in the event of a crash, or chaos will result.

❑ IMPERIOUS—arrogantly self-assured, domineering, overbearing

The *imperious* princess demanded that her servants do back flips every time they came into her presence.

❑ IMPERTINENT—rude

The *impertinent* boy stuck his tongue out at the policeman.

❑ IMPERTURBABLE—not capable of being disturbed

Due to her experience with distraught children, the counselor seemed *imperturbable*, even when faced with tantrums.

❑ IMPERVIOUS—impossible to penetrate; incapable of being affected

A good raincoat should be *impervious* to moisture.

❑ IMPETUOUS—quick to act without thinking

The *impetuous* day trader rushed to sell his stocks at the first hint of trouble, and lost $300,000.

❑ IMPIOUS—not devout in religion

The nun cut herself off from her *impious* family after she entered the convent.

❑ IMPLACABLE—inflexible, incapable of being pleased

His rage at the betrayal was so great that he remained *implacable* for weeks.

❑ IMPLANT (v.)—to set securely or deeply; to instill

The reform school sought to *implant* the virtues of law-abiding citizens in the minds of its juvenile delinquent charges.

❑ IMPLAUSIBLE—improbable, inconceivable

A skeptical man by nature, Max found his neighbor's claim that he'd seen a UFO highly *implausible*.

❑ IMPLICATE—to involve in a crime, incriminate

In an effort to save himself, the criminal *implicated* his friends in the murder.

❑ IMPLICIT—implied, not directly expressed

Implicit in Jake's request that Sheila return his keys was his desire to terminate their relationship.

❑ IMPORTUNE—to ask repeatedly, beg

The assistant *importuned* her boss with constant requests for a raise and promotion.

❑ IMPOSE—to inflict, force upon

The patriarch *imposed* his will upon his daughter, refusing to allow her to marry the butler.

❑ IMPOSING—dignified, grand

The *imposing* facade of the mansion intimidated the governess who had come to work there.

❑ IMPOTENT—powerless, ineffective, lacking strength

Mr. Cliff was *impotent* to prevent his daughter's spiralling plunge into drug addiction.

❑ IMPOUND—to seize and confine

The car was *impounded* when the Hendersons could not keep up with the payments for it.

❑ IMPOVERISH—to make poor or bankrupt

Though he had more money than he could count, Bruce did nothing to help his *impoverished* relatives.

❑ IMPRECATION—curse

Spouting violent *imprecations*, Hank searched for the man who had totally destroyed his truck.

❑ IMPREGNABLE—totally safe from attack, able to resist defeat

The fortress was *impregnable*—until, that is, the defenders allowed the Trojan Horse to enter its gates.

❑ IMPRESSIONABLE—easily influenced or affected

After attending the Spice Girls concert, the *impressionable* girl began to dress like Sporty Spice every day.

❑ IMPROMPTU—spontaneous, without rehearsal

During the interview, the Beatles suddenly decided to give an *impromptu* performance of "Love Me Do."

❑ IMPROVIDENT—without planning or foresight, negligent

The *improvident* woman spent all the money she received in her court settlement within two weeks.

❑ IMPUDENT—arrogant, audacious

The teacher raged inwardly at the *impudent* comments of his student, but kept outwardly calm.

❑ IMPUGN—to call into question, attack verbally

"How dare you *impugn* my honorable motives?" protested the lawyer on being accused of ambulance chasing.

❑ IMPULSE—sudden tendency, inclination

On *impulse*, Sarah bought a leather jacket for her boyfriend, although she couldn't really afford it.

❑ IMPULSIVE—spontaneous, unpredictable

Last Christmas she was on her way to London, but at the last minute she *impulsively* canceled the trip and went to Hawaii instead.

❑ INADVERTENTLY—unintentionally

As he was backing out of the driveway, Diego *inadvertently* ran over a rose bush.

❑ INANE—foolish, silly, lacking significance

The talk show host desperately tried to make the star's *inane* comments seem more interesting.

❑ INAUGURATE—to begin or start officially; to induct into office

The president was *inaugurated* in a lavish ceremony attended by thousands.

❑ INCANDESCENT—shining brightly

The moon had an *incandescent* glow on that romantic night we met.

❑ INCARCERATE—to put in jail; to confine

The thief was *incarcerated* for two years, but he got out on parole after six months.

❑ INCARCERATION—imprisonment

In order to avoid *incarceration*, the swindler struck a plea bargain with the district attorney's office.

❑ INCARNADINE—blood-red in color

At first glance, Theo's *incarnadine* shirt made people think he was bleeding profusely.

❑ INCARNATE—having bodily form

The serial killer was so sadistic that many people thought he might be the devil *incarnate*.

❑ INCENDIARY—combustible, flammable, burning easily

Gasoline is so *incendiary* that cigarette smoking is forbidden at gas stations.

❑ INCENSE (v.)—to infuriate, enrage

The general became thoroughly *incensed* when his subordinates failed to follow his orders.

❑ INCEPTION—beginning

Even from its *inception*, those who were involved in the plan knew that it probably wouldn't succeed.

❑ INCESSANT—continuous, never ceasing

Otis's wife complained *incessantly* about the way he sat watching TV all day instead of looking for a job.

❑ INCHOATE—imperfectly formed or formulated

As her thoughts on the subject were still in *inchoate* form, Amy could not explain what she meant.

❑ INCIPIENT—beginning to exist or appear; in an initial stage

At that point, her cancer was only *incipient* and she could still work full time.

❑ INCISIVE—perceptive, penetrating

The psychologist's *incisive* analysis of her patient's childhood helped him to understand his own behavior.

❑ INCLINATION—tendency towards

Her natural *inclination* was to refuse Max's invitation to dinner, but since he was her boss she felt obligated to accept it.

❑ INCLUSIVE—comprehensive, all-encompassing

It took 30 years, but the publisher managed to produce the most *inclusive* encyclopedia on the market.

❑ INCOGNITO—in disguise, concealing one's identity

Fearful of damaging her reputation, the politician gambled in Atlantic City *incognito*.

❏ **INCONCEIVABLE**—impossible, unthinkable

It was *inconceivable* to the dictator that his subjects could hate him, although they obviously did.

❏ **INCONSEQUENTIAL**—unimportant, trivial

The king dismissed the concerns of his horrified advisers as *inconsequential*, and decided to go ahead with his marriage to the beautiful young woman despite rumors that she was criminally insane.

❏ **INCONTROVERTIBLE**—unquestionable, beyond dispute

The fact that Harvard would be too expensive for Lisa without scholarship money was *incontrovertible*.

❏ **INCORRIGIBLE**—incapable of being corrected

The puppy was *incorrigible*; however many times he was told not to chew on his master's shoes, he persisted in doing it.

❏ **INCREDULOUS**—skeptical, doubtful

I was *incredulous* as I listened to Ishmael's wild fishing story about "the one that got away."

❏ **INCULCATE**—to teach, impress in the mind

Most parents blithely *inculcate* their children with their religious beliefs instead of allowing their children to select their own faith.

❏ **INCULPATE**—to blame, charge with a crime

His suspicious behavior after the crime tended to *inculpate* him.

❏ **INCUMBENT**—holding a specified office, often political

Incumbents often have an advantage over unknown parties in political races.

❏ **INCURSION**—sudden invasion

The army was unable to resist the *incursion* of the rebel forces into their territory.

❏ **INDEFATIGABLE**—never tired

Theresa seemed *indefatigable*, barely sweating after a 10-mile run.

❏ **INDEFENSIBLE**—inexcusable, unforgivable

"Your rudeness tonight was *indefensible*; I never want to see you again!" Amelia shouted at her boyfriend.

❏ **INDELIBLE**—permanent, not erasable

Rita was enraged when her infant daughter drew pictures on the wall in *indelible* ink.

❏ **INDICATIVE**—showing or pointing out, suggestive of

The looting of the shop was *indicative* of the general lawlessness that was taking possession of the city.

❏ **INDICT**—to accuse formally, charge with a crime

The mafioso was *indicted* for tax evasion because the FBI could not prove any of his other crimes.

❏ **INDIGENOUS**—native, occurring naturally in an area

Palm trees are *indigenous* to Florida, unlike penguins.

❏ **INDIGENT**—very poor

Because the suspect was *indigent*, the state paid for his legal representation.

❑ INDIGNANT—angry, incensed, offended

The innocent passerby was *indignant* when the police treated him as a suspect in the crime.

❑ INDOLENT—habitually lazy, idle

Her *indolent* ways got her fired from many jobs.

❑ INDOMITABLE—fearless, unconquerable

Samson was *indomitable* in battle until the treacherous Delilah cut off his hair, taking away his strength.

❑ INDUBITABLE—unquestionable

His *indubitable* cooking skills made it all the more astonishing when the Thanksgiving dinner he prepared tasted awful.

❑ INDUCE—to persuade; bring about

Tom attempted to *induce* his girlfriend to go skydiving with him, but she refused.

❑ INDUCT—to place ceremoniously in office

The pitcher was proud to be *inducted* into the Baseball Hall of Fame.

❑ INDULGE—to give in to a craving or desire

Jenny *indulged* herself with a weekend at a luxurious spa.

❑ INEBRIATED—drunk, intoxicated

Obviously *inebriated*, the best man slurred his words during his speech at the wedding.

❑ INEPT—clumsy, awkward

He was so *inept* in the garden that he dug up roses and fertilized weeds.

❑ INERT—unable to move, tending to inactivity

In the heat of the desert afternoon, lizards lie *inert*.

❑ INESTIMABLE—too great to be estimated

"The value of this acquisition to our company is *inestimable*," bragged the CEO.

❑ INEVITABLE—certain, unavoidable

With all the obstacles in their path, it was perhaps *inevitable* that their affair should end unhappily.

❑ INEXORABLE—inflexible, unyielding

The *inexorable* force of the twister swept away their house.

❑ INEXTRICABLE—incapable of being disentangled

The gum caught in the sheepdog's fur was *inextricable*, and his owner had to shave him to remove it.

❑ INFALLIBLE—incapable of making a mistake

I considered my mother to be *infallible* until she got fired from her job when I was 10.

❑ INFAMY—reputation for bad deeds

The corrupt mayor's *infamy* was legendary in the city.

❑ INFANTILE—childish, immature

The young man's *infantile* behavior in the presence of his mother annoyed his fiancée intensely.

❏ INFATUATED—strongly or foolishly attached to, inspired with foolish passion, overly in love

After seeing her picture in a fashion magazine, Lester became completely *infatuated* with the beautiful model.

❏ INFER—to conclude, deduce

I think we can *infer* from the results of this study that the quality of old-age homes needs to be improved.

❏ INFILTRATE—to pass secretly into enemy territory

The spy *infiltrated* the CIA, gaining access to highly classified information.

❏ INFINITESIMAL—extremely tiny

Infinitesimal specks of dust marred the camera lens, blotching the pictures that were taken through it.

❏ INFIRMITY—disease, ailment

Plagued by a variety of *infirmities*, the old man rarely left his bed during his final years.

❏ INFRINGE—to encroach, trespass; to transgress, violate

Koca-Cola was sued by Coca-Cola for *infringing* on its copyright.

❏ INFURIATE—to anger, provoke, outrage

Malcolm knew that his irresponsible behavior would *infuriate* his mother.

❏ INFURIATING—provoking anger or outrage

The girl had an *infuriating* habit of rudely insulting her elders.

❏ INGENIOUS—original, clever, inventive

Luther found an *ingenious* way to solve the complex math problem.

❏ INGENUOUS—straightforward, open; naive and unsophisticated

She was so *ingenuous* that her friends feared that her innocence would be exploited when she visited the big city.

❏ INGRATE—ungrateful person

When none of her relatives thanked her for the fruit cakes she had sent them, Doris condemned them all as *ingrates*.

❏ INGRATIATE—to bring oneself purposely into another's good graces

Walter *ingratiated* himself with his new coworkers by bringing them doughnuts every morning.

❏ INGRESS—entrance

Ed hoped that the mailroom job would provide him with an *ingress* into the company.

❏ INHIBIT—to hold back, prevent, restrain

Paulette was too *inhibited* to tell Rod that she resented him borrowing money and never paying her back.

❏ INIMICAL—hostile, unfriendly

Even though a cease-fire had been in place for months, the two sides were still *inimical* to each other.

❑ INIQUITY—sin, evil act

"I promise to close every den of *iniquity* in this town!" thundered the conservative new mayor.

❑ INITIATE—to begin, introduce; to enlist, induct

Jewish boys have a bar mitzvah when they are *initiated* into manhood.

❑ INJECT—to force into; to introduce into conversation

The doctor *injected* the boy with a large dose of penicillin to cure his illness.

❑ INJUNCTION—command, order

The Catholic religion has an *injunction* against the use of birth control.

❑ INKLING—hint; vague idea

Niles had had no *inkling* that he was about to be promoted, and was shocked when his manager gave him the news.

❑ INNATE—natural, inborn

Her *innate* levelheadedness will help her to withstand the enormous pressure she's under.

❑ INNATENESS—state of being natural or inborn

The *innateness* of intelligence is a topic that is under debate in today's society.

❑ INNOCUOUS—harmless; inoffensive

Some snakes are poisonous, but most species are *innocuous* and pose no danger to humans.

❑ INNOVATE—to invent, modernize, revolutionize

Coco Chanel *innovated* a popular new suit design, transforming the fashion industry.

❑ INNUENDO—indirect and subtle criticism, insinuation

Through hints and *innuendo*, the yellow journalist managed to ruin the star's reputation while ensuring that he could not be sued for slander.

❑ INNUMERABLE—too many to be counted

There are *innumerable* stars in the universe.

❑ INOPERABLE—not operable; incurable by surgery

Fred's brain cancer was *inoperable*, but drugs kept it under control.

❑ INQUEST—investigation; court or legal proceeding

At the *inquest*, it was determined that Ruby's death was an accident.

❑ INSATIABLE—never satisfied

Myrtle's *insatiable* appetite made it difficult for her to lose weight.

❑ INSCRUTABLE—impossible to understand fully

The judge's face was *inscrutable* as he read the jurors' verdict, giving no clue as to what it would be.

❑ INSENTIENT—unfeeling, unconscious

I was completely *insentient* during the operation due to the anesthetic I was given.

❑ INSIDIOUS—sly, treacherous, devious

Iago's *insidious* comments about Desdemona fuelled Othello's feelings of jealousy regarding his wife.

❏ INSINUATE—to suggest, say indirectly, imply

Brenda *insinuated* that Deirdre's brother had stolen her watch without accusing him outright.

❏ INSIPID—bland, lacking flavor; lacking excitement

The critic claimed that the soup was *insipid*, lacking any type of spice.

❏ INSOLENT—insulting and arrogant

"How dare you, *insolent* wretch!" roared the king when the peasant laughed at the sight of him stumbling into the mud.

❏ INSOLUBLE—not able to be solved or explained

When a mathematician finds the solution to a problem that others have declared *insoluble*, he is hailed as a genius.

❏ INSOLVENT—bankrupt, unable to pay one's debts

The company became *insolvent* after overinvesting in many failed projects and had to go out of business.

❏ INSTIGATE—to incite, urge, agitate

The man who had *instigated* the rebellion escaped, although all his followers were arrested.

❏ INSUBSTANTIAL—modest, insignificant

The losses we risk are *insubstantial* compared with the massive profits we stand to gain.

❏ INSULAR—isolated, detached

The inhabitants of the *insular* little village were shocked when Mrs. Malone set up a belly-dancing school in her home.

❏ INSUPERABLE—insurmountable, unconquerable

The difficulties we face may seem *insuperable*, but I'm confident that we will achieve all we set out to do.

❏ INSURGENT (adj.)—rebellious, insubordinate

The *insurgent* crew staged a mutiny and threw the captain overboard.

❏ INSURRECTION—rebellion

After the Emperor's troops crushed the *insurrection*, its leaders fled the country.

❏ INTEGRAL—central, indispensable

Paper is an *integral* part of a book.

❏ INTEGRITY—decency, honesty; wholeness

The candidate's *integrity* made him a refreshing contrast to his sleazy political opponents.

❏ INTEMPERATE—not moderate

The *intemperate* climate in the Sahara Desert makes it hard for plants that need lots of water to survive.

❏ INTER—to bury

After giving the masses one last chance to file past his remains and pay their respects, the authorities *interred* the leader's body.

❑ INTERDICT—to forbid, prohibit

The matron *interdicted* male visits to the girls' dorm rooms after midnight.

❑ INTERJECT—to interpose, insert

"We have a money-back guarantee!" shouted the salesman. "But only if you have a valid receipt!" *interjected* his assistant.

❑ INTERLOCUTOR—someone taking part in a dialogue

The tapes revealed that the drug dealer had planned a criminal act with an unidentified *interlocutor*.

❑ INTERLOPER—trespasser; meddler in others' affairs

The wolf pack rejected the lone pup as an *interloper*.

❑ INTERMINABLE—endless

By the time the *interminable* play ended, the last train home had already left.

❑ INTERMITTENT—starting and stopping

The flow of traffic was *intermittent* on the highway, but the commuters were thankful that it hadn't stopped completely.

❑ INTERNECINE—deadly to both sides

The disadvantage of *internecine* chemical weapons is that they are devastating to both sides in a conflict.

❑ INTERPOLATE—to insert; change by adding new words or material

The editor *interpolated* a few new sentences into the manuscript, and the new edition was ready to print.

❑ INTERPOSE—to insert; to intervene

The policeman *interposed* himself between the two men who were about to start fighting.

❑ INTERREGNUM—interval between reigns

During the *interregnum*, no one knew who was in charge and all hell broke loose in the country.

❑ INTERROGATE—to question formally

The secret police *interrogated* the suspected rebel for days, demanding the names of his co-conspirators.

❑ INTERSECT—to divide by passing through or across

The rambling country path was *intersected* by a busy freeway.

❑ INTERSPERSE—to distribute among, mix with

Mushrooms were *interspersed* among the bushes and clumps of moss in the shady forest.

❑ INTIMATION—clue, suggestion

Abby chose to ignore Babu's *intimation* that her essay was not as good as it could have been.

❑ INTRACTABLE—not easily managed

The problem of reforming hardened criminals has proved to be an *intractable* one.

❏ INTRAMURAL—within an institution, such as a school

Betty played on the *intramural* tennis team, although she was not good enough for the varsity team.

❏ INTRANSIGENT—uncompromising, refusing to be reconciled

The professor was *intransigent* on the deadline, insisting that everyone turn the assignment in on Friday.

❏ INTREPID—fearless

The *intrepid* hiker completed his ascent to the peak, despite the freezing winds that cut through his body.

❏ INTRINSIC—inherent, internal

The *intrinsic* value of this diamond is already considerable, and its elegant setting makes it truly priceless.

❏ INTROSPECTIVE—contemplating one's own thoughts and feelings

The *introspective* young man toured the countryside on his own, writing poetry based on his reflections.

❏ INTROVERT—someone given to self-analysis

Janet's a real *introvert*; she rarely pays attention to what the people around her are doing.

❏ INTRUSION—trespass, invasion of another's privacy

Despite the Do Not Disturb sign on their door, the Smiths had to put up with constant *intrusions* from the hotel staff.

❏ INTUITIVE—instinctive, untaught

"Riya's talent with numbers is completely *intuitive*; I never taught her a thing," bragged her mother.

❏ INUNDATE—to cover with water; overwhelm

The tidal wave *inundated* Atlantis, which was lost beneath the water.

❏ INURE—to harden; accustom; become used to

Eventually, Hassad became *inured* to the sirens that went off every night and could sleep through them.

❏ INVALIDATE—to negate or nullify

Niko's driver's license was *invalidated* after he was caught speeding in a school zone.

❏ INVECTIVE—verbal abuse

A stream of *invective* poured from Mrs. Pratt's mouth as she watched the vandals smash her ceramic frog.

❏ INVESTITURE—ceremony conferring authority

After his *investiture*, the Supreme Court justice was ready to preside at his first case.

❏ INVETERATE—confirmed, long-standing, deeply rooted

An *inveterate* gambler, Lori tried her luck at roulette every chance she got.

❏ INVIDIOUS—envious; obnoxious

It is cruel and *invidious* for parents to play favorites with their children.

❑ INVINCIBLE—invulnerable, unbeatable

At the height of his career, Mike Tyson was considered practically *invincible*.

❑ INVIOLABLE—safe from violation or assault

The relieved refugees felt *inviolable* in the camp under the protection of the U.N. troops.

❑ INVOKE—to call upon, request help

Baxter *invoked* the financial assistance of all his relatives when his business ran into serious trouble.

❑ IOTA—very tiny amount

"If I even got one *iota* of respect from you, I'd be satisfied!" raged the father at his insolent son.

❑ IRASCIBLE—easily angered

Attila the Hun's *irascible* and violent nature made all who dealt with him fear for their lives.

❑ IRIDESCENT—showing many colors

The tourists sighed at the beautiful vision of the *iridescent* tropical butterfly fluttering among the orchids.

❑ IRRESOLVABLE—unable to be resolved; not analyzable

The conflict between Catholics and Protestants in Northern Ireland seemed *irresolvable* until just recently.

❑ IRREVERENT—disrespectful, gently or humorously mocking

Kevin's *irreverent* attitude in Sunday School annoyed the priest, but amused the other children.

❑ IRREVOCABLE—conclusive, irreversible

Once he had pushed the red button, the president's decision to launch a missile was *irrevocable*.

❑ ITINERANT—wandering from place to place, unsettled

The *itinerant* tomcat came by the Johansson homestead every six months or so.

❑ ITINERARY—route of a traveler's journey

The travel agent provided her customer with a detailed *itinerary* of his journey.

J

❑ JADED—tired by excess or overuse; slightly cynical

While the naive girls stared at the spectacle in awe, the *jaded* matrons dozed in their chairs.

❑ JANGLING—clashing, jarring; harshly unpleasant (in sound)

The *jangling* of the bells of all the Santa Clauses outside the store assaulted the shoppers' ears.

❑ JARGON—nonsensical talk; specialized language

You need to master technical *jargon* in order to communicate successfully with engineers.

❑ JAUNDICE—yellowish discoloration of skin

Her *jaundice* was so advanced that her head looked like a big lemon.

❏ JAUNDICED—affected by jaundice; prejudiced or embittered

The cynical man was *jaundiced* by his past unhappy marriages, and refused to fall in love again.

❏ JETTISON—to cast off, throw cargo overboard

The sinking ship *jettisoned* its cargo in a desperate attempt to reduce its weight.

❏ JINGOISM—belligerent support of one's country

The president's *jingoism* made him declare war on other countries at the slightest provocation.

❏ JOCULAR—jovial, playful, humorous

The *jocular* old man entertained his grandchildren with jokes for hours.

❏ JUBILEE—special anniversary

At the queen's Silver *Jubilee*, the entire country celebrated her long reign.

❏ JUDICIOUS—sensible, showing good judgment

The wise and distinguished judge was well known for having a *judicious* temperament.

❏ JUGGERNAUT—huge force destroying everything in its path

The *juggernaut* of Napoleon's army surged ahead until it was halted in its tracks by the brutal winter.

❏ JUNCTURE—point where two things are joined

At this *juncture*, I think it would be a good idea for us to take a coffee break.

❏ JURISPRUDENCE—philosophy of law

An expert in *jurisprudence*, the esteemed lawyer was often consulted by his colleagues.

❏ JUXTAPOSITION—side-by-side placement

The porcelain dog was placed in *juxtaposition* with the straw dog house on the mantelpiece.

K

❏ KEEN (adj.)—having a sharp edge; intellectually sharp, perceptive

With her *keen* intelligence, she figured out the puzzle in seconds flat.

❏ KERNEL—innermost, essential part; seed grain, often in a shell

The parrot cracked the hard shell of the seed in order to get at its delicious *kernel*.

❏ KEYNOTE—note or tone on which a musical key is founded; main idea of a speech, program, etc.

The university administration asked a prominent historian to deliver the *keynote* speech at the conference.

❏ KINDLE—to set fire to or ignite; excite or inspire

With only damp wood to work with, Tilda had great difficulty in *kindling* the camp fire.

❏ KINETIC—relating to motion; characterized by movement

The *kinetic* sculpture moved back and forth, startling the museum visitors.

❑ KNELL—sound of a funeral bell; omen of death or failure

When the townspeople heard the *knelling* from the church belfry, they knew that their mayor had died.

❑ KUDOS—fame, glory, honor

The actress happily accepted *kudos* from the press for her stunning performance in the indie film.

L

❑ LABYRINTH—maze

When Peichi finally reached the center of the *labyrinth*, she realized that she had no idea how to get back to its entrance.

❑ LACERATION—cut or wound

The chopping knife slipped and slashed Frank's arm, making a deep *laceration*.

❑ LACHRYMOSE—tearful

Heather always became *lachrymose* when it was time to bid her daughter good-bye.

❑ LACKADAISICAL—idle, lazy; apathetic, indifferent

The clerk yawned openly in the customer's face, not bothering to hide his *lackadaisical* attitude.

❑ LACONIC—using few words

She was a *laconic* poet who built her reputation on using words as sparingly as possible.

❑ LAGGARD—dawdler, loafer, lazy person

The manager hesitated to fire Biff, his incompetent *laggard* of an assistant, because Biff was the CEO's son.

❑ LAMENT (v.)—to deplore, grieve

The children continued to *lament* the death of the goldfish weeks after its demise.

❑ LAMPOON—to attack with satire, mock harshly

The mayor hated being *lampooned* by the press for his efforts to make the inhabitants of his city more polite.

❑ LANGUID—lacking energy, indifferent, slow

The cat *languidly* cleaned its fur, ignoring the vicious, snarling dog chained a few feet away from it.

❑ LAP (v.)—to drink using the tongue; to wash against

The dog eagerly *lapped* up all the water in its bowl, thirsty after barking nonstop for two hours.

❑ LAPIDARY—relating to precious stones

"This ring is of no *lapidary* value; you could buy it in any cheap department store," sneered the jeweller.

❑ LARCENY—theft of property

The crime of stealing a wallet can be categorized as petty *larceny*.

❏ LARDER—place where food is stored

Dottie was horrified to discover that rats had eaten all the potatoes in her *larder*.

❏ LARGESS—generosity; gift

Because the mafia don had extended considerable *largess* to his neighbors, they supported him.

❏ LARYNX—organ containing vocal cords

The opera singer's *larynx* was damaged in the accident, spelling doom for her career.

❏ LASSITUDE—lethargy, sluggishness

The defeated French army plunged into a state of depressed *lassitude* as they trudged home from Russia.

❏ LATENT—present but hidden; potential

Milton's latent *paranoia* began to emerge as he was put under more and more stress at the office.

❏ LAUDABLE—deserving of praise

Kristin's dedication is *laudable*, but she doesn't have the necessary skills to be a good paralegal.

❏ LAXITY—carelessness

Our newspaper delivery boy's *laxity* is the reason why our paper lands in a puddle more often than not.

❏ LEERY—suspicious

After being swindled once, Ruth became *leery* of strangers trying to sell things to her.

❏ LEGERDEMAIN—trickery

The magician was skilled in the arts of *legerdemain*.

❏ LEGIBLE—readable

Gordon's chickenscratch handwriting was barely *legible*.

❏ LEGISLATE—to decree, mandate, make laws

Some congressmen make every effort to *legislate* in favor of powerful interest groups.

❏ LENIENT—easygoing, permissive

When the pitcher was fined only $50 for punching the batter, fans felt the punishment was too *lenient*.

❏ LETHARGY—indifferent inactivity

The worker sank into a state of *lethargy*, letting dozens of defective toys pass him by on the assembly line.

❏ LEVITATE—to rise in the air or cause to rise

The magician caused his assistant to *levitate* in the air, astonishing the audience.

❏ LEVITY—humor, frivolity, gaiety

At Christmas, an atmosphere of *levity* fills our office as people prepare to have fun with their families.

❏ LEXICON—dictionary, list of words

You may not find the word "supercalifragilisticexpialidocious" in the *lexicon*.

❏ LIBERAL—tolerant, broad-minded; generous, lavish

Kate's *liberal* parents trusted her, and allowed her to manage her own affairs to a large extent.

❏ LIBERATION—freedom, emancipation

After the *liberation* of the slaves, the southern plantation fell into disrepair after its entire workforce left to find paid employment.

❏ LIBERTARIAN—one who believes in unrestricted freedom

The *libertarian* refused to pay taxes to the government, as he didn't recognize its jurisdiction over him.

❏ LIBERTINE—one without moral restraint

The *libertine* took pleasure in gambling and seducing innocent youths.

❏ LICENTIOUS—immoral; unrestrained by society

Religious citizens were outraged by the *licentious* exploits of the community of artists living in the town.

❏ LIEN—right to possess and sell the property of a debtor

The bank took a *lien* on the lender's house to protect themselves in case he defaulted on his loan.

❏ LIMPID—clear, transparent

Shelley could see all the way to the bottom through the pond's *limpid* water.

❏ LINEAGE—ancestry

Manuela could trace her *lineage* back through many generations.

❏ LINGUISTICS—study of language

Her study of *linguistics* helped her to master new languages more easily.

❏ LINIMENT—medicinal liquid used externally to ease pain

Vernon rubbed the soothing *liniment* into his aching joints.

❏ LIONIZE—to treat as a celebrity

After the success of his novel, the author was *lionized* by the press.

❏ LISSOME—easily flexed, limber, agile

The *lissome* yoga instructor twisted herself into shapes that her students could only dream of.

❏ LISTLESS—lacking energy and enthusiasm

Listless and depressed after breaking up with his girlfriend, Nick spent his days moping on the couch.

❏ LITERATE—able to read and write; well-read and educated

The only *literate* man in the village, Abraham was asked to read his neighbors' letters to them.

❏ LITHE—moving and bending with ease; graceful

The dancer's movements were *lithe* and graceful, even when she was not performing.

❏ LITIGATION—the movement of a lawsuit through the court system

Mr. Prather finally won his court case after years of *litigation*.

❑ LIVID—discolored from a bruise; reddened with anger

Irving was *livid* when he discovered that someone had spilled grape juice all over his cashmere coat.

❑ LOATHE—to abhor, despise, hate

Stuart *loathed* the subject so much that he could barely stand to sit through his physics class.

❑ LOCOMOTION—movement from place to place

The *locomotion* of trains became more rapid after steam engines were replaced by electrically powered ones.

❑ LOITER—to stand around idly

The teenagers *loitered* on the corner, waiting for something to happen.

❑ LOQUACIOUS—talkative

She was naturally *loquacious*, which was a problem in situations in which listening was more important than talking.

❑ LOW (v.)—to make a sound like a cow, moo

The *lowing* of the cows woke the milkmaid from her deep slumber.

❑ LUCID—clear and easily understood

Explanations should be written in a *lucid* manner so that people can understand them.

❑ LUDICROUS—laughable, ridiculous

The scientist thought his colleague's claims were *ludicrous*, but kept quiet because he didn't want to offend his old friend.

❑ LUGUBRIOUS—sorrowful, mournful; dismal

Irish wakes are a rousing departure from the *lugubrious* funeral services most people are accustomed to.

❑ LUMBER (v.)—to move slowly and awkwardly

The bear *lumbered* towards the garbage, drooling at the prospect of the Big Mac leftovers he smelled.

❑ LUMINARY—bright object; celebrity; source of inspiration

Logan's father was a *luminary* of the New York theater world, and many sought his advice.

❑ LUMINOUS—bright, brilliant, glowing

The *luminous* moon shone right through the curtains into the bedroom.

❑ LUNAR—relating to the moon

The scientists analyzed the *lunar* rocks collected by the space shuttle crew for traces of water.

❑ LURID—harshly shocking, sensational; glowing

The politician nearly had a heart attack when he saw the *lurid* headlines about his past indiscretions.

❑ LURK—to prowl, sneak

The burglar *lurked* in the bushes until the Jeffersons had left the house, then broke in.

❑ LUSCIOUS—tasty

These *luscious* strawberries are the best I've ever tasted!

❑ LUXURIANCE—elegance, lavishness

The *luxuriance* of the couches made them an obvious choice for the palace sitting room.

❑ LYRICAL—suitable for poetry and song; expressing feeling

Ambrose's *lyrical* talents made him a gifted poet and songwriter.

M

❑ MACHINATION—plot or scheme

Tired of his enemies' endless *machinations* to remove him from the throne, the king had them executed.

❑ MACROBIOTICS—art of prolonging life by special diet of organic nonmeat substances

A devout believer in *macrobiotics*, Rosemary fed her children nothing but fruit and bran.

❑ MACROCOSM—the entire universe; a complex that is a large-scale reproduction of one of its parts

In a welfare society, the state can be considered a *macrocosm* of the family in that it takes care of the elderly and children.

❑ MAELSTROM—whirlpool; turmoil; agitated state of mind

The transportation system of the city had collapsed in the *maelstrom* of war.

❑ MAGNANIMOUS—generous, noble in spirit

Although at first he seemed mean, Uncle Frank turned out to be a very *magnanimous* fellow.

❑ MAGNATE—powerful or influential person

The entertainment *magnate* bought two cable TV stations to add to his collection of magazines and publishing houses.

❑ MAGNITUDE—extent, greatness of size

When she saw the huge leaks in her ceiling, she realized the full *magnitude* of the repairs her house needed.

❑ MALADROIT—clumsy, tactless

"So, when is your baby due?" said the *maladroit* guest to his overweight but not pregnant hostess.

❑ MALADY—illness

Elizabeth visited the doctor many times, but he could not identify her mysterious *malady*.

❑ MALAPROPISM—humorous misuse of a word

When the infant pointed to the puppy and said "Look at the fluffy," his *malapropism* delighted his parents.

❑ MALCONTENT—discontented person, one who holds a grudge

Dinah had always been a *malcontent*, so no one was surprised when she complained about the new carpet in the lobby.

❑ MALEDICTION—curse

The prince-frog looked for a princess to kiss him and put an end to the witch's evil *malediction*.

❏ MALEFACTOR—evil-doer; culprit

Many organizations are still trying to bring Nazi *malefactors* to justice.

❏ MALEVOLENT—ill-willed; causing evil or harm to others

The *malevolent* gossiper spread false rumors about people just for the pleasure of upsetting them.

❏ MALFUNCTION (v.)—to fail to work

When his computer *malfunctioned* yet again, Derek decided to throw it out and buy a new one.

❏ MALFUNCTION (n.)—breakdown, failure

The *malfunction* of the booster rocket meant that the space shuttle could not be launched on schedule.

❏ MALICE—animosity, spite, hatred

Kendra felt such *malice* towards the insurance company that she celebrated when it went bankrupt.

❏ MALINGER—to evade responsibility by pretending to be ill

A common way to avoid the draft was by *malingering*—faking an illness so as to avoid being taken by the Army.

❏ MALNUTRITION—undernourishment

The child's distended stomach and spindly limbs was a sure sign that she suffered from *malnutrition*.

❏ MALODOROUS—foul smelling

The *malodorous* beggar, who had not bathed in many months, could barely stand his own smell.

❏ MANDATORY—necessary, required

It is *mandatory* for all subway employees to wear blue uniforms while on the job.

❏ MANIFEST (adj.)—obvious

The fact that she had had plastic surgery was *manifest*, since she looked 20 years younger than she had done the week before.

❏ MANIFOLD—diverse, varied, comprised of many parts

The *manifold* tourist attractions of London make it a great place to visit.

❏ MANNERED—artificial or stilted in character

Igor was so nervous about attending a high society dinner for the first time that his behavior was *mannered* and unnatural.

❏ MANUAL (adj.)—hand operated; physical

When the power lines went down, the secretary dug out his old *manual* typewriter to type his letters.

❏ MAR—to damage, deface; spoil

Telephone poles *marred* the natural beauty of the countryside.

❏ MARGINAL—barely sufficient

Because her skills were *marginal*, Edith was not a valued employee and was paid a very low salary.

❏ MARITIME—relating to the sea or sailing

At the *maritime* museum, historic ships and sailing equipment are displayed.

❑ MARTIAL—warlike, pertaining to the military

Experts in *martial* arts know how to physically defend themselves if anyone attacks them.

❑ MARTINET—strict disciplinarian, one who rigidly follows rules

A complete *martinet*, the official insisted that Pete fill out all the forms again even though he was already familiar with his case.

❑ MARTYR—person dying for his or her beliefs

Joan of Arc became a famous *martyr* after she was burned at the stake for her beliefs.

❑ MASOCHIST—one who enjoys pain or humiliation

Only a *masochist* would volunteer to take over this nightmarish project.

❑ MASQUERADE—disguise; action that conceals the truth

I dressed up as President Nixon for last year's *masquerade* party.

❑ MATERIALISM—preoccupation with material things

The couple's *materialism* revealed itself in the way they had to buy the most up-to-date model of every consumer item.

❑ MATRICULATE—to enroll as a member of a college or university

When Suda-May *matriculates* at Yale University this coming fall, she'll move to New Haven.

❑ MATRILINEAL—tracing ancestry through mother's line rather than father's

In the *matrilineal* society, inheritances were passed on through the mother's line rather than the father's.

❑ MAUDLIN—overly sentimental

The mother's death should have been a touching scene, but the movie's treatment of it was so *maudlin* that, instead of making the audience cry, it made them cringe.

❑ MAWKISH—sickeningly sentimental

The poet hoped to charm his lover with his romantic poem, but its *mawkish* tone sickened her instead.

❑ MEDDLER—person interfering in others' affairs

Mickey is a real *meddler*, always sticking his nose in where it doesn't belong.

❑ MEDIEVAL—relating to the Middle Ages (about A.D. 500–1500)

In *medieval* times, countless Europeans died of diseases because medicine was not very far advanced.

❑ MEGALITH—huge stone used in prehistoric structures

The archaeologist wondered how the prehistoric tribe had managed to move the gigantic *megalith* to the top of the hill.

❑ MEGALOMANIA—mental state with delusions of wealth and power

Suffering from *megalomania*, the mental patient demanded that the hospital staff bow to him.

❑ MELANCHOLY—sadness, depression

The gloomy, rainy weather made James feel *melancholy*.

❑ MELODY—pleasing musical harmony; related musical tunes

The hit pop song had the same basic *melody* as Beethoven's Fifth.

❑ MENAGERIE—various animals kept together for exhibition

The lion would have eaten all the other animals in the circus *menagerie* if given the chance.

❑ MENDACIOUS—dishonest

So many of her stories were *mendacious* that I decided she must be a pathological liar.

❑ MENDICANT—beggar

"Please, sir, can you spare a dime?" begged the *mendicant* as the businessman walked past.

❑ MENTOR—experienced teacher and wise adviser

After being accepted at several colleges, Luisa asked her *mentor* which one she should choose.

❑ MERCENARY (n.)—soldier for hire in foreign countries

Because his own army was so small, the dictator was forced to hire foreign *mercenaries* to protect him.

❑ MERCENARY (adj.)—motivated only by greed

Many celebrated "explorers" were actually *mercenary* plunderers.

❑ MERCURIAL—quick, shrewd, and unpredictable

Her *mercurial* personality made it difficult to guess how she would react to the bad news.

❑ MERETRICIOUS—gaudy, falsely attractive

The casino's *meretricious* decor horrified the cultivated interior designer.

❑ MERIDIAN—circle passing through the two poles of the Earth

The explorer attempted to follow the *meridian* from the North Pole to the South Pole, but he failed when his ship ran into a solid sheet of ice and he could go no further.

❑ MERITORIOUS—deserving reward or praise

The student's performance in all subjects was so *meritorious* that I'm sure she'll be awarded a scholarship.

❑ METAMORPHOSIS—change, transformation

The *metamorphosis* of a caterpillar into a butterfly is a fascinating process.

❑ METAPHOR—figure of speech comparing two different things

The *metaphor* "a sea of troubles" suggests a lot of troubles by comparing their number to the vastness of the sea.

❑ METICULOUS—extremely careful, fastidious, painstaking

To find all the clues at the crime scene, the investigators *meticulously* examined every inch of the area.

❑ METRONOME—time-keeping device used in music

Even with the help of a *metronome*, the talentless piano student couldn't keep the rhythm as she played the simple tune.

❑ METTLE—courageousness; endurance

The helicopter pilot showed her *mettle* as she landed in the battlefield to rescue the wounded soldiers.

❏ MICROBE—microorganism

A major medical breakthrough occurred when it was discovered that *microbes* were responsible for the spread of disease.

❏ MICROCOSM—tiny system used as analogy for larger system

The social order of a beehive can serve as a *microcosm* for the social order of human society.

❏ MIGRATORY—wandering from place to place with the seasons

The *migratory* geese flew in from Canada at around the same time every year.

❏ MILITATE—to operate against, work against

Lenin *militated* against the tsar for years before he overthrew him and established the Soviet Union.

❏ MINIMAL—smallest in amount, least possible

Add only a *minimal* amount of rum to the cake, or it will overwhelm the taste of all the other ingredients.

❏ MINUSCULE—very small

Dave needed a magnifying glass to read the *miniscule* print on the lease.

❏ MIRTH—frivolity, gaiety, laughter

Vera's hilarious jokes contributed to the general *mirth* at the dinner party.

❏ MISANTHROPE—person who hates human beings

Scrooge was such a *misanthrope* that even the sight of children singing made him angry.

❏ MISAPPREHEND—to misunderstand, fail to know

The policeman *misapprehended* the situation and arrested Mark, although Peter was guilty of the crime.

❏ MISCONSTRUE—to misunderstand, fail to discover

Because I don't what I've said to be *misconstrued*, I'll distribute transcripts of my speech to all of you.

❏ MISERLINESS—extreme stinginess

Although Scrooge was a rich man, his *miserliness* prevented him from helping others who were in need.

❏ MISGIVING—apprehension, doubt, sense of foreboding

Jews had serious *misgivings* about Hitler's intentions towards them, and they fled Germany in large numbers.

❏ MISHAP—accident; misfortune

In an unfortunate *mishap*, the actress broke her arm and could not perform that night as planned.

❏ MISNOMER—an incorrect name or designation

Some feel that to call a nuclear missile a "peacemaker" is a *misnomer*.

❏ MISSIVE—note or letter

Lydia spent hours composing a romantic *missive* for Leo, which she sent off in the evening mail.

❑ MITIGATE—to soften, or make milder

A judge may *mitigate* a sentence if she decides that a person committed a crime out of need.

❑ MNEMONIC—relating to memory; designed to assist memory

The *mnemonic* "King Phillip Swiftly Came Over For Good Sushi" can help you remember the order of classificatory divisions when you study for a biology test.

❑ MOBILITY—ease of movement

The wheelchair increased Stanley's *mobility*; previously, he had been confined to his bed all day.

❑ MOCK—to deride, ridicule

Charles suspected that Toni was *mocking* him behind his back, but in fact, she respected him greatly.

❑ MODERATE (adj.)—reasonable, not extreme

"Please make sure my dish is *moderately* spiced; I like a little spice, but not too much," the customer instructed the waiter.

❑ MODERATE (v.)—to make less excessive, restrain; regulate

The engineer *moderated* the flow of electricity to the house after its fuses blew repeatedly.

❑ MOLLIFY—to calm or make less severe

Their argument was so intense that it was difficult to believe any compromise would *mollify* them.

❑ MOLLUSK—sea animal with soft body

Mollusks often develop hard shells in order to protect their soft, vulnerable bodies.

❑ MOLT (v.)—to shed hair, skin, or an outer layer periodically

The snake *molted* its skin and left it behind in a crumpled mass.

❑ MONASTIC—extremely plain or secluded, as in a monastery

The philosopher retired to his *monastic* lodgings to contemplate life free from any worldly distraction.

❑ MONOCHROMATIC—having one color

The multicolored butterfly really stood out in the *monochromatic* foliage of the clearing.

❑ MONOGAMY—custom of marriage to one person at a time

Monogamy is the accepted norm in American culture, though some members of certain religions take several wives.

❑ MONOLITH—large block of stone

The looming *monolith* dominated the horizon for miles around.

❑ MONOLOGUE—dramatic speech performed by one actor

Olivier's *monologue* in the film version of *Hamlet* is a well-known example of classical acting.

❑ MONTAGE—composite picture

The artist created a *montage* of photographs, newspaper articles, and everyday objects in her work of art.

❑ MOOT—debatable; purely academic, deprived of practical significance

Charles couldn't decide what to get Alison for her birthday, but after they broke up the issue became *moot*.

❑ MORBID—gruesome; relating to disease; abnormally gloomy

Mrs. Fletcher had a *morbid* fascination with her dead daughter, displaying photos of her everywhere.

❑ MORES—customs or manners

In accordance with the *mores* of ancient Roman society, Nero held an orgy every weekend.

❑ MORIBUND—dying, decaying

Thanks to feminism, many sexist customs are now *moribund* in this society.

❑ MOROSE—gloomy, sullen, or surly

After hearing that he had been rejected by the university of his choice, Lenny was *morose* for weeks.

❑ MORSEL—small bit of food

The timid bird darted forward and quickly grabbed the *morsel* of food from between the girl's fingers.

❑ MOTE—small particle, speck

Monica's eye watered, irritated by the *mote* of dust that had blown into it.

❑ MOTLEY—many colored; composed of diverse parts

The club was made up of a *motley* crew of people from all kinds of different backgrounds.

❑ MOTTLE—to mark with spots

Food stains *mottled* the tablecloth.

❑ MULTIFACETED—having many parts, many sided

The *multifaceted* emerald sparkled in different ways depending on which angle you saw it from.

❑ MULTIFARIOUS—diverse

Ken opened the hotel room window, letting in the *multifarious* noises of the great city.

❑ MUNDANE—worldly; commonplace

The plot of that thriller was completely *mundane*; as usual, the film ended in a huge explosion.

❑ MUNIFICENT—generous

The *munificent* millionaire donated ten million dollars to the hospital.

❑ MUNITIONS—ammunition

Soon after the *munitions* plant was blown up, the troops ran out of ammunition and surrendered.

❑ MUTABILITY—changeability

We need stable substances for this solution, and the *mutability* of this compound makes it unsuitable for our experiment.

❑ MYOPIC—nearsighted

The *myopic* old man needed a magnifying glass to read the morning paper.

❑ MYRIAD—immense number, multitude

Naomi moved to the city to take advantage of the *myriad* of modeling opportunities available to her there.

N

❏ NADIR—lowest point

As Lou waited in line to audition for the diaper commercial, he realized he had reached the *nadir* of his acting career.

❏ NARRATIVE—account, story

The police took notes as the witness gave a detailed *narrative* of the events that had taken place.

❏ NASCENT—starting to develop, coming into existence

The advertising campaign was still in a *nascent* stage, and nothing had been finalized yet.

❏ NATAL—relating to birth

The pregnant woman and her husband searched for a hospital specializing in *natal* care.

❏ NEBULOUS—vague, cloudy

The candidate's *nebulous* plans to fight crime lacked the concrete detail that skeptical voters demanded.

❏ NECROMANCY—black magic

Maya's mother forbade her to practice *necromancy* or witchcraft of any kind.

❏ NEFARIOUS—vicious, evil

Nefarious deeds are never far from an evil-doer's mind.

❏ NEGLIGENT—careless, inattentive

The court determined that Mr. Glass had been *negligent* in failing to keep his vicious dog chained up.

❏ NEGLIGIBLE—not worth considering

It's obvious from our *negligible* dropout rate that our students love our program.

❏ NEOLOGISM—new word or expression

Many *neologisms* are actually words we borrow from other languages and add to the English vocabulary.

❏ NEONATE—newborn child

The intensive care unit was filled with tiny, vulnerable *neonates* having respiratory problems.

❏ NEOPHYTE—novice, beginner

A relative *neophyte* at bowling, Seth rolled all of his balls into the gutter.

❏ NETHER—located under or below

Paul hunted for his favorite tie in the *nether* regions of the closet.

❏ NETTLE (v.)—to irritate

I don't particularly like having blue hair—I just do it to *nettle* my parents.

❏ NEUTRALITY—disinterest, impartiality

Switzerland is well known for its *neutrality* in times of international conflict.

❏ NEUTRALIZE—to balance, offset

Dr. Schwartz poured acid in the beaker to *neutralize* the basic solution.

❏ NICETY—elegant or delicate feature; minute distinction

Lani went to fancy parties all summer, enjoying the *niceties* of upper-crust society.

❏ NICHE—recess in a wall; best position for something

The thieves tucked the stolen money into a hidden *niche* in the wall.

❏ NIGGARDLY—stingy, ungenerous

Sarah received only *niggardly* praise from her jealous supervisor for her brilliant performance.

❏ NIHILISM—belief that existence and all traditional values are meaningless

Robert's *nihilism* expressed itself in his lack of concern with the norms of decent, moral society.

❏ NOCTURNAL—pertaining to night; active at night

Bats are *nocturnal* creatures, sleeping all day and emerging only at night.

❏ NOISOME—stinking, putrid

A dead mouse trapped in your walls produces a *noisome* odor.

❏ NOMADIC—moving from place to place

The *nomadic* Berber tribe travels from place to place, searching for grasslands for their herds.

❏ NOMENCLATURE—terms used in a particular science or discipline

Although I've been studying medicine for six months, I can't seem to get the hang of the *nomenclature*.

❏ NOMINAL—existing in name only; negligible

A *nominal* but far from devout Catholic, she rarely if ever went to church.

❏ NON SEQUITUR—conclusion not following from apparent evidence

The FBI agent's conclusion that Jimmy had not committed the murder was a total *non sequitur* to the incriminating evidence he'd presented.

❏ NONDESCRIPT—lacking interesting or distinctive qualities; dull

The celebrity showed up wearing sunglasses and a *nondescript* black outfit.

❏ NOTORIETY—unfavorable fame

Wayne realized from the silence that greeted him as he entered the bar that his *notoriety* preceded him.

❏ NOVICE—apprentice, beginner

Although Jen is only a *novice* at sailing, she shows great potential.

❏ NOVITIATE—state of being a beginner or novice

Women who want to enter a convent must go through a lengthy *novitiate* before they can be accepted as full-fledged nuns.

❏ NOXIOUS—harmful, unwholesome

The workers wore face masks to avoid breathing in the *noxious* chemical fumes.

❏ NUANCE—shade of meaning

The scholars argued for hours over tiny *nuances* in the interpretation of the last line of the poem.

❏ NULLIFY—to make legally invalid; to counteract the effect of

Crystal *nullified* her contract with her publisher when she received a better offer from another company.

❏ NUMISMATICS—coin collecting

Cleo picked up dozens of rare coins at the *numismatics* convention.

❏ NUPTIAL—relating to marriage

Pamela would not consent to marriage until Leland agreed to draw up a pre-*nuptial* agreement.

❏ NUTRITIVE—relating to nutrition or health

Try as he might, George could not convince us of the *nutritive* benefits of seaweed.

O

❏ OBDURATE—stubborn

The president was *obdurate* on the issue, and no amount of persuasion would change his mind.

❏ OBFUSCATE—to confuse, obscure

Benny always *obfuscates* his own arguments by using complicated words that he doesn't understand.

❏ OBLIQUE—indirect, evasive; misleading, devious

Usually open and friendly, Allie has been behaving in a curiously *oblique* manner lately.

❏ OBLITERATE—demolish, wipe out

The city center was completed *obliterated* by the atom bomb.

❏ OBLIVIOUS—unaware, inattentive

Gandhi calmly made his way through the crowd, seemingly *oblivious* to the angry rioters around him.

❏ OBSCURE (adj.)—dim, unclear; not well known

The speaker's style was so confusing that it *obscured* his main point rather than made it clear.

❏ OBSCURITY—a state of being obscure

The mayor hoped that the scandal that had almost torn the community apart would fade into *obscurity*.

❏ OBSEQUIOUS—overly submissive, brownnosing

The *obsequious* new employee complimented her supervisor's tie and agreed with him on every issue.

❏ OBSESSIVE—preoccupying, all-consuming

Jorge is *obsessive* about his work; he never leaves the office before ten at night.

❏ OBSOLETE—no longer in use

Black-and-white television is now almost completely *obsolete*.

❏ OBSTINATE—stubborn

The *obstinate* child could not be made to eat any food that he disliked.

❏ OBSTREPEROUS—troublesome, boisterous, unruly

The *obstreperous* toddler, who was always breaking things, was the terror of his nursery school.

❏ OBTRUSIVE—pushy, too conspicuous

I think that huge portrait of yourself that you hung in the hall is a bit *obtrusive*, don't you?

❏ OBTUSE—insensitive, stupid, dull, unclear

The directions were so *obtuse* that Alfred did not understand what was expected of him.

❏ OBVIATE—to make unnecessary; to anticipate and prevent

The river was shallow enough for the riders to wade across, which *obviated* the need for a bridge

❏ OCCLUDE—to shut, block

A shadow is thrown across the Earth's surface during a solar eclipse, when the light from the sun is *occluded* by the moon.

❏ ODIOUS—hateful, contemptible

While most people consider studying vocabulary an *odious* task, there are a few who find it enjoyable.

❏ OFFICIOUS—too helpful, meddlesome

The *officious* waiter butted into the couple's conversation, advising them on how to take out a mortgage.

❏ OFFSHOOT—branch

The company's main store is closing, but its *offshoots* in other areas are doing surprisingly well.

❏ OMINOUS—menacing, threatening, indicating misfortune

The sky filled with *ominous* dark clouds before the storm.

❏ OMNIPOTENT—having unlimited power

The manager clearly thinks he is *omnipotent*, the way he orders everyone around.

❏ OMNISCIENT—having infinite knowledge, all-seeing

Christians believe that because God is *omniscient*, they cannot hide their sins from Him.

❏ OMNIVOROUS—eating everything; absorbing everything

She is an *omnivorous* reader, covering everything from comic books to Plutarch.

❏ ONEROUS—burdensome

The assignment was so difficult to manage that it proved *onerous* to the team in charge of it.

❏ ONTOLOGY—theory about the nature of existence

There will probably never be a definitive *ontology* that people all over the world accept.

❏ OPALESCENT—iridescent, displaying colors

The infant, fascinated by the *opalescent* stone, stared at it for hours on end.

❏ OPAQUE—impervious to light; difficult to understand

The heavy buildup of dirt and grime on the windows almost made them *opaque*.

❏ OPERATIVE (adj.)—functioning, working

We all thought the photocopier was finally *operative*, until it broke down yet again.

❏ OPINE—to express an opinion

The talk show audience member *opined* that the guest was a pathetic excuse for a human being.

❏ OPPORTUNE—appropriate, fitting

Her investment in plastics, made just before the invention of plastic bags, was *opportune*.

❏ OPPORTUNIST—one who takes advantage of circumstances

Dozens of *opportunists* traveled to the earthquake-stricken region to sell food and water to the victims.

❏ OPPROBRIOUS—disgraceful, contemptuous

Despite his *opprobrious* addiction to gambling, the governor was re-elected once again.

❏ OPULENCE—wealth

Livingston considered his BMW to be a symbol of both *opulence* and style.

❏ ORACLE—person who foresees the future and gives advice

Opal decided to consult an *oracle* when she could not make the decision on her own.

❏ ORATION—lecture, formal speech

The class valedictorian gave an impressive *oration* on graduation day.

❏ ORATOR—lecturer, speaker

The new professor's dull tone of voice and lack of energy make her a particularly poor *orator*.

❏ ORB—spherical body; eye

Polly sighed at the sight of the lantern *orbs* glowing like small moons above the tables in the romantic restaurant garden.

❏ ORCHESTRATE—to arrange music for performance; to coordinate, organize

Though the president took all the credit, it was his wife who had actually *orchestrated* the entire event.

❏ ORDAIN—to make someone a priest or minister; to order

Stephanie sat proudly in the front row to watch her mother be *ordained* as the first female minister in the church's history.

❏ ORNITHOLOGIST—scientist who studies birds

The team of *ornithologists* devoted their research to the study of extinct species such as dodo birds.

❏ OSCILLATE—to move back and forth

The fans, *oscillating* from the ceiling, did little to cool down the humid Florida restaurant.

❏ OSSIFY—to turn to bone; to become rigid

Under certain conditions, cartilage in the body can *ossify* into bone.

❑ OSTENSIBLE—apparent

The *ostensible* reason for his visit was to borrow a book, but secretly he wanted to chat with lovely Wanda.

❑ OSTENTATIOUS—showy

The billionaire's 200-room palace was considered by many to be an overly *ostentatious* display of wealth.

❑ OSTRACISM—exclusion, temporary banishment

Larry knew that *ostracism* would be his fate when, after he made an obnoxious comment, all the other guests at the party turned their backs to him.

❑ OUSTER—expulsion, ejection

After his insane behavior at the meeting, the chairman faced an *ouster* by his fellow board members.

❑ OVERSTATE—to embellish, exaggerate

I do not want to *overstate* this, but I need you to understand the seriousness of the situation.

❑ OVERTURE—musical introduction; proposal, offer

The director received *overtures* from several big studios after his indie film success.

❑ OVERWROUGHT—agitated, overdone

The lawyer's *overwrought* voice on the phone made her clients worry about the outcome of their case.

P

❑ PACIFIC—calm, peaceful

The Pacific ocean was named for its comparatively subdued, *pacific* waves.

❑ PACIFIST—one opposed to war

For one who claimed to be a *pacifist*, Doug was surprisingly fond of weapons of war.

❑ PACIFY—to restore calm, bring peace

Nothing the king offered could *pacify* the angry princess, so he finally locked her in the dungeon.

❑ PALATIAL—like a palace, magnificent

After living in a one-room apartment for five years, Alicia thought the modest one bedroom looked downright *palatial*.

❑ PALAVER—idle talk

The journalist eagerly recorded the *palaver* among the football players in the locker room.

❑ PALEONTOLOGY—study of past geological eras through fossil remains

Janine decided to go into *paleontology* because of her interest in fossils and ancient civilizations.

❑ PALETTE—board for mixing paints; range of colors

The art instructor told the class to put only red, yellow, and blue paint on their *palettes*.

❑ PALISADE—fence made up of stakes

The tall iron *palisade* loomed menacingly over the prison.

❑ PALL (n.)—covering that darkens or obscures; coffin

A *pall* fell over the landscape as the clouds obscured the moon in the night sky.

❑ PALL (v.)—to lose strength or interest

Over time, the model's beauty *palled*, though her haughty attitude remained intact.

❑ PALLIATE—to make less serious, ease

The accused's crime was so vicious that the defense lawyer could not *palliate* it for the jury.

❑ PALLID—lacking color or liveliness

The old drugstore's *pallid* window could not compete with Wal-Mart's extravagant display next door.

❑ PALPABLE—obvious, real, tangible

As soon as Nicola disembarked from the plane in Mexico City, she noticed the *palpable* humidity.

❑ PALPITATION—trembling, shaking

Matthew hoped the *palpitations* of his hands would not betray how nervous he was to see her.

❑ PALTRY—pitifully small or worthless

Bernardo paid the ragged boy the *paltry* sum of ten cents to carry his luggage all the way to the hotel.

❑ PANACEA—cure-all

Some claim that vitamin C is a *panacea* for all sorts of illnesses, but I have my doubts.

❑ PANACHE—flamboyance, verve

Even when she has to plan them last minute, Leah always manages to pull off parties with *panache*.

❑ PANDEMIC—spread over a whole area or country

Pandemic alarm spread throughout Colombia after the devastating earthquake.

❑ PANEGYRIC—elaborate praise; formal hymn of praise

The director launched into a *panegyric* in praise of the man whose donation had kept his charity going.

❑ PANOPLY—impressive array

Corrina casually sifted through a *panoply* of job offers before finally deciding on one.

❑ PANORAMA—broad view; comprehensive picture

The tourists gazed in awe at the *panorama* of mountains and valleys lying before them.

❑ PARADIGM—ideal example, model

The ribs restaurant owner used McDonald's as a *paradigm* for the expansion of his business.

❑ PARADOX—contradiction, incongruity; dilemma, puzzle

It is a *paradox* that those most in need of medical attention are often those least able to obtain it.

❑ PARADOXICAL—self-contradictory but true

The civics teacher tried to explain to the class that *paradoxically*, rules and regulations helped to ensure freedom.

❏ PARAGON—model of excellence or perfection

She is the *paragon* of what a judge should be: honest, intelligent, hardworking, and just.

❏ PARAMOUNT—supreme, dominant, primary

It is of *paramount* importance that we make it back to camp before the storm hits, or we'll freeze to death.

❏ PARAPHRASE—to reword, usually in simpler terms

In *paraphrasing* the poet, she lost the eloquence of his style and the complexity of his message.

❏ PARASITE—person or animal that lives at another's expense

It is not in the *parasite's* interest to harm its host, because in doing so the parasite will reduce its own chances of survival.

❏ PARCH—to dry or shrivel

The *parched* traveler searched desperately for a water source.

❏ PARE—to trim

The scullery maid's hands were sore after she *pared* hundreds of potatoes for the banquet.

❏ PARIAH—outcast

The *pariah* dog hovered at the outskirts of the camp, begging for scraps.

❏ PARITY—equality

Mrs. Lutskaya tried to maintain *parity* between her children, although each claimed she gave the other preferential treatment.

❏ PARLEY—discussion, usually between enemies

The peace organization tried in vain to schedule a *parley* between Israel and Iraq.

❏ PAROCHIAL—of limited scope or outlook, provincial

It was obvious that Victor's *parochial* mentality would clash with Ivonne's liberal open-mindedness.

❏ PARODY—humorous imitation

Shana's new play is a thinly veiled *parody* of the corruption in the White House.

❏ PAROLE—conditional release of a prisoner

John hoped he would be released from Attica on *parole* for good behavior within three years.

❏ PARRY—to ward off or deflect

Kari *parried* every question the army officer fired at her, much to his frustration.

❏ PARSIMONY—stinginess

Ethel gained a reputation for *parsimony* when she refused to pay for her daughter's college education.

❏ PARTISAN (n.)—strong supporter

After speaking out at every meeting, Evelia became known as a *partisan* of her cause.

❏ PARTISAN (adj.)—biased in favor of

Though we claim to have a non-*partisan* democratic system, it is clear that decisions always boil down to party lines.

❑ PASTICHE—piece of literature or music imitating other works

The playwright's clever *pastiche* of the well-known Bible story had the audience rolling in the aisles.

❑ PATENT (adj.)—obvious, unconcealed

Moe could no longer stand Frank's *patent* brownnosing to the boss, and confronted him about it directly.

❑ PATENT (n.)—official document giving exclusive right to sell an invention

Margaret claims she had the idea for that computer system years ago but never got the *patent* for it.

❑ PATERNITY—fatherhood; descent from father's ancestors

In this week's episode, the soap opera's star refuses to reveal the *paternity* of her child.

❑ PATHOGENIC—causing disease

Bina's research on *pathogenic* microorganisms and their origins should help stop the spread of disease.

❑ PATHOS—pity, compassion

Dr. Irwin's cold lack of *pathos* for his patients got him fired from the hospital.

❑ PATRICIAN—aristocrat

Though he was born a pauper, Claudius hoped eventually to acquire a *patrician* standing in society.

❑ PATRICIDE—murder of one's father

Freud interpreted *patricide* as a manifestation of jealousy of one's father's intimacy with one's mother.

❑ PATRIMONY—inheritance or heritage derived from one's father

After the will was read, Petra asked her brother to donate his share of the *patrimony* to charity.

❑ PATRONIZE—to condescend to, disparage; to buy from

LuAnn *patronized* the students, treating them like idiots, which they deeply resented.

❑ PAUCITY—scarcity, lack

Because of the relative *paucity* of bananas in the country, their price was very high.

❑ PAUPER—very poor person

A common theme in movies is the ascension of a *pauper* up the ranks of society to financial success.

❑ PAVILION—tent or light building used for shelter or exhibitions

The caterers decorated the *pavilion* lavishly with lights, streamers, and balloons.

❑ PECCADILLO—minor sin or offense

Gabriel tends to harp on his brother's *peccadilloes* and never lets him live them down.

❑ PECULATION—theft of money or goods

The news reported the *peculation* of the Monet paintings and described their recovery by the police.

❑ PEDAGOGUE—teacher

Jesus was known as an influential *pedagogue* in his society.

❑ PEDANT—uninspired, boring academic

The professor's tedious commentary on the subject soon gained her a reputation as a *pedant*.

❑ PEDESTRIAN (adj.)—commonplace

Although the restaurant's prices were high, critics considered its food little more than *pedestrian*.

❑ PEDIATRICIAN—doctor specializing in children and their ailments

Although she was first attracted to family medicine, she became a *pediatrician* because she loved working with children.

❑ PEDIMENT—triangular gable on a roof or facade

I notice that the *pediments* on the roof are coming loose; we should get them fixed.

❑ PEER (n.)—contemporary, equal, match

Adults often blame their children's inappropriate actions on pressure from their *peers*.

❑ PEERLESS—unequaled

Hannah's hard work and dedication to this fund-raiser have been *peerless*.

❑ PEJORATIVE—having bad connotations; disparaging

The teacher scolded Mark for his unduly *pejorative* comments about his classmate's presentation.

❑ PELLUCID—transparent; translucent; easily understood

We could not determine whether the clear, *pellucid* liquid in the bottle was water or vodka.

❑ PENANCE—voluntary suffering to repent for a wrong

The aging pirate wanted to do *penance* for his crimes of days gone by.

❑ PENCHANT—inclination

Tiffany's *penchant* for rich, married men made her an object of hatred for their wives.

❑ PENDING (adj.)—not yet decided, awaiting decision

The court has been waiting for the jury to announce the verdict, but the decision is still *pending*.

❑ PENITENT—expressing sorrow for sins or offenses, repentant

The victim's family claimed that the murderer did not feel *penitent* and therefore should not have been released from prison.

❑ PENSIVE—thoughtful

Drew was a *pensive* boy who often spent time alone writing poetry.

❑ PENULTIMATE—next to last

The *penultimate* syllable in the word "later" is stressed.

❑ PENUMBRA—partial shadow

The *penumbras* of the spooky forest frightened Dorothy and her dog, Toto.

❑ PENURY—extreme poverty

The Watsons lived in *penury* after Mr. Watson lost his job at the factory.

❑ PERAMBULATOR—baby carriage

After placing her baby in the *perambulator*, Nan set out for the park.

❑ PERCIPIENT—discerning, able to perceive

The *percipient* detective saw through the suspect's lies and uncovered the truth in the matter.

❑ PERDITION—complete and utter loss; damnation

Faust brought *perdition* upon himself when he made a deal with the Devil in exchange for power.

❑ PEREGRINATE—to wander from place to place

Prehistoric man *peregrinated* from Africa to other parts of the globe.

❑ PERENNIAL—present throughout the years; persistent

Fortunately for me, these flowers are *perennial* and require no maintenance whatsoever.

❑ PERFIDIOUS—faithless, disloyal, untrustworthy

The actress's *perfidious* companion revealed all of her intimate secrets to the gossip columnist.

❑ PERFUNCTORY—done in a routine way; indifferent

The machinelike bank teller processed the transaction and gave the waiting customer a *perfunctory* smile.

❑ PERIHELION—point in orbit nearest to the sun

At *perihelion*, the Earth receives the greatest amount of sunlight.

❑ PERIPATETIC—moving from place to place

Morty claims that his *peripatetic* hot dog stand gives him the opportunity to travel all over the city.

❑ PERJURE—to tell a lie under oath

Benson *perjured* himself to protect his son, claiming that he had spent the evening with him when in fact he had not.

❑ PERMEABLE—penetrable

Karen discovered that her raincoat was *permeable* when she was drenched while wearing it in a rainstorm.

❑ PERNICIOUS—very harmful

The Claytons considered Rocky, a convicted felon, to be a *pernicious* influence on their innocent daughter.

❑ PERPETUAL—endless, lasting

Although objects may appear solid, the electrons that make up matter are actually in *perpetual* motion.

❑ PERSONIFICATION—act of attributing human qualities to objects or abstract qualities

Ellie may take the *personification* of her teddy bear a bit too far—she even shares her dessert with it.

❑ PERSPICACIOUS—shrewd, astute, keen witted

Inspector Poirot used his *perspicacious* mind to solve mysteries.

❑ PERT—lively and bold

The beauty contestant's *pert* personality and attractive appearance made her a natural choice for first prize.

❑ PERTINACIOUS—persistent, stubborn

Despite her parents' opposition, Tina *pertinaciously* insisted on continuing to date her boyfriend.

❑ PERTINENT—applicable, appropriate

The supervisor felt that his employee's complaints were *pertinent* and mentioned them in the meeting.

❑ PERTURBATION—disturbance

Grandpa sleeps so soundly that he wouldn't notice any kind of *perturbation*.

❑ PERUSAL—close examination

When you fly, your carry-on luggage is always subject to the *perusal* of customs officials.

❑ PERVERT (v.)—to cause to change in immoral way; to misuse

Charlene objected when the opposing lawyer seemed to be *perverting* the truth.

❑ PESTILENCE—epidemic, plague

The country went into national crisis when it was plagued by both *pestilence* and floods at the same time.

❑ PETULANCE—rudeness, peevishness

The child's *petulance* annoyed the teacher, who liked her young students to be cheerful and cooperative.

❑ PHALANX—massed group of soldiers, people, or things

Focusing on the importance of the *phalanx* in ancient Greece, the exhibit displayed several shields from the period.

❑ PHILANDERER—pursuer of casual love affairs

The *philanderer*, incapable of being faithful to one woman, had been through several divorces.

❑ PHILANTHROPY—love of humanity; generosity to worthy causes

The Metropolitan Museum of Art owes much of its collection to the *philanthropy* of private collectors who willed their estates to it.

❑ PHILISTINE—narrow-minded person, someone lacking appreciation for art or culture

"These *philistines* are incapable of appreciating true art!" fumed the playwright as he read the terrible reviews of his play.

❑ PHILOLOGY—study of words

Christian's love of *philology* led him to major in linguistics in college.

❑ PHLEGMATIC—calm in temperament; sluggish

The *phlegmatic* old boar snoozed in the grass as the energetic piglets frolicked around him.

❑ PHOBIA—exaggerated, illogical fear

Talia claims her *phobia* of spiders stems from the time she was bitten by one in third grade.

❑ PHOENIX—mythical, immortal bird that lives for 500 years, burns itself to death, and rises from its ashes

Though the family's house had burned down, they knew they would rise from the rubble like the proverbial *phoenix* and rebuild their lives.

❏ PHONETICS—study of speech sounds

The field of *phonetics* had interested Ilya ever since he'd conquered his speech impediment as a teenager.

❏ PHONIC—relating to sound

The CD-ROM had impressive graphics, but it needed *phonic* enhancement as well.

❏ PIETY—devoutness

The nun's *piety* inspired Anne to start going to church again.

❏ PILFER—to steal

Marianne did not *pilfer* the money for herself but rather for her sick brother, who needed medicine.

❏ PILLAGE—to loot, especially during a war

The invading soldiers *pillaged* the town for food and valuables.

❏ PINNACLE—peak, highest point of development

The whole show was excellent, but the *pinnacle* was when the skater did a backwards flip.

❏ PIOUS—dedicated, devout, extremely religious

Saul, a *pious* man, walks to the synagogue on the Sabbath and prays daily.

❏ PIQUE (n.)—fleeting feeling of hurt pride

In a fit of *pique*, the writer tossed his manuscript into the fire after his friend criticized it.

❏ PITHY—profound, substantial; concise, succinct, to the point

Martha's *pithy* comments during the interview must have been impressive, because she got the job.

❏ PITTANCE—meager amount or wage

Zack felt sure he would not be able to buy food for his family with the small *pittance* the government gave him.

❏ PLACATE—to soothe or pacify

The burglar tried to *placate* the snarling doberman by saying, "Nice doggy," and offering it a treat.

❏ PLACID—calm

Looking at Aparna's *placid* expression, no one could tell that she was inwardly seething with rage.

❏ PLAGIARIST—one who steals words or ideas

The notable scientist lost his job when he was exposed as a *plagiarist*; years before, he had copied a paper from a magazine.

❏ PLAINTIFF—injured person in a lawsuit

The lawyer asked the *plaintiff* to rise and show the court his injuries.

❏ PLAIT—to braid

Every morning before school the girl's grandmother *plaited* her long, curly hair.

❏ PLATITUDE—stale, overused expression

Although Jacob has some interesting ideas, he relies too much on *platitudes* in his writing.

❑ PLEBEIAN—crude, vulgar, low-class

The aristocrats would not lower themselves to attend a form of entertainment so *plebeian* as a movie.

❑ PLENITUDE—abundance, plenty

Every Thanksgiving our family gives thanks for our *plenitude* of good fortune.

❑ PLETHORA—excess, overabundance

Assuming that more was better, the defendant offered the judge a *plethora* of excuses.

❑ PLIANT—pliable, yielding

Only those with extremely *pliant* limbs are able to perform complex yoga moves.

❑ PLUCK (v.)—to pull strings on a musical instrument; to remove feathers from a bird

The moment she first *plucked* the strings of the Stradivarius, Nancy knew she had to have it.

❑ PLUCKY—courageous, spunky

The *plucky* young nurse dove bravely into the foxhole, determined to save the life of the wounded soldier.

❑ PLUMMET—to fall, plunge

Marvin screamed as he watched his new Ferrari *plummet* into the depths of the ravine.

❑ PLURALISTIC—including a variety of groups

The United States is a *pluralistic* society, incorporating a wide range of different groups.

❑ PLY (v.)—to use diligently; to engage; to join together

The weaver *plied* the fibers together to make a blanket.

❑ PNEUMATIC—relating to air; worked by compressed air

The rebel launched the dynamite with the help of a *pneumatic* gun.

❑ POACH—to steal game or fish; cook in boiling liquid

He knew it was illegal to *poach* the birds, but he did not have enough money to get a permit.

❑ PODIUM—platform or lectern for orchestra conductors or speakers

The audience could see Tara shaking as she walked up to the *podium*.

❑ POIGNANT—emotionally moving

Maria's speech in honor of her deceased friend was so *poignant* that there was not a dry eye at the funeral.

❑ POLAR—relating to a geographic pole; exhibiting contrast

Though Shawn and Angie are *polar* opposites in many ways, they have been happily married for ten years.

❑ POLARIZE—to tend towards opposite extremes

The leaders feared the conflict would *polarize* the group into two separate camps.

❑ POLEMIC—controversy, argument; verbal attack

The candidate's *polemic* against his opponent was vicious and small-minded rather than well reasoned and convincing.

❑ **POLITIC**—discreet, tactful

Her prudent and *politic* management of the crisis led her to be elected president the following year.

❑ **POLYGLOT**—speaker of many languages

Ling's extensive travels have helped her to become a true *polyglot*.

❑ **PONDEROUS**—weighty, heavy, large

We steeled ourselves before attempting to lift the *ponderous* bureau.

❑ **PONTIFICATE**—to speak in a pretentious manner

She *pontificated* about the virtues of being rich until we all left the room in disgust.

❑ **PORE (v.)**—to study closely or meditatively

I've *pored* over this text for over an hour, and I still can't understand it.

❑ **POROUS**—full of holes, permeable to liquids

Unfortunately, the tent was more *porous* than we thought and the rain soaked us to the bone.

❑ **PORTENT**—omen

Kylie quaked in fear as she watched a black cat cross her path, a *portent* of bad luck in the future.

❑ **PORTLY**—stout, dignified

The *portly* man wearily put on the Santa suit and set out for the mall.

❑ **POSIT**—to put in position; to suggest an idea

She *posited* the hideous vase on the mantelpiece in clear view of the guests who had given it to her.

❑ **POSTERIOR**—bottom, rear

The veterinarian injected the antibiotics into the *posterior* of the animal.

❑ **POSTERITY**—future generations; all of a person's descendants

Nadine saved all of her soccer trophies for *posterity*.

❑ **POTABLE**—drinkable

Though the water was *potable*, it tasted terrible.

❑ **POTENTATE**—monarch or ruler with great power

Alex was a much kinder person before he assumed the role of *potentate* and it went to his head.

❑ **PRAGMATIC**—practical; moved by facts rather than abstract ideals

While daydreaming gamblers think they can get rich by frequenting casinos, *pragmatic* gamblers realize that the odds are heavily stacked against them.

❑ **PRATTLE (n.)**—meaningless, foolish talk

Her husband's mindless *prattle* drove Hilary insane; sometimes, she wished he would just shut up.

❑ **PRECARIOUS**—uncertain

The mountain goat almost lost its *precarious* footing on the cliff face.

❑ **PRECEPT**—principle; law

The Supreme Court justices do their best to abide by the *precepts* of the Constitution.

❑ PRECIPICE—edge, steep overhang

The hikers stood at the *precipice*, staring down over the steep cliff.

❑ PRECIPITATE (adj.)—sudden and unexpected

Since the couple wed after knowing each other only a month, many expected their *precipitate* marriage to end in divorce.

❑ PRECIPITATE (v.)—to throw down from a height; to cause to happen

It's fairly certain that Lloyd's incessant smoking *precipitated* his early death from cancer.

❑ PRECIPITOUS—hasty, quickly, with too little caution

At the sight of the approaching helicopters, Private Johnson *precipitously* shot a flare into the air, not realizing that he was attracting the attention of enemy aircraft.

❑ PRÉCIS—concise summary of facts

The police chief reviewed the *précis* for any missing details.

❑ PRECISION—state of being precise

Molly entered the data into the computer with remarkable *precision* and speed.

❑ PRECLUDE—to rule out

The seriousness of the damage to the car *precluded* any attempt to repair it; it had to be scrapped.

❑ PRECOCIOUS—unusually advanced at an early age

The fact that Beatrice got married at age eighteen did not come as much of a shock, as she had always been *precocious*.

❑ PRECURSOR—forerunner, predecessor

It is amazing to compare today's sleek, advanced computers with their bulky, slow *precursors*.

❑ PREDATOR—one that preys on others, destroyer, plunderer

The lioness is a skilled *predator*, stalking her prey silently until it is close enough to go for the kill.

❑ PREDICAMENT—difficult situation

Because he had spent all of his pay, Bancha found himself in a miserable *predicament* when his rent bill arrived.

❑ PREDICATE (v.)—to found or base on

The new company is *predicated* on the central role of the Internet in modern international commerce.

❑ PREDICTIVE—relating to prediction, indicative of the future

The investors hung on every word of Bill Gates' *predictive* statements.

❑ PREDILECTION—preference, liking

The old woman's *predilection* for candy was evident from the chocolate bar wrappers strewn all over her apartment.

❑ PREDISPOSITION—tendency, inclination

I have a *predisposition* to be suspicious of used car salesmen, even though some of them may be honest.

❏ PREEMINENT—celebrated, distinguished

After he was awarded the Nobel Prize, Dr. Desai was recognized as a *preeminent* scholar in his field.

❏ PREFACE (n.)—introduction to a book; introductory remarks to a speech

Yumiko was thrilled that the famous Oprah Winfrey would be writing the *preface* to her book.

❏ PREMEDITATE—to consider, plan beforehand

The district attorney had to prove that the murder was *premeditated* in order to convince the jury to opt for the death penalty.

❏ PREMONITION—forewarning; presentiment

Mrs. Famuyiwa had a *premonition* that if her son were to marry this woman, he would suffer a terrible fate.

❏ PREPONDERANCE—majority in number; dominance

The *preponderance* of millionaires in his district meant that the Communist candidate stood no chance of being elected.

❏ PREPOSSESSING—attractive, engaging, appealing

The young man's *prepossessing* appearance and manner made him the most eligible bachelor at the party.

❏ PREPOSTEROUS—absurd, illogical

Hamish's *preposterous* plan to save the environment by burning all the cities to the ground made him an object of ridicule.

❏ PRESAGE—to foretell, indicate in advance

The demolition of the Berlin Wall *presaged* the fall of the Soviet Union.

❏ PRESCIENT—having foresight

Jonah's decision to sell the apartment turned out to be a *prescient* one, as its value soon dropped by half.

❏ PRESCRIBE—to set down a rule; to recommend a treatment

The doctor *prescribed* valium to the nervous patient, not realizing how addictive the drug was.

❏ PRESENTIMENT—premonition, sense of foreboding

I had a *presentiment* of doom when I saw the manager heading towards us with an angry look on his face.

❏ PRESTIDIGITATION—sleight of hand

Through some *prestidigitation*, the magician performed a seemingly impossible card trick.

❏ PRESUMPTUOUS—rude, improperly bold

"I don't want to be *presumptuous*, but why on earth did you choose red wallpaper?" said Ceci to her hosts.

❏ PRETEXT—excuse, pretended reason

Under the *pretext* that he needed a cup of coffee, Ted stood close to the managers, trying to overhear their conversation.

❑ PREVALENT—widespread

The teacher struggled to counteract the *prevalent* belief in the school that girls could give boys cooties.

❑ PREVARICATE—to lie, evade the truth

Rather than admit that he had overslept again, the employee *prevaricated*, claiming that traffic had made him late.

❑ PRIMEVAL—ancient, primitive

The archaeologist claimed that the skeleton he had uncovered was of *primeval* origin, though in actuality it was the remains of a monkey who had died at the zoo a few weeks previously.

❑ PRIMORDIAL—original, existing from the beginning

The first organisms were formed eons ago from *primordial* ooze.

❑ PRISTINE—untouched, uncorrupted

Since measures had been taken to prevent looting, the archeological site was still *pristine* when researchers arrived.

❑ PRIVATION—lack of usual necessities or comforts

The convict endured total *privation* while locked up in solitary confinement for a month.

❑ PROBITY—honesty, high-mindedness

The conscientious witness responded with the utmost *probity* to all the questions posed to her.

❑ PROCLIVITY—tendency, inclination

His *proclivity* for speeding got him into trouble with the highway patrol on many occasions.

❑ PROCRASTINATOR—one who continually and unjustifiably postpones

Don't be a *procrastinator*; do your homework now!

❑ PROCURE—to obtain

I was able to *procure* tickets to the premiere of the new *Star Wars* movie.

❑ PRODIGAL (adj.)—wasteful, extravagant, lavish

The *prodigal* son quickly wasted all of his inheritance on a lavish lifestyle devoted to pleasure.

❑ PRODIGIOUS—vast, enormous, extraordinary

The musician's *prodigious* talent made her famous all over the world.

❑ PROFANE—impure; contrary to religion; sacrilegious

His *profane* comments caused him to be banished from the temple for life.

❑ PROFICIENT—expert, skilled in a certain subject

The mechanic was *proficient* at repairing cars, but his horrible temper made it difficult for him to keep jobs for long.

❑ PROFLIGATE—corrupt, degenerate

Some historians claim that it was the Romans' decadent, *profligate* behavior that led to the decline of the Roman Empire.

❏ PROFUSE—lavish, extravagant

Although Janet was angry at Bart for forgetting her birthday, his *profuse* apologies made her forgive him.

❏ PROGENITOR—originator, forefather, ancestor in a direct line

The *progenitor* of the telephone is Alexander Graham Bell.

❏ PROGENY—offspring, children

The old photograph showed Greatgrandma Wells surrounded by her husband and all their *progeny*.

❏ PROGNOSIS—prediction of disease outcome; any prediction

Although his illness is serious, the new drugs on the market have made his *prognosis* relatively good.

❏ PROGRESSIVE—favoring progress or change; moving forward, going step-by-step

The *progressive* party pushed for reforms, while the conservatives tried to maintain the status quo.

❏ PROLIFERATE—propagate, reproduce; enlarge, expand

He only had two guinea pigs initially, but they *proliferated* to such an extent that he soon had dozens.

❏ PROLIFIC—productive, fertile

Stephen King, a *prolific* writer, seems to come out with a new book every six months.

❏ PROLOGUE—introductory section of a literary work or play

In the novel's *prologue*, the narrator of the story is introduced.

❏ PROMONTORY—piece of land or rock higher than its surroundings

The view of the valley from the *promontory* was an impressive sight.

❏ PROMULGATE—to make known publicly

The publicist *promulgated* the news of the celebrity's splendid wedding to the press.

❏ PROPENSITY—inclination, tendency

She has a *propensity* to lash out at others when under stress, so we leave her alone as much as possible.

❏ PROPINQUITY—nearness

The house's close *propinquity* to the foul-smelling pig farm made it impossible to sell.

❏ PROPITIATE—to win over, appease

The management *propitiated* the irate union by agreeing to raise wages for its members.

❏ PROPITIOUS—favorable, advantageous

"I realize that I should have brought this up at a more *propitious* moment, but I don't love you," said the bride to the groom in the middle of their marriage vows.

❏ PROPONENT—advocate, defender, supporter

A devoted *proponent* of animal rights, Rose rescued stray dogs and cats at every opportunity.

❏ PROSAIC—relating to prose; dull, commonplace

Simon's *prosaic* style bored his writing teacher to tears, and she dreaded having to mark his essays.

❏ PROSCRIBE—to condemn; to forbid, outlaw

Treason was *proscribed* in the country's constitution.

❏ PROSE—ordinary language used in everyday speech

The author's ideas were matched by his exquisite *prose* style, which was almost as refined as poetry.

❏ PROSECUTOR—person who initiates a legal action or suit

The *prosecutor*'s aggressive questioning left the defendant flustered, which weakened the defense's case.

❏ PROSELYTIZE—to convert to a particular belief or religion

The Jehovah's Witnesses went from door to door in the neighborhood, *proselytizing* enthusiastically.

❏ PROSTRATE—lying face downward, lying flat on ground

After taking a tumble down the stairs, Millie was found *prostrate* on the floor of the basement.

❏ PROTAGONIST—main character in a play or story, hero

In dramatic tragedy, the *protagonist* often brings about his own downfall.

❏ PROTEAN—readily assuming different forms or characters

The *protean* Scarlet Pimpernel could play a wide variety of different characters convincingly.

❏ PROTESTATION—declaration

Although the music students voiced their *protestation*, the school's music program was canceled.

❏ PROTOCOL—ceremony and manners observed by diplomats

Diplomats must strive to observe the correct *protocol* in their dealings with foreign heads of state.

❏ PROTRACT—to prolong, draw out, extend

Since every member of the committee had to have his say, the meeting was a *protracted* affair.

❏ PROTRUSION—something that sticks out

The carpenter noticed a *protrusion* in the piece of wood and sanded it down until it disappeared.

❏ PROVINCIAL—rustic, unsophisticated, limited in scope

Anita, a sophisticated city girl, sneered at the *provincial* attitudes of her country cousins.

❏ PROVOCATION—cause, incitement to act or respond

Poisonous snakes seldom attack without *provocation*; it is usually those who harass the snakes in some way who are bitten.

❏ PROWESS—bravery, skill

She credited her athletic *prowess* to daily practice and intense concentration.

❏ PROXIMITY—nearness

Tim was careful to put the glass out of reach, since the toddler loved to yank down objects in her *proximity*.

❏ PROXY—power to act as a substitute for another

The senile woman's niece produced a document that identified her as her aunt's *proxy* for all legal matters.

❑ PRUDE—one who is excessively proper or modest

The performance was admired by all except the *prude* in the front row, who fainted during the first sex scene.

❑ PRUDENT—careful, cautious

Considering the small size of our army, it would not be *prudent* for us to attack right now.

❑ PRURIENT—lustful, exhibiting lewd desires

The drunken sailor gave the buxom young waitress a *prurient* look.

❑ PRY—to intrude into; force open

I hesitated to ask Fern what had made her cry, since I didn't want to *pry* into her personal life.

❑ PSEUDONYM—pen name; fictitious or borrowed name

The exposé was so thoroughly damning to all parties involved that the author was forced to publish it under a *pseudonym*.

❑ PSYCHIC (adj.)—perceptive of nonmaterial, spiritual forces

Many unsuspecting fools have been robbed of their savings by people claiming to have *psychic* abilities.

❑ PUERILE—childish, immature, silly

Olivia's boyfriend's *puerile* antics are really annoying; sometimes he acts like a five-year-old!

❑ PUDGY—chubby, overweight

The *pudgy* dachshund was put on a diet when its owners realized that its large stomach was practically scraping the ground.

❑ PUGILISM—boxing

Pugilism has been praised a positive outlet for the aggressive impulses of deprived youths; on the down side, many boxers ultimately suffer brain damage from repeated blows to the head.

❑ PUGNACIOUS—quarrelsome, eager and ready to fight

The serene eighty-year-old used to be a *pugnacious* troublemaker in her youth, but she's softer now.

❑ PULCHRITUDE—beauty

The mortals gazed in admiration at Venus, stunned by her incredible *pulchritude*.

❑ PULVERIZE—to pound, crush, or grind into powder; destroy

The polar bear's awesome strength was such that a single blow from its paw would *pulverize* a human.

❑ PUMMEL—to pound, beat

The parents feared that the gorilla would *pummel* their precious baby, but instead, it brought him to safety.

❑ PUNCTILIOUS—careful in observing rules of behavior or ceremony

The *punctilious* butler made sure that all the proper conventions were observed for the important diplomatic dinner.

❑ PUNGENT—strong or sharp in smell or taste

The smoke from the burning tires was extremely *pungent*.

❑ PUNITIVE—having to do with punishment

The teacher banished Jack from the classroom as a *punitive* measure, but the boy was actually overjoyed to be missing class.

❑ PURGATION—catharsis, purification

Some religions require that converts undergo ritual *purgation* before accepting them as full-fledged members of the faith.

❑ PURGE—to cleanse or free from impurities

After *purging* his body of toxins, Roger felt healthy and refreshed.

❑ PURITANICAL—adhering to a rigid moral code

Fred was so *puritanical* that he refused to let his daughters talk to boys, let alone date them.

❑ PURPORT—to profess, suppose, claim

Brad *purported* to be an opera lover, but he fell asleep at every performance he attended.

Q

❑ QUACK—faker; one who falsely claims to have medical skill

Licenses are given to doctors so that patients can be assured that their M.D.'s are qualified professionals rather than *quacks*.

❑ QUADRILATERAL—four-sided polygon

The fortress was shaped as a *quadrilateral*, with watch towers in each of its four corners.

❑ QUADRUPED—animal having four feet

After I threw my back out, the only way I could manage to move around was to clamber about on all fours like a *quadruped*.

❑ QUAGMIRE—marsh; difficult situation

Kevin realized that he needed help to get himself out of this *quagmire*.

❑ QUALIFY—to provide with needed skills; modify, limit

Stacey needed to shave a full minute off her record in order to *qualify* for the Olympic finals.

❑ QUANDARY—dilemma, difficulty

Bill found himself in quite a *quandary* when he realized that he had promised to give the job to two different applicants.

❑ QUARANTINE—isolation period, originally 40 days, to prevent spread of disease

When cholera hit the village, it was *quarantined* to prevent the disease spreading any further.

❑ QUATERNARY—consisting of or relating to four units or members

The Rio Trio was hard pressed to come up with a new name when a fourth member turned their group into a *quaternary*.

❑ QUELL—to crush or subdue

The dictator dispatched troops to *quell* the rebellion.

❏ QUERULOUS—inclined to complain, irritable

Curtis's complaint letter received prompt attention after the company labeled him a *querulous* potential troublemaker.

❏ QUERY (n.)—question

When the congressman refused to answer her *query*, the journalist repeated it in a louder voice.

❏ QUIBBLE—to argue about insignificant and irrelevant details

Ignoring the widening crack in the dam, the engineers *quibbled* over whose turn it was to make coffee.

❏ QUICKEN (v.)—to hasten, arouse, excite

The car had been well constructed, but continuous exposure to sea air *quickened* its deterioration, and it had to be replaced.

❏ QUIESCENCE—inactivity, stillness

Bears typically fall into a state of *quiescence* when they hibernate during the winter months.

❏ QUINTESSENCE—most typical example; concentrated essence

As far as I'm concerned, Julio Iglesias is the *quintessence* of Spanish manliness.

❏ QUIVER—to shake slightly, tremble, vibrate

The *quivering* mobile unfastened from its weak nail and came crashing down.

❏ QUIXOTIC—overly idealistic, impractical

The practical Danuta was skeptical of her roommate's *quixotic* plans to build a rollercoaster in their yard.

❏ QUOTIDIAN—occurring daily; commonplace

The sight of people singing on the street is so *quotidian* in New York that passersby rarely react to it.

R

❏ RACONTEUR—witty, skillful storyteller

The *raconteur* kept all the passengers entertained with his stories during the six-hour flight.

❏ RADICAL—fundamental; drastic

Bored with her appearance, Lucinda decided to make a *radical* change and dyed her hair bright purple.

❏ RAIL (v.)—to scold with bitter or abusive language

When the teacher assigned twice as much homework as usual, his students *railed* against such an impossible work load.

❏ RALLY (v.)—to assemble; recover, recuperate

Martina's neighbors *rallied* to her side after the fire destroyed her home, collecting donations for her.

❏ RAMBLE—to roam, wander; to babble, digress

Central Park was designed to invite both open-air lounging and random *rambling* down various paths.

❑ RAMIFICATION—an implication, outgrowth, or consequence

Deb was too young to comprehend the *ramifications* of her actions at the time she committed the crime.

❑ RAMSHACKLE—likely to collapse

The homeless man lived in a *ramshackle* lean-to that had long been abandoned by its previous owners.

❑ RANCID—spoiled, rotten

The dead mouse was discovered after Brendan complained about the *rancid* odor emanating from behind the refrigerator.

❑ RANCOR—bitter hatred

Herbert was so filled with *rancor* that he could think of nothing but taking revenge on those who had humiliated him.

❑ RANT—to harangue, rave, forcefully scold

The teenager barely listened as her father *ranted* on and on about her disrespectful behavior.

❑ RAPPORT—relationship of trust and respect

Initially, they disliked one another, but working together eventually forged a *rapport* between the two men.

❑ RAPT—deeply absorbed

Surprisingly, the normally wild infant sat *rapt* during the classical music performance.

❑ RAREFY—to make thinner, purer, or more refined

The atmosphere *rarefies* as altitude increases, so the air at the top of high mountains is too thin to breathe.

❑ RASH (adj.)—careless, hasty, reckless

Lewis *rashly* jumped to the conclusion that the employee was completely incompetent after she made a small error.

❑ RATIFY—to approve formally, confirm

The Senate *ratified* the treaty after only a brief debate, much to the delight of its supporters.

❑ RATIOCINATION—methodical, logical reasoning

Reading Plato's work teaches a young person the *ratiocination* necessary to evaluate experiences.

❑ RATION (n.)—portion, share

After wolfing down her own *ration*, the soldier helped herself to the new recruit's meager portion.

❑ RATION (v.)—to supply; to restrict consumption of

The hikers had to *ration* their food so that it would last until they reached the safety of the camp.

❑ RATIONAL—logical, reasonable

Desiree offered no *rational* reasons for quitting school and taking her show on the road, which infuriated her parents.

❑ RAUCOUS—harsh sounding; boisterous

The grade school cafeteria was a *raucous* place at lunch time.

❑ RAVAGE—to destroy, devastate

Floods periodically *ravaged* the small town, but life was so pleasant there that residents refused to relocate.

❑ RAVENOUS—extremely hungry

The refugee had not had a bite of food for days and was *ravenous*.

❑ RAVINE—deep, narrow gorge

Police officers scoured the crime scene for days before finding the murder weapon buried in a *ravine*.

❑ RAZE—to tear down, demolish

The house had been *razed*: where it once stood there was nothing but splinters and bricks.

❑ REACTIONARY—marked by extreme conservatism, especially in politics

The former bra-burning hippie had turned into quite a *reactionary*, and the press dwelled on her about-face, attempting to expose her as a hypocrite.

❑ REBUFF (n.)—blunt rejection

The princess coldly *rebuffed* her suitor's marriage proposal, turning her back on him and walking away.

❑ REBUKE—to reprimand, scold

Sergeants often *rebuke* newly enlisted soldiers to teach them discipline.

❑ REBUT—to refute by evidence or argument

The moderator was careful to allow sufficient time for callers to *rebut* claims made by her guest speakers.

❑ RECALCITRANT—resisting authority or control

The *recalcitrant* mule refused to go down the treacherous path, however hard its master pulled at its reins.

❑ RECANT—to retract a statement, opinion, etcetera

The statement was so damning that the politician had no hopes of recovering his credibility, even though he tried to *recant* the words.

❑ RECAPITULATE—to review by a brief summary

After the long-winded president had finished his speech, his assistant *recapitulated* the points he had made for the press.

❑ RECEPTIVE—open to others' ideas; congenial

The leading software company was *receptive* to new ideas and fearless about making changes to incorporate new technology.

❑ RECLUSIVE—shut off from the world

Anthony's *reclusive* tendencies led him to leave the city and move into a lonely cabin in Montana.

❑ RECONDITE—relating to obscure learning; known to only a few

The ideas expressed in the ancient philosophical treatise were so *recondite* that only a few scholars could appreciate them.

❑ RECOUNT—to describe facts or events

Suspiciously, the witness changed her story when asked to *recount* the events leading up to the crime.

❑ RECRUIT (v.)—to draft, enlist; to seek to enroll

Companies often send representatives to college campuses to *recruit* bright young employees.

❑ RECTIFY—to correct

Most people would *rectify* errors they had made if they were given the opportunity.

❑ RECTITUDE—moral uprightness

Young women used to be shipped off to finishing schools to teach them proper manners and *rectitude*.

❑ RECURRENCE—repetition

The frequent *recurrence* of cancer even after it is seemingly cured makes it a particularly terrible disease.

❑ REDRESS—relief from wrong or injury

Seeking *redress* for the injuries she had received in the accident, Doreen sued the driver of the truck that had hit her.

❑ REDUNDANCY—unnecessary repetition

Let's delete a few paragraphs to cut down on the *redundancy* in this section of the book.

❑ REFECTORY—room where meals are served

The students rushed down to the *refectory* for their evening meal.

❑ REFLECTION—image, likeness; opinion, thought, impression

The vain young man admired his own *reflection* in the mirror for hours on end.

❑ REFRACT—to deflect sound or light

The crystal *refracted* the rays of sunlight so that they made a beautiful pattern on the wall.

❑ REFUGE—escape, shelter

The couple took *refuge* from the storm underneath the awning.

❑ REFURBISH—to renovate

This old house is charming, but it's kind of shabby and definitely needs to be *refurbished*.

❑ REFUTE—to contradict, discredit

The president managed to *refute* the charges against him by proving that his accuser had been bribed to lie by his enemies.

❑ REGIMEN—government rule; systematic plan

His marathon training *regimen* dictated that he had to run ten miles every morning.

❑ REGRESS—to move backward; revert to an earlier form or state

Elderly people who suffer from senility often *regress* to the early years of their childhood.

❑ REHABILITATE—to restore to good health or condition; re-establish a person's good reputation

The star checked herself into a clinic in order to *rehabilitate* herself from her drug addiction.

❑ REITERATE—to say or do again, repeat

The teacher was forced to *reiterate* the instructions because the class hadn't been listening the first time.

❑ REJOINDER—response

Patrick tried desperately to think of a clever *rejoinder* to Marcy's joke, but he couldn't.

❑ REJUVENATE—to make young again; renew

Martina looked and felt completely *rejuvenated* after her plastic surgery was completed.

❑ RELEGATE—to assign to a class, especially an inferior one

Because of his poor standardized test scores, Abe was *relegated* to a lower grade level than his peers.

❑ RELINQUISH—to renounce or surrender something

The toddler was forced to *relinquish* the toy when the girl who owned it asked for it back.

❑ RELISH (v.)—to enjoy greatly

Cameron *relished* the tasty sandwich, but he didn't like the pickle that came with it.

❑ REMEDIABLE—capable of being corrected

In the belief that the juvenile delinquent was *remediable* and not a hardened criminal, the judge put him on probation.

❑ REMEDY (v.)—to cure, correct

We can *remedy* this disastrous situation by putting our emergency backup plan into effect right now.

❑ REMINISCENCE—remembrance of past events

The old timer's *reminiscence* of his childhood was of a time when there were no cars.

❑ REMISSION—lessening, relaxation

Johnetta was relieved to discover that her cancer had gone into *remission*.

❑ REMIT—to send (usually money) as payment

Every month, the Pakistani sailors had to *remit* part of their salaries to people at home to whom they owed money.

❑ REMOTE—distant, isolated

The island was so *remote* that Chan's cell phone wouldn't operate on it.

❑ REMUNERATION—pay or reward for work, trouble, etcetera

You can't expect people to do this kind of boring work without some form of *remuneration*.

❑ RENASCENT—reborn, coming into being again

After decades of unemployment, industry in the city is *renascent* and jobs are becoming available.

❑ RENEGADE—traitor, person abandoning a cause

The *renegades* plotted in secret to overthrow the government.

❑ RENEGE—to go back on one's word

Hitler *reneged* on his promise that he would never attack the Soviet Union when his troops invaded the country during World War II.

❏ RENOUNCE—to give up or reject a right, title, person, etcetera

Edward *renounced* his right to the British throne in order to marry the divorcée, Mrs. Simpson.

❏ RENOWN—fame, widespread acclaim

Having spent her whole childhood banging on things, Jane grew up to be a drummer of great *renown.*

❏ REPAST—meal or mealtime

Ravi prepared a delicious *repast* of chicken tikka and naan.

❏ REPEAL—to revoke or formally withdraw (often a law)

The U.S. government *repealed* Prohibition when they realized that the law was not functioning as it had been intended.

❏ REPEL—to rebuff, repulse; disgust, offend

So far, the castle defenders have managed to *repel* the attackers, but they will not be able to hold out much longer.

❏ REPENT—to regret a past action

"If you don't *repent* your sins, you will rot in hell!" shouted the evangelical preacher.

❏ REPENTANT—apologetic, guilty, remorseful

After stealing from the church collection box, Ralph was *repentant* and confessed his sin to the priest.

❏ REPLETE—abundantly supplied

The gigantic supermarket was *replete* with consumer products of every kind.

❏ REPLICATE—to duplicate, repeat

If we're going to *replicate* last year's profit margins, we're going to have to work really, really hard.

❏ REPOSE—relaxation, leisure

After the stress you've endured at work recently, I hope you'll find some *repose* in this quiet village.

❏ REPRESS—to restrain or hold in

Sheila *repressed* the urge to tell the obnoxious man to shut up, as he was one of her best customers.

❏ REPREHENSIBLE—blameworthy, disreputable

Lowell was thrown out of the bar because of his *reprehensible* behavior towards the other patrons.

❏ REPRISE—repetition, especially of a piece of music

The soloist ended her aria with a *reprise* of its beautiful refrain.

❏ REPROACH—to find fault with; blame

Renee *reproached* her boyfriend for forgetting to buy her a Christmas present.

❏ REPROBATE—morally unprincipled person

If you ignore your society's accepted moral code, you will be considered a *reprobate.*

❏ REPROVE—to criticize or correct

Mrs. Hernandez *reproved* her daughter for her poor grades and ordered her to work harder in school.

❑ REPUDIATE—to reject as having no authority

The old woman's claim that she was Russian royalty was *repudiated* when DNA tests showed she was not related to them.

❑ REPULSE—repel, fend off; sicken, disgust

He thinks women can't resist him, when in actuality many of them are *repulsed* by his arrogance.

❑ REQUIEM—hymns or religious service for the dead

The musician composed a moving *requiem* in honor of the recently deceased and beloved leader.

❑ REQUITE—to return or repay

Thanks for offering to lend me $500,000, but I know I'll never be able to *requite* your generosity.

❑ RESCIND—to repeal, cancel

The car company *rescinded* the offer of an advertising contract it had made to the celebrity after he was accused of murder.

❑ RESIDUE—remainder, leftover, remnant

The fire burned everything, leaving only a *residue* of ash and charred debris.

❑ RESILIENT—able to recover quickly after illness or bad luck; able to bounce back to shape

Luckily, Ramon was a *resilient* person, and was able to pick up the pieces and move on with his life after losing his business.

❑ RESOLUTE—determined; with a clear purpose

Louise was *resolute*; she would get into medical school no matter what.

❑ RESOLVE (n.)—determination, firmness of purpose

I admire your *resolve*, but is it really a good idea to go through with the marathon in this bad weather?

❑ RESOLVE (v.)—to conclude, determine

The conflict was finally *resolved* when Wanda dropped the criminal charges against her ex.

❑ RESONATE—to echo

The cries of the bald eagle *resonated* throughout the canyon.

❑ RESPIRE—to breathe

Humans need oxygen in order to *respire*.

❑ RESPITE—interval of relief

The brief *respite* was over; once again, Bo's phone was ringing off the hook with customer complaints.

❑ RESPLENDENT—splendid, brilliant

The bride looked *resplendent* in her long train and sparkling tiara.

❑ RESTITUTION—act of compensating for loss or damage

The concentration camp survivors demanded *restitution* from the German government for their suffering.

❏ RESTIVE—impatient, uneasy, restless

The passengers became *restive* after having to wait in line for hours, and began to shout complaints at the airline staff.

❏ RESTORATIVE—having the power to renew or revitalize

Inge told all her friends about the miraculous *restorative* powers of the herbal tea.

❏ RESTRAINED—controlled, repressed, restricted

The formerly wild girl became *restrained* and serious after a month in the strict boarding school.

❏ RESUSCITATE—to revive, bring back to life

The doctor managed to *resuscitate* the heart attack victim one minute after he had stopped breathing.

❏ RETAIN—to hold, keep possession of

Britain had to give up most of its colonies, but it *retained* control over Hong Kong until very recently.

❏ RETARD (v.)—to slow, hold back

The Chinese tradition of footbinding involved *retarding* the growth of women's feet through binding them in heavy bandages.

❏ RETICENT—not speaking freely; reserved

Physically small and *reticent*, Joan Didion often went unnoticed by those upon whom she was reporting.

❏ RETINUE—group of attendants with an important person

The nobleman had to make room in his mansion not only for the princess, but also for her entire *retinue*.

❏ RETIRING—shy, modest, reserved

A shy and *retiring* man, Chuck was horrified at the idea of having to speak in public.

❏ RETORT (n.)—cutting response

It was only after Lance had left the room that Vera came up with the perfect *retort* to his insulting remark.

❏ RETRACT—to draw in or take back

After Lance had *retracted* his insulting remark, Vera decided to forgive him.

❏ RETRENCH—to regroup, reorganize

After their humiliating defeat, the troops *retrenched* back at the base to decide what to do next.

❏ RETRIEVE—to bring, fetch; reclaim

The eager labrador *retrieved* the Frisbee from the lake.

❏ RETROACTIVE—applying to an earlier time

Employee raises will be *retroactive* to the beginning of this year, although they only recently were awarded.

❏ RETROGRADE—having a backward motion or direction

The *retrograde* motion of the comet puzzled the astronomists, who had expected it to move forward.

❏ RETROSPECTIVE—review of the past

The cinema held a *retrospective* of the director Kurosawa's greatest works.

❏ REVELRY—boisterous festivity

An atmosphere of *revelry* filled the school after its basketball team's surprising victory.

❏ REVERE—to worship, regard with awe

All the nuns in the convent *revered* their wise Mother Superior.

❏ REVERT—to backslide, regress

Just when Liz thought he was finally becoming more mature, Kyle *reverted* to his childish ways.

❏ REVILE—to criticize with harsh language, verbally abuse

Resentful of the traumas she had inflicted upon him, George *reviled* his mother at every opportunity.

❏ REVITALIZE—to renew; give new energy to

The new CEO's upbeat, supportive managerial style *revitalized* the previously demoralized staff.

❏ REVOKE—to annul, cancel, call back

Jonas's green card was *revoked* when it was proven that he had illegally worked outside the country.

❏ REVULSION—strong feeling of repugnance or dislike

Rebecca was filled with *revulsion* at the stench that the rotten melon slices in her fridge gave off.

❏ RHAPSODY—emotional literary or musical work

The rock group Queen played on a long musical tradition with their song "Bohemian Rhapsody."

❏ RHETORIC—persuasive use of language

Lincoln's talent for *rhetoric* was evident in his beautifully expressed Gettysburg Address.

❏ RIBALD—humorous in a vulgar way

The court jester's *ribald* brand of humor delighted the rather uncouth king.

❏ RIDDLE (v.)—to make many holes in; permeate

The helicopter was *riddled* with bullet holes after its flight into the combat zone.

❏ RIFE—widespread, prevalent; abundant

The essay was so *rife* with grammatical errors that it had to be rewritten.

❏ RISQUÉ —bordering on being inappropriate or indecent

Some of the more conservative audience members found the *risqué* variety act offensive.

❏ ROBUST—strong and healthy; hardy

Many of those around her fell ill, but the *robust* Sharon remained healthy throughout the flu epidemic.

❏ ROCOCO—very highly ornamented

The *rococo* palace was a little too fancy for the minimalist architect's taste.

❏ ROOT (v.)—to dig with a snout (like a pig)

The trained pig *rooted* happily in the mud for truffles and even managed to swallow a few before his master grabbed them.

❑ ROSTRUM—stage for public speaking

The college lecture hall was occasionally used as a *rostrum* for political speeches.

❑ ROTUND—round in shape; fat

The *rotund* matron spent her days baking cookies and then eating a good share of them herself.

❑ RUE—to regret

I *rue* the day I agreed to take care of that evil little cat.

❑ RUMINATE—to contemplate, reflect upon

The scholars spent days at the retreat, *ruminating* upon the complexities of the geopolitical situation.

❑ RUSTIC—rural

The *rustic* cabin was an ideal setting for a vacation in the country.

S

❑ SACCHARINE—excessively sweet or sentimental

Geoffrey's *saccharine* love poems nauseated Lucy, and she wished he'd stop sending them to her.

❑ SACROSANCT—extremely sacred; beyond criticism

Many people considered Mother Teresa to be *sacrosanct* and would not tolerate any criticism of her.

❑ SAGACIOUS—shrewd

Owls have a reputation for being *sagacious*, perhaps because of their big eyes which resemble glasses.

❑ SALIENT—prominent or conspicuous

His most *salient* characteristic is his tendency to dominate every conversation in which he takes part.

❑ SALLOW—sickly yellow in color

Due to the long hours she spent working in the sweatshop, Bertha's skin looked *sallow* and unhealthy.

❑ SALUBRIOUS—healthful

Rundown and sickly, Rita hoped that the fresh mountain air would have a *salubrious* effect on her health.

❑ SALUTATION—greeting

Many people keep in touch by exchanging Christmas *salutations* once a year.

❑ SANCTION (n.)—permission, support; law; penalty

"The court cannot *sanction* this type of criminal behavior, and it must stop," declared the stern judge.

❑ SANCTUARY—haven, retreat

Seeking *sanctuary* from the bloodthirsty crowd that wanted to burn her at the stake, the accused witch banged on the gate of the convent.

❑ SANGUINE—ruddy; cheerfully optimistic

A *sanguine* person thinks the glass is half full, while a depressed person thinks it's half empty.

❑ SARDONIC—cynical, scornfully mocking

Denise was offended by the *sardonic* way in which her date made fun of her ideas and opinions.

❑ SATIATE—to satisfy

His desire for power was so great that nothing less than complete control of the country could *satiate* it.

❑ SAUNTER—to amble; walk in a leisurely manner

The plainclothes policeman *sauntered* casually down the street, hoping he would not attract attention.

❑ SAVANT—learned person

The *savant* was happy to give advice to those who were not as intellectually gifted as she was.

❑ SAVORY—agreeable in taste or smell

The banquet guests consumed the *savory* treats with pleasure.

❑ SCABBARD—sheath for sword or dagger

The knight drew his sword from its *scabbard* and prepared to attack the villain.

❑ SCALE (v.)—to climb to the top of

The army recruits *scaled* the wall as fast as they could and raced to the end of the obstacle course.

❑ SCATHING—harshly critical; painfully hot

After the *scathing* criticism her book of poems received, Alicia swore off poetry writing for good.

❑ SCENARIO—plot outline; possible situation

I think this triangle drama between you, your husband, and the hairdresser would make an interesting *scenario* for a play.

❑ SCINTILLA—trace amount

This poison is so powerful that no more of a *scintilla* of it is needed to kill a horse.

❑ SCINTILLATE—to sparkle, flash

The society hostess was famous for her great wit and *scintillating* conversation.

❑ SCOFF—to deride, ridicule

The toddler *scoffed* at the notion that cows could jump over the moon; he was too smart to believe that.

❑ SCORE (n.)—notation for a musical composition

The *score* of the film was wonderful, but the musicians who performed it were not very skilful.

❑ SCORE (v.)—to make a notch or scratch

The prisoner *scored* a mark in the door for every day he passed in captivity.

❑ SCRIVENER—professional copyist

The illiterate peasant dictated her letter to a local *scrivener*.

❑ SCRUPULOUS—restrained; honest; careful and precise

David could not have stolen Carmen's money; he's too *scrupulous* to do such a thing.

❑ SCRUTINY—careful observation

The prehistoric fossils were given careful *scrutiny* by a team of scientists.

❑ SCURRILOUS—vulgar, low, indecent

The decadent aristocrat took part in *scurrilous* activities every night, unbeknownst to his family.

❑ SECANT—straight line intersecting a curve at two points

The mathematician used the *secant* to calculate the area of the curved shape.

❑ SECEDE—to withdraw formally from an organization

When the U.N. recognized the independence of Platvia's former colony, the country angrily *seceded* from the organization.

❑ SECLUDED—isolated and remote

The hermit lived in a *secluded* cottage, far from the other villagers.

❑ SECTARIAN—narrow-minded; relating to a group or sect

Since the fall of Communism in the former Yugoslavia, its various ethnic groups have plunged into *sectarian* violence.

❑ SECULAR—not specifically pertaining to religion

Although his favorite book was the Bible, the archbishop also read *secular* works such as mysteries.

❑ SEDENTARY—inactive, stationary; sluggish

Americans, who often work in *sedentary* office jobs, are becoming more overweight and out of shape.

❑ SEDITION—behavior promoting rebellion

Li was arrested for *sedition* after he gave a fiery speech condemning the government.

❑ SEISMOLOGY—science of earthquakes

Architects in San Francisco need to be familiar with *seismology* to design earthquake-proof structures.

❑ SEMINAL—relating to the beginning or seeds of something

The professor's theory is regarded as *seminal* in the discipline, in that many other theories build upon it.

❑ SENESCENT—aging, growing old

Fearful of becoming *senescent*, Jobim worked out several times a week and ate only health foods.

❑ SENSUAL—satisfying or gratifying the senses; suggesting sexuality

Although the movie was admittedly rather *sensual*, I don't think it deserved an X rating.

❑ SENTENTIOUS—having a moralizing tone

The pastor took on a *sententious* tone when he lectured the teenage couple on their loose morals.

❑ SENTIENT—aware, conscious, able to perceive

The anaesthetic didn't work and I was still *sentient* when the surgeon made her cut, so the operation was agony for me.

❏ SEQUESTER—to remove or set apart; put into seclusion

The witness in the mafia case was *sequestered* for his own protection when it was determined that his life might be in danger.

❏ SERAPHIC—angelic, pure, sublime

Selena's sweet, *seraphic* appearance belied her nasty, bitter personality.

❏ SERENDIPITY—habit of making fortunate discoveries by chance

Rosemary's *serendipity* revealed itself in many ways, such as in her habit of finding money on the street.

❏ SERENITY—calm, peacefulness

Lisette's meditation helps her to achieve true *serenity*.

❏ SERPENTINE—serpentlike; twisting, winding

The princess fled down the seemingly endless *serpentine* staircase of the castle keep.

❏ SERRATED—saw-toothed, notched

A saw will not cut through wood if you do not use its *serrated* edge.

❏ SERVILE—submissive, obedient

As the wealthy widow screamed in rage at him, the *servile* butler apologized profusely for his mistake.

❏ SHARD—piece of broken glass or pottery

Barbara picked up the *shards* of the broken vase and attempted to glue them back together.

❏ SHEEPISH—timid, meek, or bashful

The dog sat near the mangled remains of its owner's fur coat with a guilty, *sheepish* look on its face.

❏ SHIRK—to avoid a task due to laziness or fear

The garbageman *shirked* his responsibilities by picking up the trash on only half of the streets he was supposed to cover.

❏ SIGNIFY—denote, indicate; symbolize

These ancient arrowheads I found *signify* that a Native American tribe once hunted in these woods.

❏ SIMIAN—apelike; relating to apes

Early man was more *simian* in appearance than modern man, as he was more closely related to apes.

❏ SIMPER—to smirk, smile foolishly

The spoiled girl *simpered* as her mother praised her extravagantly to the guests at the party.

❏ SINECURE—well-paying job or office that requires little or no work

The corrupt mayor made sure to set up all his relatives in lucrative *sinecures* in government offices.

❏ SINGE—to burn slightly, scorch

Martha *singed* the hairs on her arm while cooking food over the gas flame.

❏ SINUOUS—winding; intricate, complex

Thick, *sinuous* vines wound around the trunk of the tree.

❏ SKEPTICAL—doubtful, questioning

Although her parents still tried to make her believe that Santa Claus existed, the girl was *skeptical*.

❏ SKULK—to move in a stealthy or cautious manner; sneak

The private detective *skulked* behind a tree, waiting for the lovers to emerge from the motel room.

❏ SLIGHT—to treat as unimportant; insult

Pete *slighted* his old friend Matt by not inviting him to his annual Superbowl party.

❏ SLIPSHOD—careless, hasty

Because he was so stressed out, Kirk did a rather *slipshod* job on his last project.

❏ SLOTH—sluggishness, laziness

The formerly dynamic CEO sank into *sloth* upon retiring, staying in bed until 3 in the afternoon.

❏ SLOUGH—to discard or shed

The rattlesnake *sloughed* off its old skin and slithered away, shiny and new looking.

❏ SLOVENLY—untidy, messy

The cook's clothes were so stained and *slovenly* that no restaurant would hire him.

❏ SLUGGARD—lazy, inactive person

Helga's *sluggard* of a husband watches TV on the couch all day instead of looking for a job.

❏ SMELT (v.)—to melt metal in order to refine it

We could make jewelry out of this silver ore, but it would look more elegant if we *smelted* it first.

❏ SNIPPET—tiny part, tidbit

From the brief *snippet* of conversation she overheard, Ida realized that her job was in danger.

❏ SOBRIETY—seriousness

Wendell's witty comments alleviated the *sobriety* of the budget conference.

❏ SOBRIQUET—nickname

One of Ronald Reagan's *sobriquets* was "The Gipper."

❏ SODDEN—thoroughly soaked; saturated

My shoes were thoroughly *sodden* after trekking through the damp Irish bog.

❏ SOJOURN—visit, stay

After graduating from college, Iliani embarked on an extended *sojourn* in China.

❏ SOLACE—comfort in distress; consolation

Upset as she was by her poodle's death, Florence took *solace* in the fact that he had died happy.

❏ SOLARIUM—room or glassed-in area exposed to the sun

After a few hours too many in the *solarium*, Annette's skin took on an orangish shade.

❏ SOLECISM—grammatical mistake

The applicant's letter was filled with embarrassing *solecisms*, such as "I works here at 20 years."

❑ SOLICITOUS—concerned, attentive; eager

The *solicitous* waiter stood at the star's elbow throughout the meal, ready to serve her.

❑ SOLIDARITY—unity based on common aims or interests

The company's owner felt a certain *solidarity* with the striking workers because of his own humble origins.

❑ SOLILOQUY—literary or dramatic speech by one character, not addressed to others

Rachel's *soliloquy* gave the audience more insight into her thoughts than the other characters in the play had.

❑ SOLIPSISM—belief that oneself is the only reality

Arthur's *solipsism* meant that he treated other people as if they didn't exist, which tended to annoy them.

❑ SOLSTICE—shortest and longest day of the year

In Sweden, the summer *solstice* is celebrated with parties that last all night.

❑ SOLUBLE—capable of being solved or dissolved

Sugar is *soluble* in cold water, but it dissolves more easily in hot water.

❑ SOMBER—dark and gloomy; melancholy, dismal

Everyone at the funeral was wearing dark, *somber* clothes except for the little girl in the flowered dress.

❑ SOMNAMBULIST—sleepwalker

The *somnambulist* climbed out of bed, walked to the kitchen, made himself a sandwich, and suddenly woke up.

❑ SOMNOLENT—drowsy, sleepy; inducing sleep

Carter became *somnolent* after taking a couple of sleeping pills.

❑ SONIC—relating to sound

The *sonic* capabilities of the speakers were impressive, and Gerry couldn't wait to listen to his favorite CD on them.

❑ SONOROUS—producing a full, rich sound

The *sonorous* blaring of the foghorn woke Lily up at 4:30 in the morning.

❑ SOPHIST—person good at arguing deviously

The philosopher was known as a masterful *sophist*; people respected his abilities but did not trust him.

❑ SOPHISTRY—deceptive reasoning or argumentation

The politician used *sophistry* to cloud the issue whenever he was asked a tough question in a debate.

❑ SOPHOMORIC—immature and overconfident

The *sophomoric* young man was sure he would have no problems in writing the book, although there was no way he could accomplish the task.

❑ SOPORIFIC—sleepy or tending to cause sleep

The movie proved to be so *soporific* that soon loud snores were heard throughout the theater.

❑ SORDID—filthy; contemptible and corrupt

The details of the mayor's affair were so *sordid* that many people were too disgusted to read them.

❑ SOVEREIGN—having supreme power

The king did not take kindly to those who refused to recognize his *sovereign* power.

❑ SPARTAN—austere, severe, grave; simple, bare

The athlete's room was *spartan*, containing nothing but a bed and a pair of dumbbells.

❑ SPAWN—to generate, produce

The frog *spawned* hundreds of tadpoles.

❑ SPECULATION—contemplation; act of taking business risks for financial gain

If you want to ensure that you have a nest egg to retire on, you should not engage in too much wild financial *speculation*.

❑ SPECULATIVE—involving assumption; uncertain; theoretical

The theories I'm presenting are purely *speculative*, and they shouldn't be acted upon until more research has been done to test them out.

❑ SPONTANEOUS—on the spur of the moment, impulsive

Jean made the *spontaneous* decision to go to the movies instead of visiting her in-laws as she had planned.

❑ SPORADIC—infrequent, irregular

Since he followed the diet *sporadically*, lapsing into his old bad eating habits, Ed did not lose weight.

❑ SPORTIVE—frolicsome, playful

The lion roared in pain as the *sportive* lion cub bit his tail playfully.

❑ SPRIGHTLY—lively, animated, energetic

He was quite *sprightly* and active for a 98-year-old.

❑ SPUR (v.)—to prod

The rider *spurred* the horse on to leap over the tall hedge.

❑ SPURIOUS—lacking authenticity; counterfeit, false

Quoting from a *spurious* bible, the cult leader declared that all property should be signed over to him.

❑ SPURN—to reject or refuse contemptuously; scorn

When Harvey proposed to Harriet, she *spurned* him: she'd always considered him an idiot.

❑ SQUALID—filthy; morally repulsive

The *squalid* living conditions in the tenement building outraged the new tenants.

❑ SQUANDER—to waste

While I've been saving for a piano, my friend Sean has been *squandering* all his earnings on lottery tickets.

❑ STACCATO—marked by abrupt, clear-cut sounds

The *staccato* sounds of the coded radio transmissions filled the ship's cabin.

❑ STAGNANT—immobile, stale

That *stagnant* pond is a perfect breeding ground for mosquitoes; we should drain it.

❑ STAID—self-restrained to the point of dullness

The lively young girl felt bored in the company of her *staid*, conservative date.

❑ STALK (v.)—to hunt, pursue

The rock star put a restraining order on the insane woman who had *stalked* him for many years.

❑ STAND (n.)—group of trees

The Iroquois warriors hid in a *stand* of trees, waiting to ambush the approaching British soldiers.

❑ STARK—bare, empty, vacant

Nancy bought posters to liven up her *stark* new apartment, although she couldn't afford furniture.

❑ STASIS—motionless state; standstill

The rusty, ivy-covered World War II tank had obviously been in *stasis* for at least fifty years.

❑ STIFLE—to smother or suffocate; suppress

Much as she longed to express her anger at the dictator, Maria *stifled* her protests for fear of being arrested.

❑ STIGMA—mark of disgrace or inferiority

In *The Scarlet Letter*, Hester Prynne was required to wear the letter "A" on her clothes as a public *stigma* for her adultery.

❑ STILTED—stiff, unnatural

The nervous father of the bride gave a rather *stilted* speech at the wedding banquet.

❑ STINT (n.)—period of time spent doing something

After his *stint* in the Peace Corps, Tim decided to get a Ph.D. in international relations.

❑ STINT (v.)—to be sparing or frugal

Just don't *stint* on the mayonnaise in my ham sandwich, because I don't like my sandwiches to be too dry.

❑ STIPEND—allowance; fixed amount of money paid regularly

Unable to survive on her small *stipend* from the university, Joyce was forced to take out loans.

❑ STOCKADE—enclosed area forming defensive wall

As the enemy approached, the soldiers took their defensive positions behind the *stockade*.

❑ STOIC—indifferent to or unaffected by emotions

While most of the mourners wept, the dead woman's husband kept up a *stoic*, unemotional facade.

❑ STOLID—having or showing little emotion

The prisoner appeared *stolid* and unaffected by the judge's harsh sentence.

❑ STRATAGEM—trick designed to deceive an enemy

The Trojan Horse must be one of the most successful military *stratagems* used throughout history.

❑ STRATIFY—to arrange into layers

Many Indians use the concept of caste to *stratify* society into levels ranging from the "Untouchables" to the Brahmins.

❑ STRICTURE—something that restrains; negative criticism

The teenagers ignored all the parental *strictures* placed upon them and partied wildly every night.

❑ STRIDENT—loud, harsh, unpleasantly noisy

The customer's *strident* manner annoyed the shop assistant, but she managed to keep her temper.

❑ STRINGENT—imposing severe, rigorous standards

Many people found it difficult to live up to the *stringent* moral standards imposed by the Puritans.

❑ STULTIFY—to impair or reduce to uselessness

The company's leadership was *stultified* by its practice of promoting the owner's dimwitted children to powerful positions.

❑ STUNTED—having arrested growth or development

The bonsai tree's growth is intentionally *stunted* by the Japanese gardeners who cultivate it.

❑ STUPEFY—to dull the senses of; stun, astonish

The stag, *stupefied* by the bright glare of the headlights, stood right in the middle of the highway.

❑ STYLIZE—to fashion, formalize

Nellie *stylized* her wardrobe to match Princess Diana's, and everyone said they could have been sisters.

❑ STYMIE—to block or thwart

The police effort to capture the bank robber was *stymied* when he escaped through a rear window.

❑ SUAVE—smoothly gracious or polite; blandly ingratiating

Nina was a *suave* young woman who knew exactly how to act in any situation.

❑ SUBDUED—suppressed, stifled

The actor was momentarily *subdued* after the director bawled him out, but soon he was his usual confident self again.

❑ SUBJECTION—dependence, obedience, submission

The coach demanded total *subjection* from the athletes on his team.

❑ SUBJUGATE—to conquer, subdue; enslave

The Romans made a practice of *subjugating* all the peoples they conquered, often enslaving them.

❑ SUBLIME—awe-inspiring; of high spiritual or moral value

The music was so *sublime* that it transformed the rude surroundings into a special place.

❑ SUBLIMINAL—subconscious; imperceptible

Subliminal messages flash by so quickly on the TV screen that viewers are not consciously aware that they have seen them.

❑ SUBMISSIVE—tending to be meek and submit

The *submissive* wolf cringed at the feet of the alpha male, leader of the pack.

❑ SUBPOENA—notice ordering someone to appear in court

The lawyer *subpoenaed* the hostile witness, and she had to come to court and testify against her will.

❑ SUBSEQUENT—following in time or order

Elizabeth heard people discussing what a good president she would make, and *subsequently*, she couldn't stop thinking about how wonderful it would be to be president.

❑ SUBTERFUGE—trick or tactic used to avoid something

Spies who are not skilled in the art of *subterfuge* are generally exposed before too long.

❑ SUBTERRANEAN—hidden, secret; underground

Subterranean passages were dug for the subway after it was decided that there was no longer enough room for the tracks above ground in the crowded city.

❑ SUBTLE—hard to detect or describe; perceptive

The pickpocket was so *subtle* that his victims did not even realize they had been robbed until hours later.

❑ SUBVERT—to undermine or corrupt

The traitor intended to *subvert* loyal citizens of the crown with the revolutionary propaganda he distributed.

❑ SUCCINCT—terse, brief, concise

She was sought after by many talk shows, as her remarks were always *succinct* and to the point.

❑ SUCCULENT—juicy; full of vitality or freshness

The famished businessman dug into the *succulent* porterhouse steak with relish.

❑ SUFFERABLE—bearable

The only thing that made his prison term *sufferable* was his beloved pet mouse, Rodolfo.

❑ SUFFRAGIST—one who advocates extended voting rights

Suffragists eventually won voting rights for women, blacks, and other previously powerless groups.

❑ SULLEN—brooding, gloomy

The *sullen* child sat in the corner by herself, refusing to play with her classmates.

❑ SULLY—to soil, stain, tarnish, taint

Reginald was upset to discover that the child's sticky red lollipop had *sullied* his new cashmere overcoat.

❑ SUMPTUOUS—lavish, splendid

The banquet was a *sumptuous* affair, including a seven-course meal and quarts of champagne.

❑ SUPERANNUATED—too old, obsolete, outdated

The manual typewriter has become *superannuated*, although a few loyal diehards still swear by it.

❑ SUPERCILIOUS—arrogant, haughty, overbearing, condescending

She was a shallow and scornful society woman with a *supercilious* manner.

❑ SUPERFICIAL—hasty; shallow and phony

The politician was friendly, but in a *superficial*, unconvincing kind of way.

❏ SUPERFLUOUS—extra, more than necessary

The extra essays Jake included in his application were *superfluous*, as only one essay was required.

❏ SUPERSEDE—to take the place of; replace

Word 2000 will gradually *supersede* older versions of Word on office computers around the world.

❏ SUPERVISE—to direct or oversee the work of others

Among her other duties, a manager must *supervise* the work of her subordinates.

❏ SUPPLANT—replace, substitute

After his miserable performance, the raw young CEO was *supplanted* by a more experienced candidate.

❏ SUPPLE—flexible, pliant

The *supple* stalks of bamboo swayed back and forth in the wind.

❏ SUPPLICANT—one who asks humbly and earnestly

Alf is normally a cocky fellow, but he transformed himself into a *supplicant* when he begged the banker for a loan.

❏ SURFEIT—excessive amount

Because of the *surfeit* of pigs, pork prices have never been lower.

❏ SURLY—rude and bad-tempered

When asked to clean the windshield, the *surly* gas station attendant tossed a dirty rag at the customer and walked away.

❏ SURMISE—to make an educated guess

From his torn pants and bloody nose, I *surmised* that he had been in a fight.

❏ SURMOUNT—to conquer, overcome

The deaf and blind woman *surmounted* great obstacles to become a well-known trial lawyer.

❏ SURPASS—to do better than, be superior to

Ursula is a pretty girl, but her gorgeous sister *surpasses* her in beauty.

❏ SURPLUS—excess

The supermarket donated its *surplus* fruit to a local homeless shelter.

❏ SURREPTITIOUS—characterized by secrecy

The queen knew nothing of the *surreptitious* plots being hatched against her at court.

❏ SURVEY (v.)—to examine in a comprehensive way

Pampers *surveyed* families in the area to determine what they were looking for in a diaper.

❏ SUSCEPTIBLE—vulnerable, unprotected

Because of her weakened state, Valerie was *susceptible* to infection.

❏ SUSPEND—to defer, interrupt; dangle, hang

Construction of the building was *suspended* when an ancient Native American burial ground was discovered at the site.

❑ SUSTAIN—support, uphold; endure, undergo

If we can *sustain* our efforts a little longer, I'm sure our plan will succeed in the end.

❑ SWARTHY—having a dark complexion

The pale British tourist stood out like a sore thumb among the *swarthy* native Egyptians.

❑ SYBARITE—person devoted to pleasure and luxury

A confirmed *sybarite*, the young nobleman fainted at the thought of having to leave his lush palace and live in a tiny cottage.

❑ SYCOPHANT—self-serving flatterer, yes-man

Dreading criticism, the actor surrounded himself with admirers and *sycophants*.

❑ SYLLABUS—outline of a course

Ko looked at the course *syllabus* to figure out how much work he would be expected to do each week.

❑ SYMBIOSIS—cooperation, mutual helpfulness

The rhino and the tick-eating bird live in *symbiosis*; the rhino gives the bird food in the form of ticks, and the bird rids the rhino of parasites.

❑ SYMPOSIUM—meeting with short presentations on related topics

The university's English department held a *symposium* on sexual imagery in the works of D. H. Lawrence.

❑ SYNCOPATION—temporary irregularity in musical rhythm

Christine couldn't tell if the *syncopation* in the song was intentional or the result of a scratch in the CD she was playing.

❑ SYNOPSIS—plot summary

Oren wrote a one-page *synopsis* of a 55-page book.

❑ SYNTHESIS—blend, combination

The methods used in the experiment were a *synthesis* of techniques taken from biology and medicine.

❑ SYNTHETIC—artificial, imitation

The sushi in the window looked so delicious that you could hardly tell it was made out of *synthetic* materials.

T

❑ TABLEAU—vivid description, striking incident or scene

The tourists admired the famous painter's lifelike *tableau* of the Last Supper.

❑ TACIT—silently understood or implied

Although not a word had been said, everyone in the room knew that a *tacit* agreement had been made about which course of action to take.

❑ TACITURN—uncommunicative, not inclined to speak much

The clerk's *taciturn* nature earned him the nickname "Silent Sammy."

❏ TACTILE—relating to the sense of touch

She was a very *tactile* person, constantly touching the objects around her.

❏ TAINT—to spoil or infect; to stain honor

"I will not allow you to *taint* my reputation!" stormed the politician when the blackmailer threatened to expose his corruption.

❏ TAINTED—stained, tarnished; corrupted, poisoned

The lake water was *tainted* with chemicals from the factory, making it impossible to swim in or drink.

❏ TALON—claw of an animal, especially a bird of prey

A vulture holds its prey in its *talons* while it dismembers it with its beak.

❏ TANG—sharp flavor or odor

After being smoked together with the herring, the bacon had a distinctly fishy *tang*.

❏ TANGENTIAL—digressing, diverting

Your argument is interesting, but it's *tangential* to the matter at hand, so I suggest we get back to the point.

❏ TANGIBLE—able to be sensed, perceptible, measurable

The storming of the castle didn't bring the soldiers *tangible* rewards, but it brought them great honor.

❏ TANTAMOUNT—equivalent in value or significance; amounting to

Her refusal to defend herself against the accusation was *tantamount* to a confession in the eyes of the police officers.

❏ TARNISHED—corroded, discolored; discredited, disgraced

The antique silver plate was so *tarnished* that Nestor had to polish it for hours before using it.

❏ TAWDRY—gaudy, cheap, showy

The performer changed into her *tawdry*, spangled costume and stepped out onto the stage to do her show.

❏ TAXONOMY—science of classification

Certain strange species do not seem to fit into the systems of classification used in traditional *taxonomy*.

❏ TECHNOCRAT—strong believer in technology; technical expert

The *technocrat* could barely hide his disbelief and contempt as the CEO struggled to open a Word file on his computer.

❏ TEMPERANCE—restraint, self-control, moderation

The strict, religious community frowned on newcomers who did not behave with *temperance*.

❏ TEMPERED—moderated, restrained

The atmosphere at the dinner was *tempered* and calm, which made the loud young guest stand out.

❏ TEMPESTUOUS—stormy, raging, furious

Yentl tried to venture out into the *tempestuous* storm to buy food, but she was forced to return home.

❑ TENABLE—defensible, reasonable

Greg burned down his own house so that his ex-wife could not live in it, a scarcely *tenable* action in light of the fact that this also left his children homeless.

❑ TENACIOUS—stubborn, holding firm

For years, against all odds, women *tenaciously* fought for the right to vote.

❑ TENET—belief, doctrine

One of the *tenets* of the Muslim religion is that it is not acceptable to eat pork.

❑ TENSILE—capable of withstanding physical stress

Architects construct buildings using only *tensile* materials in areas which are prone to earthquakes.

❑ TENUOUS—weak, insubstantial

Francine's already *tenuous* connection to her cousins was broken when they moved away and didn't give her their new address.

❑ TEPID—lukewarm; showing little enthusiasm

Roxanne refused to take a bath in the *tepid* water, fearing that she would catch a cold.

❑ TERMINAL (adj.)—concluding, final; fatal

The boy's parents were devastated to learn that his illness was *terminal*.

❑ TERMINAL (n.)—depot, station

The railway *terminal* was filled with commuters during rush hour.

❑ TERRESTRIAL—earthly; down-to-earth, commonplace

Many "extraterrestrial" objects turn out to be *terrestrial* in origin, as when flying saucers turn out to be normal airplanes.

❑ TERSE—concise, brief, free of extra words

Her *terse* style of writing was widely praised for coming directly to the point.

❑ TESTAMENT—statement of belief; will

Guy's children couldn't believe that he had left everything to his chihuahua in his last will and *testament*.

❑ TESTIMONIAL—statement testifying to a truth; something given in tribute to a person's achievement

The defense lawyers presented many *testimonials* to the good character of the defendant during the trial.

❑ TETHER—to bind, tie

The cheetah chewed through its *tether* and ran away.

❑ THEOCRACY—government by priests representing a god

Under the leadership of Ayatollah Khomeini, who claimed to represent Allah, Iran could be characterized as a *theocracy*.

❑ THEOLOGY—study of God and religion

Priests must study *theology* at a seminary for several years before they can be ordained.

❏ THEORETICAL—abstract

The economics professor's advice was too *theoretical* for the company to put to any practical use.

❏ THERAPEUTIC—medicinal

Trent found the hot springs to be very *therapeutic* for his aches and pains, so he bathed in them often.

❏ THESAURUS—book of synonyms and antonyms

A *thesaurus* can be very useful when you can't think of the right word to use in a certain context.

❏ THESIS—theory or hypothesis; dissertation or long, written composition

Henry worked for six years on his Ph.D. *thesis* on the mating habits of African horned toads.

❏ THWART—to block or prevent from happening; frustrate

Thwarted in its attempt to get at the food inside the box, the chimp threw it to the ground in frustration.

❏ TIDINGS—news

"I bring *tidings* of great joy!" shouted the messenger to the assembled court.

❏ TIMOROUS—timid, shy, full of apprehension

A *timorous* woman, Lois relied on her children to act for her whenever aggressive behavior was called for.

❏ TINGE (v.)—to color slightly

Photographs become *tinged* with yellow as they age.

❏ TINGE (n.)—slight amount

Although she no longer loved him, Linda felt a *tinge* of jealousy when she heard that her ex-husband planned to remarry.

❏ TIRADE—long, violent speech; verbal assault

Observers were shocked at the manager's *tirade* over such a minor mistake.

❏ TITAN—person of colossal stature or achievement

Despite his odd personal habits, it can't be denied that Howard Hughes was a *titan* of industry.

❏ TOADY—flatterer, hanger-on, yes-man

The king was surrounded by *toadies* who rushed to agree with whatever outrageous thing he said.

❏ TOLERANCE—capacity to respect different values; capacity to endure or resist something

Dictators are characterized by their lack of *tolerance* for anyone who opposes them in any way.

❏ TOME—book, usually large and academic

The teacher was forced to refer to various *tomes* to find the answer to the advanced student's question.

❏ TONAL—relating to pitch or sound

Although it has interesting lyrics, the song's *tonal* problems make it unpleasant to listen to.

❏ TOPOGRAPHY—art of making maps or charts

A master in the art of *topography*, Leavenworth was hired to create maps of the coast of South America.

❏ TORPID—lethargic; unable to move; dormant

After surgery, the patient was *torpid* until the anesthesia wore off.

❏ TORRID—burning hot; passionate

The *torrid* weather dried out the rice paddies and ruined the entire crop.

❏ TORSION—act of twisting and turning

The cat executed a variety of desperate *torsions* in its attempt to escape the grip of its owner, who planned to give it a bath.

❏ TORTUOUS—having many twists and turns; highly complex

To reach the remote inn, the travelers had to negotiate a winding, *tortuous* path up the steep mountain.

❏ TOTTERING—barely standing

The *tottering* old man still managed to make his way to the corner shop every day to buy his favorite candy bar.

❏ TOXIN—poison

It's essential to keep all *toxins* away from children and animals, as they might eat them unwittingly.

❏ TRACTABLE—obedient, yielding

Though it was exhausted, the *tractable* workhorse obediently dragged the carriage through the mud.

❏ TRANSCEND—to rise above, go beyond

Yoga helps me to *transcend* the petty frustrations of everyday life and to achieve true spirituality.

❏ TRANSCENDENT—rising above, going beyond

For Wendy, the weekend with the Hari Krishnas was a truly *transcendent* experience, and she lost no time in joining their ranks.

❏ TRANSCRIPTION—copy, reproduction; record

The *transcription* of the incriminating conversation was entered into evidence in the court case.

❏ TRANSGRESS—to trespass, violate a law

After *transgressing* against every parking law in the city, Marvin had accumulated over 300 tickets.

❏ TRANSIENT (adj.)—temporary, short-lived, fleeting

The actress's moment in the spotlight proved to be *transient* when her play folded due to poor reviews.

❏ TRANSITORY—short-lived, existing only briefly

The reporter lived a *transitory* life, staying in one place only long enough to cover the current story.

❏ TRANSLUCENT—partially transparent

The man was visible through the *translucent* shower curtain.

❏ TRANSMUTE—to change in appearance or shape

In a series of stages, the caterpillar *transmuted* into a beautiful butterfly.

❏ TRANSPIRE—to happen, occur; become known

It later *transpired* that a faulty gear shift had been responsible for the horrible accident.

❑ TRAVESTY—parody, exaggerated imitation, caricature

When the pickpocket was sentenced to life in prison, many observers called it a *travesty* of justice.

❑ TREMULOUS—trembling, quivering; fearful, timid

The *tremulous* stray cat hardly dared to approach the bowl of milk the boy offered it.

❑ TRENCHANT—acute, sharp, incisive; forceful, effective

Dan's *trenchant* observations in class made him the professor's favorite student.

❑ TREPIDATION—fear and anxiety

Mike approached the door of the principal's office with *trepidation*.

❑ TRIFLING—of slight worth, trivial, insignificant

That little glitch in the computer program is a *trifling* error; in general, it works really well.

❑ TRITE—shallow, superficial

Lindsay's graduation speech was the same *trite* nonsense we've heard hundreds of times in the past.

❑ TROUNCE—to beat severely, defeat

The inexperienced young boxer was *trounced* in a matter of minutes by the seasoned champ.

❑ TROUPE—group of actors

This acting *troupe* is famous for its staging of Shakespeare's romantic comedies.

❑ TRUNCATE—to cut off, shorten by cutting

The mayor *truncated* his standard lengthy speech when he realized that the audience was not in the mood to listen to it.

❑ TRYING—difficult to deal with

Miraculously, she managed to finish the project under the most *trying* of circumstances.

❑ TRYST—agreement between lovers to meet; rendezvous

The knight arranged a secret *tryst* with the nobleman's wife deep in the forest.

❑ TUMULT—state of confusion; agitation

The *tumult* of the demonstrators drowned out the police chief's speech.

❑ TUNDRA—treeless plain found in arctic or subarctic regions

The Siberians set off across the freezing *tundra*, hoping to reach their homes before nightfall.

❑ TURBULENCE—commotion, disorder

The plane shook violently as it passed through the pocket of *turbulence*.

❑ TURGID—swollen, bloated

In the process of osmosis, water passes through the walls of *turgid* cells, ensuring that they never contain too much water.

❑ TURPITUDE—inherent vileness, foulness, depravity

The priest's affair with the teenage parishioner was considered an act of utter *turpitude*.

❑ TYRO—beginner, novice

An obvious *tyro* at salsa, Millicent received no invitations to dance.

U

❏ UBIQUITOUS—being everywhere simultaneously

Burger King franchises are *ubiquitous* in the United States, and are common in foreign countries as well.

❏ UMBRAGE—offense, resentment

The businessman took *umbrage* at the security guard's accusation that he had shoplifted a packet of gum.

❏ UNADULTERATED—absolutely pure

Only bottled waters that are *unadulterated* with chemicals can call themselves "pure."

❏ UNANIMITY—state of total agreement or unity

The *unanimity* of the council on this issue was surprising; I never thought they'd be able to agree on it.

❏ UNAPPEALING—unattractive, unpleasant

The fish dish looked so *unappealing* that Laszlo could not bring himself to taste it.

❏ UNAVAILING—hopeless, useless

Her efforts to drag her couch out of the flooding house were *unavailing*—it was simply too heavy for her.

❏ UNCONSCIONABLE—unscrupulous; shockingly unfair or unjust

The president's betrayal of the loyal employees who had worked to get him elected him was *unconscionable*.

❏ UNCTUOUS—greasy, oily; smug and falsely earnest

The *unctuous* salesman showered the rich customers with exaggerated compliments.

❏ UNDERMINE—to sabotage, thwart

Rumors of his infidelities *undermined* the star's marriage, and it eventually ended in divorce.

❏ UNDOCUMENTED—not certified, unsubstantiated

The journalist's controversial claims turned out to be completely *undocumented*, ruining his reputation.

❏ UNDULATING—moving in waves

The tourists hiked up and down the *undulating* hills of the lush countryside.

❏ UNEQUIVOCAL—absolute, certain

The jury's verdict was *unequivocal*: the sadistic murderer would be locked up for life.

❏ UNFROCK—to strip of priestly duties

The priest was *unfrocked* after it was discovered that he had broken many of his holy vows.

❏ UNHERALDED—unannounced, unexpected, not publicized

The gallant knight's arrival was *unheralded*, so the princess was surprised to discover him in the castle.

❑ UNIDIMENSIONAL—having one size or dimension, flat

The chocolate bars came off the factory conveyor belt in *unidimensional* little packages.

❑ UNIFORM (adj.)—consistent and unchanging; identical

We need to come up with a *uniform* look for our customer-service employees so that they can easily be identified as such.

❑ UNIMPEACHABLE—beyond question

His actions seem suspicious, but he's so honest that I know his motives must be *unimpeachable*.

❑ UNINITIATED—not familiar with an area of study

Uninitiated in the routines of tax assessment, the new employee had to consult his manual constantly.

❑ UNKEMPT—uncombed, messy in appearance

Sam's long hair seemed *unkempt* to his grandmother, and she told him he looked like a bum.

❑ UNOBTRUSIVE—modest, unassuming

"Servants should be *unobtrusive*, carrying out their duties quietly and efficiently," opined the countess.

❑ UNSCRUPULOUS—dishonest

The *unscrupulous* cafe owner watered down his soft drinks so that he could make a bigger profit on them.

❑ UNSOLICITED—unrequested

It is rare that *unsolicited* manuscripts are published; publishers are usually only interested in manuscripts they have requested through agents.

❑ UNWARRANTED—groundless, unjustified

The harshness of the criticism the film received was *unwarranted*, since it was really not all that bad.

❑ UNWITTING—unconscious; unintentional

Not looking where he was going, John charged into the subway car, *unwittingly* knocking down a blind man.

❑ UNYIELDING—firm, resolute

Despite her son's desperate pleas, Mrs. Young was *unyielding*: under no circumstances could he stay out after midnight.

❑ UPBRAID—to scold sharply

The teacher *upbraided* the student for scrawling graffiti all over the walls of the school.

❑ UPROARIOUS—loud and forceful

The *uproarious* soccer fans made a huge racket as they filed out of the stadium after the match.

❑ URBANE—courteous, refined, suave

The *urbane* teenager sneered at the mannerisms of his country-bumpkin cousin.

❑ USURP—to seize by force

The vice-principal was power-hungry, and threatened to *usurp* the principal's power.

❑ USURY—practice of lending money at exorbitant rates

The moneylender was convicted of *usury* for charging 50 percent interest on all his loans.

❑ UTILITARIAN—efficient, functional, useful

The suitcase was undeniably *utilitarian*, with its convenient compartments of different sizes, but it was also ugly.

❑ UTOPIA—perfect place

Wilson's idea of *utopia* was a beautiful, sunny beach on a tropical island.

V

❑ VACILLATE—to waver, show indecision

The customer held up the line as he *vacillated* between ordering chocolate or coffee ice cream.

❑ VACUOUS—empty, void; lacking intelligence, purposeless

The congresswoman's *vacuous* speech angered the voters, who were tired of hearing empty platitudes.

❑ VAGRANT—poor person with no home

Unable to afford a room for the night, the *vagrant* huddled in a sheltered doorway.

❑ VALIDATE—to authorize, certify, confirm

The Disney employee *validated* my guest pass so that I was able to enter Disney World for free.

❑ VANQUISH—to conquer, defeat

Napoleon was *vanquished* by the English at the Battle of Waterloo.

❑ VAPID—tasteless, dull

Todd found his blind date *vapid* and boring, and couldn't wait to get away from her.

❑ VARIABLE—changeable, inconstant

The weather has been so *variable* lately that I never know whether to put on a coat or shorts in the morning.

❑ VARIEGATED—varied; marked with different colors

The *variegated* foliage of the jungle allows it to support thousands of different animal species.

❑ VAUNTED—boasted about, bragged about

The much-*vaunted* new computer program turned out to have so many bugs that it had to be recalled.

❑ VEHEMENTLY—strongly, urgently

Susanne *vehemently* denied the accusation that she had cheated on the test.

❑ VENDETTA—prolonged feud marked by bitter hostility

The *vendetta* between the Montagues and the Capulets resulted in the death of Romeo and Juliet.

❑ VENERABLE—respected because of age

All of the villagers sought the *venerable* old woman's advice whenever they had a problem.

❏ VENERATION—adoration, honor, respect

In traditional Confucian society, the young treat their elders with *veneration*, deferring to the elders' wisdom.

❏ VENT (v.)—to express, say out loud

Bob *vented* his frustrations at his malfunctioning computer by throwing coffee at it, which only served to make the problem worse.

❏ VERACIOUS—truthful, accurate

Uncertain of whether her son's excuse for coming home late was *veracious*, Sue decided to check his story.

❏ VERACITY—accuracy, truth

She had a reputation for *veracity*, so everyone believed her version of the story.

❏ VERBATIM—word for word

A court stenographer's job is to take down testimony in a court case *verbatim*, making no changes whatsoever in what is said.

❏ VERBOSE—wordy

The professor's answer was so *verbose* that his student forgot what the original question had been.

❏ VERDANT—green with vegetation; inexperienced

He wandered deep into the *verdant* woods in search of mushrooms and other edible flora.

❏ VERDURE—fresh, rich vegetation

The settlers admired the *verdure* that covered the land they had bought, knowing it meant that this land was fertile.

❏ VERIFIED—proven true

Before you publish that information, I'll have to make sure that it's been *verified*.

❏ VERISIMILITUDE—quality of appearing true or real

The TV show's *verisimilitude* led viewers to believe that the characters it portrayed were real.

❏ VERITY—truthfulness; belief viewed as true and enduring

The *verity* of the situation was that Roy couldn't bear to step down and let his sons take over the company.

❏ VERMIN—small creatures offensive to humans

Laura called the exterminator to fumigate her *vermin*-infested apartment.

❏ VERNACULAR—everyday language used by ordinary people; specialized language of a profession

Preeti could not understand the local *vernacular* of the southern U.S. region in which she now resided.

❏ VERNAL—related to spring

Bea basked in the balmy *vernal* breezes, happy that winter was at last coming to an end.

❏ VERSATILE—adaptable, all-purpose

This *versatile* little gadget can be used to dice vegetables, open cans, and whip cream!

❏ VESTIGE—trace, remnant

Vestiges of the former tenant still remained in the apartment, although he hadn't lived there for years.

❏ VETO (v.)—to reject formally

Fearful that the new law would be used to reduce her powers, the president *vetoed* it.

❏ VEX—to irritate, annoy; confuse, puzzle

The old man, who loved his peace and quiet, was *vexed* by his neighbor's loud music.

❏ VIABLE—workable, able to succeed or grow

I don't think your plan to increase sales by sending free samples to every household in the city is *viable*.

❏ VIADUCT—series of elevated arches used to cross a valley

The ancient roman *viaduct* stretched across the lush green valley.

❏ VICARIOUS—substitute, surrogate; enjoyed through imagined participation in another's experience

Harriet lived *vicariously* through her daughter, listening avidly to her tales of romance and adventure.

❏ VICISSITUDE—change or variation; ups and downs

Investors must be prepared for *vicissitudes* in the market and not panic when stock prices fall occasionally.

❏ VIE—to compete, contend

The two wrestlers *vied* for the title of champion in the final match of the competition.

❏ VIGILANT—attentive, watchful

Air traffic controllers must be *vigilant* in order to ensure that planes do not collide with one another.

❏ VIGNETTE—decorative design; short literary composition

The writer's clever little *vignette* was published in a respected literary magazine.

❏ VILIFY—to slander, defame

The candidate *vilified* his opponent, accusing him of being a wife-beating liar.

❏ VIM—energy, enthusiasm

The sprightly old woman, still full of *vim* and vigor, walked four miles every day.

❏ VINDICATE—to clear of blame; support a claim

Tess felt *vindicated* when her dire predictions about the impending earthquake came true.

❏ VINDICATION—clearance from blame or suspicion

Many years after he was unjustly accused of treason, Dreyfus finally received full *vindication* from the authorities.

❏ VINDICTIVE—spiteful, vengeful, unforgiving

After her husband left her for a young model, the *vindictive* ex-wife plotted to destroy their relationship.

❏ VIRILE—manly, having qualities of an adult male

John Wayne tended to play *virile*, tough roles rather than effeminate, sensitive roles.

❑ VIRTUOSO—someone with masterly skill; expert musician

He is a *virtuoso* conductor and has performed in all the most prestigious concert halls.

❑ VIRULENT—extremely poisonous; malignant; hateful

Alarmed at the *virulent* hate mail she was receiving, the movie star decided to hire a bodyguard.

❑ VISCOUS—thick, syrupy, and sticky

The *viscous* sap trickled slowly down the trunk of the tree.

❑ VITRIOLIC—burning, caustic; sharp, bitter

Given the opportunity to critique his enemy's new book, the spiteful critic wrote an unusually *vitriolic* review of it for the *New York Times*.

❑ VITUPERATE—to abuse verbally

The crabby old man *vituperated* his wife for forgetting to buy his favorite breakfast cereal at the market.

❑ VIVACIOUS—lively, spirited

She was *vivacious* and outgoing, always ready to try something new.

❑ VIVID—bright and intense in color; strongly perceived

The *vivid* colors of the rose garden were visible from miles away.

❑ VOCIFEROUS—loud, vocal, and noisy

The prime minister continued his speech despite the *vociferous* protests of the members of parliament.

❑ VOID (adj.)—not legally enforceable; empty

The will was declared null and *void* after it was discovered that the butler had forged his wealthy employer's signature on it.

❑ VOID (n.)—emptiness, vacuum

The astronauts released their shuttle's ancillary rockets and watched them drift off into the *void*.

❑ VOID (v.)—to cancel, invalidate

Her credit card was *voided* after she failed to pay her bills for months on end.

❑ VOLITION—free choice, free will; act of choosing

Dorio gave up her property of her own *volition*; no one pressured her into anything.

❑ VOLLEY (n.)—flight of missiles, round of gunshots

The troops fired a *volley* at the enemy, but they could not be sure how many of their bullets had found their targets.

❑ VOLUBLE—speaking much and easily, talkative; glib

The *voluble* man and his silent wife proved the old saying that opposites attract.

❑ VOLUMINOUS—large, having great volume

The bride's *voluminous* train trailed several yards behind her as she walked down the aisle.

❑ VORACIOUS—having a great appetite

The *voracious* farming family consumed a huge meal after a long day of heavy labor.

❏ VULNERABLE—defenseless, unprotected; innocent, naive

The child whisked the *vulnerable* little duckling out of the raging whirlpool just in time.

W

❏ WAIVE—to refrain from enforcing a rule; to give up a legal right

Veronique *waived* her right to half of her ex-husband's property, ridding herself of everything that could remind her of him.

❏ WALLOW—to indulge oneself excessively, luxuriate

He *wallowed* in the luxurious waterbed, sighing contentedly.

❏ WAN—sickly pale

The sick child had a *wan* face, in contrast to her rosy-cheeked sister.

❏ WANTON—undisciplined, unrestrained, reckless

Instead of singling out appropriate targets for his anger, the crazed man struck out in a *wanton* manner.

❏ WARRANTY—guarantee of a product's soundness

I can't believe that the *warranty* on this radio ran out two days before it broke! Now I won't be able to get my money back!

❏ WARY—careful, cautious

The dog was *wary* of Bola at first, only gradually letting its guard down and wagging its tail when he came home at night.

❏ WAYWARD—erratic, unrestrained, reckless

The Vanderbolts' *wayward* son squandered his inheritance and got into trouble with the law.

❏ WEATHER (v.)—to endure, undergo

I'm surprised that the old shack is still standing; I never expected it to *weather* that storm last night.

❏ WHET—to sharpen, stimulate

The delicious odors wafting from the kitchen *whet* Jack's appetite, and he couldn't wait to eat.

❏ WHIMSICAL—playful or fanciful idea

The ballet was *whimsical*, delighting the children with its imaginative characters and unpredictable sets.

❏ WILY—clever, deceptive

Yet again, the *wily* coyote managed to elude the ranchers who wanted to capture it.

❏ WINDFALL—sudden, unexpected good fortune

A sudden *windfall* enabled the old woman to buy the big new house she wanted after all.

❏ WINSOME—charming, happily engaging

Dawn gave the customs officers a *winsome* smile, and they let her pass without searching her bags.

❑ WITHDRAWN—unsociable, aloof; shy, timid

Silent and *withdrawn*, Yuri was not exactly the life of the party.

❑ WIZENED—withered, shriveled, wrinkled

The *wizened* old man was told that the plastic surgery necessary to make him look young again would cost more money than he could imagine.

❑ WRIT—written document, usually in law

Writs are considered more legally valid than oral statements, as they provide a permanent record of what has been decided.

❑ WRY—amusing, ironic

Although his words sounded very serious, Del's *wry* expression clued his observers into the fact that he was only joking.

X

❑ XENOPHOBIA—fear or hatred of foreigners or strangers

Countries in which *xenophobia* is prevalent often have more restrictive immigration policies than countries which are more accepting of foreign influences.

Y

❑ YOKE (v.)—to join together

As soon as the farmer had *yoked* his oxen together, he began to plow the fields.

Z

❑ ZEALOT—someone passionately devoted to a cause

The religious *zealot* had no time for those who failed to share his strongly held beliefs.

❑ ZENITH—highest point, summit

The diva considered her triumphant performance as Carmen at the Metropolitan Opera to be the *zenith* of her career.

❑ ZEPHYR—gentle breeze

The *zephyr* blowing in from the ocean made the intense heat on the beach bearable for the sunbathers.

❑ ZOOLOGIST—scientist who studies animals

The *zoologist* spent much of his career studying the social interaction of a group of chimpanzees.

SAT Root List

Knowing roots can help you in two ways. First, instead of learning one word at a time, you can learn a whole group of words that contain a certain root. They'll be related in meaning, so if you remember one, it will be easier for you to remember others. Second, roots can often help you decode an unknown SAT word. If you recognize a familiar root, you could get a good enough idea of the word to answer the question.

❏ A, AN—not, without
amoral, atrophy, asymmetrical, anarchy, anesthetic, anonymity, anomaly

❏ AB, A—from, away, apart
abnormal, abdicate, aberration, abhor, abject, abjure, ablution, abnegate, abortive, abrogate, abscond, absolve, abstemious, abstruse, annul, avert, aversion

❏ AC, ACR—sharp, sour
acid, acerbic, exacerbate, acute, acuity, acumen, acrid, acrimony

❏ AD, A—to, towards
adhere, adjacent, adjunct, admonish, adroit, adumbrate, advent, abeyance, abet, accede, accretion, acquiesce, affluent, aggrandize, aggregate, alleviate, alliteration, allude, allure, ascribe, aspersion, aspire, assail, assonance, attest

❏ ALI, ALTR—another
alias, alienate, inalienable, altruism

❏ AM, AMI—love
amorous, amicable, amiable, amity

❏ AMBI, AMPHI—both
ambiguous, ambivalent, ambidextrous, amphibious

❏ AMBL, AMBUL—walk
amble, ambulatory, perambulator, somnambulist

❏ ANIM—mind, spirit, breath
animal, animosity, unanimous, magnanimous

❏ ANN, ENN—year
annual, annuity, superannuated, biennial, perennial

❏ ANTE, ANT—before
antecedent, antediluvian, antebellum, antepenultimate, anterior, antiquity, antiquated, anticipate

❏ ANTHROP—human
anthropology, anthropomorphic, misanthrope, philanthropy

SAT Emergency

If you don't have much time, just skim through this Root List to familiarize yourself with the component part of commonly tested SAT words.

❑ ANTI, ANT—against, opposite
antidote, antipathy, antithesis, antacid, antagonist, antonym

❑ AUD—hear
audio, audience, audition, auditory, audible

❑ AUTO—self
autobiography, autocrat, autonomous

❑ BELLI, BELL—war
belligerent, bellicose, antebellum, rebellion

❑ BENE, BEN—good
benevolent, benefactor, beneficent, benign

❑ BI—two
bicycle, bisect, bilateral, bilingual, biped

❑ BIBLIO—book
Bible, bibliography, bibliophile

❑ BIO—life
biography, biology, amphibious, symbiotic, macrobiotics

❑ BURS—money, purse
reimburse, disburse, bursar

❑ CAD, CAS, CID—happen, fall
accident, cadence, cascade, deciduous

❑ CAP, CIP—head
captain, decapitate, capitulate, precipitous, precipitate, recapitulate

❑ CARN—flesh
carnal, carnage, carnival, carnivorous, incarnate

❑ CAP, CAPT, CEPT, CIP—take, hold, seize
capable, capacious, captivate, deception, intercept, precept, inception, anticipate, emancipation, incipient, percipient

❑ CED, CESS—yield, go
cease, cessation, incessant, cede, precede, accede, recede, antecedent, intercede, secede, cession

❑ CHROM—color
chrome, chromatic, monochrome

❑ CHRON—time
chronology, chronic, anachronism

❑ CIDE—murder
suicide, homicide, regicide, patricide

❑ CIRCUM—around
circumference, circumlocution, circumnavigate, circumscribe, circumspect, circumvent

❑ CLIN, CLIV—slope
incline, declivity, proclivity

❑ CLUD, CLUS, CLAUS, CLOIS—shut, close
conclude, reclusive, claustrophobia, cloister, preclude, occlude

❑ CO, COM, CON—with, together
coeducation, coagulate, coalesce, coerce, cogent, cognate, collateral, colloquial, colloquy, commensurate, commodious, compassion, compatriot, complacent, compliant, complicity, compunction, concerto, conciliatory, concord, concur, condone, conflagration, congeal, congenial, congenital, conglomerate, conjugal, conjure, conscientious, consecrate, consensus, consonant, constrained, contentious, contrite, contusion, convalescence, convene, convivial, convoke, convoluted, congress

❑ COGN, GNO—know
recognize, cognition, cognizance, incognito, diagnosis, agnostic, prognosis, gnostic, ignorant

❑ CONTRA—against
controversy, incontrovertible, contravene

❑ CORP—body
corpse, corporeal, corpulence

❑ COSMO, COSM—world
cosmopolitan, cosmos, microcosm, macrocosm

❑ CRAC, CRAT—rule, power
democracy, bureaucracy, theocracy, autocrat, aristocrat, technocrat

❑ CRED—trust, believe
incredible, credulous, credence

❑ CRESC, CRET—grow
crescent, crescendo, accretion

❑ CULP—blame, fault
culprit, culpable, inculpate, exculpate

❑ CURR, CURS—run
current, concur, cursory, precursor, incursion

❑ DE—down, out, apart
depart, debase, debilitate, declivity, decry, deface, defamatory, defunct, delegate, demarcation, demean, demur, deplete, deplore, depravity, deprecate, deride, derivative, desist, detest, devoid

❑ DEC—ten, tenth
decade, decimal, decathlon, decimate

❑ DEMO, DEM—people
democrat, demographics, demagogue, epidemic, pandemic, endemic

❑ DI, DIURN—day
diary, quotidian, diurnal

❑ DIA—across
diagonal, diatribe, diaphanous

❑ DIC, DICT—speak
abdicate, diction, interdict, predict, indict, verdict

❑ DIS, DIF, DI—not, apart, away
disaffected, disband, disbar, disburse, discern, discordant, discredit, discursive, disheveled, disparage, disparate, dispassionate, dispirit, dissemble, disseminate, dissension, dissipate, dissonant, dissuade, distend, differentiate, diffidence, diffuse, digress, divert

❑ DOC, DOCT—teach
docile, doctrine, doctrinaire

❑ DOL—pain
condolence, doleful, dolorous, indolent

❑ DUC, DUCT—lead
seduce, induce, conduct, viaduct, induct

❑ EGO—self
ego, egoist, egocentric

❑ EN, EM—in, into
enter, entice, encumber, endemic, ensconce, enthrall, entreat, embellish, embezzle, embroil, empathy

❑ ERR—wander
erratic, aberration, errant

❑ EU—well, good
eulogy, euphemism, euphony, euphoria, eurythmics, euthanasia

❑ EX, E—out, out of
exit, exacerbate, excerpt, excommunicate, exculpate, execrable, exhume, exonerate, exorbitant, exorcise, expatriate, expedient, expiate, expunge, expurgate, extenuate, extort, extremity, extricate, extrinsic, exult, evoke, evict, evince, elicit, egress, egregious

❑ FAC, FIC, FECT, FY, FEA—make, do
factory, facility, benefactor, malefactor, fiction, fictive, beneficent, affect, confection, refectory, magnify, unify, rectify, vilify, feasible

❑ FAL, FALS—deceive
infallible, fallacious, false

❑ FERV—boil
fervent, fervid, effervescent

❑ FID—faith, trust
confident, diffidence, perfidious, fidelity

❑ FLU, FLUX—flow
fluent, affluent, confluence, effluvia, superfluous, flux

❑ FORE—before
forecast, foreboding, forestall

❑ FRAG, FRAC—break
fragment, fracture, diffract, fractious, refract

❑ FUS—pour
profuse, infusion, effusive, diffuse

❑ GEN—birth, class, kin
generation, congenital, homogeneous, heterogeneous, ingenious, engender, progenitor, progeny

❑ GRAD, GRESS—step
graduate, gradual, retrograde, centigrade, degrade, gradation, gradient, progress, congress, digress, transgress, ingress, egress

❑ GRAPH, GRAM—writing
biography, bibliography, epigraph, grammar, epigram

❑ GRAT—pleasing
grateful, gratitude, gratis, ingrate, congratulate, gratuitous, gratuity

❑ GRAV, GRIEV—heavy
grave, gravity, aggravate, grieve, aggrieve, grievous

❏ GREG—crowd, flock
segregate, gregarious, egregious, congregate, aggregate

❏ HABIT, HIBIT—have, hold
habit, cohabit, habitat, inhibit

❏ HAP—by chance
happen, haphazard, hapless, mishap

❏ HELIO, HELI—sun
heliocentric, heliotrope, aphelion, perihelion, helium

❏ HETERO—other
heterosexual, heterogeneous, heterodox

❏ HOL—whole
holocaust, catholic, holistic

❏ HOMO—same
homosexual, homogenize, homogeneous, homonym

❏ HOMO—man
homo sapiens, homicide, bonhomie

❏ HYDR—water
hydrant, hydrate, dehydration

❏ HYPER—too much, excess
hyperactive, hyperbole, hyperventilate

❏ HYPO—too little, under
hypodermic, hypothermia, hypochondria, hypothesis, hypothetical

❏ IN, IG, IL, IM, IR—not
incorrigible, indefatigable, indelible, indubitable, inept, inert, inexorable, insatiable, insentient, insolvent, insomnia, interminable, intractable, incessant, inextricable, infallible, infamy, innumerable, inoperable, insipid, intemperate, intrepid, inviolable, ignorant, ignominious, ignoble, illicit, illimitable, immaculate, immutable, impasse, impeccable, impecunious, impertinent, implacable, impotent, impregnable, improvident, impassioned, impervious, irregular

❏ IN, IL, IM, IR—in, on, into
invade, inaugurate, incandescent, incarcerate, incense, indenture, induct, ingratiate, introvert, incarnate, inception, incisive, infer, infusion, ingress, innate, inquest, inscribe, insinuate, inter, illustrate, imbue, immerse, implicate, irrigate, irritate

❏ INTER—between, among
intercede, intercept, interdiction, interject, interlocutor, interloper, intermediary, intermittent, interpolate, interpose, interregnum, interrogate, intersect, intervene

❏ INTRA, INTR—within
intrastate, intravenous, intramural, intrinsic

❏ IT, ITER—between, among
transit, itinerant, transitory, reiterate

❏ JECT, JET—throw
eject, interject, abject, trajectory, jettison

❏ JOUR—day
journal, adjourn, sojourn

❏ JUD—judge
judge, judicious, prejudice, adjudicate

❏ JUNCT, JUG—join
junction, adjunct, injunction, conjugal, subjugate

❏ JUR—swear, law
jury, abjure, adjure, conjure, perjure, jurisprudence

❏ LAT—side
lateral, collateral, unilateral, bilateral, quadrilateral

❏ LAV, LAU, LU—wash
lavatory, laundry, ablution, antediluvian

❏ LEG, LEC, LEX—read, speak
legible, lecture, lexicon

❏ LEV—light
elevate, levitate, levity, alleviate

❏ LIBER—free
liberty, liberal, libertarian, libertine

❏ LIG, LECT—choose, gather
eligible, elect, select

❏ LIG, LI, LY—bind
ligament, oblige, religion, liable, liaison, lien, ally

❏ LING, LANG—tongue
lingo, language, linguistics, bilingual

❏ LITER—letter
literate, alliteration, literal

❏ LITH—stone
monolith, lithograph, megalith

❏ LOQU, LOC, LOG—speech, thought
eloquent, loquacious, colloquial, colloquy,
soliloquy, circumlocution, interlocutor,
monologue, dialogue, eulogy, philology,
neologism

❏ LUC, LUM—light
lucid, elucidate, pellucid, translucent, illu-
minate

❏ LUD, LUS—play
ludicrous, allude, delusion, allusion, illusory

❏ MACRO—great
macrocosm, macrobiotics

❏ MAG, MAJ, MAS, MAX—great
magnify, magnanimous, magnate, magnitude, majesty, master, maximum

❏ MAL—bad
malady, maladroit, malevolent, malodorous

❏ MAN—hand
manual, manuscript, emancipate, manifest,
manumission

❏ MAR—sea
submarine, marine, maritime

❏ MATER, MATR—mother
maternal, matron, matrilineal

❏ MEDI—middle
intermediary, medieval, mediate

❏ MEGA—great
megaphone, megalomania, megaton,
megalith

❏ MEM, MEN—remember
memory, memento, memorabilia, reminisce

❏ METER, METR, MENS—measure
meter, thermometer, perimeter,
metronome, commensurate

❏ MICRO—small
microscope, microorganism, microcosm,
microbe

❏ MIS—wrong, bad, hate
misunderstand, misanthrope, misappre-
hension, misconstrue, misnomer, mishap

❏ MIT, MISS—send
transmit, emit, missive

❏ MOLL—soft
mollify, emollient, mollusk

❏ MON, MONIT—warn
admonish, monitor, premonition

❏ MONO—one
monologue, monotonous, monogamy,
monolith, monochrome

❏ MOR—custom, manner
moral, mores, morose

❏ MOR, MORT—dead
morbid, moribund, mortal, amortize

❏ MORPH—shape
amorphous, anthropomorphic, metamorphosis, morphology

❏ MOV, MOT, MOB, MOM—move
remove, motion, mobile, momentum,
momentous

❏ MUT—change
mutate, mutability, immutable, commute

❏ NAT, NASC—born
native, nativity, natal, neonate, innate, cognate, nascent, renascent, renaissance

❏ NAU, NAV—ship, sailor
nautical, nauseous, navy, circumnavigate

❏ NEG—not, deny
negative, abnegate, renege

❏ NEO—new
neoclassical, neophyte, neologism, neonate

❏ NIHIL—none, nothing
annihilation, nihilism

❏ NOM, NYM—name
nominate, nomenclature, nominal, cognomen, misnomer, ignominious, antonym,
homonym, pseudonym, synonym,
anonymity

❏ NOX, NIC, NEC, NOC—harm
obnoxious, noxious, pernicious,
internecine, innocuous

❏ NOV—new
novelty, innovation, novitiate

❏ NUMER—number
numeral, numerous, innumerable,
enumerate

❏ OB—against
obstruct, obdurate, obfuscate, obnoxious,
obsequious, obstinate, obstreperous,
obtrusive

❏ OMNI—all
omnipresent, omnipotent, omniscient,
omnivorous

❏ ONER—burden
onerous, exonerate

❏ OPER—work
operate, cooperate, inoperable

❏ PAC—peace
pacify, pacifist, pacific

❏ PALP—feel
palpable, palpitation

❏ PAN—all
panorama, panacea, panegyric, pandemic,
panoply

❏ PATER, PATR—father
paternal, paternity, patriot, compatriot,
expatriate, patrimony, patricide, patrician

❏ PATH, PASS—feel, suffer
sympathy, antipathy, empathy, apathy,
pathos, impassioned

❏ PEC—money
pecuniary, impecunious, peculation

❏ PED, POD—foot
pedestrian, pediment, expedient, biped,
quadruped, tripod

❏ PEL, PULS—drive
compel, compelling, expel, propel,
compulsion

❏ PEN—almost
peninsula, penultimate, penumbra

❏ PEND, PENS—hang
pendant, pendulous, compendium, sus-
pense, propensity

❏ PER—through, by, for, throughout
perambulator, percipient, perfunctory, permeable, perspicacious, pertinacious, perturbation, perusal, perennial, peregrinate

❏ PER—against, destruction
perfidious, pernicious, perjure

❏ PERI—around
perimeter, periphery, perihelion, peripatetic

❏ PET—seek, go towards
petition, impetus, impetuous, petulant,
centripetal

❏ PHIL—love
philosopher, philanderer, philanthropy,
bibliophile, philology

❏ PHOB—fear
phobia, claustrophobia, xenophobia

❏ PHON—sound
phonograph, megaphone, euphony, phonetics, phonics

❏ PLAC—calm, please
placate, implacable, placid, complacent

❏ PON, POS—put, place
postpone, proponent, exponent, preposition, posit, interpose, juxtaposition, depose

❏ PORT—carry
portable, deportment, rapport

❏ POT—drink
potion, potable

❏ POT—power
potential, potent, impotent, potentate,
omnipotence

❏ PRE—before
precede, precipitate, preclude, precocious,
precursor, predilection, predisposition,
preponderance, prepossessing, presage,
prescient, prejudice, predict, premonition,
preposition

❏ PRIM, PRI—first
prime, primary, primal, primeval, primordial, pristine

❏ PRO—ahead, forth
proceed, proclivity, procrastinator, profane,
profuse, progenitor, progeny, prognosis,
prologue, promontory, propel, proponent,
propose, proscribe, protestation, provoke

❏ PROTO—first
prototype, protagonist, protocol

- PROX, PROP—near
  approximate, propinquity, proximity

- PSEUDO—false
  pseudoscientific, pseudonym

- PYR—fire
  pyre, pyrotechnics, pyromania

- QUAD, QUAR, QUAT—four
  quadrilateral, quadrant, quadruped, quarter, quarantine, quaternary

- QUES, QUER, QUIS, QUIR—question
  quest, inquest, query, querulous, inquisitive, inquiry

- QUIE—quiet
  disquiet, acquiesce, quiescent, requiem

- QUINT, QUIN—five
  quintuplets, quintessence

- RADI, RAMI—branch
  radius, radiate, radiant, eradicate, ramification

- RECT, REG—straight, rule
  rectangle, rectitude, rectify, regular

- REG—king, rule
  regal, regent, interregnum

- RETRO—backward
  retrospective, retroactive, retrograde

- RID, RIS—laugh
  ridiculous, deride, derision

- ROG—ask
  interrogate, derogatory, abrogate, arrogate, arrogant

- RUD—rough, crude
  rude, erudite, rudimentary

- RUPT—break
  disrupt, interrupt, rupture

- SACR, SANCT—holy
  sacred, sacrilege, consecrate, sanctify, sanction, sacrosanct

- SCRIB, SCRIPT, SCRIV—write
  scribe, ascribe, circumscribe, inscribe, proscribe, script, manuscript, scrivener

- SE—apart, away
  separate, segregate, secede, sedition

- SEC, SECT, SEG—cut
  sector, dissect, bisect, intersect, segment, secant

- SED, SID—sit
  sedate, sedentary, supersede, reside, residence, assiduous, insidious

- SEM—seed, sow
  seminar, seminal, disseminate

- SEN—old
  senior, senile, senescent

- SENT, SENS—feel, think
  sentiment, nonsense, assent, sentient, consensus, sensual

- SEQU, SECU—follow
  sequence, sequel, subsequent, obsequious, obsequy, non sequitur, consecutive

- SIM, SEM—similar, same
  similar, verisimilitude, semblance, dissemble

- SIGN—mark, sign
  signal, designation, assignation

- SIN—curve
  sine curve, sinuous, insinuate

- SOL—sun
  solar, parasol, solarium, solstice

- SOL—alone
  solo, solitude, soliloquy, solipsism

- SOMN—sleep
  insomnia, somnolent, somnambulist

- SON—sound
  sonic, consonance, dissonance, assonance, sonorous, resonate

- SOPH—wisdom
  philosopher, sophistry, sophisticated, sophomoric

- SPEC, SPIC—see, look
  spectator, circumspect, retrospective, perspective, perspicacious, perspicuous

- SPER—hope
  prosper, prosperous, despair, desperate

- SPERS, SPAR—scatter
  disperse, sparse, aspersion, disparate

❏ SPIR—breathe
respire, inspire, spiritual, aspire, transpire

❏ STRICT, STRING—bind
strict, stricture, constrict, stringent, astringent

❏ STRUCT, STRU—build
structure, obstruct, construe

❏ SUB—under
subconscious, subjugate, subliminal, subpoena, subsequent, subterranean, subvert

❏ SUMM—highest
summit, summary, consummate

❏ SUPER, SUR—above
supervise, supercilious, supersede, superannuated, superfluous, insurmountable, surfeit

❏ SURGE, SURRECT—rise
surge, resurgent, insurgent, insurrection

❏ SYN, SYM—together
synthesis, sympathy, synonym, syncopation, synopsis, symposium, symbiosis

❏ TACIT, TIC—silent
tacit, taciturn, reticent

❏ TACT, TAG, TANG—touch
tact, tactile, contagious, tangent, tangential, tangible

❏ TEN, TIN, TAIN—hold, twist
detention, tenable, tenacious, pertinacious, retinue, retain

❏ TEND, TENS, TENT—stretch
intend, distend, tension, tensile, ostensible, contentious

❏ TERM—end
terminal, terminus, terminate, interminable

❏ TERR—earth, land
terrain, terrestrial, extraterrestrial, subterranean

❏ TEST—witness
testify, attest, testimonial, testament, detest, protestation

❏ THE—god
atheist, theology, apotheosis, theocracy

❏ THERM—heat
thermometer, thermal, thermonuclear, hypothermia

❏ TIM—fear, frightened
timid, intimidate, timorous

❏ TOP—place
topic, topography, utopia

❏ TORT—twist
distort, extort, tortuous

❏ TORP—stiff, numb
torpedo, torpid, torpor

❏ TOX—poison
toxic, toxin, intoxication

❏ TRACT—draw
tractor, intractable, protract

❏ TRANS—across, over, through, beyond
transport, transgress, transient, transitory, translucent, transmutation

❏ TREM, TREP—shake
tremble, tremor, tremulous, trepidation, intrepid

❏ TURB—shake
disturb, turbulent, perturbation

❏ UMBR—shadow
umbrella, umbrage, adumbrate, penumbra

❏ UNI, UN—one
unify, unilateral, unanimous

❏ URB—city
urban, suburban, urbane

❏ VAC—empty
vacant, evacuate, vacuous

❏ VAL, VAIL—value, strength
valid, valor, ambivalent, convalescence, avail, prevail, countervail

❏ VEN, VENT—come
convene, contravene, intervene, venue, convention, circumvent, advent, adventitious

❏ VER—true
verify, verity, verisimilitude, veracious, aver, verdict

❏ VERB—word
verbal, verbose, verbiage, verbatim

❏ VERT, VERS—turn
avert, convert, pervert, revert, incontrovertible, divert, subvert, versatile, aversion

❏ VICT, VINC—conquer
victory, conviction, evict, evince, invincible

❏ VID, VIS—see
evident, vision, visage, supervise

❏ VIL—base, mean
vile, vilify, revile

❏ VIV, VIT—life
vivid, vital, convivial, vivacious

❏ VOC, VOK, VOW—call, voice
vocal, equivocate, vociferous, convoke,
evoke, invoke, avow

❏ VOL—wish
voluntary, malevolent, benevolent, volition

❏ VOLV, VOLUT—turn, roll
revolve, evolve, convoluted

❏ VOR—eat
devour, carnivore, omnivorous, voracious

SAT Word Families List

❑ **Talkative**
   garrulous
   glib
   loquacious
   raconteur
   verbose
   voluble

❑ **Secret/Hidden**
   abscond
   alias
   arcane
   clandestine
   covert
   cryptic
   enigma
   furtive
   incognito
   inconspicuous
   lurk
   obscure
   skulk
   subterranean
   surreptitious

❑ **Not Talkative**
   concise
   curt
   laconic
   pithy
   reticent
   succinct
   taciturn

❑ **Praise**
   accolade
   adulation
   commend
   eulogize
   exalt
   extol
   laud
   lionize
   plaudit
   revere

SAT Emergency

If you're short on time, you may want to just skim these Word Families. Learning words in groups is good way to maximize your limited study time.

❏ **Criticize/Scold**
admonish
berate
castigate
censure
chastise
defame
denigrate
disdain
disparage
excoriate
malign
obloquy
rail
rebuke
reproach
reprimand
reprove
revile
upbraid
vilify

❏ **Stubborn**
intractable
mulish
obdurate
obstinate
pertinacious
recalcitrant
refractory
tenacious

❏ **Lazy/Lacking Energy**
indolent
lackadaisical
laggard
languid
lassitude
lethargic
listless
loiter
phlegmatic
sluggard
somnolent
torpid

❏ **Cowardly**
craven
diffident
pusillanimous
timid
timorous

❏ **Inexperienced**
callow
fledgling
infantile
ingenuous
neophyte
novice
tyro

❏ **Obedient**
amenable
assent
compliant
deferential
docile
pliant
submissive
tractable

❏ **Haughty/Pretentious**
affected
aloof
bombastic
grandiloquent
grandiose
magniloquent
mannered
ostentatious
pontificate
supercilious

❏ **Friendly**
affable
amiable
amicable
bonhomie
convivial
gregarious

❏ **Lucky**
auspicious
fortuitous
opportune
serendipity
windfall

❑ **Soothe**
allay
alleviate
anodyne
assuage
liniment
mitigate
mollify
pacify
palliate
placate

❑ **Hostility/Hatred**
abhor
anathema
animosity
antagonism
antipathy
aversion
contentious
deplore
odious
rancor

❑ **Stupid**
buffoon
dolt
dupe
fatuous
imbecile
inane
insipid
obtuse
simpleton
vacuous
vapid

❑ **Subservient**
fawn
grovel
obsequious
servile
subjection
sycophant
toady

❑ **Argumentative**
adversarial
bellicose
belligerent
fractious
irascible
obstreperous
pugnacious
quibble

❑ **Cautious**
chary
circumspect
discretion
leery
prudent
wary

❑ **Impermanent**
ephemeral
evanescent
fleeting
transient
transitory

❑ **Ability/Intelligence**
acumen
adept
adroit
agile
astute
cogent
deft
dexterous
erudite
literate
lithe
lucidity
sagacious
trenchant

❑ **Kind/Generous**
altruistic
beneficent
benevolent
bestow
largess
liberal
magnanimous
munificent
philanthropic

SAT Math in a Nutshell

The math on the SAT covers a lot of ground—from arithmetic to algebra to geometry.

Don't let yourself be intimidated. We've highlighted the 100 most important concepts that you'll need for SAT Math and listed them in this chapter.

You've probably been taught most of these in school already, so this list is a great way to refresh your memory.

A MATH STUDY PLAN

Use this list to remind yourself of the key areas you'll need to know. Do four concepts a day, and you'll be ready within a month. If a concept continually causes you trouble, circle it and refer back to it as you try to do the questions.

Need more help? The math reference list comes from Kaplan's *SAT Math Workbook*. For more help with the Math section of the SAT, the workbook is a great place to start.

SAT Emergency

Even if you have only a week or two to prepare for the SAT, you should read through this entire chapter—it's essential and helpful to review the major math concepts.

NUMBER PROPERTIES

1. Integer/Noninteger

Integers are **whole numbers**; they include negative whole numbers and zero.

2. Rational/Irrational Numbers

A rational number is a number that can be expressed as **a ratio of two integers. Irrational numbers** are real numbers—they have locations on the number line; they just **can't be expressed precisely as fractions or decimals**. For the purposes of the SAT, the most important **irrational numbers** are $\sqrt{2}$, $\sqrt{3}$, and π.

3. Adding/Subtracting Signed Numbers

To **add a positive and a negative**, first ignore the signs and find the positive difference between the number parts. Then attach the sign of the original number with the larger number part. For example, to add 23 and –34, first we ignore the minus sign and find the positive difference between 23 and 34—that's 11. Then we attach the sign of the number with the larger number part—in this case it's the minus sign from the –34. So, 23 + (–34) = –11.

Make **subtraction** situations simpler by turning them into addition. For example, think of –17 – (–21) as –17 + (+21).

To **add or subtract a string of positives and negatives**, first turn everything into addition. Then combine the positives and negatives so that the string is reduced to the sum of a single positive number and a single negative number.

4. Multiplying/Dividing Signed Numbers

To multiply and/or divide positives and negatives, treat the number parts as usual and **attach a minus sign if there were originally an odd number of negatives**. For example, to multiply –2, –3, and –5, first multiply the number parts: $2 \times 3 \times 5 = 30$. Then go back and note that there were three—an odd number—negatives, so the product is negative: $(-2) \times (-3) \times (-5) = -30$.

5. PEMDAS

When performing multiple operations, remember **PEMDAS**, which means **Parentheses** first, then **Exponents**, then **Multiplication and Division** (left to right), and lastly, **Addition and Subtraction** (left to

right). In the expression $9 - 2 \times (5 - 3)^2 + 6 \div 3$, begin with the parentheses: $(5 - 3) = 2$. Then do the exponent: $2^2 = 4$. Now the expression is: $9 - 2 \times 4 + 6 \div 3$. Next do the multiplication and division to get: $9 - 8 + 2$, which equals 3. If you have difficulty remembering PEMDAS, use this sentence to recall it: **P**lease **E**xcuse **M**y **D**ear **A**unt **S**ally.

6. Counting Consecutive Integers

To count consecutive integers, **subtract the smallest from the largest and add 1**. To count the integers from 13 through 31, subtract: $31 - 13 = 18$. Then add 1: $18 + 1 = 19$.

DIVISIBILITY

7. Factor/Multiple

The factors of integer n are the positive integers that divide into n with no remainder. The multiples of n are the integers that n divides into with no remainder. For example, 6 is a factor of 12, and 24 is a multiple of 12. 12 is both a factor and a multiple of itself, since $12 \times 1 = 12$ and $12 \div 1 = 12$.

8. Prime Factorization

To find the prime factorization of an integer, just keep breaking it up into factors until **all the factors are prime**. To find the prime factorization of 36, for example, you could begin by breaking it into 4×9: $36 = 4 \times 9 = 2 \times 2 \times 3 \times 3$.

9. Relative Primes

Relative primes are integers that have no common factor other than 1. To determine whether two integers are relative primes, break them both down to their prime factorizations. For example: $35 = 5 \times 7$, and $54 = 2 \times 3 \times 3 \times 3$. They have **no prime factors in common**, so 35 and 54 are relative primes.

10. Common Multiple

A common multiple is a number that is a multiple of two or more integers. You can always get a common multiple of two integers by **multiplying** them, but, unless the two numbers are relative primes, the product will not be the *least* common multiple. For example, to find a common multiple for 12 and 15, you could just multiply: $12 \times 15 = 180$.

KAPLAN

11. Least Common Multiple (LCM)

To find the least common multiple, check out the **multiples of the larger integer** until you find one that's **also a multiple of the smaller**. To find the LCM of 12 and 15, begin by taking the multiples of 15: 15 is not divisible by 12; 30 is not; nor is 45. But the next multiple of 15, 60, *is* divisible by 12, so it's the LCM.

12. Greatest Common Factor (GCF)

To find the greatest common factor, break down both integers into their prime factorizations and multiply **all the prime factors they have in common**. $36 = 2 \times 2 \times 3 \times 3$, and $48 = 2 \times 2 \times 2 \times 2 \times 3$. What they have in common is two 2s and one 3, so the GCF is $2 \times 2 \times 3 = 12$.

13. Even/Odd

To predict whether a sum, difference, or product will be even or odd, just **take simple numbers such as 1 and 2 and see what happens**. There are rules—"odd times even is even," for example—but there's no need to memorize them. What happens with one set of numbers generally happens with all similar sets.

14. Multiples of 2 and 4

An integer is divisible by 2 (which is even) if the **last digit is even**. An integer is divisible by 4 if the **last two digits form a multiple of 4**. The last digit of 562 is 2, which is even, so 562 is a multiple of 2. The last two digits form 62, which is *not* divisible by 4, so 562 is not a multiple of 4. The integer 512, however is divisible by four because the last two digits form 12, which is a multiple of 4.

15. Multiples of 3 and 9

An integer is divisible by 3 if the **sum of its digits is divisible by 3**. An integer is divisible by 9 if the **sum of its digits is divisible by 9**. The sum of the digits in 957 is 21, which is divisible by 3 but not by 9, so 957 is divisible by 3 but not by 9.

16. Multiples of 5 and 10

An integer is divisible by 5 if the **last digit is 5 or 0**. An integer is divisible by 10 if the **last digit is 0**. The last digit of 665 is 5, so 665 is a multiple of 5 but *not* a multiple of 10.

17. Remainders

The remainder is the **whole number left over after division**. 487 is 2 more than 485, which is a multiple of 5, so when 487 is divided by 5, the remainder will be 2.

FRACTIONS AND DECIMALS

18. Reducing Fractions

To reduce a fraction to lowest terms, **factor out and cancel** all factors the numerator and denominator have in common.

$$\frac{28}{36} = \frac{4 \times 7}{4 \times 9} = \frac{7}{9}$$

19. Adding/Subtracting Fractions

To add or subtract fractions, first find a **common denominator**, then add or subtract the numerators.

$$\frac{2}{15} + \frac{3}{10} = \frac{4}{30} + \frac{9}{30} = \frac{4+9}{30} = \frac{13}{30}$$

20. Multiplying Fractions

To multiply fractions, **multiply** the numerators and **multiply** the denominators.

$$\frac{5}{7} \times \frac{3}{4} = \frac{5 \times 3}{7 \times 4} = \frac{15}{28}$$

21. Dividing Fractions

To divide fractions, **invert** the second one and **multiply**.

$$\frac{1}{2} \div \frac{3}{5} = \frac{1}{2} \times \frac{5}{3} = \frac{1 \times 5}{2 \times 3} = \frac{5}{6}$$

22. Converting a Mixed Number to an Improper Fraction

To convert a mixed number to an improper fraction, **multiply** the whole number part by the denominator, then **add** the numerator. The result is the new numerator (over the same denominator). To convert $7\frac{1}{3}$, first multiply 7 by 3, then add 1, to get the new numerator of 22. Put that over the same denominator, 3, to get $\frac{22}{3}$.

23. Converting an Improper Fraction to a Mixed Number

To convert an improper fraction to a mixed number, divide the denominator into the numerator to get a **whole number quotient with a remainder**. The quotient becomes the whole number part of the mixed number, and the remainder becomes the new numerator—with the same denominator. For example, to convert $\frac{108}{5}$, first divide 5 into 108, which yields 21 with a remainder of 3. Therefore, $\frac{108}{5} = 21\frac{3}{5}$.

24. Reciprocal

To find the reciprocal of a fraction, **switch the numerator and the denominator**. The reciprocal of $\frac{3}{7}$ is $\frac{7}{3}$. The reciprocal of 5 is $\frac{1}{5}$. The product of reciprocals is 1.

25. Comparing Fractions

One way to compare fractions is to **re-express them with a common denominator**. $\frac{3}{4} = \frac{21}{28}$ and $\frac{5}{7} = \frac{20}{28}$. $\frac{21}{28}$ is greater than $\frac{20}{28}$, so $\frac{3}{4}$ is greater than $\frac{5}{7}$. Another way to compare fractions is to **convert them both to decimals**. $\frac{3}{4}$ converts to .75 , and $\frac{5}{7}$ converts to approximately .714.

26. Converting Fractions to Decimals

To convert a fraction to a decimal, **divide the bottom into the top**. To convert $\frac{5}{8}$, divide 8 into 5, yielding .625.

27. Converting Decimals to Fractions

To convert a decimal to a fraction, set the decimal over 1 and **multiply the numerator and denominator by ten raised to the number of digits to the right of the decimal point**. For instance, to convert .625 to a fraction, you would multiply $\frac{.625}{1}$ by $\frac{10^3}{10^3}$, or $\frac{1000}{1000}$. Then simplify: $\frac{625}{1000} = \frac{5 \times 125}{8 \times 125} = \frac{5}{8}$.

28. Repeating Decimal

To find a particular digit in a repeating decimal, note the **number of digits in the cluster that repeats**. If there are 2 digits in that cluster, then every second digit is the same. If there are three digits in that cluster, then every third digit is the same. And so on. For example, the decimal equivalent of $\frac{1}{27}$ is .037037037..., which is best written $.\overline{037}$. There are three digits in the repeating cluster, so every third digit is the same: 7. To find the 50th digit, look for the multiple of three just less than 50—that's 48. The 48th digit is 7, and with the 49th digit the pattern repeats with 0. The 50th digit is 3.

29. Identifying the Parts and the Whole

The key to solving most fractions and percents story problems is to identify the part and the whole. Usually you'll find the **part** associated with the verb *is/are* and the **whole** associated with the word *of*. In the sentence, "Half of the boys are blonds," the whole is the boys ("of the boys"), and the part is the blonds ("are blonds").

PERCENTS

30. Percent Formula

Whether you need to find the part, the whole, or the percent, use the same formula:

$$\text{Part} = \text{Percent} \times \text{Whole}$$

Example: What is 12% of 25?
Setup: Part = .12 × 25

Example: 15 is 3% of what number?
Setup: 15 = .03 × Whole

Example: 45 is what percent of 9?
Setup: 45 = Percent × 9

31. Percent Increase and Decrease

To increase a number by a percent, **add the percent to 100 percent**, convert to a decimal, and multiply. To increase 40 by 25 percent, add 25 percent to 100 percent, convert 125 percent to 1.25, and multiply by 40. 1.25 × 40 = 50.

32. Finding the Original Whole

To find the **original whole before a percent increase or decrease, set up an equation**. Think of the result of a 15 percent increase over x as $1.15x$.

Example: After a 5 percent increase, the population was 59,346. What was the population before the increase?
Setup: $1.05x = 59{,}346$

33. Combined Percent Increase and Decrease

To determine the combined effect of multiple percent increases and/or decreases, **start with 100 and see what happens**.

Example: A price went up 10 percent one year, and the new price went up 20 percent the next year. What was the combined percent increase?

Setup: First year: 100 + (10 percent of 100) = 110. Second year: 110 + (20 percent of 110) = 132. That's a combined 32 percent increase.

RATIOS, PROPORTIONS, AND RATES

34. Setting up a Ratio

To find a ratio, put the number associated with the word *of* **on top** and the quantity associated with the word *to* **on the bottom** and reduce. The ratio of 20 oranges to 12 apples is $\frac{20}{12}$, which reduces to $\frac{5}{3}$.

35. Part-to-Part Ratios and Part-to-Whole Ratios

If the parts add up to the whole, a part-to-part ratio can be turned into two part-to-whole ratios by putting **each number in the original ratio over the sum of the numbers.** If the ratio of males to females is 1 to 2, then the males-to-people ratio is $\frac{1}{1+2} = \frac{1}{3}$ and the females-to-people ratio is $\frac{2}{1+2} = \frac{2}{3}$. In other words, $\frac{2}{3}$ of all the people are female.

36. Solving a Proportion

To solve a proportion, **cross-multiply:**

$$\frac{x}{5} = \frac{3}{4}$$
$$4x = 3 \times 5$$
$$x = \frac{15}{4} = 3.75$$

37. Rate

To solve a rates problem, **use the units** to keep things straight.

Example: If snow is falling at the rate of one foot every four hours, how many inches of snow will fall in seven hours?

Setup:
$$\frac{1 \text{ foot}}{4 \text{ hours}} = \frac{x \text{ inches}}{7 \text{ hours}}$$
$$\frac{12 \text{ inches}}{4 \text{ hours}} = \frac{x \text{ inches}}{7 \text{ hours}}$$
$$4x = 12 \times 7$$
$$x = 21$$

38. Average Rate

Average rate is *not* simply the average of the rates.

$$\text{Average } A \text{ per } B = \frac{\text{Total } A}{\text{Total } B}$$

$$\text{Average Speed} = \frac{\text{Total distance}}{\text{Total time}}$$

To find the average speed for 120 miles at 40 mph and 120 miles at 60 mph, **don't just average the two speeds**. First figure out the total distance and the total time. The total distance is 120 + 120 = 240 miles. The times are two hours for the first leg and three hours for the second leg, or five hours total. The average speed, then, is $\frac{240}{5}$ = 48 miles per hour.

AVERAGES

39. Average Formula

To find the average of a set of numbers, **add them up and divide by the number of numbers**.

$$\text{Average} = \frac{\text{Sum of the terms}}{}$$

To find the average of the five numbers 12, 15, 23, 40, and 40, first add them: 12 + 15 + 23 + 40 + 40 = 130. Then divide the sum by 5: 130 ÷ 5 = 26.

40. Average of Evenly Spaced Numbers

To find the average of evenly spaced numbers, just **average the smallest and the largest**. The average of all the integers from 13 through 77 is the same as the average of 13 and 77:

$$\frac{13 + 77}{2} = \frac{90}{2} = 45$$

41. Using the Average to Find the Sum

Sum = (Average) × (Number of terms)

If the average of ten numbers is 50, then they add up to 10 × 50, or 500.

42. Finding the Missing Number

To find a missing number when you're given the average, **use the sum**. If the average of four numbers is 7, then the sum of those four numbers is 4 × 7, or 28.

Suppose that three of the numbers are 3, 5, and 8. These three numbers add up to 16 of that 28, which leaves 12 for the fourth number.

43. Median

The median of a set of numbers is the **value that falls in the middle of the set**. If you have five test scores, and they are 88, 86, 57, 94, and 73, you must first list the scores in increasing or decreasing order: 57, 73, 86, 88, 94.

The median is the middle number, or 86. If there is an even number of values in a set (six test scores, for instance), simply take the average of the two middle numbers.

44. Mode

The mode of a set of numbers is the **value that appears most often**. If your test scores were 88, 57, 68, 85, 99, 93, 93, 84, and 81, the mode of the scores would be 93 because it appears more often than any other score. If there is a tie for the most common value in a set, the set has more than one mode.

POSSIBILITIES AND PROBABILITY

45. Counting the Possibilities

The fundamental counting principle: If there are *m* **ways** one event can happen and *n* **ways** a second event can happen, then there are *m* × *n* **ways** for the two events to happen. For example, with five shirts and seven pairs of pants to choose from, you can put together 5 × 7 = 35 different outfits.

46. Probability

$$\text{Probability} = \frac{\text{Favorable outcomes}}{}$$

For example, if you have 12 shirts in a drawer and nine of them are white, the probability of picking a white shirt at random is $\frac{9}{12} = \frac{3}{4}$. This probability can also be expressed as .75 or 75 percent.

POWERS AND ROOTS

47. Multiplying and Dividing Powers

To multiply powers with the same base, **add the exponents and keep the same base:**

$$x^3 \times x^4 = x^{3+4} = x^7$$

To divide powers with the same base, **subtract the exponents and keep the same base:**

$$y^{13} \div y^8 = y^{13-8} = y^5$$

48. Raising Powers to Powers

To raise a power to a power, **multiply the exponents:**

$$(x^3)^4 = x^{3 \times 4} = x^{12}$$

49. Simplifying Square Roots

To simplify a square root, **factor out the perfect squares** under the radical, unsquare them and put the result in front.

$$\sqrt{12} = \sqrt{4 \times 3} = \sqrt{4} \times \sqrt{3} = 2\sqrt{3}$$

50. Adding and Subtracting Roots

You can add or subtract radical expressions **when the part under the radicals is the same:**

$$2\sqrt{3} + 3\sqrt{3} = 5\sqrt{3}$$

Don't try to add or subtract when the radical parts are different. There's not much you can do with an expression like:

$$3\sqrt{5} + 3\sqrt{7}$$

51. Multiplying and Dividing Roots

The product of square roots is equal to the **square root of the product:**

$$\sqrt{3} \times \sqrt{5} = \sqrt{3 \times 5} = \sqrt{15}$$

The quotient of square roots is equal to the **square root of the quotient:**

$$\frac{\sqrt{6}}{\sqrt{3}} = \sqrt{\frac{6}{3}} = \sqrt{2}$$

ALGEBRAIC EXPRESSIONS

52. Evaluating an Expression

To evaluate an algebraic expression, **plug in** the given values for the unknowns and calculate according to **PEMDAS**. To find the value of $x^2 + 5x - 6$ when $x = -2$, plug in -2 for x: $(-2)^2 + 5(-2) - 6 = 4 - 10 - 6 = -12$.

53. Adding and Subtracting Monomials

To combine like terms, **keep the variable part unchanged while adding or subtracting the coefficients:**

$$2a + 3a = (2 + 3)a = 5a$$

54. Adding and Subtracting Polynomials

To add or subtract polynomials, **combine like terms**.

$$(3x^2 + 5x - 7) - (x^2 + 12) =$$
$$(3x^2 - x^2) + 5x + (-7 - 12) =$$
$$2x^2 + 5x - 19$$

55. Multiplying Monomials

To multiply monomials, **multiply the coefficients and the variables separately:**

$$2a \times 3a = (2 \times 3)(a \times a) = 6a^2$$

56. Multiplying Binomials—FOIL

To multiply binomials, use **FOIL**. To multiply $(x + 3)$ by $(x + 4)$, first multiply the **F**irst terms: $x \times x = x^2$. Next the **O**uter terms: $x \times 4 = 4x$. Then the **I**nner terms: $3 \times x = 3x$. And finally the **L**ast terms: $3 \times 4 = 12$. Then add and combine like terms:

$$x^2 + 4x + 3x + 12 = x^2 + 7x + 12$$

57. Multiplying Other Polynomials

FOIL works only when you want to multiply two binomials. If you want to multiply polynomials with more than two terms, make sure you **multiply each term in the first polynomial by each term in the second.**

$$(x^2 + 3x + 4)(x + 5) =$$
$$x^2(x + 5) + 3x(x + 5) + 4(x + 5) =$$
$$x^3 + 5x^2 + 3x^2 + 15x + 4x + 20 =$$
$$x^3 + 8x^2 + 19x + 20$$

After multiplying two polynomials together, the number of terms in your expression before simplifying should equal the number of terms in one polynomial multiplied by the number of terms in the second. In the example above, you should have $3 \times 2 = 6$ terms in the product before you simplify like terms.

FACTORING ALGEBRAIC EXPRESSIONS

58. Factoring out a Common Divisor

A factor common to all terms of a polynomial can be **factored out**. Each of the three terms in the polynomial $3x^3 + 12x^2 - 6x$ contains a factor of $3x$. Pulling out the common factor yields $3x(x^2 + 4x - 2)$.

59. Factoring the Difference of Squares

One of the test maker's favorite factorables is the **difference of squares**.

$$a^2 - b^2 = (a - b)(a + b)$$

$x^2 - 9$, for example, factors to $(x - 3)(x + 3)$.

60. Factoring the Square of a Binomial

Learn to recognize polynomials that are squares of binomials:

$$a^2 + 2ab + b^2 = (a + b)^2$$
$$a^2 - 2ab + b^2 = (a - b)^2$$

For example, $4x^2 + 12x + 9$ factors to $(2x + 3)^2$, and $n^2 - 10n + 25$ factors to $(n - 5)^2$.

61. Factoring Other Polynomials—FOIL in Reverse

To factor a quadratic expression, **think about what binomials you could use FOIL on to get that quadratic expression**. To factor $x^2 - 5x + 6$, think about what First terms will produce x^2, what Last terms will produce $+6$, and what Outer and Inner terms will produce $-5x$. Some common sense—and a little trial and error—lead you to $(x - 2)(x - 3)$.

62. Simplifying an Algebraic Fraction

Simplifying an algebraic fraction is a lot like simplifying a numerical fraction. The general idea is to **find factors common to the numerator and denominator and cancel them**. Thus, simplifying an algebraic fraction begins with factoring.

For example, to simplify $\dfrac{x^2 - x - 12}{x^2 - 9}$, first factor the numerator and denominator:

$$\frac{x^2 - x - 12}{x^2 - 9} = \frac{(x - 4)(x + 3)}{(x - 3)(x + 3)}$$

Canceling $x + 3$ from the numerator and denominator leaves you with $\dfrac{x - 4}{x - 3}$.

SOLVING EQUATIONS

63. Solving a Linear Equation

To solve an equation, do whatever is necessary to both sides to **isolate the variable**. To solve the equation $5x - 12 = -2x + 9$, first get all the xs on one side by adding $2x$ to both sides: $7x - 12 = 9$. Then add 12 to both sides: $7x = 21$. Then divide both sides by 7: $x = 3$.

64. Solving "in Terms of"

To solve an equation for one variable **in terms of** another means to **isolate the one variable on one side of the equation**, leaving an expression containing the other variable on the other side of the equation. To solve the equation $3x - 10y = -5x + 6y$ for x in terms of y, isolate x:

$$3x - 10y = -5x + 6y$$
$$3x + 5x = 6y + 10y$$
$$8x = 16y$$
$$x = 2y$$

65. Translating from English into Algebra

To translate from English into algebra, **look for the key words and systematically turn phrases into algebraic expressions and sentences into equations**. Be careful about order, especially when subtraction is called for.

Example: The charge for a phone call is r cents for the first three minutes and s cents for each minute thereafter. What is the cost, in cents, of a phone call lasting exactly t minutes? ($t > 3$)

Setup: The charge begins with r, and then something more is added, depending on the length of the call. The amount added is s times the number of minutes past three minutes. If the total number of minutes is t, then the number of minutes past three is $t - 3$. So the charge is $r + s(t - 3)$.

66. Solving a Quadratic Equation

To solve a quadratic equation, put it in the "$ax^2 + bx + c = 0$" form, **factor** the left side (if you can), and set each factor equal to 0 separately to get the two solutions. To solve $x^2 + 12 = 7x$, first rewrite it as $x^2 - 7x + 12 = 0$. Then factor the left side:

$$(x - 3)(x - 4) = 0$$
$$x - 3 = 0 \text{ or } x - 4 = 0$$
$$x = 3 \text{ or } 4$$

67. Solving a System of Equations

You can solve for two variables only if you have two distinct equations. Two forms of the same equation will not be adequate. **Combine the equations** in such a way that **one of the variables cancels out**. To solve the two equations $4x + 3y = 8$ and $x + y = 3$, multiply both sides of the second equation by -3 to get: $-3x - 3y = -9$. Now add the two equations; the $3y$ and the $-3y$ cancel out, leaving: $x = -1$. Plug that back into either one of the original equations and you'll find that $y = 4$.

68. Solving an Inequality

To solve an inequality, do whatever is necessary to both sides to **isolate the variable**. Just remember that when you **multiply or divide both sides by a negative number**, you must **reverse the sign**. To solve $-5x + 7 < -3$, subtract 7 from both sides to get: $-5x < -10$. Now divide both sides by -5, remembering to reverse the sign: $x > 2$.

COORDINATE GEOMETRY

69. Finding the Distance Between Two Points

To find the distance between points, use the **Pythagorean theorem or special right triangles**. The difference between the xs is one leg and the difference between the ys is the other.

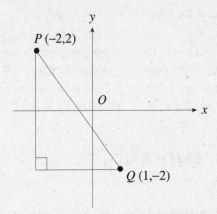

In the figure above, PQ is the hypotenuse of a 3-4-5 triangle, so $PQ = 5$.

You can also use the **distance formula**:

$$d = \sqrt{(x_1 - x_2)^2 + (y_1 - y_2)^2}$$

To find the distance between $R(3, 6)$ and $S(5, -2)$:

$$d = \sqrt{(3 - 5)^2 + [6 - (-2)]^2}$$
$$= \sqrt{(-2)^2 + (8)^2}$$
$$= \sqrt{68} = 2\sqrt{17}$$

70. Using Two Points to Find the Slope

$$\text{Slope} = \frac{\text{Change in } y}{} = \frac{\text{Rise}}{}$$

The slope of the line that contains the points $A(2, 3)$ and $B(0, -1)$ is:

$$\frac{y_A - y_B}{x_A - x_B} = \frac{3 - (-1)}{2 - 0} = \frac{4}{2} = 2$$

71. Using an Equation to Find the Slope

To find the slope of a line from an equation, put the equation into the **slope-intercept** form:

$$y = mx + b$$

The **slope is m**. To find the slope of the equation $3x + 2y = 4$, rearrange it:

$$3x + 2y = 4$$
$$2y = -3x + 4$$
$$y = -\frac{3}{2}x + 2$$

The slope is $-\frac{3}{2}$.

72. Using an Equation to Find an Intercept

To find the *y*-intercept, you can either put the equation into $y = mx + b$ (**slope-intercept**) form—in which case **b is the y-intercept**—or you can just **plug $x = 0$** into the equation and **solve for y**. To find the *x*-intercept, **plug $y = 0$** into the equation and **solve for x**.

LINES AND ANGLES

73. Intersecting Lines

When two lines intersect, **adjacent angles are supplementary and vertical angles are equal**.

In the figure above, the angles marked $a°$ and $b°$ are adjacent and supplementary, so $a + b = 180$. Furthermore, the angles marked $a°$ and $60°$ are vertical and equal, so $a = 60$.

74. Parallel Lines and Transversals

A transversal across parallel lines forms **four equal acute angles and four equal obtuse angles**.

In the figure above, line 1 is parallel to line 2. Angles *a*, *c*, *e*, and *g* are obtuse, so they are all equal. Angles *b*, *d*, *f*, and *h* are acute, so they are all equal.

Furthermore, **any of the acute angles is supplementary to any of the obtuse angles**. Angles *a* and *h* are supplementary, as are *b* and *e*, *c* and *f*, and so on.

TRIANGLES—GENERAL

75. Interior Angles of a Triangle

The three angles of any triangle add up to 180°.

In the figure above, $x + 50 + 100 = 180$, so $x = 30$.

76. Exterior Angles of a Triangle

An exterior angle of a triangle is equal to the **sum of the remote interior angles**.

In the figure above, the exterior angle labeled $x°$ is equal to the sum of the remote angles: $x = 50 + 100 = 150$.

The three exterior angles of a triangle add up to 360°.

In the figure above, $a + b + c = 360$.

77. Similar Triangles

Similar triangles have the same shape; **corresponding angles are equal and corresponding sides are proportional.**

The triangles above are similar because they have the same angles. The 3 corresponds to the 4 and the 6 corresponds to the s.

$$\frac{3}{4} = \frac{6}{s}$$

$$3s = 24$$

$$s = 8$$

78. Area of a Triangle

$$\text{Area of Triangle} = \frac{1}{2}(\text{base})(\text{height})$$

The height is the perpendicular distance between the side that's chosen as the base and the opposite vertex.

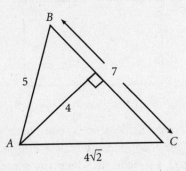

In the triangle above, 4 is the height when the 7 is chosen as the base.

$$\text{Area} = \frac{1}{2}bh = \frac{1}{2}(7)(4) = 14$$

79. Triangle Inequality Theorem

The length of one side of a triangle must be **greater than the difference and less than the sum** of the lengths of the other two sides. For example, if it is given that the length of one side is 3 and the length of another side is 7, then you know that the length of the third side must be greater than $7 - 3 = 4$ and less than $7 + 3 = 10$.

80. Isosceles Triangles

An isosceles triangle is a triangle that has **two equal sides**. Not only are two sides equal, but the angles opposite the equal sides, called base angles, are also equal.

81. Equilateral Triangles

Equilateral triangles are triangles in which **all three sides are equal**. Since all the sides are equal, all the angles are also equal. All three angles in an equilateral triangle measure 60 degrees, regardless of the lengths of sides.

RIGHT TRIANGLES

82. Pythagorean Theorem

For all right triangles:

$$(\text{leg}_1)^2 + (\text{leg}_2)^2 = (\text{hypotenuse})^2$$

If one leg is 2 and the other leg is 3, then:

$$2^2 + 3^2 = c^2$$
$$c^2 = 4 + 9$$
$$c = \sqrt{13}$$

83. The 3-4-5 Triangle

If a right triangle's leg-to-leg ratio is 3:4, or if the leg-to-hypotenuse ratio is 3:5 or 4:5, it's a 3-4-5 triangle and you don't need to use the Pythagorean theorem to find the third side. Just figure out what multiple of 3-4-5 it is.

In the right triangle shown, one leg is 30 and the hypotenuse is 50. This is 10 times 3-4-5. The other leg is 40.

84. The 5-12-13 Triangle

If a right triangle's leg-to-leg ratio is 5:12, or if the leg-to-hypotenuse ratio is 5:13 or 12:13, then it's a 5-12-13 triangle. You don't need to use the Pythagorean theorem to find the third side. Just figure out what multiple of 5-12-13 it is.

Here one leg is 36 and the hypotenuse is 39. This is 3 times 5-12-13. The other leg is 15.

85. The 30-60-90 Triangle

The sides of a 30-60-90 triangle are in a ratio of $x : x\sqrt{3} : 2x$; the Pythagorean theorem is not necessary.

If the hypotenuse is 6, then the shorter leg is half that, or 3; and then the longer leg is equal to the short leg times $\sqrt{3}$, or $3\sqrt{3}$.

86. The 45-45-90 Triangle

The sides of a 45-45-90 triangle are in a ratio of $x : x : x\sqrt{2}$.

If one leg is 3, then the other leg is also 3, and the hypotenuse is equal to a leg times $\sqrt{2}$, or $3\sqrt{2}$.

OTHER POLYGONS

87. Characteristics of a Rectangle

A rectangle is a **four-sided figure with four right angles**. Opposite sides are equal. Diagonals are equal.

Quadrilateral *ABCD* above is shown to have three right angles. The fourth angle therefore also measures 90°, and *ABCD* is a rectangle. The perimeter of a rectangle is equal to the sum of the lengths of the four sides, which is equivalent to 2(length + width).

88. Area of a Rectangle

Area of Rectangle = Length × Width

The area of a 7-by-3 rectangle is $7 \times 3 = 21$.

89. Characteristics of a Parallelogram

A parallelogram has **two pairs of parallel sides**. Opposite sides are equal. Opposite angles are equal. Consecutive angles add up to 180°.

In the figure above, s is the length of the side opposite the 3, so $s = 3$.

90. Area of a Parallelogram

Area of Parallelogram = base × height

In parallelogram *KLMN* above, 4 is the height when *LM* or *KN* is used as the base. Base × height = $6 \times 4 = 24$.

91. Characteristics of a Square

A square is a **rectangle with four equal sides**.

If *PQRS* is a square, all sides are the same length as *QR*. The perimeter of a square is equal to four times the length of one side.

92. Area of a Square

Area of Square = (Side)²

The square above, with sides of length 5, has an area of $5^2 = 25$.

93. Interior Angles of a Polygon

The **sum of the measures of the interior angles of a polygon** = $(n - 2) \times 180$, where n is the number of sides.

Sum of the Angles = $(n - 2) \times 180$

The eight angles of an octagon, for example, add up to $(8 - 2) \times 180 = 1,080$.

CIRCLES

94. Circumference of a Circle

$$\text{Circumference} = 2\pi r$$

In the circle above, the radius is 3, and so the circumference is $2\pi(3) = 6\pi$.

95. Length of an Arc

An **arc** is a piece of the circumference. If n is the degree measure of the arc's central angle, then the formula is:

$$\text{Length of an Arc} = \left(\frac{n}{360}\right)(2\pi r)$$

In the figure above, the radius is 5 and the measure of the central angle is 72°. The arc length is $\frac{72}{360}$ or $\frac{1}{5}$ of the circumference:

$$\left(\frac{72}{360}\right)(2\pi)(5) = \left(\frac{1}{5}\right)(10\pi) = 2\pi$$

96. Area of a Circle

$$\text{Area of a Circle} = \pi r^2$$

The area of the circle is $\pi(4)^2 = 16\pi$.

97. Area of a Sector

A **sector** is a piece of the area of a circle. If n is the degree measure of the sector's central angle, then the formula is:

$$\text{Area of a Sector} = \left(\frac{n}{360}\right)(\pi r^2)$$

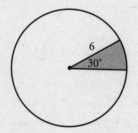

In the figure above, the radius is 6 and the measure of the sector's central angle is 30°. The sector has $\frac{30}{360}$ or $\frac{1}{12}$ of the area of the circle:

$$\left(\frac{30}{360}\right)(\pi)(6^2) = \left(\frac{1}{12}\right)(36\pi) = 3\pi$$

SOLIDS

98. Surface Area of a Rectangular Solid

The surface of a rectangular solid consists of three pairs of identical faces. To find the surface area, find the area of each face and add them up. If the length is l, the width is w, and the height is h, the formula is:

$$\text{Surface Area} = 2lw + 2wh + 2lh$$

The surface area of the box above is: $2 \times 7 \times 3 + 2 \times 3 \times 4 + 2 \times 7 \times 4 = 42 + 24 + 56 = 122$

99. Volume of a Rectangular Solid

Volume of a Rectangular Solid = *lwh*

The volume of a 4-by-5-by-6 box is

$$4 \times 5 \times 6 = 120$$

A cube is a rectangular solid with length, width, and height all equal. If *e* is the length of an edge of a cube, the volume formula is:

Volume of a Cube = e^3

The volume of this cube is $2^3 = 8$.

100. Volume of a Cylinder

Volume of a Cylinder = $\pi r^2 h$

In the cylinder above, $r = 2$, $h = 5$, so:

$$\text{Volume} = \pi(2^2)(5) = 20\pi$$

User's Guide to the CD-ROM

CONGRATULATIONS!

You've purchased the best test prep software on the market, the software that's more fun than an abacus and more educational than an overhead projector. *Higher Score on the SAT and PSAT* is the most comprehensive, instructive, and entertaining software product in the field of test prep to arrive since . . . well, since the dawn of humankind!

In This Software, You Get:

- Interactive lessons detailing the famed Kaplan methods for each section of the SAT
- Full-Length Tests and Practice Tests, so that you can try out your new skills as you move through the sessions
- A Plan detailing your personalized study plan based on your needs
- A math reference section, for reviewing mathematical concepts
- Math, vocabulary, and writing flashcards
- Games for reviewing vocabulary and math for the SAT
- Invaluable college admissions information, and more

Higher Score on the SAT and PSAT provides the tools that will help you devise your personal test-taking plan. Each test you take is closely analyzed, with detailed feedback on your strategic performance, including answers to these questions:

- Do you know when you've found the right answer?
- If you have second thoughts, should you change your answer?
- Can you recognize wrong answers?
- Are you spending too much time on questions?

Naturally, every question comes with a complete explanation. And our detailed scoring charts will track your progress on every type of question. Only *Higher Score on the SAT and PSAT* offers this range of essential features for successful test performance.

INSTALLATION AND TECH SUPPORT

Windows™ CD-ROM Version

1. Start your PC and Windows.
2. Insert the *Higher Score* CD-ROM.
3. From the Start menu, choose Run and choose d:\setup.exe (where d: is your CD-ROM drive).
4. When installation is complete, click the *Higher Score* icon to begin the program.

Macintosh® CD-ROM Version

1. Insert the CD-ROM into the drive.
2. Double-click the *Kaplan Higher Score* Install icon.
3. You will be presented with a dialog box that will let you choose Easy Install or Custom Install. If you choose Easy Install, the program will automatically install *Higher Score on the SAT and PSAT* and update your files if necessary. If you choose Custom Install, you can choose where to install the different components of the program and whether to overwrite existing versions of files.
4. When installation is complete, click the *Higher Score* icon to begin the program.

Tech Support

If you have any questions or problems that don't seem to be covered in this manual, call our tech support line at (503) 968-4058. You can speak to a tech support rep between the hours of 9 A.M. and 1 A.M. (the next day) E.S.T. Monday through Thursday, and 9:00 A.M. to 8:00 P.M. Friday through Sunday.

GETTING STARTED

Double-click on the *Higher Score* icon. Once the program is launched, a "Select User ID" dialog box will appear. If you are a first-time user, you'll need to click on the "Add New User" button and enter your name. The first time you start the program you will be given a Guided Tour to introduce some of the features. (You can skip the tour if you really want to.) You may view the Guided Tour any time by clicking on the CD on the dashboard, but it will not appear again automatically. The Guided Tour is followed by a Student Profile in which we ask for your study preferences and other information which we use to develop your customized study plan.

Navigator Help

The first time you see a submenu of the main dashboard (games, roadmap, reference computer, and admissions calendar) you will view a video featuring one of your guides describing the features of the area you're in. If you would like to replay this video at any time, click on the help button , located on the submenu screen.

The Main Interface

Main Interface

The main interface has these features:

- **Lessons:** Click on the Lesson icon (the suitcase) on the Main Menu screen to bring up the Lessons submenu; click on the desired submenu.

- **Reference and Games:** Located in the Reference Lounge, the Reference and Games area includes Games, a Vocabulary Builder, Flashcards, and the SAT FAQs (Frequently Asked Questions).

- **The Test Center:** Take Diagnostic, Practice, and Full-Length Tests, get feedback, and see how well you're doing overall.

- **Next Stop:** Clicking in the Next Stop area brings you directly to the next item on your personalized Plan.

- **Progress Bar:** The Progress Bar, located beneath the Next Stop area, lets you know how much of your Plan you've completed.

- **Admissions:** Click on the Admissions icon on the Main Menu screen for info on choosing, getting into, and paying for school, and finding schools that best suit your needs. You can also compare your scores to the average scores at over 1,000 colleges and universities, or search for scholarships based on relevant criteria.

- **Weblink:** Click on the "www" hood ornament on the car to access the award-winning Kaplan website!

The Menus

- The **File** menu lets you set up your printer and exit the program.

- The **Options** menu lets you set preferences and reset your profile.

- The **Goto** menu can take you to Lessons, Math Review, Reference, Tests, Games, the Guided Tour, Admissions, the Roadmap, College Search, and Compare Scores.

- The **Help** menu will take you to the Help system, or to the Test Tutorial.

YOUR PERSONALIZED PLAN

Your *Higher Score for the SAT and PSAT* is personalized: Your study plan is customized to your individual needs. Your plan is based on two things:

- *Your Profile*, which you fill out the first time you begin the program
- Your *Diagnostic* results

Personalized plan

We recommend that you take the Diagnostic at the beginning of your preparation, in order to truly personalize your Plan. If you prefer to skip the Diagnostic, choose the Crash Course in the Profile.

Your Plan will cover only the lessons and tests. Admissions, About the Test, and Reference material won't be included in the Plan, but don't forget to check these areas out on your own.

You may move to any item on your Plan by clicking on it. Pieces you have completed are checked (but you can always return to them by clicking again). Redoing your Profile will give you a new Plan (and remember, any previously completed work won't show up on the new Plan).

THE LESSONS

Each scored question type on the exam has its own lesson covering:

- The nuts and bolts of the section (directions, how many questions, timing)
- What you need to know
- The basic Kaplan method
- Strategies, shortcuts, tips on answering questions when you're not sure
- Time management tips

Lesson Navigation

To move to the next page in a Lesson, click the forward arrow button . To move to the previous page, click the back arrow button . You can push the replay button to replay the section you're in. Clicking on the tabs along the bottom of the screen will take you to the different sections of the lesson, or to Drills within the lesson. To quit the session and return to the Main Menu, click the Main button .

Sample Questions

Sample questions appear throughout the Lessons. Questions with answer bubbles are exercises for you to answer. Clicking directly on the bubble will show the explanation to that particular choice. When you answer questions in drills, you'll have the option of clicking the "Hint" button for some help.

REFERENCE

Reference resources are located in the Reference Lounge. Be sure to check out this area.

The Lessons emphasize the strategic part of test taking: how to approach the questions, shortcuts for finding the right answer, how to save time. To score well in math, however, you've also got to know basic arithmetic, algebra, and geometry concepts. The SAT also requires grammar knowledge. The interactive flashcards and Vocabulary Builder in the Reference area are a great way to brush up your skills. The Reference area covers all the content you might need to review for the SAT in small bite-sized pieces.

To move between the different areas of the Reference Lounge, just click on the computers on the screen.

Frequently Asked Questions

Click on the SAT/FAQ, then click highlighted links for the answers to lots of questions about the test.

Flashcards

The flashcards summarize the math, grammar, and vocabulary you need to know for the test. You can print the vocabulary flashcards by clicking on the print button on the flashcard screen. You will be presented with a dialog which gives you the option to print the current flashcard, your selected flashcards, or all flashcards.

You can view the Flashcards directly through the Main Menu (just click on the Reference Lounge and go to the Flashcards area). You can move through the Flashcards by using the left and right arrow buttons, or by clicking the math and grammar topic buttons at the bottom of the screen. These buttons will take you to the first card in that topic.

The Flip button will flip the card over so you can see the other side. You can choose to see the word or question, then flip to the definition or answer, or choose to flip from the definition or answer to the word or question by using the Word/Definition lever. Just move the lever to your desired setting.

You can select particular cards to be saved for review. When you're viewing a card you wish to select, click the Select button and the card will be added to the Selected group. When you want to look at the cards you've selected, move the Selected/All lever to the Selected position and those cards will be displayed. You can clear the selected cards by clicking Clear Selected. You can go back to the regular view by moving the lever to the All position.

Links to the Flashcards appear in math and verbal question explanations. For instance, an example involving Averages would include a link to the Averages flashcard. If you want more information on that topic, click on the highlighted text, and you'll see the flashcard on the topic. If you want the definition and a sample sentence for a highlighted vocabulary word, click on it, and the flashcard will appear.

GAMES

The Games are fun and exciting—plus, they reinforce the skills you'll need to succeed on the test! Each game is played on a 4-by-4 grid of boxes. The object is always the same: match the two boxes that are related in some way. The pieces you pair vary depending on the game you choose (Math or Verbal). Before each game, you'll receive instructions explaining what you are to match.

To make a match, first click on one box with your mouse. This will highlight the box. Then click on the box which best matches the highlighted box. To unselect a highlighted box, click on it again.

For every correct match, you will receive 20 points. For every incorrect match, you will lose 5 points.

The pieces change position during the game. You can adjust the speed of the changes (slow, medium, fast).

ADMISSIONS

Choose the Admissions icon on the Main Menu screen to get to the Admissions area and check out these features:

- **Planner:** Click on the Admissions Planner to get more information on topics like Early Decision, Essays, Financial Aid, and Recommendations. Check out the College Board website for the latest test information, dates, and fees (www.collegeboard.com).

- **Compare Schools/Schools Search:** Find schools best suited to your needs, then compare your scores to the average scores of entering freshman at hundreds of colleges and universities.

- **Search Screen:** Select items by clicking on them. You may select more than one item in a list box by using Ctrl-Click (⌘-Click on the Mac). Use Ctrl-Click (⌘-Click on the Mac) to deselect a choice. Click Search to see your results, or Cancel to resume the lesson.

- **Results Screen:** Click on a school to view its attributes. Click "Search Again" to go back to the Search screen and begin a new search. Click on Compare scores to compare your scores to the schools which resulted from your search or to all schools. Click Done to exit the Search and resume the lesson.

- **Compare Scores:** Compare your current or previous SAT scores to all schools or just the schools which resulted from your search. If you haven't entered your score in the Profile or taken a test in the software, the graph will only show the average scores of the schools you've chosen.

- **Scholarship Search:** Find scholarships best suited to your needs by choosing the Scholarship Search icon. Choose criteria such as Minimum GPA, Activities, Ethnicity, and others.

TESTING

The Test Center on your Roadmap is the place to go to start tests or get scoring information. You'll see your Plan there, plus lists of all the tests and scores available to you.

There are three kinds of tests in *Higher Score on the SAT and PSAT*:

- The Diagnostic is a half-length test that covers all the question types. We use it to develop your Plan, to give you a baseline score, and to analyze your strategic performance.

- The Practice Tests are section-length tests that cover one particular area. Use them to practice using the Lessons and to build up your stamina.

- The Full-Length Tests should be taken near the end of your preparation. Your analysis will tell you how well you're using the Lessons and give you specific advice for test day.

Beginning a Test

Before starting, you should have scrap paper and a pencil. You do not need a clock, as the program will time you.

To begin a test, click on the test you want to take in the Test Center, or click on it in your Plan. If you have already taken the test, you will have a choice of reviewing your results or resetting the test. Resetting a test will erase your previous work and allow you to retake it. You will be offered a short tutorial before beginning your first test. (If you want to see it again later, go to Help.)

The SmartGrid Option

You may choose to view the questions on the screen, or may follow along in your test booklet. If you wish to use the test booklet, then you may choose the "SmartGrid" option; in this mode, you will view only the answer grid on the screen. The disadvantage of SmartGrid is that the program will not record any question timing information.

The SmartGrid

Test Mode and Tutor Mode

You may take the Practice Tests (everything other than the Diagnostic and Full-Length Tests) either in Test Mode or in Tutor Mode. In Tutor Mode, you may see hints for the questions while taking the test, and the test is not timed. We recommend that you use Tutor Mode at the beginning of your preparation as you use strategies for the first time. You may set a default for Tutor or Test Mode through the Set Preferences Screen in the Options menu.

The Testing Screen

The Testing Screen contains a Toolbar (Control Bar) on the top, and the Question Screen on the bottom. Use the Toolbar to move from one question to another, to indicate your confidence level (Sure or Unsure), to mark questions, and to indicate when you have finished a section. The Toolbar also displays two clocks, which show the time spent per question and the time remaining in the section.

The window below the Toolbar shows the question. If the question is based on a passage, the passage will appear to the left of the question. If the question or passage is longer than the screen, scroll bars will appear to the right of the passage window.

You may view directions or relevant references during the exam through the Windows pull-down menu. Online help is also available through the Help menu. Note that the clock continues to run while you are in Help.

Navigating Through the Test

As you begin each section, the first question will be displayed. The question number and the section number are both displayed on the Toolbar.

After selecting your answer choice, use the Right Arrow button to move on to the next question. You can use the Right or Left Arrow buttons to move to the next or previous question in the section. The right arrow button will not operate once you have reached the last question in the section.

At any time you may press the Go To button to see a record of your answer choices within the section. You can then move to any question directly by clicking on the question number and pressing the Enter key.

Selecting an Answer Choice

To select an answer choice, click on the bubble to the left of the answer choice. The bubble will darken. Clicking again will unselect your choice. Selecting a new answer choice will automatically cancel your previous selection. The program will keep track of when you change answers, and whether you change from a wrong to a right answer or vice versa. (Or whether you just change from one wrong answer to another wrong one.)

Eliminating Answer Choices from Consideration

If you know an answer is wrong, you can eliminate it by clicking directly on the text of the choice itself (rather than on the bubble). A line will appear through the choice. Clicking on it again will make the line disappear. The program will track your success in eliminating wrong choices.

Note: You cannot eliminate every answer choice for a given question. To get the most accurate performance analysis, eliminate choices only as you try to identify the correct answer. Once you've chosen your answer, don't eliminate any more choices.

Marking Questions

Mark a question for later review by clicking the "Mark It" button. A check mark will appear to indicate that the question is marked. When you use the "GoTo" button to move to the Answer Grid window, Marked questions will be indicated. To return to a Marked question from the Grid, click on the line corresponding to the question and press Enter.

Confidence

Indicate your level of confidence in your response by clicking the Sure or Unsure button. Use these buttons only when you are very sure or very unsure. If you have only moderate confidence in your choice, do not click on either button.

Timing

Two clocks display the time remaining in the section and elapsed time on the current question. If you find a clock distracting, click on it to hide the time from view. Click again to restore the time. The clock runs when you are viewing questions, indicating answer choices and eliminations, accessing help, browsing through a section, and viewing the "GoTo" screen. If you are interrupted for an extended period while taking the test, you should abort the section by clicking on the erase button and begin the section again.

You will receive a warning when there are five minutes remaining in the section, and another warning when there is one minute remaining. The computer will also tell you when your time has elapsed. (To simulate real test conditions, this isn't possible during the Diagnostic or Full-Length Tests.)

Using SmartGrid

If you take a test using SmartGrid, choose your answer by clicking on the answer bubble and note your confidence level by checking the appropriate box. If you want, you may mark questions and return to them later.

To eliminate answer choices:

- For Windows users, click on the bubble with your right mouse button.
- For Macintosh users, hold down the option key while clicking on the bubble.

Grid-in questions appear in SmartGrid as boxes with a triangle next to them. Click on the triangle and a Grid-in window will appear; click on the appropriate bubbles and click on "OK" when finished.

Using Tutor Mode

If you take a Practice Test in Tutor Mode, the highlighted word Hint will appear beneath the question. To view the hint, click on the word.

Finishing a Test

Use the Erase and Finished buttons when you are through with a test (or a section of a full-length test). The Erase button will delete the information on the section you are working on. Note that it deletes the information ONLY for that one section in a full-length test. If you choose Erase during a full-length test, resuming the test will bring you back to the beginning of the same section.

Use the Finished button when you are done with a section, and want to keep the record. When you finish a practice test you may see your results and the explanations. When you finish a section in the Diagnostic or Full-Length Test, you may continue to the next section.

ANALYSIS AND PRINTING

The Analysis offered at the end of a test is one of the unique features of the *Higher Score on the SAT and PSAT* software. It allows you to evaluate the success of your test-taking strategies, and can tell you things you may not have suspected about your performance. The information is presented to you in tables, analyzing your performance by question type. For example, you can tell easily whether eliminating choices is helping you more on Critical Reading than on other question types. This allows you to compile your own personalized strategy plan for test day. In addition, bullet points highlight important points and crucial advice for your future performance. Keep in mind, of course, that the analysis is based on a small amount of data. Nevertheless, you should examine the analysis closely.

Once you finish an exam, you can view your results. The Diagnostic and Full-Length Test Analysis includes six separate screens analyzing your performance. (Each practice test has one summary analysis screen.)

Diagnostic and Full-Length Test Analysis

For the Diagnostic and Full-Length Tests, the first screen shows the different options available in Analysis Mode. The same buttons appear on each Analysis screen.

- The Main button returns you to the Main interface screen.

- The Scores button provides your raw and scaled test scores, percentile rankings, and a table containing the number of questions correct, incorrect, omitted, and not reached.

Your raw score is calculated from your number correct. It is then converted to a scaled score on the familiar 200–800 scale. On the actual exam, this scaled score is reported to schools. The scaled score is converted to a percentile ranking, which shows how you performed relative to a larger group of test takers. A score in the 65th percentile, for example, indicates that you scored higher than 65 percent of the students in the larger group.

The Scoring Table

The Scoring Table includes information on items Omitted and those Not Reached. A question that you look at but choose not to answer counts as an Omit; a question that you have not seen (or saw for less than five seconds) is considered Not Reached. Neither counts towards your score, but pay attention to the Not Reached: a significant number of Not Reached questions suggests that you have a timing problem.

The Types button gives you a bar graph showing the percentage of questions correct by Question Type. It also provides a table organized by test section, showing the percentage correct, the average time per question, and the number of questions not reached.

Using the Analysis Information

Use the information provided in the Question Type tables to determine your areas of relative strength and weakness and to plan your course of preparation leading up to Test Day. The tables also provide breakdowns of specific question subtypes, so that you can precisely focus your study where it will do the most good. In addition, these subtypes also appear in the Scoring screens, allowing you to track your progress through *Higher Score on the SAT and PSAT*.

Other Analysis Screens

The other four Analysis screens include a chart showing your strategic performance on the test, listed by question type, as well as short bullet points identifying key points and recommendations.

Sure/Unsure

Sure/Unsure analyzes your performance in terms of the confidence level you assigned to your responses. Organized by question type, it indicates the percentage correct on questions you felt relatively sure of, and the percentage correct on questions you felt unsure of.

This analysis is particularly useful because you assign the confidence rating at the moment of truth, as you are answering each question. If there is a mismatch between your expressed confidence and your performance, you will be notified by bullet-point messages. Be on the lookout not only for misplaced confidence (which can prevent you from giving a question the careful consideration it deserves) but also for a tendency to underrate your knowledge, which can lead to hesitation or even skipping questions that you might have gotten right.

Answer Changing

This screen lets you know how good you are at second-guessing your answers. A table organized by question type shows the number of times you switched from an incorrect answer to a correct one, and the number of times you switched away from the correct response.

Too much answer changing is not helpful—even if you're switching to the correct response, choosing it directly saves time. But sometimes you'll have to decide whether to go with your first instinct or with your second (or third) opinion. This analysis tracks your success at switching. If there is a trend in either direction, you'll be notified by a bullet-point message. Then you'll have a better idea whether to trust that impulse to switch on the next test you face.

Elimination

Elimination provides several types of information. On the most basic level, a table organized by question type shows the number of questions you got correct using the elimination strategy, and the number of times you eliminated the correct answer. Messages will tell you whether you generally keep the correct answer in contention when you eliminate choices, and whether you tend to select the correct choice from the remaining contenders.

Using the Elimination Strategy well is one of the most powerful ways to improve your score. Remember, indicate only those answer choices you are able to eliminate before you settle on your final choice. That way, the program can give you an accurate analysis of whether you recognize wrong choices when you see them, and whether, having successfully narrowed the field of contenders, you then go on to score points. After all, identifying wrong choices is only useful if you get the question right!

Timing

This screen gives you a table organized by question type, showing the average time you spent before settling on correct responses and on incorrect responses. It provides a listing of the five correct items and five incorrect items on which you spent the greatest amount of time. (Note that this list does not include questions with passages; those naturally take longer since you need to read the passage.) It also gives the average amount of time you spent on questions of low, moderate, and high difficulty.

Using your time wisely is essential to scoring well. Too much time spent on a difficult question can hurt your score if you don't have time to reach an easier question—and you still might not get that difficult question right! The Timing screen will tell you whether your perseverance pays off or penalizes you.

Practice Test Analysis

The Practice Test Analysis screen shows your performance on the test, and highlights your use of elimination techniques, your answer changing, your confidence, and your performance on the five longest questions. Compare your strategic performance on different tests as you proceed through them.

Printing

You can print any of the Analysis screens by moving to the screen you want to print, then clicking the Print button. To select or set up your printer, choose Printer Setup from the File menu.

EXPLANATIONS

To view explanations to a test, choose the Explain Answers button from the Analysis screen. For a multisection test, entering the explanations will enable the Explanations pull-down menu; use this menu to navigate from one section to another. Within a section, you can use the GoTo button to move quickly from one question to another. The GoTo screen in Explanations Mode has two options: the Summary view (the default) shows you the question number and whether you answered the question correctly. You can easily move to your next incorrect response by just double-clicking on the question number. Clicking the Details button in the GoTo screen shows your response, the correct response, your confidence level, the question timing, and the category of the question. You will not always need this level of detail, but it will prove handy when (for instance) you want to review all your "Unsure" questions or all questions on a particular topic.

The Explanation Window

Each Explanation Window shows the question and its explanation, as well as your answer, confidence level, eliminations, and other strategic approaches. To view passages accompanying questions or the passage explanation, use the pull-down menu. Each explanation is followed by highlighted links to the Reference area.

You may quit Explanations Mode by clicking on the Main Menu button at any point. To return to the explanations of a test you took previously, select the test from the Tests menu, and choose "Results."

Scoring

The Scoring Screens offer invaluable tools for tracking your performance through the *Higher Score on the SAT and PSAT*. The first screen shows your overall scores on the Diagnostic and Full-length Tests; each question type gets its own screen, showing your performance by category for all tests. For instance, you can track your progress on each type of reading question throughout *Higher Score on the SAT and PSAT*, and use this information to fine-tune your study plans.

Score Reports

Your performances on the Diagnostic, Practice Tests, and Full-Length Tests are charted on bar graphs. This is a visual representation of your progress through the tests. To reach the Scoring area, either click on the Scoring icon on the dashboard, or choose Scoring from the Test Center. The Scoring Overview screen compares your performance on the Full-Length Tests. If you wish to see your improvement in a particular question type, select from the buttons on the right of the screen. Each Question Type screen displays your overall progress for that question type, and further breaks down your performance by category, again using easy-to-read bar graphs.

HELP AND PREFERENCES

Help

To enter the Help system, use the "Help" pulldown menu (Windows) or the "Balloon Help" menu (Macintosh). The pulldown menu also offers the Test Tutorial.

Setting Preferences

Choosing "Set Preferences" gives you a screen with several options.

- *Smart Grid* or *On-Screen Questions*. For Diagnostic and Full-Length Tests.

- *Tutor or Test Mode*. Choose whether you want to access explanations during a Practice Test.

- *Distracting Sounds in Tests*. One of the hard parts of taking a standardized test is concentrating on the test itself and tuning out other noises. To simulate a test environment, turn on the distracting sounds.

- *College Bit*. Upon completing a lesson or test, you'll be shown a fun fact about college. To stop these from appearing, choose this option.

- *Skip Intro*. Choose whether to skip the intro movies when starting *Higher Score*.

- *Browser*. Allows you to choose a Web browser.

ACKNOWLEDGMENTS

Reading passages in these tests, as on the actual SAT, are condensed and adapted from published material. The ideas contained in them do not necessarily represent the opinions of Kaplan, Inc. To make the text suitable for testing purposes, we may in some cases have altered the style or emphasis of the original.

Kaplan, Inc. wishes to thank the following for permission to reprint excerpts from published material used with test questions appearing herein:

"Artificial Organs: Learning to Live with Risk," by Pierre M. Galletti. Reprinted with permission from *Technology Review*, copyright © 1988.

"Bound for Deep Water," by Scott A. Eckert. Reprinted with permission from *Natural History*, March, 1992. Copyright © the American Museum of Natural History, 1992.

"Drowning Dogs and the Dawn of Art," by Jared Diamond. Reprinted with permission from *Natural History*, March, 1993. Copyright © the American Museum of Natural History, 1993.

"Made of Muscle or Bone," by Karen Sandrick. Reprinted with permission from *Technology Review*, copyright © 1991.

Excerpt from *Making It* by Norman Podhoretz. Copyright © 1967 by Norman Podhoretz. Reprinted by permission of Random House, Inc.

"Proxemics in the Arab World," from *The Hidden Dimension* by Edward T. Hall. Copyright © 1966, 1982 by Edward T. Hall. Used by permission of Doubleday, a division of Bantam Doubleday Dell Publishing Group, Inc.

Excerpt from "Waiting for the Weekend" by Witold Rybczynski. Copyright © 1991 by Witold Rybczynski. Used by permission of Viking Penguin, a division of Penguin Books USA Inc.

David V. Edwards, *The American Political Experience: An Introduction to Government*, 1988, p. 471. Prentice-Hall, Inc. Englewood Cliffs, NJ 07632

Excerpt from "Architects and Power, the Natural Market for Architecture," Prof. Robert Gutman, *Progressive Architecture*, December 1992.

Excerpt from "Earth's Ozone Shield Under Threat," France Bequette, *The UNESCO Courier*, June 1990.

From *Fifth Business* by Robertson Davies, condensed from pp. 25–29 ©1970 by R Davies. Viking Penguin, Penguin USA Inc, 375 Hudson Street, NY NY 10014-3657.

Excerpt from *From Slavery to Freedom 5/E*, by John Hope Franklin. Copyright © 1947, 1956, 1967, 1974, 1980 by Alfred A. Knopf, Inc. Reprinted by permission of the publisher.

Excerpt from *A History of Women Artists* by Hugo Munsterberg. Copyright © 1975 by Hugo Munsterberg. Reprinted by permission of Clarkson N. Potter, Inc., a division of Crown Publishers, Inc.

Photo Credits:
© Archive Photos/Edwin Levick/PNI
© Culver Pictures/PNI
© Hulton Deutsch/PNI
© Magnum/Chris Steele-Perkins/PNI

"Sound Effects" provided courtesy of Dominion Entertainment, Inc.

SAT is a registered trademark of the College Entrance Examination Board, which does not endorse or sponsor this product.

Copyright © 2000 Kaplan, Inc.

Minimum System Requirements *

	Windows®	Macintosh®
Operating System:	Windows 98, 98SE, NT 4.0, 2000, ME, XP	Macintosh OS 8.1, 8.5, 8.6, 9, X (runs with OS X under Classic Mode)
CPU Type and Speed:	Pentium® 266 MHz or higher	Power PC®, G3, G4, or higher
Hard Drive Space:	15 MB	18 MB
Graphics:	640x 480 thousands of colors (millions recommended)	640x 480 thousands of colors (millions recommended)
CD-ROM Speed:	4x CD-ROM or higher	4x CD-ROM or higher
	Note: An Internet connection is required for the web features of this program.	Note: An Internet connection is required for the web features of this program.

Installation instructions are in the User's Guide.

SOFTWARE LICENSE/DISCLAIMER OF WARRANTIES

For additional technical assistance please visit the "Customer Service" area of our e website at www.kaptest.com

KAPLAN

Want a High Score on the SAT?

We've got a guide for every student need.

Higher Score Guaranteed

KAPLAN
World Leader in Test Prep

PSAT
2003 EDITION

KAPLAN
kaptest.com
SAT & PSAT
2003

KAPLAN
World Leader in Test Prep
SAT Math Workbook
FOURTH EDITION

The Procrastinator's Guide to the SAT & PSAT
Higher Score Guaranteed

KAPLAN
kaptest.com
SAT for Super Busy Students
Higher Score Guaranteed
PRACTICE TEST INCLUDED

SAT Math Map
100 Most Frequently Tested

SAT Verbal Velocity
Learn 623 Frequently Tested Words through Music, Movies, TV, Sports, History, and the News
Higher Score

The Ring of McAllister
A Score-Raising Mystery Featuring 1,046 Must-Know SAT Vocabulary Words

What Smart Girls Know about the SAT

KAPLAN
World Leader in Test Prep
SAT Verbal Workbook
FOURTH EDITION
Higher Score Gua

SAT Vocabulary Flashcards
FLIP-O-MATIC
Efficient • Brilliantly Low-Tech!

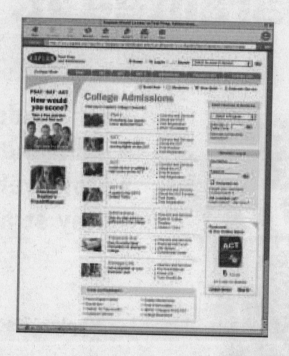